AF619164

Rough Sets in Knowledge Discovery 2

Studies in Fuzziness and Soft Computing

Editor-in-chief
Prof. Janusz Kacprzyk
Systems Research Institute
Polish Academy of Sciences
ul. Newelska 6
01-447 Warsaw, Poland
E-mail: kacprzyk@ibspan.waw.pl

Vol. 3. A. Geyer-Schulz
Fuzzy Rule-Based Expert Systems and Genetic Machine Learning, 2nd ed. 1996
ISBN 3-7908-0964-0

Vol. 4. T. Onisawa and J. Kacprzyk (Eds.)
Reliability and Safety Analyses under Fuzziness, 1995
ISBN 3-7908-0837-7

Vol. 5. P. Bosc and J. Kacprzyk (Eds.)
Fuzziness in Database Management Systems, 1995
ISBN 3-7908-0858-X

Vol. 6. E. S. Lee and Q. Zhu
Fuzzy and Evidence Reasoning, 1995
ISBN 3-7908-0880-6

Vol. 7. B. A. Juliano and W. Bandler
Tracing Chains-of-Thought, 1996
ISBN 3-7908-0922-5

Vol. 8. F. Herrera and J. L. Verdegay (Eds.)
Genetic Algorithms and Soft Computing, 1996
ISBN 3-7908-0956-X

Vol. 9. M. Sato et al.
Fuzzy Clustering Models and Applications, 1997
ISBN 3-7908-1026-6

Vol. 10. L. C. Jain (Ed.)
Soft Computing Techniques in Knowledge-based Intelligent Engineering Systems, 1997
ISBN 3-7908-1035-5

Vol. 11. W. Mielczarski (Ed.)
Fuzzy Logic Techniques in Power Systems, 1998
ISBN 3-7908-1044-4

Vol. 12. B. Bouchon-Meunier (Ed.)
Aggregation and Fusion of Imperfect Information, 1998
ISBN 3-7908-1048-7

Vol. 13. E. Orłowska (Ed.)
Incomplete Information: Rough Set Analysis, 1998
ISBN 3-7908-1049-5

Vol. 14. E. Hisdal
Logical Structures for Representation of Knowledge and Uncertainty, 1998
ISBN 3-7908-1056-8

Vol. 15. G. J. Klir and M. J. Wierman
Uncertainty-Based Information, 1998
ISBN 3-7908-1073-8

Vol. 16. D. Driankov and R. Palm (Eds.)
Advances in Fuzzy Control, 1998
ISBN 3-7908-1090-8

Vol. 17. L. Reznik, V. Dimitrov and J. Kacprzyk (Eds.)
Fuzzy Systems Design, 1998
ISBN 3-7908-1118-1

Vol. 18. L. Polkowski and A. Skowron (Eds.)
Rough Sets in Knowledge Discovery 1, 1998
ISBN 3-7908-1119-X

Lech Polkowski · Andrzej Skowron (Eds.)

Rough Sets in Knowledge Discovery 2

Applications, Case Studies and Software Systems

With 88 Figures
and 131 Tables

Springer-Verlag Berlin Heidelberg GmbH

Prof. Dr. Sc. Lech Polkowski
Institute of Mathematics
Warsaw University of Technology
Pl. Politechniki 1
00-665 Warsaw, Poland
and
Polish-Japanese Institute of Computer Techniques
Koszykowa 86
02-008 Warsaw, Poland

Prof. Dr. Sc. Andrzej Skowron
Institute of Mathematics
Warsaw University
ul. Banacha 2
02-097 Warsaw, Poland

Library of Congress Cataloging-in-Publication Data
Die Deutsche Bibliothek – CIP-Einheitsaufnahme
Rough sets in knowledge discovery / Lech Polkowski; Andrzej Skowron (eds.).
2. Applications, case studies and software systems: with 131 tables.
(Studies in fuzziness and soft computing; Vol. 19)

DOI 10.1007/978-3-7908-1883-3

Originally published by Physica-Verlag Heidelberg New York in 1998
MyCopy version of the original edition 1998

Hardcover Design: Erich Kirchner, Heidelberg

SPIN 10679055 88/2202-5 4 3 2 1 0 – Printed on acid-free paper
www.springer.com/mycopy

Foreword

The papers on rough set theory and its applications placed in this volume present a wide spectrum of problems representative to the present stage of this theory. Researchers from many countries reveal their recent results on various aspects of rough sets. The papers are not confined only to mathematical theory but also include algorithmic aspects, applications and information about software designed for data analysis based on this theory. The volume contains also list of selected publications on rough sets which can be very useful to every one engaged in research or applications in this domain and sometimes perhaps unaware of results of other authors.

The book shows that rough set theory is a vivid and vigorous domain with serious results to its credit and bright perspective for future developments. It lays on the crossroads of fuzzy sets, theory of evidence, neural networks, Petri nets and many other branches of AI, logic and mathematics. These diverse connections seem to be a very fertile feature of rough set theory and have essentially contributed to its wide and rapid expansion. It is worth mentioning that its philosophical roots stretch down from Leibniz, Frege and Russell up to Popper. Therefore many concepts dwelled on in rough set theory are not entirely new, nevertheless the theory can be viewed as an independent discipline on its own rights. Rough set theory has found many interesting real life applications in medicine, banking, industry and others.

The rough set approach seems to be of fundamental importance to AI and cognitive sciences, especially in the areas of machine learning, knowledge acquisition, decision analysis, knowledge discovery from databases, expert systems, inductive reasoning and pattern recognition. It appears to be of particular importance to decision support systems and data mining. Although rough set theory has many achievements to its credit, nevertheless several theoretical and practical problems require further attention. It is especially important to develop widely accessible, efficient software for rough set based data analysis, particularly for large collections of data. Despite of many valuable methods, based on rough set theory, for efficient generation of optimal decision rules from data, developed in recent years, more research is needed here, particularly, when quantitative attributes are involved. In this context also new discretization methods for quantitative attribute values are badly needed. Comparison with other similar methods still requires due attention, although important results have been obtained in this area. A study of the relationship between neural network and rough set approaches tends to be particularly interesting. Image and signal processing using rough sets methods are felt to be also very promising areas. Recently rough data bases and rough information retrieval have been pursued by many researchers. Last but not least, rough set computer is badly needed for many advanced applications.

The volume not only provides many very interesting results but also, no doubt, marks out future directions of developments of this domain.

Congratulations are due to Professors Lech Polkowski and Andrzej Skowron for their marvelous job.

Zdzisław Pawlak

Warsaw, February 1998

Contents

PART 2: CASE STUDIES

PART 3: HYBRID APPROACHES

APPENDIX 1: ROUGH SET BIBLIOGRAPHY

APPENDIX 2: SOFTWARE SYSTEMS

Chapter 1

Introducing the Book

Lech Polkowski[1] *and Andrzej Skowron*[2]

[1] Institute of Mathematics, Warsaw University of Technology
Pl. Politechniki 1, 00-665 Warsaw, Poland
e-mail: polk@mimuw.edu.pl
[2] Institute of Mathematics, Warsaw University
Banacha 2, 02-097 Warsaw, Poland
e-mail: skowron@mimuw.edu.pl

The collection of articles entitled **Rough Sets in Knowledge Discovery: Applications, Case Studies and Software Systems** which is presented to the reader reflects a variety of research themes pursued in Applications of Rough Set Theory to manifold real - life problems. The collection **Rough Sets in Knowledge Discovery:Applications, Case Studies and Software Systems** is divided into three Parts: APPLICATIONS (Part 1) where in consecutive chapters a discussion of theoretical principles and methods underlying specific applications of rough sets is undertaken, CASE STUDIES (Part 2) bringing forth papers illuminating applications of rough sets in various fields of expertise ranging from signal processing and image processing through information retrieval, civil engineering and industrial applications to applications in economic analysis and medical diagnosis and HYBRID APPROACHES (Part 3) consisting of chapters in which rough set techniques are either augmented or contrasted with other approaches to data analysis (e.g. discriminant analysis) or rough set - theoretic tools are enhanced by or enhance other tools of soft computing like neural networks, genetic algorithms, concurrent systems, Petri nets. The collection concludes with two Appendices. APPENDIX 1: ROUGH SET BIBLIOGRAPHY brings forth a list of about 1100 research papers devoted to Rough Set Theory and Applications collected from various sources, notably lists of papers sent by the authors represented in this volume. APPENDIX 2: SOFTWARE SYSTEMS consists of concise presentations of principal now existing software systems built on rough set theory principles.

From its inception, the Theory of Rough Sets has been developed both by theoreticians and practitioners in the context of many distinct fields of theoretical research and applications of which we mention the following, represented by papers in this collection.

Abstract approximation spaces. In standard rough set theory, objects under consideration are perceived as sets of values taken on them by some chosen a priori attributes (features) and objects having identical sets of values are regarded as indiscernible (relative to the given set of attributes). The induced indiscernibility relation is an equivalence relation which partitions the set of objects into disjoint classes of pairwise indiscernible objects. The classes of indiscernibility are exact in the sense that the membership in them is crisp: any object either is certainly in the given class or it is certainly in the complement of this class. This property extends to unions of classes. Any concept, i.e. a subset of the set of considered objects, can be approximated by exact concepts (sets) either from below or from above. The former kind of approximation leads to the lower approximation while the latter gives the upper approximation. One can perceive rough (inexact) sets as those concepts for which the two approximations differ. Replacing the pair (a set of objects, a set of attributes) with the pair (the set of objects, the induced equivalence relation(s)) leads to the concept of an approximation space. This concept has been modified in some ways e.g. by passing from equivalence relations to various kinds of similarity relations. Approximation spaces may be given a topological flavor by observing that the lower, respectively, the upper approximation operator coincides with the interior, respectively, the closure, operator with respect to the induced partition topology. This approach leads to the notion of a topological rough set.

Relations to other paradigms in analysis of uncertainty e.g. evidence (belief) theory, fuzzy set theory. Rough membership functions provide the class of membership functions generated from data tables (information /decision systems). These functions are based on frequency count of objects in indiscernibility classes meeting a given set of objects. A deep and far - reaching generalization of both rough and fuzzy set theories is provided by the paradigm of rough mereology. This theory is based on a formal rendering of the predicate " to be a part of..... in degree...." and stems from mereological theory of St. Leśniewski. Other approaches to the problem of relationships and interplay between rough set and fuzzy set theories consist in studying models equipped in graded approximation operators as well as models resulting from imposing an equivalence or similarity relation on a fuzzy universe. Interpretations of evidence theory in the framework of rough set theory giving inter alia methods for extracting belief and plausibility functors from data tables also exist in the literature. Recently, problems related to the metaphor of granularity of knowledge entered rough set literature.

Knowledge reduction. This problem has been studied from the point of view of independence of knowledge. The notion of a reduct has been proposed as a minimal set of attributes which induces the same indiscernibility relation (object classification) as the whole set of attributes. Various approaches has been proposed and undertaken for finding reducts among them boolean reasoning has been proposed as a tool for finding reducts: reducts of a data table are in one - to - one correspondence with prime implicants of a suitable boolean function. The notion of a reduct has been generalized in various contexts, viz. notions of a relative reduct as well as a dynamic reduct and an approximate reduct have been proposed. Other direction of generalization is related to the notion of a reduct in generalized approximation spaces.

Synthesis of decision algorithms. Decision rules of which a decision algorithm consists are of the form

$$\textbf{if } (a_1, v_1) \wedge (a_2, v_2) \wedge ...(a_k, v_k) \textbf{ then } (d, v)$$

where $a_1, a_2, ..., a_k$ are (conditional) attributes, d is the decision attribute, v_i is a value of the attribute a_i and v is a value of the attribute d. Many authors have discussed the problem of decision rule synthesis from data and the problem of rule evaluation. Several generalizations of (deterministic) decision rules have been discussed, like non–deterministic or probabilistic rules. Many authors have discussed the problem of decision rule synthesis from data and the problem of rule evaluation. In particular, Boolean reasoning in combination with rough set methods proved to be very useful for decision rule synthesis as well as in preprocessing of data, in particular in problems of discretization and scaling, missing values, new feature extraction, (probabilistic) pattern extraction. New methods of pattern extraction and decision rules generation from data are discussed. They are based on heuristics for extraction from data of (sub)-optimal similarity relations. These methods have been successfully applied to problems of real–life data analysis in object classification, data mining or decision support. Relationship between methods based on rough set theory and those developed by Machine Learning community have also been intensively studied.

Case studies. One of the main criterions for evaluation of the quality of new methodology in soft computing is its usefulness in analysis of real–life data. Case studies presented in the book are showing that rough set methods are successful in many areas of applications. Real–life applications of rough tools in e.g. medicine and health care, civil engineering, information retrieval, economy, marketing, industry, audio signal processing are based on proprietary software systems constructed on rough set theory lines. Rough classifiers induced by means of these systems have proved to be fully on par with other now existing in use tools for Knowledge Discovery and Data Mining. Many specific examples of the case studies are collected in Part 2 and they are presented briefly below.

Hybrid systems. It is an experience of soft computing community that hybrid systems combining different soft computing techniques in one system can often improve the quality of the constructed system. This has also been claimed in case of rough set methods that combined with neural networks, genetic algorithms and evolutionary programming, statistical inference tools or Petri nets may give better solutions. In this book we offer a number of chapters on hybrid systems showing the results which bear out this claim.To be specific: adding statistical tools can improve the quality of decision rules induced by rough set methods. Rough set based data reduction can be very useful in preprocessing of data input to neural networks. Decision algorithms synthesized by rough set methods can be used in designing neural networks. Rough set ideas can lead to new models of neurons. Optimization heuristics based on evolutionary programs can efficiently generate rough set constructs like reducts, patterns in data, decision rules. Rough set methods can be useful in specifying concurrent systems from which corresponding Petri nets can be automatically generated. Rough sets combined with fuzzy sets and Petri nets give an efficient method for designing clock information systems.

Rule induction systems. Software systems for rule induction have been developed by various authors. These systems have been applied to data analysis and real–life problems. Of many existing systems, twelve are presented in APPENDIX 2.

Introducing the articles. Part 1: APPLICATIONS begins with the chapter *Rough approximation of a preference relation in a pairwise comparison table* in which SALVATORE GRECO, BENEDETTO MATARAZZO and ROMAN SŁOWIŃSKI propose a rough set based methodology for modeling preferences in multi - criterion decision problems. They introduce new relation approximations based on a set of graded dominance relations. An illustrative example of the proposed method concerning an analysis of a regional water supply system is given.

KRZYSZTOF KRAWIEC, ROMAN SŁOWIŃSKI and DANIEL VANDERPOOTEN in the chapter: *Learning decision rules from similarity based rough approximations*, present an approach to induction of decision rules employing usage of a similarity relation instead of an equivalence (indiscernibility) relation. Algorithms for extracting a particular type of similarity relation from data are presented. The results of experiments with different data tables are reported and compared with those obtained by using other methods.

SINH HOA NGUYEN, ANDRZEJ SKOWRON and PIOTR SYNAK report in the chapter: *Discovery of data patterns with applications to decomposition and classification problems* the results of a thorough study of theoretical and applicational issues related to the technique of discovering from data the so - called templates and patterns. The former allow to cluster data into "regular" sub-domains of the universe of objects. The latter are discovered by means of optimal, in a sense, similarity relations extracted from data. Experiments reported are showing that discovered templates and patterns allow to obtain decision rules with higher quality of classification of new objects.

ZBIGNIEW RAS in the chapter: *Answering non - standard queries in distributed knowledge - based systems* presents theoretical foundations as well as related methodological issues about the system *QRAS - NC* (*Query Rough Answering System with Negative Constraints)* aimed at answering queries in distributed knowledge based systems.

JAROSŁAW STEPANIUK in : *Approximation spaces, reducts and representatives,* discusses generalized approximation spaces in which equivalence relations are replaced with more general similarity (tolerance) relations. The counterparts of standard notions and algorithms are analyzed in this new context; in particular algorithms for the generation of various types of tolerance reducts and tolerance decision rules are proposed.

NING ZHONG, JU–ZHEN DONG and SETSUO OHSUGA in their chapter: *Data mining: a probabilistic rough set approach*, propose a methodology for discovering classifiers, guised as if - then rules, in data tables which combines rough set techniques with a probabilistic ingredient in the form of some a priori probability estimates for appearance of new instances in data which are used to determine strength of induced rules.

Part 2: CASE STUDIES is devoted to applications of rough set techniques to data classification and decision algorithm induction from data in various fields of expertise.

ANDRZEJ CZYŻEWSKI in the chapter: *Soft processing of audio signals* presents a digital signal processing system employing soft computing tools, among them rough set - based algorithms, for analysis of audio signals and includes results of experiments with speaker - independent recognition of digits and noise removal from speech as well as musical signals.

KANAME FUNAKOSHI and TU BAO HO in : *An approach to information retrieval using tolerance relations* propose an information retrieval technique based on rough approximations in a suitable tolerance space defined over a collection of terms in a database. Methodological assumptions, an algorithm and a case study of retrieving relevant to the user interest documents in a real database are presented.

HITOSHI FURUTA, MICHIYUKI HIROKANE and YUKIHIRO MIKUMO introduce in the chapter: *Extraction method, by rough set theory, of rule - type knowledge from diagnostic cases of slope - failure danger levels* a technique for inducing a minimal non - contradictory decision algorithm from data about slope failure danger levels.

BOŻENA KOSTEK in : *Soft computing - based recognition of musical sounds* presents soft computing - based tools, among them rough set tools, for recognizing objects in audio material, in particular the problem of recognition of selected musical instruments is addressed and the results of experiments are reported.

ADAM MRÓZEK and LESZEK PŁONKA in the chapter: *Rough sets in industrial applications*, explain rough set based methodology for synthesis of a rough controller from experimental data tables. The approach is illustrated with examples of applications in industrial control of a rotary clinker kiln and a chemical reactor. Authors discuss the advantages of the proposed approach as well as some problems related to it. A comparison with fuzzy controllers is included.

ADAM MRÓZEK and KRZYSZTOF SKABEK discuss in: *Rough sets in economic applications* some examples of using rough sets in support of economic decision - making. They illustrate their methodology with examples on evaluating a company value, aiding bank credit policy and creating a marketing strategy of a company.

KRZYSZTOF SŁOWIŃSKI and JERZY STEFANOWSKI in: *Multistage rough set analysis of therapeutic experience with acute pancreatitis*, study a case of rough set applications in medical multi - stage diagnosis aimed at selecting sets of the most important attributes for determining the therapeutic course. Exemplary analysis of medical data is presented supported by the system *Rough Das* for reduct generation and the algorithm *LEM2* for inducing strong decision rules.

HIDEO TANAKA and YUTAKA MAEDA devote the chapter: *Reduction methods for medical data* to a case study of medical diagnosis in hepatic disease. They propose some heuristics for reducing information systems and for scaling attributes and illustrate their approach with an example from clinical practice.

SHUSAKU TSUMOTO in the chapter: *Formalization and induction of medical expert system rules based on rough set theory* introduces a system *PRIMEROSE - REX (Probabilistic Rule Induction MEthod based on ROugh SEts and Resampling methods for EXpert systems)*. He reports the results of application of PRIMEROSE - REX to some clinical databases to extract decision rules supporting the diagnosis and presents a comparison of received results with those obtained by using rules generated by some known empirical learning methods as well as rules delivered by medical experts.

DIRK Van der POEL is concerned in the chapter: *Rough sets for database marketing* with modeling of a response to marketing. He compares the performance of various tools: based on discriminant analysis, logistic regression, neural networks, C45, rough set systems *ProbRough* and *LERS*, classification and regression trees, and chi - squared automatic interaction detector on a real–life data sample and reports the results of experiments.

HUANGLIN ZENG and ROMAN SWINIARSKI propose in the chapter: *A new halftoning method based on error diffusion with rough set filtering* an averaging rough - set - based algorithm for converting a continuous tone image into a halftone image. They include a comparison of the new technique with the method based on an adaptive error diffusion.

Part 3: HYBRID APPROACHES opens up with a report: *IRIS revisited: a comparison of discriminant and enhanced rough set data analysis* by CIARÁN BROWNE, IVO DÜNTSCH and GÜNTHER GEDIGA in which the standard data set *IRIS* is analyzed by means of classical Fischer discriminant analysis as well as by means of rough set - based *ROUGHIAN* system. A comparison of the results with some early results obtained by means of rough sets is offered which points to the usefulness of adding statistical tools to rough set methods.

PAWAN LINGRAS in: *Applications of rough patterns* discusses neural networks enhanced by a rough set ingredient viz. rough neurons. Methodological analysis is presented followed by applications to pattern classification by rough Kohonen - type neural networks, to estimation of important highway traffic parameter and to time series analysis of highway traffic volume.

JAMES F. PETERS III in: *Time and clock information systems: concepts and roughly fuzzy Petri net models* proposes a new class of Petri nets: roughly fuzzy Petri nets in which new models of clock representation systems are discussed. Some applications are pointed to aimed at extracting rough fuzzy approximations from universes of fuzzy objects.

ZBIGNIEW SURAJ attempts in his chapter: *The synthesis problem of concurrent systems specified by dynamic information systems* to give an approach to concurrency based on rough set - theoretic ideas. Introducing a new notion of a dynamic information system, he proposes a method for constructing an elementary net system equivalent to a given dynamic information system in the sense that the related transition systems are isomorphic. This provides a method for synthesis of a concurrent system specified by a dynamic information system.

MARCIN SZCZUKA in: *Rough sets and artificial neural networks* presents a survey of several approaches to linking rough sets and artificial neural networks. He discusses usage of rough sets as a preprocessor of data for neural networks, networks of rough neurons as well as rough set methods for synthesis of neural networks.

JAKUB WRÓBLEWSKI in the chapter: *Genetic algorithms in decomposition and classification problems* introduces hybrid algorithms i.e. non - deterministic problem - oriented heuristics controlled by a genetic algorithm. He discusses methodological foundations and points to applications of these algorithms in solving basic rough set problems.

APPENDIX 1: ROUGH SET BIBLIOGRAPHY contains a list of about 1100 research papers in rough set theory and its applications which will prove a valuable source of information for researchers interested in this theory.

APPENDIX 2: SOFTWARE SYSTEMS consists of twelve articles describing some of the existing software tools for rule induction and classification based on rough set methods. The reader will find here brief descriptions of the following systems.

Ivo Düntsch and Günther Gediga describe **GROBIAN** - the system for rough information analysis which emphasizes non - invasive data filtering and statistical validation of approximate reducts.

Maria C. Fernandez Baizan, Ernestina Menasalvas Ruiz, José M. Peña and Borja Pardo Pastrana present **RSDM** - the system for Data Mining employing rough set methodologies.

Jerzy Grzymala - Busse describes **LERS** - the system for knowledge discovery based on rough set rule inducing techniques. Algorithms of **LERS** allow either for induction of rules in the minimal discriminant form or for induction of all potential rules hidden in data. The system handles data with missing values, is able to classify new cases and performs multiple - fold crossvalidation.

TRANCE - a system for generating rough models of data (i.e. partitions of the data into clusters representing decisions) is presented by Wojciech Kowalczyk. **TRANCE** performs the automatic search for a partition which does optimize a given measure of performance.

Andrzej Lenarcik and Zdzisław Piasta outline **ProbRough** - a system for inducing rules from data employing background knowledge in the form of prior probabilities of decisions and predefined costs of misclassifications.

Alexander Øhrn, Jan Komorowski, Andrzej Skowron and Piotr Synak present **ROSETTA** - the software system designed to support the overall knowledge discovery process from preprocessing routines through rule generation to validation of induced rules. The system offers a GUI environment allowing for interactive manipulating and processing of objects.

RSL - the Rough Set Library is a collection of routines in C language working in UNIX as well as MS - DOS or MS Windows environments written at the Institute of Computer Science of Warsaw University of Technology.

Rough Family presented by Roman Słowiński and Jerzy Stefanowski is a software package whose programs implement basic functions of the rough set approach to rule induction. The package enables rough set based analysis of data, extraction of characteristic patterns from data, induction of decision rules from learning samples, validation of rules and construction of decision algorithms. The system has facilities enabling handling uncertainty in data sets.

Zbigniew Suraj describes **TAS** - the system for automatic analysis and synthesis of models of concurrent processes discovered in data tables. **TAS** enables one to build parallel programs for decision - making based on a given decision table.

Roman Swiniarski presents **RoughFuzzyLab** - the system for data mining and knowledge discovery based on rough and fuzzy set theories and intended especially for the treatment of databases containing images.

Shusaku Tsumoto describes **Primerose** - the system for inducing probabilistic rules from databases allowing for the statistical analysis of induced rules. The system is oriented towards applications in medical knowledge discovery.

KDD - R described by Wojciech Ziarko is the system offering a comprehensive set of tools for data mining based on variable precision rough sets model proposed by the Author. The system is targeted towards market research and can be also employed in medical data analysis or sensory data analysis in control problems.

We would like to express our hope that this collection will render soft computing community, in particular rough set community, a service by bringing together articles by many leading experts in the field of rough set theory and applications which picture the state of the art in this area and its relations with other paradigms of soft computing. We would like to extend our thanks to all authors who made this collection possible by their contributions. Our special thanks go to Professors Zdzisław Pawlak and Lotfi Zadeh for their constant encouragement and support.

The Editors

PART 1:

APPLICATIONS

Chapter 2

Rough Approximation of a Preference Relation in a Pairwise Comparison Table

Salvatore Greco[1], *Benedetto Matarazzo*[1] *and Roman Słowiński*[2]

[1] Faculty of Economics, University of Catania, Corso Italia, 55, 95129 Catania, Italy
[2] Institute of Computing Science, Poznan University of Technology, 60-965 Poznan, Poland

Abstract. A methodology for using rough sets for preference modelling in multi-criteria decision problems is presented. It operates on a pairwise comparison table (PCT), i.e. an information table whose objects are pairs of actions instead of single actions, and whose entries are binary relations (graded preference relations) instead of attribute values. PCT is a specific information table and, therefore, all the concepts of the rough set analysis can be adapted to it. However, the classical rough set approximations based on indiscernibility relation do not consider the ordinal properties of the criteria in a decision problem. To deal with these properties, a rough approximation based on graded dominance relations has been recently proposed. The decision rules obtained from these rough approximations can be used to obtain a recommendation in different multi-criteria decision problems. The methodology is illustrated by an example which compares the results obtained when using the rough approximation by indiscernibility relation and the rough approximation by graded dominance relations, respectively.
Keywords: Rough set theory, Pairwise comparison table, Multi-criteria decision problems, Preference modelling, Decision rules.

1 Introduction

Solving a multi-criteria decision problem means to give the decision maker (DM) a recommendation (Roy, 1993) in terms of the best actions (choice), or of the assignement of the actions to pre-defined categories (sorting), or of the ranking of actions from the best to the worst (ranking). None of these recommendations can be elaborated before the DM provides some preferential information suitable to the preference model assumed.

There are two major models used until now for preference modelling in multi-criteria decision analysis: functional and relational ones. The functional model has been extensively used within the framework of multi-attribute utility theory (Keeney and Raiffa, 1976). The relational model has its most widely known representation in the form of an outranking relation (Roy, 1991) and a fuzzy relation (Fodor and Roubens, 1994). These models require specific preferential information more or less explicitly related with their parameters. For example, in the deterministic case, the DM is often asked for pairwise comparisons of actions, from which one can assess the substitution rates in the functional model or importance weights in the relational model (cf. Fishburn, 1967; Jacquet-Lagrèze and Siskos, 1982; Mousseau, 1993). This kind of preferential information seems to be close to the natural reasoning of the DM. He/she is typically more confident exercising his/her comparisons than explaining them. The transformation of this information into functional or relational models seems, however, less natural. According to Slovic (1975), people make decisions by searching for rules which provide good justification of their choices. So, after getting the preferential information in terms of exemplary comparisons, it would be natural to build the preference model in terms of "if ... then ..." rules. Then, these rules can be applied to a set of potential actions in order to obtain specific preference relations. From the exploitation of these relations, a suitable recommendation can be obtained to support the DM in decision problem at hand.

The induction of rules from examples is a typical approach of artificial intelligence. It is concordant with the principle of posterior rationality by March (1988) and with aggregation-disaggregation logic by Jacquet-Lagrèze (1981). The rules represent the preferential attitude of the DM and enable his/her understanding of the reasons of his/her preference. The recognition of the rules by the DM justifies their use for decision support. So, the preference model in the form of rules derived from examples, fulfils both representation and recommendation tasks (cf. Roy, 1993).

This explains our interest in the rough set theory (Pawlak, 1982, 1991), which proved to be a useful tool for the analysis of vague description of decision situations (Pawlak and Slowinski, 1994). An important advantage of the rough set approach is that it can deal with a set of inconsistent examples, i.e. objects indiscernible by condition attributes but discernible by decision attributes. Moreover, it provides useful information about the role of particular subsets of attributes in the approximation of decision classes, and prepares the ground for generation of decision rules involving relevant attributes.

Until now, however, the use of rough sets has been restricted to the sorting problems (Slowinski, 1993), i.e. to the analysis of classifications (partitions). This use is straightforward because the sorting examples can be directly put in the information table analysed by the rough set approach. In the case of choice and ranking problems, this straightforward use is not possible because the information table in its original form does not allow the representation of preference orders between actions.

To handle the ordinal character of criteria, Greco, Matarazzo and Slowinski (1995) proposed to operate the rough set approach on, so called, pairwise comparison table (PCT), i.e. a decision table whose objects are pairs of actions for which multi-criteria evaluations and a comprehensive preference relation are known.

Some aspects of the ordinal properties of the criteria are not captured, however, by the PCT. The use of an indiscernibility relation on the PCT makes problems with interpretation of the approximations of the preference relation and of the decision rules derived from these approximations. Indiscernibility permits handling inconsistency which occurs when two pairs of actions have preferences of the same strength on considered criteria, however, the comprehensive preference relations established for these pairs are not the same. When we deal with criteria, there may arrive also another type of inconsistency connected with the dominance principle: one pair of actions is characterized by some preferences on a given set of criteria and another pair has all preferences at least of the same strength, however, for the first pair we have preference and for the other – inverse preference. This is why indiscernibility relation is not able to handle all kinds of inconsistencies connected with the use of criteria. For this reason, Greco, Matarazzo and Slowinski (1996) proposed another way of defining the approximations and decision rules, which is based on the use of graded dominance relations.

The paper is structured as follows. In the next section we recall some concepts of the rough set theory used throughout the paper. Section 3 presents the PCT. In section 4 we introduce the rough approximation of a preference relation by means of the graded dominance relations defined on the PCT. Section 5 is devoted to the generation of decision rules from the rough approximation by graded dominance relations. In section 6 we investigate the exploitation of decision rules in the framework of a given multi-criteria decision problem. Section 7 presents an illustrative example. In this example we consider the rough approximation by indiscernibility relation and the rough approximation by graded dominance relations, and we compare the respective results. Section 8 groups conclusions.

2 Introductory remarks about the rough set theory

2.1 The general idea

The rough set concept proposed by Pawlak (1982, 1991) is founded on the assumption that with every object of the universe of discourse there is associated some information (data, knowledge). For example, if objects are firms submitted to a bankruptcy evaluation, their financial, economic and technical characteristics form information (description) about the firms. Objects characterized by the same description are indiscernible (similar) in view of available data. The *indiscernibility relation* generated in this way is an equivalence relation and it is the mathematical basis of the rough set theory.

Any set of indiscernible objects is called an elementary set and forms a basic granule of knowledge (atom) about the universe. Any subset Y of the universe can either be expressed precisely in terms of the granules or roughly only. In the latter case, subset Y can be characterized by two ordinary sets, called *lower and upper approximations*. These two approximations define the *rough set*. The lower approximation of Y consists of all elementary sets included in Y, whereas the upper approximation of Y consists of all elementary sets having a non-empty intersection with Y. Obviously, the difference between the upper and the lower approximations constitutes the *boundary region*, including objects which cannot be properly classified as belonging or not to Y, using the available data.

Cardinality of the boundary region says, moreover, how exactly we can describe Y in terms of available data.

If approximation concerns a partition of a finite set of objects U into classes, then one can speak, analogously, about lower and upper approximations of the partition (classification). Then, the ratio of the sum of cardinalities of lower approximations of the classes to the cardinality of set U is the *quality of approximation* of the classification or, in short, *quality of classification.*

2.2 Information table

For algorithmic reasons, information about objects will be represented in the form of an information table. The rows of the table are labelled by *objects,* whereas columns are labelled by *attributes* and entries of the table are *attribute-values.* In general, the notion of attribute differs from that of criterion, because the domain (scale) of a criterion has to be ordered according to a decreasing or increasing preference, while the domain of an attribute does not have to be ordered. We will use the notion of criterion when the preferential ordering of the attribute domain will be important in a given context. Formally, by an *information table* we understand the 4-tuple $S = \langle U, Q, V, f \rangle$, where U is a finite set of objects, Q is a finite set of *attributes,* $V = \bigcup_{q \in Q} V_q$ and V_q is a domain of the attribute q, and $f : U \times Q \rightarrow V$ is a total function such that $f(x, q) \in V_q$ for every $q \in Q$, $x \in U$, called an *information function* (cf. Pawlak, 1991).

Rough set analysis of an information table permits to find out reducts and core of the set of attributes. A *reduct* consists of a minimal subset of independent attributes ensuring the same quality of classification as the whole set. There can be more than one reduct. The intersection of all the reducts is the *core.* It represents a collection of the most important attributes, i.e. the set of all the attributes which cannot be eliminated without decreasing the quality of classification.

2.3 Decision rules derived from rough approximations

An information table can be seen as a *decision table* assuming that the set of attributes $Q = C \cup D$ and $C \cap D = \emptyset$, where set C contains, so called, *condition attributes,* and D, *decision attributes.*

From the decision table, a set of *decision rules* can be derived and expressed as logical statements "if ... then ..." relating descriptions of condition classes and decision classes. The rules are *exact* or *approximate* depending whether a description of a condition class corresponds to a unique decision class or not. Different procedures for derivation of decision rules have been proposed (e.g. by Slowinski and Stefanowski, 1992; Grzymala-Busse, 1992; Skowron, 1993; Mienko, Stefanowski, Toumi and Vanderpooten, 1996; Ziarko, Golan and Edwards, 1993).

3 Pairwise comparison table

Let A be a finite set of actions (fictious or not, feasible or not), considered in the multi-criteria decision problem at hand. The preference model is being built using a preferential information provided by the DM. This information concerns a set $B \subseteq A$ of, so called, *reference actions,* with respect to which the DM is willing to express his/her attitude through pairwise comparisons. The pairwise comparisons are considered as exemplary decisions. We are distinguishing two kinds of them:

- historical,
- simulated.

Historical examples represent actual decisions taken by the DM in the past. Simulated examples represent decisions taken by the DM on fictitious or real reference actions with the aim of using them for preference modelling.

In order to represent the preferential information, we shall use a pairwise comparison table introduced in (Greco, Matarazzo and Slowinski, 1995).

Let C be the set of criteria (condition attributes) describing the actions. For any criterion $q \in C$, let V_q be its domain and T_q a finite set of binary relations defined on V_q such that $\forall v'_q, v''_q \in V_q$ exactly one binary relation $t \in T_q$ is verified. For interesting applications it should be card$(T_q) \geq 2$, $\forall q \in C$.

Furthermore, let T_d be a set of binary relations defined on set A (comprehensive pairwise comparisons) such that at most one binary relation $t \in T_d$ is verified $\forall x, y \in A$.

The *pairwise comparison table* (PCT) is defined as information table $S_{PCT} = \langle \mathbf{B}, C \cup \{d\}, T_C \cup T_d, g \rangle$, where $\mathbf{B} \subseteq B \times B$ is a non-empty *set of exemplary pairwise comparisons of reference actions,* $T_C = \cup_{q \in C} T_q$, d is a decision corresponding to the comprehensive pairwise comparison (comprehensive preference relation), and $g : \mathbf{B} \times (C \cup \{d\}) \to T_C \cup T_d$ is a total function such that $\forall (x,y) \in \mathbf{B}$, $g[(x,y),q] \in T_q$, $\forall q \in C$, and $g[(x,y),d] \in T_d$. It follows that for any pair of reference actions $(x,y) \in \mathbf{B}$ there is verified one and only onc binary relation $t \in T_d$. Thus, T_d induces a partition of $\mathbf{B}$. In fact, information table S_{PCT} can be seen as a decision table, since the set of considered criteria C and decision d are distinguished.

In this paper, we consider S_{PCT} related to the choice and the ranking problems (Roy, 1985) and assume that the exemplary pairwise comparisons provided by the DM can be represented in terms of *binary graded preference relations* defined on V_q:

$$T_q = \{P_q^h,\ h \in H_q\},$$

where $H_q = \{h \in Z : h \in [-p_q, r_q]\}$ and $p_q, r_q \in Z^+$ $\forall q \in C$. For any pair of actions $(x,y) \in A \times A$,

$xP_q^h y$, $h > 0$, means that action x is preferred to action y by degree h with respect to criterion q,

$xP_q^h y$, $h < 0$, means that action x is not preferred to action y by degree h with respect to criterion q,

$xP_q^0 y$ means that x is similar (asymmetrically indifferent) to y with respect to criterion q.

We assume that exactly one binary relation P_q^h is verified for any q and for any pair of actions. Of course, xP_q^0x, $\forall x \in A$, and $\forall q \in C$, i.e. P_q^0 is reflexive, and $\forall x, y \in A$

$$[xP_q^h y,\ h \geq 0] \Leftrightarrow [yP_q^k x,\ k \leq 0].$$

Therefore, $\forall (x,y),(w,z) \in A \times A$ and $q \in C$:

- if $xP_q^h y$ and $wP_q^k z$, $k \geq h \geq 0$, then w is preferred to z not less than x is preferred to y with respect to criterion q;
- if $xP_q^h y$ and $wP_q^k z$, $k \leq h \leq 0$, then w is not preferred to z not less than x is not preferred to y with respect to criterion q.

The set of binary relations T_d is defined analogously; however, $xP_d^h y$ means that x is comprehensively preferred to y by degree h.

Since $q \in C$ is a criterion, i.e. there exists a function $c_q : A \to R$ such that $\forall x, y \in A$, $c_q(x) \geq c_q(y)$ means "x is at least as good as y with respect to q" (Roy, 1985), then, in order to define the set of preference relations T_q one can use a function $k_q : R^2 \to R$ satisfying the following properties $\forall x, y, z \in A$:

$$c_q(x) > c_q(y) \Leftrightarrow k_q[c_q(x), c_q(z)] > k_q[c_q(y), c_q(z)],$$

$$c_q(x) > c_q(y) \Leftrightarrow k_q[c_q(z), c_q(x)] < k_q[c_q(z), c_q(y)],$$

$$c_q(x) = c_q(y) \Leftrightarrow k_q[c_q(x), c_q(y)] = 0.$$

The function $k_q[c_q(x), c_q(y)]$ measures *the strength of* positive (when $c_q(x) > c_q(y)$) or negative (when $c_q(x) < c_q(y)$) *preference* of x over y with respect to q. Typical representatives of k_q are

$$k_q[c_q(x), c_q(y)] = c_q(x) - c_q(y)$$

and, if $c_q(z) > 0\ \forall z \in A$,

$$k_q[c_q(x), c_q(y)] = \frac{c_q(x)}{c_q(y)} - 1.$$

Other kinds of measures of the strength of preference $k_q[c_q(x), c_q(y)]$ could be used as well (see e.g. Brans and Vincke, 1985).

The strength of preference represented by k_q is then transformed into a specific binary relation P_q^h using a set of thresholds

$$\Delta_q = \{\Delta_q^h,\ h = -p_q - 1, -p_q, \ldots, -1, 1, \ldots, r_q, r_q + 1:$$

$$\Delta_q^h < 0 \text{ if } h < 0,\ \Delta_q^h > 0 \text{ if } h > 0,\ \Delta_q^h > \Delta_q^{h-1},\ \forall h > -p_q - 1\},$$

where

$$\Delta_q^{-p_q-1} = \min_{(x,y)\in A\times A} \{k_q[c_q(x), c_q(y)]\}$$

and

$$\Delta_q^{r_q+1} = \max_{(x,y)\in A\times A} \{k_q[c_q(x), c_q(y)]\}.$$

On the basis of the thresholds of the set Δ_q a set of intervals I_q is obtained:

$$I_q = \{[\Delta_q^{-p_q-1}, \Delta_q^{-p_q}), (\Delta_q^{-p_q}, \Delta_q^{-p_q+1}), \dots (\Delta_q^{r_q-1}, \Delta_q^{r_q}), (\Delta_q^{r_q}, \Delta_q^{r_q+1}]\},$$

where the extreme left and right intervals are closed on the left and on the right, respectively, and other intervals have closed or open bounds according to the condition that if an interval is open (closed) on the right, the next interval to the right (if it exists) is closed (open) on the left.

Thus we can state :

$$k_q[c_q(x), c_q(y)] \in (\Delta_q^h, \Delta_q^{h+1}) \Leftrightarrow xP_q^h y \text{ for } h \in H_q \text{ and } h > 0,$$

$$k_q[c_q(x), c_q(y)] \in (\Delta_q^{h-1}, \Delta_q^h) \Leftrightarrow xP_q^h y \text{ for } h \in H_q \text{ and } h < 0$$

and

$$k_q[c_q(x), c_q(y)] \in (\Delta_q^{-1}, \Delta_q^1) \Leftrightarrow xP_q^0 y.$$

The above definitions allow us to express any type of multiple relational preference structures (on these subject see e.g. Roberts, 1971; Cozzens and Roberts, 1982; Roubens and Vincke, 1985; Doignon *et al.*, 1986; Doignon, 1987; Tsoukias and Moreno, 1996).

4 Rough approximation by graded dominance relations

Let $H_P = \bigcap_{q \in P} H_q$, $\forall P \subseteq C$. Given $x, y \in A$, $P \subseteq C$ and $h \in H_P$, we say that x positively dominates y by degree h with respect to the set of criteria P iff $xP_q^f y$ with $f \geq h$, $\forall q \in P$. Analogously, $\forall x, y \in A$, $P \subseteq C$ and $h \in H_P$, x negatively dominates y by degree h with respect to the set of criteria P iff $xP_q^f y$ with $f \leq h$ $\forall q \in P$. Thus, $\forall h \in H_P$ every $P \subseteq C$ generates two binary relations (eventually empty) on A which will be called *P-positive-dominance of degree h*, denoted by D_{+P}^h, and *P-negative-dominance of degree h*, denoted by D_{-P}^h, respectively. The relations D_{+P}^h and D_{-P}^h satisfy the following properties:

(P1) if $(x, y) \in D_{+P}^h$ then $(x, y) \in D_{+R}^k$, $\forall R \subseteq P$ and $k \leq h$;
(P2) if $(x, y) \in D_{-P}^h$ then $(x, y) \in D_{-R}^k$, $\forall R \subseteq P$ and $k \geq h$.

In the following we consider a PCT where the decision d can have only two values on $\mathbf{B} \subseteq A \times A$:

- either x outranks y, which will be denoted by xSy or $(x, y) \in S$,
- or x does not outrank y, which will be denoted by $xS^c y$ or $(x, y) \in S^c$,

where "x outranks y" means "x is at least as good as y" (Roy, 1985). Let us remember that the minimal property verified by the outranking relation S is reflexivity (cf. Roy, 1991; Bouyssou, 1996).

We propose to approximate the binary relation S by means of the binary dominance relation D_{+P}^h. Therefore, S is seen as a rough binary relation (cf. Greco, Matarazzo and Slowinski, 1995).

The P-*lower approximation* of S (cf. Greco, Matarazzo and Slowinski, 1996), denoted by $\underline{P}S$, and the P-*upper approximation* of S, denoted by $\overline{P}S$, are respectively defined as:

$$\underline{P}S = \bigcup_{h \in H_P} \{(D^h_{+P} \cap \mathbf{B}) \subseteq S\},$$

$$\overline{P}S = \bigcap_{h \in H_P} \{(D^h_{+P} \cap \mathbf{B}) \supseteq S\}.$$

Taking into account property (P1) of the dominance relations D^h_{+P}, $\underline{P}S$ can be viewed as the dominance relation D^h_{+P} which has the largest intersection with $\mathbf{B}$ included in the outranking relation S and $\overline{P}S$ as the dominance relation D^h_{+P} including S which has the smallest intersection with $\mathbf{B}$.

Analogously, we can approximate S^c by means of the binary dominance relation D^h_{-P}:

$$\underline{P}S^c = \bigcup_{h \in H_P} \{(D^h_{-P} \cap \mathbf{B}) \subseteq S^c\},$$

$$\overline{P}S^c = \bigcap_{h \in H_P} \{(D^h_{-P} \cap \mathbf{B}) \supseteq S^c\}.$$

The interpretation of $\underline{P}S^c$ and $\overline{P}S^c$ is similar to the interepretation of $\underline{P}S$ and $\overline{P}S$. Taking into account property (P2) of the dominance relations D^h_{-P}, $\underline{P}S^c$ can be viewed as the dominance relation D^h_{-P} which has the largest intersection with $\mathbf{B}$ included in the negation of S and $\overline{P}S^c$ as the dominance relation D^h_{-P} including the negation of S which has the smallest intersection with $\mathbf{B}$.

Notice that the above definitions of rough approximations of S and S^c do not satisfy the property of complementarity, i.e. $\underline{P}S$ is, in general, non-equal to $\mathbf{B} - \overline{P}S^c$ and $\underline{P}S^c$ is, in general, non-equal to $\mathbf{B} - \overline{P}S$. This is due to the fact that S and S^c are approximated with different approximating sets: D^h_{+P} and D^h_{-P}, respectively. Nevertheless, the obtained approximations create a good basis for generation of simple decision rules.

5 Decision rules derived from rough approximations of S and S^c

We can derive a generalized description of the preferential information contained in a given PCT in terms of decision rules.

If the approximations of S and S^c were made using the classical indiscernibility relation on a PCT, then we could obtain the decision rules being statements of the following types (cf. Greco, Matarazzo and Slowinski, 1995):

- $[xP^{h_1}_{q_1}y$ and $\ldots, xP^{h_t}_{q_t}y] \Rightarrow xSy$, where $\{q_1, \ldots, q_t\} \subseteq C$, and $h_1 \in H_{q_1}, \ldots$ $h_t \in H_{q_t}$, or
- $[xP^{k_1}_{s_1}y$ and $\ldots, xP^{k_u}_{s_u}y] \Rightarrow xS^c y$, where $\{s_1, \ldots, s_u\} \subseteq C$, and $k_1 \in H_{q_1}, \ldots$ $k_u \in H_{q_u}$.

Considering approximations of S and S^c by graded dominance relations, we get the decision rules being statemens of the following types:

- D_{++}-decision rule, being a statement of the type: $xD^h_{+P}y \Rightarrow xSy$;
- D_{+-}-decision rule, being a statement of the type: *not* $xD^h_{+P}y \Rightarrow xS^cy$;
- D_{-+}-decision rule, being a statement of the type: *not* $xD^h_{-P}y \Rightarrow xSy$;
- D_{--}-decision rule, being a statement of the type: $xD^h_{-P}y \Rightarrow xS^cy$.

The constructive definition of the considered decision rules is as follows.

If

(P3) [**(P5)**] there is at least one pair $(w,z) \in \mathbf{B}$ such that $wD^h_{+P}z$ [$wD^h_{-P}z$] and wSz [wS^cz],
and
(P4) [**(P6)**] there is no $(v,u) \in \mathbf{B}$ such that $vD^h_{+P}u$ [$vD^h_{-P}u$] and vS^cu [vSu],

then $xD^h_{+P}y \Rightarrow xSy$ [$xD^h_{-P}y \Rightarrow xS^cy$] is accepted as a D_{++}-decision rule [D_{--}-decision rule].

Analogously, if

(P7) [**(P9)**] there is at least one pair $(w,z) \in \mathbf{B}$ such that *not* $wD^h_{+P}z$ [*not* $wD^h_{-P}z$] and wS^cz [wSz],
and
(P8) [**(P10)**] there is no $(v,u) \in \mathbf{B}$ such that *not* $vD^h_{+P}u$ [*not* $vD^h_{-P}u$] and vSu [vS^cu],

then *not* $xD^h_{+P}y \Rightarrow xS^cy$ [*not* $xD^h_{-P}y \Rightarrow xSy$] is accepted as a D_{+-}-decision rule [D_{-+}-decision rule].

A D_{++}-decision rule [D_{+-}-decision rule] $xD^h_{+P}y \Rightarrow xSy$ [*not* $xD^h_{+R}y \Rightarrow xS^cy$] will be called *minimal* if there is not any other rule $xD^k_{+R}y \Rightarrow xSy$ [*not* $xD^k_{+R}y \Rightarrow xS^cy$] such that $R \subseteq P$ and $k \leq h$ [$k \geq h$]. A D_{-+}-decision rule [D_{--}-decision rule] *not* $xD^h_{-P}y \Rightarrow xSy$ [$xD^h_{-P}y \Rightarrow xS^cy$] will be called minimal if there is not any other rule *not* $xD^k_{-R}y \Rightarrow xSy$ [$xD^k_{-R}y \Rightarrow xS^cy$] such that $R \subseteq P$ and $k \leq h$ [$k \geq h$].

Let us observe that, since each decision rule is an implication, the minimal decision rules represent the implications such that there is no other implication with an antecedent of at least the same weakness and a consequent of at least the same strength.

Theorem 1 (Greco, Matarazzo, Slowinski, 1996). *If*

- $xD^h_{+P}y \Rightarrow xSy$ *is a minimal* D_{++}*-decision rule, then* $\underline{P}S = D^h_{+P} \cap \mathbf{B}$*;*
- $xD^h_{-P}y \Rightarrow xS^cy$ *is a minimal* D_{--}*-decision rule, then* $\underline{P}S^c = D^h_{-P} \cap \mathbf{B}$*;*
- not $xD^h_{+P}y \Rightarrow xS^cy$ *is a minimal* D_{+-}*-decision rule, then* $\overline{P}S = D^h_{+P} \cap \mathbf{B}$*;*
- not $xD^h_{-P}y \Rightarrow xSy$ *is a minimal* D_{-+}*-decision rule, then* $\overline{P}S^c = D^h_{-P} \cap \mathbf{B}$.

6 Application of decision rules and definition of a final recommendation

The decision rules derived from rough approximations of S and S^c are then applied to a set of actions $M \subseteq A$. The application of rules obtained using the classical indiscernibility relation lead to straightforward conclusions about S and S^c for any given pair $(u, v) \in M \times M$.

If approximations are made by graded dominance relations, then the application of rules to any pair of actions $(u, v) \in M \times M$ means to state the presence (uSv) or the absence ($uS^c v$) of outranking relation using the following implications:

- if $xD^h_{+P}y \Rightarrow xSy$ is a D_{++}-decision rule and $uD^h_{+P}v$, we conclude that uSv;
- if *not* $xD^h_{+P}y \Rightarrow xS^c y$ is a D_{+-}-decision rule and *not* $uD^h_{+P}v$, we conclude that $uS^c v$;
- if *not* $xD^h_{-P}y \Rightarrow xSy$ is a D_{-+}-decision rule and *not* $uD^h_{-P}v$, we conclude that uSv;
- if $xD^h_{-P}y \Rightarrow xS^c y$ is a D_{--}-decision rule and $uD^h_{-P}v$, we conclude that $uS^c v$.

With respect to each pair of actions $(u, v) \in M \times M$, we get one of the following four states (cf. Tsoukias and Vincke 1992, 1994):

- uSv and *not* $uS^c v$, i.e. true outranking , denoted by $uS^T v$;
- $uS^c v$ and *not* uSv, i.e. false outranking, denoted by $uS^F v$;
- uSv and $uS^c v$, i.e. contradictory outranking, denoted by $uS^K v$;
- *not* uSv and *not* $uS^c v$, i.e. unknown outranking, denoted by $uS^U v$.

These four states constitute the four-valued outranking relations. They are introduced in order to underline the presence and the absence of positive and negative reasons of outranking. Furthermore, they allow to distinguish contradictory from unknown situations.

Theorem 2 (Greco, Matarazzo, Slowinski, 1996). *The application of all the decision rules obtained for a given S_{PCT} on any pair of actions $(u, v) \in M \times M$ results in the same outranking relation as obtained by the application of the minimal decision rules only.*

From Theorem 2 we conclude that the set of all decision rules is completely characterized by the set of the minimal rules. Therefore, only the latter ones are presented to the DM and applied to work out a recommendation.

Once decision rules based on indiscernibility relations or dominance relations have been applied on the set of actions M, we can define a recommendation with respect to the decision problem at hand. To this aim we can calculate a particular score for the actions of M.

Let be

$$S^{++}(x) = \text{card}\{y \in M : \text{there is at least one decision rule stating that } xSy\},$$

$S^{+-}(x) = \text{card}\{y \in M : \text{there is at least one decision rule stating that } ySx\}$,
$S^{-+}(x) = \text{card}\{y \in M : \text{there is at least one decision rule stating that } yS^cx\}$,
$S^{--}(x) = \text{card}\{y \in M : \text{there is at least one decision rule stating that } xS^cy\}$.

To each $x \in M$ we assign a *score*, called Net Flow Score,

$$S_{\text{NF}}(x) = S^{++}(x) - S^{+-}(x) + S^{-+}(x) - S^{--}(x).$$

In ranking problems, we consider the total preorder established by $S_{\text{NF}}(x)$ on M. For choice problems, the final recommendation is $x^* \in M$ such that $S_{\text{NF}}(x^*) = \max_{x \in M} S_{\text{NF}}(x)$.

The proposed scoring procedure can be considered as an extension to the four-valued logic of the well-known Copeland ranking and choice method (see Goodman, 1954; Fishburn, 1973). These procedures have been characterized by Rubinstein (1980) and Henriet (1985) and, with respect to valued binary relations, by Bouyssou (1992a and b). As a ranking procedure, it was also used in the Multiple Criteria Decision Aid method PROMETHEE II (Brans and Vincke, 1985). Recently Greco *et al.* (1997) showed that the scoring procedure based on $S_{NF}(x)$ also satisfies some desirable properties.

7 Illustrative example

Let us consider a real example concerning the problem of programming water supply systems (WSSs) for use in the countryside, called regional WSSs.

According to the methodology proposed in (Roy, Slowinski, Treichel, 1992), the programming task is decomposed into two problems:

a) setting up a priority order in which the water users should be connected to a new WSS, taking into account economic, agricultural and sociological consequences of the investment; and
b) choosing the best technical variant of the regional WSS evaluated from technical and economic viewpoints and from the viewpoint of concordance with the priority-orders of users coming from problem (a).

In this paper, we are interested in problem (b). It has already been analysed using the PREFCALC method (Jacquet-Lagrèze, 1990), which consists in estimating a utility function by an ordinal regression (Jacquet-Lagrèze and Siskos, 1982). The input data to PREFCALC is a preferential information in the form of a weak order on a small subset of reference actions B. Let us remark the methods based on the ordinal regression, like PREFCALC, do not accept preferential information being neither inconsistent with the dominance principle nor incomplete in the sense of partial ranking. On the contrary, the rough set approach can deal with both inconsistent and partial preferential information.

In the following, we will use the same preferential information in order to illustrate our approach. The DM's preferential information is given in the form of a decreasing preference order on a subset of reference actions composed of seven technical variants (see Roy, Slowinski, Treichel, 1992). The technical variants are described by four characteristics to be minimised:

- investment cost,
- operating cost,
- reliability,
- distance betweeen technical programming and socio-economic priority order of water users.

This information is presented in Table 1. It is assumed that the ranking of the actions has the following interpretation: "If x is better ranked than y, then xSy and $yS^c x$."

Action	Variant	InvestCost	OperatCost	Reliability	Distance	Ranking
a_1	Var. 27_B	274.9	29.0	4.8	358	1
a_2	Var. 25_A	292.4	26.6	2.5	390	2
a_3	Var. 11_B	264.8	25.7	8.9	392	3
a_4	Var. 2_B	252.6	28.9	7.0	331	4
a_5	Var. 15_A	286.8	26.5	11.6	421	5
a_6	Var. 10_A	290.0	29.4	10.1	393	6
a_7	Var. 19_A	293.5	27.4	13.5	408	7

Table 1. Characteristics and ranking of the reference actions belonging to the set B.

As the criteria considered in the first part of our paper are increasing with preference, the four characteristics describing the variants become criteria after taking an opposite sign.

To measure the strength of preferences, we apply the following definition of function $k_q[c_q(x), c_q(y)]$:

$$k_q[c_q(x), c_q(y)] = c_q(x) - c_q(y), \quad \forall q \in C.$$

In order to apply the rough set approach, we define the sets of possible degrees of preference: $H_q = \{-3, -2, -1, 0, 1, 2, 3\}$, $\forall q \in C$.

$\forall q \in C$ the binary preference relations have the following interpretation:

$aP_q^3 b$ (and $bP_q^{-3} a$) means that a is strongly preferred to b with respect to q,
$aP_q^2 b$ (and $bP_q^{-2} a$) means that a is preferred to b with respect to q,
$aP_q^1 b$ (and $bP_q^{-1} a$) means that a is weakly preferred to b with respect to q,
$aP_q^0 b$ (and $bP_q^0 a$) means that a is indifferent to b with respect to q.

The thresholds used for the definition of the graded preference relations P_q^h have been obtained by means of the following procedure.

Let $\mathbf{B} = B \times B$. Then, $\forall q \in C$, we fixed $\delta_q = \max_{(x,y)\in\mathbf{B}}\{c_q(x) - c_q(y)\}$. We considered the following values of the thresholds $\forall q \in C$

$$\Delta_q^3 = -\Delta_q^{-3} = 0.68\delta_q,$$
$$\Delta_q^2 = -\Delta_q^{-2} = 0.25\delta_q,$$
$$\Delta_q^1 = -\Delta_q^{-1} = 0.18\delta_q.$$

They were chosen experimentally in order to obtain a good approximation of S and S^c.

The bounds on the range of the difference between evaluations of actions by means of particular criteria are the following:

$$\Delta_q^{-4} = \min_{(x,y)\in A\times A}\{c_q(x) - c_q(y)\},$$

and

$$\Delta_q^{4} = \max_{(x,y)\in A\times A}\{c_q(x) - c_q(y)\}.$$

All the tresholds are shown in Table 2.

criteria	δ_q	Δ_q^1	Δ_q^2	Δ_q^3	Δ_q^4
c_1	40.9	7.36	10.23	27.81	83.27
c_2	3.7	.67	.93	2.52	14.99
c_3	11	1.98	2.75	7.48	12.44
c_4	90	16.2	22.5	61.2	290

Table 2. Thresholds considered for definition of graded preference relations on criteria.

Using these thresholds, we defined the following set I_q of intervals $\forall q \in C$:

$$I_q = \{[\Delta_q^{-4}, \Delta_q^{-3}],]\Delta_q^{-3}, \Delta_q^{-2}],]\Delta_q^{-2}, \Delta_q^{-1}],]\Delta_q^{-1}, \Delta_q^{1}[, [\Delta_q^{1}, \Delta_q^{2}[, [\Delta_q^{2}, \Delta_q^{3}[, [\Delta_q^{3}, \Delta_q^{4}]\}.$$

Thus $\forall q \in C$ and $\forall (x,y) \in A \times A$ we have

$$\begin{aligned}
c_q(x) - c_q(y) &\in [\Delta_q^{-4}, \Delta_q^{-3}] \Leftrightarrow xP_q^{-3}y,\\
c_q(x) - c_q(y) &\in]\Delta_q^{-3}, \Delta_q^{-2}] \Leftrightarrow xP_q^{-2}y,\\
c_q(x) - c_q(y) &\in]\Delta_q^{-2}, \Delta_q^{-1}] \Leftrightarrow xP_q^{-1}y,\\
c_q(x) - c_q(y) &\in]\Delta_q^{-1}, \Delta_q^{1}[\Leftrightarrow xP_q^{0}y,\\
c_q(x) - c_q(y) &\in [\Delta_q^{1}, \Delta_q^{2}[\Leftrightarrow xP_q^{1}y,\\
c_q(x) - c_q(y) &\in [\Delta_q^{2}, \Delta_q^{3}[\Leftrightarrow xP_q^{2}y,\\
c_q(x) - c_q(y) &\in [\Delta_q^{3}, \Delta_q^{4}] \Leftrightarrow xP_q^{3}y.
\end{aligned}$$

Let us remark that on the basis of the adopted definition of the set I_q of intervals, we have $aP_q^h b \Leftrightarrow bP_q^{-h}a$, $\forall q \in C$.

At this stage, we were able to build the PCT. Table 3 shows a part of the whole PCT. Each row of this table represents an ordered pair (a_i, a_j) with $i = 1, \ldots 6$, $j = i+1, \ldots 7$, i.e. this part of the PCT includes the pairs (a_i, a_j) such that a_i ranks better than a_j in the preference order shown in Table 1. For each pair (a_i, a_j), Table 3 shows the degree of preference of a_i over a_j with respect to each criterion, and the presence or absence of outranking, respectively S or

S^c (in fact, in this piece of PCT we have situations of presence of outranking only). Precisely, the first row of Table 3 says that: $a_1 P^2_{c_1} a_2$, $a_1 P^{-2}_{c_2} a_2$, $a_1 P^{-1}_{c_3} a_2$, $a_1 P^2_{c_4} a_2$ and $a_1 S a_2$.

Pairs	c_1	c_2	c_3	c_4	d
(a_1, a_2)	2	−2	−1	2	S
(a_1, a_3)	−1	−3	2	2	S
(a_1, a_4)	−2	0	1	−2	S
(a_1, a_5)	2	−2	2	3	S
(a_1, a_6)	2	0	2	2	S
(a_1, a_7)	2	−2	3	2	S
(a_2, a_3)	−2	−1	2	0	S
(a_2, a_4)	−3	2	2	−2	S
(a_2, a_5)	0	0	3	2	S
(a_2, a_6)	0	3	3	0	S
(a_2, a_7)	0	1	3	1	S
(a_3, a_4)	−2	3	0	−2	S
(a_3, a_5)	2	1	1	2	S
(a_3, a_6)	2	3	0	0	S
(a_3, a_7)	3	2	2	0	S
(a_4, a_5)	3	−2	2	3	S
(a_4, a_6)	3	0	2	3	S
(a_4, a_7)	3	−2	2	3	S
(a_5, a_6)	0	3	0	−2	S
(a_5, a_7)	0	1	0	0	S
(a_6, a_7)	0	−2	2	0	S

Table 3. A part of the PCT

The other rows of the PCT can be obtained from Table 3 in the following way:

- for (a_i, a_i), $i = 1, \ldots 7$, we have $a_i P^0_q a_i$ $\forall q \in C$, and $a_i S a_i$,
- for (a_j, a_i), $i = 1, \ldots 6$, $j = i+1, \ldots 7$, we have $a_j P^{-h}_q a_i$ $\forall q \in C$, and $a_j S^c a_i$, where h is the same as in $a_i P^h_q a_j$.

For instance, with respect to (a_2, a_1) we have $a_2 P^{-2}_{c_1} a_1$, $a_2 P^2_{c_2} a_1$, $a_2 P^1_{c_3} a_1$, $a_2 P^{-2}_{c_4} a_1$ and $a_2 S^c a_1$.

Considering the classical approach based on the use of the indiscernibility relation in the PCT, we obtain a quality of the approximation equal to 1, i.e. a perfect approximation. There is only one reduct composed of c_2 (operating cost) and c_3 (reliability). The same two criteria constitute the core.

Using the well known algorithm called LERS (Grzymala-Busse, 1992), for generation of decision rules from approximations of decision classes, we obtained the set of rules shown in Table 4.

Rule #	c_1	c_2	c_3	c_4	d
1		0		0	S
2			2		S
3			3		S
4		3	0		S
5		1	1		S
6		−2	−1		S
7		0	1		S
8		1	0		S
9			−2		S^c
10			−3		S^c
11		−3	0		S^c
12		−1	−1		S^c
13		2	1		S^c
14		0	−1		S^c
15		−1	0		S^c

Table 4. Decision rules generated by LERS.

Let us observe that the rules obtained from the (original) rough set approach based on indiscernibility relation present some problems with respect to their interpretation. More precisely, in Table 4, some decision rules which imply the outranking (the rules #1 to 8) are "contradicted" by examples of pairwise comparison in the PCT. Let us consider, for instance, rule #1. It says that if actions x and y were indifferent with respect to criteria c_2 and c_4, then xSy. It is reasonable to expect that if x was indifferent or better than y on c_2 and c_4, then xSy *a fortiori*. However, as can be seen from the PCT, a_3 is weakly preferred to a_2 with respect to c_2 and a_3 is indifferent to a_2 with respect to c_4, nevertheless, $a_3S^ca_2$.

Similar situations can arise with respect to the decision rules which imply the negation of the outranking (in Table 4 the rules #9 to 15). For istance, according to rule #12, if y is weakly preferred to x with respect to c_2 and c_3 then xS^cy. It is reasonable to expect that if y was at least weakly preferred to x with respect to c_2 and c_3 then xS^cy *a fortiori*. However, a_2 is preferred to a_1 with respect to c_2 and a_2 is weakly preferred to a_1 with respect to c_3, nevertheless, a_1Sa_2.

The complete list of these ambiguous situations is the following:

rule #1 with respect to the pairs (a_3,a_2), (a_4,a_1), (a_7,a_6),
rule #5 with respect to the pair (a_2,a_1),
rule #6 with respect to the pairs (a_2,a_1), (a_4,a_1), (a_5,a_3), (a_7,a_5),
rule #7 with respect to the pair (a_2,a_1),
rule #8 with respect to the pair (a_2,a_1),
rule #12 with respect to the pair (a_1,a_2),
rule #13 with respect to the pairs (a_1,a_1), (a_1,a_2), (a_1,a_4), (a_2,a_2), (a_3,a_3), (a_3,a_5), (a_4,a_4), (a_5,a_5), (a_6,a_6), (a_7,a_7),

rule #14 with respect to the pair (a_1, a_2),
rule #15 with respect to the pair (a_1, a_2).

Other paradoxical results arise from the comparison between some decision rules. E.g. rule #6 states that if y is preferred to x with respect to c_2 and y is weakly preferred to x with respect to c_3 then xSy, while rule #13 states that if x is preferred to y with respect to c_2 and x is weakly preferred to y with respect to c_3 then xS^cy. Rule #6 makes also confusion with rules #12, 14, 15, which imply negative outranking even if their requirements on the strength of preference on the considered criteria are higher.

Furthermore, let us consider the pairs of actions (a_1, a_2) and (a_4, a_1). a_4 is preferred to a_1 with a strength at least equal to the strength with which a_1 is preferred to a_2. Nevertheless a_1Sa_2 but $a_4S^ca_1$. An analogous situation arises with respect to the pairs of actions (a_1, a_4) and (a_2, a_1). These situations should be interpreted as ambiguous cases with respect to the approximations of S and S^c. However, applying the original rough set approach, quality of approximation is equal to 1, which means a perfect approximation. In general, the original rough set approach cannot discover these ambiguous cases because it does not take into account the ordering properties of criteria.

After the calculation of lower and upper approximations of S and S^c by dominance relations, we get the set of decision rules. The minimal D_{++}-decision rules are shown in Table 5, in which each row corresponds to the minimal D_{++}-decision rule $xD^h_{+P}y \Rightarrow xSy$, where P is the subset of criteria marked by "x" and h is the degree shown in the last column. Analogously, the minimal D_{--}-decision rules, D_{+-}-decision rules and D_{-+}-decision rules are shown in Tables 6, 7 and 8, respectively.

Rule #	InvestCost	OperatCost	Reliability	Distance	Degree h
1	x	x			2
2			x		2
3	x		x		1
4	x	x	x		0
5				x	3
6		x		x	1
7			x	x	1
8		x	x	x	0

Table 5. Minimal D_{++}-decision rules.

The obtained decision rules have the following interpretation:

rule #1: if x is at least preferred to y with respect to c_1 and c_2, then xSy;
rule #2: if x is at least preferred to y with respect to c_3, then xSy;

Rule #	InvestCost	OperatCost	Reliability	Distance	Degree h
9	x	x			−2
10			x		−2
11	x		x		−1
12				x	−3
13		x		x	−1
14			x	x	−1

Table 6. Minimal D_{--}-decision rules.

Rule #	InvestCost	OperatCost	Reliability	Distance	Degree h
15			x		−1
16				x	−2

Table 7. Minimal D_{+-}-decision rules.

rule #3: if x is at least weakly preferred to y with respect to c_1 and c_3, then xSy;
rule #4: if x is at least indifferent to y with respect to c_1, c_2 and c_3, then xSy;
rule #5: if x is strongly preferred to y with respect to c_4, then xSy;
rule #6: if x is at least weakly preferred to y with respect to c_2 and c_4, then xSy;
rule #7: if x is at least weakly preferred to y with respect to c_3 and c_4, then xSy;
rule #8: if x is at least indifferent to y with respect to c_2, c_3 and c_4, then xSy;
rule #9: if y is at least preferred to x with respect to c_1 and c_2, then xS^cy;
rule #10: if y is at least preferred to x with respect to the criterion c_3, then xS^cy;
rule #11: if y is at least weakly preferred to x with respect to c_1 and c_3, then xS^cy;
rule #12: if y is strongly preferred to x with respect to c_4, then xS^cy;
rule #13: if y is at least weakly preferred to x with respect to c_2 and c_4, then xS^cy;

Rule #	InvestCost	OperatCost	Reliability	Distance	Degree h
17			x		1
18				x	2

Table 8. Minimal D_{-+}-decision rules.

rule #14: if y is at least weakly preferred to x with respect to c_3 and c_4, then xS^cy;
rule #15: if y is not at most weakly preferred to x with respect to c_3, then xS^cy;
rule #16: if y is not at most preferred to x with respect to c_4, then xS^cy;
rule #17: if x is not at most weakly preferred to y with respect to c_3, then xSy;
rule #18: if x is not at most preferred to y with respect to c_4, then xSy.

The list of pairs of actions (a_i, a_j), $i = 1, \dots 7$, $j = 1, \dots 7$, supporting the minimal decision rules are presented in Table 9.

Rule #	Pairs of actions
1	(a_3,a_6) (a_3,a_7)
2	(a_1,a_3) (a_1,a_5) (a_1,a_6) (a_1,a_7) (a_2,a_3) (a_2,a_4) (a_2,a_5) (a_2,a_6) (a_2,a_7) (a_3,a_7) (a_4,a_5) (a_4,a_6) (a_4,a_7) (a_6,a_7)
3	(a_1,a_5) (a_1,a_6) (a_1,a_7) (a_3,a_5) (a_3,a_7) (a_4,a_5) (a_4,a_6) (a_4,a_7)
4	(a_1,a_1) (a_1,a_6) (a_2,a_2) (a_2,a_5) (a_2,a_6) (a_2,a_7) (a_3,a_3) (a_3,a_5) (a_3,a_6) (a_3,a_7) (a_4,a_4) (a_4,a_6) (a_5,a_5) (a_5,a_6) (a_5,a_7) (a_6,a_6) (a_7,a_7)
5	(a_1,a_5) (a_4,a_5) (a_4,a_6) (a_4,a_7)
6	(a_2,a_7) (a_3,a_5)
7	(a_1,a_3) (a_1,a_5) (a_1,a_6) (a_1,a_7) (a_2,a_5) (a_2,a_7) (a_3,a_5) (a_4,a_5) (a_4,a_6) (a_4,a_7)
8	(a_1,a_1) (a_1,a_6) (a_2,a_2) (a_2,a_5) (a_2,a_6) (a_2,a_7) (a_3,a_3) (a_3,a_5) (a_3,a_6) (a_3,a_7) (a_4,a_4) (a_4,a_6) (a_5,a_5) (a_5,a_7) (a_6,a_6) (a_7,a_7)
9	(a_6,a_3) (a_7,a_3)
10	(a_3,a_1) (a_3,a_2) (a_4,a_2) (a_5,a_1) (a_5,a_2) (a_5,a_4) (a_6,a_1) (a_6,a_2) (a_6,a_4) (a_7,a_1) (a_7,a_2) (a_7,a_3) (a_7,a_4) (a_7,a_6)
11	(a_5,a_1) (a_5,a_3) (a_5,a_4) (a_6,a_1) (a_6,a_4) (a_7,a_1) (a_7,a_3) (a_7,a_4)
12	(a_5,a_1) (a_5,a_4) (a_6,a_4) (a_7,a_4)
13	(a_5,a_3) (a_7,a_2)
14	(a_3,a_1) (a_5,a_1) (a_5,a_2) (a_5,a_3) (a_5,a_4) (a_6,a_1) (a_6,a_4) (a_7,a_2) (a_7,a_4)
15	(a_3,a_1) (a_3,a_2) (a_4,a_2) (a_5,a_1) (a_5,a_2) (a_5,a_4) (a_6,a_1) (a_6,a_2) (a_6,a_4) (a_7,a_1) (a_7,a_2) (a_7,a_3) (a_7,a_4) (a_7,a_6)
16	(a_5,a_1) (a_5,a_4) (a_6,a_4) (a_7,a_4)
17	(a_1,a_3) (a_1,a_5) (a_1,a_6) (a_1,a_7) (a_2,a_3) (a_2,a_4) (a_2,a_5) (a_2,a_6) (a_2,a_7) (a_3,a_7) (a_4,a_5) (a_4,a_6) (a_4,a_7) (a_6,a_7)
18	(a_1,a_5) (a_4,a_5) (a_4,a_6) (a_4,a_7)

Table 9. Pairs of actions supporting minimal decision rules.

Application of the decision rules to the complete set M $(= A)$ of 69 actions (variants) considered in Roy, Slowinski, Treichel (1992) results in two outranking relations S and S^c on this set. Table 10 shows the four-valued outaranking relations obtained with respect to the pairs (x_i, x_j) (x_i on the row and x_j on the column) with x_i and x_j belonging to the set of the first ten variants considered, i.e. x_1 = Var. 1_A, x_2 = Var. 1_B, x_3 = Var. 1_C, x_4 = Var. 2_A, x_5 = Var. 2_B, x_6 = Var. 2_C, x_7 = Var. 3_A, x_8 = Var. 3_B, x_9 = Var. 3_C, x_{10} = Var. 4_A.

	x_1	x_2	x_3	x_4	x_5	x_6	x_7	x_8	x_9	x_{10}
x_1	S^T	S^T	S^U	S^T	S^T	S^T	S^T	S^T	S^T	S^T
x_2	S^T	S^T	S^U	S^T	S^T	S^T	S^T	S^T	S^T	S^T
x_3	S^T	S^T	S^T	S^T	S^T	S^T	S^T	S^T	S^T	S^T
x_4	S^F	S^F	S^F	S^T	S^U	S^U	S^T	S^T	S^U	S^F
x_5	S^T	S^T	S^F	S^T	S^T	S^T	S^T	S^T	S^T	S^F
x_6	S^T	S^T	S^F	S^T	S^T	S^T	S^T	S^T	S^T	S^U
x_7	S^F	S^F	S^F	S^T	S^F	S^F	S^T	S^T	S^U	S^F
x_8	S^F	S^F	S^F	S^F	S^F	S^F	S^U	S^T	S^T	S^U
x_9	S^U	S^U	S^F	S^T	S^T	S^T	S^T	S^T	S^T	S^F
x_{10}	S^T	S^T	S^U	S^T	S^T	S^T	S^T	S^T	S^T	S^T

Table 10. Four-valued outranking relations for the first ten variants.

Exploitation of the outranking relations S and S^c obtained from application of the decision rules assigns a score to the actions and leads to the ranking shown in Table 11, where the values in each column have the following meaning: (1) investment cost, (2) operating cost, (3) reliability, (4) distance between technical programming and socio-economic priority order of users, (5) score $S_{\mathrm{NF}}(x)$ based on outranking relations S and S^c, (6) rank according to score $S_{\mathrm{NF}}(x)$.

The rough set approach gives a clear recommendation: for the choice problem it suggests to select Var.5_B having maximum score (111) and for the ranking problem it suggests the ranking presented in Table 11.

8 Conclusions

In this paper, application of rough sets to analysis of preferential information in multicriteria choice and ranking decision problems was investigated. The key concepts enabling this consideration are the PCT and the graded dominance relations. For the sake of simplicity, we were using single-graded dominance relations characterized by the same grade h for all $q \in C$; finer approximations can be obtained by considering multi-graded dominance relations characterized by vectors of grades.

As shown in the paper, the classical rough set approximations based on indiscernibility relation can be applied to the PCT, but they do not take into account the ordinal properties of the considered criteria. This drawback can be removed by considering rough approximations of the preference relations by graded dominace relations. The rough approximations by indiscernibility relation and by graded dominance relations were compared on a real world example considered

Variant #	(1)	(2)	(3)	(4)	(5)	(6)
Var. 5_B	249,33	26,78	7,468	249	111	1
Var. 5_A	245,11	27,35	7,603	249	106	2
Var. 5_C	246,64	27,22	7,644	249	104	3
Var. 1_C	251,3	27,25	7,505	311	93	4
Var. 4_C	239,66	27,86	7,107	298	93	5
Var. 4_A	239,52	28,18	7,387	298	86	6
Var. 6_C	252,44	26,5	7,247	354	86	7
Var. 6_B	255,39	26,46	7,205	354	84	8
Var. 25_B	288,3	25,72	2,508	390	82	9
Var. 25_A	292,39	26,36	2,532	390	78	10
Var. 28_C	277,87	27,62	3,861	393	73	11
Var. 28_B	280,8	27,54	3,892	393	72	12
Var. 27_C	276,65	28,9	4,736	358	70	13
Var. 27_B	274,88	29,05	4,778	358	69	14
Var. 6_A	254,44	27,66	7,52	354	66	15
Var. 2_C	256,62	28,25	6,967	331	64	16
Var. 4_B	241,33	30,22	7,266	298	63	17
Var. 1_A	253,3	28,41	7,778	311	62	18
Var. 1_B	254,99	28,58	7,881	311	59	19
Var. 28_A	279,87	28,78	4,166	393	58	20
Var. 2_B	252,64	28,9	7,002	331	55	21
Var. 27_A	275,77	29,57	4,875	358	45	22
Var. 2_A	255,08	29,64	7,131	331	35	23
Var. 14_A	265,52	24,35	9,623	355	29	24
Var. 14_B	266,57	24,07	9,562	355	24	25
Var. 14_C	266,63	24,46	9,641	355	24	26
Var. 26_D	312,76	28,5	3,862	395	23	27
Var. 9_B	280,42	28,48	8,532	310	21	28
Var. 9_A	279,09	28,75	8,596	310	20	29
Var. 26_B	314,07	28,62	4,137	395	19	30
Var. 16_B	264,85	23,37	10,125	400	8	31
Var. 11_B	264,79	25,71	8,934	392	7	32
Var. 11_A	263,28	25,89	8,976	392	5	33
Var. 17_B	262,36	23,25	10,1	429	5	34
Var. 26_C	316,86	29,41	3,862	395	5	35

Table 11. Ranking from the rough set approach.

in the literature. The results showed clearly the advantages of the rough approximations by graded dominance relations over the rough approximations by indiscernibility relation. The approach based on the former type of approximations proposes a consistent recommendation for multicriteria choice and ranking decision problems, while the approach based on the latter can lead to confusing results.

Variant #	(1)	(2)	(3)	(4)	(5)	(6)
Var. 11_C	264,51	26	8,989	392	2	36
Var. 3_C	272,44	28,89	8,013	335	1	37
Var. 29_C	290,55	28,71	5,067	437	−14	38
Var. 7_C	270,05	28,07	8,045	379	−15	39
Var. 26_A	322,79	30,49	4,093	395	−15	40
Var. 17_A	269,45	24,44	10,461	429	−20	41
Var. 9_C	288,01	30,64	9,044	310	−21	42
Var. 16_A	271,84	24,56	10,478	400	−23	43
Var. 29_A	290,05	29,61	5,249	437	−30	44
Var. 29_B	291,26	29,73	5,304	437	−34	45
Var. 10_C	280,82	26,5	9,648	393	−38	46
Var. 3_A	273,24	30,23	8,343	335	−40	47
Var. 20_A	273,56	23,13	10,808	454	−44	48
Var. 10_B	280,01	27,43	9,648	393	−47	49
Var. 7_B	273,87	29,4	8,401	379	−52	50
Var. 13_D	287,02	27,57	9,594	383	−53	51
Var. 30_C	304,51	29,25	5,282	527	−55	52
Var. 3_B	278,6	31,25	8,717	335	−56	53
Var. 13_B	288,33	27,69	9,594	383	−58	54
Var. 30_A	303,53	29,61	5,313	527	−59	55
Var. 30_B	305,84	30,33	5,519	527	−63	56
Var. 7_A	275,52	38,08	8,53	379	−71	57
Var. 15_B	282,66	25,55	11,401	421	−75	58
Var. 24_A	275,1	23,09	10,857	503	−75	59
Var. 13_C	291,12	28,48	9,869	383	−76	60
Var. 23_A	277,64	24,64	12,608	459	−79	61
Var. 10_A	290,04	29,42	10,131	393	−88	62
Var. 18_A	280,42	26,3	14,082	396	−92	63
Var. 13_A	297,05	29,56	10,077	383	−93	64
Var. 15_A	286,75	26,46	11,646	421	−93	65
Var. 22_A	278,71	24,18	13,149	499	−94	66
Var. 19_B	289,36	26,52	13,202	408	−100	67
Var. 19_A	293,46	27,43	13,478	408	−106	68
Var. 21_A	301,1	25,85	14,944	530	−128	69

Table 12. Ranking from the rough set approach (continuation).

Acknowledgement

The research of the first two authors has been supported by grant No. 96.01658. CT10 from Italian National Council for Scientific Research; the research of the third author has been supported by grant No. 8 T11C 013 13 from State Committee for Scientific Research (Komitet Badan Naukowych).

References

1. Bouyssou, D.: Ranking methods based on valued preference relations: a characterization of the net flow method. European Journal of Operational Research **60** (1992a) 61–68
2. Bouyssou, D.: A note on the sum of differences choice function for fuzzy preference relations. Fuzzy sets and systems **47** (1992b) 197–202
3. Bouyssou, D.: Outranking relations: do they have special properties?. Journal of Multi-Criteria Decision Analysis **5/2** (1996) 99–111
4. Brans, J. P., Vincke, Ph.: A preference ranking organization method. Management Science **31** (1985) 647–656
5. Cozzens, M., Roberts, F.: Multiple semiorders and multiple indifference graphs. SIAM Journal of Algebraic Discrete Methods **3** (1982) 566–583
6. Doignon, J.P.: Threshold representation of multiple semiorders. SIAM Journal of Algebraic Discrete Methods **8** (1987) 77–84
7. Doignon, J. P., Monjardet, B., Roubens, M., Vincke, Ph.: Biorder families, valued relations and preference modelling,. Journal of Mathematical Psychology **30** (1986) 435–480
8. Fishburn, P. C. Methods for estimating additive utilities. Management Science **13** (1967) 435–453
9. Fishburn, P. C.: The theory of social choice. Princeton University Press, Princeton NJ (1973)
10. Fodor, J., Roubens, M.: Fuzzy preference modelling and multicriteria decision support. Kluwer Academic Publishers, Dordrecht (1994)
11. Goodman, L. A. : On methods of amalgamation. In: R.M. Thrall, C.H. Coombs and R.L. Davis (eds.), Decision processes, Wiley, New York (1954) 39-48.
12. Greco S., Matarazzo, B., Słowiński, R.: Rough set approach to multi-attribute choice and ranking problems. ICS Research Report 38/95, Warsaw University of Technology, Warsaw (1995). Also in: G. Fandel and T. Gal (eds.), Multiple criteria decision making. Proceedings of the Twelfth International Conference, Hagen (Germany) Springer-Verlag, Berlin (1997) 318–329
13. Greco S., Matarazzo, B., Słowiński, R.: Rough approximation of a preference relation by dominance relations. ICS Research Report 16/96, Warsaw University of Technology, Warsaw (1996)
14. Greco S., Matarazzo, B., Słowiński, R., Tsoukias, A.: Exploitation of a rough approximation of the outranking relation. In: Selected papers of the Thirteenth International Conference on Multiple Criteria Decision Making, CapeTown (South Africa), Springer-Verlag, Berlin (1997)
15. Grzymala-Busse, J.W.: 'LERS - a system for learning from examples based on rough sets. In: R. Słowiński (ed.), Intelligent decision support. Handbook of applications and advances of the rough sets theory, Kluwer Academic Publishers, Dordrecht (1992) 3–18
16. Henriet, D.: The Copeland choice function - an axiomatic characterization. Social Choice and Welfare **2** (1985) 49–64
17. Jacquet-Lagrèze, E.: Systèmes de décision et acteurs multiples - contribution à une théorie de l'action pour les sciences des organisations. Thèse d'Etat, Université de Paris-Dauphine, Paris (1981)
18. Jacquet-Lagrèze, E.: Interactive assessment of preference using holistic judgements - the PREFCALC system. In: C. A. Bana e Costa (ed.), Readings in multiple criteria decision aid, Springer-Verlag, Berlin 335–350

19. Jacquet-Lagrèze, E., Siskos, J.: Assessing a set of additive utility functions for multicriteria decision-making, the UTA method. European Journal of Operational Research **10** (1982) 151–164
20. Keeney, R. L., Raiffa, H.: Decision with multiple objectives - preferences and value tradeoffs. Wiley, New York (1976)
21. March, J. G.: Bounded rationality, ambiguity, and the engineering of choice. In: D. E. Bell, H., Raiffa, A. Tversky (eds), Decision making, descriptive, normative and prescriptive interactions, Cambridge University Press, New York (1988) 33–58
22. Mienko, R., Stefanowski, J., Toumi, K., Vanderpooten, D.: Discovery–oriented induction of decision rules. Cahier du LAMSADE **141** Université de Paris - Dauphine, Paris (1996)
23. Moreno, J.A., Tsoukias, A.: On nested interval orders and semiorders. Annals of Operations Research (1996) (to appear)
24. Mousseau, V.: Problèmes liés à l'évaluation de l'importance en aide multicritère à la décision: réflexions théoriques et expérimentations. Thèse, Université de Paris-Dauphine, Paris (1993)
25. Pawlak, Z.: Rough sets. International Journal of Information & Computer Sciences **11** (1982) 341–356
26. Pawlak, Z.: Rough sets: theoretical aspects of reasoning about data. Kluwer Academic Publishers, Dordrecht (1991)
27. Pawlak, Z., Słowiński, R.: Rough set approach to multi-attribute decision analysis. European Journal of Operational Research **72** (1994) 443–459
28. Roberts, F. S.: Homogeneous families of semiorders and the theory of probabilistic consistency. J. Math. Psycho. **8** (1971) 248–263
29. Roubens, M., Vincke, Ph.: Preference modelling. Springer-Verlag, Berlin (1985)
30. Roy, B.: Méthodologie multicritère d'aide à la décision. Economica, Paris (1985)
31. Roy, B.: The outranking approach and the foundation of ELECTRE methods. Theory and Decision **31** (1991) 49–73
32. Roy, B.: Decision science or decision aid science. European Journal of Operational Research. Special Issue on Model Validation in Operations Research **66** (1993) 184–203
33. Roy, B., Słowiński, R., Treichel, W.: Multicriteria programming of water supply systems for rural areas. Water Resources Bulletin **28/1** (1992) 13–31
34. Rubinstein, A.: Ranking the participants in a tournament. SIAM Journal of Applied Mathematics **38** (1980) 108–111
35. Skowron, A.: Boolean reasoning for decision rules generation. In: J. Komorowski, Z.W. Ras, (eds.), Methodologies for Intelligent Systems, Lecture Notes in Artificial Intelligence **689** Springer -Verlag, Berlin (1993) 295–305
36. Slovic, P.: Choice between equally-valued alternatives. Journal of Experimental Psychology: Human Perception Performance **1** (1975) 280–287
37. Słowiński, R.: Rough set learning of preferential attitude in multi-criteria decision making. In: J. Komorowski, Z.W. Ras (eds.), Methodologies for Intelligent Systems, Lecture Notes in Artificial Intelligence **689** Springer-Verlag, Berlin (1993) 642–651
38. Słowiński, R., Stefanowski, J.: RoughDAS and RoughClass software implementations of the rough sets approach. In: R. Słowiński (ed.), Intelligent decision support. Handbook of applications and advances of the rough sets theory, Kluwer Academic Publishers, Dordrecht (1992) 445–456
39. Tsoukias, A., Vincke, Ph.: A survey on non-conventional preference modelling. Ricerca Operativa **61** (1992) 5–49

40. Tsoukias, A., Vincke, Ph.: A new axiomatic foundation of the partial comparability theory. Theory and Decision **39** (1995) 79–114
41. Ziarko, W., Golan, D., Edwards, D.: An application of DATALOGIC/R knowledge discovery tool to identify strong predictive rules in stock market data. In: Proc. AAAI Workshop on Knowledge Discovery in Databases, Washington D.C.(1993) 89-101.

Chapter 3

Learning Decision Rules from Similarity Based Rough Approximations

Krzysztof Krawiec[1], *Roman Słowiński*[1] *and Daniel Vanderpooten*[2]

[1] Institute of Computing Science
Poznań University of Technology
3A Piotrowo Street
60-965 Poznań, Poland

[2] University of Paris Dauphine
LAMSADE
75775 Paris Cedex 16, France

Abstract: Decision rules induced from lower approximations of decision classes are certain in the sense of covering the objects which certainly belong to the corresponding decision classes. The definition of rough approximations is originally based on an indiscernibility relation in the set of objects. The indiscernibility relation requiring strict equality of attribute values for the objects being compared is often restrictive in practical applications. This is why, we are proposing to use a more natural similarity relation to define rough approximation of decision classes. The only requirement imposed on this relation is reflexivity. The similarity relation is being derived from data. Decision rules induced from lower approximations of decision classes based on similarity are not only certain but robust in the sense of covering objects which belong to the corresponding decision classes and are not similar to objects from outside. The approach is illustrated by a simple example and it is validated on a set of benchmark examples.

Keywords: Rough sets, similarity relation, decision rules, classification tests.

1 Introduction

The rough set philosophy is founded on the assumption that with every object of the universe of discourse we associate some information (data, knowledge). Objects characterized by the same information are indiscernible in view of the available information about them. The indiscernibility relation generated in this way is the mathematical basis for the rough set theory.

Any maximal set of pairwise indiscernible objects is called an elementary set, and forms a basic granule of knowledge about the universe. Any set of objects being a union of some elementary sets is referred to as crisp (precise) - otherwise a set is rough (imprecise, vague). Consequently, each rough set has boundary-line cases, i.e. objects which cannot be classified with certainty as members of the set or of its complement.

Therefore, a rough set can be replaced by a pair of crisp sets, called the lower and the upper approximation. The lower approximation consists of all objects which surely belong to the set and the upper approximation contains objects which possibly belong to the set, with respect to the given knowledge.

Classical definitions of lower and upper approximations (see, e.g., [17, 18]) were originally introduced with reference to an indiscernibility relation which was assumed to be an equivalence relation (reflexive, symmetric and transitive). It is quite interesting to extend these concepts to the case of more general relations. In particular, considering a similarity or tolerance relation instead of an indiscernibility relation is quite relevant (see, e.g. [16, 11, 6, 13, 19, 25, 27, 30, 28]). Such relations express weaker forms of indiscernibility and, usually, are not equivalence relations. While the reflexivity property seems quite necessary to express any form of indiscernibility or similarity, the two other properties may be relaxed.

Considering a data set in the form of a decision table, a challenging task is to describe sets of objects corresponding to particular decision classes in terms of *if ... then ...* decision rules. Because of possible inconsistency in the data set, instead of describing the original decision classes, lower and upper approximations and/or boundaries of these classes can be described. Inconsistency and approximation are strictly interrelated in the rough set theory by an indiscernibility or similarity relation.

The main argument for the use of a similarity relation instead of the original indiscernibility relation is connected with the existence of quantitative attributes in the decision table. Very often, these attributes carry an uncertain information because of non adequate definition, imprecise measurement or random fluctuation of some parameters. For these reasons, the credibility of 'precise' scores of the objects on these attributes is rather low. On the other hand, in order to create a generalized description of the decision table and to discover some regularities in the data, the user may wish to translate numerical values of attributes into qualitative terms.

Therefore, when using the strict indiscernibility relation, the quantitative attributes should be discretized using some *norms* translating the attribute domains into subintervals corresponding to qualifiers: low, medium, high, etc. For example, in medicine the use of norms is quite frequent and there are many global or local conventions establishing them. In those applications, however, where the definition of norms is arbitrary and makes difficult the interpretation of decision rules, it is more natural to define a relative similarity with respect to a given value of the attribute. Moreover, the use of norms introduces an undesirable 'frontier phenomenon', when very close objects are separated by the frontier between two consecutive sub-intervals. This is the argument for the use of a similarity relation instead of the indiscernibility relation.

As lower approximations of decision classes include only those objects which belong to the corresponding decision classes without any ambiguity, the decision rules describing the lower approximations are called *certain* or *exact*. Upper approximations of decision classes include, in turn, those objects which belong to the corresponding decision classes, possibly with some ambiguity. For this reason, the decision rules describing the upper approximations are called *possible*.

The differences of upper and lower approximations of decision classes are called boundaries and include only ambiguous objects, i.e. inconsistent examples. The decision rules describing the boundaries are called *approximate.*

While certain rules indicate a univocal class assignment, possible rules may not and approximate rules do not indicate a univocal class assignment. From a practical point of view, certain rules are more interesting than possible and approximate ones. The generalized description represented by certain rules is based on examples (objects) for which there is no similar negative example (object from different class). Thus, in the sense of discernibility with boundary cases, the certain rules can be considered as robust ones.

This paper is devoted to construction of rough classifiers composed of certain rules. The definition of lower approximations of decision classes is based on the use of the most general form of the similarity relation preserving the property of reflexivity only.

The paper is organized as follows. Following [28], we first discuss the concept of similarity and present the generalized definitions of lower and upper approximations based on similarity. Then, in section 3, we consider the problem of inferring a similarity relation from data. Generation of certain and robust decision rules is discussed in section 4. A simple illustrative example explains the whole approach in section 5. Section 6 is devoted to classification tests and the final section groups conclusions.

2 Similarity relation and rough approximations

2.1 Similarity

Suppose we are given a finite non empty set U of objects, called the *universe.*

Indiscernibility reflects an equivalence between objects. This situation can be represented using a binary relation R defined on U which is reflexive, symmetric and transitive. Objects of U can be partitioned into indiscernibility (or equivalence) classes which form the basic granules of the knowledge available through R.

It is natural to extend the indiscernibility concept to take account of situations where objects are not significantly distinct. This happens in particular when the data describing objects is imprecise or, even if it is precise, when small differences are meaningless in the context of the study. This situation can be modelled using a binary relation R defined on U, which represents a certain form of *similarity.* Similarity or tolerance relations have been studied extensively (see, e.g., [34, 33, 22, 8]).

A basic difference with indiscernibility relations is that, in general, similarity relations do not give rise to a partition of the set of objects. Information about similarity can be represented using *similarity classes* for each object $x \in U$. More precisely, the similarity class of x, denoted by $R(x)$, is the set of objects which are similar to x:

$$R(x) = \{y \in U : yRx\}$$

It is clear that an object from a given similarity class may be similar to an object of another similarity class. Therefore, the basic granules of knowledge are intertwined.

Extending indiscernibility to similarity imposes to weaken some of the properties of the binary relation in terms of reflexivity, symmetry and transitivity.

The reflexivity property cannot be relaxed, since, as any object is trivially indiscernible with itself, it is, a fortiori, similar to itself.

The most controversial property is symmetry. Most authors dealing with similarity relations do impose this property. Notice, however, that the statement yRx which means '*y is similar to x*' is directional; it has a *subject* y and a *referent* x and it is not equivalent in general to the statement '*x is similar to y*' as argued by Tversky [31]. For example, in the following statement: '*a son resembles his father*' the son is the subject and the father is the referent; the inverse statement usually makes much less sense. Another example is when the similarity is based on a numerical measure ρ. If we consider that objects whose measures differ by less than a given percentage are similar we might express this in the following way: y is similar to x iff $\rho(y) \in [(1-\epsilon)\rho(x); (1+\epsilon)\rho(x)]$, where $\epsilon > 0$. In this case, we may have yRx but not xRy (e.g. if $\rho(x) = 100, \rho(y) = 90$ and $\epsilon = 0.1$). This suggests that, at least in some cases, similarity relations should not be imposed to be symmetric. In such cases, we can consider the inverse relation of R, denoted by R^{-1}. Let $R^{-1}(x)$ be the class of referent objects to which x is similar:

$$R^{-1}(x) = \{y \in U : xRy\}$$

Imposing transitivity to R is even more questionable. The reason for this is that, sometimes, a series of negligible differences cannot be propagated as shown in the famous example by Luce [12]: considering a series of cups of coffee with slightly increasing amounts of sugar, two successive cups may judged similar whereas the first and the last in the series may not.

Most extensions of the indiscernibility relation relax the transitivity property only [16, 11, 13, 19, 25, 30]. However, it may be relevant in some cases to relax also the symmetry property as shown in [27, 28].

2.2 Similarity based rough approximations

A key concept leading to the correct definition of rough approximations is the concept of ambiguity [28]. Considering a subset $X \subseteq U$ and a binary relation R defined on U, an object $x \in U$ may be ambiguous considering its membership to X in two cases.

- If $x \in X$ but there exists $y \notin X$ such that x is similar to y, in which case the information provided by R suggests to discard x from X.
- If $x \notin X$ but there exists $y \in X$ such that x is similar to y, in which case the information provided by R suggests to include x into X.

Therefore, we give the following definition based on these considerations.

Definition 1. Considering a subset $X \subseteq U$ and a binary relation R defined on U, an object $x \in U$ is *R-ambiguous* in the two following cases:

- x is an ambiguous object of type I iff

$$x \in X \quad \text{and} \quad R^{-1}(x) \cap (U \setminus X) \neq \emptyset \tag{1}$$

- x is an ambiguous object of type II iff

$$x \in U \setminus X \quad \text{and} \quad R^{-1}(x) \cap X \neq \emptyset \tag{2}$$

Considering statements (1) and (2), one can conclude that the status of any object $x \in U$ is non ambiguous in any of the following cases:

- x belongs to X without ambiguity iff

$$x \in X \quad \text{and} \quad R^{-1}(x) \subseteq X \tag{3}$$

  Such objects will be referred to as 'positive' objects.
- x does not belong to X without ambiguity:

$$x \in U \setminus X \quad \text{and} \quad R^{-1}(x) \subseteq U \setminus X \tag{4}$$

  Such objects will be referred to as 'negative' objects.

Note finally that, given $X \subseteq U$ and a binary relation R, any object $x \in U$ belongs to one and only one of the following categories:

- positive objects,
- ambiguous objects of type I,
- ambiguous objects of type II,
- negative objects.

Thus, these four categories define a partition of U.

Since reflexivity is a minimal requirement for any type of similarity relation, we assume in the following that R is reflexive.

A convenient way of describing the set of positive or ambiguous objects as a union of similarity classes is given by the following result.

Result 1 *[28]: Considering a subset $X \subseteq U$ and a binary reflexive relation R defined on U, $\bigcup_{x \in X} R(x)$ corresponds to the set of positive or ambiguous objects.*

The concept of ambiguity which leads to the definition of positive and ambiguous objects as well as Result 1 naturally suggest the following definition for rough approximations based on a reflexive binary relation R [28]:

Definition 2. Considering a subset $X \subseteq U$ and a binary reflexive relation R defined on U, the lower approximation of X, denoted by $R_*(X)$, and the upper approximation of X, denoted by $R^*(X)$, are respectively defined as follows:

$$R_*(X) = \{x \in U : R^{-1}(x) \subseteq X\} \tag{5}$$

$$R^*(X) = \bigcup_{x \in X} R(x) \tag{6}$$

3 Inferring similarity relation from data

The problem of a proper shaping of the similarity relation for a given data set is of crucial importance for the further analysis. The meaning of similarity is sometimes suggested by an expert, however, it is usually quite rough and may be used as a first approximation only. We claim that a more precise and robust definition of similarity may be inferred directly from the data (decision table). Our previous research [10] has shown that such approach is particularly useful in the framework of a 'classification perspective' (alternative to 'explanation perspective').

The data set is organised in a decision table where each row represents an object x belonging to a universe U and each column represents an *attribute* $a_k, k = 1, \ldots, n$, where n is the total number of attributes describing the objects. An element $a_k(x)$ at the intersection of object $x \in U$ and attribute a_k is a value describing x by a_k. One column of the decision table plays a particular role of a *decision attribute* or, shortly, decision, i.e. this attribute assigns objects to particular decision classes and thus it induces a partition of set U. In order to distinguish the decision attribute from the others we will call the latter ones the *conditional attributes.*

In this section, we outline an approach for estimating the parameters of the similarity relation given a decision table. The proposed algorithm is strongly local in the sense, that it computes the range of similarity for each object and each conditional attribute value of that object separately. Additionally, it takes into account assignment of objects to particular classes. Its aim is to establish rather fine-grained similarity classes on the decision table which have not to be perfectly consistent with the partition of objects into decision classes, in what it differs from some other proposals (see [26]).

Similarity is defined with respect to each object playing the role of a referent in a pair of objects being compared. Let x be a referent object and y a subject. We are considering the following definition of similarity:

$$yRx \iff a_k(y) \in [a_k(x) - \epsilon_k^-(x); a_k(x) + \epsilon_k^+(x)] \text{ for } k = 1, \ldots, n$$

where $\epsilon_k^-(x)$ and $\epsilon_k^+(x)$ denote, respectively, the lower and the upper bound of similarity for the attribute a_k and the referent x. $\epsilon_k^-(x)$ and $\epsilon_k^+(x)$ define the range of similarity around $a_k(x)$, also called the *tolerance interval.*

We will describe now the method for estimating the lower and upper bounds of similarity. For a given object x, let us denote by $C_k(x)$ the set of objects, which are currently similar to it with respect to the attribute a_k. Then, the method proceeds as shown in Fig. 1. For the given attribute a_k and an object x, the procedure tries to extend the lower and upper bounds of the tolerance interval until the violation of the stopping condition defined by the function *PurityCondition*. This search is performed twice for each object x, separately for objects y_i in the direction of smaller and greater values of the attribute a_k, until the lower and upper bounds $\epsilon_k^-(x)$ and $\epsilon_k^+(x)$, respectively, are found. The bounds are computed as the average of distances between x and two objects:

Fig. 1. The proposed algorithm for the estimation of tolerance intervals.

```
for each a_k, k = 1,...,n
    for each x ∈ U
        Estimate the lower bound of the tolerance interval:
        C_k(x) ← {x}
        i ← 1
        loop
            y_i ← arg min{a_k(x) − a_k(y_i) : y_i ∈ U \ C_k(x), a_k(y_i) ≤ a_k(x)}
            if PurityCondition(C_k(x) ∪ {y_i}) then
                C_k(x) ← C_k(x) ∪ {y_i}
                i ← i + 1
            else
                exit loop
        end loop
        ε_k^-(x) ← a_k(x) − 1/2 (a_k(y_i) + a_k(y_{i-1}))
        Perform an analogous computation for the upper bound
        of the tolerance interval, obtaining
        ε_k^+(x) ← 1/2 (a_k(y_i) + a_k(y_{i-1})) − a_k(x)
    end for
end for
```

the last one which did not violate the *PurityCondition* (y_{i-1}), and the first one which was unacceptable according to that criterion (y_i).

As the proposed approach is local in the sense that it computes the bounds of similarity for each attribute and object separately, the obtained definition of the similarity relation may be not monotonic with respect to the scale of the given attribute. That is quite unnatural, thus we force the monotonicity by performing a smoothing of the bounds of similarity. For this purpose, the objects are sorted according to the ascending value of the considered attribute a_k . Then, starting with the first object in the order, the lower bounds for consecutive objects are processed as follows. For the given object x, let $e_k^-(x)$ be the maximal value of the lower extent of tolerance interval, $a_k(y) - \epsilon_k^-(y)$, for the objects y processed so far ($a_k(y) \leq a_k(x)$). Then, if $a_k(x) - \epsilon_k^-(x) < e_k^-(x)$ (i.e. the lower bound of similarity of the object x violates the monotonicity), then $\epsilon_k^-(x)$ is set (decreased) to the value $a_k(x) - e_k^-(x)$, which ensures the monotonicity. The smoothing of upper bounds of similarity is carried out in an analoguous way.

The core of the algorithm for estimation of the tolerance intervals is the stopping condition defined by the function *PurityCondition.* Let $C_k^+(x) \subseteq C_k(x)$ be the set of all objects from $C_k(x)$ which belong to the same decision class as x (*positive examples*). In our previous study [10], we defined the stopping condition according to the share of $C_k^+(x)$ in $C_k(x)$, namely as

$$\frac{|C_k^+(x)|}{|C_k(x)|} \geq \mu, \quad \mu \in (0,1]$$

However, as the reasonable value of μ is usually close to 1, such a condition often stops prematurely the process of extending the bounds of similarity in presence of noise. For instance, with $\mu > 0.5$ the algorithm would stop if the first nearest neighbour of x, y_1, did not belong to $C_k^+(x)$, even if all remaining objects belonged to $C_k^+(x)$. As a result, the tolerance interval for x would be very small.

Thus, we define here the stopping condition more precisely, in that the required share of positive examples in $C_k(x)$ is not a constant fraction of $|C_k(x)|$. In general, a function which is convex close to the origin of the system of coordinates $|C_k(x)| \times |C_k^+(x)|$ and linear afterwards, may be used to model the required number of positive examples in $C_k^+(x)$. The stopping condition is then much more tolerant for a few nearest neighbours of x, than for the following ones.

An exemplary definition of the *PurityCondition* is shown in Fig. 2. Each black dot corresponds to a share of positive examples in $C_k(x)$ accepted by the *PurityCondition* (*PurityCondition* returns true). For other cases, *PurityCondition* returns false.

Fig. 2. An exemplary definition of the *PurityCondition*. For detailed description see text.

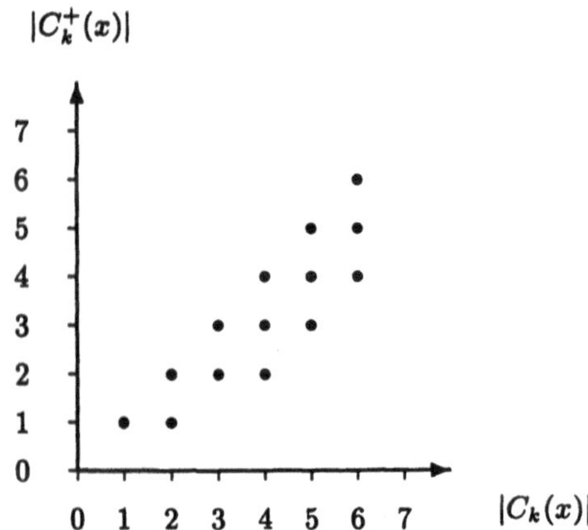

4 Generation of certain and robust decision rules

Analogously to the rough sets based on indiscernibility relation, given a decision table and a similarity relation, it is possible to induce some decision rules from that data. As already mentioned in section 1, decision rule is an '*if...then...*'

statement, i.e. it is composed of the conditional part (premise) and the decision. In this study, we are considering the rules with the premise being a conjunction of elementary conditions imposed on particular attributes, called hereafter, *selectors*. According to the similarity relation being used, a selector is a condition of the following form:

$$a_k \in [a_k(x) - \epsilon_k^-(x); a_k(x) + \epsilon_k^+(x)] \quad (7)$$

In the approach presented in this study, each rule is built starting from a particular object in the decision table, which we refer to as *base object*. An object (example) *matches* a rule, if it is similar to it in the sense of similarity relation R, i.e. if the values of particular attributes for that object belong to the corresponding intervals in the conditional part of the rule. All examples from the learning set matching a given rule constitute its *covering*. The cardinality of the covering of a rule is often referred to as *rule strength*. From a viewpoint of a particular rule, all objects covered by the rule and belonging to the same decision class as the base object are *positive*, whereas the others are *negative*.

The set of rules obtained from the decision table is usually evaluated according to two main criteria: size (the number of rules) and the predictive accuracy (usually being the accuracy of classification on some testing set). Unfortunately, those two criteria are often conflicting: a small set of rules, suitable for explanation, gives usually worse accuracy of classification than that composed of many rules which, on the contrary, is illegible. That is why many schemes of rule induction have been proposed, depending on the goal (see [7, 28]). Those proposals may be classified according to the characteristics of the resulting description:

- *Minimal description* - a minimal set of rules covering all examples from the learning set (if induced by a greedy technique it will be referred to as *minimal greedy*).
- *Exhaustive description* - all possible rules induced from the decision table.
- *Characteristic description* - the classifier is not imposed to cover all examples from the learning set; the rules which cover less than $\lambda\%$ of examples from the learning set are rejected.

In our study, we are mostly interested in the minimal and characteristic descriptions.

The algorithm for rule generation incorporates some ideas from [7, 28]. At the very beginning, the objects being subject to rule induction are sorted according to the descending size of their similarity classes $R(x)$. Then, for consecutive objects, rules are induced starting from an empty rule and adding incrementally selectors in form of (7), which are built from the values and tolerances on particular attributes for that base object. In such a way, short and general rules are induced before long and specific ones. The rules which satisfy the stopping condition (related, among others, to the above mentioned λ parameter) are inserted into the resulting classifier. Thus, as far as the process of creating the rule by adding new selectors is concerned, the proposed procedure may be characterized as a top-down approach.

After inducing a rule from an object, all objects covered by it are removed from the decision table and from the similarity classes $R(x)$. Afterwards, the objects are sorted again according to the descending size of their similarity classes and the algorithm proceeds with the next object having the largest similarity class.

The proposed procedure may be used to obtain all three types of description. The minimal description may be obtained by setting the λ parameter to 0%. Skipping the stage of removal of covered examples described above results in the exhaustive description (all possible rules). Finally, setting $\lambda > 0\%$ gives the characteristic description.

In our approach, the rule induction is influenced by an additional parameter. By common definition, a rule covers only the positive examples from the learning set, i.e. the examples belonging to the decision class indicated by the conclusive part of the rule. However, such a definition is often too restrictive and causes the process of rule building to be very sensitive to noise. In an extreme case, even a single negative example (exception) in the covering of the rule can prevent it from being induced. Thus, we release in part that condition, in that we accept rules covering at least η% of positive examples. Moreover, as we are interested in certain rules, only objects belonging to the lower approximation of decision classes are used for rule induction.

The resulting classifier may be then validated on the set of testing examples. For that purpose, every example from the testing set is checked for its matching to every rule from the classifier. Then, all the rules which match the object being classified are grouped according to the decision classes they are indicating, and, for each class, the total strength of the rules is computed. The decision is made according to the maximal total strength over all decision classes.

5 Illustrative example

For illustration of the proposed approach to rule induction from the lower approximations of decision classes based on similarity relation, let us consider an exemplary information system, containing quantitative attributes [27]. At the very beginning, we apply the algorithm described in section 3 to derive the similarity relation R from the table. The decision table together with lower and upper bounds of similarity for particular attributes and objects produced by the procedure is presented in Table 1. The information system is composed of 12 objects described by 3 attributes and representing two decision classes, $X_0 = \{x_0, x_2, x_6, x_8, x_{10}\}$ and $X_1 = \{x_1, x_3, x_4, x_5, x_7, x_9, x_{11}\}$. The similarity classes $R(x)$ induced by the similarity relation R are also shown in the table. For illustration, the upper and lower bounds of similarity estimated for attribute a_0 are graphically presented in Fig. 3.

Note that the derived relation R is not symmetric; for instance $x_3 R x_2$, but $\neg x_2 R x_3$. According to formulae (5) and (6), the lower and upper approximations of decision classes given similarity relation R are :

$$R_*(X_0) = \{x_2, x_6, x_{10}\} \qquad R^*(X_0) = \{x_0, x_1, x_2, x_3, x_6, x_8, x_{10}, x_{11}\}$$

Table 1. The exemplary decision table with lower and upper similarity bounds and induced similarity classes $R(x)$ (d = decision).

x	$\epsilon_0^-(x)$	$a_0(x)$	$\epsilon_0^+(x)$	$\epsilon_1^-(x)$	$a_1(x)$	$\epsilon_1^+(x)$	$\epsilon_2^-(x)$	$a_2(x)$	$\epsilon_2^+(x)$	d	$R(x)$
x_0	0	43	27	5	78	8	0	0	0.5	X_0	x_0, x_1
x_1	11	54	16	17	75	11	0	0	0	X_1	x_0, x_1
x_2	24	124	3	0	50	18	0	1	0	X_0	x_2, x_3
x_3	32	102	25	7	65	21	0	1	0.5	X_1	x_3, x_8, x_{11}
x_4	28	98	29	7	80	23	0.5	2	0	X_1	x_4, x_5
x_5	18	88	39	29	102	1	0.5	2	0	X_1	x_4, x_5
x_6	3	130	4	7	57	11	0	0	0	X_0	x_6
x_7	28	128	6	19	92	11	0	1	0	X_1	x_7
x_8	39	82	11	9	59	9	0	1	0	X_0	x_8
x_9	7	134	0	30	103	0	0.5	2	0	X_1	x_9
x_{10}	15	58	35	5	55	13	0	0	0	X_0	x_{10}
x_{11}	26	126	8	13	71	15	0	1	0	X_1	x_3, x_{11}

Fig. 3. Bounds of similarity for particular objects estimated for attribute a_0.

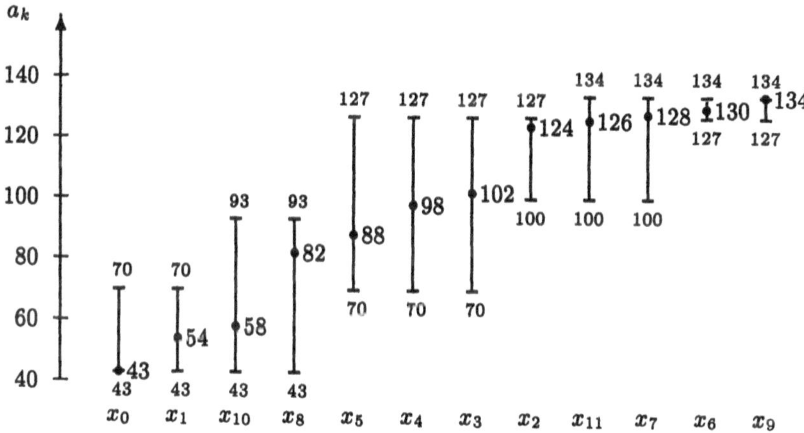

$$R_*(X_1) = \{x_4, x_5, x_7, x_9, x_{11}\} \quad R^*(X_1) = \{x_0, x_1, x_3, x_4, x_5, x_7, x_8, x_9, x_{11}\}$$

The approximations are characterized by the values of quality of approximation 0.6 and 0.71 for class X_0 and X_1, respectively. The overall quality of classification is equal to 0.67.

Based on the lower approximations of decision classes, we can induce certain rules from our exemplary decision table, using the proposed similarity relation. Suppose we are interested in perfectly discriminating rules and set the η parameter to 100%. All possible certain rules according to the procedure described in section 4, i.e. the exhaustive description, are shown in Table 2 (the duplicates have been removed for clarity). There are 13 such rules. Note, that no rule has

Table 2. The exhaustive description ('all rules' classifier) induced from the exemplary decision table. Rule numbers reflect the order of rule induction.

Rule No.	Rule strength	Base object	Rule
0	3.0	x_4	a2[1.50,2.00] $\rightarrow$ 1
1	2.0	x_4	a0[70.00,127.00] a1[73.00,103.00] $\rightarrow$ 1
2	2.0	x_4	a0[70.00,127.00] a2[1.50,2.00] $\rightarrow$ 1
3	3.0	x_4	a1[73.00,103.00] a2[1.50,2.00] $\rightarrow$ 1
4	2.0	x_6	a1[50.00,68.00] a2=0.00 $\rightarrow$ 0
5	1.0	x_6	a0[127.00,134.00] a1[50.00,68.00] $\rightarrow$ 0
6	1.0	x_6	a0[127.00,134.00] a2=0.00 $\rightarrow$ 0
7	2.0	x_7	a0[100.00,134.00] a1[73.00,103.00] $\rightarrow$ 1
8	1.0	x_7	a1[73.00,103.00] a2=1.00 $\rightarrow$ 1
9	2.0	x_9	a0[127.00,134.00] a1[73.00,103.00] $\rightarrow$ 1
10	1.0	x_9	a0[127.00,134.00] a2[1.50,2.00] $\rightarrow$ 1
11	2.0	x_{10}	a0[43.00,93.00] a1[50.00,68.00] $\rightarrow$ 0
12	2.0	x_{11}	a0[100.00,134.00] a1[58.00,86.00] $\rightarrow$ 1

been induced for object x_2, although it belongs to the lower approximation of class X_0. This phenomenon is due to the lack of symmetry of R. According to formula (5), object x_2 belongs to the lower approximation of X_0 because it is not similar to any object from outside of X_0. However, there is an object from outside of X_0, which is similar to object x_2, namely object x_3 (see Table 1). Thus, any conjunction of selectors built from object x_2 will cover some negative examples, which is unacceptable if we tend to build perfectly discriminating rules (i.e. $\eta = 100\%$).

On the other hand, building the minimal description from lower approximations of decision classes leads to the classifier composed of only four rules, presented in Table 3. Let us notice that the algorithm induces the rules from objects according to the size of their similarity classes, starting from the biggest one (object x_4 for class X_1, for instance).

Table 3. The minimal description induced from the exemplary decision table using the greedy algorithm.

Rule No.	Rule strength	Base object	Rule	Rule covering
0	2.0	6	a1[50.00,68.00] a2[0.00,0.50] $\rightarrow$ 0	x_6, x_{10}
1	3.0	4	a2[1.50,2.00] $\rightarrow$ 1	x_4, x_5, x_9
2	2.0	11	a0[100.00,134.00] a1[58.00,86.00] $\rightarrow$ 1	x_3, x_{11}
3	1.0	7	a1[73.00,103.00] a2=1.00 $\rightarrow$ 1	x_7

Let us remark that the adopted way of defining the similarity relation from examples implies the interpretation of decision rules. Precisely, if we would like to be completely coherent with the definition of the lower approximation of decision classes, a decision rule r should be tested for similarity with a new object x by checking the truth of the statement: 'r *is similar to* x'. However, this would require to define the similarity relation, and thus ϵ_k's, with respect to x which is the referent. In our method, the ϵ_k's are inferred from decision table with respect to each particular object for which the class assignment is known; but the class assignment is unknown for x.

This being so, we have to use an inverted similarity test, i.e. check the statement: 'x *is similar to* r'. In consequence, when generating the decision rules, we shall also use the inverted similarity test and thus it is possible that an object from the lower approximation of a decision class may remain not covered by any of those rules (in the example, it is the case of x_2 in 'all rules' description).

Table 4. Data sets used in experiments (Type: bot. - botanical, med. - medical, tech. - technical).

	Iris	*Glass*	*Pima*
Number of objects	150	214	768
Number of attributes	4	9	8
Number of decision classes	3	6	2
Type	bot.	tech.	med.

6 Classification test on real-world data

To verify the usefulness of the presented methodology, a computational experiment has been performed. All elements of the approach, i.e. the algorithm for estimation of tolerances, the basic elements of the rough-set theory using the similarity relation, as well as the rule induction algorithm, have been implemented in a computer program.

To obtain comparable results, the computational experiments have been carried out on well-known reference data sets *Iris* (Fisher's Iris Plant Database), *Glass* (glass identification database) and *Pima* (Pima Indians diabetes database), coming from the University of California Repository of Machine Learning Databases [14]. Obviously, to test the usefulness of the similarity relation, we selected data sets composed of quantitative attributes exclusively. Table 4 describes shortly these domains.

To fulfil the Machine Learning requirement concerning the division of data into the learning and testing set, cross validation technique (CV) has been used. Thus, a set of examples is split into ten subsets, each of the same size (as far as it is possible). Then, ten experiments are carried out; in each 'fold', nine of the ten subsets constitute the learning set, whereas the remaining one plays the role of the testing set.

It has to be pointed out that the testing set is used for the validation of the classifier only. Everything else, i.e. estimating the tolerance intervals, computing of the similarity classes, lower and upper approximations and rule induction, is done exclusively on the ground of the learning set.

As the domain knowledge concerning all the above data sets was beyond our grasp, we were obliged to use the technique described in section 3 to estimate the tolerances on particular attributes. Several additional experiments have been performed on few data sets, to assess the value of μ (see section 3). At that point, two criteria have been taken into account: the quality of classification of the resulting decision table, and the number of 'non-trivial' similarity classes, i.e. those containing at least two objects. Finally, we found out the values of μ in the range $[0.7, 0.85]$ being close to optimum, and that range has been accepted and used in the experiments described below. For the rule induction algorithm, the λ coefficient (minimal percentage of examples covered by a single rule) has been set to 1%, and η (minimal share of positive examples covered by a rule; see section 4) to $0.7 \ldots 0.9$.

Table 5. Comparison of the accuracy of classification obtained using different classifiers (results for C4.5, IBL3 and ANN quoted from [9]).

Algorithm	Description	*Iris*	*Glass*	*Pima*
C4.5		95.5±0.5	67.9±2.6	70.8±0.8
IBL3		96.7±3.8	65.4±2.6	68.2±1.4
ANN		95.3±0.8	65.0±2.1	76.4±0.8
RS with indiscernibility relation	exhaustive	81.3±0.8	32.2±0.9	65.1±0.6
	minimal	80.0±1.2	32.2±0.9	65.1±0.6
RS with Similarity relation	exhaustive	97.3±0.6	68.7±0.7	70.1±0.6
	minimal	96.7±0.6	57.5±1.7	63.5±0.8

Table 6. Detailed description of the RS classifiers.

	Description	*Iris*	*Glass*	*Pima*
Average number of rules	exhaustive	427	891	701
	minimal	12	55	28
Average number of selectors per rule	exhaustive	2.0	1.9	1.4
	minimal	1.0	1.1	1.0

Table 5 shows the accuracy of classification achieved using various classifiers. For the approach proposed in this paper, the best results obtained using the mentioned range of parameters are reported in the table (meaning the maximal value of accuracy of classification for particular data set), for both the minimal and 'all rules' descriptions. For comparison, the results for four other approaches are given: decision tree induction algorithm C4.5 [20], case-based reasoning method *Instance Based Learning 3* [1, 2], layered Artificial Neural Network (ANN) with standard, on-line 'vanilla' backpropagation learning algorithm [21]. Additionally, our approach has been tested for tolerances set to zero, to simulate the standard indiscernibility relation in RS. All the experiments have been carried out in a 10-fold cross validation framework. The accuracy of classification has been averaged over all folds, and is given in percents together with the standard deviation.

As it has been stressed in section 4, apart from the accuracy of classification, we were also sometimes interested in keeping the classifier as compact as possible. Thus, in the experiments, for each set of examples and each cross validation fold, we collected the statistical data concerning the generated rules: the average number of rules in each classifier and the average number of selectors per rule. These values are reported in Table 6, for both rule induction strategies.

The computations for the approach based on similarity relation have been performed on the Power Challenge L SGI Scalar Server, loading one 300 MFLOP processor in average. A single cycle of computation, i.e. one cross validation fold composed of tolerance estimation, generation of similarity classes and approximations, rule induction and rule verification, took from less than 1 second in the case of small data sets (*Iris*) to few minutes for larger domains (*Pima*). The greater part of the computation time is consumed by the rule induction algorithm.

7 Conclusions

In this paper, an alternative approach to rough set-based induction of decision rules is proposed. In contrast to the standard rough set approach, instead of indiscernibility relation, it incorporates simple asymmetric similarity relation, modelled by tolerance intervals. We claim that such model of similarity reflects well the human way of reasoning, and allows an easy and elegant incorporation in the framework of the rough set theory. The experiments show, that even if the detailed definition of the similarity relation is not given by an expert, it is still possible to obtain its useful estimation using the technique described in section 3.

In this work, the existing RS-based rule induction algorithms have been subject to extension, using the introduced similarity relation. In consequence, one obtains classifiers composed of tolerance rules, which, in contrast to the majority of existing RS classifiers are able to handle quantitative features, extending in this way the variety of possible applications. Moreover, the classifiers obtained using the minimal description approach offer good readability, being compact in twofold way: (i) they are composed of relatively few, strong rules, and (ii) the rules are short, being usually composed of a few (1-2) selectors (Table 6). At the same time they are certain and robust, being capable to generalize in degree which is comparable to such renowned and widely used techniques, as C4.5, IBL3 and Neural Networks (see Table 5). The entire approach is simple, being influenced by only a few well-defined and comprehensible parameters. Its implementation works relatively fast, so it may be used in an interactive framework, giving the user the possibility of 'trial-and-error' approach, in domains such as Decision Support, Machine Learning, Knowledge Discovery and Data Mining.

Acknowledgments

The computational experiments have been carried out at the Supercomputing and Networking Center of Poznań. The research of the first two authors has been supported by grant no. 8 T11C 013 13 from State Committee for Scientific Research (Komitet Badań Naukowych). Moreover, this research has been carried out within the French-Polish joint research project.

References

1. Aha, D.W.: Case-based learning algorithms. In: Proceedings of the Case-Based Reasoning Workshop, Morgan Kaufmann (1991) 147–158
2. Aha, D.W., Kibler, E., Alberk, M.K.: Instance based learning algorithms. Machine Learning **6** (1991) 37–66
3. Chan, Ch.-Ch., Grzyma'a-Busse, J.W.: On the two local inductive algorithms: PRISM and LEM2. Foundations of Computing and Decision Sciences **19/3** (1994) 185–204
4. Chmielewski, M., Grzyma'a-Busse, J.: Global Discretization of Continuous Attributes as Preprocessing for Machine Learning. In: Lin, T. Y., Wildberger, A. M. (eds.), Soft computing: rough sets, fuzzy logic, neural networks, uncertainty management, Simulation Councils, San Diego (1995) 294–301
5. Dubois, D., Prade, H.: Criteria aggregation and ranking of alternatives in the framework of fuzzy set theory. In: Zimmermann, H.J., Zadeh, L.A., Gaines, B.R. (eds.), Fuzzy sets and decision analysis. Studies in the management sciences **20** North-Holland, Amsterdam (1984) 209–240
6. Dubois, D., Prade, H.: Putting rough sets and fuzzy sets together. In: Słowiński, R. (ed), Intelligent decision support. Handbook of applications and advances of the rough set theory, Kluwer Academic Publishers, Dordrecht (1992) 203–232
7. Grzyma'a-Busse, J.W.: LERS - a system for learning from examples based on rough sets. In: Słowiński, R. (ed), Intelligent decision support. Handbook of applications and advances of the rough set theory, Kluwer Academic Publishers, Dordrecht (1992) 3–18
8. Höhle, U.: Quotients with respect to similarity relations. Fuzzy Sets and Systems **27** (1988) 31–44
9. Jelonek, J.: Generalization capability of homogenous voting classifier based on partially replicated data. In: Integrating Multiple Learned Models for Improving and Scaling Machine Learning Algorithms. Proceedings of Thirteenth National Conference on Artificial Intelligence. Portland, Oregon (1996) 47–52
10. Krawiec, K., Słowiński, R., Vanderpooten, D.: Construction of Rough Classifiers based on Application of a Similarity Relation. In: Tsumoto S., Kobayashi, S.,

Yokomori, T., Tanaka, H. (eds.), Proceedings of the Fourth International Workshop on Rough Sets, Fuzzy Sets and Machine Discovery (RSFD'96), Tokyo Nov. 6-8, Tokyo Univ. Press (1996) 23–30
11. Lin, T.: Neighborhood systems and approximation in database and knowledge base systems. In: Proceedings of the 4th International Symposium on Methodologies for Intelligent Systems (1989)
12. Luce, R.: Semi-orders and a theory of utility discrimination. In: Econometrica **24** 1956.
13. Marcus, S.: Tolerance rough sets, Čech topologies, learning processes. Bull. Polish Acad. Sci. Ser. Sci. Tech. **42/3** (1994) 471–484
14. Merz, C.J., Murphy, P.M.: UCI Repository of machine learning databases [http://www.ics.uci.edu/m̃learn/MLRepository.html]. Irvine, CA: University of California, Department of Information and Computer Science (1996)
15. Mieko, R., Stefanowski, J., Vanderpooten, D.: Discovery-oriented induction of decision rules. Cahier du LAMSADE **141** Universite de Paris-Dauphine, Paris (Septembre 1996)
16. Nieminen, J.: Rough tolerance equality. Fundamenta Informaticae **11/3** (1988) 289–296
17. Pawlak, Z.: Rough sets. Int. J. Computer and Information Sci. **11** (1982) 341–356
18. Pawlak, Z.: Rough sets: theoretical aspects of reasoning about data. Kluwer Academic Publishers, Dordrecht (1991)
19. Polkowski, L., Skowron, A., Zytkow, J.: Tolerance based rough sets. In: Lin, T.Y., Wildberger, A. M. (eds.,) Soft computing: rough sets, fuzzy logic, neural networks, uncertainty management, Simulation Councils, San Diego (1995) 55–58
20. Quinlan, J.R.: C4.5: Programs for Machine Learning. Morgan Kaufmann Publishers, San Mateo CA (1988)
21. Rumelhart, D.E., Hinton, G.E., Williams, R.J.: Learning internal representations by error propagation. In: Rumelhart, D.E., McClelland, J.L. and the PDP Research Group (eds.), Parallel distributed processing. Explorations in the microstructure of cognition, MIT Press, Cambridge MA (1986) 318–362
22. Schreider, J.A.: Equality, Resemblance and Order. Mir Publishers, Moscow (1975)
23. Shan, N., Ziarko, W.: An incremental learning algorithm for constructing decision rules. In: Ziarko, W. (ed.), Rough sets, fuzzy sets and knowledge discovery, Springer-Verlag, Berlin (1994) 326–334
24. Skowron, A.: Boolean reasoning for decision rules generation. In: Komorowski, J., Ras, Z.W. (eds.): Methodologies for Intelligent Systems. LNAI **689** Springer Verlag, Berlin (1993) 295–305
25. Skowron, A., Stepaniuk, J.: Generalized approximation spaces. In: Lin, T.Y., Wildberger, A.M. (eds.), Soft computing: rough sets, fuzzy logic, neural networks, uncertainty management, Simulation Councils, San Diego (1995) 18–21
26. Skowron, A., Polkowski, L., Komorowski, J.: Learning tolerance relations by Boolean descriptors: automatic feature extraction from data tables. In: Tsumoto S., Kobayashi, S., Yokomori, T., Tanaka, H. (eds.), Proceedings of the Fourth International Workshop on Rough Sets, Fuzzy Sets and Machine Discovery (RSFD'96), Tokyo Nov. 6-8, Tokyo Univ. Press (1996) 11–17
27. Słowiński, R., Vanderpooten, D.: Similarity relation as a basis for rough approximations. ICS Research Report 53/95. Institute of Computer Science, Warsaw University of Technology, Warsaw, 1995. Also in: Wang, P. (ed.): Advances in Machine Intelligence & Soft Computing, Bookwrights, Raleigh NC (1997) 17–33

28. Słowiński, R., Vanderpooten, D.: A generalized definition of rough approximations based on similarity. IEEE Trans. on Data and Knowledge Engineering (to appear)
29. Stefanowski, J., Vanderpooten, D.: A general two-stage approach to inducing rules from examples. In: Ziarko, W. (ed.), Rough sets, fuzzy sets and knowledge discovery, Springer Verlag, Berlin, British Computer Society, London (1994) 317–325
30. Tentush, I.: On minimal absorbent sets for some types of tolerance relations. Bull. Polish Acad. Sci. **43/1** (1995) 79–88
31. Tversky, A.: Features of similarity. Psychological Review **84/4** (1977) 327–352
32. Yao, Y., Wong, S.: Generalization of rough sets using relationships between attribute values. In: Proceedings of the 2nd Annual Joint Conference on Information Sciences, Wrightsville Beach, N.C. (1995) 30–33
33. Zadeh, L.A.: Similarity relations and fuzzy orderings. Information Sciences **3** (1971) 177–200
34. Zeeman, E.C.: The topology of brain and visual perception. In: Fort, K.M. (ed.): Topology of 3-manifolds and related topics, Prentice Hall, Englewood Cliffs N.J. (1965) 240–256

Chapter 4

Discovery of Data Patterns with Applications to Decomposition and Classification Problems

Sinh Hoa Nguyen[1], *Andrzej Skowron*[2], *Piotr Synak*[3]

[1] Institute of Computer Science,
Warsaw University, Banacha 2, 02-097 Warsaw, Poland
e-mail: hoa@mimuw.edu.pl
[2] Institute of Mathematics,
Warsaw University, Banacha 2, 02-097 Warsaw, Poland
e-mail: skowron@mimuw.edu.pl
[3] Polish-Japanese Institute of Computer Techniques
Koszykowa 86, 02-018 Warsaw, Poland
e-mail: synak@pjwstk.waw.pl

1 Introduction

Data mining community is searching for efficient methods of extracting patterns from data [20],[22],[39],[46],[45]. We study problems of extracting several kinds of patterns from data. The simplest ones are called templates. We consider also more sophisticated relational patterns extracted automatically from data.

We present several strategies searching for patterns represented by so called templates. In the simplest case the template is a "long enough" value vector of some features (attributes) supported by "sufficiently many" objects. The high computational complexity of the searching problem for optimal templates shows that it is necessary to develop efficient heuristics for extracting efficiently semi-optimal templates from large data sets. Among the discussed heuristics there are some using information about the distribution of attribute values in data tables [26] easily computable from data. We also mention some more advanced techniques based on application of genetic algorithms [25], [51]. An important class of the methods for pattern discovery from data is based on relational patterns [37]. These patterns are defined in a given data table by the optimal similarity (tolerance) relations in some preassumed classes of tolerance relations [28]. A tolerance relation is optimal if the set of parameters (with respect to the assumed quality measure) specifying this relation allows to construct the relevant data patterns for a given data table.

There are different possible applications of patterns extracted from data.

Some of them can be used to decompose large data tables [25], [28]. The set of objects supporting e.g. a given template can be treated as regular, in a sense, sub-domain of object universe because it consists of many objects sharing many common features. The large data tables can be decomposed into a binary tree of templates or patterns. Each node of the tree is related to one step of decomposition. The process of the decomposition stops when the sub-tables attached to leaves have a feasible size with respect to the existing methods of decision rules generation. We apply previously developed methods based on rough set approach (see e.g. [5], [30],[22],[30],[35]) for decision rules generation from the decision tables attached to leaves. In the process of new cases classification for any new object a path in the tree is selected by matched templates. Next the object is classified on the basis of decision rules generated from the sub-table attached to the leaf of that path.

We also discuss strategies searching for patterns (almost) included in decision classes. This process can be treated as searching for strong approximate default decision rules [22].

Our methods can also be used to search for approximate decision rule synthesis from data tables. The approximate nature of these rules is specified by some constraints. The strong decision rule can be understood like in the case of associations (see e.g. [1], [2]) but can also be characterized by some additional constraints e.g. assuming a high specificity (see e.g. [11], [21]) of the synthesized approximate decision rules guaranteed by the discovered templates or patterns. It is important to observe that relational patterns are expressed in a higher level language than templates so the former ones can lead to better generalization than the latter.

In the paper we concentrate on some efficient methods for patterns generation from data and their application to decomposition of data tables and object classification. We discuss the results of the performed computer experiments. We also investigate the complexity of the searching problem for the optimal template.

The paper consists of five parts. Introduction as well as general remarks related to the pattern discovery problem are presented in the first part. In the second part we introduce rough set preliminaries used in the paper. Methods for template generation from data tables are investigated in the third part. We also present some applications of discovered templates. In the fourth part we describe the relational pattern problem and methods for relational patterns extraction from data and their applications. The conclusions are included in the last part.

The third part of the paper is organized as follows:

In Section 3.1 we recall the template definition. We investigate the computational complexity of the template problem in Section 3.2. In Section 3.3 we show some searching methods for semi-optimal templates. The applications of templates for classification and decomposition are discussed in Section 3.4.

The fourth part of the paper is organized as follows:

In Section 4.1 we introduce some basic definitions related to patterns defined by tolerance relations. In Section 4.2 we propose a classification of methods searching for tolerance relation from data. A geometrical illustration of some tolerance relation families used for discovery of relational patterns is discussed in Section 4.3. In Section 4.4 we show some heuristics for semi-optimal tolerance relation generation. The applications of discovered from data tolerance relations are discussed in Section 4.5. The experimental results of methods based on tolerance relation are presented in the last section.

2 Preliminaries

An *information system* is defined by a pair $\mathbf{A} = (U, A)$, where U is a non-empty, finite set of *objects* called *the universe*, $A = \{a_1, \ldots, a_k\}$ is a non-empty, finite set of *attributes*, i.e. $a_i : U \to V_{a_i}$ for $i \in \{1, ..., k\}$, where V_{a_i} is called *the domain of the attribute* a_i.

The information space of A is defined by $INF_A = \prod_{a \in A} V_a$. We define the information function $Inf_A : U \to INF_A$ by $Inf_A(x) = (a_1(x), \ldots, a_k(x))$, for any $x \in U$. Any object $x \in U$ is represented by its *information vector* $Inf(x)$.

A decision table $\mathbf{A} = (U, A \cup \{d\})$, where $d \notin A$ is a distinguished attribute called *decision* and is a special case of information systems. The elements of A are called *conditions*. For $V_d = \{1, ..., r\}$, *the decision classes* are defined by

$$C_i = \{x \in U : d(x) = i\}, \text{for } i = 1, ..., r.$$

For any information system $\mathbf{A}$ and $B \subset A$, we define the B*-indiscernibility relation* $IND(B)$ by

$$x \; IND(B) \; y \Leftrightarrow \forall_{a \in B} \; a(x) = a(y).$$

Obviously, $IND(B)$ is an equivalence relation. Objects x, y satisfying relation $IND(B)$ are *indiscernible* by attributes from B. We denote by $[x]_{IND(B)} = \{y : \langle x, y\rangle \in IND(B)\}$ the equivalence class defined by the object $x \in U$.

The equivalence relation $IND(B)$ is a useful tool to approximate subsets of the universe U. For any $X \subseteq U$ one can define the lower approximation and the upper approximation of X by

$$\underline{B}X = \{x \in U : [x]_{IND(B)} \subseteq X\} \text{ and } \overline{B}X = \{x \in U : [x]_{IND(B)} \bigcap X \neq \emptyset\},$$

respectively. The pair $(\underline{B}X, \overline{B}X)$ is called the rough set of X.

3 Searching for Templates in Data Tables

3.1 Templates

Let $\mathbf{A} = (U, A)$ be an information system (decision table). A *template* T of $\mathbf{A}$ is any propositional formula $\bigwedge(a_i = v_i)$, where $a_i \in A$, $a_i \neq a_j$ for $i \neq j$, and $v \in V_{a_i}$. Assuming $A = \{a_1, ..., a_m\}$ one can represent any template

$$T = (a_{i_1} = v_{i_1}) \wedge ... \wedge (a_{i_k} = v_{i_k})$$

by the sequence $[x_1, ..., x_m]$ where on the position p occurs v_p if $p = i_1, ..., i_k$ and "*" (don't care symbol) otherwise. An object x satisfies the descriptor $a = v$ if $a(x) = v$. An object x *satisfies (matches)* the template T if it satisfies all descriptors of the template (i.e. if $x \in \|T\|_{\mathbf{A}}$ using standard notation from [40]). For any template T by $length(T)$ we denote the number of different descriptors $a = v$ occurring in T and by $fitness_{\mathbf{A}}(T)$ we denote its *fitness* i.e. the number of objects from the universe U satisfying T. If T consists of one descriptor $a = v$

only we also write $n_{\mathbf{A}}(a, v)$ (or $n(a, v)$) instead of $fitness_{\mathbf{A}}(T)$. By the *quality* of template T we often understand the number $fitness_{\mathbf{A}}(T) \times length(T)$. If s is an integer then by $Template_{\mathbf{A}}(s)$ we denote the set of all templates of $\mathbf{A}$ with fitness non-less than s.

Example : Let $\mathbf{A} = (U, A \cup \{d\})$ be a decision table as presented in Table 1. Let $T = (a_1 = 5) \wedge (a_3 = 0) \wedge (a_5 = black)$ be a template for $\mathbf{A}$ (T can be also expressed by $[5, *, 0, *, black]$). Then objects x_1 and x_4 satisfy T.

Objects	Conditional attributes					Decision
	a_1	a_2	a_3	a_4	a_5	d
$\mathbf{x}_1$	**5**	1	**0**	1.16	**black**	1
x_2	4	0	0	8.33	red	0
x_3	5	1	0	3.13	red	1
$\mathbf{x}_4$	**5**	0	**0**	3.22	**black**	1
x_5	1	0	1	3.24	red	0
Template	**5**	*	**0**	*	**black**	

Table 1. The example of the template with fitness equal to 2 and length equal to 3

3.2 Complexity of Template Problem

In this section we focus on the computational complexity of two *Template Problems*. For the first problem we are interested in the complexity of algorithms searching for the template with *maximal fitness* (*maximal length*) that has the *length* (*fitness*) at least equal to a given number L. The second problem is related to the complexity of algorithms searching for the template with *maximal quality* being a combination of the *fitness* and the *length* of template. In the first case we show that the corresponding decision problem is NP-complete and the optimization problem is NP-hard. We present also two problems equivalent to the second problem that can be useful to prove NP-hardness of this problem.

3.2.1 Templates with Maximal Fitness

The subject of this section is the computational complexity of an algorithm searching for the template with *maximal fitness*. The template is *L-optimal* if the number of objects matching it is maximal among templates with the length equal to a given number L. We show that the template decision problem is NP-complete and the optimization problem is NP-hard.

A template decision problem is defined as follows:

Template Fitness Problem (TFP)
Instance: Information system $\mathbf{A} = (A, U)$, positive integers F, L
Question: Is there a template T with the length equal to L and the fitness at least F?

The corresponding optimization problem is defined as follows:

Optimal Template Fitness Problem (OTFP)
Instance: Information system $\mathbf{A} = (A, U)$, positive integer L
Question: Find a template T with the length L and the maximal fitness.

Below we list some NP-complete problems used to show NP-completeness of the Template Fitness Problem.

Balanced Complete Bipartite Subgraph (BCBS) [10]
Instance: Bipartite undirected graph $G = (V_1 \cup V_2, E)$, positive integer $K \leq \min(|V_1|, |V_2|)$
Question: If there exist two subsets $U_1 \subseteq V_1, U_2 \subseteq V_2$ satisfying $|U_1| = |U_2| = K$ and $\{u, v\} \in E$ for any $u \in U_1, v \in U_2$?

The BCBS problem is NP-complete [10]. We consider a modified version of BCBS problem called *Complete Bipartite Subgraph* (CBS) problem. We will show that the BCBS problem can be polynomially reduced to the CBS problem, so the NP-completeness of the CBS problem will follow immediately once BCBS problem has been proved to be NP-complete.

Complete Bipartite Subgraph (CBS)
Instance: Bipartite undirected graph $G = (V_1 \cup V_2, E)$, positive integer $K_1 \leq |V_1|, K_2 \leq |V_2|$
Question: If there exist two subsets $U_1 \subseteq V_1, U_2 \subseteq V_2$ such that $|U_1| = K_1$, $|U_2| \geq K_2$ and $\{u, v\} \in E$ for any $u \in U_1, v \in U_2$?

Theorem 1. *The CBS problem is NP-complete.*

Proof. It is easy to see that CBS $\in$ NP, since a non-deterministic algorithm needs only to guess the subsets $U_1 \subseteq V_1$ and $U_2 \subseteq V_2$ with $|U_1| = K_1, |U_2| \geq K_2$ and to check in polynomial time if the subgraph defined on $U_1 \cup U_2$ is complete, i.e. $u \in U_1, v \in U_2$ implies $\{u, v\} \in E$.

Let $G|_{U_1 \cup U_2}$ denote the subgraph of G being the restriction of G to $U_1 \cup U_2$. We say that the subgraph $G|_{U_1 \cup U_2}$ has the size (K_1, K_2) if $|U_1| = K_1, |U_2| = K_2$.

We will transform BCBS to CBS. Let a graph G along with an integer K be an instance of BCBS. For CBS, we consider the same graph G with parameters $K_1 = K_2 = K$. It is obvious that the graph G has a complete subgraph $G|_{U_1 \cup U_2}$ such that $|U_1| = K_1$ and $|U_2| \geq K_2$ if and only if it contains a complete subgraph $G|_{U_1 \cup U_2}$, where $|U_1| = K_1$ and $|U_2| = K_2$. We obtain in this way the polynomial reduction of BCBS to CBS. □

Now we show that CBS can be polynomially reduced to TFP. Hence from the NP-completeness of CBS the NP-completeness of the TFP will follow.

Theorem 2. *TFP and CBS are polynomially equivalent.*

Proof. First we show that TFP is polynomially reducible to CBS. Let an information system $\mathbf{A} = (U, A)$ and positive integers $L \leq |A|, F \leq |U|$ be given as an arbitrary instance of the TFP, where L denotes the length of template to be found out and matched by at least F objects. We shall construct a bipartite graph $G = (V_1 \cup V_2, E)$ and parameters K_1, K_2 such that G has a complete subgraph of the size (K_1, K_2) if and only if there exists in $\mathbf{A}$ a template with the length L being matched by at least F objects. The graph $G = (V_1 \cup V_2, E)$ is constructed as follows: V_1 is the set of objects U and V_2 is the set of all attribute values. Formally vertex sets of the graph G are defined by

$$V_1 = \{u : u \in U\} \text{ and } V_2 = \{(a = v) : a \in A, v \in V_a\}$$

Any vertex $u \in V_1$ is connected with the vertex $(a = v) \in V_2$ iff $a(u) = v$. We recall that a template is a descriptor conjunction of the form

$$T = \bigwedge_{a \in B} (a = v), where B \subseteq A$$

Hence every template can be treated as a subset of V_2. One can observe that if T is a template with length L and fitness F and $U_1 \subseteq V_1$ is a set of objects matching T then the subgraph $G|_{U_1 \cup T}$ is a complete bipartite graph with $|U_1| = F$ and $|T| = L$. Conversely, any complete bipartite subgraph $G|_{U_1 \cup T}$, where $U_1 \subseteq V_1, |U_1| = F$ and $T \subseteq V_2, |T| = L$ defines exactly one template T with length L and fitness F. The illustration of the graph G and a complete subgraph $G|_{U_1 \cup T}$ is shown in Figure 1. The straight lines represent edges of the graph G and bold lines represent edges of the complete subgraph $G|_{U_1 \cup T}$ defining the template T where U_1 is the set of objects matching it.

We conclude that the graph G has a complete subgraph of size (F, L) if and only if an information system $\mathbf{A}$ has a template T with the length L and the fitness F. One can see that the graph G can be constructed in polynomial time from an information system $\mathbf{A}$. Therefore the answer to TFP can be obtained from the answer to BCS in time $O(1)$. Hence the graph G with parameters $K_1 = F, K_2 = L$ is a corresponding instance for CBS.

Conversely, we show that CBS can be transformed polynomially into TFP. We assume that a bipartite graph $G = (V_1 \cup V_2, E)$ and positive integers K_1, K_2 are given as an arbitrary instance of CBS. We shall construct an information system $\mathbf{A}$ and parameters F, L such that the system $\mathbf{A}$ has a template of the length L and the fitness at least equal to F if and only if there is a complete subgraph of G with the size (K_1, K_2). First, we define the information system $\mathbf{A} = (U, A)$. The object set U is equal to the vertex set V_1 and attribute set A is equal to the vertex set V_2, formally $U = V_1$ and $A = V_2$. Any attribute $a \in A$ is a function $a : U \to V_a$ defined by

$$a(u) = \begin{cases} 0 & \text{if } (u, a) \in E \\ v_{a,u} & \text{otherwise} \end{cases}$$

For a given object u and a given attribute a, the value $v_{a,u}$ is defined as follows: Let $U_a \subseteq V_1$ be the set of all vertices not connected with the vertex a. We

A	a	b	c
u_1	1	Y	0
$\mathbf{u_2}$	**2**	**N**	0
$\mathbf{u_3}$	**2**	**N**	0
u_4	3	Y	0
$\mathbf{u_5}$	**2**	**N**	1

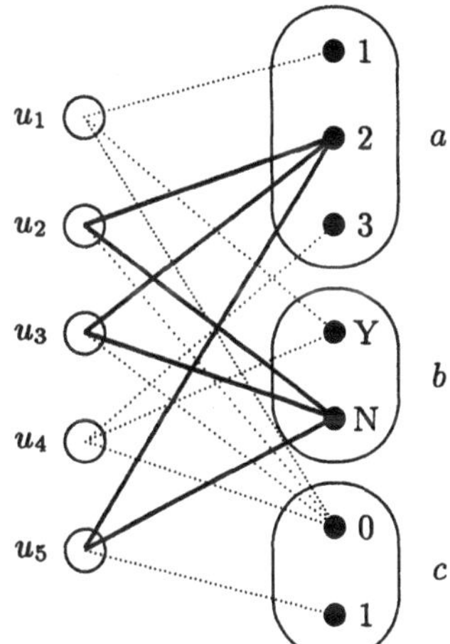

Fig. 1. The bipartite graph generated from the table and the subgraph corresponding to the template: $(a = 2) \wedge (b = N)$

assume that $|U_a| = m$ and vertices from U_a are ordered by $u_{a,1}, u_{a,2}, ..., u_{a,m}$. Hence if $(u, a) \notin E$ then $u = u_{a,i}$ for some $i \in \{1, ..., m\}$. We take in this case $v_{a,u} = i$ (i.e. $a(u) = i$). In Figure 2 we give an example of a bipartite graph G and the corresponding information system $\mathbf{A}$. One can observe that the information system $\mathbf{A}$ can be constructed in polynomial time from a bipartite graph G. We can also see that every template T of fitness greater than 1 is of the form $T = \bigwedge\{(a = 0) : \text{for some } a \in A\}$. Therefore it determines exactly one bipartite subgraph $G|_{U_1 \cup U_2}$, where $U_1 \subseteq V_1$ is the set of objects matching the template T and $U_2 \subseteq V_2$ is a set of attributes occurring in T, i.e. $U_2 = \{a : aoccuresinT\}$. Hence the table $\mathbf{A} = (U, A)$ with the parameters $F = K_1$, $L = K_2$ is a corresponding instance for TFP. We obtain in this way the polynomial transformation of CBS into TFP. □

Corollary 3. *The TFP is NP-complete.*

Proof. CBS is polynomially reducible to $TFP \in NP$. Hence NP-completeness of TFP results from NP-completeness of CBS. □

Now we observe that TFP is not harder than the OTFP, which along with the fact that TFP is NP-complete, constitutes a proof that the optimization problem is NP-hard.

Theorem 4. *If $P \neq NP$ then OTFP is NP-hard.*

Proof. Suppose $S[\mathbf{A}, L]$ is a subroutine that calculates for an information system $\mathbf{A}$ a template of length L with the maximal fitness. Then the decision

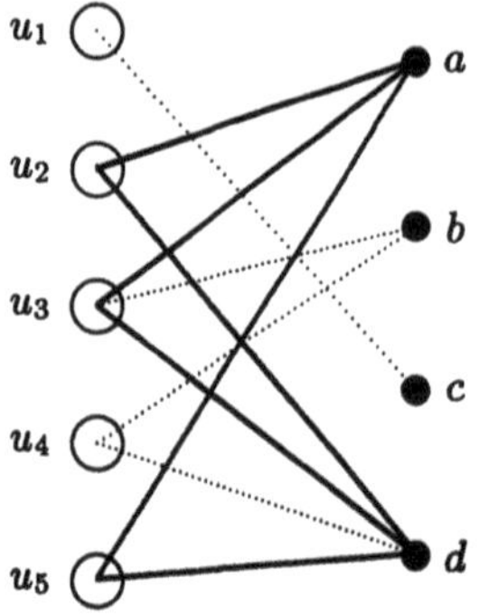

A	a	b	c	d
u_1	1	1	0	1
u_2	0	2	1	0
u_3	0	0	2	0
u_4	2	0	3	0
u_5	0	3	4	0

Fig. 2. The table constructed from the bipartite graph and corresponding template: $(a = 0) \wedge (d = 0)$.

problem TFP with the instance: **A** - information system, L - template length, F - template fitness could be solved as follows: We call subroutine $S[\mathbf{A}, L]$ to compute the template T with the length L and the maximal fitness. One can see that if $fitness(T) < F$ the answer for the decision problem is negative, i.e. does not exist any template with length L and fitness at least F. Otherwise (i.e. $fitness(T) \geq F$), the answer for the decision problem is positive, i.e. there exists a template with length L and fitness at least F.

Hence TFP could be solved in polynomial time if $S[\mathbf{A}, L]$ were a polynomial time subroutine for the OTFP. From the NP-completeness of TFP it follows that OTFP is NP-hard and cannot be solved by any polynomial time algorithm unless $P = NP$. □

We can observe that the Complete Bipartite Subgraph problem is symmetrical i.e. if we exchange the roles of the parameters K_1, K_2 we obtain again a NP-complete problem. Hence the Template Fitness Problem with exchanged roles of fitness and length of a template is NP-complete, too. We obtain therefore the following two results:

Corollary 5. *Given an information system* $\mathbf{A} = (A, U)$ *and positive integers* F, L. *The decision problem of checking if there exists a template* T *with fitness equal to* F *and length at least* L *is NP-complete.*

Corollary 6. *Given an information system* $\mathbf{A} = (A, U)$ *and positive integer* F. *The optimization problem of searching for a template* T *(if any) with fitness* F *and maximal length is NP-hard.*

3.2.2 Templates with Maximal Quality

In the previous section we considered computational complexity of algorithms searching for optimal template, i.e. template of length (fitness) at least equal to a given number L and with maximal fitness (maximal length). The quality of the template can be defined either to be equal to the product of fitness and length of to be equal to the sum of them. In this section we focus on computational complexity of Template Problem in this new sense. The template is *optimal* if its quality is maximal. We present two problems relative to the mentioned above problems.

Template Quality Problem can be formulated as a following decision problem:

Template Quality Problem (TQP)
Instance: An information system $\mathbf{A} = (U, A)$, an integer K
Question: Does there exist a template for $\mathbf{A}$ with the quality higher than K?

One can show that TQP with the quality measure defined by

$$quality(T) = fitness(T) + length(T)$$

can be solved in polynomial time.

However, if we are using a template quality definition:

$$quality(T) = fitness(T) \times length(T)$$

the problem seems to be *NP-complete*, but it is still open. Similarly the following optimalization problem seems to be *NP-hard*:

Optimal Template Quality Problem (OTQP)
Instance: An information system $\mathbf{A} = (U, A)$
Question: Find a template T of the best quality (i.e. maximal $fitness(T) \times length(T)$).

Below we present two different equivalent formulations of OTQP that could be useful in proving its *NP-hardness*.

Labelled Subgraph Problem (LSP)
Input: A complete labelled indirected graph $G = (V, E, e)$ with labelling function $e : E \to 2^X$ having the following properties:

1. $\bigcup_{u,v \in V} e(u, v) = X$
2. $\forall_{u,v,w \in V} e(u, v) \cap e(v, w) \subseteq e(u, w)$.

Output: Find $V' \subseteq V$, such that $|V'| \cdot \left| \bigcap_{u,v \in V'} e(u, v) \right|$ is maximal.

Lemma 7. *LSP is polynomially equivalent to OTQP.*

Proof. For a given complete graph $G = (V, E)$, labelled with subsets of a given set X and satisfying conditions 1-2 we construct an information system $\mathbf{A} = (U, A)$. Let $A = X$ and $U = V$. For any $v \in V$ we construct a new object x_v. The values of attributes on objects can be found using the following algorithm:

If $a \in A$ then by $G_a = (V, E_a)$ we denote a subgraph of G defined by $\{u, v\} \in E_a$ iff $a \in e(u, v)$ for any $u, v \in V$. Let us assign different non-negative integers to different connected components of G_a. We put $a(u) = i$ iff u is in the ith connected component of G_a. It is easy to observe that connected components of G_a are complete graphs and any template T with nonempty set of satisfying it objects can be described by

$$T = \bigwedge\{(a = i_a) : a \in A'\}$$

for some $A' \subseteq A$ where i_a is the number assigned to a connected component of G_a.

For any $V' \subseteq V$ let us consider the set A' of all a such that V' is a connected component of G_a. Let i_a be the number assigned to V'. We define a template $T_{V'} = \bigwedge\{(a = i_a) : a \in A'\}$. We have

$$|V'| \cdot \left| \bigcap_{u,v \in V'} e(u, v) \right| = length(T_{V'}) \cdot fitness_{\mathbf{A}}(T_{V'}).$$

Therefore $|V'| \cdot \left| \bigcap_{u,v \in V'} e(u, v) \right|$ is maximal iff $length(T_{V'}) \cdot fitness_{\mathbf{A}}(T_{V'})$ is maximal.

Example: Let $X = \{a, b, c\}$ and $G = (V, E, e)$ be a complete labelled graph as in Figure 3.

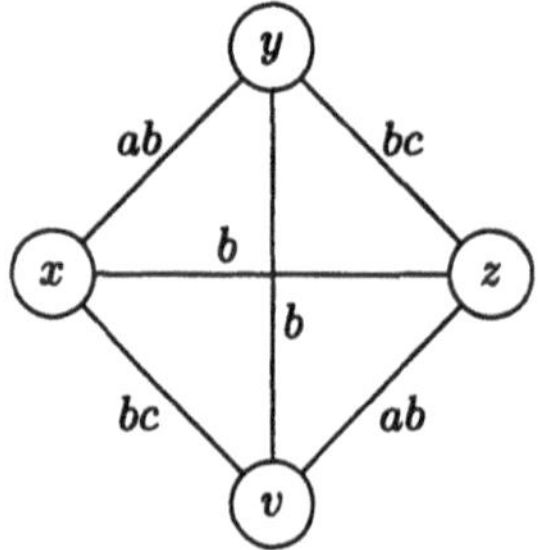

A	a	b	c
x	0	0	1
y	0	0	0
z	1	0	0
v	1	0	1

Fig. 3. The complete labelled graph and the corresponding information system

Applying our algorithm we obtain the information system on the right hand side of the Figure 3.

The time complexity of the algorithm constructing an information system from a given graph is of order $O(n^2m)$, where $n = |V|$ and $m = |X|$.

Similarly, for any information system $\mathbf{A} = (U, A)$ one can construct a complete labelled graph $G = (V, E, e)$, where $V = U$

$$e(u, v) = \{a \in A : a(u) = a(v)\}.$$

Then any template T of $\mathbf{A}$ defines the subset $V_T = \{x : x \text{ satisfies } T\}$ of V and the number $fitness_{\mathbf{A}}(T) \cdot l(T)$ is equal to $|V_T| \cdot \left| \bigcap_{u,v \in V_T} e(u, v) \right|$. One can also easily see that for any template T we have $fitness(T) \cdot l(T)$ is maximal iff $|V_T| \cdot \left| \bigcap_{u,v \in V_T} e(u, v) \right|$ is maximal. □

Another problem polynomially equivalent to the Optimal Template Problem is the following:

Uniform Submatrix Problem
Input Matrix $C_{m \times n}$
Output Find a permutation of columns and rows of C such that C contains largest *uniform block* with the largest size i.e. block containing only one value (by the *size* of a block we mean the number of its columns times the number of its rows).

3.3 Methods for Template Generation

We propose in this section some effective heuristics extracting (semi-)optimal templates from data. We also present some template searching strategies which do not use the decision attribute (unsupervised methods). However one can see that proposed methods are universal and one can easily adopt them to obtain the template searching methods using decision attribute (supervised methods).

3.3.1 Finding Templates Using Weights

Object weight algorithm

The idea of the method is based on an observation that any object set $U_1 \subseteq U$ *generates* some set $T(U_1)$ of templates matching all objects from U_1. Let T_{U_1} denote the template with maximal length among all templates belonging to $T(U_1)$. We define the *local quality* of the template T_{U_1} to be the product of cardinality of U_1 and the length of the template T_{U_1} (i.e. $card(U_1) \times length(T_{U_1})$). The template T_{U_1} is called *locally optimal* if its local quality is maximal. The goal of this method is to search for a subset U_1 such that the template T_{U_1} generated by U_1 is locally optimal. Intuitively, the object set U_1 generates a template with a high quality if objects in the set U_1 are similar. For that purpose we are computing for all objects in the information system some appropriate weights reflecting their potential ability to be "good" generators for a semi-optimal template. We use a greedy algorithm to compute the object set U_1. We start from empty set $U_1 = \emptyset$. Each time objects are chosen randomly with respect to their weights and appended to the set U_1. For a new set U_1 the template T_{U_1} and its local quality is calculated. If the quality of T_{U_1} is better - the algorithm continues, otherwise - the decision depends on value of a control variable. The algorithm uses a mechanism of so called "mutation" i.e. some objects are selected to be removed once upon a time. It allows to avoid the local extrema. Below we presents some useful similarity measures that describe object weights.

- *Weights of objects reflecting potential similarity of objects*
  Let $\mathbf{A} = (U, A)$ and $x \in U$. For any $y \in U$, we calculate

$$g_{x,y} = |\{a \in A : a(x) = a(y)\}|$$

  i.e. the number of attributes that have the same value on x and y. This number reflects the "closeness" of y to x. Then, for any attribute $a \in A$, we calculate

$$w_a(x) = \sum_{y:a(x)=a(y)} g_{x,y}$$

  and finally the weight

$$w(x) = \sum_{a \in A} w_a(x).$$

  We have

$$w(x) = \sum_{y} g_{x,y}^2$$

- *Weights of objects derived from attribute value frequency*
  Let $\mathbf{A} = (U, A)$ and $x \in U$. Then for any $a \in A$ we define

$$w_a(x) = n_{\mathbf{A}}(a, a(x)) \text{ and } w(x) = \sum_{a \in A} w_a(x).$$

  Our experiments show that these weights allow for quite satisfactory clustering of objects into templates while more "naive" values of weights decrease the quality of results.

Attribute weight algorithm

The idea is very similar to "object weights" method, however, appropriate weights are being attached to all attributes in the decision table. Within an attribute each attribute value has its own weight, too. In the process of searching for templates, first the attribute and then the attribute value are being chosen randomly with respect to their weights. Each time new attribute and attribute value are chosen, fitness of obtained template is calculated. If the new template is better then the algorithm continues, otherwise it depends on the control variable. The algorithm uses a mechanism of "mutation" i.e. with some frequency a randomly chosen fixed attribute value in the template is being changed to "don't care" (*) value. It allows to avoid local extrema of the quality function.

Algorithm (Attribute Weight)

1. Initialize $T = [*, *, ..., *]$;
2. $i = 1$; $k = 1$; $fitness = 0$;
3. **while** criterion not satisfied
   (a) Randomly choose $r \in [0, 1)$;
   (b) **if** ($r < w_{\mathbf{A}}(a_i)$ **and** $T[i] = *$) **then**
      Choose an integer $l \in \{1, ..., |V_{a_i}|\}$ such that
      $$\sum_{k=1}^{l-1} w_{\mathbf{A}}^{a_i}(v_k^{a_i}) \leq r \leq \sum_{k=1}^{l} w_{\mathbf{A}}^{a_i}(v_k^{a_i});$$
      $T[i] = v_l^{a_i}$;
      Calculate $new\_fitness$ for T;
      if $new\_fitness \leq fitness \times fit\_coeff$ **then**
         $T(i) = *$;
      else
         $fitness = new\_fitness$; Store(T);
      endif
   (c) **if** $k = mutation\_coeff$ **then**
      change randomly chosen value of *template*;
      $k = 0$;
      endif
   (d) $i = i + 1$; $k = k + 1$;
   (e) **if** $i = n$ **then** $i = 1$;
   endwhile

Let $\mathbf{A} = (U, A), m = |U|, n = |A|$. One can order the attribute values of $a \in A$ according to the value $n_{\mathbf{A}}(a, v)$ for any $a \in A$. Then by v_i^a we denote the i-th value of attribute a in that order. The value v_1^a is then the most often occurring value of a in A. We randomly choose the order between values v and u if $n_{\mathbf{A}}(a, v) = n_{\mathbf{A}}(a, u)$. For any attribute $a \in A$ we define

$$w_{\mathbf{A}}(a) = \frac{m}{\sum_{i=1}^{|V_a|} i \cdot n_{\mathbf{A}}(a, v_i^a)}.$$

Hence $w_{\mathbf{A}}(a) \in (0, 1]$. For any value u of attribute a, we can define the weight of u by

$$w_{\mathbf{A}}^a(u) = \frac{n_{\mathbf{A}}(a, u)}{m}.$$

We have $w_{\mathbf{A}}^a(u) \in (0, 1]$ and $\sum_{v \in V_a} w_{\mathbf{A}}^a(v) = 1$ for any $a \in A$.

One can be interested in searching for templates with possibly smaller fitness but with a high number of fixed attribute values. In such case the initial template can be set by performing operations from Step 3.a. to Step 3.e. In other cases the most important factor may be the quality of template without taking into account the length of templates. Relatively to this the initial template can be set with "don't care" (*) values. The *fitness_coeff* and *mutation_coeff* have to be set experimentally. They allow for obtaining different kinds of templates: with smaller or higher number of fixed attributes.

3.3.2 Template Extraction by Max Methods

Algorithm (Max I)
Input: An information system $\mathbf{A} = (U, A)$, where $n = |U|, m = |A|$ and an integer s.
Output: A template T from $Template_{\mathbf{A}}(s)$ with semi-maximal length.
begin

1. $T = \emptyset$;
2. **while** ($length(T) < m$ **and** $fitness_{\mathbf{A}}(T) > s$) **do**
   (a) **for** $a \in A$
   Sort objects from U with respect to values of a;
   Determine the value v_a that $n_{\mathbf{A}}(a, v_a) = \max_{v \in V_a}\{n_{\mathbf{A}}(a, v)\}$;
   endfor
   (b) Choose $a = v_a$ that $n_A(a, v_a) = \max_{b \in A \setminus A(T)} \{n_{\mathbf{A}}(b, v)\}$, where $A(T)$ is the set of attributes occurring in T;
   (c) $U =$ The set of objects from U matching the template $a = v_a$;
   (d) $A = A \setminus \{a\}$; $T = T \cup \{a = v_a\}$;
   endwhile

end

The purpose of this method is to search for as long as possible templates with fitness not less than certain lower bound s. We propose a heuristic called "*Max method*". The algorithm starts with null template e.g. template with length equal to 0. The template is extended by successive additions of descriptors of form $a = v_a$ until fitness of the template is not less than the fixed value s and the template can be extended. If the current template T consists of $i - 1$ variables then the i-th descriptor is chosen as follows: we search among attributes not occurring in the template T for an attribute a and a suitable value v_a such that the fitness of the new template $T \cup (a = v_a)$ is maximal. The construction of the template can be realized efficiently as follows: Let T be the template with i-1 variables and let $\mathbf{A}_{i-1} = (U_{i-1}, A_{i-1})$ where U_{i-1} is the set of objects matching the template T and A_{i-1} consists of all attributes from A not occurring in the template. The algorithm sorts objects from U_{i-1} with respect to the values of any attribute. Among sorted values of all attributes it chooses the attribute a and the value v with maximal $fitness_{\mathbf{A}_{i-1}}(a = v)$. Details of our method are presented in the description of Algorithm Max I.

The described algorithm allows to construct large template efficiently but it generates only one template. We present a modification of the Max I algorithm to obtain more than one template. Instead of choosing the descriptor with the largest fitness we consider all descriptors constructed in Step 2.a and choose one from them randomly according to a certain probability. Then the candidate descriptor $a = v_a$ is chosen to be added to T with a probability:

$$P(a = v_a) = \frac{n_{\mathbf{A}}(a, v_a)}{\sum\limits_{v \in V_a} n_{\mathbf{A}}(a, v)}.$$

The Algorithm Max I can be modified as follows:

Algorithm (Max II)
  $T = \emptyset$;
  while ($l(T) < m$ **and** $fitness_{\mathbf{A}}(T) < s$) **do**
    for $a \in A$
      Sort objects from U with respect to the values of a;
      Determine the value v_a that $n_{\mathbf{A}}(a, v_a) = \max\limits_{v \in V_a}\{n_{\mathbf{A}}(a, v)\}$;
    endfor
    Choose randomly the descriptor $a = v_a$ with the probability

$$P(a = v_a) = \frac{n_{\mathbf{A}}(a, v_a)}{\sum\limits_{v \in V_a} n_{\mathbf{A}}(a, v)}.$$

    U = The set of objects from U matching template $a = v_a$;
    $A = A \setminus \{a\}$;
    $T = T \cup \{a = v\}$;
  endwhile

Both algorithms take $O(m^2 n log n)$ time in worst case.

3.3.3 Finding Template Using Genetic Algorithms

Genetic algorithms are a class of metaheuristics based on the Darwinian principle of natural selection. In the problem of template generation a hybrid algorithm (see [51]) was successfully used. The algorithm bases on a simple heuristic procedure:

Step 1: Get an object x_0 as a base object.
Step 2: Let σ be a permutation of attributes.
Step 3: Consider a set of templates of the form: $T_1 = (a_{\sigma_1} = v_{\sigma_1}); T_2 = (a_{\sigma_1} = v_{\sigma_1}) \wedge (a_{\sigma_2} = v_{\sigma_2}), etc.$, where v_i denotes a value of i-th attribute on x_0.
Step 4: Choose the best template among T_1,...,T_n. This is a result generated by permutation σ.

This simple heuristic generates good templates. However, the result depends on a base object x_0 and a permutation σ. The object x_0 is chosen randomly, whereas the optimal permutation is generated by an order-based genetic algorithm. A fitness function of a permutation σ is proportional to the quality of the best template generated by σ.

3.3.4 Generalized Templates

The idea of a template may be extended to so called *generalized templates* i.e. templates of the form

$$GT = (a_{i_1} = v_{i_1} \vee ... \vee a_{i_1} = v_{i_n}) \wedge ... \wedge (a_{j_k} = v_{j_1} \vee ... \vee a_{j_k} = v_{j_m}).$$

The main difference is that instead of one-value we have many-valued positions of GT. We say that an object x satisfies the generalized descriptor $a = v_1 \vee ... \vee a = v_m$ if the value of a on x belongs to the set $\{v_1, ..., v_m\}$. An object x satisfies the generalized template GT if it satisfies all descriptors in GT. Another extension of this idea may be realized by templates with non-discrete descriptors i.e.

$$a \in [v_{i_1}, v_{i_2}] \vee ... \vee a \in [v_{m_1}, v_{m_2}].$$

In case of generalized templates GT one may modify the length of a descriptor from GT by

$$l(a) = \begin{cases} \frac{1}{k} & \text{if } a \text{ occured in a template} \\ 0 & \text{otherwise} \end{cases}$$

for any $a \in A$, the number k is equal to ***length*** of the generalized descriptor of a. By ***quality*** of a generalized descriptor of a we mean the product of $l(a)$ and the number of matching it objects. Using the function l one can easily modify fitness and length functions of generalized template. By $fitness_{\mathbf{A}}(GT)$ of GT we understand the number of objects satisfying GT and the length of GT we define by

$$length(GT) = \sum_{a \in A} l(a).$$

The ***quality*** of template GT is defined by $fitness_{\mathbf{A}}(GT) \times length(GT)$.

To find the generalized template with (semi-)maximal quality we can adopt the methods proposed in Section 3.3. One of the simplest strategy is a modified version of Max method. For any attribute $a \in A$ instead of searching for a value matching the maximal number of objects one can extract a set of values S_a so that the quality of the generalized descriptor defined by a and values from S_a is maximal. The set S_a is chosen from subsequences of a sorted list of all values V_a defined on a. The subsequence S_a is ***optimal*** if the quality of the descriptor $\bigvee\{a = v : v \in S_a\}$ is maximal. Starting from empty template $GT = \emptyset$, the scheme presented below describes a process of GT generation

Step 1: For any attribute $a \in A$ compute the optimal set S_a.
Step 2: Choose an attribute a and the corresponding to a set of values S_a such that the quality of the descriptor $p = \bigvee\{a = v : v \in S_a\}$ is maximal.
Step 3: Append descriptor p to GT; remove a from A. Compute the quality of GT.
Step 4: Repeat Step 1 to Step 3 until the set A is empty.
Step 5: Among generated templates choose the best one i.e. a template with maximal quality.

3.3.5 Experimental Results

Our methods for template generation were implemented and tested on several data tables of different size. Max methods show to be robust, it generates usually good templates in short time. In addition we can control the fitness and length of templates extracted by this method. However the object weight and attribute weight algorithm generate the templates with various values of fitness and lengths, sometime it found out templates with very high quality. Below we present the qualities of templates generated by methods proposed in Section 3.3. In Table 2 the quality of template is described by the product of the fitness (the first number) and the length (the second number).

Table Size (obj×attr)	Genetic Algorithm	Object Weight	Attribute Weight	Max I Method	Max II Method
471×33	240×3	200×4	216×4	216×4	219×4
	215×4	142×6	142×3	104×8	157×6
		301×2	301×2	30×11	47×10
225×490	86×8	94×27	74×36	153×12	91×13
	156×5	39×95	33×105	44×65	62×20
	122×10	14×210	14×210	20×120	10×73
15534×16	13929×2	13930×2	13930×2	13930×2	13930×2
	7868×3	6877×3	7869×3	7869×3	7869×3
		530×7	358×9	680×8	1227×7

Table 2. Results of template generation methods. The qualities of template T is represented by $fitness(T) \times length(T)$

3.4 Template Application

3.4.1 Templates and Initial Classification Process

The notion of a decision template may be useful for fast, initial classification of new objects. If the object matches one of the templates generated for the decision class C, we may assume C to be the appropriate decision for this object. The example presented below shows, that in many cases information hidden in templates is sufficient for classification.

Tested database: Satellite Image Data (4435 training objects, 2000 testing objects, 36 attributes). Training time: 1203 sec., classification of testing objects: 12 sec. Results (on testing objects):

37% classified correctly
6% classified incorrectly
2% classified to more than one decision class
52% not classified
99.97% of training objects classified correctly.

Due to the high rate of "not classified" objects we cannot use this technique as separate classification method. On the other hand, the low rate of incorrectly classified objects and the short training time (in comparison with other expert systems) make it interesting additional technique. The high rate of "not classified" objects is related to the "sharpness" of the notion of a template. To classify objects in a more flexible way, we should introduce a notion of similarity of objects with respect to a template. The similarity of attribute values is a function $d(v_i, v_j)$, which takes values between 0 and 1 (1 - values equal or nearly equal, 0 - values completely different). An example of such a function is:

$$d(v_1, v_2) = \frac{|v_1 - v_2|}{|v_{max} - v_{min}|}$$

where v_{max} and v_{min} are extreme values of attribute. The similarity function may take more complicated form (e.g. exponential, partially discrete), and may be different for each attribute.

Suppose that we have similarity measures d_i: $V_i \times V_i \rightarrow [0,1]$ defined on values of all attributes a_i. Let $D(x, T)$ be the measure of similarity of an object x to a template T, defined as follows:

$$D(x, T) = \prod_{i: v_i \neq " * "} d_i(a_i(x), v_i)^{p_i}$$

where v_i is a value of $i - th$ attribute in template T,

p_i is an accuracy parameter associated with the value v_i of attribute a_i in template T.

The similarity measure D takes values between 0 and 1. Now, when we obtain a new object x, we can compute the value $D(x, T)$ for any template T in the covering set. Then we can find the closest template and the decision class associated with it. The new object x is classified as belonging to this decision class.

The notion of similarity is very useful, when the description of new object is incomplete i.e. when values of some attributes are missing. The similarity rate of these blank fields and attribute values in the template may either be constant or be depedent from the probability distribution of values in the training database(see e.g. [35]).

3.4.2 Descriptions of Decision Classes

In this section we outline a general searching scheme for approximate description of decision classes built from templates. Suppose that we are given a decision table **A**. We are interested in the description of its $i - th$ decision class by a set of decision rules i.e. by the decision algorithm for this class.

One possibility is to search for a set of templates covering the decision class, i.e. most objects from the class match one of templates while as few as possible objects from other classes match them. Algorithms for template generating can be adapted to this new kind of a template: one can simply change the formula for the template fitness (see Section 3.3) [51]. Strategy of choosing templates can also depend on the estimation of how promising these templates can be for the construction of the decision class approximation by application of different operators like grouping, generalization, contraction. Hence, a more general strategy can be described as follows

Step 1: We produce a set of templates.

Step 2: We combine the templates obtained in Step 1 into groups and apply some operations of generalization and/or contraction. The grouping procedures are executed after templates are chosen. In this step the following principles should be observed:

(i) Two templates covering almost the same objects from the class and almost disjoint on objects not belonging to the class should be separated by grouping procedures;

(ii) The family of intersections of different templates in one group should not be "close" to the partition of the decision class into one element sets.

Groups of templates are received as the results of these procedures. Different approximate coverings of the decision class are constructed by applying generalization to these groups. Next, the grouping procedures are executed again as a pre-processing for contraction. The process continues until a description of the decision class with a sufficient quality is constructed; otherwise, the construction process is estimated as unsuccessful and it is redone starting from some previous construction level by applying another grouping, generalization or contraction strategies. The generalization operator may be understood in the simplest cases as the union of objects matching one of the templates, alternatively as a minimal template including all the templates. The contraction, in the simplest case, can be defined as the intersection of the templates. For both operators, one may take into account e.g. weights attached to the attributes. One may also employ additional techniques using tolerance relation or non crisp template description. We repeat Step 2 until the quality of obtained decision algorithm is sufficiently good.

Step 3: If the quality of the decision algorithm is not satisfactory then we repeat from Step 1 else we can use the algorithm (maybe after some post-processing) as the approximate definition of the i-th decision class.

The quality of decision algorithm obtained by this method depends on how it fits the decision class, and also on its complexity - we tend to produce rules with as simple as possible description. We are working on the implementation of this general strategy by using genetic programming.

3.4.3 Template and Decomposition Problem

The main task of decomposition problem is to search for a partition the large data table into sub-tables of feasible sizes. It means that these sub-tables should be not too large to be analyzed by existing algorithms and at the same time they should be not too small for assuring sufficient generality of decision rules extracted from them. We also optimize (minimize) the number of generated sub-tables. In addition, we want to reach sub-tables with some degree of a regularity. The presented below methods are ones of possible solution for these requirements.

Binary Decomposition Tree (BDT)

Performed experiments have shown that the idea of templates may be successfully used for the decomposition of large data tables. Let A be a data table, the easiest strategy can be presented as follows:

Step 1: Find the best (generalized) template T in A.
Step 2: Divide A into two sub-tables: $A(T)$ containing all objects satisfying T, $A(\neg T) = A - A(T)$.
Step 3: If obtained sub-tables are of feasible sizes (i.e. existing rough set methods can be efficiently used) then stop else repeat $1 - 3$ for all "too large" sub-tables.
Step 4: Calculate decision rules for obtained sub-tables.

This algorithm results with a binary tree of sub-tables with corresponding sets of decision rules for sub-tables in the leaves of the tree.

Decomposition by Minimal Set Covering

In previous section we have presented the method of decomposing the data table into disjoint sub-tables. In this section we propose another approach for this problem. Namely partition is defined by some optimal set of sub-tables that cover the whole (or majority part of) data table. The **optimal** cover set can be defined by different strategies. In this paper we consider cover sets with minimal cardinality.

One can observe that every object determines some *best* template covering it i.e. the template matched by this object and having maximal quality. In consequence every template defines some set of objects matching it. Therefore any object $u \in U$ can be treated as a *generator* for some sub-table of objects similar to u and covering u. The object is called a *representative generator* if it is similar to "many" other objects. One can use the object similarity measures presented e.g. in Section 3.3.1 to classify representative generators. Following the idea of approximating algorithm for the minimal set cover presented in [7] the searching process for optimal cover set of a given table can be described as follows:

Step 1: Choose the most representative generator $u \in U$ and construct the "good" template T_u matched by u. One can modify the heuristics proposed in Section 3.3 to construct such templates. Let U_1 be a sub-table matching T_u.
Step 2: Remove U_1 from U; Repeat Step 1 for remaining objects until the set U is empty.

The set of sub-tables generated by presented above algorithm create a sub-minimal set covering the data table. The set of corresponding templates defines a decomposition description of the data table into a minimal number of sub-tables.

3.4.4 Templates and Classification Problem

New Case Classification by Binary Decomposition Tree

Suppose we have a binary tree created in the process of decomposition (BDT method) as described in Section 3.4.3. Let x be a new object and $A(T)$ be a sub-table containing all objects matching T, we evaluate x starting from the root of the tree as follows:

Step 1: If x matches template T found for A then go to sub-tree related to $A(T)$ else go to sub-tree related to $A(\neg T)$.
Step 2: If x is at the leaf of the tree then go to 3 else repeat $1-2$ substituting $A(T)$ (or $A(\neg T)$) for A, respectively.
Step 3: Apply decision rules calculated [22],[35],[5] for sub-table attached to the leaf to classify x.

Presented above algorithm uses the binary decision tree, however it should not be misled with C4.5 [35], ID3 [21] and other algorithms using decision trees. The difference is that the above algorithm splits the object domain (universe) into sub-domains and for a new case we search for the most similar (from the point of view of the templates) sub-domain. Then rough set methods, C4.5, etc., may be used for the classification of this new case relatively to the matched sub-domain. In computer experiments we used generalized templates and attribute weight algorithm to create a binary decomposition tree. For Satellite Image [23] data we obtained a tree of depth 3. Sub-domains of the training table of size from 200 to 1000 objects have been found during the tree construction. By evaluating the testing table using the constructed tree we have obtained at leaves testing sub-domains of size from 100 to 500 objects. Applying the decision rules [5] corresponding to the sub-domains we have obtained the overall quality of classification 82,6%. This is due to the fact that there are leaves containing exceptions i.e. objects that do not match any (or very few) found template. Such leaves are in some sense chaotic and have worse quality of classification (about 70-80%) that decrease the overall score. However in many leaves of the tree the local quality of classification was much higher (about 90%). That means that using templates we have found some good, uniform sub-domains with strong, reliable rules.

New Case Classification by Minimal Set Covering

Another approach for new object classification is based on sub-tables covering the domain. We know that every sub-table from a cover set binds a template matching it. Assume $\{T_1, T_2, ..., T_m\}$ is a set of templates defining the cover set then a new object x can by classified as follows:

Step 1: Use well known methods [22],[35],[5],[29] to generate decision rules for any sub-table from the cover set.
Step 2: Classify x to proper sub-tables by matching it to templates from $\{T_1, T_2, ..., T_m\}$.
Step 3: Use decision rules of sub-tables found in Step 2 to classify x.

Below we present experimental results for some data tables chosen from U.C. Irvine repository [23]. In our experiments we used the discretization method (see e.g. [29]) to generate decision rules for sub-tables. We show the classification results of two testing methods.

In the first method, called *Global method*, we generate decision rules for the entire input training data and classify the new object using these decision rules.

In the second method, called *Local method*, first we decompose the input data table into sub-tables and the new object is classified according to the scheme described above.

Experimental result show the advantage of the local method, which at first searches for groups of the similar objects matched the same templates, then among similar objects extracts the decision rules. The decision rules generated by local methods in majority of cases are simpler and better than rules extracted by global method. Together with extracted templates, the *local* decision rules create the strong *global* rules for the whole data table.

Data Set	Obj_No	Attr_No	Training Set	Testing Set	Global Method	Local Method
Australian	690	14	621	69(CV10)	79,71%	83,67%
Diabetes	768	8	704	64(CV12)	67,85%	70%
Glass	214	9	172	42(CV5)	66,45%	66,45%
Heart	270	13	240	30(CV9)	74 %	76,67%
Iris	150	5	120	30(CV5)	95,66%	97,33%
Sat. Image	4435	36	4435	2000	81,80%	83,6%

Table 3. Classification quality: Global and Local Method

4 Searching for Relational Patterns in Data Tables

In previous sections we have suggested to search for patterns in the form of templates. Using them it was possible to decompose a given table into a family of sub-tables corresponding to these patterns and to create sub-domains of a given space of objects.

In this section we consider patterns defined by tolerance relations. These patterns correspond to some (semi-)optimal tolerance relations extracted from data. In this way we propose to search for (semi-)optimal tolerance relations from data in predefined classes of tolerance relations rather than by assuming apriori their form (as it is often done when clustering methods are used [3]).

In searching for tolerance relations from data we follow a method proposed in [37] based on rough sets. We propose a method of searching for (semi-)optimal tolerance relation (with respect to the number of the pairs of objects with the same decision from this relation) by transforming this problem to a problem of approximate description of some regions in affine space R^k, where k is equal to the number of (conditional) attributes.

We consider several classes of tolerance relation. Any class is characterized by a first order formula and some parameters which are tuned up in the optimization process. For any of these classes we propose strategies searching for semi-optimal tolerance relation in it i.e. described by a maximal set of object pairs having the same decision. We illustrate how the extracted patterns can be used for cluster construction and classification of new objects.

4.1 Basic Notions

The indiscernibility relation is a useful tool of rough set theory, but in many cases it is not sufficient, in particular, when we deal with real value attributes. In this case almost every object can differ from another on a particular attribute. The equivalence classes divide universe into tiny classes not enough general. The standard rough set approach [P84] can be generalized by assuming any type of binary relation (on attribute values) instead of the equivalence relation (see e.g. [17], [38], [47]).

In this paper we consider a relation which is *reflexive* and *symmetric*. This kind of relation is called *tolerance relations*. Formally a relation $\tau \subseteq U \times U$ is a tolerance relation on the set U iff

- $\forall_{x \in U}\ \langle x, x \rangle \in \tau$; (reflexivity)
- $\forall_{x,y \in U}\ (\langle x, y \rangle \in \tau \Rightarrow \langle y, x \rangle \in \tau)$; (symmetry)

Having a tolerance relation one can extend an object *indiscernibility* to similarity.

For a given decision table $\mathbf{A} = (U, A \cup \{d\})$ where $A = \{a_1, \ldots, a_k\}$, any object is characterized by attribute values. First we define tolerance relations in $INF_A \times INF_A$, where $INF_A = \prod_{a \in A} V_a$ and V_a is the domain of the attribute $a \in A$. We use the tolerance relation τ_A on INF_A to determine the tolerance relation in $U \times U$ by

$$\forall_{x,y \in U}\ \{\langle x, y \rangle \in \tau \Leftrightarrow \langle Inf_A(x), Inf_A(y) \rangle \in \tau_A\}$$

The tolerance relation τ defines tolerance classes for any $x \in U$

$$[x]_\tau = \{y \in U : \langle x, y \rangle \in \tau\}$$

We say, that the tolerance relation τ *identifies* objects x and y if $\langle x, y \rangle \in \tau$; otherwise we say that it *discerns* them.

One can define the lower approximation and the upper approximation of any subset $X \subseteq U$ with respect τ to by

$$\underline{\tau(X)} = \{x \in U : [x]_\tau \subseteq X\}; \quad \overline{\tau(X)} = \{x \in U : [x]_\tau \cap X \neq \emptyset\},$$

respectively.

We consider a local tolerance relation $\tau_a \subseteq V_a \times V_a$ for any attribute a of a decision table $\mathbf{A}$. To define a relation τ_a we use *similarity measures* for the attribute a. We assume any similarity measure $\delta_a : U \times U \to \Re^+ \cup \{0\}$, (for the attribute $a \in A$) is satisfying the following conditions:

- the value of $\delta_a(x,y)$ depends on the values $a(x)$ and $a(y)$ only;
- $\delta_a(x,x) = 0$;
- $\delta_a(x,y) = \delta_a(y,x)$;

The *parametric local relation* $\tau_a(\varepsilon_a)$ can be defined by $\langle x,y\rangle \in \tau_a(\varepsilon_a) \Leftrightarrow \delta_a(x,y) < \varepsilon_a$, where ε_a is a threshold and δ_a is a similarity measure.

Hence, a *global tolerance relation* $\tau \subseteq U \times U$ can be defined by

$$\langle x,y\rangle \in \tau \Leftrightarrow \Psi_R(\delta_{a_1}(x,y), \delta_{a_2}(x,y), \ldots, \delta_{a_k}(x,y)) = \textbf{true} \tag{1}$$

where $\Psi(\xi_1, \xi_2, ..., \xi_k)$ is an open formula of first order logic and Ψ_R is its realization in a relational structure of real numbers such that $\Psi_R(0,0,\ldots,0) = \textbf{true}$.

By C_k we denote the set $\{\langle r_1, r_2, ..., r_k\rangle \in R^k : 0 \le r_i \text{ for } i = 1,...,k\}$. Any relation τ defined by (1) determines a subset $\overline{\tau} \subseteq C_k$ equal to

$$\{(r_1, r_2, ..., r_k) \in C_k : \Psi_R(r_1, r_2, ..., r_k) = \textbf{true}\}.$$

One can define different tolerance relations using different formulas

$$\Psi(\xi_1, \xi_2, ..., \xi_k)$$

We list some basic families of parameterized tolerance relations considered in the paper:

1. $\langle x,y\rangle \in \tau_1(\varepsilon) \Leftrightarrow \max_{a_i\in A}\{\delta_{a_i}(x,y)\} \le \varepsilon$
2. $\langle x,y\rangle \in \tau_2(\varepsilon_1, ..., \varepsilon_k) \Leftrightarrow \bigwedge_{a_i\in A}[\delta_{a_i}(x,y) \le \varepsilon_i]$
3. $\langle x,y\rangle \in \tau_3(w_1, ..., w_k, w) \Leftrightarrow \sum_{a_i\in A} w_i \cdot \delta_{a_i}(x,y) + w \le 0$
4. $\langle x,y\rangle \in \tau_4(w_1, ..., w_k, w) \Leftrightarrow \sum_{a_i\in A} w_i \cdot \delta^2_{a_i}(x,y) + w \le 0$
5. $\langle x,y\rangle \in \tau_5(\varepsilon) \Leftrightarrow \min_{a_i\in A}\{\delta_{a_i}(x,y) \le \varepsilon\}$
6. $\langle x,y\rangle \in \tau_6(\varepsilon_1, ..., \varepsilon_k) \Leftrightarrow \bigvee_{a_i\in A}[\delta_{a_i}(x,y) \le \varepsilon_i]$
7. $\langle x,y\rangle \in \tau_7(w) \Leftrightarrow \prod_{a_i\in A} \delta_{a_i}(x,y) \le w$

where $\delta_{a_i}(x,y)$ is a predefined similarity measure for $i = 1,...,k$ and ε_i, ε,w_i, w are real numbers, called *parameters*.

A tolerance relation $\tau \subseteq U \times U$ is *consistent* with a decision table $\mathbf{A} = (U, A \cup \{d\})$ if

$$\langle x,y\rangle \in \tau \Rightarrow (d(x) = d(y)) \vee (\langle x,y\rangle \in IND_A)$$

for any objects $x, y \in U$.

The tolerance relation is *inconsistent* if it is not consistent.

One can see that if a tolerance relation is consistent with the decision table $\mathbf{A}$ then it contains only pairs of objects with the same generalized decision, however *inconsistent* tolerance may contain the pairs of objects with different generalized decisions.

The relation τ is *optimal* in the family $\mathcal{T}$ for a given $\mathbf{A}$ if τ contains the *maximal number* of pairs of objects among tolerance relations from $\mathcal{T}$ consistent with $\mathbf{A}$.

A tolerance relation $\tau \subseteq U \times U$ is U_1*-consistent*, where $U_1 \subseteq U$ if

$$\langle x,y\rangle \in \tau \Rightarrow (d(x) = d(y)) \vee (\langle x,y\rangle \in IND(A))$$

for any objects $x \in U_1, y \in U$. We denote by τ_{U_1} the U_1*-consistent* tolerance relation.

4.2 Extraction of Global Tolerance Relations in Data Tables

4.2.1 Basic Similarity Measure

For a decision table $\mathbf{A} = (U, A \cup \{d\}$ we consider tolerance relations constructed from some *predefined similarity measures* on attribute values. In this section we list some basic similarity measures often used to define the tolerance relations (see [16]). We distinguish two kinds of similarity measures: for attributes with *numeric values* and for attributes with *categorical values.*

In the first case the similarity measure δ_a:$U \times U \rightarrow \Re^+ \cup \{0\}$ for attribute $a \in A$ can be defined by:

1. $\delta_a(x,y) = |a(x) - a(y)|$, where $x, y \in U$ or
2. $\delta_a(x,y) = \frac{|a(x)-a(y)|}{|a_{max}-a_{min}|}$, where $x, y \in U$ and a_{max}, a_{min} denote the minimum and maximum values of attribute a.

In the categorical attribute case the similarity measure δ_a can be defined by

$$\delta_a(x,y) = \sum_{k \in V_d} \frac{\left|Card(C_k \cap [x]_{IND(a)}) - Card(C_k \cap [y]_{IND(a)})\right|}{Card(C_k)},$$

where C_k denotes the k-th decision class and V_d denotes the set of decision values.

4.2.2 Classification of Searching Methods for Tolerance Relations

We discuss three methods for tolerance relation construction from a given decision table $\mathbf{A} = (U, A \cup \{d\})$, called *global, local,* and *categorical method.* Any of these methods generates tolerance relations of different types. The choice among these methods depends on the chosen application problem.

The global method extracts from the whole space of object pairs $U \times U$ the optimal tolerance relation describing similarity between objects from one decision class. This method gives a simple description of the tolerance relation. The relation computed by global method determines global similarities of all pairs of objects. A limitation of a global method is space and time complexity of the searching process.

The second strategy of tolerance relation generation, called *local method,* is searching for the optimal tolerance relations τ_x where $x \in U$. We restrict the searching space to $\{x\} \times U$ while constructing the tolerance relation τ_x. The tolerance relation τ_x is optimal for a given object x if τ_x discerns x from all objects with decisions different from $d(x)$ and at the same time it identifies x with the maximal number of objects with the same decision $d(x)$. In the local method we do not examine the whole space of object pairs, but only pairs of objects that contain a given object x. Therefore the local method saves time and space complexity. Tolerance relations generated by local methods describe well the similarity of a given object to another but they do not describe the global similarities for the decision table.

The *categorical method* extracts a tolerance relation optimal with respect to a given decision class. The tolerance relation τ_C is optimal for given decision class C if it discern objects from C from all objects not belonging to C and at the same time τ_C identifies the maximal number of pairs of objects from C. For construction of τ_C one should examine the set $C \times U$ only. This method is more expensive than local method with respect to time and space complexity but the tolerance relation generated by this method describes well the similarities of the group of objects characteristic for a given decision.

Global Method

Let $\mathbf{A} = (U, A \cup \{d\})$ be a decision table and let δ_a be the similarity measure for any attribute $a \in A$. The problem of extracting a tolerance relation is a searching problem for the parameters such that the tolerance relation defined by these parameters returned as output from the searching process is *optimal*. Our goal is to search for a global tolerance relation that ***discerns*** between all pairs of objects with different decisions and ***identifies*** (makes similar) maximal number of pairs of objects with the same decision.

In the first stage of tolerance relation construction, we define the new decision table called the ***similarity table***, which consists of information about the object similarity calculated from similarity measures. The ***universum*** of the similarity table is defined by the set of all pairs of objects from table **A** and the ***attribute values*** are the values of the similarity measure function for pairs of objects. The new table has a binary decision. The decision value for any pair of objects is equal to 0 if its objects have the same decision in the original table **A**, and 1 otherwise. Formal definition of a similarity table **B** from table **A** and the set of similarity measures $\{\delta_a\}_{a \in A}$ is presented below

$$\mathbf{B} = (U', A' \cup \{D\}), \text{ where } U' = U \times U$$
$$A' = \left\{a' : U' -> \Re^+\right\} : a'(<x, y>) = \delta_a(x, y),$$
$$D(x, y) = \begin{cases} 0 \text{ if } d(x) = d(y) \\ 1 \text{ otherwise} \end{cases}$$

The searching problem for the *optimal* tolerance relation of table **A** among relations from a given class of tolerance relations can be considered as the problem of decision rule extraction from the decision table **B**. We are interested in the decision rules describing the decision class of **B** with decision 0, i.e. the class associated with pairs of objects of the table **A** with the same decision in **A**. Our goal is to search for the rule of the form $\Psi\left(a_1'(u), a_2'(u), \ldots, a_k'(u)\right) \Rightarrow (D = 0)$ satisfied by as many as possible objects $u \in U'$.

Local Method

The local method constructs relative tolerance relations. Let $\mathbf{A} = (U, A \cup \{d\})$ be a decision table and let δ_a be a similarity measure for any attribute $a \in A$. For a given object x the local method extracts the tolerance relation τ_x optimal with respect to x. The goal is to search for a tolerance relation discerning x from all objects with decisions different from $d(x)$ and identifying the maximal number of objects with the decision $d(x)$. Analogously to the global method we construct a new decision table, which contains an information about the similarity of the object x to other objects. The new table $\mathbf{B}_x$ is defined from $\mathbf{A}$ and the set of similarity measures $\{\delta_a\}_{a\in A}$ as follows

$$\mathbf{B}_x = (U', A' \cup \{D\}) \text{ where } U' = \{x\} \times U$$
$$A' = \left\{a' : U' \to \Re^+\right\} : a'(<x,y>) = \delta_a(x,y),$$
$$D(x,y) = \begin{cases} 0 \text{ if } d(x) = d(y) \\ 1 \text{ otherwise} \end{cases}$$

The searching problem for the *optimal* tolerance relation relatively to the given object x and a table $\mathbf{A}$ can be transformed to the problem of decision rule extraction from the decision table $\mathbf{B}_x$. Again our goal is to search for the rule of the form $\Psi\left(a_1'(u), a_2'(u), \dots, a_k'(u)\right) \Rightarrow (D = 0)$ satisfied by as many as possible objects $u \in U'$. One can see that using this method we do not consider all pairs of objects but only pairs containing a given object x. Hence the size of the table $\mathbf{B}_x$ is linear relatively to the size of table $\mathbf{A}$. Therefore the local method needs less memory than global method.

Categorical Method

The last method extracts the optimal tolerance relation relatively to the given decision class C (C-optimal tolerance relation, in short). For this purpose we construct the similarity table $\mathbf{B}$ that contains an information about the similarity of objects from decision class C to objects from U. Given the decision table $\mathbf{A} = (U, A \cup \{d\})$ the similarity table $\mathbf{B}_C$ is defined as follows:

$$\mathbf{B}_C = (U', A' \cup \{D\}), \text{ where } U' = C \times U$$
$$A' = \left\{a' : U' -> \Re^+\right\} : a'(<x,y>) = \delta_a(x,y),$$
$$D(x,y) = \begin{cases} 0 \text{ if } d(x) = d(y) \\ 1 \text{ otherwise} \end{cases}$$

The searching problem for C-optimal tolerance relation for table $\mathbf{A}$ can be transformed to the problem of decision rule extraction from the decision table $\mathbf{B}_C$. Our goal is to search for the rule of the form $\Psi\left(a_1'(u), a_2'(u), \dots, a_k'(u)\right) \Rightarrow (D = 0)$ satisfied by as many as possible objects $u \in U'$.

4.3 Geometrical Interpretation of Tolerance Relations

In this section we show that some families of tolerance relations have clear geometrical interpretations, i.e. they can be represented in a straightforward way by subsets of a real affine space R^k. Therefore the searching problem for a semi-optimal tolerance relation τ can be reduced to searching for an approximate description of the corresponding subset of real affine space R^k.

For a decision table $\mathbf{A} = (U, A \cup \{d\})$ with k conditional attributes and a set $\{\delta_{a_i}\}_{a_i \in A}$ of predefined similarity measures we build the similarity table $\mathbf{B} = (U', A' \cup \{D\})$ constructed from decision table $\mathbf{A}$ and the set $\{\delta_{a_i}\}_{a_i \in A}$ of similarity measures. Every object u of the table $\mathbf{B}$ can be represented by a point $p(u) = \left[a_1'(u), ..., a_k'(u)\right] \in R^k$ of one of two categories "white" or "black". A point $p(u) \in R^k$ is "white" iff $\left\{u_0 \in U' : p(u_0) = p(u)\right\}$ is non-empty and it consists of objects with the decision D equal to 0; otherwise $p(u)$ is "black". Below we present a geometrical interpretations of some standard tolerance relations. As a similarity measures we take the functions: $\delta_{a_i}(x, y) = |a_i(x) - a_i(y)|$ for any attribute $a_i \in A$. We take as an example a table with two attributes representing the quantity of vitamin A and C in apples and pears.

Vit.A	Vit.C	Fruit	Vit.A	Vit.C	Fruit
1.0	0.6	Apple	2.0	0.7	Pear
1.75	0.4	Apple	2.0	1.1	Pear
1.3	0.1	Apple	1.9	0.95	Pear
0.8	0.2	Apple	2.0	0.95	Pear
1.1	0.7	Apple	2.3	1.2	Pear
1.3	0.6	Apple	2.5	1.15	Pear
0.9	0.5	Apple	2.7	1.0	Pear
1.6	0.6	Apple	2.9	1.1	Pear
1.4	0.15	Apple	2.8	0.9	Pear
1.0	0.1	Apple	3.0	1.05	Pear

Table 4. Apple and pear data

We want to extract the similarities of fruits of one category. The data about apples and pears are shown in Figure 4.

Below we present a geometrical interpretations of some standard tolerance relations in the space of pairs of objects from the fruit table.

1. First we consider a tolerance relation defined by:

$$\langle x, y \rangle \in \tau_1(\varepsilon) \Leftrightarrow \max_{a_i \in A} \{\delta_{a_i}(x, y)\} \leq \varepsilon$$

where ε is a non-negative real number. The relation $\tau_1(\varepsilon)$ defines the following subset $\overline{\tau_1(\varepsilon)} \subseteq R^k$:

$$\overline{\tau_1(\varepsilon)} = \{(r_1, ..., r_k) \in C_k : 0 \leq r_i \leq \varepsilon \text{ for } i = 1, ..., k\}.$$

Hence $\overline{\tau_1(\varepsilon)}$ is a **hypercube** with edges of length ε, this hypercube is attached to the origin O of axes (Figure 5a).

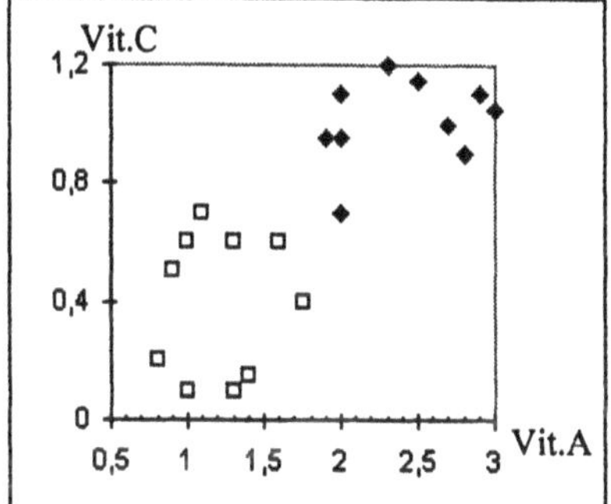

a) The set of apples and pears

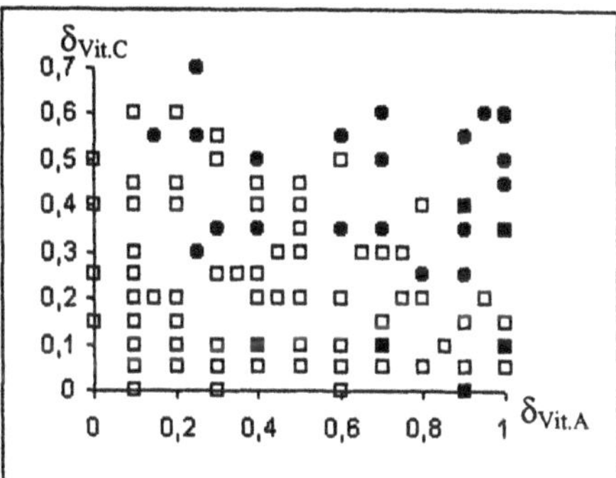

b) The set of fruit pairs

Fig. 4. Visual of data

By $\mathcal{T}_1$ we denote the family of all tolerance relations $\tau_1(\varepsilon)$ where ε is a positive real.

2. The second relation, called the *descriptor conjunction*, is defined by formula

$$\langle x, y\rangle \in \tau_2(\varepsilon_1, ..., \varepsilon_k) \Leftrightarrow \bigwedge_{a_i \in A} [\delta_{a_i}(x, y) \leq \varepsilon_i]$$

where $\varepsilon_1, ..., \varepsilon_k$ are non-negative real numbers. The relation $\tau_2(\varepsilon_1, ..., \varepsilon_k)$ defines the following subset $\overline{\tau_2(\varepsilon_1, ..., \varepsilon_k)} \subseteq R^k$:

$$\overline{\tau_2(\varepsilon_1, ..., \varepsilon_k)} = \{(r_1, ..., r_k) \in C_k : 0 \leq r_i \leq \varepsilon_i \text{ for } i = 1, ..., k\}$$

$\overline{\tau_2(\varepsilon_1, ..., \varepsilon_k)}$ is an **interval** in R^k with boundaries $\varepsilon_1, \varepsilon_2, ..., \varepsilon_k$; it is attached to the origin O of axes (Figure 5b).

By $\mathcal{T}_2$ we denote the family of all tolerance relations of the form $\tau_2(\varepsilon_1, ..., \varepsilon_k)$.

3. The relation τ_3, called the *linear combination*, is defined by

$$\langle x, y\rangle \in \tau_3(w_1, ..., w_k, w) \Leftrightarrow \sum_{a_i \in A} w_i \cdot \delta_{a_i}(x, y) + w \leq 0$$

where $w_1, ..., w_k, w$ are real numbers. The relation $\tau_3(w_1, ..., w_k, w)$ defines the following subset $\overline{\tau_3(w_1, ..., w_k, w)} \subseteq R^k$

$$\overline{\tau_3(w_1, ..., w_k, w)} = \left\{(r_1, ..., r_k) \in C_k : \sum_{i=1}^{k} w_i \cdot r_i + w \leq 0\right\}$$

Hence $\overline{\tau_3(w_1, ..., w_k, w)}$ is a region in C_k under the hyperplane $H : \sum_{i=1}^{k} w_i \cdot x_i + w = 0$ (Figure 6a). By $\mathcal{T}_3$ we denote the family of all tolerance relations of the form $\tau_3(w_1, ..., w_k, w)$.

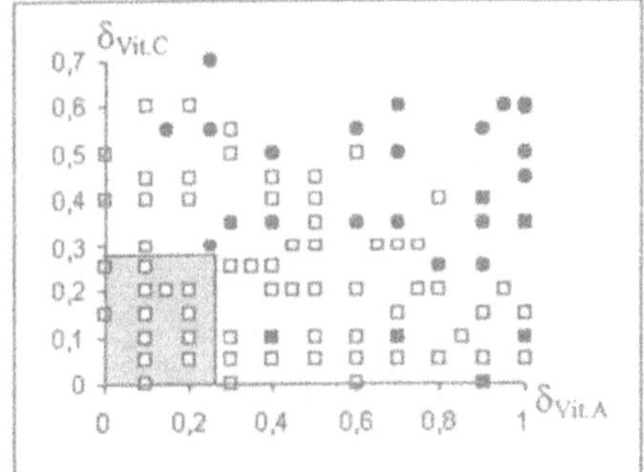

a) Tolerance relation $\Im_1$

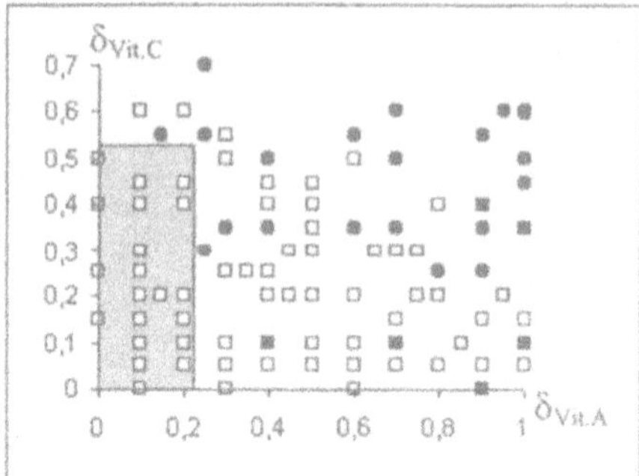

b) Tolerance relation $\Im_2$

Fig. 5. Tolerance Relation Interpretation

4. A linear combination can be extended to the higher order combination. For example one can consider a tolerance relation τ_4 defined by the *square combination of similarity measures*

$$\langle x, y\rangle \in \tau_4 (w_1, ..., w_k, w) \Leftrightarrow \sum_{a_i \in A} w_i \cdot \delta^2_{a_i} (x, y) + w \leq 0$$

where $w_1, ..., w_k, w$ are real numbers. The relation $\tau_4 (w_1, ..., w_k, w)$ defines the following subset $\overline{\tau_4 (w_1, ..., w_k, w)} \subseteq R^k$:

$$\overline{\tau_4 (w_1,...,w_k, w)} = \left\{(r_1, ..., r_k) \in C_k : \sum_{i=1}^{k} w_i \cdot r_i^2 + w \leq 0\right\}$$

Hence $\overline{\tau_4 (w_1, ..., w_k, w)}$ is a region in C_k bounded by **ellipsoid** (Figure 6b). By $\mathcal{T}_4$ we denote the family of all relations of the form $\tau_4 (w_1, ..., w_k, w)$

5. The next relation called "*min*" is defined by the formula

$$\langle x, y\rangle \in \tau_5 (\varepsilon) \Leftrightarrow \min_{a_i \in A} \{\delta_{a_i} (x, y)\} \leq \varepsilon,$$

where ε is a non-negative real. The set $\overline{\tau_5 (\varepsilon)}$ is equal to:

$$\bigcup_{i=1}^{k} \{(r_1, ..., r_k) \in C_k : r_i \leq \varepsilon\}$$

Hence $\overline{\tau_5 (\varepsilon)}$ is a **sum of bands** with boundaries $x_i = 0$ and $x_i = \varepsilon$ for $i = 1, ..., k$.
By $\mathcal{T}_5$ we denote the family of all tolerance relations of the form $\tau_5 (\varepsilon)$.

6. The tolerance relation τ_6 is defined by a disjunction of atomic formulas

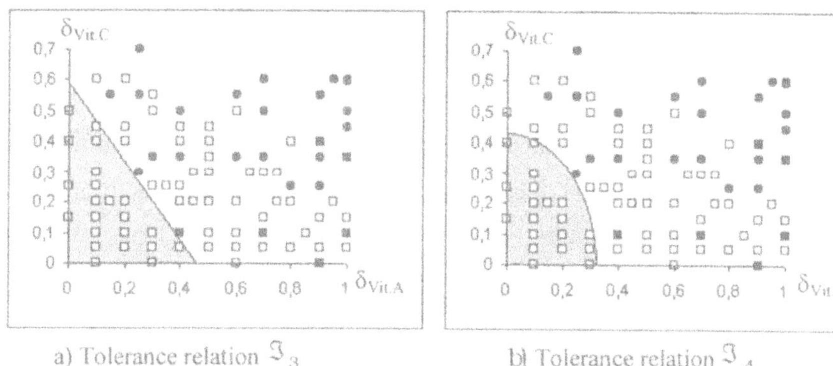

Fig. 6. Tolerance Relation Interpretation

$$\langle x, y \rangle \in \tau_6 (\varepsilon_1, ..., \varepsilon_k) \Leftrightarrow \bigvee_{a_i \in A} [\delta_{a_i} (x, y) \leq \varepsilon_i],$$

where $\varepsilon_1, ..., \varepsilon_k$ are non-negative real numbers. This relation is a generalization of the relation "*min*" (Figure 7a).

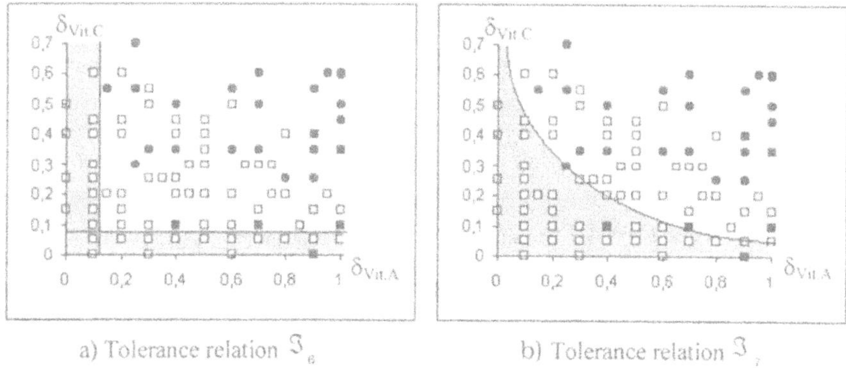

Fig. 7. Tolerance Relation Interpretation

7. Our last example is a tolerance relation defined by

$$\langle x, y \rangle \in \tau_7 (w) \Leftrightarrow \prod_{a_i \in A} \delta_{a_i} (x, y) \leq w,$$

where w is a non-negative real. The set $\overline{\tau_7(w)}$ is equal to

$$\{(r_1, ..., r_k) \in C_k : r_1 \times ... \times r_k \leq w\}$$

Hence it is a region in C_k bounded by **hyperboloid** (Figure 7b).

4.4 Heuristics for Tolerance Relation Generation

Time complexity of the searching problem for optimal tolerance relation parametrized by k parameters for a set of n objects is $O(n^k)$ because we have to test all possible values of parameter vector, where the number of possible values for one parameter is usually $O(n)$. This time is not feasible, when the dimension of the problem is large (the number of points n and the dimension k of the space are large). We show, that the approximations of some tolerance relations can be constructed if its geometrical description is known. Below we present heuristics for two important tolerance relation classes.

4.4.1 Searching for Description Conjunction

The first example of tolerance relation class is a *descriptor conjunction*, i.e.

$$\langle x, y\rangle \in \tau(\varepsilon_1, ..., \varepsilon_k) \Leftrightarrow \bigwedge_{a_i \in A} [\delta_{a_i}(x, y) \leq \varepsilon_i]$$

We have

$$\overline{\tau(\varepsilon_1, ..., \varepsilon_k)} = \{(r_1, ..., r_k) \in C^k : 0 \leq r_i \leq \varepsilon_i \text{ for } i = 1, ..., k\} \quad (2)$$

One can see that for given $\varepsilon_1, ..., \varepsilon_k$, the set (2) is included in the interval $I(\varepsilon_1, ..., \varepsilon_k)$ from R^k. Our goal is to search for parameters $\varepsilon_1, ..., \varepsilon_k$ such that the interval $I(\varepsilon_1, ..., \varepsilon_k)$ consists of "white" points only and, at the same time, of as many as possible of them. Starting from the empty interval of the form $I(0, \infty, ..., \infty)$ we gradually augment the one chosen parameter, for example ε_1, and at the same time decrease one of the remaining parameter so, that the interval $I(\varepsilon_1, ..., \varepsilon_k)$ still consists of one kind of points and it contains as many as possible points. The idea of the algorithm is illustrated in Figure 8. In this example we show the two-dimensional intervals with parameters $\varepsilon_1, \varepsilon_2$. In every step of the algorithm we augment the first parameter ε_1 and decrease the second parameter ε_2 to obtain the new interval $I(\varepsilon_1, \varepsilon_2)$.

Details of the algorithm are presented below

Algorithm (Description conjunction)
Input: The set of labeled points from $V_{a'_1} \times V_{a'_2} \times \ldots \times V_{a'_k} \subset R^k$
Output: The set $\{\varepsilon_i \in V_{a'_i} : i = 1..k\}$ of parameters for a (semi-)optimal interval
begin
Sort values of lists $V_{a'_1}, \ldots, V_{a'_k}$ in an increasing order;
$\varepsilon_1 = 0, \varepsilon_2 = \infty, \ldots, \varepsilon_k = \infty$;
repeat
$\varepsilon_1 = v$, where v is the first element from the list $V_{a'_1}$ such that there exists black point p with coordinate $a'_1(p) = v$;
for ($i \in \{2, .., k\}$)
Set $\varepsilon_i = v_i$, where $v_i = \min \left\{\varepsilon_i, a'_i(p)\right\}$ so, that the interval $I(\varepsilon_1, \ldots, \varepsilon_k)$ with the modified parameters ε_1 and ε_i still contains only "white" points from R^k;
m_i = number of "white" points in the new interval $I(\varepsilon_1, \ldots, \varepsilon_k)$;
endfor
Choose in the set of computed parameters ε_i and values v_i the parameter ε_{i_0} and the value v_{i_0} corresponding to the interval $I(\varepsilon_1, \ldots, \varepsilon_k)$ with the maximal number m_{i_0} of "white" points contained in it;
$\varepsilon_{i_0} = v_{i_0}$;
$V_{a'_1} = V_{a'_1} \setminus \{v\}$;
until $(V_{a'_1} = \emptyset)$
Among generated intervals, choose the interval $I(\varepsilon_1, \ldots, \varepsilon_k)$ with the maximal number of "white" points from R^k. In this way we obtain the semi-optimal parameters $\{\varepsilon_1, \ldots, \varepsilon_k\}$.
end (Algorithm)

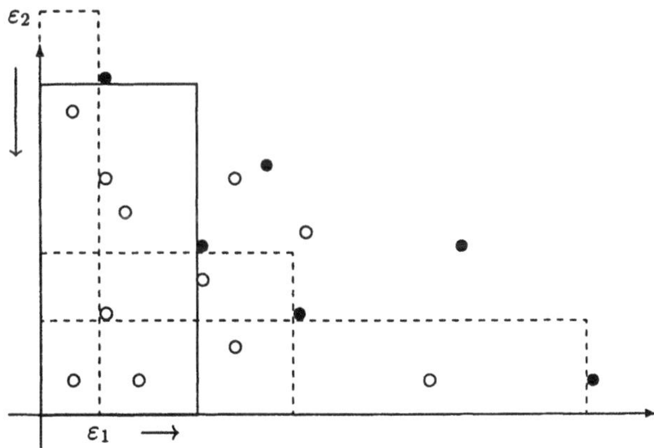

Fig. 8. Interpretation of an algorithm searching for an optimal interval $I(\epsilon_1, \epsilon_2)$

4.4.2 Searching for Linear Combination (hyperplane)

Let us consider a *linear combination* defined by the formula

$$[\langle x, y\rangle \in \tau(w_1,...,w_k, w)] \Leftrightarrow \sum_{i=1}^{k} w_i \cdot \delta_{a_i}(x, y) + w \leq 0$$

We have

$$\overline{\tau(w_1, ..., w_k, w)} = \left\{(r_1, ..., r_k) \in C_k : \sum_{i=1}^{k} w_i \cdot r_i + w \leq 0\right\}$$

For given parameters $w_1, ..., w_k, w$ the formula (4.4.2) describes the set points with positive coordinates that are below the hyperplane $H = \sum_{i=1}^{k} w_i \cdot x_i + w = 0$. This hyperplane is determined by $(k+1)$ parameters. We are interested in the hyperplanes having non-negative intersections with all axes of the space R^k. Hence $w_i > 0$ for any i and $w < 0$. Any hyperplane divides the space into two half-spaces. Our goal is to search for a hyperplane H such, that the half-space below the hyperplane H contains only "white" points and the number of these points is as large as possible. Searching for the optimal hyperplane H, we randomly choose a hyperplane $H = \sum_{i=1}^{k} w_i \cdot x_i + w$. After that we try to rotate this hyperplane by fixing k parameters, for example $w, w_1, ..., w_{j-1}, w_{j+1}, ..., w_k$ and modifying only one parameter w_j. We would like to find a value of w_j such that the modified hyperplane determines a new partition of set of objects. From the equation of hyperplane H we have $w_j = \frac{-\sum_{i \neq j} w_i \cdot x_i - w}{x_j}$. Any point $p_0 = [x_1^0, x_2^0 ... x_k^0] \in C^k$ is below H iff $H(p_0) < 0$ i.e. $w_j < \frac{-\sum_{i \neq j} w_i \cdot x_i^0 - w}{x_j^0}$ and it is above H iff $w_j > \frac{-\sum_{i \neq j} w_i \cdot x_i^0 - w}{x_j^0}$.

Let $S_j(p_0) = \frac{-\sum_{i \neq j} w_i \cdot x_i^0 - w}{x_j^0}$, where $p_0 = [x_1^0, x_2^0 ... x_k^0]$. We construct a set

$$S = \left\{S_j(p_0) : p_0 = \left[a_1'(u), ..., a_k'(u)\right] \text{ for any } u \in U'\right\} \tag{3}$$

Any value $w_j > 0$ chosen from S determines a new hyperplane defining a new partition of the set of points. For any defined hyperplane we translate it until the points below hyperplane are all "white". Among constructed hyperplanes we choose the best. The idea of the algorithm is illustrated in Figure 9. In our example we show two-dimensional hyperplane (straight line) defined by parameters w, w_1, w_2. In every step of the algorithm, we first rotate the initally chosen line by modifying w_1 and fixing w, w_2, then translate it to the "good" position to obtain the new hyperplane $H(w, w_1, w_2)$.

The algorithm is presented as follows:

Algorithm (Linear combination)
Input: The set of labeled points of the space R^k.
Output: The set of parameters $\{w, w_1, ..., w_k\}$ of the semi-optimal hyperplane $H(w, w_1, ..., w_k)$.
begin
$H(w, w_1, ..., w_k)$ = randomly chosen hyperplane;
for (any $j = 1..k$)
Construct the set S defined in (3) and sort S in increasing order;
for (any positive $v \in S$)
$w_j = v$;
Translate $H(w, w_1, ..., w_k)$ to a *good* position i.e. with all "white" points below it and calculate the number of these white points. The *fitness* of the hyperplane is equal to this number.
endfor
endfor
Among *good* hyperplanes we choose a hyperplane with maximal fitness.
end (algorithm)

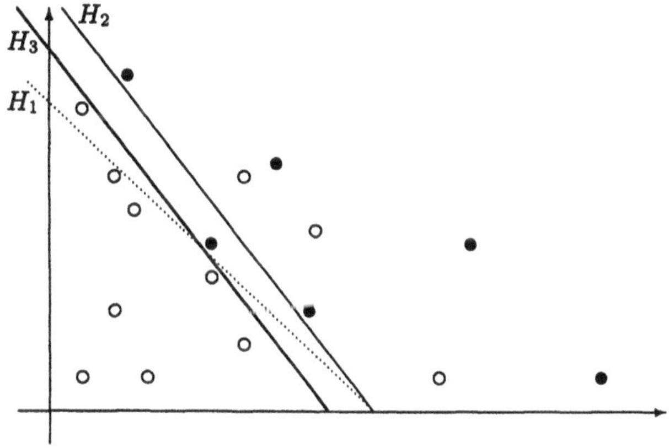

Fig. 9. H_1 - an randomly chosen hyperplane; H_2 - after rotation; H_3 - after translation.

4.5 Relational Pattern Applications

4.5.1 Clustering Problem

The goal of the clustering problem is to group objects, that are classified as similar by tolerance relation. The question is, how to group objects into "homogenous" clusters, that means the clusters containing maximal number of objects from one decision class and minimal number of objects from another classes. The quality of a cluster depends on the number of objects from a given decision class and the number of objects from other decision classes that belong to the cluster. The cluster is becoming better if the former number is larger and latter number is smaller. We will show how we can construct the clusters with good quality by heuristics based on tolerance relation. We consider two cases of tolerance relations: *consistent* and *inconsistent*.

First we focus on application of *consistent* tolerance relations to the clustering problem. Let $\mathbf{A} = (U, A \cup \{d\})$ be a decision table. For this table one can compute a *consistent* tolerance relation τ (by *global method*) or tolerance relation family $\{\tau_{x_0}\}$ for every object $x_0 \in U$ (by *local method*) or tolerance family $\{\tau_D\}$ for every decision class D (by *categorical method*). For the tolerance τ we define transitive closure τ^* by

$$\tau^k = \{(x,y) : \exists_z \ (x,z) \in \tau^{k-1} \wedge (z,y) \in \tau\}$$
$$\tau^* = \bigcup_{k \geq 0} \tau^k$$

The x_0-transitive closure $\tau^*_{x_0}$ for the relative tolerance $\tau_{x_o}$is defined by

$$\tau^k_{x_0} = \{(x_0,y) : \exists_z \ (x_0,z) \in \tau^{k-1}_{x_0} \wedge (z,y) \in \tau_z\}$$
$$\tau^*_{x_0} = \bigcup_{k \geq 0} \tau^k_{x_0}$$

The D-transitive closure τ^*_D for decision class D is defined by

$$\tau^k_D = \{(x,y) : \exists_z \ (x,z) \in \tau^{k-1}_D \wedge (z,y) \in \tau_{D_z}, \text{for } x \in C, z \in D_z\}$$
$$\tau^*_D = \bigcup_{k \geq 0} \tau^k_D$$

The cluster C can be defined as the object set $[x]_{\tau^*}$ (or $[x]_{\tau^*_x}$ or $[x]_{\tau^*_D}$) for some object $x \in U$. The object x is called a *generator* of the cluster C.

The clusters of the universe U can be constructed in a straightforward way by the following algorithm.

```
Algorithm (Clustering I)
repeat
    Choose randomly an object x ∈ U;
    C_i = [x]_{τ*} (or [x]_{τ*_x}, [x]_{τ*_{d(x)}}),
    U = U \ C_i;
    i = i + 1;
until U = ∅
```

One can see that clusters determined by the algorithm are disjoint and they contain the objects with the same decision. We can observe also that clusters generated by consistent tolerance relations do not depend on the generator.

In more general case we have to deal with *inconsistent* tolerance relation. We recall the tolerance relation is inconsistent if it contains the pairs of objects with different decisions. The cluster C is defined by $C = [x]_{\tau^k}$ (or $[x]_{\tau^k_x}$ or $[x]_{\tau^k_D}$, where $x \in D$) for some generator $x \in U$ and some positive number k. We can see that cluster C may contain different decisions. The quality of cluster in this case depends on the generator x and on the number k. The "good" generator corresponds the object x defining $[x]_{\tau^k}$ $([x]_{\tau_x^k}, [x]_{\tau_D^k})$ with the best quality among all objects from U. We extend its tolerance class by successive iteration of tolerance $\tau^k (k = 1, 2...)$. After every step of extension we examine the quality of the new class. If the quality of the cluster rapidly decreases we stop the process of extension with the current value of the parameter k, otherwise we continue the process.We extract in this way the tolerance τ^k. The improved method of searching for good clusters is presented in the Algorithm *Clustering II.*

Algorithm (Clustering II)
repeat
1. Search for $x \in U$ with the best quality of $[x]_\tau$ $([x]_{\tau_x}, [x]_{\tau_{d(x)}})$;
2. Search for $C_i = [x]_{\tau^k}$ (*or* $[x]_{\tau_x^k}, [x]_{\tau_{d(x)}^k}$), where $x \in U$ is an object obtained from previous step;

   The number k in Step 2 is computed as follows: for $k =$ $1, 2...$ *we construct the cluster* $[x]_{\tau^k}$ *as an extension of the cluster* $[x]_{\tau^{k-1}}$ *and investigate the quality of the obtained cluster.*
3. $U = U \setminus C_i$; $i = i + 1$;

until $U = \emptyset$

We can use those clusters for classification of new cases in different ways. One example of classification strategy is presented below:

Step 1: Every cluster C_i is characterized by its *center* $\mathbf{c}_i$ and its *mass* $\mathbf{m}_i$ (Number of objects belonging to the cluster C_i);
Step 2: Define the distance function d based on tolerance relation;
Step 3: For a new object x, the number $p_i(x) = \frac{m_i}{d(c_i, x)}$ is a gravitation power measure of the cluster C_i influencing the new object x. The new case x is classified to the cluster with the maximal gravitation power $p_i(x)$.

4.5.2 Decomposition Problem

The goal of the decomposition problem is to divide the large table into smaller ones. In the decomposition problem we are interested in finding the simple patterns that describe these sub-tables. We want to obtain such sub-tables that may give credible decision rules. Intuitively the sub-table is good if it is described by a simple pattern and it contains many objects but it omits some decision classes. As the quality of a sub-table we can take a function of its cardinality and the number of decision classes intersected with it.

Let $\mathbf{A} = (U, A \cup \{d\})$ be a decision table. We compute for a table $\mathbf{A}$ a tolerance relation τ (by *global method*) or tolerance relation family $\{\tau_x\}$ for every object $x \in U$ (by *local method*) or tolerance family $\{\tau_D\}$ for every decision class

D (by *categorical method*). Every sub-table T is defined by $T = [x]_\tau$(or $[x]_{\tau_x}$ or $[x]_{\tau_D}, x \in D$) for some object $x \in U$. The question is how to choose the object x that the sub-table generated by tolerance class $[x]_\tau$ (or $[x]_{\tau_x}$ or $[x]_{\tau_D}, x \in D$) is good. A natural answer is: x is the object that $[x]_\tau$ has the best quality. Below we present the decomposition algorithm:

repeat
 Searching for $x \in U$ with the best quality of $[x]_\tau$ (or $[x]_{\tau_x}$or $[x]_{\tau_D}$);
 $T_i = [x]_\tau$(or $[x]_{\tau_x}$ or $[x]_{\tau_D}$);
 $U = U \setminus T_i$;
until $U = \emptyset$

One can see that every sub-table $T = [x]_\tau$ (or $[x]_{\tau_x}$ or $[x]_{\tau_{d(x)}}$) is described by a simple pattern defined by the object x and the tolerance relation $\tau(\tau_x, \tau_D)$. Having the decomposing of a given table into sub-tables we can classify the new object x according the scheme proposed in Section 3.4.4.

4.5.3 Classification by Nearest Neighbour Method

For a given tolerance τ and any object x one can define the set of neighbours of x in the tolerance sense. The set of neighbors of x can be defined gradually as follows:

$$NN_1(x) = \{y : y \; \tau \; x\}$$
$$NN_k(x) = \left\{y : \bigvee_{z \in NN_{k-1}(x)} x\tau z \wedge z\tau y\right\}$$

Having a set of neighbours of the object x, one can classify x using different strategies, for example one can take a majority rule as the standard criterion. Classification process of new objects is presented below

Step 1: Construct the set of neighbours $NN_k(x)$ of x for some k. We choose the value k in such way that the set $NN_k(x)$ contains no less then M objects from training set.

Step 2: Use M nearest neighbours of x to vote for the decision value on x. The object x is classified to the decision class supported by the maximal number of objects from the $NN_k(x)$.

4.6 Experimental Results

The classification methods using tolerance relations have been implemented. The results of experiments are presented in Table 5. To classify a new object we first divide a data table into clusters, which are defined by tolerance classes with *maximal extension*. Next using discretization method proposed in [29] we compute the decision rules for all clusters. A new object is classified according to the decision rules generated for clusters covering a new object. In case of decision conflict we use a majority rule to classify an object. We have tested efficiency of two classification algorithms. The first algorithm generates clusters using tolerance relation defined by *conjunction of descriptions*. The second algorithm employs the tolerance relation of *linear combination* form to generate clusters. Good classification result show that object similarity is one of very important tool to extract hidden pattern in data.

Data set	No. of Objects	No. of Attributes	Accuracy Rates	
			Conjunction	Linear Combination
Australian	690	14	80.72%	82.46%
Diabetes	768	8	76.03%	74.3%
Glass	214	9	72.8%	69%
Heart	270	13	79.62%	81.4%
Iris	150	4	96.67%	95.7%
Sat. Image	4435	36	85.65%	82.9%

Table 5. Classification results by tolerance relations

5 Conclusions

We have presented some efficient methods for pattern generation from data and a general scheme for approximate description of decision classes based on different notions of patterns. An interesting aspect of our approach is that on the one hand searching methods are oriented towards uncertainty reduction in constructed descriptions of decision classes but on the other hand uncertainty in temporary synthesized descriptions of decision classes is the main "driving force" for the searching methods. The results of computer experiments are showing that the presented methods for template generation are promising even for large tables; however, much more additional work should be done on strategies for the construction of approximate decision class descriptions e.g. on the basis of the general mereological scheme [33]. The presented results also create a step for further experiments and research on adaptive decision system synthesis.

Acknowledgments This work has been supported by the grant #8T11C01011 from Polish National Committee for Scientific Research (Komitet Badań Naukowych) and by the ESPRIT project 20288 CRIT-2.

References

1. Agrawal, R., Imielinski, T., Suami, A.: Mining assocation rules between sets of items in large datatabes. In: ACM SIGMOD. Conference on Management of Data, Washington DC (1993) 207–216

2. Agrawal, R., Mannila, H., Srikant, R., Toivonen, H., Verkamo, A.I.: Fast discovery of assocation rules. In: V.M. Fayad, G. Piatetsky–Shapiro, P. Smyth, R. Uthurusamy (eds.), Advanced in Knowledge Discovery and Data Mining, AAAI/MIT Press (1996) 307-328
3. Bezdek, J.: A sampler of non-neural fuzzy models for clustering and classification. In: Tutorial at the Fourth European Congress on Intelligent Techniques and Soft Computing, Aachen, Germany, September 2–5 (1996)
4. Bezdek, J.C., Chuah, S., Leep, D.: Generalized k-nearest neighbour rule. In: Fuzzy Sets and Systems **18/3** (1986) 237–256
5. Bazan, J., Skowron, A., Synak, P.: Dynamic reducts as a tool for extracting laws from decision tables. In: Z. W. Ras, M. Zemankova (eds.), Proceedings of the Eighth Symposium on Methodologies for Intelligent Systems, Charlotte, NC, October 16-19, Lecture Notes in Artificial Intelligence **869**, Springer-Verlag (1994) 346–355
6. Cattaneo, G.: Generalized rough sets. Preclusivity fuzzy-intuitionistic (BZ) lattices. Studia Logica **58** (1997) 47–77
7. Cormen, T.H., Leiserson, C.E., Rivest, R.L. (eds.): Introduction to algorithms. The MIT Press/McGraw Hill, Cambridge, MA (1990) 974–978
8. Davis, L.(ed.): Handbook of genetic algorithms. Van Nostrand Reinhold, New York (1991)
9. Goldberg, D.E.: GA in search, optimisation, and machine learning. Addison-Wesley, New York (1989)
10. Garey, M.R., Johnson, D.S.: Computers and interactability. A guide to the theory of NP-completeness. W.H. Freeman and Company, New York (1979)
11. Grzymala–Busse, J.: A new version of the rule induction system LERS. In: Fundamenta Informatice **31/1** (1997) 27–39
12. Holland, J.H.: Adaptation in natural and artificial systems. The MIT Press, Cambridge, MA (1992)
13. Hu, X., Cercone, N.: Rough set similarity based learning from databases. In: Proc. of The First International Conference of Knowledge Discovery and Data mining, Montreal, Canada, August 20–21 (1995) 162–167
14. Koza, J.R.: Genetic programming: On the programming of computers by means of the natural selection, The MIT Press, Cambridge, MA (1992)
15. Krętowski, M., Stepaniuk, J., Polkowski, L., Skowron, A.: Data reduction based on rough set theory. In: Y. Kodratoff, G. Nakhaeizadeh, and Ch. Taylor (eds.), Proceedings of the Workshop on Statistics, Machine Learning and Knowledge Discovery in Data Bases, April 25–27, Crete, Greece (1995) 210–215; see also: ICS Research Report **13/95**, Warsaw University of Technology (1995)
16. Krętowski, M., Stepaniuk, J.: Selection of objects and attributes a tolerance rough set approach. In: Proceedings of Poster Session of the Ninth International Symposium on Methodologies for Intelligent Systems (ISMIS'96), Zakopane, Poland, June 9–13, Oak Ridge Laboratory (1996) 169–180
17. Krawiec, K., Słowiński, R., Vanderpooten, D.: Construction of rough classifiers based on application of a similarity relation. In: S. Tsumoto, S. Kobayashi, T. Yokomori, H. Tanaka, and A. Nakamura (eds.): Proceedings of the Fourth International Workshop on Rough Sets, Fuzzy Sets, and Machine Discovery (RSFD'96), The University of Tokyo, November 6–8 (1996) 23–30
18. Lin, T.Y.: Neighborhood system and approximation in database and knowled base systems. In: Proc. of The Fourth International Symposium on Methodologies of Intelligent System (1989)

19. Marcus, S.: Tolerance rough sets, Cech topologies, learning processes. Bulletin of the Polish Academy of Sciences, Technical Sciences **42/3** (1994) 471–487
20. Mannila, H., Toivonen, H., Verkamo, A. I.: Efficient algorithms for discovering association rules. In: U. Fayyad and R. Uthurusamy (eds.): AAAI – Workshop on Knowledge Discovery in Databases, Seattle, WA (1994) 181-192
21. Michalski, R., Mozetic, I., Hong, J., Lavrac, N.: The multi-purpose increamental learning system AQ15 and its testing application to three medical domains. In: Proc. of the Fifth National Conference on AI, (1986) 1041–1045
22. Mollestad, T., Skowron, A.: A rough set framework for data mining of propositional default rules. In: Z.W. Ras, M. Michalewicz (eds.), Ninth International Symposium on Methodologies for Intelligent Systems (ISMIS-96), Zakopane, Poland, June 9–13, Lecture Notes in Artificial Intelligence **1079**, Springer-Verlag, Berlin (1996) 448–457
23. Murthy, S., Aha, D.: UCI repository of machine learning data tables. `http://www/ics.uci.edu/ mlearn`.
24. Nguyen, S. Hoa., Nguyen, T.Trung., Skowron, A., Synak, P.: Knowledge discovery by rough set methods. In: Nagib C. Callaos (ed.), Proceedings of the International Conference on Information Systems Analysis and Synthesis (ISAS'96), July 22–26, Orlando, USA (1996) 26–33
25. Nguyen, S. Hoa., Polkowski, L., Skowron, A., Synak, P., Wróblewski J.: Searching for approximate description of decision classes. In: S. Tsumoto, S. Kobayashi, T. Yokomori, H. Tanaka, and A. Nakamura (eds.): Proceedings of the Fourth International Workshop on Rough Sets, Fuzzy Sets, and Machine Discovery (RSFD'96), The University of Tokyo, November 6–8 (1996) 153–161
26. Nguyen, S. Hoa, Skowron, A., Synak, P.: Rough sets in data mining: approximate description of decision classes. In: Proceedings of the Fourth European Congress on Intelligent Techniques and Soft Computing (EUFIT'96), September 2–5, Aachen, Germany, Verlag Mainz, Aachen (1996) 149–153
27. Nguyen, H. Son, Skowron, A.: Quantization of real value attributes: rough set and boolean reasoning approach. In: P.P. Wang (ed.), Second Annual Joint Conference on Information Sciences (JCIS'95), Wrightsville Beach, North Carolina, 28 September – 1 October (1995) 34–37
28. Nguyen, S. Hoa, Skowron, A.: Searching for relational patterns in data. In: J. Komorowski, J. Żytkow, (eds.), The First European Symposium on Principle of Data Mining and Knowledge Discovery (PKDD'97), June 25–27, Trondheim, Norway, Lecture Notes in Artificial Intelligence **1263**, Springer-Verlag, Berlin (1997) 265–276
29. Nguyen, S. Hoa, Nguyen, H. Son: Some efficient algorithms for rough set methods. In: Proceedings of the Sixth International Conference, Information Procesing and Management of Uncertainty in Knowledge–Based Systems (IPMU'96), July 1-5, Granada, Spain (1996) 1451–1456
30. Pawlak, Z.: Rough classification. In: International Journal of Man–Machine Studies **20** (1984) 469–483
31. Pawlak, Z.: Rough sets. Theoretical aspects of reasoning about data, Kluwer Academic Publishers, Dordrecht (1991)
32. Polkowski, L., Skowron, A., Żytkow, J.: Tolerance based rough sets. In: T.Y. Lin, A.M. Wildberger (eds.): Soft Computing: Rough Sets, Fuzzy Logic, Neural Networks, Uncertainty Management, Knowledge Discovery, Simulation Councils, Inc., San Diego, CA (1995) 55–58

33. Polkowski, L., Skowron, A.: Rough mereological approach to knowledge-based distributed AI. In: J.K. Lee, J. Liebowitz, Y.M. Chae (eds.): Critical Technology. Proc. of The Third World Congress on Expert Systems, Seoul, Cognisant Communication Corporation, New York (1996) 774–781
34. Polkowski, L., Skowron, A.: Rough mereology: A new paradigm for approximate reasoning, Journal of Approximate Reasoning (1996) **2/4** 333–365
35. Quinlan, J.R.: C4.5: Programs for machine learning. Morgan Kaufmann, San Mateo, CA (1993)
36. Stepaniuk, J.: Similarity based rough sets and learning. In: S. Tsumoto, S. Kobayashi, T. Yokomori, H. Tanaka, and A. Nakamura (eds.): Proceedings of the Fourth International Workshop on Rough Sets, Fuzzy Sets, and Machine Discovery (RSFD'96), The University of Tokyo, November 6–8 (1996) 18–22
37. Skowron, A., Polkowski, L., Komorowski, J.: Learning tolerance relation by boolean descriptions: Automatic feature extraction from data tabes. In: S. Tsumoto, S. Kobayashi, T. Yokomori, H. Tanaka, and A. Nakamura (eds.): Proceedings of the Fourth International Workshop on Rough Sets, Fuzzy Sets, and Machine Discovery (RSFD'96), The University of Tokyo, November 6–8 (1996) 11–17
38. Skowron, A., Stepaniuk, J.: Tolerance approximation spaces. In: Fundamenta Informaticae **27/2,3** (1996) 245–253
39. Piatetsky-Shapiro, G.: Discovery, analysis and presentation of strong rules. In: G. Piatetsky-Shapiro and W.J. Frawley (eds.): Knowledge Discovery in Databases, AAAI/MIT (1991) 229–247
40. Skowron, A.; Synthesis of adaptive decision systems from experimental data. In: Aamodt., A, Komorowski., J. (eds.): Proceedings of the Fifth Scandinavian Conference on Artificial Intelligence (SCAI'95), May 29–31, 1995, Trondheim, Norway, IOS Press, Amsterdam (1995) 220–238
41. Skowron, A., Polkowski, L.: Rough mereological foundations for analysis, synthesis, design and control in distributive system. In: P.P. Wang (ed.), Second Annual Joint Conference on Information Sciences (JCIS'95), Wrightsville Beach, North Carolina, 28 September – 1 October (1995) 346–349
42. Skowron, A., Rauszer, C.: The discernibility matrices and functions in information systems. in: R. Słowiński (ed.): Intelligent Decision Support – Handbook of Applications and Advances of the Rough Sets Theory, Kluwer Academic Publishers, Dordrecht (1992) 331–362
43. Smyth, P., Goodman, R.M.: Rule introduction using information theory. In: G. Piatetsky-Shapiro and W.J. Frawley (eds.): Knowledge Discovery in Databases, AAAI/MIT (1991) 159–176
44. Tentush, I.: On minimal absorbent sets for some types of tolerance relations. In: Bulletin of the Polish Academy of Sciences **43/1** (1995) 79–88
45. Toivonen, H., Klemettinen, M., Ronkainen, P., Hatonen, P., Mannila, H.: Pruning and grouping discovered association rules. In: Familiarisation Workshop on Statistics, Machine Learning and Knowledge Discovery in Databases – MLNET, Heraklion, Crete, April (1995) 47–52
46. Uthurusamy, H., Fayyad, V.M., Spangler, S.: Learning useful rules from inconclusive data. In: G. Piatetsky-Shapiro and W.J. Frawley (eds.): Knowledge Discovery in Databases, AAAI/MIT (1991) 141–157
47. Yao, Y.Y., Wong, S.K.M., Lin, T.Y.: A review of rough set models. In: T.Y. Lin, N. Cercone (eds.): Rough Sets and Data Mining. Analysis of Imprecise Data, Kluwer Academic Publishers, Boston, Dordrecht (1997) 47–75

48. Windham, M.P.: Geometric fuzzy clustering algorithms. Fuzzy Sets and Systems **3** (1983) 271–280
49. Wróblewski, J.: Finding minimal reducts using genetic algorithms. In: P.P. Wang (ed.), Second Annual Joint Conference on Information Sciences (JCIS'95), Wrightsville Beach, North Carolina, 28 September – 1 October (1995) 186–189
50. Wróblewski, J.: Theoretical foundations of order-based genetic algorithms. In: Fundamenta Informaticae **28/3-4** Kluwer Academic Publishers, Dordrecht (1996) 423–430
51. Wróblewski, J.: Genetic algorithm in decomposition and classification problems. (in this book)
52. Ziarko, W.: Rough sets, fuzzy sets and knowledge discovery. In: Workshops in Computing, Springer–Verlag & British Computer Society, Berlin, London (1994)

Chapter 5

Answering Non-Standard Queries in Distributed Knowledge-Based Systems

Zbigniew W. Ras

University of North Carolina
Department of Comp. Science
Charlotte, N.C. 28223, USA
ras@uncc.edu

Abstract. In this paper we present a query answering system for solving non-standard queries in a distributed knowledge based system (DKBS). Our system is different from solving queries on a conventional distributed database or cooperative database in the sense that it discovers rules, if needed, and uses them to resolve unknown attributes. In [12], the rules used to resolve unknown attributes are discovered directly from the tables (relational databases) either locally or on remote sites. In this paper, the rule discovery process is dependent on descriptions of objects which will never be stored in our system (they either do not exist or we have no interest in storing them). Such descriptions are called either locally-negative (l-negative) or globally-negative (g-negative) terms. L-negative terms refer to the situation when only a local site of DKBS is taken into cosideration. If any site of DKBS is considered for storing the data, we use g-negative terms instead.

1 Introduction

By a distributed knowledge-based system (DKBS) we mean a collection of autonomous knowledge-based systems called agents which are capable of interacting with one another. Each agent is represented by an information system (collection of data) with structured attributes, a knowledge-based system (collection of rules and negative terms), and a query answering system based on Client/Server schema.

Each agent can be a source of a non-standard query. We will consider two types of queries:

- queries asking for objects in a local information system satisfying a given description (o-queries),
- queries asking for rules describing a local attribute value in terms of a group of local attributes (r-queries)

By a local query for a given agent we mean a query entirely built from values of attributes local for that agent. Otherwise, a query is called global (non-standard). To resolve a local o-query, we use a cooperative approach similar to the one proposed by Chu [1], Gaasterland [2], and others. In order to resolve a global o-query for a site i (called a client), information systems at other sites (called servers) have to be contacted. To be more precise, the client site will search for servers which can resolve unknown attribute values used in a global o-query. Such servers will try to discover approximate descriptions of these unknown attribute values, from their information systems, in a form of rules and if they succeed, they will send these descriptions to the client site. These sets of rules are sound at the sites they have been discovered (they can only overlap on g-negative terms) but clearly they do not have to be sound at the client site. If more than one server site sends these rules to the client site, then the new set of rules at the client site has to be checked for consistency. If the result is negative, then this set of rules has to be repaired. The repair algorithm is successful if condition parts of initially inconsistent rules overlap at the client site only on g-negative and l-negative terms.

The query answering system at the client site is using these newly discovered and repaired (if needed) rules to resolve a global o-query. In a case of a local r-query, we use a modified LERS system (the overlaps on both g-negative and l-negative condition parts of the rules are allowed).

Our system is different from solving queries on a conventional relational database or from solving queries in a cooperative information system ([1],[2]) in the sense that it uses rules discovered on remote servers to resolve unknown attributes.

2 Basic Definitions

In this section, we introduce the notion of an attribute tree, an information system which is a generalization of Pawlak's system [10], an information system with negative constraints (called nc-system), a distributed information system (DIS), and finally we give definitions of local and global queries for one of the sites of DIS.
To simplify some definitions, attributes and attribute values are called attributes in this paper.
By an attribute tree we mean a pair $(V, \leq)$ such that:

- $(V, \leq)$ is a partially ordered set of attributes,
- $(\forall a, b, c \in V)[(a \leq b \wedge c \leq b) => (a \leq c \vee c \leq a)]$,
- $(\forall a, b \in V)(\exists c \in V)(c \leq a \wedge c \leq b)$,
- $(\forall a)[$ a has minimum two children or a is a leaf$]$.

We say here that b is a child of a if $\sim (\exists c)[c \neq a \wedge c \neq b \wedge a \leq c \leq b]$.

Let $(V, \leq)$ and $(U, \leq)$ are attribute trees. We say that $(U, \leq)$ is a subtree of $(V, \leq)$ if $U \subseteq V$ and $(\forall a \in U)(\forall c \in V)(a \leq c \Rightarrow c \in U)$.

Information system S is defined as a sequence $(X, V, \leq, f)$, where X is a set of objects, V is a set of attributes and f is a classification function. We assume that:

- $V = \bigcup\{V_i : i \in I\}$ and $(V_i, \leq)$ is an attribute tree for any $i \in I$,
- $V_i \cap V_j = \emptyset$ for any $i, j \in I$,
- $f : X \times I \longrightarrow 2^V$ where $(f(x,i), \leq)$ is a subtree of $(V_i, \leq)$ for any $i \in I$.

Clearly card(I) is equal to the number of maximal subtrees in $(V, \leq)$. We interpret I as the set of attribute names in the system S. The root of the tree $(f(x,i), \leq)$ gives the value of the attribute i for an object x and the set $f(x,i)$ gives all possible values of the attribute i for x. If $(\exists x)[f(x,i) = V_i]$, then the value of the attribute i for an object x in S is unknown.

Example 1. Let us assume that the value $f(x, color)$ of the attribute x is represented by the Figure 1 given below.

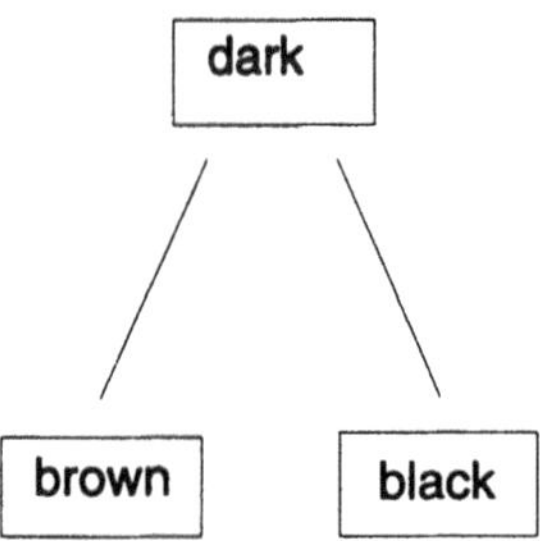

Fig. 1. Value of the attribute color for object x

In this case the color of x is dark and it can be either brown or black. □

With each information system $S = (X, V, \leq, f)$, we link a formal language $L(S)$ called a description language or query language (see [7]). If only the attributes of S are taken as the descriptors of $L(S)$, then $L(S)$ is called local for S (see [7], [12]). If descriptors of $L(S)$ contain some attributes which are not from S, then $L(S)$ is not local. In this paper, we mainly deal with query languages which are not local (we call them global for S).

Let us be more precise. By a set of S-terms for $S = (X, V, \leq, f)$, $V = \bigcup\{V_i : i \in I\}$ we mean a least set T_S such that:

- if $v \in V_i$ then $(i, v) \in T_S$, for any $i \in I$
- if $t_1, t_2 \in T_S$ then $(t_1 + t_2), (t_1 * t_2), \sim t_1 \in T_S$.

We say that:

- S-term t is *atomic* if it is of the form (i, w) or $\sim (i, w)$ where $w \in V_i$,
- S-term t is *positive* if it is of the form $\prod\{(i, w) : w \in V_i\}$,

- S-term t is *primitive* if it is of the form $\prod\{t_j : t_j \text{ is atomic }\}$,
- S-term is in *disjunctive normal form* (DNF) if $t = \sum\{t_j : j \in J\}$ where each t_j is primitive.

By a local o-query for S we mean any element in T_S which is in DNF. Informally, o-query $t \in T_S$ can be read as:

find all objects in X which descriptions are consistent with query t.

By a local r-query (called in this paper r-query) for S we mean either a pair $((i,w),I_1)$ or $(\sim (i,w),I_1)$, where $i \in I - I_1$ and $I_1 \subset I$. Correspondingly, we can read such r-queries as:

describe (i,w) in terms of attributes from I,
describe $\sim (i,w)$ in terms of attributes from I.

Before we give the semantics (interpretation J_S) of local o-queries for S and r-queries for S, where $S = (X,V,\leq,f)$, we introduce function $\bar{f}$. Let us assume that $S = (X,V,\leq,f)$ is an information system, where $V = \bigcup\{V_i : i \in I\}$. Then, function $\bar{f}$ is defined by two conditions below:

- $\bar{f} : X \times I \longrightarrow 2^V$,
- $\bar{f}(x,i)$ is a root of the tree $(f(x,i),\leq)$.

The set $\{\bar{f}(x,i) : i \in I\}$ contains values of attributes which conjunct gives the most specific description of x which is known by the agent represented by S.

By an S-rule we mean either a pair $[(i,w),t]$ or $[\sim (i,w),t]$, where t is an S_1-term in DNF and $S_1 = (X,\bigcup\{V_j : j \in I - \{i\}\},\leq,f)$.

Now, let us assume that $S = (X,V,\leq,f)$, $V = \bigcup\{V_i : i \in I\}$ and $v \in V_i$. By $Ant(v,i)$ we mean the smallest subset of $Neg(v,i) = \{w \in V_i :\sim (w \leq v) \& \sim (v \leq w)\}$ such that:

if $w_1 \in Neg(v,i)$, then $(\exists w_2 \in Ant(v,i))(w_2 \leq w_1)$.

Example 2. Let us assume that V_{color} = {*dark*, *bright*, *brown*, *black*, *gray*, *yellow*, *white*, *blue*} is a set of values of the attribute *color* both represented by Figure 2.

Then, *Ant*(*blue*, *color*) = {*white*, *yellow*, *dark*}. □

Terms t_1, t_2 are called contradictory if:

- there is (i,w_1) which is a subterm of t_1,
- there is (i,w_2) which is a subterm of t_2,
- the set $\{w_1,w_2\}$ is an antichain in $(V_i,\leq)$.

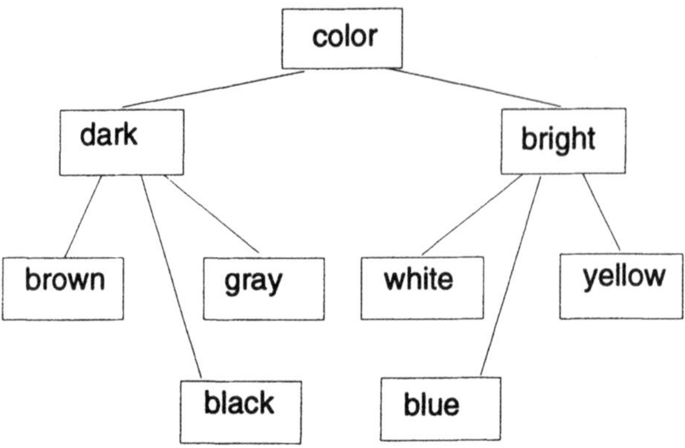

Fig. 2. Structured attribute *color*.

The interpretation J_S of local o-queries for S in $S = (X, V, \leq, f)$, $V = \bigcup\{V_i : i \in I\}$ is given below:

- $J_S((i,v)) = \{x \in X : v \leq \bar{f}(x,i)\}$,
- $J_S(\sim (i,v)) = \bigcup\{\{x \in X : w \leq \bar{f}(x,i)\} : w \in Ant(v,i)\}$,
- if t_1, t_2 are S-terms, then

  $J_S(t_1 + t_2) = J_S(t_1) \cup J_S(t_2)$,

  $J_S(t_1 * t_2) = J_S(t_1) \cap J_S(t_2)$.

Assume now that $r = [t_1, t_2]$, where $t_2 = \prod\{t_j : j \in J_1\}$, is an S-rule. We say that:

- r is valid in S if $J_S(t_2) \subset J_S(t_1)$,
- r is simple if t_2 is positive,
- r is optimal if r is valid and simple and there is no other valid and simple rule $[t_1, t_3]$ in S, such that

  $t_3 = \prod\{s_k : k \in J_2\}$,

  $(\forall k \in J_2)(\exists j \in J_1)(s_k \leq t_j)$,

  $(\forall j \in J_1)(\exists k \in J_2)(s_k \leq t_j)$.

By an information system with negative constraints (nc-system) we mean a pair (S, N), where $S = (X, V, \leq, f)$, is an information system and N is a set of primitive terms called negative constraints for S. A term t is a negative constraint for S if $J_S(t) = \emptyset$.

Let q be a local r-query for a nc-system (S, N). By nc-interpretation of local r-queries in (S, N) we mean any function J_S satisfying three conditions below:

- if $q = ((i, w), I_1)$, then $J_S(q)$ is a non-empty set of optimal S-rules describing (i, w) in terms of values of attributes from $\bigcup\{V_j : j \in I_1\}$,

- if $q = (\sim (i, w), I_1)$, then $J_S(q)$ is a non-empty set of optimal S-rules describing $\sim (i, w)$ in terms of values of attributes from $\bigcup\{V_j : j \in I_1\}$,
- if $((i, w_1), t_1) \in J_S(q_1)$, $((i, w_2), t_2) \in J_S(q_2)$, $w_1 \neq w_2$ then either $(\exists t \in N)(t$ is a subterm of $t_1 * t_2)$ or terms t_1, t_2 are contradictory.

We say that J_S is standard if:

- for any antichain $\{v_1, v_2\} \subset V_i$, $J_S(v_1) \cap J_S(v_2) = \emptyset$,
- $(\forall v \in V_i)[X - J_S(v) = \bigcup\{J_S(u) : u \in Ant(v, i)\}]$.

The class of standard *nc*-interpretations is the simplest class for which the results presented in [13], [14] (including completeness theorem) are naturally extended. In this paper we plan to outline the methodology for answering *o*-queries and *r*-queries in a distributed information system. We assume here that each system (agent) knows, according to his experience, both locally-negative terms and globally-negative terms. As we have mentioned earlier, a $locally-negative\ term$ refers to the situation when objects consistent with that term either do not exist or will never be stored at the client site. Similarly, a $globally - negative$ $term$ refers to the situation when objects consistent with that term either do not exist or will never be stored at any site of our distributed information system.

We begin with the definition below:

By a distributed information system we mean a pair $DS = (\{(S_k, N_k)\}_{k \in K}, L)$ where:

- $S_k = (X_k, V_k, \leq, f_k)$ is an information system for any $k \in K$,
- $N_k = N_{l_k} \cup N_{g_k}$ is a set of negative constraints for S_k,
- N_{l_k} is a set of locally-negative constraints for S_k,
- N_{g_k} is a set of globally-negative constraints for S_k,
- $(\forall k1, k2 \in K)[N_{g_{k1}} = N_{g_{k2}}]$,
- L is a symmetric, binary relation on the set K,
- K is a set of sites.

We assume here that $V_k = \bigcup\{V_{<k,i>} : i \in I_k\}$.

Systems $(S_{k1}, N_{k1}), (S_{k2}, N_{k2})$ are called neighbors in a distributed information system DS if $(k1, k2) \in L$. The transitive closure of L in K is denoted by L^*.

Before we introduce *o*-queries and *r*-queries for a distributed information system DS, we generalize first the definition of S_k-terms. By a set of DS-terms for $DS = (\{(S_k, N_k)\}_{k \in K}, L)$ we mean a least set T_{DS} such that:

- if $v \in \bigcup\{V_k : k \in K\}$ then $v \in T_{DS}$,
- if $t_1, t_2 \in T_{DS}$ then $(t_1 + t_2), (t_1 * t_2), \sim t_1 \in T_{DS}$.

By *o*-query for DS we mean any element in T_{DS} which is in DNF.

By r-query for DS we mean either a pair $((i,w),I)$ or $(\sim (i,w),I)$, where $i \in \bigcup\{I_k : k \in K\} - I$ and $I \subset \bigcup\{I_k : k \in K\}$.

We say that r-query (either $((i,w),I)$ or $(\sim (i,w),I)$) for DS is k-local, if $i \in I_k$ and $I \subset I_k$. We say that r-query (either $((i,w),I)$ or $(\sim (i,w),I)$) for DS is k-global, if $I \subset I_k$. So, in a case of k-global queries the attribute i does not have to belong to I_k. In this paper we are only interested in r-queries which are either k-local or k-global.

Similarly, o-queries for DS built from elements in V_k are called k-local. All other o-queries for DS are called global. Global r-queries are initiated by agents only when they have to answer global o-queries. The interpretation J_{DS} of global o-queries at site k of DS was given for instance in [13] and [14]. In this paper we assume that our system DS is cooperative in the sense of Chu [1] or Gaasterland [2]. It means that if the interpretation of o-query at site k is giving us an empty set, we generalize first the local attribute values listed in o-query to answer it. If we still fail to answer the query at site k, then we contact servers at other sites of DS.

Assume now that $DS = (\{(S_k, N_k)\}_{k \in K}, L)$. Let q be r-query for DS which is k-local. An nc-interpretation J_{DS} of q in $S = S_k$ is defined below:

- if $q = ((i,w),I)$, then $J_{DS}(q)$ is a non-empty set of optimal S-rules describing (i,w) in terms of attributes from I,
- if $q = (\sim (i,w),I)$, then $J_{DS}(q)$ is a non-empty set of optimal S-rules describing $\sim (i,w)$ in terms of values of attributes from I,
- if $((i,w_1),t_1),((i,w_2),t_2) \in J_{DS}(q)$, $w_1 \neq w_2$ then either $(\exists t \in N_k)$(t is a subterm of $t_1 * t_2$) or terms t_1, t_2 are contradictory.

Assume now that q is r-query for DS which is k-global. It means that we can not resolve our r-query at site k or saying another words any nc-interpretation J_{DS} is not defined for q. In this case the client program at site k will search for servers which can resolve the query q. If such a server is found, the nc-interpretation J_{DS} at site k will be replaced by a new nc-interpretation linked with that server.

3 Distributed Knowledge-Based System

In this section, we show how to construct rules and dictionaries (knowledge-bases). Next, we show how to use them to improve nc-interpretations of o-queries for DS at site k.

Let us take an information system (S_k, N_k), where $(X_k, V_k, \leq, f_k)$, $X_k = \{a1, a3, a4, a6, a8, a9, a10, a11\}$, $V_k = \{H, h1, h2, E, e1, e2, F, f1, f2, f3, G, g1,$-$g2, g3, K, k1, k2, L, l1, l2\}$, $I_k = \{i1, i2, i3, i4, i5, i6\}$, and f_k is defined by Table 1.

We assume here that: $H \leq h1$, $H \leq h2$, $E \leq e1$, $E \leq e2$, $F \leq f1$, $F \leq f2$, $F \leq f3$, $G \leq g1$, $G \leq g2$, $G \leq g3$, $K \leq k1$, $K \leq k2$, $L \leq l1$, $L \leq l2$. System S_k represents one of the sites of DS. A knowledge-base which is basically

X_k	$i1$	$i2$	$i3$	$i4$	$i5$	$i6$
$a1$	$h1$	$e1$	$f2$	$g1$	$k1$	$l1$
$a3$	$h2$	$e1$	$f1$	$g1$	$k1$	$l1$
$a4$	$h1$	$e1$	$f2$	$g2$	$k1$	$l1$
$a6$	$h2$	$e2$	$f3$	$g3$	$k2$	$l2$
$a8$	$h2$	$e2$	$f2$	$g2$	$k2$	$l2$
$a9$	$h1$	$e1$	$f1$	$g1$	$k1$	$l2$
$a10$	$h2$	$e1$	$f2$	$g2$	$k2$	$l2$
$a11$	$h1$	$e1$	$f2$	$g1$	$k1$	$l1$

Table 1. Information System S_k

seen as a set of rules is added to each site of DS. A pair (information system, knowledge-base), is called a knowledge-based system. In [12], we proposed, so called, standard interpretation of rules and gave a strategy to construct rules which are optimal (not reducible).

Now, to recall our strategy, let us assume that information system represented by Table 1 is used to generate rules describing $e1, e2$ in terms of $\{f1$, $f2$, $f3$, $g1$, $g2$, $k1$, $k2$ $\}$. Following Grzymala-Busse in [4], $f3 * g3 * k2 \to e2$ is a certain rule and $f2 * g2 * k2 \to e2$ is a possible one in S_k. Similarly, $f1 * g1 * k1 + f2 * g1 * k1$ $+ f2 * g2 * k1 \to e1$ is a certain rule and $f2 * g2 * k2 \to e1$ is a possible rule in S_k. Now, assuming that S_k is not changing (we are not allowed to make any updates or add new tuples), we optimize the rules in S_k. As a result, we get two generalized certain rules: $f3 \to e2$ and $k1 \to e1$. The generalization process for possible rules is not trivial unless we want to generalize our rule $f2*g2*k2 \to e2$ to $\mathbf{1} \to e2$. We should also notice that the generalization process for certain rules allows us to create rules $f3 \to e2$ and $k1 \to e1$ which will become contradictory (no longer certain) if the term $f3 * k1$ does not belong to N_k. To prevent the last problem, we can change the optimization process for rules.

Let us assume that $\{u1, u2\}$ is an antichain in V_k such that $(\exists u \in V_k)(u \leq u1 \wedge u \leq u2)$ and $t1 \to u1$, $t2 \to u2$ are certain rules in (S_k, N_k), where S_k $= (X_k, V_k, \leq, f_k)$ and $N_k = N_{g_k} \cup N_{l_k}$. We say that these rules are k-locally sound if $J_S(t_1 * t_2) = \emptyset$ for any nc-system (S, N_k). We say that these rules are k-globally sound if $J_S(t_1 * t_2) = \emptyset$ for any nc-system (S, N_{g_k}).

Now, let us assume that $\{u1, u2\}$ is an antichain in V_k such that $(\exists u \in V_k)(u \leq u1 \wedge u \leq u2)$, $t1 \to u1$ is a certain rule, and $t2 \to u2$ is a possible rule in (S_k, N_k). We again say that these rules are k-locally sound if $J_S(t_1 * t_2) = \emptyset$ for any nc-system (S, N_k). We also say that these rules are k-globally sound if $J_S(t_1 * t_2) = \emptyset$ for any nc-system (S, N_{g_k}).

From this time on, we will allow only those generalizations which are preserving local soundness of rules on the client site and global soundness on the server sites. In [7] and [12], we described the process of building such rules when the set of negative constraints was empty. In both papers, we have used similar representation for certain and possible rules. Namely, we have defined them as triples $[u, t_1, t_2]$, where $t_1 \rightarrow u$ represents a certain rule and $t_1 + t_2 \rightarrow u$ represents a possible one.

X_m	$i1$	$i2$	$i3$	$i4$	$i5$
$a1$	$f2$	c1	$d1$	e1	$g1$
$a6$	$f2$	c1	$d2$	e3	$g2$
$a7$	$f1$	c2	$d1$	e3	$g1$
$a11$	$f1$	c1	$d2$	e3	$g1$
$a13$	$f1$	c2	$d2$	e3	$g1$
$a14$	$f1$	c2	$d1$	e3	$g2$
$a15$	$f1$	c1	$d1$	e3	$g1$

Table 2. Information System S_m

Let us assume that we have information system (S_m, N_m), where $S_m = (X_m, V_m, \leq, f_m)$, $X_m = \{a1, a6, a7, a11, a13, a14, a15\}$, $V_m = \{C, c1, c2, E, e1, e2, e3, D, d1, d2, F, f1, f2, G, g1, g2, \}$, $I_m = \{i1, i2, i3, i4, i5\}$, and f_m is defined by Table 2.

We assume here that: $F \leq f1$, $F \leq f2$, $G \leq g1$, $G \leq g2$, $E \leq e1$, $E \leq e2$, $E \leq e3$, $C \leq c1$, $C \leq c2$, $D \leq d1$, $D \leq d2$. System (S_m, N_m) represents one of the sites of DS. Now, employing similar strategy to the one described in [12], we can generate two globally sound rules from (S_m, N_m): $[d1, e1, f1{*}e3]$ and $[d2, f2{*}e3, f1{*}e3]$. These rules can be added to the knowledge-base KB_k assigned to the site k of our distributed information system because $N_{g_m} = N_{g_k}$. If KB_k is empty, then (S_k, N_k) is extended to a knowledge-based system $((S_k, N_k), KB_k)$. If KB_k is not empty then the k-local soundness of any two rules in KB_k have to be checked. If the rules are not k-locally sound, then they have to be repaired following a strategy similar to the one described in [11].

Let us assume that $((S_k, N_k), KB_k)$ represents one of the sites of a distributed knowledge-based system DS, $S_k = (X_k, V_k, \leq, f_k)$ and J_{S_k} is the interpretation of queries from $L(S_k)$ in S_k. By a standard interpretation of global queries (elements of $L(DS)$) at site k, we mean function M_k such that:

- $M_k(\mathbf{0}) = \emptyset$, $M_k(\mathbf{1}) = X_k$,
- for any $w \in V_k$, $M_k(w) = J_{S_k}(w)$,
- for any $w \notin V_k$, $M_k(w) = \{x \in X_k : (\exists t, s \in L(S_k))([w, t, s] \in KB_k \wedge x \in J_{S_k}(t)\}$,
- for any $w \notin V_k$, $M_k(\sim w) = \{x \in X_k : (\exists t, s \in L(S_k))([w, t, s] \in KB_k \wedge x \notin J_{S_k}(s)\}$,
- for any global query t, $M_k(t) = J_{S_k}(t)$.

Let us go back to Table 2. Clearly, we can also generate the following rules from S_m:

$[g1, e1 + c1 * f1, c2 * f1 * e3]$,
$[g2, f2 * e3, c2 * f1 * e3]$.

These rules are globally sound and can be added to KB_k. If they are added to KB_k, they may change the local nc-interpretation M_k of global queries at site k. There is one problem, attributes $c1, c2$, listed in the descriptions of both rules, are not local for a site k. So, we can either interpret them as empty sets of objects or ask other sites of DS for k-global rules describing $c1$ and $c2$.

To conclude our discussion, assume that M_k is retrieving empty set when asking for a local nc-interpretation of a local attribute. In this case, we can go to a parent of this attribute (our attributes are represented as trees) and check if M_k retrieves any objects for that parent node. There is a possibility that the empty set will not be retrieved. Also, by generalizing queries we may retrieve some objects which are not interesting for the user. Clearly, it makes sense to give a chance to the user to make him decide if objects retrieved by the client system are useful or useless. If queries contain foreign attributes, then the client will search for server systems which can resolve these attributes. The use of negative constraints gives us the possibility to search for more compact representation of rules and improves the time complexity of the query answering system.

Conclusion

This paper presents a methodology and theoretical foundations of QRAS-NC (Query Rough Answering Systems with Negative Constraints) which first version is implemented at UNC-Charlotte on a cluster of SPARC workstations.

References

1. Chu, W.W., Chen, Q., Lee, R.: Cooperative query answering via type abstraction hierarchy. In: S. M. Deen (ed.), Cooperating knowledge-based systems, North Holland (1991) 271–292
2. Gaasterland, T., Godfrey, P., Minker, J.: An overview of cooperative answering. Journal of Intelligent Information Systems **1** (1992) 123–158
3. Grice, H.: Logic and conversation. In: P. Cole, J. Morgan (eds.), Syntax and semantics, Academic Press, New York (1975)
4. Grzymala-Busse, J.: Managing uncertainty in expert systems. Kluwer Academic Publishers, Dordrecht (1991)
5. Kryszkiewicz, M., Ras, Z.W.: Query rough-answering system for CKBS. In: Tsumoto S., Kobayashi, S., Yokomori, T., Tanaka, H. (eds.), Proceedings of the Fourth International Workshop on Rough Sets, Fuzzy Sets and Machine Discovery (RSFD'96), Tokyo Nov. 6-8, Tokyo Univ. Press (1996) 162–167
6. Lipski, W., Marek, W.: On information storage and retrieval systems. In: Mathematical foundations of computer science. Banach Center Publications **2** Warsaw (1977) 215–259

7. Maitan, J., Ras, Z.W., Zemankova, M.: Query handling and learning in a distributed intelligent system. In: Z.W. Ras (ed.), Methodologies for Intelligent Systems **4** North Holland (1989) 118–127
8. Michalski, R.S.: Pattern recognition as rule-guided inductive inference. IEEE Transactions on Pattern Analysis and Machine Intelligence PAMI-2 **4** (July 1980)
9. Pawlak, Z.: Rough sets and decision tables. In: Proceedings of the Fifth Symposium on Computation Theory. Lecture Notes in Computer Science **208** (1985) 118–127
10. Pawlak, Z.: Mathematical foundations of information retrieval. CC PAS Reports **101** Warsaw (1973)
11. Ras, Z.W.: Dictionaries in a distributed knowledge-based system. In: Proceedings of Concurrent Engineering: Research and Applications Conference, Pittsburgh, August 29-31. Concurrent Technologies Corporation (1994) 383–390
12. Ras, Z.W.: Collaboration control in distributed knowledge-based systems. In: Information Sciences Journal **96/3/4** (1997) 193–205
13. Ras, Z.W.: Cooperative knowledge-based systems. In: Intelligent Automation and Soft Computing Journal **2/2** (1996) 193–202
14. Ras, Z.W.: Resolving queries through cooperation in multi-agent systems. In: T.Y. Lin, N. Cercone (eds.), Rough sets and data mining, Kluwer Academic Publishers (1997) 239–258

Chapter 6

Approximation Spaces, Reducts and Representatives

Jarosław Stepaniuk

Institute of Computer Science
Bialystok University of Technology
Wiejska 45A, 15-351 Bialystok, Poland
e-mail: jstepan@ii.pb.bialystok.pl

Abstract. The main objective of this chapter is to discuss different approaches to searching for optimal approximation spaces. Basic notions concerning rough set concept based on generalized approximation spaces are presented. Different constructions of approximation spaces are described. The problems of attribute and object selection are discussed.

1 Introduction

Rough set theory was proposed [21, 22] as a new approach to processing of incomplete data.

Suppose we are given the finite non-empty set U of objects, called the universe. Each object of U is characterized by a description, for example a set of attribute values. In standard rough sets [21, 22] introduced by Pawlak an equivalence relation (reflexive, symmetric and transitive relation) on the universe of objects is defined based on the attribute values. In particular, this equivalence relation is constructed based on the equality relation on attribute values.

Many attempts were made to resolve limitations of this approach and many authors proposed interesting extensions of the initial model (for example see [35, 36, 38, 24, 14, 11, 32, 34, 39, 42]). It was observed that considering a similarity relation instead of an indiscernibility relation is quite relevant. The similarities between objects can be represented by a function forming for every object the class of objects which are not noticeably different in terms of the available description. The objects of the universe are often described by a finite set of m attribute values. In this case, for every object, the global similarity class is usually obtained by aggregating local similarity classes corresponding to particular attributes a_i, where $i = 1, ..., m$ [11, 12]. A global similarity relation can be also computed by aggregation of similarity relations for particular attributes [38, 14]. Computation of a similarity relation can be also done for all objects and attributes at the same time [19].

One of the problems we are interested in is the following: given a subset $X \subseteq U$, define X in terms of the similarity classes defined by attributes.

We discuss an approach based on generalized approximation spaces introduced in [32, 33, 34]. There are several modifications of the original approximation space definition [22].

The first one concerns the so called uncertainty function. Information about an object, say x is represented by its attribute value vector. The set of all objects with similar (to attribute value vector of x) value vectors creates the similarity class $I(x)$. In [22] all objects with the same value vector create the indiscernibility class. The relation $y \in I(x)$ is in this case an equivalence relation. We consider a more general case when it can be any relation.

The second modification of approximation space definition introduces a generalization of a rough membership function [23]. We assume that to answer a question whether an object x belongs to an object set X we have to answer a question whether $I(x)$ is in some sense included in X. Hence we take as a primitive notion a rough inclusion function rather than rough membership function. Our approach allows us to unify different cases considered in [22, 48, 9].

One of the problems related to practical applications of rough set methods is whether the whole set of attributes is necessary and if not, how to determine the simplified and still sufficient subset of attributes equivalent to the original. Significant results in this area have been achieved in [31]. The problem of finding reducts is transformable to the problem of finding prime implicants of a monotone Boolean function. This problem is known to be NP-hard, but many heuristics are presented for the computation of one prime implicant.

In this paper we discuss definitions of a reduct for a single object and for all objects of information system with similarity classes defined for all objects [34]. We also consider definitions of a reduct for a single object, for a decision class and for all objects of a decision table. The definitions have a property that, like in the standard rough set model [22, 31] and in the variable precision rough set model [48, 15], the set of prime implicants of a corresponding discernibility function is equivalent to the set of reducts.

In some sense dual to the problem of attribute set reduction is the problem of object number reduction (selection). In the standard rough set approach it seems that the first idea is to take one element from every equivalence class defined by a set of attributes. When we consider overlapping similarity classes the above idea should be modified. We discuss equivalence of the problem of object number reduction to the problem of prime implicants computation for a suitable Boolean function.

The paper is organized as follows. In Section 2 generalized approximation spaces are discussed. Basic notions concerning the rough set concept based on generalized approximation spaces are presented. In Section 3 different constructions of approximation spaces (similarity relations) are described. In Section 4 attribute reduction problems are discussed. In Section 5 a computation of adequate representative objects is investigated. Some illustrative examples are included.

2 Approximation Spaces

In the standard rough set model knowledge is formally represented by an equivalence relation IND (called ***indiscernibility relation***) defined on a certain universe of objects U. The pair (U, IND) is called an approximation space. The approximation space provides an approximate characterization of any subset X of U.

In this section we present a more general definition of approximation space [32, 34] which can be used for example for the similarity based rough set model and the variable precision rough set model.

An approximation space is a system $AS = (U, I, \nu)$, where

- U is a non-empty set of objects,
- $I : U \longrightarrow P(U)$ is an uncertainty function ($P(U)$ denotes the set of all subsets of U),
- $\nu : P(U) \times P(U) \longrightarrow [0, 1]$ is a rough inclusion function.

An uncertainty function defines a neighborhood of every object x.

The rough inclusion function defines the value of inclusion between two subsets of U. In [34, 29], the following conditions were formulated for the rough inclusion function:

- $\nu(X, X) = 1$ for any $X \subseteq U$,
- $\nu(X, Y) = 1$ implies $\nu(Z, Y) \geq \nu(Z, X)$ for any $X, Y, Z \subseteq U$,
- $\nu(\emptyset, X) = 1$ for any $X \subseteq U$.

Example 1. **The standard rough set model.**

In the classical definition of an approximation space [22], we consider a pair (U, IND), where U is a non-empty set and IND is an equivalence relation on U. The classical approximation space corresponds to the approximation space $AS = (U, I, \nu)$, where

- $\{I(x) : x \in U\}$ creates a partition of U ($(x, y) \in IND$ if and only if $I(x) = I(y)$),
- $\nu(X, Y) = \begin{cases} \frac{card(X \cap Y)}{card(X)} & \text{if } X \neq \emptyset \\ 1 & \text{if } X = \emptyset \end{cases}$ for any $X, Y \subseteq U$.

Definitions of the lower and the upper approximations can be written as follows:

$L(AS, X) = \{x \in U : \nu(I(x), X) = 1\}$ and
$U(AS, X) = \{x \in U : \nu(I(x), X) > 0\}$.

Example 2. **The variable precision rough set model.**

A modification of the standard rough set model is presented in [48, 9] for the so called variable precision rough set model. The approximation spaces $AS_{l,u} = (U, I, \nu(f_{l,u}))$, where $0 \leq l < u \leq 1$ are defined in the same way as before with only one exception, namely the rough inclusion is defined by $\nu(f_{l,u})(X, Y) = f_{l,u}\left(\frac{card(X \cap Y)}{card(X)}\right)$, where $f_{l,u}$ is a function such that $f_{l,u}(t) = \begin{cases} 0 & \text{if } 0 \leq t \leq l \\ \frac{t-l}{u-l} & \text{if } l < t < u \\ 1 & \text{if } \quad t \geq u \end{cases}$.

The set approximations are defined by
$L(AS_{l,u}, X) = \{x \in U : \nu(f_{l,u})(I(x), X) = 1\}$ and
$U(AS_{l,u}, X) = \{x \in U : \nu(f_{l,u})(I(x), X) > 0\}$.

Example 3. **The similarity based rough set model.**

If the uncertainty function I defines a similarity relation (at least reflexive relation) not being an equivalence relation then there is a variety of possibilities to define the lower and the upper set approximations.

Let AS be an approximation space and let an intended relation $r \subseteq U \times U$. The lower and the upper approximation of $X \subseteq U$ in AS (relatively to r) are defined by
$L_r(AS, X) = \{x \in U : \forall y ((x, y) \in r \to \nu(I(y), X) = 1)\}$ and
$U_r(AS, X) = \{x \in U : \forall y ((x, y) \in r \to \nu(I(y), X) > 0)\}$, respectively.
There are different possible choices for r [34], for example:

- r_1 is the identity relation,
- $(x, y) \in r_2$ if and only if $y \in I(x)$,
- $(x, y) \in r_3$ if and only if $y \in \bigcap\{I(z) : x \in I(z)\}$.

In this case we have $L_{r_3}(AS, X) \subseteq L_{r_2}(AS, X) \subseteq L_{r_1}(AS, X)$ and

$$U_{r_3}(AS, X) \subseteq U_{r_2}(AS, X) \subseteq U_{r_1}(AS, X).$$

It depends on particular application which type of set approximation to choose.

Example 4. **Approximation spaces in information retrieval problem.**

We consider generalized approximation spaces in information retrieval problem [6]. At first, to determine an approximation space, we choose the universe U as the set of all keywords. Let DOC be a set of documents, which are described by keywords. Let $key : DOC \longrightarrow P(U)$ be a function mapping documents into sets of keywords. Denote by $c(x_i, x_j)$, where $c : U \times U \longrightarrow \{0, 1, 2, \ldots\}$ the frequency of co-occurrence between two keywords x_i and x_j i.e. $c(x_i, x_j) = card(\{doc \in DOC : \{x_i, x_j\} \subseteq key(doc)\})$.

We define the uncertainty function I_θ depending on a threshold

$$\theta \in \{0, 1, 2, \ldots\}$$

as follows: $I_\theta(x_i) = \{x_j \in U : c(x_i, x_j) \geq \theta\} \cup \{x_i\}$. The rough inclusion function is defined in the standard way:

$$\nu(X, Y) = \begin{cases} \frac{card(X \cap Y)}{card(X)} & \text{if } X \neq \emptyset \\ 1 & \text{if } X = \emptyset \end{cases}.$$

A query is defined as a set of keywords. Different strategies of information retrieval based on the lower and the upper approximations of queries and documents are investigated in [6].

We define some basic notions of the rough set theory in the case of generalized approximation spaces.

Let $AS = (U, I, \nu)$ be an approximation space and let $\{X_1, \ldots, X_r\}$ be a classification of objects (i.e. $\{X_1, \ldots, X_r\} \subseteq U$, $\bigcup_{i=1}^{r} X_i = U$ and $X_i \cap X_j = \emptyset$ for $i \neq j$, where $i, j = 1, \ldots, r$).

The positive region of the classification $\{X_1, \ldots, X_r\}$ with respect to the approximation space AS is defined as

$$POS\left(AS, \{X_1, \ldots, X_r\}\right) = \bigcup_{i=1}^{r} L\left(AS, X_i\right).$$

The quality of approximation of the classification $\{X_1, \ldots, X_r\}$ in the approximation space AS is defined as

$$\gamma\left(AS, \{X_1, \ldots, X_r\}\right) = \frac{card\left(POS\left(AS, \{X_1, \ldots, X_r\}\right)\right)}{card\left(U\right)}.$$

This coefficient expresses the ratio of the number of all AS-correctly classified objects to the number of all objects in U.

3 Searching for Optimal Approximation Spaces

In this section we consider problem of searching for an adequate approximation space. We mainly consider problem of searching for adequate uncertainty function in an approximation space. The search for proper uncertainty function is crucial and the most difficult task related to decision algorithm synthesis based on uncertainty functions.

The general problem can be formulated as follows:

Input. A decision table $(U, A \cup \{d\})$.

Output. An approximation space (U, I_A, ν) with an adequate uncertainty function $I_A : U \longrightarrow P(U)$.

We present different possibilities for constructing an uncertainty function. We should start with some information about attribute values for all attributes. In the standard rough set approach only information if two values are equal or not is necessary. In more general situation, we also need quantitative information how different is one value of attribute with respect to other value.

For every subset $B \subseteq A$ we define the following equivalence between similarity relation and uncertainty functions:

$(x_j, x_i) \in SIM(B)$ if and only if $x_j \in I_B(x_i)$.

Different approaches to searching for uncertainty function/similarity relation are presented in the literature (see e.g. [38, 14, 19, 11, 12]).

In further analysis we will consider two stages of searching for proper uncertainty function.

In the first stage, for each attribute uncertainty function is defined and in the second stage such functions are combined for the set of all attributes.

3.1 Local Uncertainty Functions based on Attribute Values Metrics

One approach to searching for an uncertainty function is based on the assumption that there are given some metrics (distances) on attribute values. Distance and similarity are closely related. Relations obtained on attribute values by using metrics are reflexive and symmetrical i.e. they are tolerance relations. For review of different metrics defined on attribute values see [45]. Here we only present two examples of such metrics.

The Value Difference Metric (VDM) was introduced [40] to provide an appropriate distance function for nominal attributes. A simplified version of VDM (without weighting schemes) defines the distance between two values v and v' of an attribute a as:

$$vdm_a(v,v') = \sum_{i=1}^{r(d)} \left(P(d=i|a=v) - P(d=i|a=v')\right)^2,$$

where $r(d)$ is a number of decision classes and

$$P(d=i|a=v) = \frac{card(x \in U : d(x) = i, a(x) = v)}{card(x \in U : a(x) = v)}.$$

Using the distance measure VDM, two values are considered to be closer if they have more similar classifications. For example, if an attribute color has three values red, green and blue, and the application is to identify whether or not an object is an apple, red and green would be considered closer than red and blue because the former two both have correlations with decision apple.

If this distance function is used directly for continuous attributes, the values can all potentially be unique. Some approaches to the problem of using VDM on continuous attributes are presented in [45].

We can also use some other distance function for continuous attributes, for example

$$diff_a(v,v') = \frac{|v-v'|}{\max_a - \min_a},$$

where $\max_a$ and $\min_a$ are the maximum and minimum value, respectively, for the attribute $a \in A$.

Let $\delta_a : V_a \times V_a \longrightarrow [0,\infty)$ be a given distance function on attribute values, where V_a is a set of all values for attribute $a \in A$.

We can define the following uncertainty function

$$y \in I_a^{\varepsilon_a}(x) \text{ if and only if } \delta_a(a(x), a(y)) \leq \varepsilon_a,$$

where $\varepsilon_a \geq 0$ is a given real number.

3.2 Searching for Parameters of Uncertainty Functions

Different methods of searching for parameters of proper uncertainty functions / similarity relations are discussed for example in papers [11, 12, 19, 29], [14, 38].

In papers [38, 14] a genetic algorithm was applied for searching for adequate similarity relation (uncertainty function) of the type $I_A(x) = \bigcap_{a \in A} I_a(x)$.

In this subsection we present problem of finding the optimal uncertainty function relation and sketch its effective solution based on genetic algorithms. The problem is formulated as follows:

Input.
decision table $(U, A \cup \{d\})$
distance measures $\delta_a : V_a \times V_a \longrightarrow [0, \infty)$ for all $a \in A$.
Output. An approximation space $AS = (U, I_A, \nu)$, where
$y \in I_A(x)$ if and only if for every $a \in A$ $\delta_a(a(x), a(y)) \leq \varepsilon_a$ and $\{\varepsilon_a : a \in A\}$ is an optimal set of thresholds. The optimization can be carried out with respect to different conditions. Actually we would like to obtain maximization of the following function:

$$\frac{card(\{(x,y) \in U \times U : I_A(x) = I_A(y), d(x) = d(y)\})}{card(\{(x,y) \in U \times U : d(x) = d(y)\})} + \gamma(AS, \{d\}).$$

First part of the objective function responds for an increase in the number of connections. But we are interested only in connections between objects with the same decision. Hence the second part of the function is introduced to prevent shrinking of the positive region of partition. So the function tries to find out some kind of balance between enlarging $\{(x,y) \in U \times U : I_A(x) = I_A(y)\}$ and preventing the shrinking of the positive region $POS(AS, \{d\})$.

If we decrease the value of ε_a then the $I_a(x_i)$ will not change or become larger. So starting from $\varepsilon_a = 0$ and increasing the value of threshold we can using above property find all values when $I_a(x_i)$ changes. We can create lists of such thresholds for each $a \in A$. We can throw out some threshold values and do not take them under consideration. Next we can check all possible combinations of thresholds to find out the best for our purpose. Of course it will be a long process, because in the worst case, the number of combinations is equal:

$$\frac{1}{2} \prod_{a \in A} \left(card(V_a)^2 - card(V_a) \right) + 1.$$

So it shows that we need some heuristics to find, maybe not the best of all, but very good solution in reasonable time. We use genetic algorithms for this purpose. For more details see [38, 14].

3.3 Strict, Weak and Epsilon-Indiscernibility Relations

In this subsection we assume that values of all condition attributes are real numbers which means that $V_a \subset (-\infty, \infty)$, where $a \in A$.

In papers [35, 36] strict and weak indiscernibility relations were considered which can define some kind of uncertainty functions.

Let $\{[c_0^a, c_1^a), \ldots, [c_{k_a}^a, c_{k_a+1}^a)\}$ be a partition of V_a into subintervals, where k_a is some integer and $\min_a = c_0^a < c_1^a < \ldots < c_{k_a}^a < c_{k_a+1}^a = \max_a$.

Discretization can lose much of the important information available in the continuous values. For example, two values in the same discretized range are considered equal even if they are located on opposite ends of the range.

Therefore, for every cut point c_i^a in [36] a threshold value t_i^a is defined. An enlarged subinterval is defined as $\left[c_i^a - t_i^a, c_{i+1}^a + t_{i+1}^a\right]$.

The threshold values are limited from the top by the requirement that no more than two enlarged subintervals may overlap in the whole set of values of a given attribute a i.e. $c_i^a + t_i^a < c_{i+1}^a - t_{i+1}^a$.

Two objects x and y are considered as strictly indiscernible with regard to an attribute a if their values $a(x)$ and $a(y)$ belong to only one enlarged subinterval which is the same for both values.

We can define the following uncertainty function (strict indiscernibility relation):

$$y \in I_a^s(x) \text{ if and only if } \exists_{c_i^a, c_{i+1}^a \in V_a} \left(c_i^a + t_i^a \leq a(x), a(y) \leq c_{i+1}^a - t_{i+1}^a\right).$$

Let us observe that the strict indiscernibility relation is in general not reflexive.

Objects x and y are weakly indiscernible by an attribute a if and only if $a(x)$ and $a(y)$ belong to the same enlarged subinterval.

We can define the following uncertainty function (weak indiscernibility relation):

$$y \in I_a^w(x) \text{ if and only if } \exists_{c_i^a, c_{i+1}^a \in V_a} \left(c_i^a - t_i^a \leq a(x), a(y) \leq c_{i+1}^a + t_{i+1}^a\right).$$

In some cases it is natural to consider relations defined by ε-indiscernibility [11]. In such way we can obtain relations which need not be symmetrical. We can define the following uncertainty function (ε-indiscernibility relation):

$$y \in I_a^\varepsilon(x) \text{ if and only if } |a(y) - a(x)| \leq \alpha_a * a(x) + \beta_a.$$

where α_a, β_a are some parameters [11] which completely characterize the similarity for the particular attribute a. Searching for parameters α_a, β_a is done independently for every attribute $a \in A$. Linear regression is used for estimation of parameters.

In [12] a more general type of ε-indiscernibility is defined. We can describe this uncertainty function as follows:

$$y \in I_a^{\varepsilon\pm}(x) \text{ if and only if } a(x) - \varepsilon_a^-(x) \leq a(y) \leq a(x) + \varepsilon_a^+(x),$$

where $\varepsilon_a^-, \varepsilon_a^+ : U \longrightarrow V_a$. We assume that ε_a^- and ε_a^+ are some functions which satisfy so called *PurityCondition* [12].

3.4 Aggregation of Local Uncertainty Functions

In this subsection we present general methods of aggregating uncertainty functions defined with respect to single attributes. The usual approach in the standard rough set model is based on the intersection operator. This means that uncertainty function for the whole set of condition attributes is defined as $I_A(x) = \bigcap_{a \in A} I_a(x)$.

We assume that the operator combining partial uncertainty functions (for particular attributes) is defined by monotone Boolean function with variables corresponding to attributes.

Example 5. Let $A = \{a_1, \ldots, a_m\}$ be a set of attributes and let $a_1^*, \ldots, a_m^*$ be Boolean variables corresponding to attributes $a_1, \ldots, a_m$, respectively.

- A global uncertainty function is obtained as the intersection of all local uncertainty functions ($I_A(x) = \bigcap_{a \in A} I_a(x)$), this process is described by the conjunction of all variables:

$$f^{\wedge}(a_1^*, \ldots, a_m^*) = \bigwedge_{i=1}^{m} a_i^*.$$

- A global uncertainty function is obtained as the union of all local uncertainty functions: $I_A(x) = \bigcup_{a \in A} I_a(x)$, then we consider the disjunction of Boolean variables i.e.

$$f^{\vee}(a_1^*, \ldots, a_m^*) = \bigvee_{i=1}^{m} a_i^*.$$

- If we allow that two objects are globally similar if and only if they are similar with respect to at least $m-1$ attributes (dissimilarity on one attribute is not important), then we consider the following Boolean function:

$$f^{\vee\wedge}(a_1^*, \ldots, a_m^*) = \bigvee_{i=1}^{m} \bigwedge_{j \neq i} a_j^*.$$

4 Approximation Spaces and Reducts

One of the problems related to practical applications of rough set methods is whether the whole set of attributes is necessary and if not, how to determine the simplified and still sufficient subset of attributes equivalent to the original one. Significant results in this area have been achieved in [31]. The problem of finding reducts is transformable to the problem of finding prime implicants of a monotone Boolean function.

In this section we discuss a generalization of the standard reduct notion when uncertainty function is defined.

The computation of all types of reducts is based on generalized discernibility matrix. Discernibility matrix was introduced in [31]. In this paper we consider dissimilarity instead of discernibility.

Let (U, A) be an information system. By the generalized discernibility matrix we mean the square matrix $(c_{x,y})_{x,y \in U}$ where

$$c_{x,y} = \{a \in A : y \notin I_a(x)\}.$$

Let us observe that such generalized discernibility matrix may be non – symmetrical.

Let (U, A) be an information system such that $A = \{a_1, \ldots, a_m\}$. We assume that $a_1^*, \ldots, a_m^*$ are Boolean variables corresponding to attributes $a_1, \ldots, a_m$, respectively. Let $f(a_1^*, \ldots, a_m^*)$ be a monotonic Boolean function corresponding to aggregation of local uncertainty functions. Let $x, y \in U$ be two objects. A Boolean function $f_{x,y}(a_1^*, \ldots, a_m^*)$ is obtained using function $f(a_1^*, \ldots, a_m^*)$ and set of attributes $c_{x,y}$ by the following procedure:

1. Boolean connectives are changed from $\wedge$ to $\vee$ and vice versa.
2. For all Boolean variables, if $a \notin c_{x,y}$, then a^* is replaced by 0. We use the following laws of simplification: $a^* \vee 0 \equiv a^*$ and $a^* \wedge 0 \equiv 0$.

Example 6. Let us assume that there be three attributes i.e. $A = \{a, b, c\}$. Let the aggregation of local uncertainty functions be obtained by $I_A(x) = (I_a(x) \cup I_b(x)) \cap (I_a(x) \cup I_c(x)) \cap (I_b(x) \cup I_c(x))$. This fact one can express by the Boolean function $f(a^*, b^*, c^*) = (a^* \vee b^*) \wedge (a^* \vee c^*) \wedge (b^* \vee c^*)$. Let in a discernibility matrix for some objects $x, y \in U$ $c_{x,y} = \{a, b\}$. In this case we obtain $f_{x,y}(a^*, b^*, c^*) = (a^* \wedge b^*) \vee (a^* \wedge 0) \vee (b^* \wedge 0) \equiv (a^* \wedge b^*) \vee 0 \vee 0 \equiv a^* \wedge b^*$.

4.1 Information Systems and Reducts

In this subsection we discuss computation of reducts in information systems.

Reduct computation can be translated to computing prime implicants of a Boolean function. The type of reduct controls how the Boolean function is constructed.

In the case of reducts for an information system, there are determined the minimal sets of attributes that preserve dissimilarity of all objects from one another. Thus the full similarity relation is considered. A resulting reduct is therefore a minimal set of attributes that enables one to introduce the same similarity relation on the universe as the whole set of attributes does.

In the case of object-related reducts we consider the dissimilarity relation relative to each object. For each object, there are determined the minimal sets of attributes that preserve dissimilarity of that object from all others. Thus we construct a Boolean function by restricting the conjunction to only run over the row corresponding to a particular object x of the discernibility matrix (instead of over all rows), hence we obtain the discernibility function related to object x. The set of all prime implicants of this function determines the set of reducts of A related to the object x. These reducts reveal the minimum amount of information needed to preserve dissimilarity of x from all other objects.

In the following definitions we present more formally notions of both types of reducts.

Definition 1. A subset $B \subseteq A$ is called a reduct of A for an object $x \in U$ if and only if

1. $I_B(x) = I_A(x)$.
2. For every proper subset $C \subset B$ the first condition is not satisfied.

Definition 2. A subset $B \subseteq A$ is called a reduct of A if and only if

1. For every $x \in U$ $I_B(x) = I_A(x)$.
2. For every proper subset $C \subset B$ the first condition is not satisfied.

In the following theorems we present equivalence between reducts and prime implicants of suitable Boolean functions.

Theorem 3. *For every object $x \in U$ we define the following Boolean function*

$$g_{A,x}(a_1^*, \ldots, a_m^*) = \bigwedge_{y \in U} f_{x,y}(a_1^*, \ldots, a_m^*).$$

The following conditions are equivalent:

1. *$\{a_{i_1}, \ldots, a_{i_k}\}$ is a reduct for object $x \in U$ in information system (U, A).*
2. *$a_{i_1}^* \wedge \ldots \wedge a_{i_k}^*$ is a prime implicant of the Boolean function $g_{A,x}$.*

Theorem 4. *We define the following Boolean function*

$$g_A(a_1^*, \ldots, a_m^*) = \bigwedge_{x,y \in U} f_{x,y}(a_1^*, \ldots, a_m^*).$$

The following conditions are equivalent:

1. *$\{a_{i_1}, \ldots, a_{i_k}\}$ is a reduct for information system (U, A).*
2. *$a_{i_1}^* \wedge \ldots \wedge a_{i_k}^*$ is a prime implicant of the Boolean function g_A.*

4.2 Decision Tables and Reducts

In this subsection we present methods of attribute set reduction in decision tables.

If we consider a decision table instead of an information system, this translates to a modification of the discernibility function constructed for information system. Since we do not need to preserve dissimilarity between objects with the same decision, we can delete those expressions from the discernibility function that preserve dissimilarity between objects within the same decision class. A resulting reduct is thus a minimal set of attributes that enables one to make the same decisions as the whole set of attributes allows for.

In the case of computing object-related reducts in a decision table, decision rules can be also computed at the same time for reasons of efficiency. It was observed that object-related reducts will typically produce shorter rules, that may subsequently be potentially more noise tolerant.

The third useful type of a relative reduct is a so called decision class related reduct. If we are especially interested in characterization of some decision class, then it is useful to compute reducts for that class.

Let $(U, A \cup \{d\})$ be a decision table. In the following definitions we present more formally all types of reducts.

Definition 5. A subset $B \subseteq A$ is called a relative reduct of A for an object $x \in U$ if and only if

1. $\{y \in U : y \in I_B(x), d(y) = d(x)\} = \{y \in U : y \in I_A(x), d(y) = d(x)\}$.
2. For every proper subset $C \subset B$ the first condition is not satisfied.

Definition 6. A subset $B \subseteq A$ is called a relative reduct of A for a decision class X_i if and only if

1. $L(AS(B), X_i) = L(AS(A), X_i)$.
2. For every proper subset $C \subset B$ the first condition is not satisfied.

Definition 7. A subset $B \subseteq A$ is called a relative reduct of A if and only if

1. $POS(AS(B), \{d\}) = POS(AS(A), \{d\})$.
2. For every proper subset $C \subset B$ the first condition is not satisfied.

In the following theorems we obtain an equivalence between relative reducts and prime implicants of suitable Boolean functions.

Theorem 8. *For every object $x \in U$ we define the Boolean function*

$$g_{A\cup\{d\},x}(a_1^*, \ldots, a_m^*) = \bigwedge_{y\in U, d(y)\neq d(x)} f_{x,y}(a_1^*, \ldots, a_m^*).$$

The following conditions are equivalent:

1. *$\{a_{i_1}, \ldots, a_{i_k}\}$ is a relative reduct for object $x \in U$ in decision table*
$$(U, A \cup \{d\}).$$
2. *$a_{i_1}^* \wedge \ldots \wedge a_{i_k}^*$ is a prime implicant of the Boolean function $g_{A\cup\{d\},x}$.*

Theorem 9. *We define the Boolean function*

$$g_{A\cup\{d\},X_i}(a_1^*, \ldots, a_m^*) = \bigwedge_{x,y\in U, d(y)\neq d(x)=i} f_{x,y}(a_1^*, \ldots, a_m^*).$$

The following conditions are equivalent:

1. *$\{a_{i_1}, \ldots, a_{i_k}\}$ is a relative reduct of for decision class X_i.*
2. *$a_{i_1}^* \wedge \ldots \wedge a_{i_k}^*$ is a prime implicant of the Boolean function $g_{A\cup\{d\},X_i}$.*

Theorem 10. *We define the Boolean function*

$$g_{A\cup\{d\}}\left(a_1^*,\ldots,a_m^*\right) = \bigwedge_{x,y\in U, d(y)\neq d(x)} f_{x,y}\left(a_1^*,\ldots,a_m^*\right).$$

The following conditions are equivalent:

1. $\{a_{i_1},\ldots,a_{i_k}\}$ *is a relative reduct of* A.
2. $a_{i_1}^* \wedge \ldots \wedge a_{i_k}^*$ *is a prime implicant of the Boolean function* $g_{A\cup\{d\}}$.

Now we discuss a heuristic [38, 14] which can be applied for computation of relative reducts without explicitly using discernibility function. But the presented method can be obviously applied to discernibility function simplification.

To find one relative reduct we build a discernibility matrix. Next we make reduction of superfluous entries in such matrix. We set an entry to be empty if it is a superset of another non-empty entry. At the end of this process we obtain the set $COMP$ of the so called components. From the set of components the described type of reduct can be generated by applying Boolean reasoning. We present heuristics for computing one reduct of the considered type with the minimal number of attributes. These heuristics can produce sets which are supersets of considered reducts but the heuristics are much more efficient than the general procedure.

First we introduce a notion of a minimal distinction. By a minimal distinction (*md*, in short) we understand a minimal set of attributes sufficient to discern between two objects. Let us observe that the minimal component *com* consists of minimal distinctions and *card*(*com*) is equal or greater than *card*(*md*). We say that *md* is indispensable if there is a component composed of only one *md*. We include all attributes from the indispensable *md* to R. Then from $COMP$ we eliminate all these components which have at least one *md* equal to *md* in R. It is important that the process of selecting attributes to R will be finished when the set $COMP$ is empty. We calculate for any *md* from $COMP$:

$c(md) = w_1 * c_1(md) + w_2 * c_2(md)$, where

$c_1(md) = \left(\frac{card(md\cap R)}{card(md)}\right)^p$ and

$c_2(md) = \left(\frac{card(\{com\in COMP: \exists_{md'\subset com} md'\subset(R\cup md)\})}{card(COMP)}\right)^q.$

For example, we can assume $p = q = 1$.

The first function is a "measure of extending" of R. Because we want to minimize cardinality of R, we are interested in finding *md* with the largest intersection with actual R. In this way we always add to R an almost minimal number of new attributes. The second measure is used to examine our profit after adding attributes from *md* to R. We want to include in R the most frequent *md* in $COMP$ and minimize $COMP$ as much as possible. When $c_2(md) = 1$, then after "adding this *md*" to R we will obtain a pseudo-reduct i.e. a superset of a reduct.

5 Approximation Spaces and Representatives

In this section we discuss the problem of proper representative object selection from data tables.

The general problem can be described as follows:

Given a set of objects U, the reduction process of U consists in finding a new set $U' \subset U$. The objects which belong to the set U' are chosen for example by using an evaluation criterion. The main advantage of the evaluation criterion approach is that a simple evaluation criterion can be defined which ensures a high level of efficiency. On the other hand, the definition of the evaluation criterion is a difficult problem, because in the new data set some objects are dropped and only a good evaluation criterion preserves the effectiveness of the knowledge acquired during the subsequent learning process.

There are many methods of adequate representative selection (see for example [4, 7, 18, 41, 38, 14]).

In the standard rough set model representatives can be computed from every indiscernibility class. In this section we discuss representative selection based on generalized approximation spaces and Boolean reasoning. This approach was suggested in [29, 41].

We assume that $AS = (U, I_A, \nu)$ is an approximation space, where $U = \{x_1, \ldots, x_n\}$ is a set of objects and let $x_1^*, \ldots, x_n^*$ be Boolean variables corresponding to objects $x_1, \ldots, x_n$, respectively.

5.1 Representatives in Information Systems

Definition 11. Let (U, A) be an information system. A subset $U' \subseteq U$ is a minimal set of representatives if and only if the following two conditions are satisfied:

1. For every $x \in U$ there is $y \in U'$ such that $x \in I_A(y)$.
2. For every proper subset $U" \subset U'$ the first condition is not satisfied.

In the next theorem we obtain a characterization of minimal sets of representatives.

Theorem 12. *We define the Boolean function*

$$g_{(U,A)}(x_1^*, \ldots, x_n^*) = \bigwedge_{x_i \in U} \bigvee_{x_j \in I_A(x_i)} x_j^*.$$

The following conditions are equivalent:

1. *$\{x_{i_1}, \ldots, x_{i_k}\}$ is a minimal set of representatives.*
2. *$x_{i_1}^* \wedge \ldots \wedge x_{i_k}^*$ is a prime implicant of the Boolean function $g_{(U,A)}$.*

5.2 Representatives in Decision Table

In decision tables we also consider the decision in computation of minimal sets of representatives.

Definition 13. Let $(U, A \cup \{d\})$ be a decision table. A subset $U' \subseteq U$ is a relative minimal set of representatives if and only if the following two conditions are satisfied:

1. For every $x \in U$ there is $y \in U'$ such that $x \in I_A(y)$ and $d(x) = d(y)$.
2. For every proper subset $U" \subset U'$ the first condition is not satisfied.

We can formulate a similar theorem for computation of representatives in a decision table as with computation of relative reducts.

Theorem 14. *Let $ST(x_i) = \{x_j \in U : x_j \in I_A(x_i), d(x_i) = d(x_j)\}$. We define the Boolean function*

$$g_{(U, A \cup \{d\})}(x_1^*, \ldots, x_n^*) = \bigwedge_{x_i \in U} \bigvee_{x_j \in ST(x_i)} x_j^*.$$

The following conditions are equivalent:

1. *$\{x_{i_1}, \ldots, x_{i_k}\}$ is a relative minimal set of representatives.*
2. *$x_{i_1}^* \wedge \ldots \wedge x_{i_k}^*$ is a prime implicant of the Boolean function $g_{(U, A \cup \{d\})}$.*

Below we sketch an algorithm for computation of one set of representatives with minimal or near minimal number of elements.

The main difference between finding out one set of representatives and one relative reduct is in the way in which we calculate and interpret components. In case of the relative set of representatives we do not build the discernibility matrix, but we replace it by a similar table containing for any object x_i all objects similar to x_i and with the same decision:

$ST(x_i) = \{x_j \in U : x_j \in I_A(x_i), d(x_i) = d(x_j)\}$.

After reduction, we obtain components as essential entries in ST. For $COMP$ we can apply the algorithm used to compute a reduct assuming $card(md) = 1$. We add to the constructed relative absorbent set any object which is the most frequent in $COMP$ and then eliminate from $COMP$ all components having this object. This process terminates when $COMP$ is empty. For more details see [38, 14].

6 Conclusions

In the standard rough set model, an equivalence relation is used to define an approximation space. In this paper we have presented a generalization of the approximation space notion to cover some of its modifications, for example the similarity based rough set model and the variable precision rough set model. We point out the role of searching for proper uncertainty functions. Adequate uncertainty functions are important for extracting laws from decision tables. We also discuss problems of attribute and object reduction in the case of generalized approximation spaces. The rough set methods combined with Boolean reasoning techniques have been used to develop efficient tools for extracting important attributes and objects from data tables.

7 Acknowledgments

The author would like to thank Professor Andrzej Skowron for valuable discussions.

This work has been supported by the grant 8T11C01011 from the State Committee for Scientific Research (Komitet Badan Naukowych).

References

1. Bryniarski E., Wybraniec-Skardowska U.: Generalized Rough Sets in Contextual Spaces. In: T. Y. Lin, N. Cercone (eds.), Rough sets and data mining. Analysis of imprecise data, Kluwer Academic Publishers, Boston (997) 339–354
2. Cattaneo G.: Generalized rough sets. Preclusivity fuzzy-intuitionistic (BZ) lattices. Studia Logica **58** (1997) 47–77
3. Cattaneo G.: Mathematical foundations of roughness and fuzziness (manuscript). University of Milan (1997)
4. Dasarathy B. V. ed.: Nearest neighbor pattern classification techniques. IEEE Computer Society Press (1991)
5. Dubois D., Prade H.: Similarity versus preference in fuzzy set-based logics. In: E. Orlowska (ed.), Incomplete information: rough set analysis, Springer-Verlag (Physica Verlag), Chapter 14 (1997)
6. Funakoshi K., Ho T. B..: Information retrieval by rough tolerance relation. In: In: Tsumoto S., Kobayashi, S., Yokomori, T., Tanaka, H. (ed.), Proceedings of the Fourth International Workshop on Rough Sets, Fuzzy Sets and Machine Discovery (RSFD'96), Tokyo Nov. 6-8 (1996) 31–35
7. Gemello R., Mana F.: An Integrated characterization and discrimination scheme to improve learning efficiency in large data sets, Proceedings of the Eleventh International Joint Conference on Artificial Intelligence, Detroit MI, 20-25 August (1989) 719–724
8. Hu X., Cercone N.: Rough sets similarity-based learning from databases. In: Proceedings of the First International Conference on Knowledge Discovery and Data Mining, Montreal, Canada, August 20-21 (1995) 162–167
9. Katzberg J. D., Ziarko W.: Variable precision extension of rough sets. Fundamenta Informaticae **27** (1996) 155–168
10. Konikowska B.: A logic for reasoning about similarity. In: E. Orlowska (ed.), Incomplete information: rough set analysis, Chapter 15 (1997)
11. Krawiec K., Slowinski R., Vanderpooten D.: Construction of rough classifiers based on application of a similarity relation. In: In: Tsumoto S., Kobayashi, S., Yokomori, T., Tanaka, H. (ed.), Proceedings of the Fourth International Workshop on Rough Sets, Fuzzy Sets and Machine Discovery (RSFD'96), Tokyo Nov. 6-8 (1996) 23–30
12. Krawiec K., Slowinski R., Vanderpooten D.: Learning of decision rules from similarity based rough approximations (this book)

13. Kretowski M., Polkowski L., Skowron A., Stepaniuk J.: Data reduction based on rough set theory. In: Y. Kodratoff, G. Nakhaeizadeh, Ch. Taylor (eds.), Proceedings of the International Workshop on Statistics, Machine Learning and Knowledge Discovery in Databases, Heraklion April 25-27 (1995) 210–215
14. Kretowski M., Stepaniuk J.: Selection of objects and attributes, a tolerance rough set approach. In: Proceedings of the Poster Session of Ninth International Symposium on Methodologies for Intelligent Systems, Zakopane Poland,June 10-13 (1996) 169–180
15. Kryszkiewicz M.: Maintenance of reducts in the variable precision rough set model. In: T. Y. Lin, N. Cercone (eds.), Rough sets and data mining analysis of imprecise data, Kluwer Academic Publishers, Dordrecht (1997) 355–372
16. Marcus S.: Tolerance rough sets, Cech topologies, learning processes. Bull.Polish Acad. Sci. Ser. Sci. Tech. **42/3** (1994) 471–487
17. Michalewicz Z.: Genetic algorithms + data structures = evolution programs, Springer-Verlag, Berlin (1996)
18. Michalski R. S., Larson J. B.: Selection of most representative training examples and incremental generation of VL1 hypotheses. Report **867** Department of Computer Science University of Illinois at Urbana-Champaign (1978)
19. Nguyen S. H., Skowron A.: Searching for relational patterns in data. In: Proceedings of the First European Symposium on Principles of Data Mining and Knowledge Discovery (PKDD'97) Trondheim, Norway, June 25-27 Lecture Notes in Artificial Intelligence **1263** (1997) 265–276
20. Nieminen J.: Rough tolerance equality. Fundamenta Informaticae **11** (1988) 289–296
21. Pawlak Z.: Rough sets. International Journal of Computer and Information Science **11** (1982) 341–356
22. Pawlak Z.: Rough sets: theoretical aspects of reasoning about data, Kluwer Academic Publishers, Dordrecht (1991)
23. Pawlak Z., Skowron A.: Rough membership functions. In: M. Fedrizzi, J.Kacprzyk, R. R. Yager (eds.), Advances in the Dempster-Shafer theory of evidence, John Wiley and Sons, New York (1994) 251–271
24. Polkowski L., Skowron A., Zytkow J.: Tolerance based rough sets. In: T.Y.Lin, A.M.Wildberger (eds.), Soft Computing Simulation Councils, San Diego (1995) 55–58
25. Pomykała J. A.: Approximation operations in approximation space, Bull. Polish Acad.Sci.Ser. Sci. Math. **35** 653–662
26. Pomykała J. A.: On definability in the nondeterministic information system. Bull. Polish Acad. Sci.Ser. Sci. Math., **36** 193–210
27. Skowron A.: Data filtration: a rough set approach. In: W. Ziarko (ed.), Rough sets, fuzzy sets and knowledge discovery, Springer-Verlag, Berlin (1994) 108–118
28. Skowron A.: Extracting laws from decision tables. Computational Intelligence **11/2** (1995) 371–388
29. Skowron A., Polkowski L.: Synthesis of decision systems from data tables. In: T. Y. Lin, N. Cercone (eds.), Rough sets and data mining. Analysis of imprecise data, Kluwer Academic Publishers, Boston (1997) 259–299
30. Skowron A., Polkowski L., Komorowski J.: Learning tolerance relations by Boolean descriptors: automatic feature extraction from data tables. In: Tsumoto S., Kobayashi, S., Yokomori, T., Tanaka, H. (ed.), Proceedings of the Fourth International Workshop on Rough Sets, Fuzzy Sets and Machine Discovery (RSFD'96), Tokyo Nov. 6-8 (1996) 11–17

31. Skowron A, Rauszer C.: The Discernibility matrices and functions in information systems. In: R. Słowiński (ed.), Intelligent decision support. Handbook of applications and advances of rough sets theory, Kluwer Academic Publishers, Dordrecht (1992) 331–362
32. Skowron A., Stepaniuk J.: Generalized approximation spaces. In: Proceedings of the Third International Workshop on Rough Sets and Soft Computing, San Jose, November 10-12 (1994) 156–163
33. Skowron A., Stepaniuk J.: Generalized approximation apaces. In: T.Y.Lin, A.M.Wildberger (eds.), Soft computing, Simulation Councils, San Diego (1995) 18–21
34. Skowron A., Stepaniuk J.: Tolerance approximation spaces. Fundamenta Informaticae **27** (1996) 245–253
35. Słowiński R.: A Generalization of the indiscernibility relation for rough sets analysis of quantitative information. Revista di Matematica per le Scienze Economiche e Sociali **15/1** (1992) 65–78
36. Słowiński R.: Strict and weak indiscernibility of objects described by quantitative attributes with overlapping norms. Foundations of Computing and Decision Sciences **18** (1993) 361–369
37. Słowiński R., Vanderpooten D.: Similarity relation as a basis for rough approximations. Warsaw University of Technology, Institute of Computer Science Research Report **53** (1995)
38. Stepaniuk J., Kretowski M.: Decision system based on tolerance rough sets. In: Proceedings of the Fourth International Workshop on Intelligent Information Systems, Augustow, Poland, June 5-9 (1995) 62–73
39. Stepaniuk J.: Similarity based rough sets and learning. In: Tsumoto S., Kobayashi, S., Yokomori, T., Tanaka, H. (ed.), Proceedings of the Fourth International Workshop on Rough Sets, Fuzzy Sets and Machine Discovery (RSFD'96), Tokyo Nov. 6-8 (1996) 18–22
40. Stanfill C., Waltz D.: Toward memory-based reasoning. Communications of the ACM **29** (1986) 1213–1228
41. Tentush I.: On minimal absorbent sets for some types of tolerance relations. Bull. Polish Acad. Sci. Ser. Sci. Tech. **43/1** (1995) 79–88
42. Yao Y. Y., Lin T. Y.: Generalization of rough sets using modal logic. Intelligent Automation and Soft Computing **2** (1996) 103–120
43. Yao Y. Y., Wong S. K. M., Lin T. Y.: A review of rough set models. In: T. Y. Lin, N. Cercone (eds.), Rough sets and data mining. Analysis of imprecise data, Kluwer Academic Publishers, Boston (1997) 47–75
44. Vakarelov D.: Information systems, similarity relations and modal logic. In: E. Orlowska (ed.), Incomplete information: Rough set analysis, Springer - Verlag (Physica Verlag), Berlin (1997) Chapter 16
45. Wilson D. A., Martinez T. R.: Improved heterogeneous distance functions. Journal of Artificial Intelligence Research **6** (1997) 1–34
46. Wybraniec-Skardowska U.: On a generalization of approximation space. Bull. Polish Acad. Sci. Ser. Sci. Math. **37** (1989) 51–61
47. Zadeh L. A.: Similarity relations and fuzzy orderings. Information Sciences **3** (1971) 177–200
48. Ziarko W.: Variable precision rough sets model. Journal of Computer and Systems Sciences **46/1** (1993) 39–59

Chapter 7

Data Mining: A Probabilistic Rough Set Approach

Ning Zhong, Ju-Zhen Dong,[1] *and Setsuo Ohsuga*[2]

[1] Department of Computer Science and Systems Engineering, Faculty of Engineering, Yamaguchi University, Tokiwa-Dai, 2557, Ube 755, Japan
E-mail: {zhong, dong}@ai.csse.yamaguchi-u.ac.jp

[2] Department of Information and Computer Science, School of Science and Engineering, Waseda University, 3-4-1 Okubo Shinjuku-Ku, Tokyo 169, Japan
E-mail: ohsuga@ohsuga.info.waseda.ac.jp

Abstract. This paper introduces a new approach for mining *if-then* rules in databases with uncertainty and incompleteness. The approach is based on the combination of *Generalization Distribution Table (GDT)* and the *Rough Set* methodology. A GDT is a table in which the probabilistic relationships between concepts and instances over discrete domains are represented. By using a GDT as a hypothesis search space and combining the GDT with the rough set methodology, noises and unseen instances can be handled, biases can be flexibly selected, background knowledge can be used to constrain rule generation, and *if-then* rules with strengths can be effectively acquired from large, complex databases in an incremental, bottom-up mode. In this paper, we focus on basic concepts and an implementation of our methodology.

1 Introduction

Using the *rough set* theory introduced by Pawlak as a methodology of data mining is effective in practice [20, 19]. The process of data mining based on the rough set methodology is that of knowledge reduction in such a way that the decision specified could be made by using minimal set of conditions. The process of knowledge reduction is similar to the process of generalization in a hypothesis search space. Mitchell formalized this view of *generalization as search* in his development of *version-space* in the machine learning community, that is, the learning task is to search a hypothesis space, subject to constraints imposed by the training instances, to determine plausible generalizations [7, 8]. It is well known that *version-space* is a typical bottom-up, incremental approach, in which learning a concept is possible not only when instances are input simultaneously but also when they are given one by one. However, it is difficult to handle noisy and incomplete data, and it is weak in mining rules from very large, complex databases.

In this paper, we propose a new approach for mining *if-then* rules in databases with uncertainty and incompleteness. We first outline the rough set methodology for data mining. Then we define a Generalization Distribution Table (GDT), which is an extension of version-space, as a hypothesis search space for generalization. Furthermore, we combine the GDT with the rough set methodology for mining *if-then* rules from databases. We focus on basic concepts and an implementation of our methodology.

2 The Rough Set Methodology to Data Mining

In the rough set methodology to data mining, a database is regarded as a decision table, which is denoted $T = (U, A, C, D)$, where U is universe of discourse, A is a family of equivalence relations over U, and $C, D \subset A$ are two subsets of attributes that are called condition and decision attributes, respectively [20].

The process of data mining is that of simplifying a decision table and generating minimal decision algorithm. In general, an approach for decision table simplification consists of the following steps:

1. Computation of reducts of condition attributes that is equivalent to elimination of some column from the decision table.
2. Elimination of duplicate rows.
3. Elimination of superfluous values of attributes.

A representative approach for the problem of reducts of condition attributes is the one to represent knowledge in the form of a discernibility matrix [14, 20]. The basic idea can be briefly presented as follows:

Let $T = (U, A, C, D)$ be a decision table, with $U = \{u_1, u_2, \ldots, u_n\}$. By a *discernibility matrix* of T, denoted $M(T)$, we will mean $n \times n$ matrix defined thus:

$$m_{ij} = \{a \in A : a(u_i) \neq a(u_j)\ \} \text{ for } i, j = 1, 2, \ldots, n.$$

Thus entry m_{ij} is the set of all attributes that discern objects u_i and u_j.

Based on the rough set methodology, several researchers have been working on some advanced topics such as generating approximate or probabilistic rules, discretization of continuous valued attributes, approximate reasoning in parallel-distributed systems [16, 5, 13, 15].

3 Generalization Distribution Table

The central idea of our methodology is to use *Generalization Distribution Table (GDT)*, as a hypothesis search space for generalization, in which the probabilistic relationships between concepts and instances over discrete domains are represented [21, 22, 23, 24]. A GDT is a table that consists of three components: the possible instances, the possible generalizations for instances, and the probabilistic relationships between the possible instances and the possible generalizations.

The *possible instances*, which are denoted in columns in a GDT, are all possible combinations of attribute values in a database, and the number of the possible instances is

$$\prod_{i=1}^{m} n_i, \tag{1}$$

where m is the number of attributes, n is the number of different data values in each attribute.

The *possible generalizations* for instances, which are denoted in rows in a GDT, are all possible generalizations for all possible instances, and the number of the possible generalizations is

$$\prod_{i=1}^{m}(n_i + 1) - (\prod_{i=1}^{m} n_i) - 1. \tag{2}$$

The *probabilistic relationships* between the possible instances and the possible generalizations, which are denoted as the elements t_{ij} in a GDT, are the probabilistic distributions for describing the strength of the relationship between every possible instance and every possible generalization.

If we do not use any prior background knowledge, the initial values of the probabilistic distributions (i.e., the prior probability distributions) are equiprobable and are defined by Eq. (3),

$$p(PI_j|PG_i) = \frac{1}{N_{PG_i}}, \tag{3}$$

where PI_j is the jth possible instance in all possible instances, PG_i is the ith possible generalization in all possible generalizations for the jth instance, and N_{PG_i} is the number of the possible instances for the ith possible generalization, i.e.,

$$N_{PG_i} = \prod_{j}^{m} n_j, \tag{4}$$

where $j = 1, \ldots, m$, and $j \neq$ the attribute that is contained by the ith possible generalization (i.e., j just contains the attributes expressed by the wild card as shown in Table 1).

The probability distributions defined by Eq. (3) will be dynamically updated according to the real data in a database, and the posterior probability distributions will converge to the real ones.

Furthermore, background knowledge can be used as a bias to constrain the possible instances and the prior probabilistic distributions. This issue will be further discussed in Sections 4.5 and 7.

Table 1 is an example of the GDT created for a sample database as shown in Table 2, in which three attributes, $a, b, c,$

$a \in \{a_0, a_1\}$, $b \in \{b_0, b_1, b_2\}$, $c \in \{c_0, c_1\}$,

Table 1. The Generalization Distribution Table for a sample database shown in Table 2

(Note: in the GDT, the elements that are not displayed are all zero.)

	a0b0c0	a0b0c1	a0b1c0	a0b1c1	a0b2c0	a0b2c1	a1b0c0	a1b0c1	...	a1b2c1
*b0c0	1/2						1/2		...	
*b0c1		1/2						1/2	...	
*b1c0			1/2						...	
*b1c1				1/2					...	
*b2c0					1/2				...	
*b2c1						1/2			...	1/2
a0*c0	1/3		1/3		1/3				...	
a0*c1		1/3		1/3		1/3			...	
a1*c0							1/3		...	
a1*c1								1/3	...	1/3
a0b0*	1/2	1/2							...	
a0b1*			1/2	1/2					...	
a0b2*					1/2	1/2			...	
a1b0*							1/2	1/2	...	
a1b1*									...	
a1b2*									...	1/2
**c0	1/6		1/6		1/6		1/6		...	
**c1		1/6		1/6		1/6		1/6	...	1/6
b0	1/4	1/4					1/4	1/4	...	
b1			1/4	1/4					...	
b2					1/4	1/4			...	1/4
a0**	1/6	1/6	1/6	1/6	1/6	1/6			...	
a1**							1/6	1/6	...	1/6

Table 2. A sample database

No	a	b	c	d
u1	a0	b0	c1	y
u2	a0	b1	c1	y
u3	a0	b0	c1	y
u4	a1	b1	c0	n
u5	a0	b0	c1	n
u6	a0	b2	c1	n
u7	a1	b1	c1	y

are used. Thus, the number of the possible instances for this example is 12. Furthermore, "*" in Table 1, which specifies a wild card, denotes the generalization for instances. For example, the generalization $\{*b_0c_1\}$ for the instance $\{a_0b_0c_1\}$ means the attribute a is unimportant for describing a concept. And the number of the possible generalizations is 23.

4 Data Mining based on the GDT and Rough Sets

Based on the preparation in the above sections, this section describes the basic methodology of mining *if-then* rules, which is based on the combination of the GDT and rough sets.

4.1 Rule Representation and Condition/Decision Attributes

Let $T = (U, A, C, D)$ be a decision table, U a universe of discourse, A a family of equivalence relations over U, and $C, D \subset A$ two subsets of attributes that are called condition and decision attributes, respectively.

The learned rules are typically expressed in

$$X \rightarrow Y \text{ with } S. \qquad (X \in C, Y \in D)$$

That is, "a rule $X \rightarrow Y$ has a strength S in a given decision table T". Where X denotes the conjunction of the conditions that a concept must satisfy, Y denotes a concept that the rule describes, and S is a "measure of strength" of which the rule holds.

The example shown in Table 2 is, in fact, a decision table in which $U = \{u_1, u_2, \ldots, u_7\}$, condition attributes $C = \{a, b, c\}$, a decision attribute $D = \{d\}$.

Usually, the decision attributes are not used to create the GDT, but are used to distinguish contradictory rules and different concepts (classes).

4.2 Rule Strength

We define the strength S of a rule $X \rightarrow Y$ in a given decision table T as follows:

$$S = p \times (1 - r). \tag{5}$$

From Eq. (5) we can see that the strength S of a rule is affected by the following two factors:

1. The probabilistic relationships between the possible instances and their generalization, p.
2. The rate of noises, r. It shows the quality of classification, that is, how many instances as the conditions that a rule must satisfy can be classified into some class.

Here we would like to describe in detail the first factor stated above. The second factor will be discussed in next section.

The prior probability distributions between the possible instances and their generalizations are given by Eq. (3). The posterior probability distributions could be defined as follows:

$$p(PG_i) = \sum_j (p(PI_j|PG_i)),$$

where PG_i is the ith possible generalization, PI_j is the jth possible instance, $p(PI_j|PG_i)$ is the prior probability distribution defined in Eq. (3), and j is the sequence number of the observed instances relating to the ith possible generalization.

Since $p(PI_j|PG_i)$ is a constant for each significance instance j, the above equation can be re-written as below:

$$p(PG_i) = \frac{1}{N_{PG_i}} \times N_{ins-rel,i} \tag{6}$$

where $N_{ins-rel,i}$ is the number of the observed instances satisfying the ith generalization.

It merits our attention that Eq. (6) is not suitable for duplicate instances. Hence the duplicate instances should be handled before using this equation.

From the GDT, we can see that a generalization is 100% true if and only if all of instances belonging to this generalization appear.

Let us again use the example shown in Table 2. We can see that both $\{a_0b_1\}$ and $\{b_1c_1\}$ are generalizations for the instance $\{a_0b_1c_1\}$ as shown in Figure 1. Their strengths can be calculated in Eq. (5). If the noise rate, r, is 0, the strengths are

$$S(\{a_0b_1\}) = 0.5, \qquad S(\{b_1c_1\}) = 1,$$

respectively. In other words, if either $\{a_0b_1c_0\}$ or $\{a_0b_1c_1\}$ appears, the probability of the generalization $\{a_0b_1\}$ is 0.5. If both $\{a_0b_1c_0\}$ and $\{a_0b_1c_1\}$ appear, the probability of the generalization $\{a_0b_1\}$ is 1.

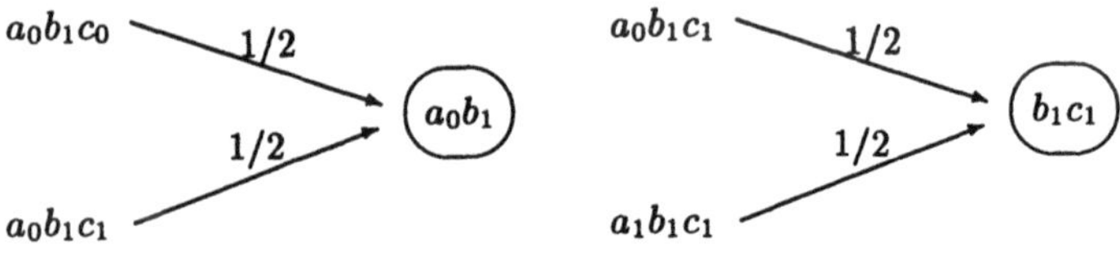

Fig. 1. Probability of a generalization rule

4.3 Contradictory Rules and Noises

We say that *contradictory rules* are the ones that have the conjunction of the same conditions that the rules must satisfy, but describe different concepts with nearly same strength.

For example, the rules, which are learned from a sample database as shown in Table 2,

$a_1 \wedge b_1 \to y$ with $(S = 0.5)$
$a_1 \wedge b_1 \to n$ with $(S = 0.5)$,

are contradictory rules because they have the same condition $a_1 \wedge b_1$ and describe different concepts y and n, with same strength $S = 0.5$.

Furthermore, if the strength of the rule belonging to y is much larger than the strength of the rule belonging to n, the rule belonging to n can be regarded as a *noise*. The rate of noises can be defined by Eq. (7).

$$r = \frac{N_{ins-rel} - N_{ins-class}}{N_{ins-rel}}, \tag{7}$$

where $N_{ins-rel}$ is the number of the observed instances relating to some case of generalization, $N_{ins-class}$ is the number of the instances relating to some case of generalization and belonging to a class. We distinguish the following two cases according to the ratio of Eq. (7):

- If the ratio is 0, there is not noisy data for the classification, that is, all instances relating to some case of generalization belong to same class.
- If the ratio is far from 0, we conclude that there are noisy data in the database for the classification.

A user can specify an allowed noise rate as the threshold value. Thus, the rules with the larger rates than the threshold value will be deleted.

4.4 Simplifying a Decision Table by Using the GDT

In Section 2, we observed that the process of data mining based on the rough set methodology is that of simplifying a decision table and generating a minimal decision algorithm. In this section, we propose a method for simplifying a decision table by using the GDT. The method of computing the reducts of condition attributes in our approach, in principle, is equivalent to the discernibility matrix method [14, 20], but we do not remove dispensable attributes. This is because

- The greater the number of dispensable attributes, the more difficult it is to acquire the best solution;
- Some values of a dispensable attribute may be indispensable for some values of a decision attribute.

By using the GDT, it is obvious that one instance can be expressed by several possible generalizations, and several instances can be expressed by one possible generalization.

For example, the instance $\{a_0b_1c_1\}$ can be expressed by $\{a_0b_1\}$, $\{a_0c_1,\}$ $\{b_1c_1\}\ldots$, or $\{c_1\}$ as shown in Figure 2. Both instances $\{a_0b_1c_1\}$ and $\{a_1b_1c_1\}$ can be expressed by $\{b_1c_1\}$. If a generalization contains the instances with different classes, we say that the generalization is *contradictory* [3] and it cannot be used to generate a rule. In contrast, if a generalization contains several instances with the same class, we can use this generalization to substitute for these instances.

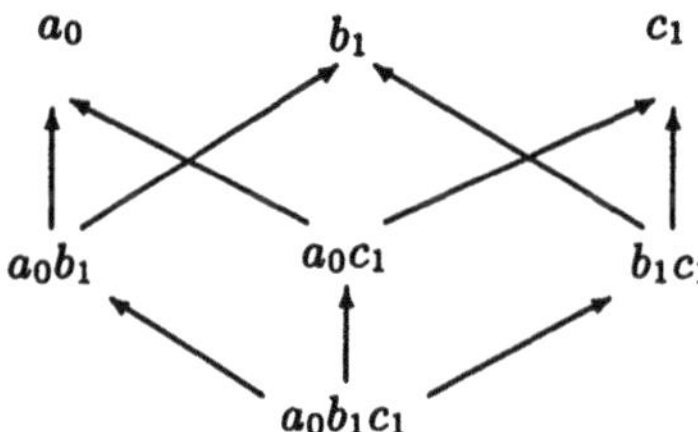

Fig. 2. The relationships among generalizations

Figure 2 gives the relationship among generalizations. We can see that every generalization in upper levels contains all generalizations related to it in lower levels. That is,

$$\{a_0\} \supset \{a_0b_1\}, \{a_0c_1\} \supset \{a_0b_1c_1\}.$$

In other words, $\{a_0\}$ can be specialized into $\{a_0b_1\}$ and $\{a_0c_1\}$ only. In contrast, $\{a_0b_1\}$ and $\{a_0c_1\}$ can be generalized into $\{a_0\}$. If the rule $\{a_0\} \rightarrow y$ is true, the rules $\{a_0b_1\} \rightarrow y$ and $\{a_0c_1\} \rightarrow y$ are also true.

In order to acquire a consistent decision algorithm, we have to ensure that all of its decision rules are true. Proposition 1 can be used to check whether a decision rule is true or not [20].

Proposition 1:

Let $T = (U, A, C, D)$ be a decision table, where C is the condition attribute set and D is the decision attribute set. A decision rule $\phi \rightarrow \psi$ in a decision algorithm is true in T, where ϕ is C-formula and ψ is D-formula, if and only if for any decision rule $\phi' \rightarrow \psi'$ in a decision algorithm, (ϕ' is C-formula and ψ' is D-formula), $\phi = \phi'$ implies $\psi = \psi'$. □

[3] Here we assume that the threshold value for the noise rate is 0.

Consider again the database shown in Table 2. Let us check whether the generalizations $\{a_0c_1\}$ and $\{b_1\}$ can be used as conditions to discern decision attribute {d}. The following rules

$$\begin{array}{ll} a_0c_1 \rightarrow y & \{u_1, u_2, u_3\} \\ a_0c_1 \rightarrow n & \{u_5, u_6\} \\ b_1 \rightarrow y & \{u_2, u_7\} \\ b_1 \rightarrow n & \{u_4\} \end{array}$$

are contradictory, because the rules have the same ϕ' in the left and different ψ' in the right. That is, the generalizations $\{a_0c_1\}$ and $\{b_1\}$ contain the instances belonging to different decisions y and n. Hence, we are unable to discern decisions y and n by means of the generalizations (conditions).

It is clear that if a generalization for some instances is contradictory, the related generalizations in upper levels than this generalization are also contradictory. That is, as shown in Figure 3, if $\{a_0c_1\}$ is a contradictory generalization for the instance $\{a_0b_1c_1\}$, the generalizations $\{a_0\}$ and $\{c_1\}$ for$\{a_0c_1\}$ are also contradictory. Hence, for the instance $\{a_0b_1c_1\}$, the generalizations $\{a_0c_1\}, \{b_1\}, \{a_0\}$, and $\{c_1\}$ are contradictory. Thus, only the generalizations $\{a_0b_1\}$ and $\{b_1c_1\}$ can be used.

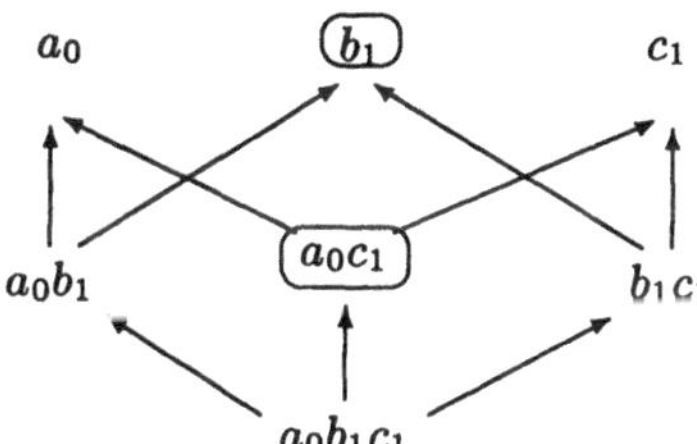

the generalization for instances with different classes

Fig. 3. A result of generalizing the instance $a_0b_1c_1$ with the instances in the class n.

This result is the same as the one of the discernibility matrix method when no noise exists in the database. Let G_- be contradictory generalizations, G_T be all possible consistent generalizations obtained from a discernibility matrix. Clearly, $G_T = \overline{G_-}$. That is,

$$G_T = \{b_1\} \cap (\{a_0\} \cup \{c_1\}) = \{b_1a_0\} \cup \{b_1c_1\}$$

$$\begin{aligned} \overline{G_-} &= \overline{\{a_0c_1\} \cup \{b_1\}} = \overline{\{a_0c_1\}} \cap \overline{\{b_1\}} = \{b_1\} \cap (\{a_0\} \cup \{c_1\}) \\ &= \{b_1a_0\} \cup \{b_1c_1\}. \end{aligned}$$

For the database with noises, the generalization that contains instances with different classes should be checked. If a generalization contains more instances belonging to a class than those belonging to other classes, and the noise rate is smaller than a threshold value, the generalization is regarded as a consistent generalization of that class. Otherwise, the generalization is contradictory. Furthermore, if two generalizations in the same level have different strengths, the one with larger strength will be selected first.

4.5 Search Control and Biases

Since our approach for data mining is based on the search in a GDT, *search control* is to limit or direct its search through *biases*. The biases are divided into the following three types corresponding to three components of the GDT defined in Section 3.

The first type of biases is related to the possible generalizations in a GDT. It is used to decide which concept description should be first considered. To get the best concept descriptions, all possible generalizations should be considered, but not all of them need to be considered at the same time. We divide possible generalizations (concept descriptions) into several levels of generalization according to the number of the wild cards in a generalization, and the greater the number of the wild cards, the higher the level. For example, all possible generalizations shown in Table 1 are divided into two levels of generalization, that is,

$$Level_1 \in \{*b_0c_0, *b_0c_1, \ldots, a_1b_2*\}$$
$$Level_2 \in \{**c_0, **c_1, \ldots, a_1**\}.$$

Thus, we can see that any generalization in a lower level is properly contained by one or more generalizations in an upper level. As default, our approach prefers more general concept descriptions in an upper level to more specific ones in a lower level. However, if needed, we can use a meta control to alter the bias into preferring more specific descriptions to more general ones.

The second type of biases is related to the probability values denoted in t_{ij} in a GDT. It is used to adjust the strength of the relationship between an instance and a generalization. If no prior background knowledge as a bias is available, as default, we consider that the possibility of which all possible instances appear is equiprobable, as shown in Table 1, to create the prior distribution of a GDT. However, a bias such as background knowledge and/or meta knowledge can be used while creating a GDT, and the probability distribution can be dynamically revised for acquiring the posterior distribution.

The third type of biases is related to the possible instances in a GDT. In our approach, the strength of the relationship between every possible instance and every possible generalization depends on a certain extent how to create and define the possible instances. Background knowledge can be used as a bias to constrain the possible instances so that the more refined result can be obtained (see Section 7).

4.6 Rule Selection

There are several possible ways for rule selection. For example,

- Select the rules that contain as many instances as possible;
- Select the rules in the levels as high as possible according to the first type of biases stated above;
- Select the rules with larger strengths.

Here we would like to describe a method of rule selection for our purpose as follows:

- Since our purpose is to simplify the decision table, the rules that contain less instances will be deleted if a rule that contains more instances exists.
- Since we prefer simpler results of generalization (i.e., more general rules), we first consider the rules corresponding to an upper level of generalization.
- The rules with larger strengths are first selected as the real rules.

5 The Learning Process

Since mining rules can be viewed as a process of generalization, the learning process is that of choosing the best generalization rules. We first find the contradictory rules and delete them, and then select the rules with larger strengths as the rules mined. The main steps of the learning process are as follows:

Step 1. Suppose the set of instances, which is stored in a database, $U = \{u_1, u_2, \ldots, u_n\}$, is given. Before learning, one or more GDTs are created and the prior distribution is generated in Eq. (3).
In fact, this step can be omitted because the prior distribution of a generalization is calculated by the number of attribute values as we explained in Eq. (4). Let $\{A_1, A_2, \ldots, A_m\}$ be condition attributes, and $N_{A_1}, N_{A_2}, \ldots, N_{A_m}$ be the number of the different values in each attribute, respectively. Thus, the prior distribution of the generalization with two attribute values is

$p(\{A_i A_j\}) = \prod_{k \neq i,j} \frac{1}{N_{A_k}}$,

if we do not use any prior background knowledge for this calculation.

Step 2. Handle duplicate instances as shown in Table 3, so that the probability of generalization can be calculated correctly.

Step 3. Find out all generalizations with other instances for each instance. Then, all of the generalizations are divided into two sets G_+ and G_- according to the rate of belonging to some class. Here G_+ contains all consistent generalizations, and G_- contains all contradictory generalizations.
Figure 4 shows a result of generalizing for the instance $\{a_0 b_1 c_1\}$. That is,

Table 3. Handling duplicate instances

No.	abc	d
u1,u3,u5	a0b0c1	y, y, n
u2	a0b1c1	y
u7	a1b1c1	y
u4	a1b1c0	n
u6	a0b2c1	n

$$G_+ = \{b_1c_1\}$$
$$G_- = \{\{a_0c_1\}, \{b_1\}\}.$$

Here $\{b_1\}$ is the generalization with the class n and belongs to G_-, $\{b_1c_1\}$ is the generalization with the class y and belongs to G_+.

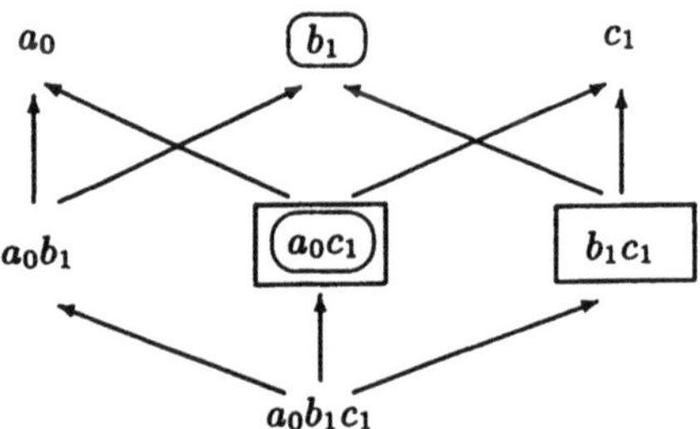

the generalization for instances with the same class
the generalization for instances with different classes

Fig. 4. The generalizations of $\{a_0b_1c_1\}$

Both of the rates of $\{a_0c_1\}$ belonging to the classes, y and n, are 2/4, because within the four instances satisfying the generalization $\{a_0c_1\}$, two of them belong to the class n, and two others belong to the class y. Thus, $\{a_0c_1\}$ is contradictory and should belong to G_-. Furthermore, if a user does not specify the threshold value, as default, all of generalizations belonging to different classes are contradictory. Otherwise the generalizations with larger rates than the threshold value are contradictory.

Let m be the number of attributes, n be the number of instances, the complexity of the algorithm in this step is $O(m \times n^2)$.

Finding all generalizations for one instance with other instances requires $n - 1$ steps. Checking if the same generalizations exist and classifying them into G_- and G_+ require $\frac{n \times (n-1)}{2}$ steps. Computing the intersection of two instances requires at most m steps to compare all attribute values. Hence, the cost is at most $O(m \times n^2)$.

Step 4. Acquire the consistent generalizations by $\overline{G_-}$, and the result is denoted in G_T. That is, $G_T = \overline{G_-}$.
For example, if $G_- = \{a_0c_1\} \cup \{b_1\}$ for the instance $\{a_0b_1c_1\}$,

$$\begin{aligned} G_T &= \overline{G_-} = \overline{\{a_0c_1\} \cup \{b_1\}} = \overline{\{a_0c_1\}} \cap \overline{b_1} \\ &= \{b_1\} \cap \{a_0 \cup c_1\} = \{a_0b_1\} \cup \{b_1c_1\}. \end{aligned}$$

Step 5. Revise the probability distribution of the generalizations in G_T that contains one of the generalizations in G_+ in Eq. (6).

Step 6. Select the generalizations by using one of the methods stated in Section 4.6 as the mined rules corresponding to some instances.
For example, if we use the method of selecting the rules with larger strengths, the unique candidate is $\{b_1c_1\}$ for the instance $\{a_0b_1c_1\}$. Thus the rule is $\{b_1c_1\} \to y$ with $S = 1$.

Step 7. Go back to *Step 3* until all of instances are handled.

Let the threshold value for the noise rate be 0, the learning result for the sample database shown in Table 2 is shown in Table 4.

Table 4. Rules learned from the sample database shown in Table 2

No	abc	d	G_T	rules
u1,u3,u5	a0b0c1	y,y,n	-	-
u2	a0b1c1	y	a0c1,b1c1	b1c1 → y, 1
u7	a1b1c1	y	c1, b1c1	b1c1 → y, 1
u4	a1b1c0	n	c0	c0 → n, 0.167
u6	a0b2c1	n	b2	b2 → n, 0.25

6 Prediction of Unseen Instances

One of the main advantages of our approach is that it can predict unseen instances because the search space based on the GDT considers all possible combination of the observed instances (i.e., the seen instances). Thus, the uncertainty of a rule including the prediction of possible instances can be explicitly represented in the strength S.

We can see that Eq. (5), which is used to define the strength of a rule, can be divided into two parts. The first part is

$$p(PG_i)$$

that is used to describe the strength of a rule and including the prediction for unseen instances. For example, based on the result of learning by using the method stated in Section 5, the rule

$r_{1.1} : b_2 \rightarrow n$ with $p = 0.25$

can be acquired by generalizing the instance, $\{a_0 b_2 c_1\}$. The reason why the strength of the rule is 0.25 is that we only observed one of four kinds of possible instances, which can be generalized into b_2 in the database shown in Table 2. In other words, we did not observe other kinds of possible instances, $\{a_0 b_2 c_0\}$, $\{a_1 b_2 c_0\}$, $\{a_1 b_2 c_1\}$, in this database. Furthermore, if the instances, $\{a_0 b_2 c_0\}$, $\{a_1 b_2 c_0\}$, $\{a_1 b_2 c_1\}$, are added to the database, then we revise the probability distribution into 1 in Eq. (6).

We argue that the prediction for the unseen instances is an important function for concept learning and data mining from real-world databases. In most cases, the set of instances collected in a database represents a part of all possible instances. This is reasonable, because we expect to learn rules without first collecting every possible instance (like physicians to learn how to diagnose diseases without first having seen every possible patient) [12]. However, it also means that the learning task is ill-posed, because for previous inductive approaches, without some other source of constraint, there is no way to know the instances of describing a concept that has never before been observed. Our approach based on the Generalization Distribution Table and the rough set methodology provides a possibility for predicting the unseen instances and for explicitly representing the strength of a rule including the prediction. In other words, our approach tries to find the descriptions of concepts not only by the instances observed during learning but also by unseen instances.

7 An Example

Some of databases such as postoperative patient, earthquack, weather, mushroom, cancer have been tested for our approach. We would like to use the earthquack database as an example [17].

In the earthquake database, there are 15 condition attributes and 1 decision attribute, and 155 instances. The features represented by the condition attributes are as follows:

$C_1, C_2, \ldots, C_8$ — represent 8 sites, and each takes one of the values $(1, 2, 3, 4, 5)$ indicating a very low, low, average, high, very high level, according to the measured rates of radon emanation from "boukoal" detectors.
$C_9, C_{10}, \ldots, C_{13}$ — represent 5 climatic factors, respectively. And each also takes one of the values (levels) $(1, 2, 3, 4, 5)$.
C_9 — the atmospheric pressure
C_{10} — the duration of sunshine
C_{11} — the air temperature

C_{12} — the relative humidity
C_{13} — the rainfall.

The last two attributes C_{14}, C_{15} are also climatic attributes, but they take only the values 1 or 2 to indicate if there exists some frost or not, respectively.

C_{14} — indicates frost at ground level
C_{15} — indicates two centimeters below ground level.

The unique decision attribute is d, takes the value 1 or 2.

d — the risk level of seismic activity
$d = 1$: the magnitude on the Richter scale is ≤ 1.5
$d = 2$: the magnitude on the Richter scale is > 1.5.

Table 5. Rules for d = 1

No	rules	strengths
R_1	$C_1 = 3$	$p = 1/(5^{12} * 2^2) * 34$
R_2	$C_1 = 4$	$p = 1/(5^{12} * 2^2) * 26$
R_3	$C_1 = 5$	$p = 1/(5^{12} * 2^2) * 27$
R_4	$C_2 = 2$	$p = 1/(5^{12} * 2^2) * 48$
R_5	$C_4 = 4$	$p = 1/(5^{12} * 2^2) * 28$
R_6	$C_6 = 1$	$p = 1/(5^{12} * 2^2) * 25$
R_7	$C_8 = 5$	$p = 1/(5^{12} * 2^2) * 23$
R_8	$C_{10} = 5$	$p = 1/(5^{12} * 2^2) * 27$
R_9	$C_{12} = 2$	$p = 1/(5^{12} * 2^2) * 35$
R_{10}	$C_2 = 5, C_{15} = 2$	$p = 1/(5^{12} * 2) * 16$
R_{11}	$C_4 = 2, C_{14} = 2$	$p = 1/(5^{12} * 2) * 38$
R_{12}	$C_5 = 3, C_{15} = 2$	$p = 1/(5^{12} * 2) * 46$
R_{13}	$C_7 = 5, C_{14} = 2$	$p = 1/(5^{12} * 2) * 15$
R_{14}	$C_9 = 3, C_{14} = 2$	$p = 1/(5^{12} * 2) * 35$
R_{15}	$C_3 = 3, C_5 = 3$	$p = 1/(5^{11} * 2^2) * 16$
R_{16}	$C_5 = 3, C_6 = 5$	$p = 1/(5^{11} * 2^2) * 16$

In Table 5 and Table 6, we present a result. The threshold value for the noise rate is 0, and we prefer the rules that are supported by as many instances as possible. Note that the strengths described in the 3'th column of Table 5 and Table 6 are the posterior probability distributions calculated in Eq. (6). $R_1, R_2, \ldots, R_{14}$, and $M_1, M_2, \ldots, M_5$ are rules that must be selected. The rules R_{15}, R_{16} have the same strength for covering the instance 17.

instance 17: R_{15}, R_{16}

Table 6. Rules for d = 2

No	rules	strengths
M_1	$C_1 = 2, C_2 = 4, C_3 = 2, C_5 = 2$	$p = 1/(5^9 * 2) * 3$
M_2	$C_1 = 2, C_2 = 4, C_5 = 2, C_{10} = 2$	$p = 1/(5^8 * 2^2) * 3$
M_3	$C_2 = 4, C_4 = 5, C_{13} = 4$	$p = 1/(5^{10} * 2^2) * 2$
M_4	$C_3 = 2, C_6 = 3, C_{10} = 2, C_{12} = 4$	$p = 1/(5^9 * 2^2) * 3$
M_5	$C_8 = 2, C_{11} = 1, C_{12} = 5, C_{14} = 1$	$p = 1/(5^{10} * 2) * 2$

Furthermore, we can get two groups of minimal decision rules described as follows:

$$R_1 \cup R_2 \cup ... \cup R_{13} \cup R_{14} \cup R_{15} \rightarrow d(1)$$
$$M_1 \cup M_2 \cup ... \cup M_5 \rightarrow d(2)$$

and

$$R_1 \cup R_2 \cup ... \cup R_{13} \cup R_{14} \cup R_{16} \rightarrow d(1)$$
$$M_1 \cup M_2 \cup ... \cup M_5 \rightarrow d(2)$$

Here we would like to describe how to use background knowledge as a bias to constrain the possible instances in a GDT. For example, if we use a background knowledge,

> *"when the air temperature is very high, it is not possible there exists some frost at ground level",*

then we do not consider the possible instances that are contradictory with this background knowledge in all possible combination of different attribute values in a database for creating a GDT. Thus, we can get the more refined result by using background knowledge in the learning process stated in Section 5. This example shows that our approach is a *soft* one that can use background knowledge as a bias for controlling the creation of a GDT and the discovery process.

8 Concluding Remarks

In this paper, we presented a new approach based on Generalization Distribution Table (GDT) and the rough set methodology for mining *if-then* rules from databases. We described basic concepts and an implementation of our methodology. Main features of our approach can be summarized as follows:

- It can learn *if-then* rules from very large, complex databases in an incremental, bottom-up mode;
- It can predict unseen instances and represent explicitly the uncertainty of a rule including the prediction of possible instances in the strength of the rule;

- It can effectively handle noisy data, missing data and data change;
- It can flexibly select biases for search control;
- It can use background knowledge as a bias for controlling the creation of a GDT and the discovery process.

Some issues on real-world applications have not yet been solved in our approach. Discretization of continuous attributes is one among them. Like many algorithms developed in the machine learning community, our approach focuses on learning in nominal attribute space. However, since many real-world classification tasks exist that involve continuous attributes, discretization of continuous attributes must be used as a step of pre-processing in our approach. Recently, discretization of continuous attributes has received significant attention in the machine learning community and some researchers have investigated about this [18, 13, 1, 10]. These results can be combined with our approach as a step of pre-processing.

Acknowledgements

The authors would like to thank the anonymous reviewers for their valuable comments.

References

1. Dougherty, J., Kohavi, R., Sahami, M.: Supervised and unsupervised discretization of continuous features. In: Proc. 12th Inter. Conf. on Machine Learning (1995) 194-202.
2. Gordon, D.F., DesJardins, M.: Evaluation and selection of biases in machine learning. Machine Learning **20** (1995) 5–22
3. Hirsh, H.: Generalizing version spaces. Machine Learning **17** (1994) 5–46
4. Langley, P.: Elements of machine learning, Morgan Kaufmann Publishers (1996)
5. Mollestad, T., Skowron, A.: A rough set framework for data mining of propositional default rules. In: Z.W. Ras and M. Michalewicz (eds.), Ninth International Symposium on Methodologies for Intelligent Systems (ISMIS-96), Zakopane, Poland, June 9–13, Lecture Notes in Artificial Intelligence **1079**, Springer–Verlag, Berlin (1996) 448–457
6. Michalski, R.S., Carbonell, J.G., Mitchell, T.M.: Machine learning - An artificial intelligence approach, **1-3** Morgan Kaufmann Publishers (1983, 1986, 1990)
7. Mitchell, T.M.: Version spaces: A candidate elimination approach to rule learning. In: Proc. 5th Int. Joint Conf. Artificial Intelligence, (1977) 305–310
8. Mitchell, T.M.: Generalization as search. Artificial Intelligence **18** (1982) 203–226
9. Ohsuga, S.: Symbol processing by non-symbol processor. In: Proc. 4th Pacific Rim International Conference on Artificial Intelligence (PRICAI'96) (1996) 193–205
10. Pfahringer, B.: Compression-based discretization of continuous attributes. In: Proc. 12th Inter. Conf. on Machine Learning (1995) 456–463

11. Piatetsky-Shapiro, G., Frawley, W.J. (eds.): Knowledge discovery in databases. AAAI Press and The MIT Press, (1991)
12. Shavlik, J.W., Dietterich, T.G. (eds.): Readings in machine learning. Morgan Kaufmann Publishers, San Mateo, CA (1990)
13. Shan, N., Hamilton, H.J., Ziarko, W., Cercone, N.: Discretization of continuos valued attributes in classification systems, In: S. Tsumoto, S. Kobayashi, T. Yokomori, H. Tanaka, and A. Nakamura (eds.): Proceedings of the Fourth International Workshop on Rough Sets, Fuzzy Sets, and Machine Discovery (RSFD'96), The University of Tokyo, November 6–8 (1996) 74–81
14. Skowron, A., Rauszer, C.: The discernibility matrices and functions in information systems. In: R. Słowiński (ed.): Intelligent Decision Support – Handbook of Applications and Advances of the Rough Sets Theory, Kluwer Academic Publishers, Dordrecht (1992) 331–362
15. Skowron, A., Suraj, Z.: A parallel algorithm for real–time decision making: A rough set approach. Journal of Intelligent Information Systems **7** (1996) 5–28
16. Skowron, A., Polkowski, L.: Synthesis of decision systems from data tables. In: T.Y. Lin, N. Cercone (eds.): Rough Sets and Data Mining. Analysis of Imprecise Data, Kluwer Academic Publishers, Boston, Dordrecht (1997) 259–299
17. Teghem, J., Charlet J.-M.: Use of 'rough sets' method to draw premonitory factors for earthquakes by emphasing gas geochemistry: The case of a low seismic activity context, in Belgium. In: R. Słowiński (ed.): Intelligent Decision Support – Handbook of Applications and Advances of the Rough Sets Theory, Kluwer Academic Publishers, Dordrecht (1992) 165–179
18. Lin, T.Y.: Neighborhood systems - A qualitative theory for fuzzy and rough sets. In: P.P. Wang (ed.), Advances in Machine Intelligence and Soft Computing **4** (1996) 132–155
19. Lin, T.Y., Cercone, N. (eds.): Rough sets and data mining: Analysis of imprecise data. Kluwer Academic Publishers, Boston, Dordrecht (1997)
20. Pawlak, Z.: Rough sets – Theoretical aspects of reasoning about data. Kluwer Academic Publishers, Dordrecht (1991)
21. Zhong, N. Ohsuga,S.: Using generalization distribution tables as a hypotheses search space for generalization. In: S. Tsumoto, S. Kobayashi, T. Yokomori, H. Tanaka, and A. Nakamura (eds.): Proceedings of the Fourth International Workshop on Rough Sets, Fuzzy Sets, and Machine Discovery (RSFD'96), The University of Tokyo, November 6–8 (1996) 396–403
22. Zhong, N., Fujitsu, S., Ohsuga, S.: Generalization based on the connectionist networks representation of a generalization distribution table. In: Proc. First Pacific-Asia Conference on Knowledge Discovery and Data Mining (PAKDD-97), World Scientific (1997) 183–197
23. Zhong, N., Dong, J.Z., Ohsuga, S.: Discovering rules in the environment with noise and incompleteness. In: Proc. 10th International Florida AI Reaserch Symposium (FLAIRS-97), Special Track on Uncertainty in AI (1997) 186–191
24. Zhong, N., Dong, J.Z., Ohsuga, S.: Soft techniques to rule discovery in data. In: Proceedings of the Fifth European Congress on Intelligent Techniques and Soft Computing (EUFIT'97), September 8–11, Aachen, Germany, Verlag Mainz, Aachen (1997) 212–217

PART 2:

CASE STUDIES

Chapter 8

Soft Processing of Audio Signals

Andrzej Czyżewski

Technical University of Gdansk, Faculty of Electronics, Telecommunications and Informatics, Sound Engineering Department, 80-952 Gdansk, Poland

1 Introduction

The aim of the presented research is to develop and to test some digital signal processing systems applicable to modern telecommunications. A special feature of the elaborated systems is the improvement in performance of audio signal processing algorithms obtained through the use of some soft computing methods based on rough sets, fuzzy logic and neural networks. The engineered and tested digital signal processing systems enabled some comparative studies of the effectiveness of algorithms based on soft computing. The results of speaker-independent recognition of digits and of noise removal from speech and music signals will be presented. Some general conclusions concerning the application of intelligent decision systems to real-time signal processing will be added.

2 Recognition of isolated words

The first investigated system was a speaker-independent system for man-machine voice interfacing using a small vocabulary containing digits. The cepstrum trajectory tracking method was implemented to feature vector extraction from speech signal [8]. Some intelligent decision systems were tried including a neural network algorithm completed by a fuzzy logic classification procedure, with rough set method permitting the derivation of decision rules for the recognition of speech patterns.

2.1 Feature extraction

The input speech signal was sampled with a sampling frequency equal to 22.05 kHz and quantized using 8-bit linear quantization. The density of envelope peaks of the speech signal was analyzed in order to determine the word boundaries [8]. The implemented feature extraction method allows for the determination of cepstral coefficients calculated using a non-linear frequency scale (the mel scale) that are particularly applicable to the presented experiments. In order to determine these parameters, the spectrum is calculated based on the typical

Hamming window procedure and 256-point DFT (Discrete Fourier Transform) computation. Subsequently, the mel-frequency cepstrum coefficients (MFCC) are determined for each packet on the basis of the following equation [2]:

$$M_i = \sum_{k=1}^{F} X_k \cos\left[i(k-0.5)\pi/F\right] \tag{1}$$

where: X_k –is a result of DFT calculation as follows :

$$X_k = \sum_{n=0}^{N-1} x(n)e^{-j2\pi k\frac{n}{N}} = \sum_{n=0}^{N-1} x(n)[\cos(2\pi k\tfrac{n}{N}) - j\sin(2\pi k\tfrac{n}{N})]$$

and: F is the number of filters,

i- number of the cepstrum coefficient,

k - number of the frequency subband,

N - number of points in the Hamming window (equal to 256),

$x(n)$- is the result of the convolution of speech samples and nth point of the Hamming window,

$j = \sqrt{-1}$

The number of filters F was set to 20. Consequently, the results of spectral analysis X_k were located in 20 frequency subbands on the mel-frequency scale. The feature vector also consists of two other parameters reflecting the time-domain characteristics of the signal. These are: the density of local time-envelope peaks and the relative amplitude midpoint value $p_A$defined as follows:

$$p_A = \frac{\sum_i iA_i}{\sum_i A_i} \tag{2}$$

where: i - segment number,

A_i- relative average amplitude for segment i;

Similarly to the mel-cepstrum coefficients, the above parameters are independent of the signal energy. The parameters calculated for individual signal packets (sets of 256 samples) may be expressed by trajectories reflecting parameter evolutions in the whole segment containing a certain number of packets. Consequently, each parameter is to be represented by its i-point evolutionary path based on the orthogonal system:

$$T_i = \sum_{j=1}^{n} P_j \cos\left[i(j-0.5)\pi/n\right] \tag{3}$$

where: i- number of trajectory coefficient ($i = 1, 2, .., 6$),

j- segment number,

n - number of segments in the whole utterance,

P_j- parameter calculated for the jth segment.

It should be noted that after the calculation of trajectory coefficients, the information relating to utterance time duration is no longer exploited. Hence, this way of parametrization comprises also the time-normalization of speech patterns.

2.2 Training the neural network

First, a computer model of a fully connected, feed forward neural network (perceptron model) was employed for testing [1]. The number of layers was set to 3. The hyperbolic tangent function was selected as a transfer function of neurons. A modified back-propagation algorithm was implemented at the training stage. The voice patterns taken from 10 subjects were employed for the network training. In order to improve this algorithm, it was completed with the fuzzy logic-based decision procedure described in the next paragraph.

2.3 Fuzzy logic-based decision procedure

The neural network applied to recognition of digits may have 10 outputs. In this case it is expected that the output will fire which number is associated with a particular digit. Ideally, the state of this output should be logical '1' while the remaining outputs show logical '0'. However, in practice the network is also generating another type of vectors on its output, consisting of elements having real-type values. That is why the fuzzy decision block was added at the outputs of the neural network. The final decision comes from the fuzzy logic module using the following set of rules:

if (Y_1=1 AND Y_2=0 ANDY_3=0 AND...Y_{10}=0) then digit=one
if (Y_1=0 AND Y_2=1 AND Y_3=0 AND...Y_{10}=0) then digit=two
....
if (Y_1=0 ANDY_2=0 ANDY_3=0 AND...Y_{10} = 1)then digit=ten

The knowledge base was built up according to the assumption that fuzzy set boundaries might be described by simple trapezoid membership functions. This assumption is justified by current technology solutions which offer integrated fuzzy processors that usually implement triangular, trapezoid or bell-type membership functions.

The data for the fuzzy knowledge base was acquired from the neural net outputs during the recognition tests performed with the participation of 20 speakers (10 voices exploited at the training stage and 10 new voices). The collection of network responses obtained in such a way reflects the fuzziness of results of classifications made by this algorithm when performing both speaker dependent and speaker-independent recognition tests. As was mentioned above, these responses were subjected to further processing in order to obtain fuzzy sets with trapezoid boundary functions outlined in Fig. 1.

The membership functions are related to the estimated probability density function chosen to describe boundaries of these sets. The membership function parameters a and b seen in Fig. 1 are to be found using the data acquired in the described tests. The computing of 2nd and of 4th order central moments is based on the following relationships:

$$M_2 = \int_{-\infty}^{+\infty} x^2 p(x) dx = Aa^3 \left(\frac{2}{3} - \frac{a}{2b} \right) \tag{4}$$

$$M_4 = \int_{-\infty}^{+\infty} x^4 p(x) dx = Aa^5 \left(\frac{2}{5} - \frac{a}{3b}\right) \tag{5}$$

The membership function center value A was calculated considering the identity:

$$\int_{-\infty}^{+\infty} p(x) = 1 \tag{6}$$

thus it is equal:

$$A = \frac{b}{2ab - a^2} \tag{7}$$

The 10 fuzzy sets obtained using this method represent separate classes related to digit patterns. The sets proved to not be disjointed, however one of the decision rules firing in each recognition test qualifies every pattern to one of these sets. The decision is made on the basis of calculations using principles of fuzzy logic. Hence, during subsequent speech recognition tests each neural network output vector is to be associated with the reference set for which the fuzzy rule has acquired the highest value.

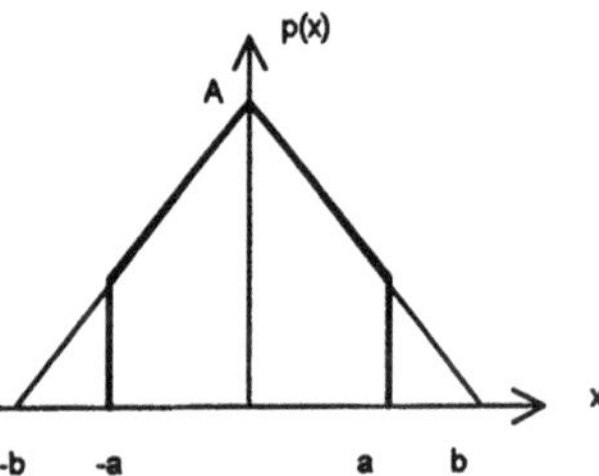

Fig. 1 Estimated probability density forming the membership function.

2.4 Rough set approach

A fundamental notion of the rough set-based learning system is the need to discover dependencies between given features of a problem to be classified. Consequently, this system is applicable to speech recognition [3][7].

The basic concepts related to rough set theory are extensively covered in a rich assortment of literature. One of the most basic definitions in the rough set system is the rough measure of the rule μ_{RS}. This measure associated with each rule is defined as follows:

$$\mu_{RS} = \frac{|X \cap Y|}{|Y|} \tag{8}$$

where: X- is the concept, and Y- the set of examples described by the rule.

A new parameter was defined for the purpose of the presented investigations allowing one to optimize the rule generation process, e.g. in speech recognition tasks. This parameter was called the rule strength r and is defined as follows:

$$r = c(\mu_{RS} - n_{\mu}), \tag{9}$$

$$n_{\mu} \in < 0, 1) \tag{10}$$

where: c - number of cases supporting the condition part of the rule,
n_{μ}- neutral point of the rough measure.

The neutral point n_{μ} of the rough measure μ_{RS} is one of the parameters of the rule generation system to be set experimentally by its operator during the testing of the system. This parameter allows the regulation of the influence of possible rules on the process of decision making. This results from the fact, that the decision system is designed in such a way, that each derived rule is assigned a value called rule strength r that reflects the degree of confidence to the rule. Correspondingly, the decision is influenced mostly by strong rules assigned higher values of r and less by rules having lower values of r. When the neutral point of the rough measure n_{μ} is set to 0, the rule strength is proportional to the rough measure μ_{RS} providing the typical descriptor of rule quality. However, owing to the parameter defined as the neutral point of the rough measure, the decision system can be tuned experimentally. For example if n_{μ} will be selected as equal to μ_{RS} , then rules having rough measure $\mu_{RS} = n_{\mu}$ will be not taken into consideration during the decision making (the rule strength $r = 0$). In the same time, it becomes possible that some rules will be assigned a negative value of rule strength (the rule weakens the decision related to this case) or some rules can be biased over other ones through the setting of n_{μ} to some values of the range $< 0, 1)$. The value of n_{μ} is selected experimentally after building the knowledge base of the system.

The knowledge base is built up during the training phase in such a way that the objects corresponding to each category are collected in the proper class. Consequently, 10 sets containing parameters representing each digit are created with regard to voice patterns taken from speakers involved in the system training. Subsequently, minimum and maximum values of consecutive parameters are calculated for each class. These values are used to determine ranges of individual parameters serving as attributes for the decision system. The ranges form the basis for subsequent redefinition of attributes in order to replace float type numbers by the quantized ones. Several methods of attribute quantization are known from the literature [7][9][15]. The algorithm using an adaptable quantization of attributes was proposed by the author and his colleague [7]. The principle of this approach consists in analyzing the individual class contents in opposition to the remaining ones. The Quantization of Attributes procedure produces vectors representing attributes for each Concept. This procedure transforms parameter values into range representations. The quantization order (number of ranges for each parameter) is incremented until new contrary cases are no longer produced. The individual approach to attributes procedure permits finding the smallest number of an attribute range for which it remains valuable to the decision procedure (specific). This attribute is then added to the set of reducts [7].

A newer version of the system for speech recognition uses another method for scaling of attribute values based on the statistical approach to the determination of ranges of non-linear feature vector parameters [8]. The Behrens-Fisher statistics served as a tool for the determination of division points while determining the attribute ranges basing on the clustered parameter values. The Behrens-Fisher statistics is defined as follows:

$$V = \frac{\overline{X} - \overline{Y}}{\sqrt{S_1^2/n + S_2^2/m}} \tag{11}$$

where:

$$\overline{X} = \frac{1}{n}\sum_{i=1}^{n} X \ ,$$

$$\overline{Y} = \frac{1}{m}\sum_{i=1}^{m} Y_i$$

are arithmetic averages of observed parameter values X_i i Y_i and:

$$S_1^2 = \frac{1}{n-1} \cdot \sum_{i=1}^{n} (X_i - \overline{X})^2, \ S_2^2 = \frac{1}{m-1} \cdot \sum_{i=1}^{m} (Y_i - \overline{Y})^2$$

are estimators of variances of the corresponding random variables; n, m - cardinalities of test sets of populations X and Y.

In the case of the fixed cardinalities n and m the statistics serves as a distance measure between the compared classes for the individual parameters (in most cases $n = m$). The possibility to discern between patterns is more probable for the pairs giving higher values of this statistics. Lower dispersion and bigger differences between average values are calculated on the basis of data considered as random tests, while the whole population is of normal distribution. In order to find the discriminator it is necessary to use distribution estimators of the examined parameters. Provided these estimated distributions are having the same dispersions, the discriminator value may be calculated on the basis of the following equation:

$$d_{xy} = \frac{\overline{X} + \overline{Y}}{2} \tag{12}$$

d_{xy} - discriminator value,

$\overline{X}$, $\overline{Y}$ - are arithmetic averages of observed parameter values X_i and Y_i. For the case of unequal dispersions the discriminator should be closer the mean value of this distribution which is having lower dispersion, thus the following term is to be fulfilled:

$$P(x > d_{xy}) = P(y < d_{xy}) \tag{13}$$

where:
$P(x > d_{xy})$ - probability that the random variable x fulfils the term: $x > d_{xy}$
$P(y < d_{xy})$ - probability that the random variable y fulfils the term: $y < d_{xy}$

Assuming that the *a priori* probabilities of random events x and y are equal to each other, the above term guarantees the lowest probability of making the wrong decision. The need to fulfil the above term demands the estimation of the value d_{xy}:

$$d_{xy} = \frac{\overline{X}S_2 + \overline{Y}S_1}{S_1 + S_2} \tag{14}$$

For the data basis containing k classes, the number of the possible pairs to be compared is equal to:

$$p = \frac{k \cdot (k-1)}{2} \tag{15}$$

Subsequently, the values calculated for the above pairs are used for the quantization of feature vector parameters. The values are described by the corresponding statistics, providing a measure of significance for such comparisons. The number of ranges resulting from the quantization procedure may be limited arbitrarily, due to the need to observe the computational costs. The need to reduce the number of ranges occurs when the number of generated pairs is exceeding the assumed quantization order. This reduction may be realized on the basis of one of the following procedures:

1. Constant quantization - imposing the same number of ranges for each feature vector parameter. The values are selected from the calculated discriminators, for which the calculated statistics V is giving the highest results,

2. Variable quantization - practically leading to different quantization of each feature vector parameter. The division values are selected for which the statistics V is exceeding the selected threshold.

As it was revealed by experimental procedures, various discretization techniques can bear on results of speech recognition (the differences up to 10% in recognition accuracy were observed depending on the discretization technique). The variable quantization allowed to achieve best speech recognition scores.

The rough set decision algorithm uses rules that are to be found during the system training. Speech patterns selected for training are initially processed in order to extract feature vectors. Subsequently, the adaptable algorithm for quantization of attribute values is executed and rules are generated on the basis of the decision table using a rough set algorithm [7][8]. The leave-one out model validation technique was exploited. Correspondingly, it was found experimentally [7][8] that the settings of the rough set decision systems should be selected as follows: maximum rule length: 4, minimum allowable rough measure μ_{RS}= 0.5, neutral point of the rough measure n_{μ}= 0.6. This selection found experimentally for the constructed speech recognition system compromises both satisfying recognition scores and reasonable computational demands.

2.5 Comparative studies of speech recognition effectiveness

A series of tests and comparative studies were performed in order to optimize parameters of the feature extraction procedure and decision system settings. Finally, three speech recognition systems were prepared, diversified as to the decision algorithm employed. These are:

1. three-layer perceptron with one-bit threshold quantization of output neuron state,
2. three-layer perceptron supported with fuzzy logic decision rules,
3. rough set expert system.

Speech patterns were recorded digitally in the workstation hard disk, edited, parametrized using trajectory representations and parameter values were quantized to become the range representations (attributes). All above systems were trained with speech material collected from 10 speakers (8 male and 2 female). Digits pronounced by another 10 speakers (also 8 male and 2 female) served as the test material.

The number of neurons in the hidden layer of the neural network was selected as equal to 1/2 of the amount of input neurons (equal to 30) and the number of outputs was equal to 10, i.e. each output was assigned to the recognition of one of the digits.

The rule generation procedure induced over 1600 rules of diversified rough set measures in the range of <0.5, 1>. Subsequently, these rules were used for processing speech patterns recorded by 10 new speakers, pronouncing digits.

Tab.1 Results of experiments with unknown voices
(90 MHz Unix workstation)

Method	Right class.	Wrong class.	Error rate	Training time
neural net	86	6 (+8 none)	6 (14)	8h:13 min.
net +fuzzy	93	7	7	8h:15 min.
rough set	92	8	8	34 min.

As is seen from Tab. 1, the fuzzy logic decision procedure supporting the neural network learning algorithm improved speech recognition results meaningfully. The rough set algorithm recognition scores are similar to the results obtained with the neural network algorithm extended with a fuzzy logic-based decision system. However, the time needed for the training was many times shorter in this case. The speed of processing of new examples during the recognition phase is similar in both cases and the decision comes after a several second delay needed to process the feature vectors derived from an utterance representation.

3 Rough set-based filtration of noisy sound

Variety of digital signal processing methods applicable to the removal of noise are known from the literature. Often, the algorithms were derived from classic speech processing techniques, and radar or seismic signal processing methods. The collection of methods based on the mathematical model approach to the problem of restoration of recorded or transmitted audio may be completed with learning algorithm implementations. The separation of signal from noise is also important to hearing aid performance. As it results from experiments conducted by the author, learning algorithms provide a powerful tool when implemented to the elimination of noise. First, the neural networks were applied to the detection and to the removal of impulse distortions [5][14]. Next, the rough set approach to the separation of signal and noise in old audio recordings and in telecommunication channels was investigated [10][17]. Moreover, the rough set method was employed to the automatic selection of speech components in hearing prostheses [12]. The rough set approach to the removal of noise will be briefly discussed in this paragraph.

3.1 The audio signal analysis-synthesis model

The main idea of intelligent signal filtration proposed with regard to the presented experiments consists of the following main steps:

· spectral analysis of the signal,

· discerning eligible signal components from noise using an intelligent decision algorithm,

· resynthesis of a new signal on the basis of the selected components.

The analysis model based on the McAulay-Quatieri analysis-resynthesis procedure was utilized in these experiments [4]. It allows one to make the resynthesis on the basis of a finite number of sinusoidal components represented by the sum:

$$x(n) = \sum_{k=1}^{J} a_k \cos(\omega_k n + \phi_k) \tag{16}$$

where:

$x(n)$ - the reconstructed signal,

J- number of sinusoidal components forming the segment,

$a(k)$ - amplitude of kth spectrum component,

ω_k - angular frequency of kth component,

ϕ_k - phase of kth component.

The synthesis parameters are considered time-variant, so their values must be updated frequently by analyzing small consecutive signal blocks. The 256-sample packets are slightly overlapped (overlap fold: 32-samples). The spectral representation obtained in effect of the above procedures can be filtered through the use of some intelligent threshold operations and subsequently resynthesized employing the additive synthesis based on the inverse Fourier transform.

3.2 Intelligent threshold operations

The parameters describing signal patterns are to be determined on the basis of processing of consecutive packets containing samples and on the basis of subjective assessments provided by the expert, operating the system at the training stage. The intelligent procedure which will be described below may be completed by some non-intelligent threshold algorithms which are not described here [17].

The knowledge is collected in this noise reduction system in the form of a rule base. The rules are constructed as follows:

< chain of condition attributes > ==> < expert opinion >

The system uses the following condition attributes:

1. settings defined by the operator for the entire pattern (approximately 3 second portion of audio signal):

c- relative cut-off threshold of the spectral components (magnitude-domain filtration),

f_p - initial frequency of preemphasis [Hz],

p - preemphasis slope [dB/oct.].

2. parameters to be calculated by the system:

m_1, m_2, m_3 - three statistical parameters of signal representation determined on the basis of processing of sample packets. These parameters represent the first three central moments of the average spectrum of the whole pattern, according to the following definitions:

$$m_1 = \frac{\sum_{i=1}^{n} i \cdot A_i}{\sum_{i=1}^{n} A_i}, \tag{17}$$

where m_1 represents the spectral centroid;

$$m_2 = \frac{\sum_{i=1}^{n} (i - m_1)^2 \cdot A_i}{\sum_{i=1}^{n} A_i} \tag{18}$$

where: m_2 is the second central moment (variance) of the spectrum reflecting the distribution of the spectral energy in relation to the spectrum 'gravity center';

$$m_3 = \frac{\sum_{i=1}^{n} (i - m_1)^3 \cdot A_i}{\sum_{i=1}^{n} A_i} \tag{19}$$

where: m_3 is the third central moment reflecting the degree of symmetry of the spectrum in relation to the gravity midpoint (e.g. for a symmetrical spectral shape $m_3 = 0$).

The remaining denotations are as follows:

A_i *-ith* line of the average spectrum,

n - number of spectral lines.

d_1, d_2, d_3 - parameters describing the speed of signal decay in the whole pattern (usually resulting from the presence of reverberation). The decay rapidity is determined on the basis of the averaged speed of level decrease in some subbands of the whole audio band, calculated according to the following relationship:

$$d_r = \frac{1}{j} \cdot \sum_{i=1}^{j} (L_{r,i} - L_{r,i-1}), \tag{20}$$

where:

$L_{r,i}$ - signal level in packet i in relation to packet $i-1$ within the subband r. Practically, 3 subbands were used: 0-1kHz; 1-5.5kHz; 5.5-11kHz, thus $r \in \{1, 2, 3\}$,

j - is the number of sample packets in the whole pattern.

The need to preemphasize higher components of the frequency band results from the natural decrease in energy of audio signals at the upper part of the frequency band. Consequently, the signal should be emphasized in upper frequency band, starting from a certain frequency f_p (the rising slope of the filter selected equal to p [dB/oct.]). Both parameters, namely f_p and p, provide two variables to be regulated by the human operator during experiments.

The parameters: $c, f_p, p, m_1, m_2, m_3, d_1, d_2,$and d_3 providing attributes of the decision system are quantized i.e. they are represented by ranges instead of continuous values. For example: p (preemphasis slope) can be represented by the following ranges:

(0-3); (3-6); (6-12) [dB/oct.]

The remaining attributes are quantized in such a way, that individual parameters are represented by a few values (resolution limited to 3 - 5 ranges has been found to be appropriate during the testing). The non-linear relationship between the integer values representing the ranges and the real parameter values is not an obstacle to the rough set decision system, provided the chosen values of parameters are discernible and specific as to their influence on the expert's decisions. Practically, the quantized attributes are represented by the numbers 1, 2, 3,...5 showing to which of the numbered ranges the current value of the related parameter falls.

The rules only that are related to the positive assessment of pattern quality are taken into account (concept selection). Next, the rules selected in such a way are processed. The processing consists of changing c, h, f_p, and p previously used as condition attributes to the decision attributes. Consequently, the new rules appear after such a transformation, e.g. as follows:

$[m1 = 1]\&[m2 = 2]\&[m3 = 0]\&[d1 = 0]\&[d2 = 1]\&[d3 = 0] => [c = 1]$
$[m1 = 1]\&[m2 = 2]\&[m3 = 0]\&[d1 = 0]\&[d2 = 1]\&[d3 = 0] => [h = 2]$
$[m1 = 1]\&[m2 = 2]\&[m3 = 0]\&[d1 = 0]\&[d2 = 1]\&[d3 = 0] => [f_p = 2]$
$[m1 = 1]\&[m2 = 2]\&[m3 = 0]\&[d1 = 0]\&[d2 = 1]\&[d3 = 0] => [p = 0]$

The above listed rules can provide decisions allowing one to automatically regulate settings of the noise reduction system. As is seen, the condition attributes now represent quantized values *calculated* on the basis of the individual signal packets, while the decision attributes may be used directly to *regulate* the parameters of the noise reduction procedure when processing these packets. The values m_1, m_2 and m_3 can be determined from a single packet while d_1, d_2 and d_3 use data contained in the two consecutive packets. Usually, the rule list is much longer than the exemplary one presented above, and comprises practically all found configurations of attributes.

The regulation of the threshold is controlled by three main decision attributes as follows:

1. spectral filtration cut-off threshold $c \in \{0, 1, 2, 3, 4\}$;
2. coefficient k_i related to the preemphasis (boost of the high frequency range) defined as follows:

$$k_i = 1 \; for \; i \leq \frac{m \cdot f_p}{f_s} \tag{21}$$

$$k_i = \frac{1}{\left(\frac{i \cdot f_s}{m \cdot f_p}\right)^{\frac{p}{6}}} \; for \; i > \frac{m \cdot f_p}{f_s}$$

where:
f_s - sampling frequency (22.05 kHz),
m - number of samples in a single packet (256),
i - ith spectral line related to the frequency $f_i = i \cdot \frac{f_s}{m}$,
f_p - initial preemphasis frequency, $f_p \in \{0, 1, 2\}$,
p - preemphasis slope [dB/octave], $p \in \{0, 1, 2\}$.

3. hysteresis coefficient $h \in \{0, 1, 2, 3\}, 0 \leq h < 1$. If this coefficient is set to a non-zero value then it relates the cut-off threshold of spectral components to its level in the preceding packet. This feature is realized by the use of the function of level of the cut-off threshold of the preceding packet $f_d(i)$, defined as follows:

$$f_d(i) = \begin{cases} -h \; for & A'_i > t_p(i) \\ 0 \; for \; A'_i < t_p(i) \wedge \left(A'_{i-1} > t_p(i) \vee A'_{i+1} > t_p(i)\right) \\ h \; for \; A'_i < t_p(i) \wedge A'_{i-1} < t_p(i) \wedge A'_{i+1} < t_p(i) \end{cases} \tag{22}$$

where: A'_i - magnitude of the i-th spectral line of the preceding packet,

$t_p(i)$ - threshold set in the preceding packet;

The cut-off threshold $t(i)$ is calculated, based on the following relationship employing the above defined parameters:

$$t(i) = \bar{A}_i \cdot c \cdot k_i (1 + f_d(i)) \quad (23)$$

where:

$\bar{A}_i = \frac{1}{n_h} \sum_{i=1}^{n_h} \frac{A_i}{k_i}$ - spectral magnitude averaged for the whole sample packet,

n_h- index of the spectrum line at the upper boundary of the frequency band $n_h = \frac{m}{2}$.

As results from the above equation, the current value of spectral filtration threshold is determined by the average spectral magnitude and by the coefficients regulated by the rough set decision system. These coefficients (decision attributes associated with the winning rules) influence some basic signal features, namely level (through the use of the parameter c), spectral characteristics (through the use of the preemphasis parameter k) and shape of time envelope (through the use of the parameter h). In turn, the collection of components obtained by threshold filtration depends on the calculated threshold values. Correspondingly, three decision categories (classes) were defined:

1. noisy sound (threshold too low),
2. pure sound (threshold proper),
3. poor sound (threshold too high).

The expressions above, correspond to subjective assessments of the effect of filtration of spectral components used for the resynthesis of the sound. When the threshold is too low, then noise or hiss is clearly audible. When the threshold is too high, then many eligible components are removed, so the resulting sound is clean, but poor. The proper threshold corresponds to the removal of noise without discarding too many eligible signal components (pure sound case).

The learning procedure which produces the rules consists of:

(a) selecting some short fragments of the recording,

(b) setting the parameter values (c, h, f_p, p) by the operator, and

(c) subjectively assessing the effect of the threshold procedure after the resynthesis.

In this way the knowledge base is built with regard to a human expert's subjective assessment of the individual examples.

3.3 Experiments with the rough set-based noise filtration

Practically, it is sufficient to choose some examples corresponding to the most characteristic fragments of an audio signal to be restored. Typically up to 5 % of the whole material is chosen and assessed on the basis of 3 second portions. After execution of some preliminary tests, the following attribute values were found experimentally to have a noticeable effect on the quality of the processed sound:

$attr.1 = c_s; s \in < 0, 1, 2, 3, 4 >, \; c_s \in \{0.2, 0.4, 0.6, 0.8, 1.0\}$

$attr.2 = h_s; s \in < 0, 1, 2, 3 >,\ h \in \{0.2, 0.4, 0.6, 0.8\}$;

$attr.3 = f_p; s \in < 0, 1, 2 >,\ f_p \in \{0.4, 1.0, 3.0\}$ –expressed in[kHz];

$attr.4 = p_s; s \in < 0, 1, 2 >,\ p \in \{3, 6, 12\}$ –expressed in[dB/oct.];

$attr.5$ to $10 \Rightarrow m_1, m_2, m_3, d_1, d_2, d_3$- calculated by the algorithm using signal packets and automatically quantized.

The generated rules represent relevant decision classes labelled as *noisy*, *pure* and *poor* sound. Next the rule base is processed with regard to the concept *pure sound*. Consequently, the new rules for c, h, f_p and p are defined on the basis of current values of parameters $m_1, m_2, m_3, d_1, d_2, d_3$ which are automatically calculated when the new material is processed. In this way the knowledge base is built up to be applicable to the selected fragments (certainly) and to the rest of the recording (possibly). The generalization capabilities of the rough set method proved to work well also with material not employed to the training.

In an exemplary experiment the rule set was derived automatically by the learning procedure on the basis of 10 characteristic fragments of the audio material sampled at 22.05 kHz, each with time duration of 3 seconds or about 260 of 256-sample packets. From the analysis, 441 rules were generated of various rough measures (μ_{RS}) reflecting the degree of confidence for each rule.

The acquired rule base was then used for the automatic determination of thresholds for all packets of the whole recording. For a typical analyzed signal packet many rules are firing, some of them certain (rough measure equal to 1) and some uncertain. The spectral filtering threshold is updated according to the parameters associated with the winning rule. Some examples illustrating the magnitude threshold filtration are shown in Fig. 2. More detailed description of the designed algorithms and obtained results is to be found in literature [12][17].

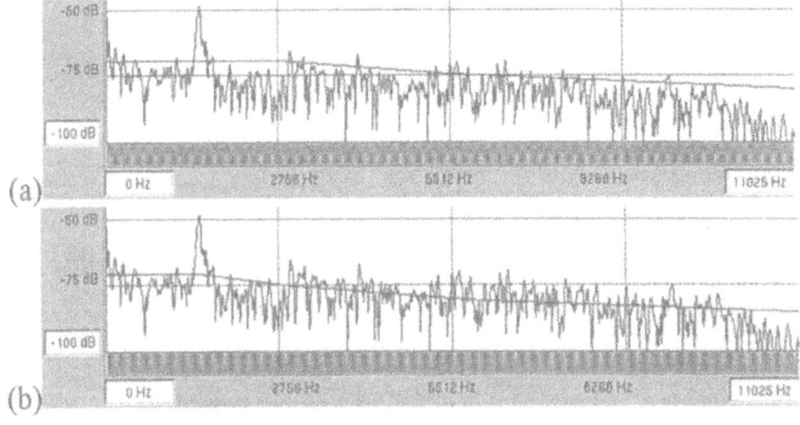

Fig. 2 Spectral threshold filtration of noisy sound controlled by the rough set-based algorithm (a) too high threshold case, (b) proper threshold case.

4 Perceptual compression of noisy audio data

The concept of perceptual coding is based on the masking phenomena in the critical bands of hearing. The critical bands concept is derived from the well-proven phenomenon that the human auditory system processes sounds as a bank of band-pass filters which analyze a broad spectral range in some independent subbands. The presence of a tone in a critical band (acting as a masker) may cause other tones falling into this critical band or neighboring bands to not be perceived. The effectiveness of such a masking depends mainly on the level of the masker. The masking phenomena in critical bands are widely used for the compression of audio data [13].

The perceptual noise reduction and simultaneous data compression algorithm consists of two separate procedures: the algorithm of noise samples analysis and the algorithm of perceptual signal filtering. First, samples of noise are taken from a silent passage of a recording or transmission and are analyzed. In turn, the intelligent perceptual filter takes a sound affected by noise and automatically updates the masking threshold levels. The decision regarding the update is made by an intelligent inference engine by virtue of the statistical information on the noise characteristics and the spectral contents of the currently analyzed frame. Fuzzy logic [6], neural networks[11] and rough sets [18] are employed to assess the similarities between the currently analyzed frame and the collected noise patterns. Because of space limitations, in this paper only the rough set -based inference engine implementation will be shown.

Intelligent perceptual coding algorithm A general flowchart of the intelligent perceptual coding system is shown in Fig. 3.

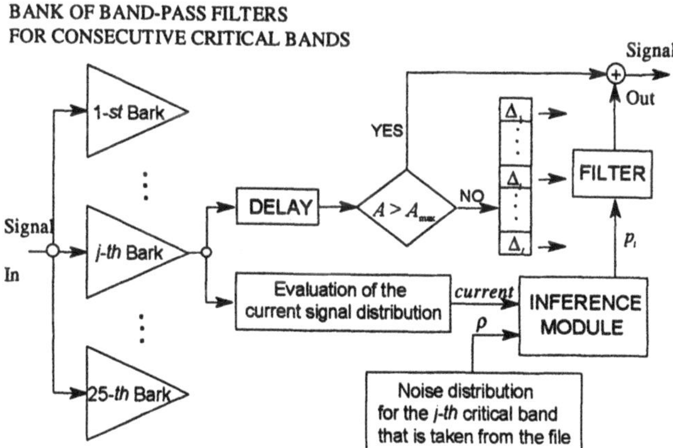

Fig. 3 Flowchart of the perceptual noise reduction system

For the cbth critical band and its noise patterns, the density ρ denotes the percentage of spectral components whose magnitudes belong to the ith interval Δ_i. In the kth moment of time, this percentage may be expressed as follows:

$$\rho(\Delta_i, t_j) = \left|\frac{k_n(\Delta_i, t_j)}{X}\right|_{j=k} \quad ; \quad i = 1, ..., I \tag{24}$$

where:

$X-$ is the number of intervals of spectral magnitude which varies depending on the frequency band

Δ_i - interval of values from the ranges: $[(i-1)\cdot\Delta,(i+1)\cdot\Delta]$of spectral magnitudes.

$k_n(\Delta_i, t_j)$ - number of noise components with magnitude values which belong to the ith interval Δ_i

For the maximum value MAX of spectral magnitudes in the cbth critical band, it may be written:

$$\lceil MAX \rceil = \Delta_i \cdot I \tag{25}$$

where: I - number of intervals Δ_i into which the whole range of spectral magnitudes is divided.

The measure *current* of the values of signal spectral elements is given as follows:

$$current(\Delta_i, t_j) = \left|\frac{k_s(\Delta_i, t_j)}{X}\right|_{j=k} \quad ; \quad i = 1, 2, ..., I; \; j, k = 1, 2, ..., \tag{26}$$

where: $k_s(\Delta_i, t_j)$ - number of signal components in which magnitude values belong to the ith interval Δ_i.The pair $< MAX(cb), \rho(cb) >$ defines the characteristics of noise in the cbth critical band. Thus, these values for consecutive subbands are stored in a file as a noise reference pattern. The pair $< MAX(cb), current(cb) >$ characterizes properties of a signal portion.

Application of rough sets In the cbth critical band, all spectral magnitudes that surpass $MAX(cb)$ are qualified for resynthesis. The others are analyzed in $I(cb)$intervals. The number of components in a single interval Δ_i of spectral magnitude is compared to that of the noise characteristics. Thus, the expert system generates the value (pcb, i) which represents the grade of similarity of the current signal portion to noise. This value is then used as a probability limit for the removal of noisy components. Consequently, the spectral components are cut-off with the probability of (pcb, i) or pass to the resynthesis with the probability $1-(pcb, i)$. As the above results indicate, the role of the expert system is to assess the grade of similarity between signal portions and reference noise patterns on the basis of previously computed parameters, and to produce the coefficients (pcb, i). This task may be realized by a rough set-based decision system.

The results of noise reduction with this method proved to be satisfactory [18]. It is possible to reduce non-stationary noise found in sounds transmitted through telecommunication channels. The maximum level of noise possible to remove was as high as -30 dB with respect to signal level. This method allows one also to compress audio data files without degrading the subjective quality of sound. Compression ratios 1:6 were found acceptable in some subjective listening tests.

In all experiments the rough set system was used. The system was developed and implemented at the Technical University of Gdansk [7].

5 Conclusions

Problems related to the application of soft computing methods to the analysis and processing of audio data were presented considering only some exemplary applications, namely the speaker-independent recognition of digits and the removal of noise from audio recordings or transmission. These operations illustrate the usefulness of this non-standard approach to problem solving in digital signal processing. The implementation of a soft computing approach is desirable when it is not possible to build an exact mathematical model to describe the examined phenomena. This situation describes many practical areas in digital signal processing. Consequently, algorithms based on neural networks, rough sets and fuzzy logic should be implemented more widely to this domain.

A comparison of the effectiveness of various methods (neural networks, rough sets, fuzzy logic) shows that they can be equally effective in some applications or that some of them can outperform the others in some specific tasks. The combining of some of these methods also brought positive results.

Fuzzy logic applications in digital signal processing proved to be very promising because of the simplicity of such an approach. However, the computational cost of the defuzzyfying procedure, typically made with the centroid method, must be taken into consideration in some real-time digital signal processing applications.

In the case of rough sets, the computational cost of the training phase is generally lower than for neural networks because the neural network is trained with consecutive examples, and the rough set algorithm simultaneously processes the whole collection of examples. Moreover, the back-propagation algorithm is iterative, while the rough set algorithm scans the database to derive rules based on combinations of reduced attributes. The performance of fully trained algorithms based on rough sets are comparable to neural networks and are generally faster than in the case of fuzzy logic. Generally, each of the investigated intelligent decision systems proved to be applicable to the solving of some vital problems in the domain of digital processing of audio signals.

Acknowledgments The presented research was sponsored by the State Committee for Scientific Research, Warsaw, Poland, partially within the framework of Grant No. 8 S 503 021 06 (1995) and of Grant No. 8 T11D 021 12 (1997). I am indebted to Mr. Rafal Krolikowski and to Dr. Andrzej Kaczmarek for their help in the software preparation.

References

1. Czyzewski, A., Kaczmarek, A.: Multilayer knowledge base system for speaker-independent recognition of isolated words. In: W. Ziarko (ed.): Rough Sets, Fuzzy Sets and Knowledge Discovery (RSKD'93). Workshops in Computing, Springer-Verlag & British Computer Society, London, Berlin (1994) 387–394
2. Bon, K. Sy, Horowitz, M.: A statistical causal model for the assessment of dysarthric speech and the utility of computer-based speech recognition. In: IEEE Trans. on Biomed. Eng. **40/12** (1993)
3. Zhao, Z.: A rough set approach to speech recognition. The Master Thesis guided by W. Ziarko, Dept. of Computer Science, Regina University, Regina, Saskatchewan (1992)
4. McAulay, R.J., Quatieri, T.F.: Speech analysis synthesis based on a sinusoidal representation. In: IEEE Trans. Acoust., Speech, Signal Processing **34** (1986)
5. Czyzewski, A.: Some methods for detection and interpolation of impulsive distortions in old audio recordings. In: IEEE ASSP Workshop on Application of Signal Processing to Audio and Acoustics, New York, USA (1995)
6. Czyzewski, A., Królikowski, R.: Simultaneous noise reduction and data compression in old audio recordings. In: 101st Audio Engineering Society Convention **4337**, Los Angeles, November (1996)
7. Czyzewski, A., Kaczmarek, A.: Speech recognition based on rough sets and neural networks. In: T.Y. Lin, A.M. Wildberger (eds.): Soft Computing: Rough Sets, Fuzzy Logic, Neural Networks, Uncertainty Management, Knowledge Discovery, Simulation Councils, Inc., San Diego, CA (1995) 97–100
8. Czyzewski, A.: Speaker–independent recognition of digits - experiments with neural networks, fuzzy logic and rough sets. In: Journal of Intelligent Automation and Soft Computing (Autosoft) **2/2** (1996) 133–146
9. Kostek, B.: Rough set and fuzzy set methods applied to acoustic analyses. In: Journal of Intelligent Automation and Soft Computing (Autosoft) **2/2** (1996) 147-160
10. Czyzewski, A.: Mining knowledge in noisy audio data. In: E. Simoudis, J. Han, and U. Fayyad (eds.), Second International Conference on Knowledge Discovery and Data Mining, Proceedings (KDD'96), August 2–4, Portland, Oregon, USA, AAAI Press, Menlo Park (1996) 220-225
11. Czyzewski, A., Krolikowski, R.: New methods of intelligent filtration and coding of audio. In: 102nd Audio Engineering Society Convention **4482**, Munich, Germany (1997)
12. Czyzewski, A., Kostek, B.: Rough set–based filtration of sound applicable to hearing prostheses. In: S. Tsumoto, S. Kobayashi, T. Yokomori, H. Tanaka, and A. Nakamura (eds.): Proceedings of the Fourth International Workshop on Rough Sets, Fuzzy Sets, and Machine Discovery (RSFD'96), The University of Tokyo, November 6–8 (1996) 168–175

13. Pena, A.S.: A theoretical approach to a generalized auditory model for audio coding and objective perceptual assessment. In: 96th AES Convention **3802**, Amsterdam (1994)
14. Czyzewski, A.: Artificial intelligence–based processing of old audio recordings. In: 97th Audio Engineering Society Convention **3885**, San Francisco (1994)
15. Nguyen, H.S., Nguyen, S.H.: Discretization of real value attributes for control problems. In: Proceedings of the Fourth European Congress on Intelligent Techniques and Soft Computing (EUFIT'96), September 2–5, Aachen, Germany, Verlag Mainz, Aachen (1996) 188–191
16. McAulay, R.J., Quatieri, T.F.: Speech analysis synthesis based on a sinusoidal representation. In: IEEE Trans. Acoust., Speech, Signal Processing **34** (1986)
17. Czyzewski, A.: New learning algorithms for the processing of old audio recordings. In: 99th Audio Engineering Society Convention 4078, New York (1995)
18. Czyzewski, A., Krolikowski, R., Application of intelligent decision systems to the perceptual noise reduction of audio signals. In: Proceedings of the Fifth European Congress on Intelligent Techniques and Soft Computing (EUFIT'97), September 8–11, Aachen, Germany, Verlag Mainz, Aachen (1997) 188-192

Chapter 9

A Rough Set Approach to Information Retrieval

Kaname Funakoshi, Tu Bao Ho

Japan Advanced Institute of Science and Technology
Tatsunokuchi, Ishikawa, 923-12 JAPAN

Abstract. In this paper we introduce another approach to information retrieval based on rough set theory, but instead of equivalence relations we adopt tolerance relations. We define a tolerance space by employing the co-occurrence of terms in the collection of documents and an algorithm for matching the user query. An illustrative example is provided that shows the application potential of the approach.

Keywords: intelligent information retrieval, tolerance relation.

1 Introduction

Conventional information retrieval (IR) systems do exact match of documents involving the same elements to the user query as most of them use the Boolean operations. Boolean operations are simple but they do not always provide good responses to the user's interest [Fr1]. There have been attempts to improve information retrieval quality by doing inexact match with different techniques (e.g., probabilistic, vector space, clustering, intelligent retrieval). Intelligent matching strategies for information retrieval often use concept analysis requiring semantic calculations [Ka1], [Ch1].

Rough set theory, a mathematical tool to deal with vagueness and uncertainty introduced by Pawlak in early 1980s [Pa1], has been successful in many applications. In this theory each subset of a universe is approximated by a pair of ordinary sets called *lower* and *upper approximations*, determined by *equivalence relations* in the universe. The idea of using rough sets in information retrieval has been addressed by several researchers, e.g., Raghavan and Sharma [RS1], Srinivasan [Sr1], [Sr2]. However, the requirement of reflexive, symmetric and transitive properties in equivalence relations, which is suitable in many application domains, seems too strict in the fields of natural language processing and information retrieval where the transitive property is not always satisfied. Several authors, e.g., Skowron and Stepaniuk [SS1], Yao and his collaborators [Ya1], have recently generalized models of rough sets by using *tolerance relations* that are suitable to domains in which the transitive property does not hold.

In this paper we present an approach to information retrieval based on the rough set theory but we adopt tolerance relations instead of equivalence relations. The core of this work is a way of determinating a tolerance relation and a matching algorithm based on the rough tolerance inclusions. The model, hereafter called *tolerance rough set model*, has been implemented and tested as a system on workstations and the World Wide Web. We present a case-study with the database of articles in Journal of the Japanese Society for Artificial Intelligence.

2 Preliminaries

2.1 Information Retrieval Systems

Information retrieval systems can be formulated as a quadruple

$$\mathcal{S} = (\mathcal{T}, \mathcal{D}, \mathcal{Q}, \alpha) \tag{1}$$

where $\mathcal{T} = \{t_1, t_2, \ldots, t_M\}$ is a set of index *terms* (e.g., keywords); $\mathcal{D} = \{d_1, d_2, \ldots, d_N\}$ is a set of *documents* each $d_j \subseteq \mathcal{T}$; $\mathcal{Q} = \{Q_1, Q_2, \ldots, Q_P\}$ is a set of queries each $Q_k \subseteq \mathcal{T}$; and $\alpha : \mathcal{Q} \times \mathcal{D} \rightarrow \Re^+$ is a ranking function that evaluates the relevance between a query and a document. In a general form a document d_j can be denoted as a set of index term-weight pairs

$$d_j = (t_{j_1}, w_{j_1}; t_{j_2}, w_{j_2}; \ldots; t_{j_n}, w_{j_n}) \tag{2}$$

where $t_{j_r} \in \mathcal{T}$ and $w_{j_r} \in [0,1]$, $r = 1, \ldots, n$, reflect the relative importance of terms t_{j_r} in d_j. A query $Q \in \mathcal{Q}$ can also be denoted as a set of index term-weight pairs

$$Q = (t_{q_1}, w_{q_1}; t_{q_2}, w_{q_2}; \ldots; t_{q_m}, w_{q_m}) \tag{3}$$

where $t_{q_s} \in \mathcal{T}$ and $w_{q_s} \in [0,1], s = 1, \ldots, m$. The information retrieval task is to yield a set $A = \{d_{a_1}, d_{a_2}, \ldots, d_{a_n}\} \subseteq \mathcal{D}$ to the query Q with a ranking order of $\alpha(Q, d_{a_i})$.

Most information retrieval systems use Boolean operations for searching large document collections. While Boolean operations for information retrieval systems [Wa1] have been criticized, improving their retrieval effectiveness has been difficult [Fr1]. Intelligent matching strategies for information retrieval often uses concept analysis requiring semantic calculations at different levels [Ka1].

2.2 Tolerance Spaces

Among the three properties of an equivalence relation R in a universe U of objects used in rough set theory (reflexive: xRx; symmetric: $xRy \rightarrow yRx$; transitive: $xRy \wedge yRz \rightarrow xRz$), the transitive property does not hold in certain application domains, in particular natural language processing and information retrieval. We take an illustration from the Roget's thesaurus where each word

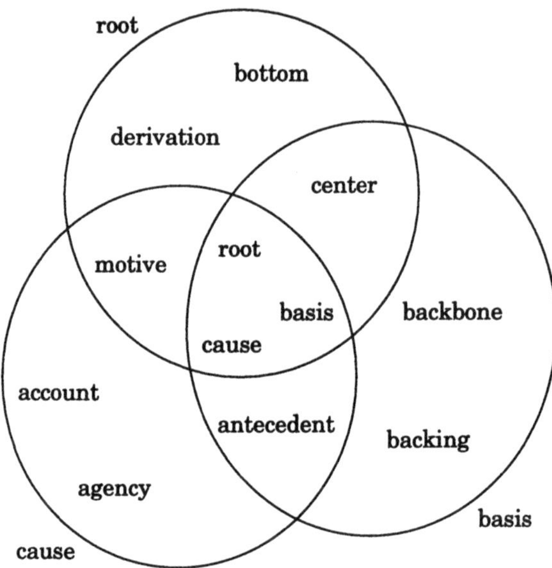

Fig. 1. Overlapping classes of terms *root, cause* and *basis*

is associated with a class of related words. These classes are not disjoint (equivalence classes) but overlapping, as those for three words *root, cause* and *basis* illustrated in Figure 1.

Generalized approximation spaces using tolerance relations which are only reflexive and symmetric have been investigated in [Ni1], [SS1], [Ya1]. These generalized spaces are called *tolerance spaces.* In [SS1], a tolerance space is a system expressed by a quadruple $\mathcal{R} = (U, I, \nu, P)$, where U is a non-empty set of objects, $I : U \to \mathcal{P}(U)$ is an uncertainty function, $\nu : \mathcal{P}(U) \times \mathcal{P}(U) \to [0,1]$ is a vague inclusion and $P : I(U) \to \{0,1\}$ is a structurality function.

The uncertainty function I on U is any function satisfying the condition $x \in I(x)$ and $y \in I(x)$ iff $x \in I(y)$ for any $x, y \in U$. This function corresponds to a relation $\mathcal{I} \subseteq U \times U$ understood as $x\mathcal{I}y$ iff $y \in I(x)$. $\mathcal{I}$ is a tolerance relation because it satisfies the properties of reflexivity and symmetry.

The vague inclusion $\nu : \mathcal{P}(U) \times \mathcal{P}(U) \to [0,1]$ defines the value of inclusion between two subsets $X, Y \subseteq U$, according to the vagueness β $(0 \leq \beta < 0.5)$. If $t = |X \cap Y|/|X|$, the value of vague inclusion $\nu_\beta(X,Y)$ can be expressed as

$$\nu_\beta(X,Y) = \begin{cases} 0, & \text{if } 0 \leq t \leq \beta \\ f(t), & \text{if } \beta \leq t \leq 1-\beta \\ 1, & \text{if } 1-\beta \leq t \leq 1 \end{cases} \tag{4}$$

where $f(t)$ is any monotonous function in $\beta \leq t \leq 1 - \beta$.

Finally, $P : I(U) \to \{0,1\}$ classifies $I(x)$ for each $x \in U$ into two classes – structural subsets $(P(I(x)) = 1)$ and non-structural subsets $(P(I(x)) = 0)$. We use only structural tolerance subsets for lower and upper approximations.

In the tolerance space $\mathcal{R}$, the lower approximation $\mathcal{L}_{\mathcal{R}}$ and the upper approximation $\mathcal{U}_{\mathcal{R}}$ for any $X \subseteq U$ are defined as

$$\mathcal{L}_{\mathcal{R}}(X) = \{x \in U | P(I(x)) = 1 \ \ \& \ \ \nu_{\beta}(I(x), X) = 1\} \tag{5}$$

$$\mathcal{U}_{\mathcal{R}}(X) = \{x \in U | P(I(x)) = 1 \ \ \& \ \ \nu_{\beta}(I(x), X) > 0\} \tag{6}$$

The basic problem of using tolerance spaces in any application is how to determine suitably I, ν and P.

3 A Rough Tolerance Relation Based Method

3.1 Determination of the Rough Tolerance Space

The essence of the method is how to determine suitably I, ν and P for information retrieval problem. First of all, to define a tolerance space $\mathcal{R}$, we choose the universe U as the set $\mathcal{T}$ of all terms in the database $\mathcal{D}$.

$$U = \{t_1, t_2, \ldots, t_M\} = \mathcal{T} \tag{7}$$

The key notion used in the method is the co-occurrence of terms in all documents from the database. Denote by $c(t_i, t_j)$ the frequency of co-occurrence between two terms t_i and t_j. We define the uncertainty function I depending on a threshold θ as follows

$$I_{\theta}(t_i) = \{t_j | c(t_i, t_j) \geq \theta\} \cup \{t_i\} \tag{8}$$

The relation $c(t_i, t_j)$ defined above is both reflexive and symmetric, so that the function I satisfies the requirements of uncertainty function of $\mathcal{R}$. This function corresponds to a tolerance relation $\mathcal{I} \subseteq U \times U$ that $t_i \mathcal{I} t_j$ iff $t_j \in I_{\theta}(t_i)$. We say that $I_{\theta}(t_i)$ is the tolerance class of term t_i. We also denote by $c(t_i, t_i)$ the number of occurrences for term t_i in the database $\mathcal{D}$. The vague inclusion function ν is defined as

$$\nu(X, Y) \ \ = \ \ |X \cap Y| / |X| \tag{9}$$

The membership function for $t_i \in \mathcal{T}, X \subseteq U$ is defined by

$$\mu(t_i, X) = \nu(I_{\theta}(t_i), X) \ \ = \ \ |I_{\theta}(t_i) \cap X| / |I_{\theta}(t_i)| \tag{10}$$

Suppose that the universe $\mathcal{T}$ is closed during the retrieval process, i.e., the query Q consists of only keywords from $\mathcal{T}$. Under this assumption we can consider all tolerance classes of index terms as structural subsets. i.e., $P(I_{\theta}(t_i)) = 1$ for any $t_i \in \mathcal{T}$.

In the tolerance space $\mathcal{R} = (U, I, \nu, P)$ with the above definitions, the lower tolerance approximation $\mathcal{L}_{\mathcal{R}}$ and the upper tolerance approximation $\mathcal{U}_{\mathcal{R}}$ for any subset $X \subseteq \mathcal{T}$ are defined by

$$\mathcal{L}_{\mathcal{R}}(X) = \{t_i \in \mathcal{T} \ | \ P(I_{\theta}(t_i)) = 1 \ \ \& \ \ \nu(I_{\theta}(t_i), X) = 1\} \tag{11}$$

$$\mathcal{U}_{\mathcal{R}}(X) = \{t_i \in \mathcal{T} \ | \ P(I_{\theta}(t_i)) = 1 \ \ \& \ \ \nu(I_{\theta}(t_i), X) > 0\} \tag{12}$$

3.2 Rough Tolerance Matching of Documents

The matching between the user query and documents can be carried out by checking different levels of rough inclusion (involving equality and overlap) between their tolerance lower and upper approximations. The rough inclusions between two sets defined in [Pa1] for equivalence relations are extended to tolerance relations. There are 12 levels of inclusions between two sets that can appear while matching the set of terms in the user query Q to the set of terms in each documents d_j.

(1) Definability: This level is certainly the best match but occurs rarely

$$Q = d_j \qquad [1\text{-}1]$$

(2) Rough equalities: For any pair of sets X, Y, if $\mathcal{L}_\mathcal{R}(X) = \mathcal{L}_\mathcal{R}(Y)$ then X and Y are called ***roughly lower equal*** and denoted by $X \underset{\sim}{-} Y$. Similarly, if $\mathcal{U}_\mathcal{R}(X) = \mathcal{U}_\mathcal{R}(Y)$ then X and Y are called ***roughly upper equal*** and denoted by $X \simeq Y$. When X and Y are both roughly lower and upper equal, they are called ***roughly equal*** and denoted by $X \approx Y$. While matching Q and d_j, the following cases may occur

$$Q \approx d_j, \quad Q \underset{\sim}{-} d_j, \quad Q \simeq d_j \qquad [2\text{-}1, 2\text{-}2, 2\text{-}3]$$

(3) Rough inclusions: For any pair of sets X, Y, if $\mathcal{L}_\mathcal{R}(X) \subseteq \mathcal{L}_\mathcal{R}(Y)$ then X is called ***roughly lower included*** in Y. If $\mathcal{U}_\mathcal{R}(X) \subseteq \mathcal{U}_\mathcal{R}(Y)$ then X is called ***roughly upper included*** in Y. If X is both roughly lower and upper included in Y then X is called ***roughly included*** in Y. While matching Q to d_j the following cases may occur

$$Q \underset{\sim}{\tilde{\subset}} d_j, \quad Q \underset{\sim}{\subset} d_j, \quad Q \tilde{\subset} d_j \qquad [3\text{-}1, 3\text{-}2, 3\text{-}3]$$

(4) Rough inclusions (opposite of 3): Other situations may occur as in *(3)* but the role of Q and d_j are inversed

$$d_j \underset{\sim}{\tilde{\subset}} Q, \quad d_j \underset{\sim}{\subset} Q, \quad d_j \tilde{\subset} Q \qquad [4\text{-}1, 4\text{-}2, 4\text{-}3]$$

(5) Rough overlaps: Finally, it may happen that the tolerance lower and upper approximations of Q and d_j are overlapping

$$\mathcal{L}_\mathcal{R}(Q) \cap \mathcal{L}_\mathcal{R}(d_j) \neq \emptyset, \quad \mathcal{U}_\mathcal{R}(Q) \cap \mathcal{U}_\mathcal{R}(d_j) \neq \emptyset \qquad [5\text{-}1, 5\text{-}2]$$

Denote by A_{11}, A_{21},..., A_{52} the sets of all documents satisfying conditions [1-1], [2-1],..., [5-2], respectively, when matching them against Q. It means that

$$A_{kl} = \{d_j \in \mathcal{D} \mid d_j \text{ satisfies condition } [k\text{-}l] \text{ in matching } Q\} \qquad (13)$$

The relevance to Q of documents in sets A_{11}, A_{21}, A_{22}, A_{23}, A_{31}, A_{32}, A_{33}, A_{41}, A_{42}, A_{43}, A_{51}, A_{52} is decreasing in this order of these sets. We call this order ***relevance rank***. This rank shows that A_{11} is the set of the most relevant documents to Q, and so on.

Essentially, our answer to the user query Q is a sequence of ordered sets in $\mathcal{A}$ obtained in matching all document $d_j \in \mathcal{D}$ with Q. The corresponding matching algorithm is formulated in Table 1.

```
Algorithm Matching(Q, D)
  begin
    A11 ← ∅, A21 ← ∅, ..., A52 ← ∅
    if Q ≠ ∅ then
    begin
      for j = 1 to |D| do
      begin
        if dj ≠ ∅ then
        begin
          if Q = dj then A11 ← A11 ∪ {dj}                              [1-1]

          if L_R(Q) ≠ ∅ then
            if L_R(Q) = L_R(dj) then A22 ← A22 ∪ {dj}                  [2-2]
              if U_R(Q) = U_R(dj) then A21 ← A21 ∪ {dj}                [2-1]
            if U_R(Q) = U_R(dj) then A23 ← A23 ∪ {dj}                  [2-3]

            if L_R(Q) ⊆ L_R(dj) then A32 ← A32 ∪ {dj}                  [3-2]
              if U_R(Q) ⊆ U_R(dj) then A31 ← A31 ∪ {dj}                [3-1]
            if U_R(Q) ⊆ U_R(dj) then A33 ← A33 ∪ {dj}                  [3-3]

          if L_R(dj) ≠ ∅ then
            if L_R(dj) ⊆ L_R(Q) then A42 ← A42 ∪ {dj}                  [4-2]
              if U_R(dj) ⊆ U_R(Q) then A41 ← A41 ∪ {dj}                [4-1]
            if U_R(dj) ⊆ U_R(Q) then A43 ← A43 ∪ {dj}                  [4-3]

          if L_R(Q) ∫ L_R(dj) ≠ ∅ then A51 ← A51 ∪ {dj}                [5-1]
          if U_R(Q) ∫ U_R(dj) ≠ ∅ then A52 ← A52 ∪ {dj}                [5-2]
        end
      end
    end
  end
```

Table 1. Rough tolerance inclusion matching algorithm

3.3 Secondary Ranking on Rough Overlaps

The matching algorithm in subsection 3.2 provides a discrete ranking of answer documents like fuzzy set models which differs from other ranking methods [Bo1]. This discrete ranking has a disadvantage in the levels of rough overlaps [5-1] and [5-2] because it sometimes yields documents with different degrees of relevance in A_{51} and A_{52}. To overcome this limitation we construct a secondary ranking of documents in these two levels by dividing them into subgroups each of which contains documents with the same degree of relevance in rough tolerance model.

The secondary ranking is obtained by applying the vague inclusion function ν defined in (9). In fact, each document d_j in A_{51} or A_{52} is assigned to one of

$|Q|+1$ subgroups depending on the value of

$$\nu(Q,d_j) = \frac{|Q \cap d_j|}{|Q|} \tag{14}$$

We consider that documents in each of these $|Q|+1$ subgroups have the same degree of relevance as they have the same number of common keywords with the query Q.

4 Implementation and a Case Study

4.1 Implementation on the Web

This method has been implemented in a system in the X Window on workstations. Figure 1 shows the overview of the system.

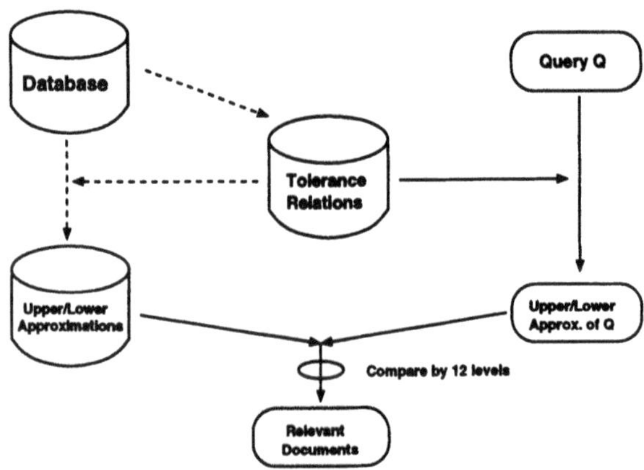

Fig. 2. Overview of the system components

The first phase determines tolerance spaces of documents. After creating and/or updating the database $(\mathcal{D}, \mathcal{T})$, the system calculates co-occurrencies of all terms from the database regarding different values of θ (from 1 to 5), and determines the tolerance classes of terms. Then the system determines the upper and lower approximations for each term. In the second phase of retrieval, when a query is encountered, the system calculates its upper and lower approximations based on information obtained in the first phase, and the system determines the twelve levels of matching by using the rough tolerance inclusions as described in the algorithm and yields a answer to the user query.

4.2 A Case Study

We illustrate the method by a case-study of retrieving relevant documents in the database of the Journal of Japanese Society for Artificial Intelligence (JSAI) after its first ten years of publication (1986-1995) for the user query. This database consists of 802 documents as partially described in Table 2 and there are in total 1823 keywords (number of tolerance classes).

Document	*List of Keywords*
d_1	object-oriented language, AI programming language, knowledge representation, non-determinism
d_2	knowledge-based system, object model, machine design
d_3	knowledge acquisition, learning, trouble-shooting system, expert system, knowledge extraction rules
d_4	knowledge representation, line drawing interpretation, production system, meta level, certainty factor
$\vdots$	$\vdots$
d_{802}	computer vision, multiagent system, intelligent agent, integration scheme

Table 2. Papers from Journal of Japanese Society for Artificial Intelligence

Consider an example where the query $Q = \{t_{19}, t_{234}, t_{235}\}$. With $\theta = 2$, the system outputs $\mathcal{U}_{\mathcal{R}}(Q) = \{t_{11}, t_{19}, t_{160}, t_{203}, t_{234}, t_{235}\}$ and $\mathcal{L}_{\mathcal{R}}(Q) = \{t_{234}, t_{235}\}$. It gives the answer at three levels $A_{31} = \{d_{81}\}, A_{51} = \{d_{363}, d_{798}\}$ and A_{52} with 105 documents. For the same query, using the Boolean AND operation we obtain only one document $A = \{d_{81}\}$, and using the Boolean OR operation we obtain 12 documents in the same level $A = \{d_7, d_{14}, d_{81}, d_{85}, d_{91}, d_{114}, d_{211}, d_{361}, d_{363}, d_{420}, d_{534}, d_{798}\}$.

Cardinal of $I(x)$	$\theta = 1$	$\theta = 2$	$\theta = 3$	$\theta = 4$
1	96	1645	1763	1800
2	85	114	37	11
3	176	28	9	1
4	391	11	3	1
5	432	3	1	0
Average	6.296	1.667	1.038	1.009
σ	6.569	0.748	0.250	0.115

Table 3. Distribution of tolerance class size for different values of θ

Table 3 shows the distribution of tolerance class size as θ varies from 1 to 4. Columns from 2 to 5 contain statistics regarding values of θ, and each row indicates the numbers of tolerance classes with the corresponding cardinal, respectively. For example, when $\theta = 1$, there are 96 tolerance classes with cardinal 1, and 1645 tolerance classes with cardinal 2, etc. The final two rows indicate the average and the dispersion of tolerance class size, respectively.

The system is being implemented on the World Wide Web. Its testing version can be seen at the address http://trumpet.jaist.ac.jp:8000/ir/test.html. The system is easy to use, just by entering the query (currently by the index of key words) and obtaining the suggested papers as shown in Figure 3. The user can also change values of the threshold θ to find different answers according to his or her interest (the smaller value of θ the bigger set of retrieved papers).

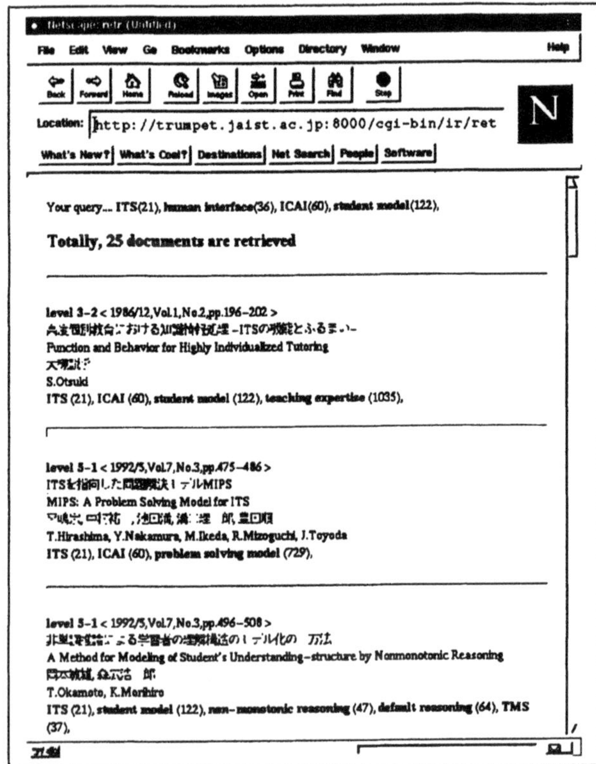

Fig. 3. Information Retrieval by Tolerance Relations on the World Wide Web

4.3 Evaluation

Generally, it is difficult to evaluate the retrieval effectiveness since the relevance judgments are subjective and unreliable. Two common measures of *precision* (P) and *recall* (R) are defined as follows

$$P = \frac{|REL \cap A|}{|A|} \qquad R = \frac{|REL \cap A|}{|REL|} \tag{15}$$

where $REL \subseteq \mathcal{D}$ is a set of all relevant document in the database to a query, and $A \subseteq \mathcal{D}$ is union of documents retrieved at the level being considered and documents at all levels ranked before this level regarding the relevance rank. For example, to calculate the precision or recall of the level [2-3] we have $A = A_{11} \cup A_{21} \cup A_{22} \cup A_{23}$. In a large scale database one does not know all elements of $REL(Q)$ but in this testing system for JSAI documents we choose manually the relevant documents for a number of twenty queries. A more careful evaluation of the rough tolerance model is being carried out and reported in [HF1]. We report here a preliminary comparative evaluation.

Method		P	R
Boolean	AND	1.000	0.062
	OR	0.413	0.814
Rough	layer 2	1.000	0.010
(average)	layer 3	0.797	0.131
	layer 4	0.707	0.168
	layer 5 (positive)	0.425	0.822
	layer 5 (zero)	0.057	0.876

Table 4. Retrieval results by Boolean operations and rough tolerance method

Table 4 gives an evaluation of precision and recall for Boolean retrieval and the rough tolerance model. In this table, the "layer" stands for a group of retrieval levels, i.e., the "layer 2" stands for the levels [2-1], [2-2] and [2-3], and so on. The precision obtained by AND operation is the same as that of rough equalities (layer 2). The precision and recall obtained by OR operation is nearly equal to that of rough overlaps (layer 5). Rough tolerance model's precision and recall in layers 3 and 4 lie in between those of AND and OR operations. It shows that the rough tolerance model can give answers better than Boolean operations. One main advantage of rough tolerance model in comparison with Boolean model is that it is able to yield documents with keywords which do not appear in the query but relate semantically to keywords in the query.

5 Conclusion

We have presented a rough set approach to information retrieval in which instead of using equivalence relations in conventional rough set theory we employ tolerance relations. We have determined a suitable tolerance space for the information retrieval, and a matching algorithm that is essentially based on rough tolerance inclusions.

We feel that the following works are worth to pursue: First, it is most important to carry out an evaluation of the method and its comparison with existing ones based on public document databases in the information retrieval community. Second, it is the question of an efficient matching when document databases are large. Third, as the rough tolerance model depends on some parameters, especially θ, it is expected to have an automatic adjustment of these parameter for obtaining reasonable sets of relevant documents. Fourth, as this model can be used only for documents with keywords, an associated technique for extracting keywords from documents when necessary will increase the application potential of the model and system.

Acknowledgements

This work is supported partially by grants from Kokusai Electric Co., Ltd. The authors would like to thank Trong Dung Nguyen for helpful discussions.

References

[BC1] Belkin, N.J., Croft, W.B.: Retrieval techniques. Annual Review of Information Science and Technology **22** (1989) 109–145

[Bo1] Bookstein, A.: Probability and fuzzy–set applications to information retrieval. Annual review of information science and technology **20** (1985) 117–151

[Ch1] Chen, H.: Machine learning for information retrieval: Neural Networks, Symbolic Learning, and Genetic Algorithms. Journal of the American Society for Information Science **46/3** (1995) 194–216

[Fr1] Frakes, W.B.: Introduction to information storage and retrieval systems. In: W.B. Frakes and R. Baeza-Yates (eds.): Information Retrieval: Data Structures & Algorithms, Prentice Hall (1992) 1–27

[HF1] Ho, T.B., Funakoshi, K.: Information retrieval using rough sets. Journal of Japanese Society for Artificial Intelligenc (submitted)

[Fa1] Fox, E., et al.: Extended boolean models. In: W.B. Frakes, R. Baeza-Yates (eds.), Information Retrieval: Data Structures & Algorithms, Prentice Hall, (1992) 393–418

[Ha1] Harman, D. et al.: Inverted files. In: W.B. Frakes, R. Baeza-Yates (eds.), Information Retrieval: Data Structures & Algorithms, Prentice Hall (1992) 28–43

[Ka1] Kantor, P.B.: Information retrieval techniques. Annual Review of Information Science and Technology **29** (1994) 53–90

[Ni1] Nieminen, J.: Rough tolerance equality and tolerance black boxes. Fundamenta informaticae **11** (1988) 289–296

[Pa1] In Pawlak, Z.: Rough sets: Theoretical aspects of reasoning about data. Kluwer Academic Publishers, Dordrecht (1991)

[RS1] Raghavan, V.V., Sharma, R.S.: A framework and a prototype for intelligent organisation of information. The Canadian Journal of Information Science **11** (1986) 88–101

[SS1] Skowron, A., Stepaniuk, J.: Generalized approximation spaces. In: T.Y. Lin (ed.): Proceedings of the Third International Workshop on Rough Sets and Soft Computing (RSSC'94), San Jose State University, San Jose, California, USA, November 10–12 (1994) 156–163

[Sr1] Srinivasan, P.: Intelligent information retrieval using rough set approximations. Information Processing & Management **25/4** (1989) 347–361

[Sr2] Srinivasan, P.: The importance of rough approximations for information retrieval. International Journal of Man-Machine Studies **34/5** (1991) 657–671

[Wal] Wartik, S.: Boolean operations. In: Frakes, W.B. and Baeza-Yates, R. (eds.),: Information Retrieval: Data Structures & Algorithms, Prentice Hall (1992) 264–292

[Yal] Yao, Y.Y., Li, X., Lin, T.Y. and Liu, Q.: Representation and classification of rough set models. In: T.Y. Lin (ed.): Proceedings of the Third International Workshop on Rough Sets and Soft Computing (RSSC'94), San Jose State University, San Jose, California, USA, November 10–12 (1994) 630–637

Chapter 10

Extraction Method Based on Rough Set Theory of Rule-Type Knowledge from Diagnostic Cases of Slope-Failure Danger Levels

Hitoshi Furuta[1] , *Michiyuki Hirokane*[1] *and Yukihiro Mikumo*[2]

[1] Kansai University, Osaka 569-11, Japan
[2] NEWJEC Inc, Osaka 542, Japan

1 Introduction

The failure of slopes caused by heavy rains in the typhoon and *baiu* seasons has taken tolls of lives and done damages all over country [1] [2]. To prevent such disaster, it is necessary to take appropriate measures against slope failure at appropriate spots at appropriate times. Preventive works of such structures as are capable of preventing slope failure have to be chosen, slopes surveyed thoroughly, geology, soil properties, costs of civil engineering works, scenery, and so on taken into account [3]. Slopes requiring such works and their danger levels of failure should be evaluated synthetically, and appropriate spots and times of such works should be determined. Accordingly, it is important to estimate the danger levels of slope failure with accuracy of a certain degree, which also helps to minimize the damages by slope failure.

Slope failure occurs under complex action of various factors, and a number of methods of diagnosing danger levels of slope failure have been proposed; i.e., a method in which a few of the various factors are highlighted [4], a statistical method [5], a dynamic method [6], and so on. However, in municipal disaster prevention programs, diagnoses of the danger levels of slope failure have been performed based on experiential knowledge of experts, without using any such methods. It can be mentioned as the background of the prevalence of diagnoses based on experiential knowledge of experts that incorporating experts' experiential knowledge in the diagnostic methods proposed to date is difficult and also no established methods are available.

Besides, diagnostic methods of such danger levels have been proposed by agencies and institutions [7] [8] [9]. However, experiential knowledge of experts is required to use any such method, and hence not every civil engineer can use such methods easily.

Under the circumstances, researches into the application of the expert system, or ES, have been performed in order to establish diagnostic methods on the basis of experiential knowledge of experts [10] [11]. In these researches, diagnostic systems have been constructed, vagueness, or fuzziness, in experiential knowledge of experts taken into the systems by using the fuzzy theory. However, in applying the fuzzy theory to diagnoses, it is necessary to solve the very difficult and important matter of which factors the theory should be applied to. If the theory is applied to all factors of slope failure and they are included in a diagnostic system, the system may turn out to be of low reliability in diagnosing danger levels [12].

The present paper explains the basic concept of the rough set theory [13] [14], which has recently drawn attention as a technique to handle experiential knowledge contained in observation results by experts, and describes a method of applying the rough set theory to the acquirement of such experiential knowledge. For this purpose, the authors applied the rough set theory to diagnostic cases, by experts, of the danger levels, or decision attributes, of slopes alongside roads and removed conditional attributes and classes of each conditional attribute insignificant in the diagnoses to extract minimal decision algorithm which was still capable of making diagnoses equal to those by experts. The conditional attributes retained in the minimal decision algorithm can be considered the same as the conditional attributes to which the experts attached particular importance in their diagnoses. The significance of the conditional attributes retained in the minimal decision algorithm is discussed, and a method of deriving rules from the algorithm for the construction of ES's is proposed.

2 Rough Set Theory

The concept of rough set theory was first introduced by Zdzislaw Pawlak in 1982 [15], and one of its essential merits is its direct relation to classification problems [16]. When one is to make judgement based on several pieces of information obtained by observation, one tries to classify objects with respect to decision attribute in accordance with various conditional attributes contained in the information. If objects are classified into one and the same class, one can not distinguish them and treats them as identical practically. For instance, when one is supposed to classify the shapes of slopes and if a single conditional attribute of height is given, one can not distinguish such slopes as have one and the same height of 5m, and treats the slopes as identical practically. In the same way, one treats slopes 7m high as identical practically. This indistinguishability is the most fundamental concept of the rough set theory. On the other hand, knowledge is generally used to distinguish and classify such things, and one's knowledge becomes more refined as one gains experience. Namely, to understand and judge things, it is necessary to distinguish them exactly. As described below, when one is given enough additional distinctive conditional attributes, they enable one to distinguish things which otherwise can not be distinguished.

Let $U = \{X_1, X_2, X_3, X_4, X_5\}$ and $\{height, gradient\}$ be a set of slopes and a set of conditional attributes, respectively, and let A represent the latter. Then, let us consider the mapping below:

$$f : U \times A \quad \longrightarrow \quad V \tag{1}$$

where V is a set of values of conditional attributes. For example, if the conditional attribute of "*height*" of the slope X_1 has value of 5m, then this fact can be expressed as follows:

$$f\{X_1, height\} = 5m \tag{2}$$

Then, if the following definitions are made for the relations R_1 and R_2

$$(x, y) \in R_1 \Longleftrightarrow f(x, height) = f(y, height) \tag{3}$$

$$(x, y) \in R_2 \Longleftrightarrow f(x, gradient) = f(y, gradient) \tag{4}$$

the following conditions for any of x, y, and $z \in U$ hold:

$$Reflexive\ \ law : x \equiv x \tag{5}$$

$$Symmetric\ \ law : x \equiv y \quad \Longrightarrow \quad y \equiv x \tag{6}$$

$$Transitive\ \ law : x \equiv y,\ \ y \equiv z \quad \Longrightarrow \quad x \equiv z \tag{7}$$

Accordingly, R_1 and R_2 are equivalence relations on U. Here, the classification or partition of R_1, i.e., the set of equivalence classes of R_1 called the quotient set of U for R_1 (U/R_1) is

$$U/R_1 = \{\{X_1, X_2\}, \{X_3, X_4, X_5\}\} \tag{8}$$

In the same way, the set of equivalence classes of R_2 (U/R_2) is

$$U/R_2 = \{\{X_1, X_3\}, \{X_2, X_4, X_5\}\} \tag{9}$$

Namely, in the partition of the conditional attribute of "*height*," the equivalence class of the value of 5m is $\{X_1, X_2\}$, and X_1 and X_2 can not be distinguished from each other. In the same way, $\{X_3, X_4, X_5\}$ is the class of slopes 7m high. In the partition of the conditional attribute of "*gradient*," the equivalence class of the value 30 is $\{X_1, X_3\}$, and X_1 and X_3 can not be distinguished from each other. In the same way, $\{X_2, X_4, X_5\}$ is the class of slopes of gradient of 45.

Then, let us consider the intersection ($U/R_1 \cap U/R_2$) of the set of equivalence classes of R_1 and the set of equivalence classes of R_2, as indicated below. In other words, we distinguish the five slopes based on the basis of conditional attributes "*height*" and "*gradient*."

$$\{X_1, X_2\} \cap \{X_1, X_3\} = \{X_1\} \tag{10}$$

$$\{X_1, X_2\} \cap \{X_2, X_4, X_5\} = \{X_2\} \tag{11}$$

$$\{X_3, X_4, X_5\} \cap \{X_1, X_3\} = \{X_3\} \tag{12}$$

$$\{X_3, X_4, X_5\} \cap \{X_2, X_4, X_5\} = \{X_4, X_5\} \tag{13}$$

The expression (10) indicates that X_1 is a slope 5m high and 30 slant; (11), that X_2 is a slope 5m high and 45 slant; (12), that X_3 is a slope 7m high and 30 slant. Thus, the three slopes could be distinguished by the set of conditional attibutes A. On the other hand, the expression (13) indicates that both the slopes, X_4 and X_5, are 7m high and 45 slant, and thus the two slopes can not be distinguished by the set of conditional attributes A. In this way, the slopes other than $\{X_4, X_5\}$ could be distinguished more particularly by increasing the number of distinctive conditional attributes. From this point of view, the concept of rough set theory is proposed as a practical method to deal with decision-making problems.

3 Diagnostic Cases by Experts

Used in the present study to extract experiential knowledge of experts were 32 diagnostic cases of slopes mainly of state alongside roads. These diagnoses of the danger levels were performed by experts in accordance with the diagnostic method prepared by Expressway Investigation Board [9]. Removing indistinctive conditional attributes in the diagnostic method, the authors put into Table 1 12 conditional attributes such as (1) failure spots and (2) signs of failure. Each conditional attribute is provided with classes. For example, the conditional attribute of (1) failure spots is provided with four classes: 1) large-scale failure spot, 2) many failure spots, 3) a few failure spots, and 4) none. Danger ranks, a, b, c and d, are assigned to the classes of each conditional attribute. The danger ranks of all the conditional attributes of each slope are quantified, its total score is calculated, and its global danger level, A, B or C, is determined. Table 2 shows the class Nos. of the conditional attributes and the global danger levels of the 32 slopes diagnosed by the experts. For instance, the No.1 slope is classified into the class 2) of the conditional attribute (1) and the class 1) of the conditional attribute (2), and its danger level is diagnosed as "A." In other words, this table shows the relation between the class Nos. of the conditional attributes of each slope and its danger level, or decision attribute, and such relations and such a table are called "decision rules" and "a decision table," respectively.

4 Extraction of Minimal Decision Algorithm

4.1 Subordination of Danger Levels to Conditional Attributes

First of all, it was necessary to check whether the danger levels were compatible with 12 conditional attributes in Table 2 which shows the summary of the diagnostic results by experts. The decision rules of all the slopes were examined to find non-deterministic rules; i.e., slopes which were classified into one and the same class under every conditional attributes but were assigned different danger levels. Non-deterministic rules were not found in Table 2, and hence the danger levels proved subordinative to the conditional attributes. If non-deterministic rules are found in such a decision table, it means that the number of conditional attributes in the decision table is not sufficient and new conditional attributes have to be added to the existing ones. In the process of extracting minimal decision algorithm, it is necessary for the time being to make trial and error to rectify non-deterministic rules, if any, and make a decision table free of contradictions.

On the other hand, the slopes 7 and 8 were governed by one and the same rule. This was also true of the slopes 28 and 29. In such a case, it suffices to remove one slope and consider only the other. Accordingly, the slopes 8 and 29 which are marked with "*" were removed from Table 2 to obtain a new decision table.

Table 1. Conditional attributes of slope-failure danger levels

Conditional attributes	Classification of individual situations	Danger ranks
(1) Failure spots	1) Large-scale failure spot	a
	2) Many failure spots	b
	3) A few failure spots	c
	4) None	d
(2) Signs of failure	1) Signs such as subsidence, crack and displacement	a
	2) None	b
(3) Unstable soil mass such as talus	1) Thick	a
	2) Thin	c
	3) None	d
(4) Rock heavily weathered or deteriorated	1) Heavy weathering and catchment topography	a
	2) Heavy weathering and deterioration	c
	3) No heavy weathering or deterioration	d
(5) Shuttered zone	1) Shuttered zone	b
	2) None	d
(6) Gradient of slope	1) Overhanging	a
	2) Over 35	b
	3) 25 – 35	c
	4) Below 25	d
(7) Gully	1) Gully	b
	2) None	d
(8) Valley-like depression on slope	1) Outlet of valley-like depression above the road	a
	2) Surface soil or weathered soil in the depression thicker than surroundings	b
	3) Valley-like depression	c
	4) No valley-like depression	d
(9) Topography of ground on top of slope	1) Concave (Catchment topography)	b
	2) Flat	c
	3) Convex	d
(10) Configuration of cross section of slope	1) Overhanging	a
	2) Flat part in the upper area of the slope	b
	3) Turning point of gradient upward or downward	c
	4) Other than the above	d
(11) Water logging	1) Large quantity of water logging	b
	2) Seepage of water logging	c
	3) None	d
(12) Cutting of slope for road construction	1) Cutting of thick unstable soil	b
	2) Cutting of bedrock heavily weathered	c
	3) Cutting of bedrock non-weathered	d

Table 2. Observation data for diagnosis of slope-failure danger levels

Slopes	Conditional attributes (1)	(2)	(3)	(4)	(5)	(6)	(7)	(8)	(9)	(10)	(11)	(12)	Danger levels
1	2	1	1	2	2	2	2	4	2	2	3	1	A
2	4	2	1	2	2	2	2	4	2	2	2	1	B
3	3	2	2	3	2	2	2	4	3	4	3	2	C
4	4	2	1	2	1	3	2	2	2	3	3	3	B
5	3	2	1	1	2	2	2	4	1	3	3	1	A
6	3	1	1	1	2	2	2	4	3	2	1	1	A
7	4	2	2	2	2	2	2	4	2	4	3	3	C
8	4	2	2	2	2	2	2	4	2	4	3	3	C *
9	3	1	1	2	2	4	2	3	1	4	3	3	B
10	3	1	1	3	2	4	2	3	1	4	3	3	B
11	4	2	1	3	2	4	2	4	2	3	3	3	C
12	4	2	1	3	2	4	2	3	1	3	3	3	B
13	4	2	1	3	2	2	2	4	2	3	1	1	B
14	3	2	2	3	2	2	1	4	1	4	2	3	B
15	4	2	1	3	2	4	1	4	2	4	3	3	C
16	4	2	1	3	2	2	2	4	3	4	1	1	B
17	4	1	1	3	2	4	2	3	1	3	2	3	B
18	3	2	1	3	2	2	1	4	2	3	3	1	B
19	4	2	1	3	2	2	2	4	2	3	3	1	C
20	4	2	1	3	2	3	2	3	1	3	3	3	B
21	3	1	1	3	2	2	2	4	2	3	3	3	B
22	4	2	2	3	2	2	2	4	3	3	3	3	C
23	4	2	2	3	2	3	1	4	1	3	3	3	C
24	4	1	1	2	2	4	2	3	1	4	3	1	B
25	4	2	2	1	1	2	2	4	1	4	1	1	A
26	4	2	2	2	2	2	1	3	1	4	1	1	B
27	4	1	2	3	2	2	2	4	3	4	3	3	C
28	2	1	1	1	1	2	2	4	2	4	3	1	A
29	2	1	1	1	1	2	2	4	2	4	3	1	A *
30	2	1	1	1	2	2	1	4	3	3	3	2	A
31	3	1	1	2	2	2	1	4	1	3	2	1	A
32	4	2	2	2	2	2	2	4	3	3	3	2	C

4.2 Reduction of Conditional Attributes

Next, it was necessary to find conditional attributes insignificant in the diagnoses. A number of conditional attributes were removed each time, and it was checked whether any contradiction occured or not in the decision table (Table 2 minus the slopes 8 and 29). Table 3 shows an example, where the conditional attributes (8) and (9) are removed, and the decision rules of the slopes 11 and 12 which are marked with "*" are contradictory to each other, which proves that the danger level of each of the slopes 11 and 12 is subordinative to one or both of the conditional attributes (8) and (9), and the two conditional attributes can not be removed simultaneously. The number of the combinations of the conditional

Table 3. Decision table after conditional attributes (8),(9) are removed

Slopes	Conditional attributes										Danger levels
	(1)	(2)	(3)	(4)	(5)	(6)	(7)	(10)	(11)	(12)	
1	2	1	1	2	2	2	2	2	3	1	A
2	4	2	1	2	2	2	2	2	2	1	B
3	3	2	2	3	2	2	2	4	3	2	C
4	4	2	1	2	1	3	2	3	3	3	B
5	3	2	1	1	2	2	2	3	3	1	A
6	3	1	1	1	2	2	2	2	1	1	A
7	4	2	2	2	2	2	2	4	3	3	C
9	3	1	1	2	2	4	2	4	3	3	B
10	3	1	1	3	2	4	2	4	3	3	B
11	4	2	1	3	2	4	2	3	3	3	C *
12	4	2	1	3	2	4	2	3	3	3	B *
13	4	2	1	3	2	2	2	3	1	1	B
14	3	2	2	3	2	2	1	4	2	3	B
15	4	2	1	3	2	4	1	4	3	3	C
16	4	2	1	3	2	2	2	4	1	1	B
17	4	1	1	3	2	4	2	3	2	3	B
18	3	2	1	3	2	2	1	3	3	1	B
19	4	2	1	3	2	2	2	3	3	1	C
20	4	2	1	3	2	3	2	3	3	3	B
21	3	1	1	3	2	2	2	3	3	3	B
22	4	2	2	3	2	2	2	3	3	3	C
23	4	2	2	3	2	3	1	3	3	3	C
24	4	1	1	2	2	4	2	4	3	1	B
25	4	2	2	1	1	2	2	4	1	1	A
26	4	2	2	2	2	2	1	4	1	1	B
27	4	1	2	3	2	2	2	4	3	3	C
28	2	1	1	1	1	2	2	4	3	1	A
30	2	1	1	1	2	2	1	3	3	2	A
31	3	1	1	2	2	2	1	3	2	1	A
32	4	2	2	2	2	2	2	3	3	2	C

attributes to be removed for the examination was calculated by the following formula:

$$\sum_{k=1}^{12} \binom{12}{k} = 4094 \tag{14}$$

Every combination was removed from Table 2 minus the slopes 8 and 29, and it was checked whether any contradiction occured or not among the decision rules.

Table 4 shows the nine combinations of conditional attributes, Case-1 to 9, each of which consists of the minimum number of conditional attributes but still is able to diagnose every slope without contradiction. Case-1 taken as an example renders a description of how to extract the minimal decision algorithm follows.

Table 4. Combinations of conditional attributes

Cases	Conditional attributes
Case-1	(1) (2) (8) (9) (11)
Case-2	(1) (3) (4) (8) (11)
Case-3	(1) (3) (4) (9) (11)
Case-4	(1) (3) (8) (9) (11)
Case-5	(1) (4) (8) (9) (11)
Case-6	(1) (4) (8) (10) (11)
Case-7	(1) (4) (8) (11) (12)
Case-8	(1) (8) (9) (10) (11)
Case-9	(1) (8) (9) (11) (12)

The conditional attributes other than those of (1), (2), (8), (9), and (11) of Case-1 were removed from Table 2 minus slopes 8 and 29 to obtain a new table. In this table, a pair of the slopes 1 and 28, a group of the slopes 7, 11, 15, and 19, and so on were governed by one and the same rule each, and the slopes of each pair or group were removed except one to obtain Table 5.

4.3 Reduction of Classes of Conditional Attributes

Finally, it was necessary to examine the classes of the conditional attributes in Table 5. The class Nos. of each conditional attribute were removed one by one to see whether any contradiction occurred or not. If the class No. of a conditional attribute of a slope is removed in such a decision table and contradiction occurs, the class No. proves significant in the diagnosis of the slope. If not, it proves insignificant in the diagnosis. For example, when the class No. 2) of the conditional attribute (1) of the slope 1 has been removed in Table 5, we can obtain a new decision table, or Table 6. In this table, the slope 1 is assigned 1), 4), 2), and 3) in the columns of the conditional attributes (2), (8), (9), and (11) and its danger level is diagnosed as "A," while the slope 21 is assigned the same Nos. in the columns of the same conditional attributes but its level lebel is diagnosed as "B." Thus, contradiction has been brought about between the decision rules of the slopes 1 and 21 which are marked with "*", proving that the class No. 2) of the conditional attribute (1) of the slope 1 is significant in the diagnosis of the slope 1 and hence can not be removed.

By removing the class Nos. one by one as mentioned above, a new decision table was obtained. Notwithstanding many class Nos. removed, this table contains

Table 5. Decision table based on the conditional attributes in Case-1

Slopes	Conditional attributes (1)	(2)	(8)	(9)	(11)	Danger levels
1	2	1	4	2	3	A
2	4	2	4	2	2	B
3	3	2	4	3	3	C
4	4	2	2	2	3	B
5	3	2	4	1	3	A
6	3	1	4	3	1	A
7	4	2	4	2	3	C
9	3	1	3	1	3	B
12	4	2	3	1	3	B
13	4	2	4	2	1	B
14	3	2	4	1	2	B
16	4	2	4	3	1	B
17	4	1	3	1	2	B
18	3	2	4	2	3	B
21	3	1	4	2	3	B
22	4	2	4	3	3	C
23	4	2	4	1	3	C
24	4	1	3	1	3	B
25	4	2	4	1	1	A
26	4	2	3	1	1	B
27	4	1	4	3	3	C
30	2	1	4	3	3	A
31	3	1	4	1	2	A

no contradiction and is capable of making diagnoses equal to those by Table 5. Besides, in this table, a pair of the slopes 1 and 30, a group of the slopes 9, 12, 17, 24, and 26, and so on were governed by one and the same rule each, and accordingly the slopes of each pair or group were removed except one to obtain a new decision table, or Table 7. This table contains no single conditional attribute or class removable without causing contradiction and is called "minimal decision algorithm."

In the same way, we can find the minimal decision algorithm in each of Case-2 to 9 in Table 4. It can be said that the five conditional attributes of each case shown in Table 4 are all indispensable for its minimal decision algorithm.

5 Evaluation of Minimal Decision Algorithm

Figure 1 shows the frequencies of appearance in Table 4 of each of the conditional attributes which are required by the minimal decision algorithm mentioned above. The conditional attribute (1) is required by every case's minimal decision

Table 6. Decision table after class No. 2 of (1) for the slope 1 are removed

Slopes	Conditional attributes (1)	(2)	(8)	(9)	(11)	Danger levels
1	–	1	4	2	3	A *
2	4	2	4	2	2	B
3	3	2	4	3	3	C
4	4	2	2	2	3	B
5	3	2	4	1	3	A
6	3	1	4	3	1	A
7	4	2	4	2	3	C
9	3	1	3	1	3	B
12	4	2	3	1	3	B
13	4	2	4	2	1	B
14	3	2	4	1	2	B
16	4	2	4	3	1	B
17	4	1	3	1	2	B
18	3	2	4	2	3	B
21	3	1	4	2	3	B *
22	4	2	4	3	3	C
23	4	2	4	1	3	C
24	4	1	3	1	3	B
25	4	2	4	1	1	A
26	4	2	3	1	1	B
27	4	1	4	3	3	C
30	2	1	4	3	3	A
31	3	1	4	1	2	A

algorithm, its appearance frequency being nine. On the other hand, the conditional attribute (2) is required by Case-1's minimal decision algorithm alone, its appearance frequency being one. If we rank the conditional attributes in the descending order of the appearance frequency, it turns out as follows: (1) failure spots, (11) water logging, (8) valley- like depression on slope, (9) topography of ground on top of slope, and (4) rock heavily weathered or deteriorated.

The conditional attribute (1) relates to slope histories. Two slopes adjacent to each other can be considered to have similar geology and soil properties, unless there is some extreme change of the geologic structure between the slopes. Accordingly, if there is a failure spot nearby, the slope is most probably regarded to have a high danger level of failure. A spot where minute changes of distances between contour lines continue or a spot where vegetation is different from that of its surroundings is indicative of slope failure [17]. Thus, the conditional attribute (1) for failure histories is one of the important conditional attributes in diagnoses of danger levels of slope failure.

The conditional attribute (11) relates to water logging. As suggested by the

Table 7. Minimal decision algorithm in Case-1

Slopes	Conditional attributes					Danger levels
	(1)	(2)	(8)	(9)	(11)	
1	2	–	–	–	–	A
2	–	–	–	2	2	B
3	–	2	–	3	3	C
4	–	–	2	–	–	B
5	3	–	4	1	3	A
6	–	1	–	–	1	A
7	4	–	4	–	3	C
9	–	–	3	–	–	B
13	–	–	–	2	1	B
14	–	2	–	–	2	B
16	–	2	–	3	1	B
18	3	–	–	2	–	B
25	–	–	4	1	1	A
27	4	–	–	3	3	C
31	–	1	4	–	2	A

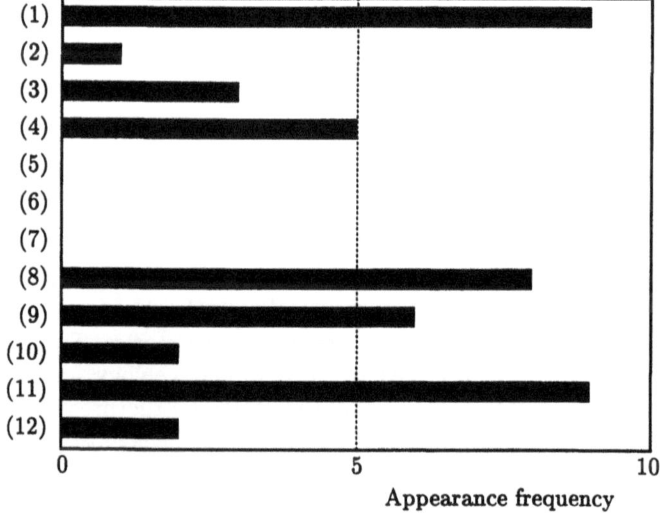

Figure 1. Appearance frequency of conditional attributes

fact that slope failure often occurs under localized heavy rains, water such as rain and drainage is an important conditional attribute of slope failure. Any of the conditional attributes (8), (9), and (4) has a class or classes for catchment topographies of grounds on top of slopes. Known for a long time as a conditional attribute of slope failure is a topography in which water such as rain water and drainage is collected to the area on top of a slope [17]. Thus, the conditional attributes (11), (8), (9), and (4) all relating to water paths can be considered important conditional attributes in diagnoses of danger levels of slope failure.

6 Derivation of Rules

The minimal decision algorithm mentioned above can be described easily by rules such as "*IF* conditional part (conditional attribute) *THEN* conclusive part (danger level, or decision attribute)." The minimal decision algorithm of Case-1 shown in Table 7 can be described by the 15 rules shown in Table 8. The rules 1 and 2 express the decision rules of the slopes 1 and 2, respectively. The rule 15 represents the decision rule of the slope 31.

Table 8. Rule-type description example of the minimal decision algorithm in Case-1

Rule No.	Rule-type description	
1	*IF* (1)=2)	*THEN* Danger level=A
2	*IF* (9)=2) *and* (11)=2)	*THEN* Danger level=B
3	*IF* (2)=2) *and* (9)=3) *and* (11)=2)	*THEN* Danger level=C
4	*IF* (8)=2)	*THEN* Danger level=B
5	*IF* (1)=3) *and* (8)=4) *and* (9)=1) *and* (10)=3)	*THEN* Danger level=A
6	*IF* (2)=1) *and* (11)=1)	*THEN* Danger level=A
7	*IF* (1)=4) *and* (8)=4) *and* (11)=3)	*THEN* Danger level=C
8	*IF* (8)=3)	*THEN* Danger level=B
9	*IF* (9)=2) *and* (11)=1)	*THEN* Danger level=B
10	*IF* (2)=2) *and* (11)=2)	*THEN* Danger level=B
11	*IF* (2)=2) *and* (9)=3) *and* (11)=1)	*THEN* Danger level=B
12	*IF* (1)=3) *and* (9)=2)	*THEN* Danger level=B
13	*IF* (8)=4) *and* (9)=1) *and* (11)=1)	*THEN* Danger level=A
14	*IF* (1)=4) *and* (9)=3) *and* (11)=3)	*THEN* Danger level=C
15	*IF* (2)=1) *and* (9)=4) *and* (11)=2)	*THEN* Danger level=C

For instance, the decision rule of the slope 1 in Table 7 indicates that if a slope is classified into the class 2) of the conditional attribute (1), its danger level is "A." This can be described by a rule below:

$$IF\ \ (1)=2)\ \ THEN\ \ DangerLevel = A \tag{15}$$

The decision rule of the slope 2 indicates that its danger level is "B" when both the conditions are met at the same time, one condition being that a slope is classified into the class 2) of the conditional attribute (9) and the other being that the slope is classified into the class 2) of the conditional attribute (11). This can be described by a rule below:

$$IF\ \ (9) = 2)\ and\ (11) = 2)\ \ THEN\ \ DangerLevel = B \tag{16}$$

To determine danger levels of conclusive parts by using an ES constructed on the basis of the above rules, it is necessary to check whether every condition in each rule is satisfied or not. As for the rule 1, it has to be checked whether the slope is classified into 2) of (1) or not. As for the rule 2, it has to be checked whether the slope is classified into 2) and 2) under (9) and (11), respectively. The total number of conditions to be checked in the 15 rules of Case-1 shown in Table 8 is 35. On the other hand, the decision tables of the minimal decision algorithm were also extracted for Case-2 to 9, and the numbers of rules and the total numbers of conditions to be checked of all the cases are summarized in Table 9.

Table 9. Total number of rules and conditions to be checked

Cases	Total number of rules	Total number of conditions
Case-1	15	35
Case-2	12	26
Case-3	16	37
Case-4	15	32
Case-5	15	32
Case-6	15	35
Case-7	15	35
Case-8	18	42
Case-9	17	39

Rules for the construction of ES should be so described that their number can be minimized for the sake of knowledge renewal and so on. Besides, conditions to be checked also should be so described that their number can be minimized for the sake of speedy reasoning. Accordingly, efficient renewal of knowledge and speedy reasoning become possible if an ES is constructed on the basis of the rules derived from the minimal decision algorithm of Case-2.

7 Closing Statement

The relevant information about the decision rules based on rough set methods was introduced and the application method of the theory to decision-making problems was described. Then, discussed was the method of extracting experiential knowledge of expert from the diagnostic results of danger levels of slope failure as the decision tables of minimal decision algorithm. Further discussed was a method to derive rule-type knowledge necessary for the construction of ES from the minimal decision algorithm.

Main findings of the present study are as follows:

a. Minimal decision algorithm could be extracted from the diagnostic results of slope failure by experts, and conditional attributes significant in the diagnoses were identified. They related to water logging, catchment topographies of grounds on top of slopes, and failure histories of slopes which have been considered important from long ago.
b. The conditional attributes indispensable for the minimal decision algorithm were the same as those regarded as important from long ago. Accordingly, conditional attributes which we attach particular importance to can be identified by extracting minimal decision algorithm from diagnostic results by an engineer, and his skills can be evaluated.
c. The decision table stipulates what decision to make when a certain condition is met. Almost all decision-making problems can be formulated by such decision tables.
d. By removing a conditional attribute or attributes each time in a decision table and seeing whether any contradiction will occur or not, we can evaluate whether the removed conditional attribute or attributes are significant in the diagnoses or not.
e. Because rough set theory starts from the problem of how to express the set of decision attributes by the set of paired conditional attributes and classes, the rough set theory can be used as a method to acquire knowledge from existing diagnostic cases in the field of civil engineering.

References

[1] Editional department of execution technique: Total of recently torrential rain. Execution Technique **5** (1972) (in Japanese)

[2] Takei, A., Kobashi, S., Nakayama, M., et al.: Landslide, slope failure and debris flow. In: Prediction and Countermeasures, Association of Kajima Pub., (1993) (in Japanese)

[3] Ishikawa, Y., Furuzeki, J., Sasaki, Y., et al.: Soil attack – *Soil disaster*, Geotech note, J. of Japanese Geotechnical Society, (1995) (in Japanese)

[4] Suzuki, M. et al.: Dangerous rainfall which soil disaster may be happened. J. of New Erosion Control **110**, (1995) (in Japanese) 1–7

[5] Kobashi, S.: Problems in classifying the danger levels of slope failure. J. of Landslide **10/3**, (1995) (in Japanese) 8–14

[6] Okimura, T., Ichikawa, R.: Prediction method of the slope-failure danger levels based on the numerical topographic features model. J. of Japan Society of Civil Engineers **358**, (1995) (in Japanese) 69–75

[7] Sand arrestation section of ministry of construction: Manual of countermeasure works for slope failure. In: Conference of Landslide and Slope Failure, (1983) (in Japanese)

[8] Forestry Agency: Investigation point in the dangerous area of slope failure, (1982) (in Japanese)
[9] Expressway Investugation Board: Study on investigation method in preventing landslide and slope failure, (1977) (in Japanese)
[10] Okimura, T., Hirokane, M. et al.: Diagnosis of the slope-failure danger levels based of fuzzy expert system. In: Kansai Branch of Japan Society of Civil Engineers, (1992) (in Japanese) 77–82
[11] Nishi, K., Furukawa, K., Nakagawa, K.: An evaluation system for slope-failure possibility factors using fuzzy set theory. J. of Japan Society of Civil Engineers **445/III-18**, (1992) (in Japanese) 109–118
[12] Terano, K., Asai, K., Sugano, M.: Introduction to Fuzzy System, Ohmu Pub., (1987) (in Japanese)
[13] Pawlak, Z.: Rough sets – Theoretical aspects of reasoning about data, Kluwer Acadenic Pub., (1991)
[14] Ziarko, W. (ed.): Rough Sets, Fuzzy Sets and Knowledge Discovery (RSKD'93). Workshops in Computing, Springer–Verlag & British Computer Society, London, Berlin (1994)
[15] Pawlak, Z.: Rough sets. International J. of Computer and Information Science **11** (1982) 341–356
[16] Matsumura, H.: Introduction to set theory, Asakura Pub., (1966) (in Japanese)
[17] Okuzono, S.: One hundred point in preventing soil disaster, Association of Kajima pub., (1986) (in Japanese)

Chapter 11

Soft Computing-Based Recognition of Musical Sounds

Bozena Kostek

Technical University of Gdansk, Faculty of Electronics, Telecommunications and Informatics, Sound Engineering Dept., 80-952 Gdansk, Poland

1 Introduction

Due to the development of multimedia technology and digital transmission of signals, there is rapid growth in the amount of audio data stored on various computer sites. Consequently, the problem is to find methods allowing one to explore a huge collection of data in order to find needed information in an effective way.

Actually, the problem is to recognize objects in audio material. One can discern two kinds of tasks that are different from one another. The first is related to the automatic recognition of musical timbre, which means that the aim is to recognize the sounds of various musical instruments. The second task concerns recognition of musical phrases, which means trying to find a concrete musical piece based on a melody line. The difference between these two approaches lies in the kind of applied analysis, because when recognizing musical timbre we must perform acoustic analyses of a signal [7], [10] while in the second case we have to take into account the musicological analysis of the material [8], [14]. The level of difficulty is similar in both cases. The first task concerns the recognition of some dozens of musical instruments, but the analysis aiming to discern particular sounds is very difficult. The analysis of musical phrases is more simple because we may deal with a very economical representation, namely the scores, but on the other hand the number of possible melodies is infinite. The most challenging problem is to follow the melody line performed by an instrument, based on the acoustical analysis of the sound produced by this instrument and then to recognize a musical piece. Tasks related to the first approach are described in the next paragraphs.

2 Parametric Representation of Acoustical Signals

The first task related to the automatic recognition of musical instruments consists of building a knowledge base in which information on musical sound patterns is to be included. However, because of the redundancy that characterizes acoustical signals, parametrization is needed which results in the creation of feature vectors. Therefore, the decision process is based on a set of parameters that are characteristic for most of musical instrument sounds. Parameters that are extracted from musical sounds can be divided into two groups: parameters derived from the time domain characteristics and parameters based on the spectral domain. For the purpose of transformation into the frequency domain the DFT (Discrete Fourier Transform) method is the most often used. However, there are some other transformations that allow analysis in the frequency domain, such as cosine transform, Walsh-Hadamard Transform, McAulay & Quatieri Transform [15], Gabor Transform and Wavelet Transform [5]. Some of the parameters derived from these analyses may describe both domains at the same time, thus belonging to the time-frequency set representation. There also exist parameters that are related to the time domain, but that are extracted from the frequency domain. The correlation parameters and the parametrs based on cepstral analysis may be included in this group. A specific group of parameters aiming to represent separately the instrument body features and those characteristic for the excitation is based on the LPC (Linear Predictive Coding) analysis, a technique well known in the speech processing domain.

The choice of parameters and their number is crucial for the effectiveness and efficient time usage of automatic classification processes.

2.1 Time Domain Parameters

Generally, the musical signal time domain characteristics may be represented by the ADSR model (see Fig. 1), which is a linear approximation of the envelope of a musical sound. This time-domain representation is depicted as consecutive sound phases - namely Attack, Decay, Sustain and Release - that may be described in terms of their energy and time relationships. Even if the Release phase is not taken into account, the other three are sufficient to resynthesize the original sound. The main difficulties are related to the appropriate detection of the attack phase beginning. Theoretically, the attack phase may be defined as the phase between the silence and the sound steady-state. In practice, it is very rare that some kind of noise is not present at the beginning of the sound recording. So, the main task is to detect whether the attack transient has already begun or whether it is still only a background noise.

Unfortunately, not all instruments may be represented by an ADSR model. For example, the sounds of some string instruments do not have a steady-state phase. Additionally, the starting transient duration differs for sounds from the same instrument and, obviously, for sounds from various instruments. The shortest duration for attack transients ranges from 15 to 35ms and is characteristic of the staccato way of playing on wind (double-reed) instruments. On the other hand, the longest duration of this phase is obtained for such instruments as flute (wind group) or contrabass (string group) while playing legato.

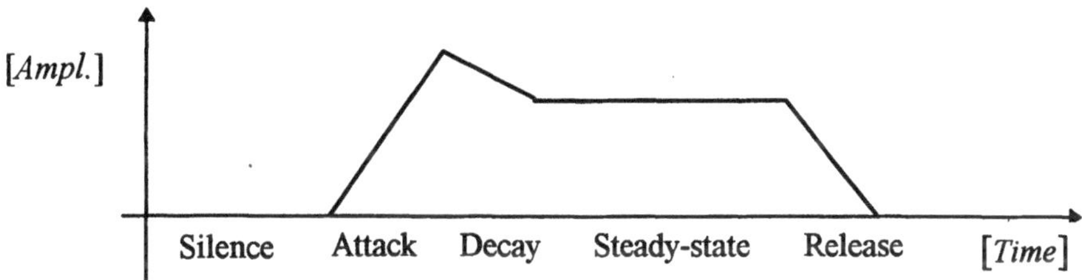

Fig. 2.1 Linear approximation of musical signal envelope.

It should be remembered that starting transients are the most important phase for the subjective recognition of musical sounds. It is known from the numerous experiments that when the attack is removed, the sound is no longer recognizable and, moreover, that some instrument sounds (trumpet and violin, for example) may not be distinguished between each other. In order to represent transient states, some parameters should be introduced. The signal level versus time is defined as:

$$I(t) = a \int_{t-\frac{T}{2}}^{t+\frac{T}{2}} u^2(\tau)\, d\tau \tag{1}$$

where: T - width of the time window, a - normalization coefficient.

Another parameter represents the amplitude envelope (or instantaneous amplitude) described by the following expression:

$$O(t) = \sqrt{u^2(t) + \hat{u}^2(t)} \tag{2}$$

where: $\hat{u}\,(t)$- Hilbert's Transform of the signal $u(t)$, calculated as:

$$\hat{u}(t) = \frac{1}{\pi} \int_{-\infty}^{\infty} \frac{u(\tau)}{t-\tau} d\tau \tag{3}$$

A parameter that is directly extracted from the time signal structure is the proposed transient midpoint t_0 (see Fig. 2.2) [7].

The value of t_0 is calculated according to the formula:

$$t_0 = \frac{M_1}{M_0} = \frac{a+b}{2} \tag{4}$$

where: M_1 is the first-order statistical moment:

$$M_1 = \int_{-\infty}^{\infty} tf(t)\,dt = \left(b^2 - a^2\right)\frac{h}{2} \tag{5}$$

In order to normalize, the signal energy M_0 is calculated according to the following equation:

$$M_0 = \int_{-\infty}^{\infty} f(t)\,dt = (b-a)\frac{h}{2} \tag{6}$$

where: h is an energy increment versus time.

The envelope rising time may be found by the calculation of the second central moment:

$$t_{ris} = b - a = \sqrt{\frac{12M_2}{M_0}} \tag{7}$$

where:

$$M_2 = \int_{-\infty}^{\infty} (t-t_0)^2 f(t)\,dt = \frac{(b-a)^3 h}{12} = (b-a)^2\frac{M_0}{12} \tag{8}$$

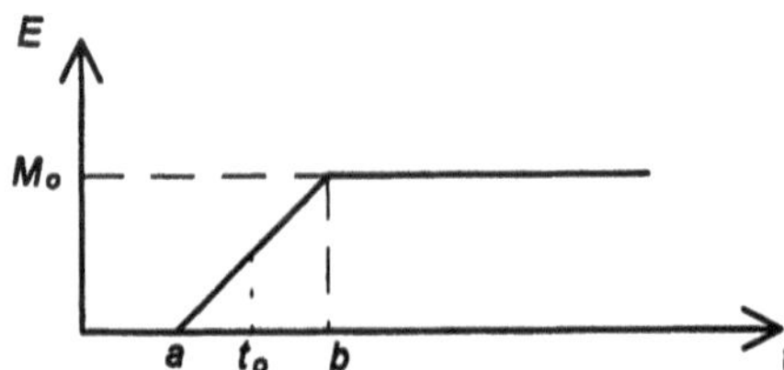

Fig. 2.2 Time envelope of the simplified transient model: a - transient starting point, b - transient ending point, M_0 - energy of the steady-state, t_0 - transient midpoint.

There are two more phases that should be taken into account, namely the phase of energy decreasing from the local maximum and the subsequent phase of energy increasing from the local minimum to the energy of the steady-state (see Fig. 2.1).

The subsequent time parameters are often used in the speech domain and are connected to the analysis of the so-called zero-crossing rate. For a signal $u = u(t)$, the zero-crossing function is defined as:

$$P(u,t) = \begin{Bmatrix} 1 - if\ there\ are\ signals\ u(t)\ that\ fulfil\ (1),(2)\ and\ (3); \\ 0 - otherwise. \end{Bmatrix} \quad (9)$$

where:

$$\begin{array}{l} (1)\ u(t) \cdot u(t - \Delta t) < 0 \\ (2)\ |u(t)| > \alpha\ and\ |(t - \Delta t)| < \alpha,\ where: \alpha << \overline{u} \\ (3)\ |u(t)| > \alpha\ for\ \ t_0 < t < t_0 + \Delta t\ and\ \Delta t = \frac{1}{f_{sampling}} \end{array} \quad (10)$$

Parameter $\alpha (\alpha \neq 0)$ is an assumed threshold.

Estimation of the spectral properties of broadband signals can be obtained using a representation based on the short-time average zero-crossing rate. Since high frequencies imply high zero-crossing rates and low frequencies imply low zero-crossing rates, there is a strong correlation between zero-crossing rate and energy distribution with frequency. This criterion is defined according to the following equation:

$$\overline{\rho_0(t)} = \frac{1}{T} \int_{t-\frac{T}{2}}^{t+\frac{T}{2}} \rho_0(\tau)\, d\tau \quad (11)$$

The basic algorithms for the determination of a zero-crossing require a comparison of signs of pairs of successive samples in assumed time intervals. The distribution of such intervals is defined by the function $R(t)$:

$$R(t) = \sum_{j=1}^{J} \delta(t - t_j) \quad (12)$$

where: $\delta(t)$ - Dirac's delta, $j = 1, 2, ...J$ (J - number of zero-crossings) and t_j - time interval between the pair of $j - 1$ and j (in segment T), additionally:

$$T = \sum_{j=1}^{J} t_j \quad (13)$$

The factor that differentiates the ideal signal model from real sound recordings is the amplitude variation of the steady-state phase. As the amplitude of the musical signal varies with time, the signal energy provides a convenient representation that reflects these amplitude variations. Variances representing these fluctuations should be also considered, thus these two parameters may be included in the feature vector.

2.2 Frequency Domain Parameters

The feature vectors containing the time domain parameters should be completed by adding the spectral properties. On the basis of the sound spectrum, many other parameters may be determined. The spectrum components midpoint value fm may be calculated using the following formula:

$$f_m = \frac{\int_0^{f_{max}} f \cdot E(f)\, df}{\int_0^{f_{max}} E(f)\, df} = r_f \frac{\sum_{i=1}^{I} i \cdot E_i}{\sum_{i=1}^{I} E_i} \tag{14}$$

where: r_f - parameter characterizing the resolution of the FFT analysis, E_i - energy of i-th component for the frequency equal to $r \cdot f_i$, f_{max} - upper limit of the analyzed frequency band, I - highest spectral component ($I \approx f_{max}/r_f$) [7].

The spectral centroid, also called *Brightness* (B) is defined as:

$$B = \frac{\sum_{n=1}^{N} n \cdot A_n}{\sum_{n=1}^{N} A_n} \tag{15}$$

where: A_n - amplitude of the *n-th* harmonic, N - total number of harmonics.

There are other parameters which describe the shape of the spectrum in the steady-state phase, such as the even (h_{ev}) and odd (h_{odd}) harmonic content in the signal spectrum:

$$h_{ev} = \sqrt{\frac{\sum_{k=1}^{M} A_{2k}^2}{\sum_{n=1}^{N} A_n^2}}, \quad h_{odd} = \sqrt{\frac{\sum_{k=2}^{L} A_{k-1}^2}{\sum_{n=1}^{N} A_n^2}} \tag{16}$$

where: $M = entier(N/2)$, $L = entier(N/2+1)$, A_n, N - as before.

Formants are also parameters connected to speech analysis which indicate local maxima of the spectrum. It is obvious that their physical interpretation in musical acoustics corresponds to resonances of the instrument body.

In the literature, another approach to the estimation of the sound spectral domain based on polynomials may be found. This approach seems to be especially justified in the case of a rich sound spectrum. The applied approximation is based on minimizing the mean-square error in the range of the analyzed spectrum [6]. An illustration of such an approach is shown in Fig. 2.3. It is seen that the 5*th* order of the approximating polynomial may be assumed as sufficient in both shown instrument cases.

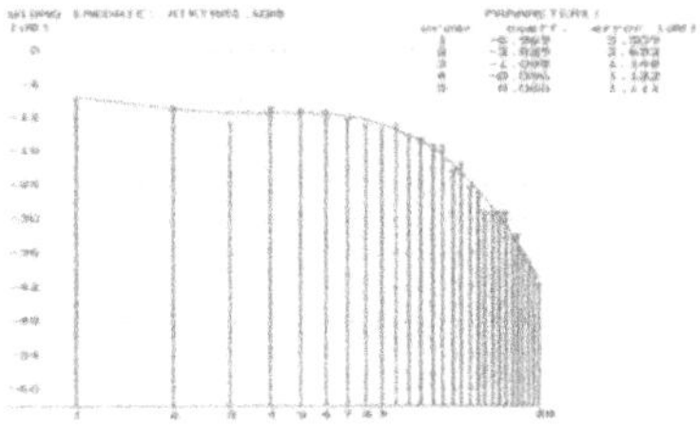

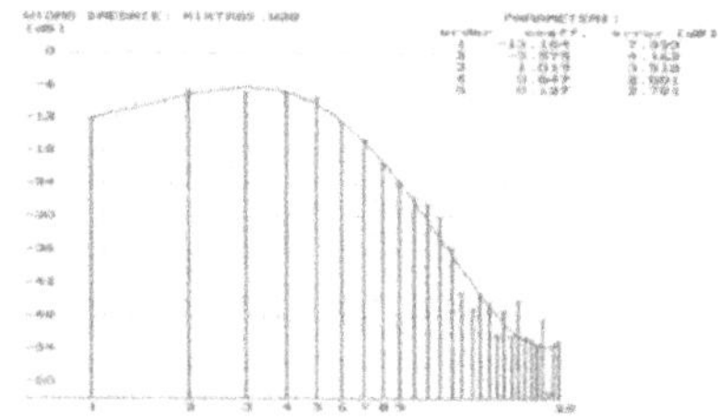

Fig. 2.3 Sound spectra approximated by the 5*th* order polynomial.

2.3 Other Parameters

It is convenient to correlate time-related properties with those of the frequency-domain. The group of parameters, called the Tristimulus, shows graphically the time-dependent behavior of musical timbre [16]. In the Tristimulus method, loudness values measured at 5ms intervals are converted into three co-ordinates, based on loudness of (1) the fundamental (N_1), (2) the group containing partials from 2 to 4 (N_2) and (3) the group containing partials from 5 to $N(N_3)$, where N is the highest significant partial. The values of N_2 and N_3 are calculated according to the formula:

$$N_{2(3)} = 0.85N_{\max} + 0.15N_i \tag{17}$$

where: N_{max} - component having the maximum loudness within the given group of harmonics.

Then parameters x, y, z are derived from the following formulae:

$$x = \frac{N_3}{N}; \quad y = \frac{N_2}{N}; \quad z = \frac{N_1}{N}; \tag{18}$$

where:

$$N = \sum_{i=1}^{3} N_i \tag{19}$$

This procedure allows a graph to be drawn that shows simply the time-dependent behavior of the starting transients with relation to the steady-state.

However, the harmonic energy or amplitude values may be taken into account instead of loudness for classification purposes [9]. Therefore, three parameters are extracted for the above defined spectrum subbands, namely the first (T_1), second (T_2) and third (T_3) modified Tristimulus parameters according to the formulas:

$$T_1 = A_1 / \sum_{n=1}^{N} A_n^2, \quad T_2 = \frac{\sum_{n=2}^{4} A_n^2}{\sum_{n=1}^{N} A_n^2}, \quad T_3 = \frac{\sum_{n=5}^{N} A_n^2}{\sum_{n=1}^{N} A_n^2} \tag{20}$$

where: A_n, N - as defined before. Additionally, the following condition is to be imposed to the above defined parameters:

$$T_1 + T_2 + T_3 = 1 \tag{21}$$

As most of the presented parameters do not have stable values within the chromatic scale of an instrument, the applicability of other criteria has been verified, such as the cepstrum coefficients defined by the following expression [9]:

$$W_c[k] = \sum_{i=1}^{n} E_i \cos(\frac{\pi}{n}(i - 0.5) \cdot k) \tag{22}$$

where: $W_c[k]$ - *k-th* cepstrum coefficient, E_i - energy of *i-th* harmonic expressed in [dB],

or parameters that are related to the frequency of *n-th* harmonic, namely: normalized frequency deviation defined in the following formula [2]:

$$\frac{\Delta F_n(t)}{n f_1} = \frac{F_n(t)}{n f_1} - 1 \tag{23}$$

where: f_n - frequency of *n-th* harmonic, f_1 - fundamental frequency.

It is a convenient way to display certain properties of a signal by using its statistical representation. For that purpose, autocorrelation (K_{An}, K_{fn}) and cross-correlation functions (K_{Amn}, K_{fmn}) are often defined:

$$K_{An}(k) = \left[(M-k)\,\sigma_{An}^2\right]^{-1} \sum_{r=0}^{M-k-1} L_n(r) \cdot L_n(k+r), \tag{24}$$

$$K_n(k) = \left[(M-k)\,\sigma_{Fn}^2\right]^{-1} \sum_{r=0}^{M-k-1} \Delta F_n(r) \cdot \Delta F_n(k+r) \tag{25}$$

where: $k = 0, 1, ..., M/2$, σ_{A_n}, σ_{F_n} are standard deviations respectively for the signal amplitude and frequency, k is the time lag, having a maximum value of $M/2$,

$$K_{Amn}(k) = \left[(M-k)\,\sigma_{Am}^2 \sigma_{An}^2\right]^{-1} \sum_{r=0}^{M-k-1} L_m(r) \cdot L_n(k+r) \tag{26}$$

$$K_{fmn}(k) = \left[(M-k)\,\sigma_{Fm}^2 \sigma_{Fn}^2\right]^{-1} \sum_{r=0}^{M-k-1} \Delta F_m(r) \cdot \Delta F_n(k+r) \tag{27}$$

where: σ_{A_m}, σ_{A_n} and σ_{F_m},σ_{F_n} are standard deviations between the *n-th* and *m-th* amplitudes and frequencies of signal harmonics, respectively [1].

These functions provide information on the relationships between signal amplitudes and frequencies and are very useful in determining the signal periodicity.

There are more parameters that may be derived using various approaches to the musical signal analysis. Consequently, the sound feature extraction is a multi-dimensional process.

3 Experiments and Results

The data contained in the constructed musical signal database were obtained using sounds recorded on CD's which were edited at McGill University [10]. Complete chromatic scales from the standard playing range of essentially all non-percussive instruments of the modern orchestra are included in these records. Additionally, a database named SHARC [18], [9], containing information about the FFT domain of 24 orchestra instruments was used in further analyses. The FFT-based data contains a choice of all notes from the chromatic scale that is characteristic of a chosen instrument.

The starting point in this work was the selection of a short fragment corresponding to the starting transient and sound steady-state portion for each note. Next, editing and analyses using FFT transform were performed. The FFT analyses were done for 1024 sample frames with 700 samples overlap. Digital 16-bit stereo recordings at 44.1 kHz sampling frequency were used, and the Hamming window was applied to analyses. Subsequently, calculation of parameters was initiated. Parameters that were extracted are based both on time and frequency domains, and combine all described approaches. However, only those parameters that were checked during preliminary tests are included in the following investigations.

Therefore the feature vector consisted of 14 parameters:

- parameters with regard to the fundamental: rising time of the first harmonic expressed in periods denoted as P_1, energy of the first harmonic calculated for the steady state (T_1), T_1 at the end of the attack divided by T_1 for the steady-state denoted as P_2;

- parameters with regard to the mid frequency partials: rising time of II, III and IV harmonics expressed in periods (P_3), energy of II, III and IV harmonics calculated for the steady state (T_2), T_2 at the end of the attack divided by T_2 for the steady-state (P_4);

- parameters connected to high frequency partials: rising time of the remaining of harmonics expressed in periods (P_5), energy of the remaining harmonics calculated for the steady state (T_3), T_3 at the end of the attack divided by T_3 for the steady-state (P_6);

- parameters describing the relationships between fundamental, mid and high frequency partials in terms of time delays: delay of II, III and IV harmonic with relation to the fundamental during the attack (P_7), delay of the remaining harmonics with relation to the fundamental during the attack (P_8);

- parameters connected with the even/odd properties of spectrum: (h_{ev}, h_{odd});
- brightness of the sound (B);
- normalized pitch of the sound (P_t):

$$P_t = i/I \tag{28}$$

where: I - number of notes (sounds) available for a parametrized instrument, i - number of the parametrized sound; sounds are numbered from 1 to I.

Parameter P_t, depending on the sound pitch, does not allow distinction between instruments but shows the position of the sound within the musical range of a parametrized instrument. It is important because of timbre changes within the chromatic scale of instruments. Parameters connected to high frequency partials (especially B) depend on the pitch because the higher the sound, the smaller the number of its harmonics in the spectrum. It is quite obvious since analysis range is always the same, whereas the fundamental frequency is increasing and higher frequency partials start to exceed the analysis range.

3.1 Experiments with Artificial Neural Networks

The goal of the experiments was to study the possibility of identifying selected classes of instruments using a neural network in order to verify the effectiveness of the extracted sound parameters. A multi-layer neural network of the feedforward type was used in the experiments. The number of neurons in the initial layer was equal to the number of elements of the parameters vector. In turn, each neuron in the output layer was matched to a different class of instrument, and so their number was equal to the number of classes of instruments used in the experiment. The number of hidden neurons was arbitrarily adopted as 15. The error back-propagation (EBP) method based on the delta learning rule was used in the experiment [13].

The training of the neural network was carried out using the EBP method several times. Each time, different initial conditions as well as training parameters were adopted. The training process constant (η) and the momentum term (α) were changed dynamically during the course of the training. They were later used to evaluate the progress of the training process. Additionally, the number of iterations necessary to make the value of the cumulative error drop below the assumed threshold value was observed. The training of the network and its testing was carried out on the basis of the feature vector described previously.

Table 1 Format of feature vectors

P_t T_2 T_3 P_1 P_2 P_3 P_4 P_5 P_6 P_7 P_8 B h_{odd} h_{ev}

To train the neural network, parameter vectors of 4 classes of instruments were selected: bass trombone, trombone, english horn, contrabassoon. In general, 2 types of sets were formed: the first encompassing all parameter vectors (type

ALL), and the second one containing about 70% of all vectors (type 70_PC). The vectors included in the set type 70_PC were chosen at random, however, it was attempted to maintain a uniform distribution. Below in Table 2, the number of parameter vectors for the given class of instruments in the training set type 70_PC with regard to the size of the class is shown. This relation is expressed as a percentage. Additionally, indexes of vectors that were excluded from the set type 70_PC are shown.

Table 2 Representation of the training set type 70_PC.

Instrument	Class 70_PC Size	Excluded Vectors
bass trombone	18/25 - 72%	2,7,10,14,18,21,23
trombone	22/32 - 68.75%	1,4,7,10,15,18,22,26,29,30
english horn	21/30 - 70%	3,5,8,12,16,19,22,27,30
contrabassoon	22/32 - 68.75%	3,6,8,11,14,19,22,25,28,31

Network Training The training was continued up to the moment when the value of the cumulative error dropped below 0.01. This value was adopted arbitrarily in order to prevent a possible case of network over-training. Three network training processes were conducted, with a diagram of the training phase presented in Fig. 3.1. The adopted descriptions have the following respective meanings: variables *range_V* and *range_W* give information on the range of values of elements of matrices V and W. Matrices V and W are sets of synaptic weights respectively: from the input layer toward the hidden one and from the hidden toward the output layer. In the first case (1), matrices of network weights were initiated at random, with values not exceeding the range (-0.2, 0.2), while in the second case (2) this range decreased to values within (-0.1, 0.1). Diagram (3) in Fig. 3.1 has a range of random weight initialization identical to diagram (2). However, these routines differ from one another because the values of the weights during random initialization are different each time. The purpose of training procedures (2) and (3) is to compare the process of training convergence within the same type of training set.

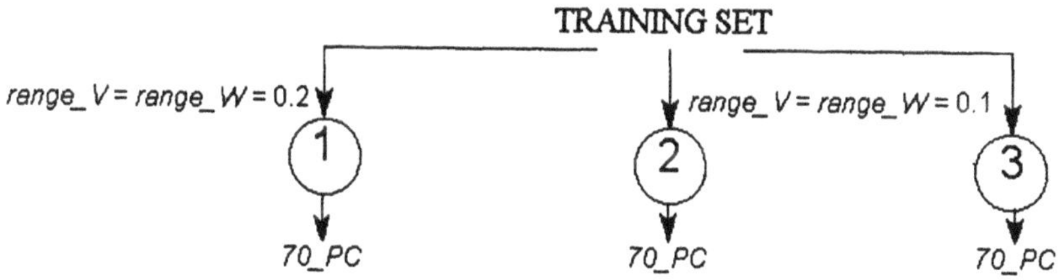

Fig. 3.1 Diagram of the training phase

Training Process No. 1 Since a stereo sound constituted the basis for calculating the parameters of musical sounds, the same parameters were calculated separately for the left and the right channels. However, the testing phase will be presented only on the left sound channel. For the training set LEFT.1_70PC, the following initial conditions were adopted: unipolar activation function of the neuron, random initialization of values of elements of matrices V and W ranging from -0.2 to 0.2, training with the momentum method applied, η= 0.05, and α= 0.45. In this training routine, the network converged quickly to the error level of 0.07 - 0.06. Further growth of required accuracy (decreasing the assigned threshold value of error) caused a drastic prolongation of the training period due to the small value of the training coefficient. It is worth emphasizing that in the proximity of the error value of 0.02 - 0.01 the term η was increased many times, causing the previously mentioned high error oscillations and, finally, the attainment of required accuracy.

Training Process No. 2 The following initial conditions were adopted in the case of the LEFT.2_70PC training set: unipolar activation function of the neuron, random initialization of values of elements of weight matrices covering the range (-0.1, 0.1), training with the momentum term, η= 0.05 and α= 0.4. The training process was sharply stopped because the value of admissible error decreased below 0.05. Initially, the training proceeded very rapidly and attained the assigned boundary error of 0.1 - 0.7 within only several thousand of iterations. As the accuracy of training was increased, the number of necessary iterations was growing.This was due to the fact that the speed of training η was very low ($\sim$0.005) and at the same time the momentum term α was reaching a high value ($\sim$0.5). Close to the error value of 0.02, the value of η was increased ten times to evoke higher error oscillations. The result was that after about 250 iterations the accuracy of the training dropped below 0.02. On the other hand, close to the value of 0.01 the speed of training was reduced twice (0.01 $\rightarrow$ 0.005) in order to reduce the error generated and allow going below the boundary value of 0.01. However, it did not succeed. The error generated increased and only by evoking higher error oscillations (η was increased twenty times) was the training terminated.

Training Process No. 3 The following initial conditions were adopted in the case of the LEFT.3_70PC training set: unipolar activation function of the neuron, random initialization of values of elements of weight matrices covering the range (-0.1, 0.1), training with the momentum term, η= 0.05, and α= 0.5. Despite fast initial convergence of network training, the value of parameter η was reduced to 0.003 at app. 0.08 error. This small value excluded a great magnitude of error oscillations during the training, but again this happened at the expense of the training speed. It was also tested if this parameter could be increased, but it turned out that the training process in this case was unstable. It was only at 0.02 accuracy that η could be increased several times, which decisively speeded up the final termination of the training.

Testing Phase In the testing phase the purpose was to test the effectiveness relation between identifying new objects by the network as it relates to network training accuracy. It is worth observing that the effectiveness of the network does not determine the quality of the trained network. Good quality can be understood as a feature of the network that causes the *k-th* neuron at the output to generate a high value with relation to the values of outputs of the remaining neurons (e.g. 0.8 to ~0.005) for a given vector at the input. In order to determine the recognition quality, all outputs of neurons were observed when the vectors from the *k-th* class were being presented. The values of the neuron outputs were treated as deviations from the expected value of 0. Variance could then be a measure of the quality of the trained network. The bigger the variance calculated for particular neuron outputs, the stronger the classifications for particular classes are. This parameter is computed on the basis of the following formula:

$$Var_k = \frac{1}{N_k} \sum_{i=1}^{N_k \Sigma} o_i^2 \tag{29}$$

where: Var_k - value of variance for *k-th* neuron, N_k - number of parameter vectors, members of the *k-th* class and not present in the training set, o_i - output of the *i-th* neuron for *k-th* feature vector.

The above considerations will be shown on the basis of the test conducted on type LEFT_30PC. The recognition effectiveness (the number of correct and wrong responses expressed as percentages (pos/neg [%])) for the chosen testing set is presented in Table 3. The visible change of recognition effectiveness happened upon changing the accuracy of the network from 0.1 to 0.09. Despite a further increase in accuracy, the effectiveness remained at the same level - 97.22%, i.e. only one vector was wrongly classified. Upon the presentation of the vectors of the particular classes it can be observed that the quality of identifying new objects was growing slightly, together with a reduction in the cumulative error E_{max}.

Table 3 Recognition effectiveness for instruments: bass trombone (I), trombone (II), english horn (III), contrabassoon (IV).

Instr.	I	II	III	IV	Score
E_{max}	pos/neg	pos/neg	pos/neg	pos/neg	pos/neg [%]
0.1	100/0	70/30	100/0	20/80	66.44/30.56
0.09	100/0	100/0	100/0	90/10	97.22/2.78
0.05	100/0	100/0	100/0	90/10	97.22/2.78
0.01	100/0	100/0	100/0	90/10	97.22/2.78

For the purpose of presenting the values of variances, two classes of instruments were selected, namely: bass trombone (Tab. 4) and trombone (Tab. 5). The first of these instruments was identified with much better effectiveness than the other one.

Table 4 Variances in neuron outputs upon presentation of vectors of the class bass trombone.

E_{max}	bass trombone	trombone	english horn	contrabassoon
0.1	0.3597468	0.0060959	0.0026676	0.0606067
0.09	0.9647862	0.0027156	0.0000044	0.0003433
0.05	0.9721547	0.0023566	0.0000030	0.0002217
0.01	0.9856030	0.0032118	0.0000008	0.0000564

Table 5 Variances in neuron outputs upon presentation of vectors of the class trombone.

E_{max}	bass trombone	trombone	english horn	contrabassoon
0.1	0.0059164	0.3968045	0.0432925	0.0353321
0.09	0.0000000	0.8179480	0.0014706	0.0222385
0.05	0.0000000	0.8198924	0.0019054	0.0180781
0.01	0.0000000	0.8223629	0.0029912	0.0090919

The best recognition effectiveness scores for the particular training procedures of the test were compiled in Table 6. The consecutive columns signify: the test routine (name of the training and testing set), classification effectiveness expressed as percentages and numbers, and respective values of E_{max}.

Table 6 Compilation of the best classifications.

Test routine	Testing set	pos/neg [%]	pos/neg	E_{max}
LEFT.1_70PC	LEFT_30PC	97.22/ 2.78	35/1	(0.09 - 0.01)
LEFT.1_70PC	RIGHT_ALL	99.16 /0.84	118/1	(0.09 - 0.02)
LEFT.2_70PC	LEFT_30PC	97.22/ 2.78	35/1	0.02; 0.01
LEFT.2_70PC	RIGHT_ALL	98.32 /1.68	117/2	0.1; 0.09
LEFT.3_70PC	LEFT_30PC	94.44 /5.56	34/2	(0.1 - 0.01)
LEFT.3_70PC	RIGHT_ALL	98.32/ 1.68	117/2	(0.1 - 0.07)

Tab. 6 shows that recognition effectiveness during the experiments was very high and was always above 90%. The number of unrecognized vectors was 1 or 2. The results obtained show that in only some experiments (with various initial training parameters) were certain vectors not correctly identified. Hence, the presumption that data in these very vectors may be incorrectly acquired. It should be remembered that the parametrized signals were sounds recorded in real conditions, i.e. as a part of a musical performance. Therefore phenomena such as musical articulation or differentiated dynamic with all features specific for an individual musician are included in the signal and resulted in signal modulation, amplitude overshoots, etc. This may cause a certain kind of "non-adaptation" to the engineered algorithms in some cases in which only three models of the relation between Attack-Decay-Sustain phases in a sound were assumed. What becomes evident is a way of testing the correctness of parametrization. If the wrongly classified vectors are always the same for a statistically large number of examined networks, then it is these vectors that should be subjected to verification.

3.2 Experiments with Rough Sets

A decision system based on rough set theory [17] was engineered at the Technical University of Gdansk [4]. It consists of learning and testing algorithms. During the first phase rules are derived that are the basis for the second phase performance. The generation of decision rules starts from rules of length equal to 1, then the system generates rules of length equal to 2, etc. The maximum rule length may be determined by the user. The system induces both possible and certain rules. It is assumed that the rough set measure for possible rules should exceed the value 0.5. Moreover, only such rules are taken into account: which were preceded by any shorter rule operating on the same parameters. The system produces rules in the following form:

$$(param\_1) = (val\_1) \wedge ... \wedge (param\_k) = (val\_k) => (instr\_i) \qquad (30)$$

Additionally, the so-called neutral point (p) has an influence on the strength of the rule (r), with the last one defined as [4]:

$$r = c(\mu_{rs} - p) \qquad (31)$$

where: c- number of cases conforming to the rule, μ_{rs}- the rough set measure, should be set by the user. This parameter controls the process of decision making by means of influencing the strength of possible rules. This results from the fact, that the decision system is designed in such a way, that for each derived rule is assigned a value called rule strength r that reflects the degree of confidence to the rule. Correspondingly, the decision is influenced mostly by strong rules with higher values of r and less by rules having lower values of r depending on the value of the neutral point of the rough measure p. Owing to the parameter defined as the neutral point of the rough measure, the decision system can be tuned by its operator. For example setting $p = 0.5$ causes that rules having rough measure equal to 0.5 are considered as having decision strength zero (they do not influence decision).

A rough set measure of the rule describing concept X is the ratio of the number of all examples from the concept X

$$\mu_{rs} = \frac{|X \cap Y|}{|Y|} \qquad (32)$$

where: X- is the concept, and Y- the set of examples described by the rule.

The next step is a testing phase in which the leave-one-out procedure is performed. During *j-th* experiment, the *j-th* object is removed from every class contained in the database. Then the learning procedure is performed on remaining objects, and the result of classification of the omitted objects by produced rules is recorded.

Attribute Discretization Parameters gathered in the created databases are of real values. Since produced rules contain parameter values, this therefore creates several problems. First of all, since spectra of sounds differ within the musical range of instruments, sounds are characterized by differentiated parameter values for each. It may be also assumed that different sound recording conditions influence the parametrization results. Therefore, the number of rules produced will be very large and they will contain specific values. That is why the number of parameter values should be limited to a few values, and thus the discretization procedure is needed.

Generally speaking, discretization can be performed in two ways:

- parameter values can be clustered together into a few groups, forming intervals, and each group of values will be considered as one new value,

- parameter domain can be divided into intervals and each parameter value belonging to the same interval will take the same new value.

After the quantization process is finished, parameters are no longer real-valued.

Quantization can be performed on each parameter separately or on all parameter values at the same time. The former way of quantization is called local, and the latter one is called global quantization. Globalization of local quantization methods is also possible [6].

The following methods have so far been implemented at the TU Gdansk [4], [12], [10]: (1) Equal Interval Width Method (EIWM) - parameter domain is divided into intervals of the same width; number of intervals is chosen by the experimenter. This method belongs to the local category; (2) Variable Statistical Quantization - in the VSQ method, n discriminators d_{xy} are assigned (where n is a limit of intervals specified by a user), then discriminators with the Behrens-Fisher statistic value V smaller than a specified threshold are deleted; (3) Maximum Gap Clusterization Method (MGCM) - number of intervals n is also chosen by the experimenter, n maximal gaps between sorted parameter values are searched and parameter domain is divided into intervals, choosing points from these gaps as division points of the parameter domain [14], [11]. This is also a local method; (4) Clusterization (CLUSTER) based on statistical parameters of distance between pairs of neighboring parameter values; value O_g serves as a criterion of value concatenating [12]:

$$O_g = a \cdot E(O) + b \cdot D^2(O) + c \cdot Min(O) + d \cdot Max(O) + e \cdot 1 \tag{33}$$

where: O - interval between parameter values, E - mean value, D^2 - variance, $a, b, c, d, e \in R$ - coefficients defined by an experimenter.

If the interval between neighboring parameter values is smaller than O_g, they are joined and make an interval [12]. This is also a local method; every parameter can be quantized into another number of intervals; (5) Method based on the Boolean reasoning approach - proposed by Skowron and Nguyen [19], the Boolean function is used as a tool to determine the best division points for each parameter domain. This is a global method; every parameter can be quantized into another number of intervals.

The first mentioned method - (EIWM) - is the simplest and fastest one to perform. However, this method neglects the distribution of parameter values; EIWM is most appropriate in case of linear data distribution. The second method - VSQ - takes the statistical properties of a set of data into account. The MGCM method - is also quite simple, but it takes into account clusters of parameter values. The next method, (CLUSTER), allows a flexible choice of system parameter values clustering into intervals. Coefficients used in this method change the number of intervals created during the quantization process. The last mentioned Boolean quantization method is a global one. In this method, division points for parameters domain are chosen in such a way that every division point separates as many classes (instruments) as possible. The quantization process does not have to divide every parameter domain. If the database contain a small number of classes and many parameters, some of them will not be quantized at all.

In Fig. 3.2, values for the previously defined parameter, namely brightness (B) are shown for the trombone before and after the discretization process has been performed. As is seen in the figure, the character of this parameter is not changed after the discretization process.

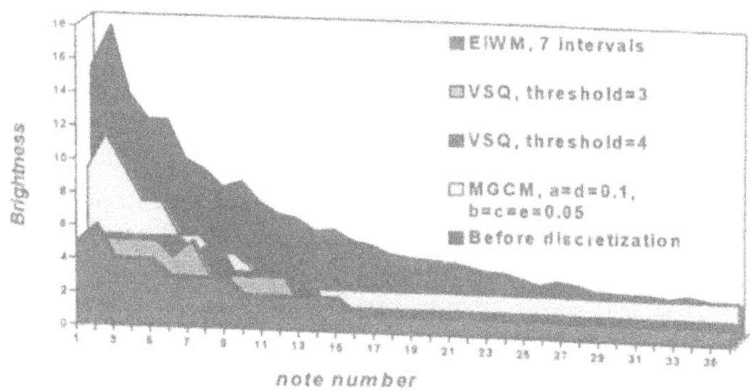

Fig. 3.2 Parameter *Brightness* (B) before and after the discretization process

After the division of parameter domains, a process of replacing the original values of input data by the number of the interval to which a selected parameter value belongs is started. Consequently, the representation of parameters by properly selected ranges instead of numbers is the essence of the above procedure. Such conversion of the parameter values into ranges results in memory saving during the learning phase.

Exemplary Results In the experiments, 15 classes containing parameters of 20 instruments were created. These instruments represent the wind group.

The most important criterion of the discretization method is its accuracy rate, computed after finishing training-and-test procedures for every experiment. For the EIWM method used in the experiments, a recognition score of 81% was obtained, assuming the neutral point equals 0.6, the rough set measure equals 0.7 and the length of rules equals 3. Such accuracy has been obtained in experiments when all mentioned instruments were tested. Below, some exemplary rules and classification scores obtained for the musical timbre database are presented (see Table 7).

Exemplary rules:

If [A7 = 0] $\wedge$ [A10 = 3] $\wedge$ [A14 = 1] then [CLASS No. 5]

If [A6 = 0] $\wedge$ [A11 = 2] $\wedge$ [A14 = 3] then [CLASS No. 6]

If [A8 = 0] $\wedge$ [A9 = 1] $\wedge$ [A14 = 0] then [CLASS No. 7]

where: A - attribute (parameter), A=1,...,14 for 15 classes (instruments), the discretization method applied: EIWM with the division into 5 intervals numerated from 0 to 4.

Table 7. Recognition scores [%] (training set containing 15 classes, EIWM - division into 5 intervals; VSQ method, the threshold value = 1.4, the maximum length of rules = 3).

Quantization Method	5 intervals	6 intervals	7 intervals
EIWM, neutral point 0.6	81.5	81.7	79.4
EIWM, neutral point 0.3	79.6	79.9	82.6
VSQ, neutral point 0.6	88	91	89.1
VSQ, neutral point 0.3	78.2	77.8	79.4

In the next experiments some of the tested instruments were disregarded and the same four instruments as in the experiment with NN's were taken into account. Tests results are included in Tab. 8. As is seen from Tab. 8, the overall recognition accuracy is greater than 80% in almost all cases. Also, results were improved if the rough set measure was declared as equal to 0.7. When only certain rules were taken into account the overall recognition score became smaller. However, there is so far no clear indication for optimum system settings. Additionally, in comparison to tests based on neural networks, the rough set-based system was not as efficient in the instrument classification task as NNs. However, it should be remembered that the recognition accuracy depends on the choice of the discretization method.

Table 8. Recognition scores obtained for various system settings.

Quantization Method	Rule length	μ_{rs}	p	Score [%]
EIWM/quant. order =5	3	0.5	0.5/0.7	75/39
EIWM/quant. order =5	3	0.7	0.5/0.7	84/85
EIWM/quant. order =5	4	0.5	0.5/0.7	71/42
EIWM/quant. order =5	4	0.7	0.5/0.7	78/80
EIWM/quant. order =7	3	0.7	0.5/0.7	74/75
VSQ/ quant. order =7	3	0.7	0.5/0.7	78/77
VSQ/ quant. order =7	3	0.7	0.5/0.7	75/74

4 Conclusions

In this paper, two applications of soft computing algorithms to musical acoustics were presented. Methods for sound parameter calculations were quoted. As musical timbre depends on both time domain characteristics and the frequency of a sound, parameters were therefore extracted with regard to both domains. Further, feature vectors, related respectively to musical sounds were derived forming a database. The created database was then tested by the engineered algorithms. For purposes of the classification of musical sounds artificial neural networks and the rough set-based system were applied.

Results of the experiments show high effectiveness for classification of musical instruments by neural networks. The obvious advantage of this type of classifier is the fact that there is no need for quantization of parameter values included in the feature vector. There is no doubt that a certain disadvantage of this type of testing is a huge amount of work needed to complete the training phase.

The rough set-based approach seems to be very valuable for testing the "the quality" of parameters. This method provides an appropriate tool for checking various sets of parameters, and thus in preliminary tests some of the described parameters were eliminated. The recognition scores obtained in the tests show high effectiveness for the rough set algorithm.

The usefulness of soft computing techniques for these types of applications seems all the greater as the feature vectors included in the musical database encompass representations of consecutive sounds in the chromatic scale. In this case, high instability of designated parameters is observed, because the presence of non-linearity related to differentiated articulations and dynamics of musical sounds affects the stability of parameters. However, the network ability to generalize, the discretization procedure and the inclusion of possible rules in the rough set-based algorithm allow a correct classification of the objects being tested.

The following more general conclusions may be derived from the performed

- there are no universal parameters related to all musical instruments, thus they must be selected on the basis of compromise,
- "effectiveness" of parameters used as condition attributes depends on a discretization method, therefore this aspect should be more thoroughly tested,
- a learning approach to musical data analysis is generally justifiable.

Acknowledgments: The research was sponsored by the Committee for Scientific Research, Warsaw, Poland, Grant No. 8 T11C 028 08.

References

1. Ando, S., Yamaguchi, K.: Statistical study of spectral parameters in musical instrument. J. Acoust. Soc. Am. **94/1** (1993) 37–45
2. Beuachamp, J.W.: Unix workstation software for analysis, graphics, modification, and synthesis of musical sounds. In: 94th AES Conv., preprint 3479, J. Audio Eng. Soc. (Abstr) **41/5** May (1993)
3. Chmielewski, M. R., Grzymala-Busse, J. W.: Global discretization of continuous attributes as preprocessing for machine learning. In: T.Y. Lin (ed.): Proceedings of the Third International Workshop on Rough Sets and Soft Computing (RSSC'94), San Jose State University, San Jose, California, USA, November 10–12, (1994) 474–480
4. Czyzewski, A., Kaczmarek, A.: Speaker-independent recognition of isolated words using rough sets. In: P.P. Wang (ed.), Second Annual Joint Conference on Information Sciences (JCIS'95), September 28 – October 1, Wrightsville Beach, North Carolina, USA (1995) 397–400
5. Evangelista, G.: Pitch-synchronous wavelet representations of speech and music signals. IEEE Trans. Signal proc. **41/12** (1993) 3313-3330
6. Kostek, B., Kaczmarek, A.: Listening tests in the computer modelled pipe organ sound. In: 93rd AES Conv., preprint 3393, J. Audio Eng. Soc. (Abstr) **40/12** December (1992)
7. Kostek, B., et al.: Artificial approach to the detection of events in musical signal. In: 96th AES Conv., preprint 3822, J. Audio Eng. Soc. (Abstr) **42/5** May (1994)
8. Kostek, B.: Computer based recognition of musical phrases using the rough set approach. In: Joint Conf. on Inform. Sciences, NC, USA, 28 September–1 October (1995)
9. Kostek, B.: Feature extraction methods for the intelligent processing of musical signals. In: 99th AES Conv., preprint 4076, J. Audio Eng. Soc. (Abstr) **43/12** December (1995)
10. Kostek, B., Wieczorkowska, A.: Study of parameter relations in musical instrument patterns. In: 100th Audio Eng. Soc. Conv., May 1996 J. Audio Eng. Soc. (Abstr) **44/7/8** (1996)
11. Kostek, B., Szczerba, M.,: Parametric representation of musical phrases. In: 101st Audio Eng. Soc. Conv., preprint 4337, Los Angeles, 8-11 November (1996)
12. Kostek, B.: Rough set and fuzzy set methods applied to acoustical analyses. J. Intelligent Automation and Soft Computing **2/2** (1996) 147–160
13. Kostek, B., Krolikowski, R.: Application of artificial neural networks to the recognition of musical sounds. Archives of Acoustics **22/1/2** (1997)
14. Kostek, B.,: Computer-based recognition of musical phrases using the rough set approach. Information Sciences (1997) (to appear)
15. McAulay, R., Quatieri, T.: Speech analysis/synthesis based on sinusoidal representation. IEEE Trans. Acoust., Speech, Signal Proc. **34** (1986) 744–754
16. Pollard, H. F., Jansson, E. V.: A tristimulus method for the specification of musical timbre. Acustica **51** (1982)
17. Pawlak, Z.,: Rough sets. International J. Information and Computer Sciences **11/5** (1982)
18. Sandell, G.J.,: SHARC – sandell harmonic archive. In: Database of Musical Timbre Information (on NeXT computers) (1994)
19. Skowron, A., Nguyen, H. Son: Quantization of real value attributes: Rough set and boolean reasoning approach. In: P.P. Wang (ed.), Second Annual Joint Conference

on Information Sciences (JCIS'95), September 28 – October 1, Wrightsville Beach, North Carolina, USA (1995) 34–37; see also: ICS Research Report **11/95**, Warsaw University of Technology (1995); see also: Bulletin of International Rough Set Society **1/1** (1996) 5–16

Chapter 12

Rough Sets in Industrial Applications

Adam Mrózek and Leszek Płonka

Institute of Theoretical and Applied Computer Science
Polish Academy of Sciences
ul. Bałtycka 5, 44–100 Gliwice, Poland

1 Introduction

The design and implementation of industrial control systems often relies on quantitative models. At times, however, we encounter problems for which such models do not exist or are difficult and expensive to obtain. In such cases it is often possible to consult human experts to create qualitative models. This approach is the cornerstone of the application of fuzzy logic to the synthesis of control systems [3]. Another approach consists in observing human operators of plants and processes and discovering rules governing their actions. The behavior of operators can often be specified by ***decision tables***, defined as sets of ***decision rules*** coupled with rule selection mechanisms. Rough set theory [10, 11] can be used to generate such tables from ***protocols of control***, containing the decisions of human operators [8].

2 Operators' Inference Models

From an operator's point of view, the controlled plant is characterized by [8]:

- *control goals space*, defined by the variables characterizing control goals,
- *observation space*, defined by measurable and observable variables,
- *control space*, characterized by measurable and controllable variables.

Observation space coordinates are defined as those parameters of the plant which the operator observes and evaluates, because he is convinced that they are directly related to the control goal.

Determination and analysis of the current situation is the starting point for the operator's evaluation whether the control goal has been reached or not. This is implied by the fact that the control goal is expressed by the operator with an appropriate configuration of measurable and observable variables.

The coordinates of the control goals space are the notions used by the operator which describe the degree in which the control goal is attained. The values of the notions are established on the basis of the configuration of the coordinates' values of current situation. Hence there exists a close correspondence between the observation space and the control goals space.

On the one hand, current situation of the controlled plant in the observation space may be mapped onto the goal space. On the other hand, the control goals may be mapped onto the observation space by partitioning or covering the space of observation. Regions of the observation space determined by the partition or covering are called *characteristic states* of the plant.

The coordinates of the control space are those parameters of the plant whose values are determined by the operator in the process of decision making with the control goal in mind. The operator determines certain typical configurations of the values of the measurable and controllable variables in the control space. For technologically imposed control conditions, this results from the commonsense rules or individual preferences of the operator.

Appropriate sets of measurable and controllable variables are called *characteristic controls*. The operator's inference model consists of:

- decomposition of the observation space into areas called *characteristic states* of the plant,
- decomposition of the control space into areas called *characteristic controls*,
- assignment of a proper characteristic control to every characteristic state.

The model defined above implies the following phases of the *operator's decision process*:

- evaluation of the current situation within the observation space,
- assignment of this situation to the proper characteristic state of the plant,
- selection and realization of the proper characteristic control within the control space,
- return to the beginning.

3 Knowledge Representation

A plant operator's inference model defines a set of conditions which should be satisfied before initiating a set of actions. A natural way to represent the plant operator's knowledge is to construct a set of decision rules (conditional productions) of the form

IF {conditions} **THEN** {decisions}

Rule-based systems have been used for years to solve many practical problems. They have many useful features, e.g.:

- ability to model the expert's knowledge in a natural way,
- modularity of the organization of the knowledge base,
- stability of the knowledge-base, i.e., ease of gradual development without the necessity of introducing radical changes to the architecture.

An advantage of rule-based systems is that decision rules can be obtained in several ways:

- Through interviews with problem domain experts. This approach is used in the example presented in Sect. 9.3.
- By means of learning from examples. First, data containing experts' decision along with conditions that prompted them to make those decisions are collected and then various learning methodologies are used to infer general decision rules covering as much of the original data set as possible. Example applications of this approach to decision rule derivation are described in Sect. 9.1 and Sect. 9.2.
- From discretized quantitative plant models. Complex quantitative plant models can be discretized and stored in a tabular format, e.g., in order to speed up the computations. In such circumstances, decision tables serve as lookup tables that allow for an accelerated generation of control signals.

We have adopted rough set theory as a method of data analysis and decision rule generation.

4 Rough Set Theory

Rough set theory is an extension of classical set theory because it incorporates classification knowledge into the set model. It may also be viewed as a mathematical tool for analyzing incomplete or imprecise information and discovering dependencies in data. The dependencies are represented in the form of decision rules that may be used to build computer knowledge bases.

In rough set theory, sets of decision rules are called decision tables and have the form shown in Fig. 1 ($c_1, \ldots, c_k$ denote the condition attributes; $d_1, \ldots, d_n$ denote the decision attributes; $v^i_{c_j}$ denote the values of the condition attributes and $v^i_{d_j}$ denote the values of the decision attributes).

	Condition attributes					*Decision attributes*				
Rule number	c_1	...	c_j	...	c_k	d_1	...	d_j	...	d_n
1	$v^1_{c_1}$	...	v^1_{cj}	...	$v^1_{c_k}$	$v^1_{d_1}$	...	$v^1_{d_j}$	...	$v^1_{d_n}$
$\vdots$	$\vdots$	$\vdots$	$\vdots$	$\vdots$	$\vdots$	$\vdots$	$\vdots$	$\vdots$	$\vdots$	$\vdots$
N	$v^N_{c_1}$	...	v^N_{cj}	...	$v^N_{c_k}$	$v^N_{d_1}$	...	$v^N_{d_j}$	...	$v^N_{d_n}$

Fig. 1. Rough set decision table

5 Knowledge Acquisition and Verification

Knowledge acquisition is the process of capturing experts' or plant operators' domain knowledge or behavior.

The first stage of knowledge acquisition consists in recording the decisions of a plant operator in the form of data tables containing the operator's decisions along with conditions that prompted him to make those decisions, interviewing a domain expert, or building a tabular representation of a mathematical model.

The second stage consists in analyzing the data contained in the table. The following formal aspects of tables can be tackled with the rough set approach:

- completeness (every combination of the values of condition attributes has a corresponding decision),
- consistency (every combination of the values of condition attributes has only one corresponding decision),
- redundancy (every combination of the values of condition attributes occurs at most once).

The objective of the analysis stage is to derive decision rules from the data. There are several general-purpose data analysis and rule generation software packages based on the rough set methodology, e.g., DataLogic [13], LERS [3], and KDD-R [17].

6 Dynamic Knowledge Bases

Reactive systems interact with their environment, i.e., respond to events occurring in the outside world. The behavior of such systems typically depends not only on the present inputs but also on the past sequence of events. To model reactive systems it is therefore necessary to specify both their dynamics (states and state transitions) and the actions in each state. Reactive systems are often *real-time*, i.e., they control real-world processes and objects, like industrial assembly lines, power plants, airplanes, spaceships, etc. The behavior of such systems not only must be functionally correct but also the results must be produced on time. A failure to respond before a deadline may have serious consequences.

6.1 Finite State Machines

Finite state machines abstract the behavior of dynamic systems. They are automata whose outputs are determined by both by their current and their past inputs, i.e., state machines contain memory, which is represented in the form of states. A state machine can be in only one out of a given number of states at any time. In any given state, certain combinations of inputs (called *events*) will cause the machine to change its state and generate outputs (called *actions*). Both the new output and the new state are functions of the current state and the inputs. State machines are often represented graphically as *state transition diagrams*.

6.2 Integration of State Machines and Decision Tables

A controller utilizing pure decision tables is not capable of modeling the dynamic behavior of real-world systems. Since state machines are widely used for reactive system specification, it is necessary for a specification method based on decision tables to be integrated with state machine descriptions.

In our approach, the decision tables define the behavior of the controller in each state and are responsible for state changes. Each state of the state machine has an associated decision table that defines the combinational actions in this state [6], as shown in Fig. 2. This leads to *dynamic knowledge bases*, in which the active sets of rules are determined by the state of the state machine.

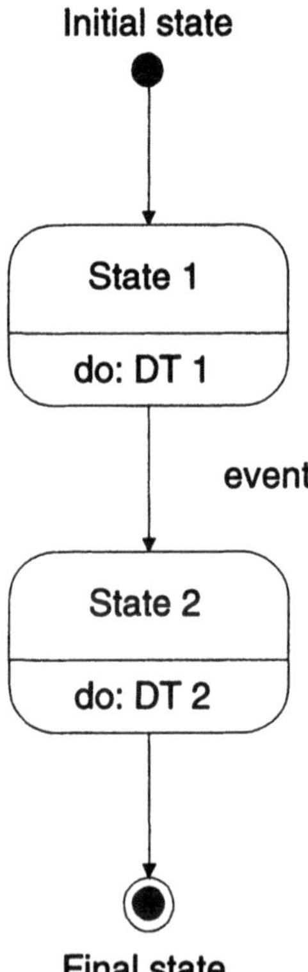

Fig. 2. State machine and decision tables

7 Rough Controller Synthesis Methodology

We have proposed a methodology of rough controller synthesis [8]. The goal of the methodology is to provide a systematic framework, comprising methods, techniques and tools, for building rough control systems. In particular, such a methodology must provide a framework for knowledge acquisition, representation, verification and implementation.

Our approach is shown in Fig. 3. It is characterized by the following features:

1. The data come from a human operator of a real-world system (or its simulator), a domain expert or a mathematical model.
2. The data (examples of an operator's decisions, decision rules provided by an expert or derived from a model) are analyzed by means of rough set theory.
3. A rule base, represented as a decision table, is generated from the data.
4. The rule base is downloaded into a rough controller or a smart network (network of rough controllers) and executed.

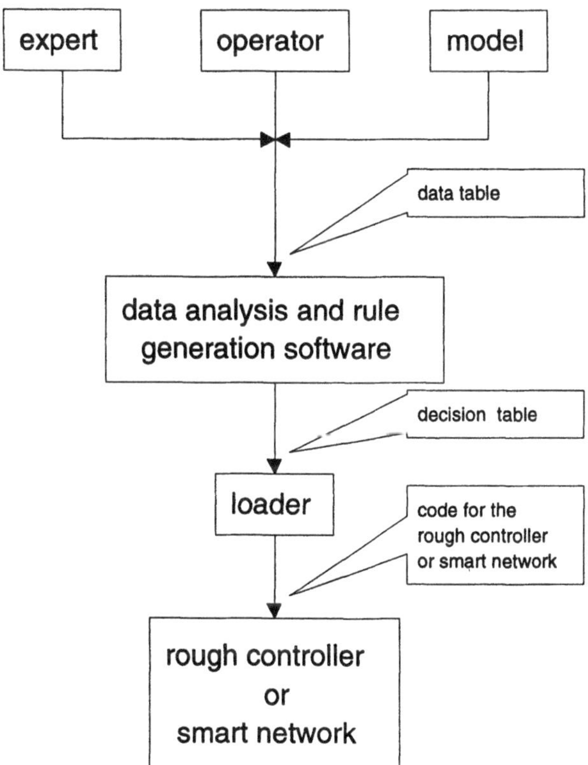

Fig. 3. Rough controller synthesis framework

7.1 Rough Controller

The "rough controller" is a hardware processor of decision tables. Its basic structure was introduced in [6] and is shown in Fig. 4.

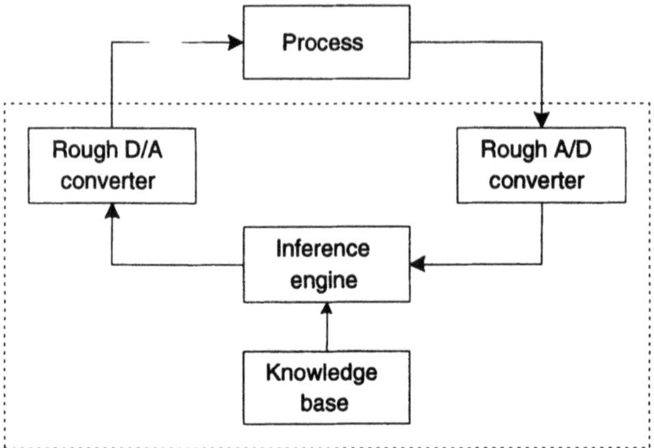

Fig. 4. Rough control system

The synthesis of the rough controller comprises the following aspects:

- synthesis of its hardware and software structure for an implementation of a rule-oriented knowledge base, rule selection mechanism and an interface to the controller's environment,
- implementation of software tools supporting the development of the knowledge base.

Our implementation of the rough controller is based on the 68HC16Z1 [6] embedded controller. A personal computer hosts the development environment which serves to prepare the decision rules to be used for control. Generated rules are downloaded to the controller over a communication link and executed.

In our implementation, the controller consists of the following subsystems:

Rough analog-to-digital converter performs the discretization and classification of the input signals.

Inference engine is responsible for the evaluation of the decision tables. It finds productions whose conditions are satisfied and performs actions specified by their decisions.

Decision table-oriented knowledge base contains conditional productions organized into decision tables.

Rough digital-to-analog converter obtains decision attributes from the rough inference engine and converts them into output signals.

The structure of the controller's software is shown in Fig. 5. It consists of the following subsystems:

Kernel supports the basic functions of the controller, such as process management, interrupt handling and device control.

Monitor is a set of supervisory procedures which control the A/D and D/A conversion, signal classification and declassification and the inference process.

Knowledge base stores the knowledge about control expressed in the form of decision tables.

Communication layer provides the data exchange capabilities.

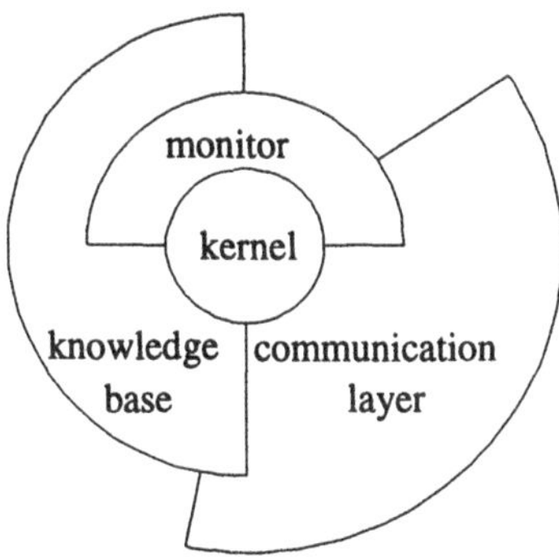

Fig. 5. Software subsystems of the rough controller

7.2 Smart Network

Progress made by semiconductor technology lead to the advent of low cost embedded controllers placed close to sensors and actuators and connected by a network. In such systems a central computer is no longer needed to execute the control algorithm as it is distributed over many "smart" devices. Since the nodes of the network have large autonomy, they can make decisions on their own or consult them with other network nodes, as well as adapt their behavior to changing conditions. Network devices are often capable of play-and-plug operation, i.e., after connecting to the network they can determine the configuration of the system, their localization and role, the role of other network devices, send their parameters to other nodes and start working. This migration of "intelligence" towards sensors leads to new opportunities in the design of control systems. In this paper we show how the rule-based approach can help in the design of smart networks.

The advantages of smart distributed systems over centralized ones are the following:

- lower cost of the wiring,
- lower cost of the processing units,
- ability to locally execute part of the control algorithm,

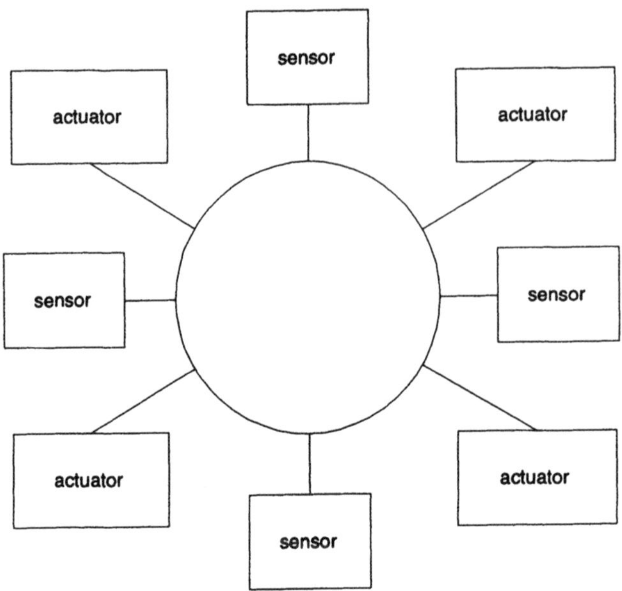

Fig. 6. Smart network

- reduced data transfers,
- increased immunity to failures (due to redundancy),
- easier reconfigurability,
- plug-and-play operation.

Various aspects of smart control networks are presented in [12].

Knowledge Base Decomposition The architecture of a smart network is always determined by the given set of sensors and actuators making up the system and does not depend on the contents of the rule-oriented knowledge base defining its behavior. In order to build a smart network, the knowledge base must be distributed between the nodes of the network, so that the network will be equivalent to a centralized system with the same knowledge base. In our approach, the smart sensors perform the measurements and classification of the input signals, i.e., the values of the condition attributes $c_1 \dots c_k$ and send them to the smart actuators. Each actuator corresponds to some decision attribute $d_1 \dots d_n$ (or a subset of decision attributes) and it is equipped with "its part" of the knowledge base. It uses that knowledge as well as the values of the condition attributes to carry out the actions specified by the decision attributes. The idea of knowledge base decomposition is illustrated in Fig. 7.

Communication Scheme Every actuator has to know the system state as well as the states of the sensors in order to execute its part of the algorithm correctly. This can be achieved with message passing. In our approach, the sensors

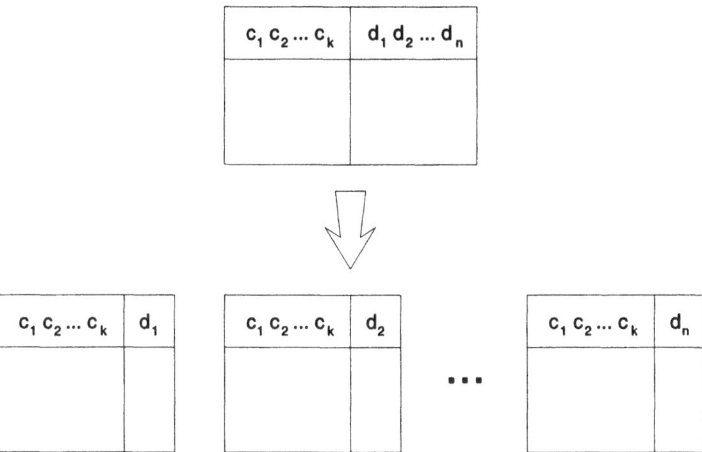

Fig. 7. Knowledge base decomposition

notify the actuators about their state changes by message broadcasts so that the actuators have up-to-date information and are able to generate correct control signals. This interaction scheme is said to be event-driven (because the actuators do not have to poll the sensors for their state and thus consume the available bandwidth but rather are updated by the sensors when necessary) and status-based [12] (because sensors do not actually send commands to specific actuators but only state information). Selected actuator (or actuators) also generate and distribute state transitions commands.

From the above discussion it can be seen that the basic set of protocol commands consists of just one element – `SensorEvent(sensor_id, data)` – used by sensors to distribute events informing of their new state.

8 A Brief Comparison of Rough, Fuzzy and Rough-Fuzzy Controllers

The rough controller is in fact a processor of decision tables. It has a simple hardware implementation and may be very fast. The main problem of rough controller synthesis is attribute value discretization. In some cases it is possible to use some automatic method, other cases require a heuristic approach and expert knowledge. Decision rules may be derived automatically from examples or supplied by a domain expert.

Fuzzy logic controllers require the decision rules and membership functions of the linguistic variables to be defined by domain experts. The defuzzification process may limit the processing speed because it is rather time consuming. However, fuzzy logic control is already a mature technology and many development systems as well as hardware solutions are available.

The rough-fuzzy approach [1] uses elements of rough set theory to *objectively* create membership functions and then uses fuzzy logic to carry out the inference process. The rough-fuzzy membership functions are not smooth and consequently the controller is less accurate, though much faster, than the fuzzy logic controller.

9 Examples

This section contains examples of the application of the proposed methodology to the synthesis of control systems.

9.1 Rotary Clinker Kiln

The rotary clinker kiln is used to produce clinker from slurry, which is one of the basic steps during cement production. The kiln is shown in Fig. 8.

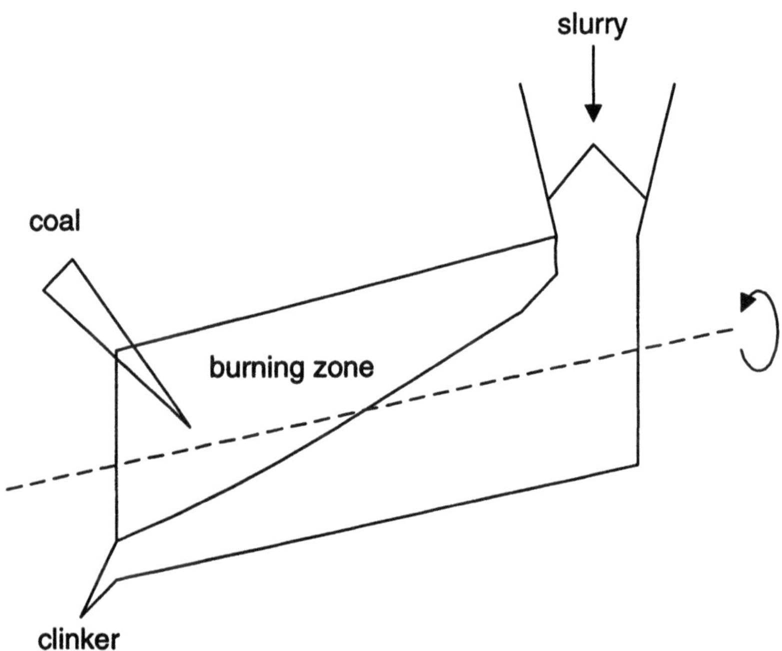

Fig. 8. Rotary clinker kiln

The kiln is controlled by a human operator (stoker) whose goal is to stabilize the temperature in the burning zone. This goal may be achieved by controlling certain decision attributes:

d_1 – number of kiln revolutions per minute,

d_2 – coal consumption, as measured by the number of revolutions of the coal worm per minute.

The operator's decisions are based on several condition attributes:

c_1 – burning zone color,
c_2 – clinker granulation,
c_3 – color inside the kiln,
c_4 – burning zone temperature,
c_5 – derivative of the burning zone temperature.

The domains of the condition attributes are the following:

$$
\begin{aligned}
V_{c_1} &= \{\text{scarlet}, \text{dark\_pink}, \text{bright\_pink}, \text{definitely\_bright\_pink}, \text{rosy\_white}\} \\
V_{c_2} &= \{\text{fine}, \text{fine\_with\_lumps}, \text{distinct\_granulation}, \text{lumps}\} \\
V_{c_3} &= \{\text{dark\_streaks}, \text{no\_dark\_streaks}\} \\
V_{c_4} &= \{1380\text{–}1400, 1400\text{–}1420, 1420\text{–}1440, 1440\text{–}1480, 1480\text{–}1500\} \\
V_{c_5} &= \{\text{slow\_increase}, \text{fast\_increase}, \text{slow\_decrease}, \text{fast\_decrease}\}
\end{aligned}
$$

The domains of the decision attributes are the following:

$$
\begin{aligned}
V_{d_1} &= \{0.9 \text{ rpm}, 1.22 \text{ rpm}\} \\
V_{d_2} &= \{0 \text{ rpm}, 15 \text{ rpm}, 20 \text{ rpm}, 40 \text{ rpm}\}
\end{aligned}
$$

Table 1 contains the protocol of control performed by a stoker during one shift. For simplicity, numbers have been substituted for the linguistic values of the attributes.

Rough set theory makes it possible to analyze the data in Table 1 and generate decision rules that will be used to implement a computer controller of the rotary clinker kiln. The set of equivalence classes of relation $D^\star$ is as follows:

$$\tilde{D} = \{S_1, S_2, S_3, S_4, S_5\}$$

where

$$
\begin{aligned}
S_1 &= \{1, 2, 9, 10, 11, 12, 13, 14, 29, 33, 34, 35, 41, 42, 43\} \\
S_2 &= \{3, 4, 5, 6, 7, 8, 21, 22, 23, 24, 30, 31, 36, 38, 39\} \\
S_3 &= \{15, 16, 17, 32, 40\} \\
S_4 &= \{18, 19, 20, 37\} \\
S_5 &= \{25, 26, 27, 28\}
\end{aligned}
$$

It can be shown that $C \xrightarrow{1} D$, unfortunately attributes c_1, c_2, c_3 are not useful for computer control because the operator's assistance is needed to determine

time	c_1	c_2	c_3	c_4	c_5	d_1	d_2
t_1	1	1	2	2	1	2	4
t_2	1	1	2	2	1	2	4
t_3	2	1	2	2	2	2	3
t_4	2	1	2	3	2	2	3
t_5	2	2	2	3	2	2	3
t_6	2	2	2	3	4	2	3
t_7	2	2	2	2	2	2	3
t_8	2	2	2	2	2	2	3
t_9	1	2	2	2	1	2	4
t_{10}	1	1	2	2	1	2	4
t_{11}	1	1	2	2	1	2	4
t_{12}	1	1	1	2	1	2	4
t_{13}	1	1	2	2	2	2	4
t_{14}	1	1	2	2	2	2	4
t_{15}	2	1	2	3	1	2	2
t_{16}	2	2	2	3	3	2	2
t_{17}	3	2	2	3	1	2	2
t_{18}	3	2	2	4	2	2	1
t_{19}	3	3	2	4	2	2	1
t_{20}	3	3	2	4	2	2	1
t_{21}	3	3	2	4	1	2	3
t_{22}	2	3	2	2	2	2	3
t_{23}	2	2	2	2	2	2	3
t_{24}	2	2	2	2	2	2	3
t_{25}	1	1	1	2	4	1	4
t_{26}	1	1	1	2	4	1	4
t_{27}	1	1	1	2	4	1	4
t_{28}	1	1	1	2	4	1	4
t_{29}	1	1	2	2	1	2	4
t_{30}	2	1	2	2	2	2	3
t_{31}	1	1	2	2	1	2	4
t_{32}	1	1	2	2	1	2	4
t_{33}	2	1	2	2	2	2	3
t_{34}	2	1	2	3	2	2	3
t_{35}	2	2	2	3	2	2	3
t_{36}	2	2	2	3	4	2	3
t_{37}	2	2	2	2	2	2	3
t_{38}	2	2	2	2	2	2	3
t_{39}	1	2	2	2	1	2	4
t_{40}	1	1	2	2	1	2	4
t_{41}	1	1	2	2	1	2	4
t_{42}	1	1	1	2	1	2	4
t_{43}	1	1	2	2	2	2	4

Table 1. Protocol of control for the rotary clinker kiln

their values. However, we can attempt to create a decision table using only attributes c_4 and c_5 which can be measured by a computer (see Table 2). This table is non-deterministic and can be decomposed into two tables, one of which is deterministic and the other is totally non-deterministic (see Table 3 and Table 4). It turns out that the deterministic table used to control the rotary clinker kiln yields better control quality than an experienced human operator [7].

Rule	c_4	c_5	d_1	d_2
1	2	1	2	4
2	2	2	2	3
3	2	3	2	4
4	3	2	2	3
5	3	1	2	2
6	4	2	2	1
7	3	4	2	4
8	3	4	2	3
9	4	1	2	2
10	4	1	2	3
11	4	4	2	3
12	2	4	1	4
13	2	4	2	4

Table 2. Non-deterministic decision table containing only measurable attributes

Rule	c_4	c_5	d_1	d_2
1	2	1	2	4
2	2	2	2	3
3	2	3	2	4
4	3	2	2	3
5	3	1	2	2
6	4	2	2	1
11	4	4	2	3

Table 3. Deterministic part of the decision table

9.2 The Inverted Pendulum

The inverted pendulum problem consists in stabilizing a pole hinged in a vehicle and rotating freely, by pushing the vehicle to the left or right (see Fig. 9). It

Rule	c_4	c_5	d_1	d_2
7	3	4	2	4
8	3	4	2	3
9	4	1	2	2
10	4	1	2	3
12	2	4	1	4
13	2	4	2	4

Table 4. Non-deterministic part of the decision table

poses serious problems for control methods, so it is a good benchmark of their performance. The basic difficulty is the inherent instability and nonlinearity of the system. Classical methods attempt model linearization around 0^0, however this approach works only for small deflection angles [?]. Erecting the pendulum up from the pendent position is not possible at all in linear control theory.

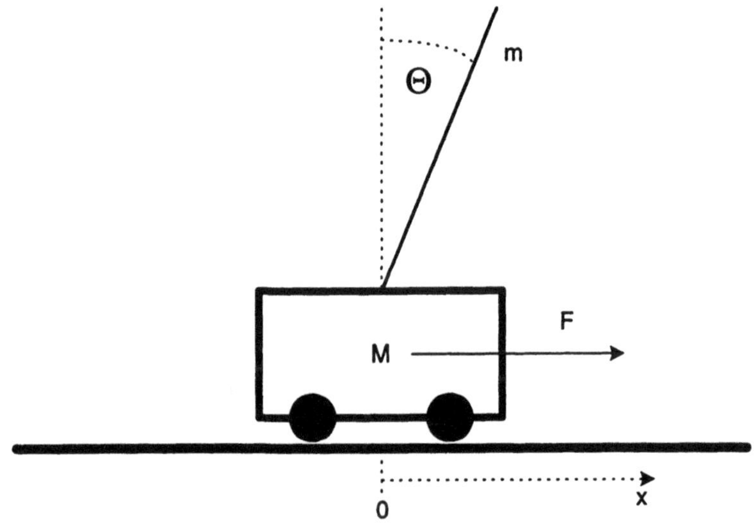

Fig. 9. Inverted pendulum

Our objective was to derive decision rules capable of swinging up and stabilizing the inverted pendulum from actions of a human operator of the system.

We began by building a computer simulator of the inverted pendulum system using equations. The simulator has the following functions:

- it displays the vehicle and the pole attached to it in a graphical window,

- it reacts to the operator pressing the arrow keys (left/right) on the keyboard by acting with force F on the vehicle,
- it recomputes θ, $\dot{\theta}$, x and $\dot{x}$ every simulation time step (typically 0.005 sec) and moves the vehicle accordingly,
- it stores tuples $(\theta, \dot{\theta}, F)$ in a disk file for later processing.

Pressing an arrow key is equivalent to applying a constant force pushing the vehicle to the left or right. In each computation step the state of the system is updated. After a few steps (typically five) $\dot{x}$ is set to zero, i.e., the vehicle is stopped. This behavior, somewhat similar to using an idealized step-motor, was chosen because it was rather difficult to control the system manually when the vehicle was allowed to continue its inertial motion.

In our system, we assumed the following domains of model parameters:

- $\theta \in [-180^0, 180^0]$,
- $x \in [0, 1]$,
- $F \in \{\text{POSITIVE}, \text{NEGATIVE}, \text{ZERO}\}$.

Knowledge Acquisition In the experiments that followed, the vehicle was controlled by a human operator whose goal was to balance the pole attached to the vehicle in an upright position. Various initial positions of the pole were tried, e.g., pendent or slightly deflected from vertical. A record of control was collected in each experiment in the form of a data table containing tuples $(\theta, \dot{\theta}, F)$ in its rows. A fragment of a sample data table is shown in Fig. 10.

θ	$\dot{\theta}$	F
1.8145	10.9504	POSITIVE
1.7561	12.4141	POSITIVE
0.0333	3.9719	ZERO
0.0134	3.9702	ZERO
-0.0064	3.9699	ZERO
-0.0223	2.3721	NEGATIVE
-0.0301	0.7751	NEGATIVE

Fig. 10. Fragment of a data table for the inverted pendulum stabilization problem

The data collected were later analyzed with DataLogic/R rough set theory-based tool [13] and decision rules were created. Rows of the data table were treated as objects; θ and $\dot{\theta}$ were condition attributes and F was a decision attribute.

The parameters controlling rule generation in DataLogic/R were set as follows:

- the domain of θ was discretized non-uniformly (more densely in the vicinity of 0^0),

– the domain of $\dot{\theta}$ was discretized uniformly,

In the course of experiments it turned out that the discretization of the domain of θ was very important. We defined the "cut points" manually, dividing the domain of θ into 0.02^0 intervals in the vicinity of 0^0 and larger intervals at a greater distance from 0^0.

We carried out two kinds of experiments. In the first one, the starting position of the pendulum was $\theta = -10^0$, $\dot{\theta} = 0$ (the pendulum was slightly deflected from vertical). Our goal was to stabilize it in the vertical position $(0, 0)$. In the second kind of experiments the initial position was $\theta = 180^0$, $\dot{\theta} = 0$ (the pendulum was motionless in the pendent position). The initial horizontal position of the vehicle was always $x = 0.5$ and $\dot{x} = 0$.

In the experiment consisting in erecting the pole from a position slightly deflected from vertical (-10^0) and stabilizing it in the upright position the following rules were generated from the data table (in these rules `theta` stands for θ and `d_theta` stands for $\dot{\theta}$):

```
IF { theta > 0.15 AND -3.70 < d_theta AND d_theta <= 11.25) OR
     theta > 0.60 OR
     theta > 0.40 AND -4.85 < d_theta AND d_theta <= 11.25  OR
     theta > 0.02 AND -3.70 < d_theta AND d_theta <= 3.20   OR
     theta > 0.15 AND 11.25 < d_theta AND d_theta <= 14.70  OR
     theta > 0.20 AND (d_theta <= -23.25 OR d_theta > 11.25 }
THEN { F = POSITIVE }

IF { theta <= -7.50 OR
     theta <= -0.02 AND -3.70 < d_theta AND theta <= 0.90   OR
     theta <= -1.60 AND -3.70 <d_theta AND d_theta <= 11.25 OR
     -4.70 < theta AND theta <= -0.06 AND (d_theta <= 0.90  OR
     d_theta > 23.90) OR
     theta <= -1.60 AND 11.25 < d_theta AND d_theta <= 17.00 }
THEN { F = NEGATIVE }

OTHERWISE F = ZERO
```

Some of the obtained rules were non-deterministic. They were examined manually and a decision was made as to which value they should produce.

In another experiment the goal was to swing up the pendulum from the pendent position (180^0) and stabilize it in the upright position. Also in this case we were able to obtain decision rules closely modeling the actions of the operator.

The rules obtained in both cases are very simple and only one presentation by the human operator producing about 300 examples was needed to create them.

Knowledge Utilization The rules derived from the observation table were subsequently used for automatic control of the inverted pendulum. In these experiments, the human operator was substituted by a "rough controller," i.e., a system evaluating the rules and selecting a value for the decision attribute F. The values of $(\theta, \dot{\theta})$ were collected to evaluate the performance of the controller.

The behavior of a dynamic system can be examined using a phase portrait, showing two state variables of a system as a function of time. In the case of the inverted pendulum system, θ and $\dot{\theta}$ are the state variables.

Phase portraits of the system are shown in Figs. 11, 12 and 13. Simulation results show that the controller does achieve its goal. The system eventually approaches state $(0, 0)$, though, due to the roughness of the rules, the equilibrium point cannot be reached asymptotically.

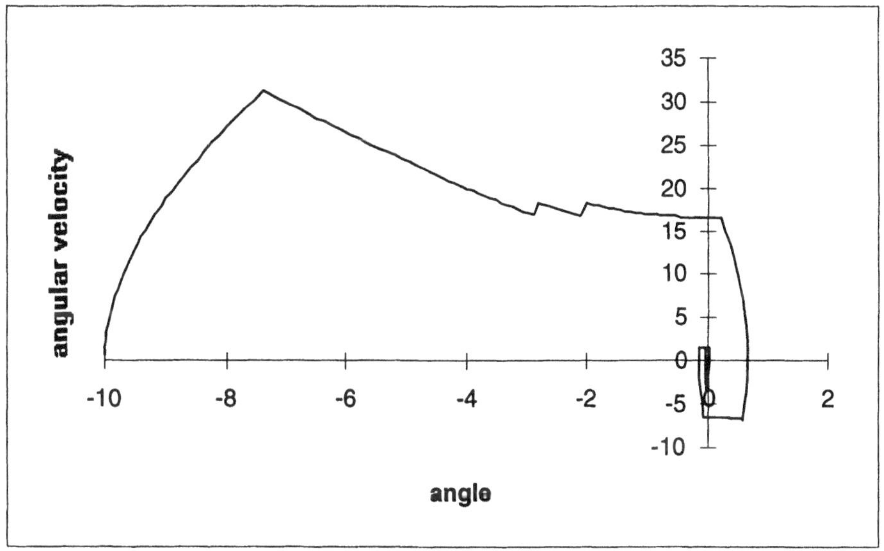

Fig. 11. Phase portrait of the system (initially the pendulum was slightly deflected from vertical)

9.3 Chemical Reactor

A simplified version of an industrial chemical reactor is shown in Fig. 14. It consists of a vat equipped with a number of sensors and actuators:

- sensors:
  - level sensors l_1 and l_2,
  - thermometer T,
  - acidity meter pH,
  - flow meter F.
- actuators:

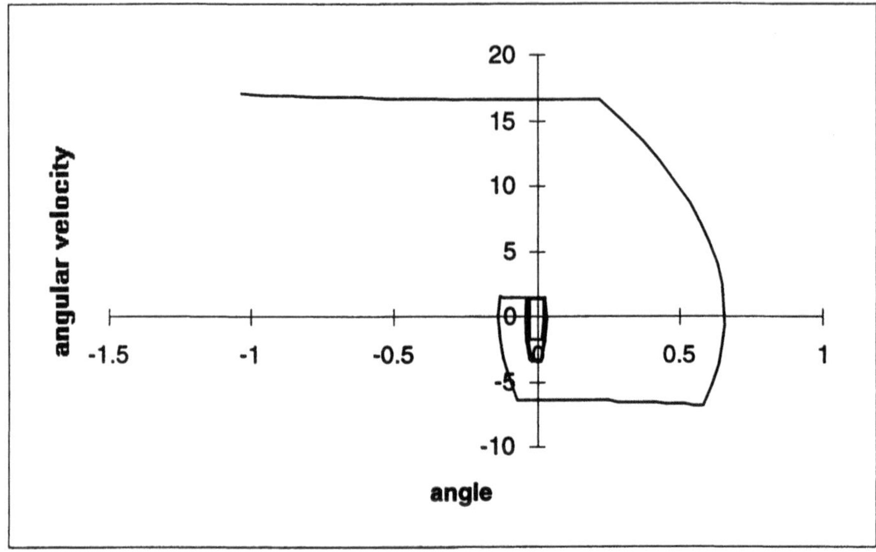

Fig. 12. Phase portrait of the system near $(0, 0)$

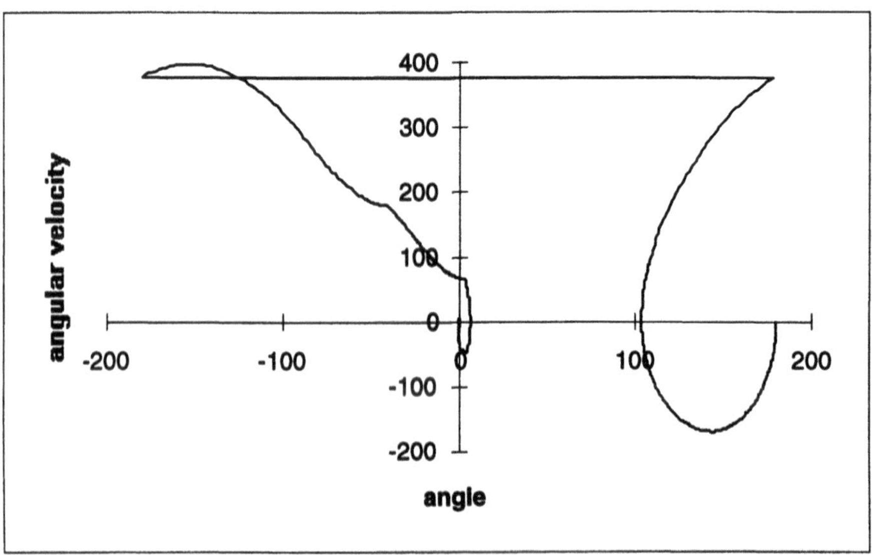

Fig. 13. Phase portrait of the system (initially the pendulum was in the pendent position)

- input valves v_1, v_2 and v_3,
- output valve v_4,
- stirrer S.

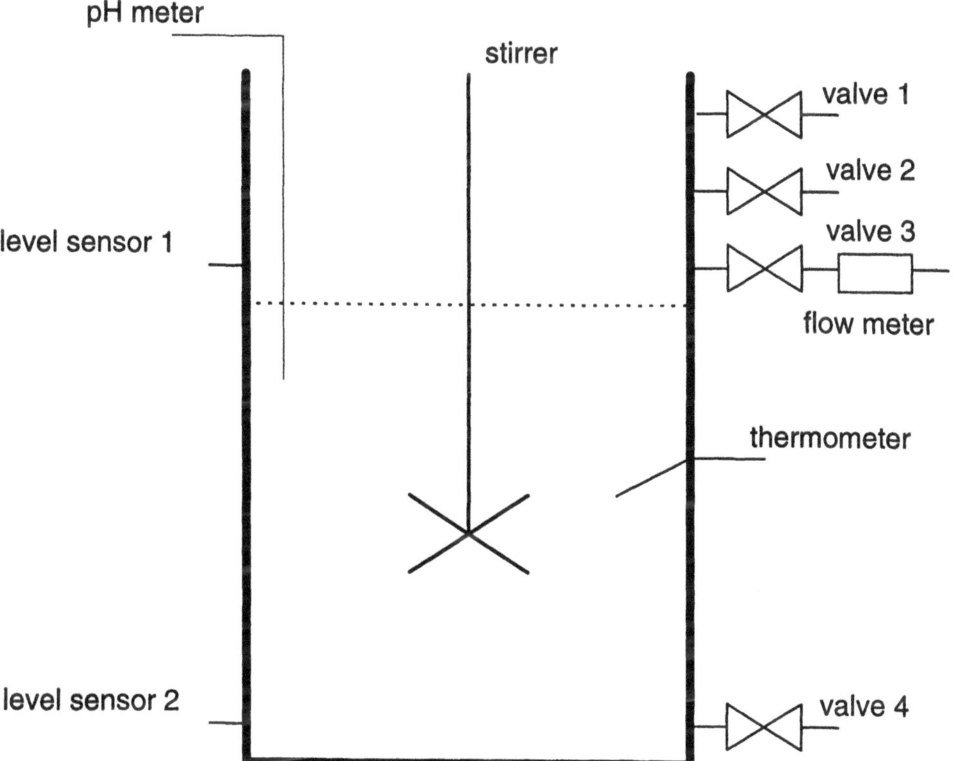

Fig. 14. Schematic of the reactor

The control algorithm can very briefly be described as follows:

1. When the operator starts the process, the valve v_1 is opened and the vat is filled with concentrate.
2. When the vat is full, a certain amount (computed by the system) of a sulphuric acid is added through the valve v_2 and the process begins. This phase is called "dosing."
3. During dosing, the acidity of the contents of the vat and the amount of the added reagent are measured by the flow meter f. Based on those data, certain corrective actions are taken in order to bring the acidity to the desired range.
4. The reaction takes the time t_R to complete. If the acidity of the contents after the reaction is less than required then another correction phase is entered.

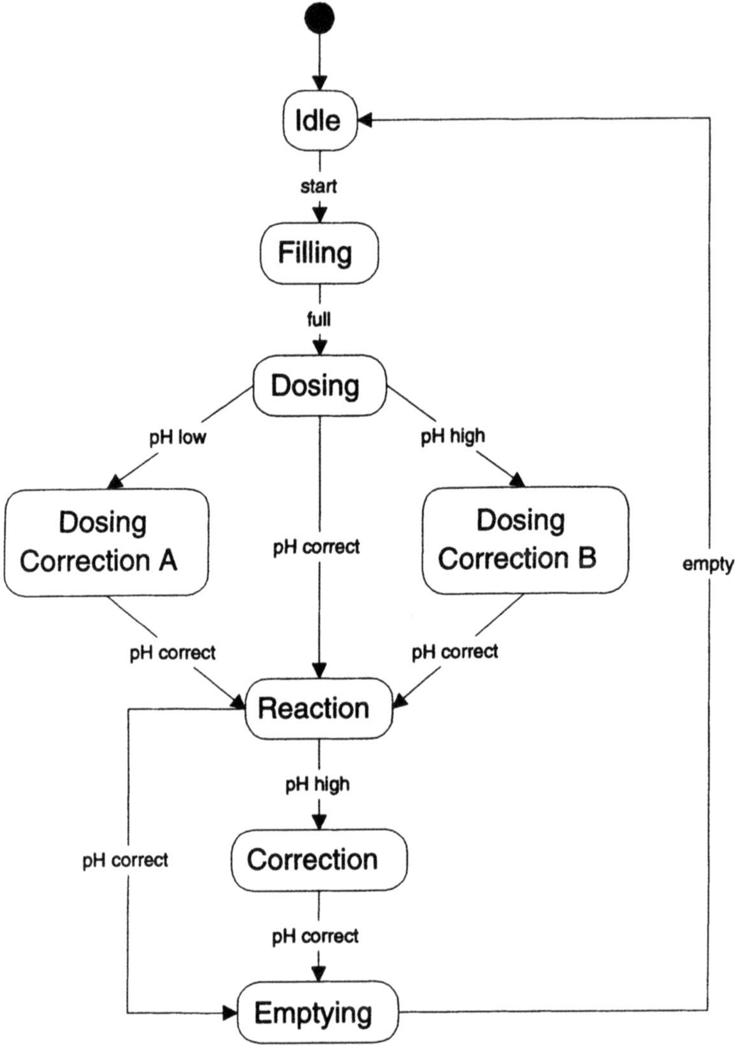

Fig. 15. State transition diagram for the chemical reactor controller

5. When the reaction and correction are over, the vat is emptied through valve v_4.

During the requirements specification phase, the models shown in Figs. 15 and 16 were created. The dynamics of the process was modeled by a state transition diagram and the desired actions of the controller in each state were modeled by decision tables associated with each state.

Smart Network Design The reactor controller can be implemented as a smart network. We have identified the following objects to be implemented as smart

State	oper.	l_1	l_2	pH	Flow	Temp	Time	v_1	v_2	v_3	v_4	s	Next state
Idle	stop							off	off	off	off	R_0	Idle
Idle	start							off	off	off	off	R_F	Filling
Filling		inactive						on	off	off	off	R_F	Filling
Filling		active						off	off	off	off	R_D	Dosing
Dosing				$< pH_1$	< 100%	correct		off	on	off	off	R_D	Dosing
Dosing				$< pH_1$	100%	correct		off	on	off	off	R_D	Correct. A
Dosing				$\in [pH_1, pH_3]$	< 100%	correct		off	on	off	off	R_R	Dosing
Dosing				$\in [pH_1, pH_3]$	100%	correct		off	off	off	off	R_R	Reaction
Dosing				$> pH_3$	< 100%	correct		off	on	off	off	R_D	Correct. B
Dosing				$> pH_3$	100%	correct		off	on	off	off	R_D	Correct. B
Dosing						too high		off	off	off	off	R_D	Dosing
Correct. A				$\geq pH_2$	120%	correct		off	off	off	off	R_R	Reaction
Correct. A				$< pH_2$	< 120%	correct		off	on	off	off	R_R	Correct. A
Correct. A				$\geq pH_2$	< 120%	correct		off	off	off	off	R_D	Reaction
Correct. A				$< pH_2$	120%	correct		off	off	off	off	R_R	Reaction
Correct. A						too high		off	off	off	off	R_D	Correct. A
Correct. B					90%	correct		off	off	off	off	R_R	Reaction
Correct. B					< 90%	correct		off	on	off	off	R_D	Correct. B
Correct. B						too high		off	off	off	off	R_D	Correct. B
Reaction							$< t_R$	off	off	off	off	R_R	Reaction
Reaction				$\geq pH_1$			$> t_R$	off	off	off	off	R_R	Correction
Reaction				$< pH_1$			$> t_R$	off	off	off	off	R_D	Emptying
Correction				$\geq pH_1$				off	off	on	off	R_R	Correction
Correction				$< pH_1$				off	off	off	off	R_D	Emptying
Emptying			active					off	off	off	on	R_D	Emptying
Emptying			inactive					off	off	off	off	R_0	Idle

Fig. 16. Decision table for the chemical reactor controller

sensors and actuators:

- operator console,
- level sensors 1 and 2,
- thermometer,
- pH meter,
- flow meter,
- valves 1 through 4,
- stirrer.

Each of the actuators must be equipped with its part of the knowledge base.

10 Conclusions

Our experience with rough set theory suggests that it constitutes a feasible approach to control. Nonetheless, several problems may be expected:

- The rules reflect the behavior of the human operator. For this reason, they also reflect all the errors as well as non-deterministic (contradictory) decisions the operator makes during training. Non-deterministic rules must be examined and a decision must be made as to what to do about them.
- As with other methods utilizing the "learning from examples" approach, a sufficiently large data base needs to be collected to ensure completeness of the obtained model.
- Discretization of the domains of the attributes is very important and must be done carefully. In many cases, discretization will require some experimentation.
- Control quality may sometimes be unsatisfactory due to discretization.

- As with all real-world control systems, verification and testing are required to ensure correct operation and safety.

In our view, the approach presented in the paper is often superior to alternative methods (i.e., both classical control theory-based and knowledge-based, like fuzzy logic and neural networks) because it:

- utilizes rules coming from control experience, i.e., derived from observation tables and optimized automatically,
- provides accuracy of control as good as that of the human operators,
- controllers are very fast and have simple hardware implementations.

An additional advantage of rough set theory, important from the software engineering point of view, is that both the decision rules and the inference process can be validated and tested more easily than in the case of, e.g., fuzzy or neural models [12].

Acknowledgements

We wish to express our gratitude to REDUCT Systems, Inc., P.O. Box 3570, Regina, Saskatchewan, Canada for an evaluation copy of DataLogic/R rough set theory-based data analysis software package which was applied to derive the decision rules used in the inverted pendulum example. We also thank Andrzej Podeszfa, SCS Design Ltd., Barlickiego 1, 44–100 Gliwice, Poland, for his cooperation on the chemical reactor example.

References

1. Cannon, R.H: Dynamics of physical systems. McGraw-Hill, New York (1967)
2. Czogała, E., Mrózek, A., Pawlak, Z.: The idea of a rough fuzzy controller and its application to the stabilization of a pendulum–car system. Fuzzy Sets and Systems **72** (1995) 61–63
3. Hirota, K. (ed): Industrial applications of fuzzy technology. Springer–Verlag, Tokyo (1993)
4. Grzymała-Busse, J.: LERS – A system for learning from examples based on rough sets. In: Słowiński, R. (ed): Intelligent Decision Support – Handbook of Applications and Advances of Rough Sets Theory, Kluwer Academic Publishers, Dordrecht (1992) 3–18
5. Lin, C.E., Sheu, Y.R.: A hybrid–control approach for pendulum–car control. IEEE Transactions on Industrial Electronics **30** (1992) 208–214
6. Motorola Inc.: MCU16 reference manual (1992)
7. Mrózek, A., Płonka, L., Winiarczyk, R., Majtan, J.: Rough sets for controller synthesis. In: T.Y. Lin (ed.): Proceedings of the Third International Workshop on Rough Sets and Soft Computing (RSSC'94), San Jose State University, San Jose, California, USA, November 10–12, (1994) 498–505
8. Mrózek, A.: Rough sets and dependency analysis Among attributes in computer implementations of expert's inference models. International Journal of Man–Machine Studies **30** (1989) 457–473

9. Mrózek, A., Płonka, L., Kedziera, J.: The methodology of rough controller synthesis. In: Proceedings of the Fifth IEEE International Conference on Fuzzy Systems FUZZ-IEEE'96, September 8–11, New Orleans, Louisiana (1996) 1135–1139
10. Pawlak, Z.: Rough sets. International Journal of Information and Computer Science **11** (1982) 341–356
11. Pawlak, Z.: Rough sets - Theoretical aspects of reasoning about data. Kluwer Academic Publishers, Dordrecht (1991)
12. Płonka, L., Mrózek, A.: Requirements specification with decision tables and rough sets. Bulletin of the Polish Academy of Sciences (to appear)
13. Raji, R.S.: Smart networks for control. IEEE Spectrum, June (1994) 49–55
14. REDUCT System, Inc.: DataLogic/R reference manual, Regina, Canada (1992)
15. Szladow, A.J., Ziarko, W.: Knowledge-based process control using rough sets. In Słowiński, R. (ed.): Intelligent Decision Support - Handbook of Applications and Advances of the Rough Sets Theory, Kluwer Academic Publishers, Dordrecht (1992)
16. Zadeh, L.A.: Fuzzy sets. Information and Control **8**, (1965) 338–353
17. Zadeh, L.A.: Fuzzy logic, neural networks, and soft computing. Communications of the ACM **37** (1994) 77–84
18. Ziarko, W., Shan, N.: KDD-R: A comprehensive system for knowledge discovery using rough sets. In: T.Y. Lin (ed.): Proceedings of the Third International Workshop on Rough Sets and Soft Computing (RSSC'94), San Jose State University, San Jose, California, USA, November 10–12 (1994) 164–173

Chapter 13

Rough Sets in Economic Applications

Adam Mrózek and Krzysztof Skabek

Institute of Theoretical and Applied Computer Science
Polish Academy of Sciences
ul. Bałtycka 5, 44–100 Gliwice, Poland

1 Introduction

Making economic decisions is indeed a very interesting and perspective domain for many applications of methods and tools of computer science. However, economic decision problems are difficult to formalize. First of all it results from their complex character and great number of parameters describing their evolution, inexplicitness and incompleteness of available information as well as shortage of explicit criteria explaining economic decisions. Thus in economic decisions we often use intuition and knowledge which is accumulated in the process of creative generalization of practical experiments and observation results or empirical analysis. The same should be obviously considered during development of computer systems which support the process of making economic decisions.

A question appears: what methods and computer tools will be useful to adopt and represent in a computer the whole available knowledge about economic decision problems and how to render it effectively, e.g. by means of suitable computer systems supporting economic decisions.

The rough approach to economic decision problems has been already studied e.g. in [SłowZop95, Piasta, BazSkSy94a].

In the article [VPoel97] an interesting comparison of different approaches with the analysis of marketing data for large data bases was presented. This analysis aims at proving the advantages of particular methods, such as statistics, machine learning, rough sets, etc.

The main purpose of this article is proving that the analysis of large data bases by means of rough set theory can be effectively conducted even by relatively little experienced persons, e.g. graduate students.

Focusing on three exemplary economic decision problems concerning: companies evaluation, credit policy of a bank and marketing strategy of a company, we present below the use of rough set theory [Pawlak82, Pawlak91] in stated above decision making problems. The extensions of rough sets theory, helpful in stated below economic data analyses are described in [PiaLen, Słow92, LenPia94, BazSkSy94b, BazSkSy94c].

2 Synthesis of a Computer Support System

The synthesis of a computer system supporting economic decisions (CSSED) can be decomposed into subtasks:

- knowledge acquisition,
- knowledge representation within a computer,
- rendering the knowledge accessible during interaction between user and computer.

2.1 Knowledge Acquisition

Solution of the knowledge acquisition problem demands the proper description of economic decision problems as well as representation of specific economic decisions.

It is accepted that an economic decision problem is described by: finite parameter set $C = \{c_1, c_2, \ldots, c_k\}$ called further *condition attributes*, finite parameter set $D = \{d_1, d_2, \ldots, d_p\}$ called further *decision attributes*, and determined *domains* (ranges of values) respectively:

$$V_C = \bigcup_{c_i \in C} V_{c_i} \text{ for condition attributes} \tag{1}$$

and

$$V_D = \bigcup_{d_j \in D} V_{d_j} \text{ for decision attributes.} \tag{2}$$

Such description of an economic decision problem causes that its solution consists in determination of condition attribute values and, on this ground, setting values on particular decision attributes. Such a process of solving economic decision problems can be represented as a decision protocol. Fig. 1 shows the structure of this decision protocol.

Rule number	*Condition attributes*					*Decision attributes*				
	c_1	...	c_j	...	c_k	d_1	...	d_j	...	d_n
1	$v^1_{c_1}$	...	v^1_{cj}	...	$v^1_{c_k}$	$v^1_{d_1}$	...	$v^1_{d_j}$	...	$v^1_{d_n}$
⋮	⋮	⋮	⋮	⋮	⋮	⋮	⋮	⋮	⋮	⋮
N	$v^N_{c_1}$	...	v^N_{cj}	...	$v^N_{c_k}$	$v^N_{d_1}$	...	$v^N_{d_j}$	...	$v^N_{d_n}$

Fig. 1. Rough set decision table

It is easy to notice that decision protocol in Fig. 1 contains decision rules. They can be denoted as conjunction of elementary conditions. For j-th decision we have:

$$\begin{aligned} &\text{if} \quad \{(c_1 = v^j_{c_1}) \,\&\, (c_2 = v^j_{c_2}) \,\&\ldots\&\, (c_k = v^j_{c_k})\} \\ &\text{then} \left\{\left(d_1 = v^j_{d_1}\right) \&\ldots\& \left(d_l = v^j_{d_l}\right) \&\ldots\& \left(d_p = v^j_{d_p}\right)\right\} \end{aligned} \tag{3}$$

Having the suitable decision protocol (containing e.g. expert decisions solving definite economic problem) the problem of knowledge acquisition can be reduced to the problem of generation of all different decision rules in the form (3) based on such protocol.

We can use for this purpose efficient software tools based on rough set theory as e.g. LERS [GrzBus92], DataLogic [DL92]. The main function of these tools is the transformation of data bases (expressed in a form of decision protocols or semantically equivalent decision tables) into the form of a reduced decision rule base (a knowledge base).

2.2 Rule Knowledge Base Representation

Knowledge representation is a formal way of knowledge projection in order to efficiently store and process it in a computer memory.

In the discussed case we consider the decision rules representation in the form (3), useful for its efficient processing by a computer system.

The decision rule representation was accepted in the form (3) and written in Prolog which, as a language of logic based on facts and rules, appeared to be suitable for this purpose [ClMel84]. From a formal point of view so-called "pure" Prolog is a computer implementation of predicate calculus [Rob65].

In Prolog a predicate consists of a name and a finite number of arguments that are called terms. A term can be an alphanumeric constant as well as numeric variable (beginning with capital letter) and correctly constructed expressions. After the substitution of the constants for variable predicate we obtain a sentence that is true or false. Predicate or its negation is called literal. Also clauses are very important in predicate calculus; they are disjunctions of literals.

In predicate calculus the knowledge base consist of a set of facts and rules. Fact is a sentence consisting of a single predicate. For example, we can treat the note in form:

```
ind3 (acceptable).
```

as a fact in knowledge base.

It expresses the fact that "economic indicator designated by number 3 assumes an acceptable value". In this case "ind3" is the predicate name whereas the constant "acceptable" is the term. Prolog makes possible recording in the knowledge base not only the facts but also the information about relations between the facts in the form of rules that are called Horn clauses [ClMel84]. For example, a rule written in Prolog has the form:

```
credit (standard) :- ind2 (acceptable), ind6 (acceptable).
```

This notation means that we can allow "the standard credit *if* the economic indicator designated by number 2 has an acceptable value *and at the same time* the economic indicator designated by number 6 has an acceptable value".

Prolog Horn clauses accept also usage possibility of condition alternatives (noted by ";") and disjunction at the same time [ChLee73]. During the decision rule analysis in the form (3) it is not difficult to notice the possibility of its natural representation in the form of an adequate Prolog Horn clause.

2.3 Prolog Inference Engine

Prolog as a language of logic is favorable for implementations of inference systems. Prolog inference engines are based on search strategies. A built-in unification mechanism as well as inference based on the resolution principle [Rob65] are also helpful during the inference process.

The most important features of expert systems are easy to implement in Prolog [Merritt89]. These are:

- backward chaining,
- forward chaining,
- rule representation of data,
- explanations.

Because of a small semantic gap between Prolog code and logical specification of the knowledge base and the inference engine, implementations of computer systems supporting economic decision can be more concise than they might be with another language.

Although the expert systems written by means of conventional languages, such as C, have often a better performance, the Prolog code makes expert systems close to a logical specification of a program and thus easy to modify.

With the inference engine described above, on the ground of facts and rules written in knowledge base, Prolog automatically generates answers resulting logically from these facts and rules.

2.4 User Interface

For a user, the most important part of a computer system supporting decisions is a user interface. Interactive program environments [FanDai93] become nowadays an indispensable tool for solving complicated problems related to its development.

For this purpose either intelligent communication algorithms or modern interactive methods can be used. Intelligent communications algorithms make it possible to transform computer requirements to the human way of reasoning in the process of making decisions whereas modern interactive methods allow a user an efficient communication with a computer. In this way a human is able to watch individual stages of the decision process performed by the computer, influence their run and obtain, except the final problem solution, intermediate information of various type.

The main components of the computer system supporting economic decision (*CSSED*) are presented in Figure 2.

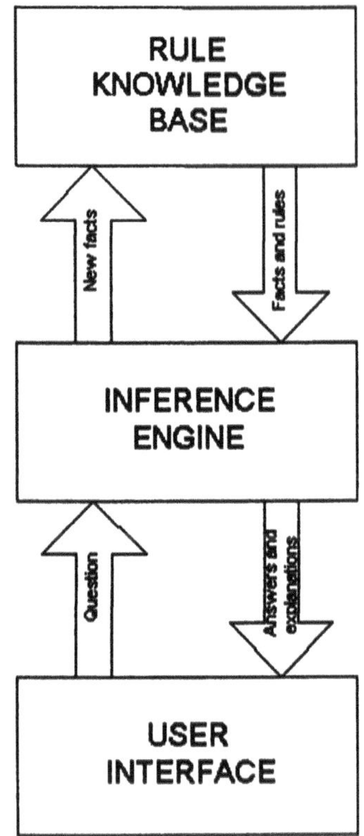

Fig. 2. Main components of *CSSED*

3 Examples

The examples of economic decision problems presented below intend to point at the elements of rough set theory as a formal tool that can be efficiently used in synthesis of appropriate computer systems supporting their solution.

A selection of economic decision problems related to: companies evaluation, credit policy of bank and marketing strategy of a company was taken from master theses [Kraw95, Skabek96, Buzala95] of three students of Silesian Technical University and of International Silesian Trade School in Katowice.

This allowed to analyze that matter deeply and comprehensively along with the place and role of rough set theory elements in acquisition and representation of knowledge concerning their solutions and a practical evaluation of usability of the realized computer systems.

3.1 Companies Valuation – the Economic Decision Problem

The necessity of companies evaluation has existed and been widely applied in economical practice of countries with well developed capital market for many years. Such situation has arisen in Poland only a short time ago [KSow93].

The main purpose of companies evaluation methods depends on a system of accepted estimators. Thanks to that system it is possible to communicate on a capital market. It results from a subjective character of a company value which is only an opinion and may be very differentiated according to the intention of a valuator as well as his methods to apply and parameters to pay attention to [BrilMai90].

Companies evaluation is therefore a very complex problem. There are three fundamental factors that make that problem difficult to formalize:

- multicomplexity – how to estimate the value of so complex object as a company;
- shortage of explicit criteria – resulting from excess of parameters describing the state of a company;
- heterogenity of parameters – parameters having quantitative, qualitative and mixed character may appear.

In this context it is not difficult to notice the place and role of an appropriate computer system supporting companies evaluation.

Acquisition and Knowledge Sources. The analysis is focused on data concerning 171 companies quoted at the Paris Stock Exchange. The data were taken from a CD system called DIANE *(Disque d'Information et d'Analyse d'Enterprises)* which is used in Banque Populaire Toulouse - Pyrenées (France). Thanks to the kindness of Banque Populaire Toulouse - Pyrenées the data were rendered accessible to students during their internships.

Condition Attributes. Parameters used to describe situation of a company are called condition attributes. They consist of such components as: balance, profit and loss account, income and expenditure account, economic indicators and another economic data.

To every condition attribute its own domain, i.e. value set, has been assigned. The condition attribute domains are either finite value sets or they are ranges of values that divide the whole domain into partitions. The majority of domains has been conventionally divided into seven intervals that correspond with intuitive division into values: "very little", "little", " intermediate–less", "intermediate", "intermediate–more", "many", "very many", applied in practice. Dispositions of values resulting from the above example are left-hand asymmetric and correspond with the division: 40–35–35–25–20–10–6. It means that if the companies are sorted according to the value of the given attribute then the interval "very little" consists of the least forty values and the interval "little" consists of the following thirty five values, etc. Some domains of condition attributes did not require such detailed fragmentation.

Selection of condition attributes:

c_1 – Activity Domain (ACTIVITY) – can assume the following values: Building Industry, Chemistry, Power Industry, Metallurgy, etc.

c_2 – Establishment Year (ESTABLISHMENT) – analysed companies were established in the years 1800 - 1980. This period was divided into intervals by years: 1900, 1940 and 1970;

c_3 – Market Extent (MARKET) – can assume three values: regional, domestic, international;

c_4 – Net Immaterial Immovables (NII) – domain: 0 to 297 963 KF (thousands of francs), interval: 50KF, 450KF, 2600KF, 10000KF, 70000KF, 200000KF;

c_5 – Stock (STOCK) – domain: 0 to 2674600KF, interval: 1000, 6400, 54000, 240000, 420000, 1500000 KF;

c_6 – Outstandings (OUTSTAND) – domain: 0 to 1747800KF, interval: 600, 3300, 20400, 92000, 171500, 500000 KF;

c_7 – Pecuniary Resources in Cash (CASH) – domain: 5 to 79709KF, interval: 1000, 3300, 10500, 24000, 51000, 205000 KF;

c_8 – Sum Of Assets and Liabilities (BALANCE_SUM) – domain: 32 to 12653800KF, interval: 70000, 250000, 500000, 1000000, 2100000, 7000000 KF;

c_9 – Own Funds (OWN_FUNDS) – domain: –172329 to 9911185KF, interval: 50000, 150000, 300000, 550000, 1000000, 4000000 KF;

c_{10} – Original Capital (ORIGINAL_CAPITAL)– domain: 1521 to 7147913KF, interval: 32500, 61000, 120000, 300000, 600000, 2000000 KF;

c_{11} – Long-term Loans (LONG_LOANS) – domain: 0 to 6798302KF, interval: 5500, 23000, 63000, 150000, 365000, 1500000 KF;

c_{12} – Short-term Loans (SHORT_LOANS) – domain: 0 to 429800KF, interval: 583, 6903, 20682, 93658, 200000 KF;

c_{13} – Liabilities (LIAB) – domain: 0 to 2217000KF, interval: 2000, 15000, 50000, 150000, 342806, 1000000 KF;

c_{14} – Incomes from Sales, Production, Turnovers (TURNOVER)–domain: 0 to 22831400KF, interval: 2600, 30000, 165000, 500000, 1500000, 5000000 KF;

c_{15} – Merchandise Margin (MARGIN)–domain: 0 to 770642KF, interval: 10000, 60000, 400000 KF;

c_{16} – Manufacturing Costs Of Sold Goods (CONSUMPTION) – domain: –50174 to 2480960KF, interval: 0, 115, 5587, 46066, 460045, 1500000 KF;

c_{17} – Value Added (VAL_ADD) – domain: 99 to 14194400KF, interval: 3000, 12000, 66000, 180000, 600000, 2500000 KF;

c_{18} – Man Cost (MAN_COST) – domain: 0 to 951987KF, interval: 1500, 5500, 30000, 100000, 200000, 600000 KF;

c_{19} – Taxes (TAXES) – domain: 0 to 7088200KF, interval: 300, 1400, 3500, 10000, 30000, 100000 KF;

c_{20} – Basic Activity Result (ACT_RESULT) – domain: –111056 to 528469KF, interval: –2700, 200, 7400, 23000, 45000, 120000 KF;

c_{21} – Profit or Loss in an Account Year (PROFIT_LOSS) – domain: –4140253 to 1160516KF, interval: 1300, 6000, 17000, 38000, 73000, 300000 KF;

c_{22} – Self-financing Capacity (SFCAP) – domain: –208117 to 1426668KF, interval: 2000, 11000, 20000, 35000, 100000, 500000 KF;

c_{23} – Acting Capital (ACT_CAPITAL) – domain: –50530 to 3959314KF, interval: 0, 40000, 110000, 300000, 800000, 1700000 KF;

c_{24} – Acting Capital – Cash (ACT_CAPITAL_CASH) – domain: –353803 to 2432634KF, interval: –1000, 0, 10000, 80000, 200000, 7000000 KF;

c_{25} – Appraisal Depreciation (DEPR) – domain: 0 to 92%, interval: 1, 20, 40, 60, 80 %;

c_{26} – Current Ratio (CURRENT) – domain: 0 to 14200, interval: 0, 1, 5, 12, 100;

c_{27} – Liquidity Ratio (LIQUID) – domain: 0 to 14200, interval: 0, 1, 5, 12, 100;
c_{28} – Number Of Employees (EMPLOYEES) – domain: 0 to 5056, interval: 0, 10, 200, 500, 1000;
c_{29} – Inventory Turnover (INV_TURN) – domain: 0 to 545, interval: 10, 50, 100;
c_{30} – Accounts Receivable Turnover (AREC_TURN) – domain: 0 to 30096, interval: 10, 30, 70, 120;
c_{31} – Accounts Payable Turnover (APAY_TURN) – domain: 0 to 503, interval: 10, 30, 70, 120;
c_{32} – Net Assets Value (NET_ASSETS) – domain: –172329 to 9849371KF, interval: 0, 50000, 200000, 600000, 1200000, 2400000 KF;

The set of condition attributes contains all attributes described above and is designated as $C = \{c_1, c_2, c_3, \dots, c_{32}\}$.

Decision Attributes. Selection of decision attributes is the same as the answer to the question: "How to estimate a company value". The answer to this question turns out in practice to be not so simple and explicit. Multiplicity of approaches and methods concerning the problem of companies evaluation origins from this fact [KSow93, NoGlo94].

Generally we can mention:

- property methods,
- methods based on cash flows,
- methods based on profitability,
- methods using Goodwill Value,
- stock exchange evaluation,

Each of these methods has its drawbacks and highlights as well as certain requirements for credibility and representativeness of used data, usefulness in the synthesis of computer system supporting companies evaluation.

Taking into consideration the above mentioned fact as well as the suggestions of French experts from Banque Populaire Toulouse - Pyrenées it was assumed that the set of decision attributes consists of three elements: *Stock Exchange Value*, *Goodwill Value* and *Price-Earning Ratio* (PER).

As *Stock Exchange Value* of a company we mean the average share price within the last three years multiplied by their number.

Goodwill Value of a company is a property value of a company increased by a immaterial value corresponding to the ability to generate incomes higher than the average. This value can be also negative – it means that the company is worth less than its property.

As *Price-Earning Ratio* of a company we mean the number that multiplies the profit of a company (the most frequently it is the average profit within the last three years) to obtain the profit value [BrilMai90, Del94, GuiLen94]. For companies that bring the loss Price-Earning Ratio assumes zero value.

The considered decision attributes are:

d_1 – *Stock Exchange Value* – domain 775 to 17151476KF, intervals 50000, 100000, 250000, 400000, 1000000, 3000000, 8000000 KF;
d_2 – *Goodwill Value* – domain –9302022 to 16319698KF, intervals –20000, 0, 20000, 100000, 500000, 1500000, 3000000 KF;

d_3 – *Price-Earning Ratio* – domain 0 to 247, intervals 4, 8, 15, 30, 80.

The set of decision attributes contains three attributes described above and is designated as $D = \{d_1, d_2, d_3\}$.

Rough Sets in Data Analysis. According to the suggestions of experts the following course of data analysis process was taken:

1. Determination of dependence between particular decision attributes from the set D and all condition attributes from the set C;
2. Determination of dependence between particular decision attributes from the set D and selected by experts condition attributes from the set C; experts use values of these attributes during companies evaluation;
3. Determination of particular condition attributes influence (from the set C) on companies classification generated by values of decision attributes from the set D;
4. Acquisition of the resultant rule knowledge base that contains minimal sets of decision rules for companies classification according to assumed values of decision attributes.

The DataLogic program [DL92] was used in analysis of selected data coming from 171 companies. The input data of that program were sets of conditions and decision attribute values in the form of a table. Information about the data was recorded in 2 files:

- file with **.tbl* extension contains condition and decision attribute values;
- file with **.typ* extension contains: names of particular conditions and decision attributes, their type e.g. integer, interval of assumed values and likely its division.

The results of data analysis of 171 companies were published in [Kraw95]. Some of them are introduced below. They characterize the usefulness of such a way of data analysis in order to gain the results having great applied importance.

Referring to the notions of rough set theory we obtain:

- the dependence of decision attribute $d_1 \in D$ on set C of condition attributes that have the value of approximation quality coefficient equal to 1 ($\gamma_C(\{d_1\}) = 1$),
- the dependence of decision attribute $d_2 \in D$ on set C of condition attributes that have the value of approximation quality coefficient equal to 1 ($\gamma_C(\{d_2\}) = 1$),
- the dependence of decision attribute $d_3 \in D$ on set C of condition attributes that have the value of approximation quality coefficient equal to 1 ($\gamma_C(\{d_3\}) = 1$),

From the semantic point of view it indicates that by means of known values of all condition attributes from set C we can explicitly classify each of 171 examined companies into the adequate interval connected with the values of decision attributes i.e. *Stock Exchange Value, Goodwill Value, Price-Earning Ratio.*

The most interesting result, also from experts' point of view, is the positive answer to the question whether the discussed value set of condition attributes allows in the explicit way for the classification of companies according to the classes determined by them i.e.: "to be in the same interval of Stock Exchange Price", "to be in the same interval of Goodwill Value", "to be in the same interval of Price-Earning Ratio".

Experts were convinced that values of the condition attributes which they used really allow analysis and the market value estimation of examined companies. The reaction of experts was positive. They were interested in the suggested approach particularly after the obtained results of the data analysis had appeared to be adequate to experts' intuition.

The following experts' suggestions concerned the dependence of decision attributes from set D on subsets of condition attributes from set C examined in companies evaluation process.

In case of decision attribute experts first pointed at the following subset of condition attributes $A = \{c_1, c_2, c_3\}$.

For the dependency $A \to d_3$ it was calculated:

$$\gamma_A(\{d_3)\} = 0.33$$

From the semantic point of view it indicates that only every third Price-Earning Ratio value out of all available values can be explained by means of knowledge represented in the set A of condition attributes. Taking into consideration only the values of these three condition attributes can lead in practice to the incorrect companies classification caused by adopted Price-Earning Ratio.

After extending this set to $A_1 = \{c_1, c_2, c_3, c_9, c_{21}, c_{32}\}$ for the dependency $A_1 \to d_3$ it was calculated:

$$\gamma_{A_1}(\{d_3)\} = 0.92$$

Then the subset B of condition attributes ($B = \{c_1, c_2, c_4, c_9, c_{21}, c_{32}\}$) for the decision attribute $d_2 \in D$ and for the dependency $B \to d_2$ was taken into consideration and it was calculated:

$$\gamma_B(\{d_2)\} = 0.93$$

Remaining analogous results of analyses obtained by means of DataLogic were published in [Kraw95]. From the semantic point of view these results mean that in case of companies classification consistent with the condition attribute values set by experts, a significant reduction of condition attribute number – occuring in the resultant decision rules – must be taken into account.

For instance, the relative reduct of condition attributes from set C with regard to the decision attribute $d_1 \in D$ (i.e. Stock Exchange Price) calculated by DataLogic is the set $C_1 \subset C$ in the form of

$$C_1 = \{c_2, c_4, c_6, c_7, c_8, c_9, c_{10}, c_{11}, c_{12}, c_{14}, c_{18}, c_{19}, c_{20}, c_{21}, c_{22}, c_{23}, c_{24}, c_{29}, c_{32}\}$$

Remaining condition attributes from set C do not have any influence on companies classification consistent with the intervals of Stock Exchange Price settled by experts.

For the decision attribute $d_1 \in D$ (i.e. Stock Exchange Price) DataLogic generated 88 decision rules. They give the full partition of the input data set. It means that each out of 171 considered companies can be explicitly classified into one of the intervals of Stock Exchange Price. Ten exemplary decision rules for Stock Exchange Price belonging to the interval [767, 5000] KF generated by DataLogic has got the form:

```
Decision ::  PRICE ==> <767.00, 5000.00>

1. [PROFIT_LOSS <= 1300.00] & [WCAPITAL_CASH <= -1000.00] &
   & [LONG_LOANS <= 5500.00 OR LONG_LOANS > 1 500 000.00]

Decision ::  PRICE ==> <5000.00, 50000.00>

2. [PROFIT_LOSS <= 1300.00] & [0.00 < NET_ASSETS <= 50000.00] &
   & [10000.00 < WCAPITAL_CASH <= 200000.00]
3. [PROFIT_LOSS <= 1300.00] & [0.00 < WCAPITAL <= 110000.00] &
   & [BALANCE_SUM <= 70000.00] & [-1000.00 < WCAPITAL_CASH <= 200000.00]
4. [NET_ASSETS <= 0.00 OR NET_ASSETS > 1200000.00] &
   & [BALANCE_SUM <= 250000.00]
5. [SFCAP <= 11000.00 OR SFCAP > 100000.00] &
   & [ACT_RESULT <= -2700.00 OR ACT_RESULT > 7400.00] &
   & [NET_ASSETS <= 0.00 OR NET_ASSETS > 1200000.00] &
   & [10000.00 < WCAPITAL_CASH <= 200000.00]
6. [BALANCE_SUM <= 70000.00] & [10000.00 < WCAPITAL_CASH <= 200000.00]
7. [OWN_FUNDS <= 150000.00] & [PROFIT_LOSS <= 1300.00] &
   & [0.00 < WCAPITAL <= 110000.00]
   & [50000.00 < NET_ASSETS <= 1200000.00]
   & [10000.00 < WCAPITAL_CASH <= 200000.00]
8. [OWN_FUNDS <= 150000.00] & [SFCAP <= 11000.00 OR SFCAP > 100000.00] &
   & [0.00 < WCAPITAL <= 110000.00] &
   & [ACT_RESULT <= -2700.00 OR ACT_RESULT > 7400.00] &
   & [NET_ASSETS <= 0.00 OR NET_ASSETS > 50000.00] &
   & [BALANCE_SUM <= 250000.00] & [10000.00 < WCAPITAL_CASH <= 200000.00]
9. [OWN_FUNDS <= 150000.00] & [PROFIT_LOSS <= 1300.00] &
   & [SFCAP <= 11000.00 OR SFCAP > 100000.00] &
   & [NET_ASSETS <= 50000.00 OR NET_ASSETS > 1200000.00] &
   & [WCAPITAL_CASH <= -1000.00 OR WCAPITAL_CASH > 200000.00]
10.[OWN_FUNDS > 150000.00] & [11000.00 < SFCAP <= 100000.00] &
   & [ACT_RESULT <= -2700.00 OR ACT_RESULT > 7400.00] &
   & [BALANCE_SUM <= 250000.00] & [10000.00 < WCAPITAL_CASH <= 200000.00]
```

For example the decision rule 1 means that Stock Exchange Price of the company belongs to the interval [767 KF, 5000 KF] when: its profit is lower than 1300 KF, its acting capital reduced by cash is negative and indebtedness is lower than 5500 KF or higher than 1 500 000 KF. The decision rule 7 means that Stock Exchange

Price of the company belongs to the interval [5000 KF, 50000 KF] when: its own funds are not higher than 150000 KF, its profit is higher than 1300, its acting capital is higher than 0 and lower than 110000, its profit is lower than 1300 KF, its net assets value is higher than 50000 and lower than 1200000 and finally its acting capital reduced by cash belongs to the interval [10000, 20000].

In case of the decision attribute $d_2 \in D$, i.e. Goodwill Value, DataLogic generated 93 decision rules.

For the decision attribute $d_3 \in D$, i.e. Price-Earning Ratio, DataLogic generated 81 decision rules.

DataLogic also enables to analyze the influence volume of condition attributes (existing in the decision rule) on the final decisions i.e. relevant values of decision attributes. The exemplary influence volume of condition attributes in case of above shown decision rules concerning Stock Exchange Price is presented below.

```
* Attribute Strength Report *

Decision Attribute: PRICE  ==> <767.00, 5000.00>     Coverage ==> 100%

Attribute                                        Max. Loc. Str.

PROFIT_LOSS                                         0.78
WCAPITAL_CASH                                       0.76
LONG_LOANS                                          0.75
```

From the semantic point of view the above report implies that companies classification to the first interval of Stock Exchange Price value relies mainly on: their Profit Values, Working Capital and Cash as well as Long-term Loans.

Values of the remaining condition attributes existing in this decision rule (i.e. Capital and Assets Value) are not so important in this case. The report can be also interpreted as follows (experts' interpretation):

- in case of a small (and thus not expensive) company its whole value is proportional to the profit which it brings – the company assets are usually limited and do not influence Stock Exchange Price;
- in case of a large company a negative profit (loss) reduces company value; it is automatically deepened by heavy indebtedness.

```
Decision Attribute: PRICE  ==> <5000.00, 50000.00>     Coverage ==> 100%

Attribute                                        Max. Loc. Str.

NET_ASSETS                                          0.57
OWN_FUNDS                                           0.57
BALANCE_SUM                                         0.52
PROFIT_LOSS                                         0.52
SFCAP                                               0.45
ACT_CAPITAL                                         0.39
```

```
ACT_CAPITAL_CASH                                  0.36
ACT_RESULT                                        0.32
```

In this case, apart from profitability, the capital size and pecuniary resources management have the main influence on the price.

```
Decision Attribute:
PRICE  ==> <50000.00, 100000.00>      Coverage ==> 100%

Attribute                                    Max. Loc. Str.

BALANCE_SUM                                       0.55
SFCAP                                             0.49
PROFIT_LOSS                                       0.49
ORIGINAL_CAPITAL                                  0.44
ACT_CAPITAL_CASH                                  0.43
TAXES                                             0.42
ACT_RESULT                                        0.39
ACT_CAPITAL                                       0.37
OUTSTAND                                          0.31
```

```
Decision Attribute:
PRICE  ==> <100000.00, 250000.00>     Coverage ==> 100%

Attribute                                    Max. Loc. Str.

OWN_FUNDS                                         0.57
BALANCE_SUM                                       0.41
NII                                               0.29
ACT_RESULT                                        0.26
ESTABLISHMENT                                     0.25
ORIGINAL_CAPITAL                                  0.24
SFCAP                                             0.24
PROFIT_LOSS                                       0.23
INV_TURN                                          0.23
ACT_CAPITAL_CASH                                  0.22
```

```
Decision Attribute:
PRICE  ==> <3000000.00, 8000000.00>     Coverage ==> 100%

Attribute                                    Max. Loc. Str.

OWN_FUNDS                                         0.66
NET_ASSETS                                        0.65
PROFIT_LOSS                                       0.65
TURNOVER                                          0.54
```

SFCAP	0.53
LONG_LOANS	0.40

In decisions considered above, the attributes to which experts paid a special attention appeared the most important.

Decision Attribute:
PRICE ==><8000000.00, 17300000.00> Coverage==>100%

Attribute	Max. Loc. Str.
ACT_CAPITAL	0.98
LONG_LOANS	0.98

In case of the interval of the most expensive companies there is a certain unpredictability or even wrong reasoning. The value of a company cannot be higher simply because it has more long–term loans. This rule proves that the most expensive companies cannot be evaluated only by means of the available economic attributes. Possibly the governmental allocations and the activity domain have an influence on the price. As we have already mentioned the results of full data analysis about 171 companies using DataLogic were published in [Kraw95].

Representation, Utilization and Verification of the Obtained Decision Rules. Rule knowledge base generated by DataLogic and related to companies classification in regard of: Stock Exchange Price, Goodwill Value, Price-Earning Ratio contains 21 kits of decision rules. The number of separate rules existing in these kits reaches 240. As DataLogic enables to record the generated decision rules in C language code, it was easy to convert them into the adequate clauses in Prolog.

So prepared rule knowledge base completed by suitable Prolog inference engine makes a core of computer system supporting companies evaluation process.

The usefulness of generated decision rule sets for companies evaluation was examined thoroughly by experts [LE95]. Below we present the results of such analysis for a selected company.

The economic parameters of an exemplary company are the following:

Activity Domain (ACTIVITY)	– transport (16)
Establishment Year (ESTABLISHMENT)	– 1910
Market Extent (MARKET)	– domestic (2)
Net Immaterial Immovables (NII)	= 182 KF
Stock (STOCK)	= 0
Outstandings (OUTSTAND)	= 9466 KF
Pecuniary Resources in Cash (CASH)	= 5333 KF
Sum Of Assets and Liabilities (BALANCE_SUM)	= 69372 KF
Own Funds (OWN_FUNDS)	= 43369 KF
Original Capital (ORIGINAL_CAPITAL)	= 4890 KF
Long-term Loans (LONG_LOANS)	= 1672 KF
Short-term Loans (SHORT_LOANS)	= 0
Liabilities (LIAB)	= 7998 KF
Incomes from Sales, Production, Turnovers (TURNOVER)	= 40230 KF
Merchandise Margin (MARGIN)	= 0
Manufacturing Costs Of Sold Goods (CONSUMPTION)	= 0
Value Added (VAL_ADD)	= 16854 KF
Man Cost (MAN_COST)	= 13396 KF
Taxes (TAXES)	= 2878 KF
Basic Activity Result (ACT_RESULT)	= 7676 KF
Profit or Loss in an Account Year (PROFIT_LOSS)	= 3787
Self-financing Capacity (SFCAP)	= 11174 KF
Acting Capital (ACT_CAPITAL)	= -253 KF
Acting Capital – Cash (ACT_CAPITAL_CASH)	= -5586 KF
Appraisal Depreciation (DEPR)	= 63 %
Current Ratio (CURRENT)	= 1.2
Liquidity Ratio (LIQUID)	= 1.2
Number Of Employees (EMPLOYEES)	= 44
Inventory Turnover (INV_TURN)	= 0 days
Accounts Receivable Turnover (AREC_TURN)	= 73 days
Accounts Payable Turnover (APAY_TURN)	= 149 days
Net Assets Value (NET_ASSETS)	= 43187 KF

As a result of the inference three intervals were obtained:

- *Price-Earning Ratio* belongs to the interval [8, 15]; 25th rule; when the profit is 3787 KF it gives the interval [30296 KF, 56805 KF] of company value;
- *Goodwill Value* belongs to the interval [0 KF, 20000 KF]; 37th rule; when Net Assets Value is 43187 KF it gives the interval [43187 KF, 61187 KF] of company value;
- *Stock Exchange Value* belongs to the interval [50000 KF, 100000 KF]; 15th rule; taking the conjunction of the above intervals we obtain (approximately) the interval [44000 KF, 57000 KF] which is the requested interval of company value.

Using the same company parameters experts obtained the interval [43559 KF, 44044 KF]. This interval of company value is in great part similar to the interval obtained in rough analysis.

Summary. The companies evaluation problem is still open even in case of well developed countries having the long lasting market tradition.

For this reason the attempts of developing and computer implementating of such tools that support companies evaluation process still should be undertaken.

Inexplicitness and incompleteness conditioned our selecting of rough set theory elements as a formal tool helpful in suitable computer system synthesis. An additional fact favorable for the expediency of rough set theory selection is that the weight of particular decision attributes is variable in time or - - in other words – estimation of company evaluation changes. From the computer science point of view the computer system supporting companies evaluation process based on this theory is data driven and hence, by its very nature, it is a nondeterministic system. Some of condition attributes may not be used in the current decision rules but it does not mean that they will not be used at all in future.

The approach to explain one knowledge in terms of another one or – in other words – classification of new facts by means of facts already gathered in the rule knowledge base is quite different from the approach typical for statistics. During their synthesis it is unnecessary to base on large representative data samples or expect from their population fulfilling certain conditions (e.g. stationarity). Because of its specific character and variable in time diverse market and political conditions, the problem cannot be analyzed and solved by means of methods adequate for statistics.

3.2 Bank Credit Policy – the Economic Decision Problem

Granting credits to individuals or businesses belongs to the fundamental duties and functions of modern banks. Such activity of banks includes a certain level of risk. That risk results from the difficulties of explicit determination of so called *credit capacity* of a debtor i.e. the possibility of credit repayment including payable interest [Debski94]. At the stage of credit terms negotiations the contrary interests of banks and debtors occur.

A bank is obviously interested in accommodation of a profitable credit and intends to rate a credit capacity of debtor in honest complete and credible way. A debtor is usually interested in obtaining a high and cheap credit. He would try to present his credit capacity as favorably as possible.

This contrast of bank and debtor interests as well as incompleteness, inexplicitness, uncertainty of available information and difficulties with selection of the parameters and criteria allowing for objective credit capacity evaluation make the credit decision problem difficult to formalize.

This fact conditioned the attempt of synthesis of computer system supporting economic decision based on rough set theory elements at the stage of knowledge acquisition and representation. Particular description of such synthesis was presented in [Skabek96]. Some components of this work illustrating the usefulness and efficiency of rough set theory elements utilization are described below.

Knowledge Sources and Acquisition. From the formal point of view the bank crediting process consists of two partial problems:

- preparing the premises for decision making i.e. honest complete and credible valuation of debtor's credit capacity;
- opening the credit up to the certain limit and on the condition that minimize a risk.

The knowledge about solution of this problem must concern solutions of both partial problems. Taking advantage of accessible publications, possibilities of discussion with experts and observations of credit decisions made by banks in real conditions allow for knowledge acquisition conduct. It was particularly described in [Skabek96].

The following economic indexes useful in valuation of credit capacity have been accepted [SieJach93, Bed93]:

- **Net Profitability Ratio**

$$\text{Ind1} = \frac{\text{Net Profit}}{\text{Sale Value}} 100\%$$

- **Current Ratio**

$$\text{Ind2} = \frac{\text{Current Assets}}{\text{Current Liabilities} + \text{Short-term Credit}}$$

- **Quick Ratio**

$$\text{Ind3} = \frac{\text{Current Assets} - \text{Stock}}{\text{Current Liabilities}}$$

- **Accounts Receivable Turnover Ratio**

$$\text{Ind4} = \frac{\text{Average Accounts Receivable}}{\text{Net Sale}} 365$$

- **Inventory Turnover Ratio**

$$\text{Ind5} = \frac{\text{Average Stock}}{\text{Net Sale}} 365$$

- **Exceeded Payables Ratio**

$$\text{Ind6} = \frac{\text{Exceeded Accounts Payables}}{\text{Total Payables}}$$

- **Equity Ratio**

$$\text{Ind7} = \frac{\text{Outside Capital}}{\text{Ownership Capital}}$$

- **Ownership Capital Ratio**

$$\text{Ind8} = \frac{\text{Ownership Capital}}{\text{Total Assets}}$$

- **Interest Coverage Ratio**

$$\text{Ind9} = \frac{\text{Interest}}{\text{Sale}} 100\%$$

Condition and decision attributes as well as their domains were determined with a help of experts' suggestions and economic indexes described above. The data were recorded in a relevant economic decision protocol making basis of knowledge acquisition process. General scheme of decision protocol was presented in Fig. 1.

Condition Attributes. Here are the selected condition attributes:

c_1 – Net Profitability Ratio – noted as *Ind1*, domain: $\{acceptable, unacceptable\}$
c_2 – Net Profitability Ratio tendency – domain: $\{increase, decrease\}$
c_3 – Net Profitability Ratio in comparison with the other companies of a branch – domain: $\{high, low\}$
c_4 – Current Ratio – noted as *Ind2*, domain: $\{acceptable, unacceptable\}$
c_5 – Quick Ratio – noted as *Ind3*, domain: { *acceptable, unacceptable* }
c_6 – Accounts Receivable Turnover Ratio – noted as *Ind4*, domain: { *acceptable* , *unacceptable* }
c_7 – Inventory Turnover Ratio – noted as *Ind5*, domain: {*acceptable, unacceptable* }
c_8 – Exceeded Payables Ratio – noted as *Ind6*, domain: $\{acceptable, unacceptable\}$
c_9 – Equity Ratio – noted as *Ind7*, domain: $\{acceptable, unacceptable\}$
c_{10} – Ownership Capital Ratio – noted as *Ind8*, domain: $\{acceptable, unacceptable\}$
c_{11} – Ownership Capital Ratio tendency – domain: $\{increase, decrease\}$
c_{12} – Interest Coverage Ratio – noted as *Ind9*, domain: $\{acceptable, unacceptable\}$

In this way we obtained the set C of condition attributes $C = \{c_1, c_2, \ldots, c_{12}\}$.

Decision Attributes. Risk rating applied by crediting banks in practice allows to classify credits into the following groups [Skabek96]:

Group 1 – ordinary credit.
Group 2 – observed credit.
Group 3 – doubtful credit.

Accordingly to the above classification, it was assumed that the only decision attribute is the credit risk group. Finally we obtained the single element set D of decision attributes ($D = \{d_1\}$). The above mentioned groups of risk make the domain of the set D.

Establishing of a condition and decision attribute set has explicitly determined the structure of a relevant decision protocol. This protocol was helpful in data acquisition process.

Recorded in protocol cases of making credit decisions have arisen from practical bank consultations (they took place during the student internships) and from available specialistic publications [SieJach93, Bed93]. The complete data set contains 512 rules and is described in [Skabek96].

Knowledge Reduction. The data set has been reduced by means of DataLogic [DL92].

The main function of this program is reducing data sets into the form of decision rules. The process of generating decision rules consists of the following stages:

- reduct searching,
- redundant attributes exclusion,
- redundant record reduction.

The complete decision table consisted of 512 items. After the reduction process the knowledge base included 150 decision rules.

Three condition attributes (c_2, c_3 and c_{11}) would appear to be unneccessary and in case of such knowledge base they could be removed. The reason of such situation is that these attributes consider the tendency and the comparison with the other companies of the branch, values of which already exist in the set of attributes. However, because of a possibility of the knowledge base extension, they remained as parameters in the program. As the application makes possible to record new cases in the knowledge base, these parameters may become useful during the system exploitation.

The particular decisions included the following numbers of rules:

- DOUBTFUL — 55 rules,
- OBSERVED — 81 rules,
- ORDINARY — 14 rules.

The exemplary decision rules for each decision category are presented below:

```
Decision :: Dec==> DOUBTFUL
===========================
    1 |     |    |[C8=NOT] & [C9=NOT] & [C7=NOT] & [C12=NOT]
      | OR
    2 |     |    |[C8=NOT] & [C9=NOT] & [C12=NOT] & [C5=NOT] & [A10=NOT]
      | OR
    3 |     |    |[C8=NOT] & [C4=NOT] & [C9=NOT] & [C10=NOT]
      | OR
    4 |     |    |[C8=NOT] & [C1=NOT] & [C9=NOT] & [C12=NOT] & [C10=NOT]
      | OR
    5 |     |    |[C8=NOT] & [C4=NOT] & [C9=NOT] & [C7=NOT]
      | OR        ...


Decision :: Dec==> OBSERVED
===========================
   56 |     |    |[C8=NOT]&[C4=ACC]&[C1=ACC]&[C7=ACC]&[C5=ACC]&[C10=NOT]
      | OR
   57 |     |    |[C8=ACC]&[C4=ACC]&[C6=ACC]&[C1=ACC]&[C9=NOT]&[C12=NOT]
      | OR
   58 |     |    |[C8=ACC]&[C1=ACC]&[C9=NOT]&[C7=ACC]&[C12=NOT]&[C5=ACC]
      | OR
   59 |     |    |[C8=ACC]&[C4=ACC]&[C6=ACC]&[C1=NOT]&[C12=NOT]&[A5=ACC]
      | OR
   60 |     |    |[C8=NOT]&[C4=NOT]&[C6=ACC]&[C1=ACC]&[C9=ACC]&[C7=ACC]
      | OR        ...


Decision :: Dec==> ORDINARY
===========================
  137 |     |    |[C10=ACC]&[C7=ACC]&[C9=ACC]&[C5=ACC]&[C1=ACC]&[C4=ACC]&
      |     |    |[C6=ACC]
      | OR
  138 |     |    |[C10=ACC]&[C8=ACC]&[C7=ACC]&[C9=ACC]&[C5=ACC]&[C1=ACC]&
      |     |    |[C4=ACC]
      | OR
```

```
139 |     |     |[C10=ACC]&[C8=ACC]&[C7=ACC]&[C9=ACC]&[C1=ACC]&[C4=ACC]&
    |     |     |[C6=ACC]
    | OR
140 |     |     |[C8=ACC]&[C7=ACC]&[C12=ACC]&[C9=ACC]&[C1=ACC]&[C4=ACC]&
    |     |     |[C6=ACC]
    | OR
141 |     |     |[C8=ACC]&[C7=ACC]&[C12=ACC]&[C9=ACC]&[C5=ACC]&[C1=ACC]&
    |     |     |[C6=ACC]
    | OR      ...
```

The complete set of decision rules is published in [Skabek96].

In the rough analysis the attribute strength report is also very important. For our decision table the report is as follows:

```
                 ******** Attribute Strength Report  ********

Decision Attribute :Dec

Decision : Dec==> DOUBTFUL     Coverage ==> 100.00%
====================================================

         Attribute          Max.Loc.Str
         ===========        =============
         C8                   0.31
         C4                   0.29
         C1                   0.28
         C9                   0.27
         C7                   0.27
         C6                   0.25
         C12                  0.25
         C5                   0.20
         C10                  0.17


Decision : Dec==> OBSERVED     Coverage ==> 100.00%
====================================================

         Attribute          Max.Loc.Str
         ===========        =============
         C8                   0.24
         C4                   0.24
         C6                   0.22
         C1                   0.22
         C9                   0.21
         C7                   0.20
         C12                  0.19
         C5                   0.14
         C10                  0.10
```

```
Decision : Dec==> ORDINARY     Coverage ==> 100.00%
=====================================================
```

Attribute	Max.Loc.Str
C10	0.39
C8	0.39
C7	0.39
C12	0.35
C9	0.35
C5	0.35
C1	0.35
C4	0.31
C6	0.22

From the analysis of the attribute strength it appears that the remaining attributes have approximately equal volume (the highest difference reaches 17%). It means that the particular attributes have a similar influence on the final decision.

3.3 Marketing Strategy of a Company – the Economic Decision Problem [Buzala95]

Marketing is a capacious term related to the way of thinking and acting which contains – among others – the application of tool and method sets in studies and formation of the companies surrounding, their structure and internal organisation in order they could achieve a success on a difficult and fluctuating consumer market.

In literature the various definitions of the term *marketing* are encountered. In [Kotler89] we are confronted with so called *modern approach* (sensu largo) – marketing is defined there as a human activity attempting to satisfy consumer's wishes and needs through the exchange processes.

Classical approach (sensu stricto) published in [Meffert86] describes marketing as a proper planning, coordinating and controlling of all company activities orientated towards current and future market.

The definition published in [GRW94] explains marketing as an integrated set of tools and activities connected with research and market creation and based on market conduct rules.

Above cited definitions point at complexity and complicated character of a proper marketing policy of a company and making marketing decision can be assumed as the problem difficult to formalise.

The commented master thesis deals with utilisation of rough set theory elements in acquisition, analysis and representation of knowledge related to one, precise marketing decision i.e. drafting an advertising budget of a company. This is due to the fact that its author was concentrating on one of marketing strategy elements – the tools and instruments of analysis and affecting the consumer market by means of advertising.

Some of acquired results have been listed below. The usefulness and effectiveness of the proposed approach in the process of synthesis of a proper computer system, supporting selected marketing decisions, is, in our opinion, unquestionable.

Knowledge Sources and Acquisition. The results of long standing marketing research concerning advertising campaigns of different products has been rendered by "Pentor" (*The Institute of Opinion and Market Research*) and then employed in student internships. Precisely, they were the standard, typical data gathered by the companies leading the advertising campaigns of their own products i.e.:

- a sort of product – connected with the branch of business,
- a stage in the product life cycle – connected with its phase i.e. market launch, expansion, position strengthening,
- sales volume,
- advertising expenditure – the total sum and its distribution into several advertisement, types i.e. TV, radio, press, billboard advertising as well as direct promotion,

These data supported the process of condition attributes, decision attributes and their domain determination.

Condition Attributes. The following condition attributes and their domains have been selected:

c_1 – branch of business, *domain:* food, cosmetics, chemicals, tobacco, household supplies, furniture, clothing, cars etc.
c_2 – stage, *domain:* market launch, expansion, position strengthening
c_3 – turnover, *domain:* sales volume in PLN
c_4 – increase, *domain:* interval [-1,1]; the numbers in this interval signify the percentage alteration of the sales volume
c_5 – share, *domain:* interval [0,1]; the numbers in this interval signify the percentage share of expenses for advertising in a branch.

The obtained set of condition attributes has got the form:

$$C = \{c_1, c_2, c_3, c_4, c_5\}$$

Decision Attributes. Decision attribute $d = budget$ is the essential decision attribute. This attribute consist of two components: $d_1 = sum$ and $d_2 = division$. Previously to giving an explanation of such structure the definition of decision attributes d_1 and d_2 is presented:

d_1 – sum; *domain:* interval [0,1]; the numbers in this interval signify the percentage share of the sum assigned for advertising within the sale product value.
d_2 – division; *domain:* shares' sequence of each media type in advertising budget for a given period or – in other words – the number in the interval [0,1].

Assuming that the position in character sequence signifies the concrete medium and that the character (letter) in this position signifies the share (the number in the interval [0,1]) of particular media in the global advertising expenditures, we obtain a new decision attribute $d = budget$ which exists as a composition of decision attributes d_1 and d_2. That connection is defined in Tab. 1.

Table 1. Components of the decision

Position in the sequence	1	2	3	4	5	6
Meaning	sum d_1	TV	Press	Billboards	Radio	Promotion
Representation	letter	letter	letter	letter	letter	letter

The letters and their meaning for particular attributes are defined in Tab. 2.

Table 2. Intervals of the decision attributes

$d_1 = sum$		$d_2 = division$	
letter	interval	letter	interval
A	[0, 0.01)	A	[0, 0.2)
B	[0.01, 0.025)	B	[0.2, 0.4)
C	[0.025, 0.04)	C	[0.4, 0.6)
D	[0.04, 0.06)	D	[0.6, 0.8)
E	[0.06, 0.09)	E	[0.8, 1.0)
F	[0.09, 0.12)		
G	[0.12, 0.15)		
H	[0.15, 0.2)		
I	[0.2, 0.25)		
J	[0.25, 0.4)		
K	[0.4, 0.6)		
L	[0.6, 1.0)		

Note: The intervals presented in Tab. 2 consider experts' notes.

For instance the sequence **BCDDAC** representing values of decision attribute d can be interpreted as follows:
The value of d_1 belongs to the interval B i.e. [0.01, 0.025].
The value of $d_2.TV$ belongs to the interval C i.e. [0.01, 0.025].
etc.

Here the stage of decision attributes' determination reaches its final. Single-element decision attribute set $D = \{d\}$ has been obtained.

The structure of the decision protocol in a form of a relevant questionnaire directed to a company conducting advertising campaign of a certain product has been defined through determination of sets C and D of condition attributes. The knowledge acquisition process is particularly described in [Buzala95].

Rough Sets in Data Analysis. 19 decision rules were generated by DataLogic using the model of input decision protocol. Generated decision rules are published in [Buzala95].

The exemplary decision rule has got the form:

```
Decision ::  BUDGET ==> ECBABB

7 | | |[0.05 <= SHARE <= 0.08]
  |  OR
8 | | |[TURNOVER <= 3401] & [0.05 <= SHARE <= 0.09]
  | OR
9 | | |[STAGE = UGR] & [TURNOVER <= 3401] & [0.09 <= SHARE <= 0.13]
  | OR
10| | |[STAGE = UGR] & [0.12 <= SHARE <= 0.13]
```

The influence volume of the particular condition attribute rules affecting a decision attribute value was examined by means of DataLogic for all generated decision rules.

In case of above decision rule we obtained:

```
* Attribute Strength Report *

Decision ::  BUDGET ==> ECBABB

Attribute                                           Max. Loc. Str.

STAGE                                                   0.77
TURNOVER                                                0.47
SHARE                                                   0.40
```

The interpretation of the semantic influence of a relevant condition attribute values on a decision attribute values is obvious. The influence analysis results of the condition attribute values are published in [Buzala95].

Usefulness of the Rule Knowledge Base. The generated decision rules were implemented in experimental computer system supporting selected marketing decisions [Buzala95]. To verify the usefulness of these rules several tests were conducted (in presence of domain experts). Tests relied on inputing data to the system in the form described in Tab. 3.

Table 3. Format of input data

Data	*Intervals of values*
Branch of business	The selection among proposed options
Stage in the product life cycle	The selection among proposed options
Turnover value in the current month	Integer value in the interval [500000, 10000000] PLN
Expected turnover raise in the following month	Real value in the interval [-1,1]
Share in expenses for advertising expenditures of the whole branch in the current month	Real value in the interval [0,1]

Table 4. Format of output data

The results	*The intervals*
Sum for advertising expenditures in the following month	Integer value in the interval [500000, 10000000] PLN
Share of TV advertising expenses in the total sum	Real value in the interval [0,1]
Share of press advertising expenses in the total sum	Real value in the interval [0,1]
Share of billboards advertising expenses in the total sum	Real value in the interval [0,1]
Share of radio advertising expenses in the total sum	Real value in the interval [0,1]
Share of promotion expenses in the total sum	Real value in the interval [0,1]
Contents of the decision rule(s) supporting the decision	Logical sentence containing the conjunction of intervals of condition attribute values for the determined value of decision attribute.
Lack of rule in the rule knowledge base relevant to the given values of condition attributes	Message "LACK OF DECISION RULES FOR THE ENTERED DATA"

When the system finds the relevant decision rule in the rule knowledge base it generates the result that has the structure described in Tab. 4.

For instance for the following values of condition attributes:

type of product:	food
Stage in product life cycle:	expansion
Turnover value in the current month:	2 400 000 PLN
Expected turnover rise in the following month:	0.06 (6%)
Share of advertising expenditures in the food branch in the current month:	0.023 (2.3%)

then the relevant rule was found in the rule knowledge base and the following values were assigned to the decision attribute d (according to its structure):

Advertising expenditures in the following month:	[144 000, 216 000] PLN
Proposed percentage partition of this sum into the particular advertising media:	
TV:	[0.6, 0.8]
Press:	[0, 0.2]
Billboards:	[0, 0.2]
Radio:	[0, 0.2]
Promotion:	[0.4, 0.6]

Note: The concrete decision that assigns the particular values to the given ranges belongs obviously to experts.

Experts confirmed on the basis of the rule knowledge base that the generated decision attributes values were correct and adequate to their intuition in all available cases.

Rough Sets in the Marketing Research Results Analysis. Revealing to the student the results of various and long standing marketing research – conducted by "Pentor" – allowed for a practical verification of the rough set theory usefulness in the large data sets analysis.

Traditionally, the large data sets assembled in different research were analysed by means of tools and methods typical for mathematical statistics.

Received results of such analysis were dependent on the quality of supplied data, so – among others – on their representative character (in the context of examined opinion or fact), credibility, completeness etc.

The conclusions formulated on the basis of acquired results had also the character of a statistical representation e.g. common, average opinion expressed by the majority of respondents. Frequently the conclusions formulated in this way had a limited area of applications.

This was an inspiration for the simultaneous use of methods and tools typical for mathematical statistics and rough set theory in the analysis of assembled data sets. The acquired results were then compared and interpreted.

Chips in the Public Opinion Analysis. The survey was conducted in order to compare three brands of chips. The points awarded by respondents to the features of examined chips have been used in this analysis.

Examined chip brands were compared in pairs. Respondents were supposed to try chips from the first unmarked package and rate their particular features. The same procedure was repeated with the second and third unmarked package of chips. Finally every questioned person answered the question "which chips tasted better?" Each pair of chips has been tested 100 times, so 300 people have taken part in research.

A structure of adequate protocols with recorded results of chips rating consisted of 30 condition atributes and one decision atribute representing answers to the question: "which chips tasted better?"

Here is the list of a condition attributes and their domains:

A_1 – Sex of respondent – *domain:* male, female;
A_2 – Age of respondent – *domain:* 10–15, 16–25, 26–35, 36–45;
A_3 – Has he taken part in consumer tests? – *domain:* yes, no;
A_4 – Does he eat salty chips? – *domain:* yes, no;
A_5 – How often does he eat chips? – *domain:* often, average, rarely;
A_6 – Chips of whose producer does he eat most frequently? – *domain:* Chio Chips, Star Chips, Ruffles, Crunchips/Bahlsen, Fritos;
A_7, A_{19} – What is his general opinion about chips – *domain:* negative, neutral, positive;
A_8, A_{20} – What does he think about the chip's form – *domain:* dislikes, neutral, likes;
A_9, A_{21} – What does he think about their colour – *domain:* too bright, OK, too dark;
A_{10}, A_{22} – What does he think about their thickness – *domain:* too thin, OK, too fat;
A_{11}, A_{23} – What does he think about their hardness – *domain:* too soft, OK, too hard;
A_{12}, A_{24} – What does he think about their crispness – *domain:* not enough crispy, OK, too crispy;
A_{13}, A_{25} – What does he think about their taste – *domain:* don't taste well, neutral, tasty;
A_{14}, A_{26} – What does he think about their potato flavor – *domain:* dislikes, neutral, likes;
A_{15}, A_{27} – What does he think about their saltness – *domain:* not enough salty, OK, too salty;
A_{16}, A_{28} – What are the chip's consumption sensations – *domain:* too fat, OK, not enough fat;
A_{17}, A_{29} – What does he think about the faint-taste – *domain:* intolerable, neutral, tolerable;
A_{18}, A_{30} – What does he think about their size – *domain:* too big, OK, too small;

Condition atributes $A_7 - A_{18}$ concern the first tasted chips and atributes $A_{19} - A_{30}$ the second ones.

For a distinction the chips were marked: CHIP1, CHIP2, CHIP3.

By means of Datalogic program the assembled data were analysed and the results of this analysis were published in [Buzala95].

Some of them have been presented below in order to illustrate the effectiveness and usefulness of instruments based on elements of rough set theory and analysis of large data kits.

The most interesting seemed to be the results of CHIP1 and CHIP3 comparison.

Below we presented the relevant decision rules generated by DataLogic as well as analysis results of the influence volume of particular attribute values on respondent's preferences.

The relevant decision rules for CHIPS1 are the following:

```
Decision :: Dec==> 1
```

```
=========================

  1 | | |[A16>=2] & [A27<>2]
  | OR
  2 | | |[A16>=2] & [A23<=1 or A23>=3] & [A6<=2 or A6>=5]
  | OR
  3 | | |[A16>=2] & [A23>=3]
  | OR
  4 |[A16>=2] & [A11=2] & [A1 <>2] & [A2<=1 or A2>=3] & [A6<=2]
  | OR
  5 | | |[A1=2] & [A2=2] & [A6<=2 or A6>=5]
  | OR
  6 | |[A16>=2] & [A11=2] & [A23=2] & [A2=2] & [3<=A6<=4]
  | OR
  7 | | |[A16<=2] & [A11 <>2] & [A17=3] & [A2=3]
  | OR
  8 | | |[A17=3] & [A1=2] & [A2<=1 or A2>=4] & [A6>=5]
```

```
   ********   Attribute Strength Report ********

Decision : Dec==> 1
=========================

    Attribute   Max. Loc. Str
    =========   ================

    A16             0.47
    A27             0.45
    A11             0.43
    A17             0.41
    A23             0.33
    A2              0.17
    A6              0.13
    A1              0.09
```

```
   ********   Rule Strength Report ********

Decision : Dec==> 1
=========================

   1       18    1,3,4,18,24,25,28,36,38,52,58,60,64,71,80,88,92,99
   2       10    2,13,24,26,28,33,34,36,38,50
   3        9    2,3,4,33,34,36,38,50,53
   4        5    36,42,68,86,92
   5        5    33,50,67,80,88
   6        4    10,32,76,82
   7        2    3,75
   8        2    47,85
```

The relevant decision rules for CHIPS2 are the following:

```
Decision :: Dec==> 2
========================

  9 | | |[A16<2]
  | OR
  10| | |[A27=2] & [A17<>3] & [A23=2]
  | OR
  11| | |[A27=2] & [A11<>2] & [A23=2] & [A2<=1 or A2>=4]
  | OR
  12| | |[A27=2] & [A11<>2] & [A1=2]
  | OR
  13| | |[A27=2] & [A1=2] & [A2<=1 or A2>=3] & [A6<=4]
  | OR
  14| | |[A27=2] & [A11=2] & [A2<=1 or A2>=3] & [3<=A6<=4]
  | OR
  15| | |[A27=2] & [A1=2] & [A2=3]
  | OR
  16| | |[A27=2] & [A23<=2] & [A2=2] & [A6<=2]
  | OR
  17| | |[A27=2] & [A1<>2] & [A23=3] & [A6>=5]
  | OR
  18| | |[A27=2] & [A23<=1] & [A6<=4]


   ********   Attribute Strength Report ********

Decision : Dec==> 2
=========================

    Attribute   Max. Loc. Str
    =========   ================


    A16             0.50
    A27             0.41
    A11             0.39
    A17             0.38
    A23             0.32
    A2              0.15
    A6              0.11
    A1              0.07


   ********   Rule Strength Report ********

Decision : Dec==> 1
```

========================

9	30	11,19,20,23,29,30,62,63,66,69,70,72,73,74,77,78,79,81, 83,84,87,89,90,91,93,94,95,96,97,100
10	26	5,8,9,12,15,23,29,30,31,45,59,62,65,66,70,72,74,77,78, 89,90,91,93,95,96,100
11	19	6,8,9,15,16,31,35,51,55,56,57,62,66,72,74,77,91,96,100
12	14	15,16,23,27,29,31,35,56,62,70,77,91,93,96
13	18	14,15,16,17,22,29,35,37,43,56,61,62,70,77,83,84,91,93
14	10	7,37,41,44,45,46,48,83,84,89
15	7	29,37,39,40,70,93,98
16	3	49,81,90
17	2	9,54
18	2	21,69

On the basis of the decision table Datalogic generates a file consisting of three principal parts:

1. Block of decision rules.
2. Block describing the local influence volume of particular attributes on a specific decision (Attribute Strength Report).
3. Block of decision rules description presenting the numbers of objects sustaining the particular rules in a decision table.

To interpret the acquired results two different methods are in question:

- the analysis of block (2) appears to be crucial in case the factors determining a particular rule need to be described;
- the analysis of blocks (1) and (3) appears to be crucial when the answer to the question: "What are the rating criteria of respondents taking part in the survey? What determines their answers?" is expected;

A data analysis conducted with the help of first method is trivial. For the particular decision, the attributes according to their influence volume are read out (Max.Loc.Str.). Then we review the block of decision rules subject to the particular attribute from the block of local volume influence description. Next we read the value assumed by the attribute in the decision rules and then interpret it according to the following rules:

- as a representative value we assent this one which is supported by min. 80% objects where the particular attribute appears having assumed such a value (if less than 80% objects – the alternative attribute value should be given); this indicates that mainly these attribute values which strongly appear in the decision rules should be attended;
- in order to control the number of objects supporting the particular attribute value the analysis of block of decision rules description can be used – the numbers of all objects supporting particular rules will be found there;
- in case of a contradictory attribute value of each decision appearance a standard statistical distribution can be found and the frequency of particular attribute values occurrence can be confronted (a situation of this type might

be encountered if respondents are hesitant or a phenomenon of weak dependence appears).

As a result we obtained the comparison of concrete attribute values ordered by their influence volume on the decision. The values of the influence volume factor belong to the interval [0,1] and they are given with the accuracy of hundredth parts. Here we have a hundred-points scale estimating the influence volume of the given attribute value. The value of this factor determines an extent of decreasing approximation accuracy of the given decision after removing a certain attribute from the condition value set.

The second method consists in the selection of a rule with the strongest support according to the description block of decision rules.

The rules connected with decision no. 1: **CHIP1 ARE BETTER**

Rule no.1: acceptance: 18 cases
(CHIP1 grease: greasy enough or not enough) &
(CHIP3 saltness: not enough salty or too salty)

Rule no.2: acceptance: 10 cases
(CHIP1 grease: greasy enough or not enough) &
(CHIP3 hardness: too hard or too soft) &
(consumers: Chio Chips, Star Chips, Fritos)

The rules connected with decision no.2: **CHIP3 ARE BETTER**

Rule no.9: acceptance: 30 cases
(CHIP1 grease: too greasy)

Rule no.10: acceptance: 26 cases
(CHIP3 saltness: salty enough) &
(CHIP1 faint taste: unsuitable or suitable) &
(CHIP3 hardness: hard enough)

Rule no.13: acceptance: 18 cases
(CHIP1 saltness: salty enough) &
(respondents: woman in the age : 10-15 or 26-45) &
(consumers: Chio Chips, Star Chips, Ruffles, Bahlsen)

In this way we received the set of factors determinating respondent's choice. The most interesting are the biggest groups, that's why the most supported decision rules should be selected for the purpose of interpretation.

Thanks to above presented interpretation methods the conclusions allowing to take several marketing decisions can be drawn. In the examined case the conclusion is followed by obvious decision: CHIP1 must be less greasy. The other conclusions concerning saltness, hardness and faint taste are also very important to the producer commissioning research. Information about age and sex of the respondents – in connection with their preferences – should determine a decision at whom the advertisements should be aimed.

Referring to the analysis of the same data by means of methods and tools of mathematical statistics it has been acknowledged that standard statistic analysis has not given the answer to the question: "Why 64% respondents preferred CHIP3 and 36% respondents preferred CHIP1".

Meanwhile, as it has been proved above the data analysis conducted by DataLogic indicates that CHIP1 were definitely rejected because of its greasiness.

Such conclusion may have great practical importance for the further production.

Summary. The results described above point at the usefulness of methods and software tools based on rough set theory elements in data analysis connected with supporting decisions.

It considers especially:

- generating decision rules that may be then used in a computer system supporting marketing decisions;
- analysis of the marketing examination results in an alternative way to the traditional methods and tools based on mathematical statistics.

Rough set theory allows to search the decision rules in the gathered data even if they are incomplete and not representative to investigated opinions or phenomena. If decision rules are included in analysed data then they will be detected even if they are inexact and incomplete.

A possibility of new decision rules search still exists during the analysis of new data. The rules are inserted in the existing rule knowledge base.

This approach allows to consider the fact - often existing in practice - that some of condition attributes can change their strength in time and such situation can vary in future unless they are the components of generated decision rules at the moment. Analysis of such data may make them occur in generated new decision rules based on these data.

4 Final Remarks

The presented above examples concerned first of all the problem of decision rules acquisition. These decision rules are enclosed within data describing the selected economic problems.

Hence at the stage of accumulating data we aim especially at fulfilling the condition of their representativeness with respect to the analysed economic decision problem.

We used here a pragmatic concept of data representativeness. We mean such data collecting that covers all known to experts cases of economic decision problems.

Therefore the obtained rule knowledge bases have an open character. This fact also influences the practical estimation of the usefulness of generated decision rules. We were mainly concentrated to answer the basic question: whether specified sets of condition attributes cover their potentially possible values in case of solving a concrete economic decision problem.

References

[BazSkSy94a] Bazan, J., Skowron, A., Synak, P.: Market data analysis: A rough set approach. In: ICS Research Report **6/94**, Warsaw University of Technology (1994)

[BazSkSy94b] Bazan, J., Skowron, A., Synak, P.: Discovery of decision rules from experimental data. In: T.Y. Lin (ed.): Proceedings of the Third International Workshop on Rough Sets and Soft Computing (RSSC'94), San Jose State University, San Jose, California, USA, November 10–12 (1994) 526–533

[BazSkSy94c] Bazan, J., Skowron, A., Synak, P.: Dynamic reducts as a tool fos extracting laws from decision tables. In: Z. W. Ras, M. Zemankova (eds.), Proceedings of the Eighth Symposium on Methodologies for Intelligent Systems, Charlotte, NC, October 16-19, Lecture Notes in Artificial Intelligence **869**, Springer-Verlag (1994) 346–355

[Bed93] Bednarski, L., Borowiecki, R., Duraj, J., Kurtys, E., Waśniewski, T., Wersty, B.: Economic analysis in a company, Wydawnictwo Akademii Ekonomicznej we Wrocławiu, Wrocław (1993) (in Polish)

[BrilMai90] Brilman, J., Maire, C.: Manuel d'evaluation des entreprises. Les Editions d'Organisation, Paris (1990)

[Buzala95] Buzała, S.: Rough sets in marketing decisions. The Master Thesis, Silesian Technical University, Gliwice (1995) (in Polish)

[ChLee73] Chang, C.R., Lee, R.C.T.: Symbolic logic and mechanical theorem proving, Academic Press (1973)

[ClMel84] Clocksin, W., Mellish, C.: Programming in Prolog, (2nd ed.) Berlin B.R.D., Springer–Verlag (1984)

[Debski94] Debski, W.: Bank risk. Bank i Kredyt **10** (1994) (in Polish)

[Del94] Delenda, J.F.: Achat et vente d'entreprise. Belfond, Paris (1994)

[FanDai93] Fan Dai: Centralized, application oriented graphical interaction control using an example of planning robotic tasks. Computer & Graphics **17/2** (1993) 155–163

[GRW94] Garbarski, L., Rutkowski, I., Wrzosek, W.: Marketing. Państwowe Wydawnictwo Ekonomiczne, Warszawa (1994) (in Polish)

[GrzBus92] Grzymała–Busse, J.: LERS – A system for learning from examples based on rough sets. In: R. Słowiński (ed.): Intelligent Decision Support – Handbook of Applications and Advances of Rough Sets Theory, Kluwer Academic Publishers, Dordrecht (1992) 3–18

[GuiLen94] Guillon,P.M., Lengaigne, J.J.: Mémento les professions. Patrimoine Management & Technologies, Bulogne (1994)

[LenPia94] Lenarcik, A., Piasta, Z.: Rough classifiers. In: W. Ziarko (ed.): Rough Sets, Fuzzy Sets and Knowledge Discovery (RSKD'93). Workshops in Computing, Springer–Verlag & British Computer Society, London, Berlin (1994) 298–316

[KSow93] Kamela–Sowińska, A.: The object of pricing in privatization. Rachunkowość **3** (1993) (in Polish)

[Kotler89] Kotler., Ph.: Marketing management. Prentice Hall, New York (1989)

[Kraw95] Krawczyk, R.: Computer system supporting companies valuation. The Master Thesis, Silesian Technical University, Gliwice (1995) (in Polish)

[LE95] Les Echos: Le Quotidien de l'Economie **16875** (1995)

[Meffert86] Meffert., H.: Marketing. Gabler, Wiesbaden (1986)

[Merritt89] Merritt, D.: Building experts systems in Prolog. Springer–Verlag, New York (1989)

[NoGlo94] Nogalski, B., Głowacki, K.: The value and price of a company – interpretation dilemmas. Przeglad organizacji **5** (1994) (in Polish)

[Pawlak82] Pawlak, Z.: Rough sets. International Journal of Information and Computer Science **11** (1982) 341–356

[Pawlak91] Pawlak, Z.: Rough sets. Theoretical aspects of reasoning about data, Kluwer Academic Publishers, Dordrecht (1991)

[Piasta] Piasta, Z.: Data mining and knowledge discovery in marketing and financial databases with rough classifiers. Wydawnictwo Akademii Ekonomicznej we Wrocławiu, Wrocław (to appear) (in Polish)

[PiaLen] Piasta, Z., Lenarcik, A.: Learning rough classifiers from large databases with missing values. (in this book)

[DL92] REDUCT System, Inc.: DataLogic/R reference manual, Regina, Canada (1992)

[Rob65] Robinson, J.A.: A machine oriented logic based on the resolution principle. Journal Assoc. Comp. Mach. **12** (1965) 23–41

[SieJach93] Sierpińska, M., Jachna, T.: The company evaluation according to international standards, Wydawnictwo Naukowe PWN, Warszawa (1993) (in Polish)

[Skabek96] Skabek, K.: Computer system supporting credit decisions. The Master Thesis, Silesian Technical University, Gliwice (1996) (in Polish)

[Słow92] Słowiński, R. (ed.): Intelligent Decision Support – Handbook of Applications and Advances of the Rough Sets Theory. Kluwer Academic Publishers, Dordrecht (1992)

[SłowZop95] Słowiński, R., Zopounidis, C.: Application of the rough set approach to evaluation of bankruptcy risk. International J. Intelligent Systems in Accounting, Finance & Management **4/1** (1995) 27–41

[VPoel97] Van den Poel, D.: Rough sets for database marketing (in this book)

Chapter 14

Multistage Rough Set Analysis of Therapeutic Experience with Acute Pancreatitis

Krzysztof Słowiński[1] *and Jerzy Stefanowski*[2]

[1] Clinic of Traumatology, K.Marcinkowski University of Medical Sciences in Poznań, 1/2 Długa Street, 61-848 Poznań, Poland,
E-mail: slowik@rose.man.poznan.pl

[2] Institute of Computing Science, Poznań University of Technology, 3A Piotrowo Street, 60-965 Poznań, Poland,
E-mail: Jerzy.Stefanowski@cs.put.poznan.pl

Abstract. The rough set approach has been applied to analyse a multistage decision process concerning the treatment of acute pancreatitis with peritoneal lavage. The clinical experience has been represented by two kinds of information systems: system A, classifying patients described by pre-lavage attributes, and five systems B, classifying patients described by attributes of the course of multistage lavage. From the medical point of view, the analysis of these information systems has aimed at identifying subsets of the most important attributes for results of the patient's treatment and discovery of decision rules representing cause-and-effect dependencies between attributes. Achieving these aims have been facilitated by using two following rough set based strategies: adding to the core the attributes of the highest increase of discriminatory power and approach to inducing the satisfactory set of strong decision rules.

1 Introduction

Medical experience concerning either diagnosing or treatment of diseases is often recorded in data sets called information systems. An information system contains a set of objects (patients, cases, etc.) described by the set of attributes (i.e. features characterising them). These attributes are usually divided into two groups: *condition attributes* referring to data coming from anamnesis and/or medical tests; and *decision attributes* referring to diagnosis, the course of treatment or the effect of therapy. The second group of attributes induces the partition of patients into disjoint family of decision classes.

Such records may have different practical importance for the physicians. So, the information systems are analysed in order to find and select the most important and valuable data elements for the medical interpretation. Typical tasks in the analysis of the medical data, in particular concerning the problems of diagnosing and/or treatment of a given disease, are the following:

- looking for cause-effect dependencies between condition and decision attributes,
- identification of the most important attributes for the patients' classification,
- determining the relationships between values of the most important attributes and the patients' classification.

Several data analysis methods are used to solve the above tasks. Statistical methods seem to be the most popular tools in bio-medical sciences. For instance, one of the simplest, standard and statistical way is to apply classical Fisherian discriminant analysis (see, e.g. [5, 6]). However, the range of other techniques available to solve the same problem is quite large and comprises, newer discriminant analysis developments including methods for mixtures of continuous and discrete features, machine learning methods, neural networks, fuzzy mathematics, rough sets, etc.

One of these possible data analysis methods is the *rough set theory* introduced by Z.Pawlak [12, 13]. In last years, the authors and their co-operators successfully applied the rough set based approach to several medical problems, see e.g. [2, 15, 21, 22, 23, 24, 25, 29, 30]. In particular, the analysis of clinical experience with *highly selective vagotomy* (see, e.g. its different aspects [2, 15, 7, 21]) has been one of the first successful real life application of the rough set theory and has given a methodological framework for other applications, even in other domains. The further medical applications undertaken by other researchers have also confirmed the usefulness of the rough set theory for the analysis of medical information systems.

Such elements of the rough set theory as the *approximations of objects' classification*, the *quality of these approximations* and notions of *reducts* could help in evaluating the importance of attributes. Moreover, combination of the rough set theory with *rule induction techniques* gives the representation of the important dependencies in the form of *decision rules* which are easy to interpret and produce a qualitative characterization and explanation of regularities in data.

All above medical applications of the rough set theory refer, however, to the analysis of data sets represented in one information system. It means that from the methodological point of view all analysed data are stored in one, global table where one part contains input/condition information about patients and the second part contains patients' classification referring either to the diagnosis of the patient's status or to the result of treatment.

On the other hand, the treatment of some medical diseases has a *multistage character*. Its specificity consists in performing some therapeutic actions depending on the evaluation of the patients' status in each stage. Then, the results of the treatment are observed. The procedure is continued in next stages (or sometimes modified) depending on the patient's clinical response. This kind of treatment is a *multistage decision process*. Each stage of this process is characterized by its specific data set. Therefore, the analysis of this medical problem should consists in considering rather the sequence of information systems referring to consecutive stages than taking into account one global information system only.

The aim of the following paper is to show on the real-life example that the rough set theory can be also applied to the analysis of the multistage medical treatment processes.

Peritoneal lavage in *acute pancreatitis* has been chosen as an example of such a multistage process. Peritoneal lavage is a kind of peritoneal dialysis used in addition to non-operative treatment of acute pancreatitis [3]. The lavage is performed in stages; at each stage a fixed volume of isotonic dialysate fluid is introduced to the peritoneum through a thin catheter and after some time it is drained.

In this paper, an experience with peritoneal lavage is represented by two kinds of information systems:

- system A, classifying patients described by pre-lavage attributes (i.e. anamnesis, etiology, clinical examination and biochemistry of the serum),
- and family of five systems B, classifying patients described by attributes of the course of the multistage lavage (i.e. biochemistry of the serum and evacuated liquid).

In both kinds of systems the classifications of patients correspond to the number of stages which have been carried out to obtain a satisfactory result of treatment. However, the system A classifies patients according to therapeutic effort (measured in a number of stages in peritoneal lavage), while system B classifies patients from the view point of decisions concerning next stages of the treatment.

From the medical point of view, the analysis of the above information systems tends to identify subsets of the most important attributes for results of the patient's treatment and discover decision rules representing cause-and-effect dependencies between attributes. The results of the performed analysis tell the physician which attributes and their values should be taken into account for evaluation of the patient status and support the decision concerning continuation of the treatment with the next stages of peritoneal lavage.

The data about patients with acute pancreatitis treated with peritoneal lavage have been collected in the Department of Surgery at the F.Raszeja Memorial Hospital in Poznan. It must be stressed that the analysis was limited to 29 patients only. We are aware of difficulties of analysing such a data set. However, from the medical point of view the severe acute pancreatitis is not frequent illness. Moreover, we took into account patients having the complete set of data about their examination before lavage and during the lavage treatment. These patients were not directed to surgical operations.

The paper is organised as follows. In the next section more details on peritoneal lavage in acute pancreatitis are given. In section 3, basic information about chosen methodology is given. The definition of all information systems is given in section 4. Then, in the next two following sections, the results of their analysis are presented. Conclusions and discussion are grouped in the final section.

2 Peritoneal lavage

Peritoneal lavage for acute pancreatitis was initially reported by Wall in 1965 [32]. The technique of this treatment can be summarized in the following way [3]. After a small incision in the midline below the umbilicus is made, a trocar with a peritoneal dialysis catheter is introduced into the peritoneal cavity towards the rectal fossa. The catheter is kept in a place by superficial skin sutures and is attached to the dialysis tubing. The bottles containing the isotonic dialysate fluid are heated to body temperature and one litre is instilled into the peritoneal cavity. After 30-40 minutes the peritoneal cavity is drained. If the liquid amylase level is higher than 1000 I.U., a new instillation is started. This procedure is continued depending on the patient's clinical response and analytical results [8].

The therapeutic efficacy of the peritoneal lavage has generally been attributed to the removal of toxic materials contained in the peritoneal exudate in acute pancreatitis [19]. It is clear that their removal, even incomplete, by peritoneal lavage is associated with immediate and significant clinical improvement and with a decrease in early mortality from severe acute pancreatitis [17, 18]. More than twenty years of experience in peritoneal lavage have shown it to be a safe and efficient complement of the traditional treatment, which resulted in a small number of complications [8, 17].

However, it is still an open question how to describe the severity of the patient's state in the course of the multistage lavage process, i.e. what is the set of attributes which should be taken into account for evaluation of the lavage process.

3 Brief information about the rough sets and rules induction techniques

The rough set theory, originally introduced by Z.Pawlak [12], is here chosen as a basic tool to analyse multistage treatment of acute pancreatitis.

From the rough set theory point of view, the analysis is connected with examining *dependencies between attributes* in the defined information systems. More precisely, similarly to previous medical applications [22, 21, 24], the following elements of rough set theory are used:

- creating classes of *indiscernibility relations* (atoms) and building *approximations* of the objects' classification,
- evaluating the ability of attributes to approximate the objects' classification; the measure of the *quality of approximation of the classification*, defined as the ratio of the number of objects in the lower approximations to the total number of objects, is used for this aim,
- discovering *cores* and *reducts* of attributes (a reduct is the minimal subset of attributes ensuring the same quality of the classification as the complete set of attributes; a core is an intersection of all reducts in the information system),

– examining the *significance* of attributes by observing changes in the quality of approximation of the classification caused by removing or adding given attributes.

Here, we do not give formal descriptions of these elements. All necessary definitions of basic concepts of the rough set theory can be found in, e.g. [13, 26, 14, 33].

Results obtained in some of the previous applications (see, e.g., [24, 29, 30]) have shown that is not always possible to solve all tasks of the data analysis by direct use of above basic elements of the rough set theory only. In particular, it refers to the problems of analysing discovered reducts and identifying the most significant attributes for the patients' classifications (see, e.g., the discussion in [29]). For some information systems the number of possible reducts is extremely high, the core is often empty or very small.

In the following study, we use the heuristic strategy based on adding to the core, the attributes of the highest increase of discriminatory power. This strategy does not need so many computations as other strategies. It is based on an observation that experts or the analysts are more interested in finding one or a few reducts only instead of computing all ones. Additionally the discovery of such reducts should be performed in a convincing way, and based on the measure easily controlled and interpreted by the human. These postulates are incorporated in the considered strategy which has been already used successfully for several real life problems (see, e.g. [22, 29, 25]).

In this strategy, the core of attributes is chosen as a starting reduced subset of attributes. It usually ensures lower quality of approximation of the objects' classification than all attributes. A single remaining attribute is temporarily added to the core and the influence of this adding on the change of the quality of approximation is examined. Such an examination is repeated for all remaining attributes. The attribute with the highest increase of the quality of classification is chosen to be added to the reduced subset of attributes. Then, the procedure is repeated for remaining attributes. It is finished when an acceptable quality of the classification is obtained. If there are ties in choosing attributes, several possible ways of adding are checked.

The next important methodological issue refers to *discovery of decision rules.* Decision rules are represented as logical statements expressed in the following form:

$$IF\ (a_1 = v_1)\&(a_2 = v_2)\& \ldots \&(a_n = v_n)\ THEN\ decision_j$$

The formula $(a_i = v_i)$ is called the *elementary condition* of the rule where a_i is the ith condition attribute, v_i is its value. The $decision_j$ is a disjunction of *elementary decision* formulae, i.e. $(d = v_1) \wedge \ldots \wedge (d = v_s)$, where d is a decision attribute, v_l its value $(l = 1, \ldots, s)$.

If s=1, i.e. decision part consists of one elementary decision formula, then the decision rule is *exact.* In this case, the elementary decision indicates decision class represented by the objects belonging to the lower approximation of this class. If s >1, then the rule is called *approximate*, i.e. the elementary decisions indicate decision classes represented by objects belonging to the common boundary region of these classes. Approximate rules are consequences of an approximate description of decision classes. It means that using the available information, one is unable to distinguish whether some objects (from the boundary region) belong to a given decision class or not.

To evaluate the discovered rules the measure of the rule ***strength*** is used [10]. It is the number of objects in the information system whose description satisfies the condition part of the rule (we say, objects *covered* by the rule). In the case of approximate rules, the strength is calculated for each possible decision class separately. Strong rules are usually more general, i.e. their condition parts are shorter and less specialised. Generally, the analysts are interested in discovering the strongest rules (see discussions in [10, 16, 28]).

Algorithms for induction of decision rules from information systems use a machine learning principle [9]. Several algorithms were presented by Grzymala-Busse [1, 4], Pawlak [13], Skowron [20], Ziarko and Shan [34], Stefanowski and Vanderpooten [31, 10].

The existing rule induction algorithms can use one of three following strategies:

- induction of a ***minimal set*** of rules covering all objects from an information system,
- induction of an ***exhaustive set*** of decision rules,
- induction of a ***satisfactory set*** of rules.

The first strategy is focused on describing all input objects using the minimum number of necessary rules. The exhaustive set of rules consists of all possible decision rules which can be generated from a given information system. This set of the rules is looked for if one wants to learn all rule patterns hidden in the data see.

The third strategy gives as a result the set of decision rules which satisfy given a priori user's requirements. For example, the user can prefer to get strongest decision rules.

In the following study the main attention is put on learning all important rule dependencies characterizing multistage decision process. Moreover, the number of analysed patients is quite small. These are the reasons that we have decided to use mainly the third and partly the second strategy instead of inducing the minimal set of rules only.

To induce the required sets of decision rules we used either the algorithm LEM2 [4] or the procedure Explore described in [10]. These procedures are implemented as a part of Rough Family software package [11]. All rough set calculations were made using RoughDAS system [27].

4 Definition of information systems

Two kinds of information systems describing 29 patients treated with peritoneal lavage in acute pancreatitis, were defined. They are called information systems A and B, respectively. The system A is composed of diagnostic data collected before the lavage, whereas the family of five systems B describes the peritoneal lavage treatment stage by stage. In all systems, classification of patients is made from the viewpoint of the number of instillations performed until the cure.

In the next paragraph, the attributes used in information systems are defined. Then, in the two paragraphs these systems are characterized.

4.1 Domains of attributes

Table 1 lists the attributes used in information systems A and B. The definition of their domains follows from clinical experience. In the case of quantitative attributes defined on real value scales their original domains are *discretized* into finite set of subintervals according to clinical norms. These discretized subintervals are interpreted in qualitative terms as 'low', 'medium', 'high' and 'very high' values. The values of discretized quantitative attributes and values of qualitative attributes are then coded for simplicity by following numbers 1,2,3,4.

Table 1. Domains of attributes

Symbol	Attribute	Coded values			
		1	2	3	4
a_1	sex	female	male	–	–
a_2	abdominal pain	no	yes	–	–
a_3	vomiting	no	yes	–	–
a_4	fever (°C)	37	(37,39]	>39	–
a_5	etiology	other	biliary	alcohol	–
a_6	abdominal swelling	no	yes	–	–
a_7	peritoneal symptoms	no	yes	–	–
a_8	peristalsis	no	yes	–	–
a_9	serum amylase level (I.U.)	≤1500	(1500,2500]	(2500,3500]	>3500
a_{10}	serum bilirubin level ($\mu mol/l$)	≤17.1	(17.1,51.3]	(51.3,85.5]	>85.5
a_{11}	volume of drained liquid (l)	≤0.300	(0.300,0.700]	>0.700	–
a_{12}	drained liquid amylase level (I.U.)	≤1500	(1500,2500]	(2500,3500]	>3500
a_{13}	drained liquid bilirubin level ($\mu mol/l$)	≤17.1	(17.1,51.3]	(51.3,85.5]	>85.5
a_{14}	drained liquid protein level (g/l)	≤0.5	(0.5,1.5]	(1.5,2.5]	>2.5
a_{15}	number of erythrocytes in drained liquid ($10^{12}/l$)	≤0.001	(0.001,0.005]	(0.005,0.01]	>0.01
a_{16}	number of leukocytes in drained liquid ($10^9/l$)	≤0.5	(0.5,2]	(2,5]	>5

In systems B, in addition to the attributes being listed, attributes a_{17} and a_{18} are used, showing the increase (positive or negative) of attributes a_{12} (amylase level in drained liquid) and a_{16} (number of leukocytes in drained liquid) between two successive lavage stages (instillations). The increase is defined in terms of new codes of the values taken by a_{12} and a_{16}, i.e.:

$$a_{17} = \begin{cases} 0 \text{ if } a_{12}(\text{stage } i) - a_{12}(\text{stage } i-1) \leq -1 \\ 1 \text{ if } a_{12}(\text{stage } i) - a_{12}(\text{stage } i-1) = 0 \\ 2 \text{ if } a_{12}(\text{stage } i) - a_{12}(\text{stage } i-1) \geq 1 \end{cases}$$

$$a_{18} = \begin{cases} 0 \text{ if } a_{16}(\text{stage } i) - a_{16}(\text{stage } i-1) \leq -1 \\ 1 \text{ if } a_{16}(\text{stage } i) - a_{16}(\text{stage } i-1) = 0 \\ 2 \text{ if } a_{16}(\text{stage } i) - a_{16}(\text{stage } i-1) \geq 1 \end{cases}$$

4.2 Information system A - pre-lavage diagnostic data

Information system A is presented in Table 2. The attributes $a_1 \div a_9$ concern anamnesis, etiology, clinical examination and serum amylase level before the lavage.

The patient's classification is defined using three following decision classes:

class 1: one or two instillations,
class 2: three or four instillations,
class 3: more than four instillations.

The definition of decision classes refers to the number of instillations performed until obtaining the good result of treatment (the greatest recorded number of instillations for analysed patients was equal to 7).

4.3 Information systems B - data from multistage peritoneal lavage

Information systems B describe the course of the treatment in five stages. Each stage refers to the stage after the corresponding instillation. The first of systems B, i.e. defined for the first instillations (see Table 3), is described by two attributes concerning the serum analysis and six attributes referring to the drained liquid analysis.

The next information systems B (stages 2 - 5) corresponding to the next four instillations (see tables 4 $\div$ 7) are defined in a different way. The main part of attributes is still the same - these are the six attributes concerning the drained liquid analysis (i.e. attributes $a_{11} \div a_{16}$) while the two others are two incremental attributes $a_{17} \div a_{18}$.

In all systems B, the patients are divided into three decision classes according to the decision about next necessary instillations:

class 1: no more next instillations,
class 2: one or two next instillations,
class 3: more than two next instillations.

Table 2. Information system A

Patient number	a_1	a_2	a_3	a_4	a_5	a_6	a_7	a_8	a_9	Decision class
1	1	2	2	2	1	1	1	2	4	1
2	2	2	2	2	1	2	2	1	3	3
3	2	2	2	2	3	2	2	1	4	2
4	2	2	2	1	3	1	1	2	1	1
5	2	2	2	2	2	1	1	1	2	2
6	2	2	2	1	1	1	2	1	4	1
7	2	1	1	2	3	2	2	1	1	2
8	1	2	2	1	1	1	1	2	4	2
9	1	2	1	1	2	1	1	2	4	1
10	1	2	2	2	2	2	1	2	1	2
11	2	2	2	1	3	1	1	1	1	1
12	1	2	2	2	2	2	2	1	3	2
13	1	2	2	2	1	2	1	1	4	2
14	2	2	1	1	3	1	2	1	2	2
15	2	2	2	2	1	1	1	1	1	1
16	1	2	2	3	2	2	2	1	1	1
17	2	2	2	2	3	1	2	1	2	1
18	2	2	2	2	3	1	2	1	1	2
19	1	2	2	1	3	1	2	1	3	1
20	2	2	2	2	1	1	2	2	1	1
21	2	2	2	2	1	1	1	2	1	1
22	1	2	2	1	2	1	1	2	2	1
23	1	2	2	1	1	1	1	1	1	1
24	1	2	2	1	2	1	1	1	1	1
25	2	2	2	2	3	1	1	1	4	3
26	2	2	2	1	3	2	2	1	1	1
27	2	2	1	2	3	2	1	2	3	2
28	2	2	1	2	3	2	2	1	3	1
29	2	2	2	2	1	2	2	1	4	2

One can notice that the number of patients decreases from Table 3 to Table 7. It is connected with the character of the multistage lavage process. If in any stage of the treatment the patient belongs to the first decision class, it means that his clinical status has improved and no more next instillations are necessary. So, the process of lavage treatment is finished for such a recovered patient and as a result he is not included in information systems referring to next stages. To indicate this therapeutic effect, we maintain the original numbering of patients in all stages.

Table 3. Information system B - Stage 1

Patient	Attributes								Decision
number	a_9	a_{10}	a_{11}	a_{12}	a_{13}	a_{14}	a_{15}	a_{16}	class
1	4	1	2	1	1	1	1	1	2
2	3	1	3	4	1	1	3	2	3
3	4	2	2	3	1	1	1	1	3
4	1	1	2	1	1	1	1	1	3
5	2	3	2	2	1	3	4	2	3
6	4	4	1	4	1	4	3	1	3
7	1	1	1	1	1	1	2	4	3
8	4	1	2	1	1	1	1	1	3
9	4	1	2	1	1	2	1	1	3
10	1	1	2	3	1	1	2	1	3
11	1	1	2	1	1	4	1	1	3
12	2	1	2	2	1	1	2	2	3
13	2	3	2	1	1	3	2	2	3
14	2	1	1	1	1	1	2	1	2
15	1	1	3	1	1	1	1	1	2
16	1	1	1	1	1	2	1	1	1
17	2	1	1	2	1	1	1	1	2
18	1	1	1	1	1	3	4	2	2
19	3	1	2	3	1	2	1	1	3
20	1	4	1	1	1	1	1	1	3
21	1	1	2	1	1	1	2	1	3
22	2	1	1	1	1	1	1	1	2
23	1	2	2	1	1	3	2	1	3
24	1	1	2	1	1	1	1	1	3
25	4	2	3	1	1	2	4	1	2
26	1	1	3	1	1	2	3	2	3
27	3	2	2	4	1	3	1	1	3
28	3	1	2	1	1	1	3	1	2
29	4	1	2	2	2	2	2	2	2

5 Analysis of information system A

Let us consider the classification of patients defined in the information system A. Table 8 presents the accuracy of approximation of all decision classes by the set of first nine attributes $a_1 \div a_9$.

As it can be noticed in Table 8, all decision classes are definable, i.e. precisely characeterized by nine attributes. The quality of approximation of classification is equal to 1. The information system A is selective as all atoms are singletons.

Table 4. Information system B - Stage 2

Patient	Attributes								Decision
number	a_{11}	a_{12}	a_{13}	a_{14}	a_{15}	a_{16}	a_{17}	a_{18}	class
1	2	1	1	2	2	1	2	2	1
2	3	2	1	2	2	1	1	1	3
3	2	3	1	2	1	1	2	2	2
4	2	1	1	1	2	1	2	2	3
5	2	1	1	3	2	4	1	3	2
6	1	1	1	1	1	1	1	2	3
7	2	1	1	1	3	4	2	2	3
8	2	1	1	1	1	1	2	2	3
9	2	1	1	2	1	1	2	2	2
10	2	1	1	1	1	1	1	2	3
11	1	1	1	2	1	1	2	2	3
12	2	2	1	1	2	1	2	2	3
13	2	1	1	3	4	1	2	2	3
14	2	1	1	2	3	4	2	3	2
15	2	4	1	2	2	3	3	3	2
17	2	1	1	1	2	2	2	2	1
18	2	2	1	1	2	1	1	2	3
19	1	1	1	1	1	1	2	2	3
20	2	1	1	1	4	2	2	3	3
21	2	2	1	1	3	2	3	3	1
22	1	2	2	4	2	1	3	2	3
23	3	1	1	2	1	1	2	2	2
24	3	4	2	4	4	1	3	2	2
25	3	1	1	1	2	3	2	4	3
26	3	4	1	4	2	3	2	3	3
27	2	1	1	1	3	1	2	2	2
28	2	1	1	2	3	2	1	2	2
29	2	1	1	1	1	1	2	2	2

5.1 Looking for reducts and the core in system A

First, we looked for the core of attributes, and then we computed all reducts. The core is composed of two attributes: a_4 (fever) and a_9 (serum amylase level). It ensures the quality of approximation of classification equal to 0.24 (only the first decision class has lower approximation different than 0).

Using standard option of the RoughDAS system [27], we found four following reducts: $\{a_4, a_5, a_7, a_8, a_9\}$, $\{a_1, a_3, a_4, a_7, a_8, a_9\}$, $\{a_4, a_5, a_6, a_8, a_9\}$, $\{a_4, a_5, a_6, a_7, a_9\}$.

All reducts ensure the same quality of classification as the complete set of attributes.

Table 5. Information system B - Stage 3

Patient number	Attributes a_{11}	a_{12}	a_{13}	a_{14}	a_{15}	a_{16}	a_{17}	a_{18}	Decision class
2	3	2	1	2	2	1	1	1	3
3	2	3	1	2	1	1	2	2	2
4	2	1	1	1	2	1	2	2	3
5	2	1	1	3	2	4	1	3	2
6	1	1	1	1	1	1	1	2	3
7	2	1	1	1	3	4	2	2	3
8	2	1	1	1	1	1	2	2	3
9	2	1	1	2	1	1	2	2	2
10	2	1	1	1	1	1	1	2	3
11	1	1	1	2	1	1	2	2	3
12	2	2	1	1	2	1	2	2	3
13	2	1	1	3	4	1	2	2	3
14	2	1	1	2	3	4	2	3	2
15	2	4	1	2	2	3	3	3	2
17	2	1	1	1	2	2	2	2	1
19	1	1	1	1	1	1	2	2	3
20	2	1	1	1	4	2	2	3	3
21	2	2	1	1	3	2	3	3	1
23	3	1	1	2	1	1	2	2	2
24	3	4	2	4	4	1	3	2	2
25	3	1	1	1	2	3	2	4	3
26	3	4	1	4	2	3	2	3	3
27	2	1	1	1	3	1	2	2	2
28	2	1	1	2	3	2	1	2	2
29	2	1	1	1	1	1	2	2	2

5.2 Selection of a set of the most important attributes

As we obtained more than one reduct, we decided to analyse precisely the components of reducts, in order to evaluate which reduced subset of attributes should be selected for further analysis of the information system A. Let us notice that attribute a_2 (abdominal pain) does not occur in any of reducts. Then, we used the procedure of adding to the core, the attributes of the highest increase of discriminatory power (described in section 3). The partial listing of the steps of adding attributes in this strategy is presented in Table 9. The selected subsets are marked with bold fonts. The final selection is the subset $\{a_4, a_5, a_7, a_8, a_9\}$. Let us also notice that besides the core, the selected attributes a_5, a_7, a_8, occur in all reducts more frequent than other attributes.

To sum up, the most important attributes in system A are the following:
attr. 4 - fever
attr. 5 - etiology
attr. 7 - peritoneal symptoms

Table 6. Information system B - Stage 4

Patient number	Attributes a_{11}	a_{12}	a_{13}	a_{14}	a_{15}	a_{16}	a_{17}	a_{18}	Decision class
2	3	2	1	2	2	1	1	1	3
3	2	3	1	2	1	1	2	2	2
4	2	1	1	1	2	1	2	2	3
5	2	1	1	3	2	4	1	3	2
6	1	1	1	1	1	1	1	2	3
7	2	1	1	1	3	4	2	2	3
8	2	1	1	1	1	1	2	2	3
9	2	1	1	2	1	1	2	2	2
10	2	1	1	1	1	1	1	2	3
11	1	1	1	2	1	1	2	2	3
12	2	2	1	1	2	1	2	2	3
13	2	1	1	3	4	1	2	2	3
19	1	1	1	1	1	1	2	2	3
20	2	1	1	1	4	2	2	3	3
21	2	2	1	1	3	2	3	3	1
23	3	1	1	2	1	1	2	2	2
24	3	4	2	4	4	1	3	2	2
26	3	4	1	4	2	3	2	3	3
27	2	1	1	1	3	1	2	2	2

Table 7. Information system B - Stage 5

Patient number	Attributes a_{11}	a_{12}	a_{13}	a_{14}	a_{15}	a_{16}	a_{17}	a_{18}	Decision class
2	3	2	1	2	2	1	1	1	3
4	2	1	1	1	2	1	2	2	3
6	1	1	1	1	1	1	1	2	3
7	2	1	1	1	3	4	2	2	3
8	2	1	1	1	1	1	2	2	3
10	2	1	1	1	1	1	1	2	3
11	1	1	1	2	1	1	2	2	3
12	2	2	1	1	2	1	2	2	3
13	2	1	1	3	4	1	2	2	3
19	1	1	1	1	1	1	2	2	3
20	2	1	1	1	4	2	2	3	3
21	2	2	1	1	3	2	3	3	1
23	3	1	1	2	1	1	2	2	2
26	3	4	1	4	2	3	2	3	3
27	2	1	1	1	3	1	2	2	2

Table 8. Accuracies of approximations of decision classes in system A

Decision class X_i	Number of patients card(X_i)	Lower approximation card($\underline{Q}X_i$)	Upper approximation card($\bar{Q}X_i$)	Accuracy $\mu_Q X_i$
1	16	16	16	1.0
2	11	11	11	1.0
3	2	2	2	1.0

attr 8 - peristalsis
attr. 9 - serum amylase level

Table 9. Steps in adding attributes to the core for information system A

The current reduced subset of attributes	Added attribute	Quality of approx. after adding attribute
4,9	1	0.41
	2	0.28
	3	0.38
	5	**0.69**
	6	0.41
	7	0.52
	8	0.41
4,5,9	1	0.79
	2	0.69
	3	0.69
	6	0.86
	7	**0.93**
	8	0.93
4,5,7,9	1	0.93
	2	0.93
	3	0.93
	6	1.00
	8	**1.00**

5.3 Discovery of decision rules in reduced information system A

Further analysis of system A consists in determining the relationships between values of the most important attributes and the patients' classification, i.e. looking for representation of these relationships in the form of decision rules. As the most important attributes were selected, we decided to induce decision rules from the reduced information system (i.e. composed of $\{a_4, a_5, a_7, a_8, a_9\}$). As it has been discussed in section 3, there are three main strategies to induce decision rules: induction of a minimal set of rules, an exhaustive set of rules, and a *satisfactory set* of decision rules. The number of considered objects is quite limited, so we used all strategies for comparative point of view. Summary of information about discovered rules is presented in Table 10.

Table 10. The sets of decision rules induced from system A

Strategy	Classification	number of rules	aver. length rule	support of the strongest of the rule	aver. strength of rules
minimal set LEM2	all classes	17	2.71	5	2.00
	class X_1	8	2.38	5	2.63
	class X_2	7	3.14	3	1.57
	class X_3	2	2.50	1	1.00
all rules	all classes	50	2.82	5	1.56
	class X_1	27	2.67	5	1.81
	class X_2	20	3.00	3	1.30
	class X_3	3	3.00	1	1.00
satisfactory rules (Explore)	all classes	10	2.50	5	2.80
	class X_1	6	2.50	5	3.67
	class X_2	1	2.00	3	3.00
	class X_3	3	3.00	1	1.00

Using the LEM2 algorithm to induce the minimal set of rules led to 17 rules which are composed of: two rules stronger than 4, three rules with the strength equal to 3, four rules with strength 2, and 8 rules supported by single patients. The relatively high number of rules supported by one or two cases is a kind of difficulty in interpreting their syntax and their clinical meaning. This is a reason that we decided to use an approach to get satisfactory set of rules. To choose stronger rules we used the following threshold values for minimal number of supporting examples: - 3 patients for decision class 1 and 2; - 1 patient for decision class 3 (for this class there are no stronger rules). The discovered decision rules are listed below (each rule is additionally described by the set of covered objects):

rule 1. if $(a_4 = 1) \wedge (a_9 = 1)$ then $(d = 1)$ $\{4, 11, 23, 24, 26\}$
rule 2. if $(a_4 = 1) \wedge (a_5 = 2)$ then $(d = 1)$ $\{9, 22, 24\}$
rule 3. if $(a_5 = 1) \wedge (a_9 = 1)$ then $(d = 1)$ $\{15, 20, 21, 23\}$
rule 4. if $(a_7 = 1) \wedge (a_8 = 1) \wedge (a_9 = 1)$ then $(d = 1)$ $\{11, 15, 23, 24\}$
rule 5. if $(a_4 = 1) \wedge (a_7 = 1) \wedge (a_8 = 1)$ then $(d = 1)$ $\{11, 23, 24\}$
rule 6. if $(a_4 = 2) \wedge (a_5 = 1) \wedge (a_8 = 2)$ then $(d = 1)$ $\{1, 20, 21\}$
rule 7. if $(a_4 = 2) \wedge (a_5 = 2)$ then $(d = 2)$ $\{5, 10, 12\}$

rule 8. if $(a_5 = 2) \wedge (a_9 = 3)$ then $(d = 3)$ {2}
rule 9. if $(a_5 = 3) \wedge (a_7 = 1) \wedge (a_9 = 4)$ then $(d = 3)$ {25}
rule 10. if $(a_4 = 2) \wedge (a_5 = 3) \wedge (a_8 = 1)$ then $(d = 3)$ {25}

6 Analysis of information systems B

Let us consider the classification of patients during multistage peritoneal lavage treatment represented in five information systems B. For each of these systems we used standard rough set operations. Table 11 summarizes the accuracy of approximation of decision classes, quality of classification for each of considered systems.

Table 11. Accuracies of approximations of decision classes and quality of classification for five stages of treatment - systems B

Stage	Quality	class X_i	card(X_i)	card($\underline{Q}X_i$)	card($\bar{Q}X_i$)	Accuracy
		1	1	1	1	1.0
I	0.93	2	9	8	10	0.8
		3	19	18	20	0.9
		1	3	3	3	1.0
II	0.93	2	15	14	16	0.88
		3	10	9	11	0.82
		1	6	5	9	0.56
III	0.84	2	12	10	14	0.72
		3	7	6	10	0.60
		1	4	3	7	0.43
IV	0.79	2	14	11	15	0.73
		3	1	1	1	1.0
		1	8	6	10	0.6
V	0.93	2	7	5	9	0.56
		3	–	–	–	–

6.1 Reducts and cores of attributes for particular stages

Then, we found all reducts and cores for consecutive stages (instillations) of treatment. They are as follows:
Stage I

- reducts: $\{a_9, a_{11}, a_{12}, a_{14},\}$, $\{a_9, a_{10}, a_{11}, a_{14}, a_{16}\}$, $\{a_9, a_{10}, a_{11}, a_{14}, a_{15}\}$, $\{a_9, a_{10}, a_{11}, a_{13}, a_{14}\}$
- the core: $\{a_9, a_{11}, a_{14}\}$

Stage II

- reducts: $\{a_{11}, a_{14}, a_{15}, a_{16}, a_{17}\}$
- the core: $\{a_{11}, a_{14}, a_{15}, a_{16}, a_{17}\}$

Stage III

- reducts: $\{a_{14}, a_{15}, a_{16}, a_{17}, \}$, $\{a_{12}, a_{15}, a_{16}, a_{17}, a_{18}\}$, $\{a_{12}, a_{14}, a_{15}, a_{17}, a_{18}\}$, $\{a_{11}, a_{14}, a_{15}, a_{17}, a_{18}\}$
- the core: $\{a_{15}, a_{17}\}$

Stage IV

- reducts: $\{a_{11}, a_{14}, a_{15}, a_{17}, a_{18}\}$, $\{a_{11}, a_{12}, a_{14}, a_{15}, a_{17}\}$
- the core: $\{a_{11}, a_{14}, a_{15}, a_{17}\}$

Stage V

- reducts: $\{a_{11}, a_{14}, a_{15}, a_{17}\}$ $\{a_{11}, a_{14}, a_{16}, a_{17}, a_{18}\}$, $\{a_{11}, a_{12}, a_{15}, a_{16}, a_{17}\}$, $\{a_{11}, a_{12}, a_{14}, a_{16}, a_{18}\}$, $\{a_{11}, a_{12}, a_{14}, a_{15}\}$
- the core: $\{a_{11}\}$

Similarly to the information system A, we had many reducts for each system B (each stage). For this reason, we tried again to find acceptable subsets of the most important attributes, one per stage for further analysis of multistage treatment process. We used the strategy of adding to the core, the attributes of the highest increase of discriminatory power. Since the part of system B corresponding to stage I differs from other stages, where two additional 'incremental' attributes (a_{17} and a_{18}) are used, we considered stage I independently from systems corresponding to stages II-V.

Using this strategy, we found the reduct set composed of the following attributes:
attr. 9 - serum amylase level,
attr. 11 - volume of drained liquid,
attr. 12 - drained liquid amylase level,
attr. 14 - drained liquid protein level.

6.2 Identification of attributes characterizing the course of the treatment

The course of treatment by peritoneal lavage is described by the systems B which correspond to stages II, III, IV and V. We repeated the strategy of adding attributes to cores for each stage. The selected reducts are the following:

- Stage II: $\{a_{11}, a_{14}, a_{15}, a_{16}, a_{17}\}$,
- Stage III: $\{a_{12}, a_{14}, a_{15}, a_{17}, a_{18}\}$,
- Stage IV: $\{a_{11}, a_{14}, a_{15}, a_{17}, a_{18}\}$, $\{a_{11}, a_{12}, a_{14}, a_{15}, a_{17}\}$ [3],

[3] Both reducts can be obtained while adding attributes to the core

– Stage V: $\{a_{11}, a_{14}, a_{15}, a_{17}\}$.

We think that it is important to generalize results obtained in each of stages. So, we tried to discover the common subset of attributes which would ensure acceptable quality of classification for each of stages. We analysed the structure of all reducts for stages II-IV in order to discover some repeating attribute patterns. We noticed that: the subset $\{a_{11}, a_{14}, a_{15}, a_{17}, a_{18}\}$ is the only reduct occurring in more than one stage; the reduct $\{a_{11}, a_{14}, a_{15}, a_{17}\}$ is a subset of two other reducts; and the reduct $\{a_{14}, a_{15}, a_{16}, a_{17}\}$ is a subset of one reduct in another stage. Then we performed the analysis of frequency of the attributes in the most acceptable reduct. The distribution of the attributes is presented in Table 12. The most frequent attributes are a_{11}, a_{14}, a_{15} and a_{17}. On contrary, attributes a_{11} and a_{14} are the less frequent.

Table 12. The most frequent attributes in chosen reducts for stages II-V

Attribute	a_{11}	a_{12}	a_{13}	a_{14}	a_{15}	a_{16}	a_{17}	a_{18}
Number of reducts	3	2	0	4	4	1	4	2

Taking into account all these partial results led us to choosing the following attributes (common for all stages II-V) which best describe the course of multi-stage treatment:
attr. 11 - volume of drained liquid,
attr. 14 - drained liquid protein level,
attr. 15 - number of erythrocytes in drained liquid,
attr. 17 - change of amylase level in drained liquid.

6.3 Discovery of decision rules

In further analysis of multistage treatment we reduced the systems B using the selected attributes in previous section, i.e. the subset $\{a_9, a_{11}, a_{12}, a_{14}\}$ for stage I, and the common subset $\{a_{11}, a_{14}, a_{15}, a_{17}\}$ for stages II-V.

As it has been discussed in previous sections we focused on using the strategy for inducing satisfactory set of decision rules. As some of information systems contained inconsistencies we generated only certain, i.e. exact, decision rules (exact rules were stronger and easier to interpret). To choose 'interesting' rules we defined the following threshold values for minimal number of supporting examples (patients):

Stage I : 3 for decision class 2 and 3; 1 for class 1.
Stage II : 2 for decision class 2 and 3; 1 for class 1.
Stage III : 2 for decision class 1 and 2; 1 for class 3.
Stage IV : 1 for decision class 1 and 3; 2 for class 2.

Stage V : 2 for decision class 1 and 2.

The discovered decision rules are listed below:

Stage I

rule 1. if $(a_{12} = 3)$ then $(d = 3)$ $\{3, 10, 19\}$
rule 2. if $(a_{12} = 4)$ then $(d = 3)$ $\{2, 6, 27\}$
rule 3. if $(a_9 = 2) \wedge (a_{10} = 1)$ then $(d = 2)$ $\{14, 17, 22\}$
rule 4. if $(a_9 = 1) \wedge (a_{10} = 2)$ then $(d = 3)$ $\{4, 10, 11, 21, 23, 24\}$
rule 5. if $(a_9 = 2) \wedge (a_{10} = 2) \wedge (a_8 = 1)$ then $(d = 1)$ $\{5, 12, 13\}$
rule 6. if $(a_{10} = 2) \wedge (a_{14} = 3)$ then $(d = 1)$ $\{5, 13, 23, , 27\}$
rule 7. if $(a_{10} = 1) \wedge (a_{14} = 2)$ then $(d = 1)$ $\{16\}$

Stage II

rule 1. if $(a_{11} = 1)$ then $(d = 3)$ $\{6, 11, 18, 21\}$
rule 2. if $(a_{14} = 1) \wedge (a_{17} = 3)$ then $(d = 1)$ $\{20\}$
rule 3. if $(a_{15} = 3) \wedge (a_{17} = 3)$ then $(d = 1)$ $\{20\}$
rule 4. if $(a_{11} = 2) \wedge (a_{15} = 4)$ then $(d = 3)$ $\{13, 19\}$
rule 5. if $(a_{11} = 3) \wedge (a_{15} = 2)$ then $(d = 3)$ $\{2, 24, 25\}$
rule 6. if $(a_{14} = 1) \wedge (a_{17} = 1)$ then $(d = 3)$ $\{6, 10\}$
rule 7. if $(a_{14} = 4) \wedge (a_{17} = 1)$ then $(d = 3)$ $\{13, 19\}$
rule 8. if $(a_{14} = 2) \wedge (a_{15} = 3)$ then $(d = 2)$ $\{14, 27\}$
rule 9. if $(a_{11} = 2) \wedge (a_{14} = 2) \wedge (a_{15} = 1)$ then $(d = 2)$ $\{3, 9\}$

Stage III

rule 1. if $(a_{11} = 1)$ then $(d = 2)$ $\{5, 16, 17\}$
rule 2. if $(a_{14} = 1) \wedge (a_{17} = 1)$ then $(d = 2)$ $\{1, 2, 17\}$
rule 3. if $(a_{14} = 2) \wedge (a_{17} = 3)$ then $(d = 2)$ $\{16, 20\}$
rule 4. if $(a_{15} = 3) \wedge (a_{17} = 2)$ then $(d = 3)$ $\{6\}$
rule 5. if $(a_{14} = 4) \wedge (a_{15} = 1) \wedge (a_{17} = 2)$ then $(d = 3)$ $\{10\}$
rule 6. if $(a_{11} = 2) \wedge (a_{14} = 2) \wedge (a_{17} = 2)$ then $(d = 2)$ $\{15, 24\}$

Stage IV

rule 1. if $(a_{11} = 1)$ then $(d = 2)$ $\{5, 10\}$
rule 2. if $(a_{14} = 4)$ then $(d = 2)$ $\{10, 16\}$
rule 3. if $(a_{15} = 2)$ then $(d = 2)$ $\{5, 12\}$
rule 4. if $(a_{17} = 3)$ then $(d = 2)$ $\{6, 15\}$
rule 5. if $(a_{14} = 3)$ then $(d = 1)$ $\{4\}$
rule 6. if $(a_{15} = 4)$ then $(d = 1)$ $\{17\}$
rule 7. if $(a_{11} = 2) \wedge (a_{14} = 2)$ then $(d = 2)$ $\{6, 12, 13, 14\}$
rule 8. if $(a_{11} = 3) \wedge (a_{14} = 2)$ then $(d = 3)$ $\{19\}$

Stage V

rule 1. if $(a_{17} = 1)$ then $(d = 2)$ $\{2, 4, 12, 15\}$
rule 2. if $(a_{15} = 2) \wedge (a_{17} = 2)$ then $(d = 1)$ $\{3, 13\}$
rule 3. if $(a_{14} = 1) \wedge (a_{17} = 2)$ then $(d = 2)$ $\{4, 12\}$

It is interesting to generalize experience acquired from analysing sets of decision rules in each stage. We looked for interesting rule patterns that repeat in consecutive stages of the treatments. For instance, one can notice that the rule pattern *if* $(a_{11} = 1)$ *then* $(d = 3)$ repeats in stages II and III. However, it 'moves' from the decision class $(d = 3)$ in stage II to the decision class $(d = 2)$ in stage III. Similar regularity between the above stages can be also noticed for other rules, e.g. *if* $(a_{14} = 1) \wedge (a_{17} = 1)$ *then* $(d = 3)$. Other repeating rule pattern can also be discovered in pairs of next stages - in particular between III and IV.

We should also comment that such regularities could be noticed only for satisfactory sets of rules. The minimal sets of rules induced from information systems B (what is not reported in this paper) did not indicate such patterns.

7 Discussion and conclusions

The results of analysis of the information system A showed that while examining a patient suspected of having acute pancreatitis one should pay special attention to the following factors: fever a_4, history of alcohol taking a_5, cholelithiasis a_5, peritoneal symptoms a_7, correct bowel movement (peristalsis a_8), amylase level in serum a_9. The high quality of classification for this set of attributes confirmed that the diagnostic criteria used by us were sufficient to recognize the acute pancreatitis.

The additional diagnostic and prognostic criteria are characteristic values of important attributes from information systems B obtained stage by stage during peritoneal lavage process. These attributes are the following: volume of drained liquid a_{11}, protein level in drained liquid a_{14}, number of erythrocytes in drained liquid a_{15} and increase of amylase level (positive or negative) in drained liquid a_{17}. Patient's status is depended on the results of peritoneal drained liquid analysis and the number of peritoneal lavages which are needed to the patient's final recovery. The character of these dependencies is contained in the decision rules. This representation is abbreviated but compressive owing to the presence of important attributes - which are the record of our experience in this way of treatment.

An analysis of stage by stage decision rules can inform in the exact case if the next peritoneal lavage is necessary or if the treatment can be finished. This fact has a special meaning in such cases where the patients status has been improved, the peritoneal signs ceased and the value of important attributes in the drained liquid are still high. An analysis of decision rules in the stage by stage algorithms (induced from information systems B) allow us to discover the following regularity observed during peritoneal lavage - after each stage of peritoneal lavage the volume of drained liquid is increased. One should think that in the severe period of acute pancreatitis a great amount of dialyzing fluid is absorbed from peritoneum to the circulatory system.

On this basis we can additionally estimate the lack of fluids and compensate it properly. In the following peritoneal lavage the level of proteins in drained liquid were - in 50% the same, in 25% higher, in 25% lower. It can represent the different dynamics of inflammatory process in the peritoneum during the acute pancreatitis.

Stage by stage the number of erythrocytes and leukocytes in drained liquid decreases which is important to clinical practice ('clarity' of drained liquid). For the patients who needed increased number of peritoneal lavage the level of amylase in drained liquid decreased slowly and even increased in the first two stages of lavage.

Perhaps, due to small number of patients, the therapeutic suggestions resulting from sets of decision rules for both information systems cannot be considered as obligatory. However, these rules are clearer than the original information systems and facilitate the exploitation of recorded clinical experience to decide in doubtful situations and to plan the prospective studies about acute pancreatitis.

Let us briefly comment methodological conclusions. The key point of this study consists in analysing the multistage medical decision process. Each stage of this process is characterized by its own information system. In comparison to previous medical application (i.e. one stage decision processes) this analysis has been focused on studying the sequence of five information systems referring to consecutive stages of the treatment. We have shown that the use of the strategy of adding, to the core, of the attributes of the highest increase of discriminatory power led to finding the acceptable reduced set of attributes which is common for all stages. Moreover, the approach to inducing the satisfactory set of rules can give the strong decision rules which characterize main dependencies between lavage process and the patient's status.

To sum up, this application shows that the rough set theory can be applied to analyse multistage medical decision processes.

Acknowledgments

Research of the second author of this paper was partly supported from the KBN grant no. 8-T11C 013 13.

References

1. Chan C.C., Grzymala-Busse J.W.: On the two local inductive algorithms: PRISM and LEM2. Foundations of Computing and Decision Sciences **19/4** (1994) 185–204
2. Fibak, J., Pawlak, Z., Slowinski, K., Slowinski, R.: Rough sets based decision algorithm for treatment of duodenal ulcer by HSV. Bull. Polish Acad. Sci. Ser. Sci. Biol. **34/10/12** (1986) 227–246
3. Gjessing J.: Peritoneal dialysis in severe acute hemorrhaigic pancreatitis. Acta Chirurgica Scandinavica **133** (1967) 645–647
4. Grzymala-Busse J.W.: LERS - a system for learning from examples based on rough sets. In: R. Słowiński (ed.): Intelligent Decision Support – Handbook of Ap-

plications and Advances of the Rough Sets Theory, Kluwer Academic Publishers, Dordrecht (1992) 3–18
5. Hand, D.J.: Discrimination and classification. Wiley, New York (1981)
6. Krusińska E., Słowiński R., Stefanowski J.: Discriminant versus rough sets approach to vague data analysis. Applied Stochastic Models and Data Analysis 8 (1992) 43–56
7. Krusińska E., Stefanowski J., Stromberg J.E.: Comparability of newer and classical data analysis techniques. Application in medical domain classification. In: Didey E. et al. (eds.), New approaches in classification and data analysis, Springer - Verlag (series Studies in Classification, Data Analysis and Knowledge Organization) (1993) 644–652
8. McMahon M.J., Pickford J., Playforth M.J.: Early prediction of severity of acute pancreatitis using peritoneal lavage. Acta Chirurgica Scandinavica **146** (1980) 171–175
9. Michalski R.S.: A theory and methodology of inductive learning. In: R.S. Michalski, J.G. Carbonell and T.M. Mitchell (eds), Machine learning: an artificial intelligence approach, Morgan Kaufman, San Mateo (1983) 83–134
10. Mienko R., Stefanowski J., Toumi K., Vanderpooten D.: Discovery-oriented induction of decision rules. Cahier du Lamsade **141** Paris, Universite de Paris Dauphine (septembre 1996)
11. Mienko R., Slowinski R., Stefanowski J., Susmaga R.: RoughFamily - software implementation of rough set based data analysis and rule discovery techniques. In: S. Tsumoto, S. Kobayashi, T. Yokomori, H. Tanaka, and A. Nakamura (eds.): Proceedings of the Fourth International Workshop on Rough Sets, Fuzzy Sets, and Machine Discovery (RSFD'96), The University of Tokyo, November 6–8 (1996) 437–440
12. Pawlak Z.: Rough sets. Int. J. Computer and Information Sciences **11** (1982) 341–356
13. Pawlak Z.: Rough sets. Theoretical aspects of reasoning about data. Kluwer Academic Publishers, Dordrecht (1991)
14. Pawlak Z., Grzymala-Busse J., Słowiński R., Ziarko, W. : Rough sets. Communications of the ACM **38/11** (1995) 89–95
15. Pawlak Z., Słowiński K., Słowiński R.: Rough classification of patients after highly selected vagotomy for duodenal ulcer. International J. Man-Machine Studies **24** (1986) 413–433
16. Piatetsky-Shapiro G.: Discovery, analysis and presentation of strong rules. In: Piatetsky-Shapiro G. and Christopher Matheus (eds.), Knowledge discovery in databases, AAAI/MIT Press (1991) 229–247
17. Ranson J.H., Rifkind K.M., Turner J.W.: Peritoneal signs and nonoperative peritoneal lavage in acute pancreatitis. Surgery, Gynecology and Obstetrics **143** (1976) 209–219
18. Ranson J.H., Spencer F.C.: The role of peritoneal lavage in severe acute pancreatitis. Annals of Surgery **187** (1978) 565–575
19. Rosato E.F., Mullis W.F., Rosato F.E.: Peritoneal lavage therapy in hemorrhagic pancreatitis. Surgery **74** (1973) 106–111
20. Skowron A.: Boolean reasoning for decision rules generation. In Komorowski J., Ras Z. (eds.), Methodologies for Intelligent Systems. LNAI **689** Springer-Verlag, Berlin (1993) 295–305
21. Słowiński, K.: Rough classification of HSV patients. In Słowiński R. (ed.), Intelligent decision support. Handbook of applications and advances of the rough sets

theory, Kluwer Academic Publishers, Dordrecht (1992) 363–372
22. Słowiński K., Słowiński R., Stefanowski J.: Rough sets approach to analysis of data from peritoneal lavage in acute pancreatitis. Medical Informatics **13** (1988) 143–159
23. Słowiński, K., El. Sanossy Sharif: Rough sets approach to analysis of data of diagnostic peritoneal lavage applied for multiple injuries patients. In: W. Ziarko (ed.): Rough Sets, Fuzzy Sets and Knowledge Discovery (RSKD'93). Workshops in Computing, Springer–Verlag & British Computer Society, London, Berlin (1994) 420–425
24. Słowiński, K., Stefanowski, J., Antczak, A., Kwias, Z.: Rough set approach to the verification of indications for treatment of urinary stones by extracorporeal shock wave lithotripsy (ESWL). In: T.Y. Lin, A.M. Wildberger (eds.): Soft Computing: Rough Sets, Fuzzy Logic, Neural Networks, Uncertainty Management, Knowledge Discovery, Simulation Councils, Inc., San Diego, CA (1995) 93–96
25. Słowiński, K., Stefanowski, J.: On limitations of using rough set approach to analyse non-trivial medical information systems. In: S. Tsumoto, S. Kobayashi, T. Yokomori, H. Tanaka, and A. Nakamura (eds.): Proceedings of the Fourth International Workshop on Rough Sets, Fuzzy Sets, and Machine Discovery (RSFD'96), The University of Tokyo, November 6–8 (1996) 176–184
26. Słowiński R. (ed.), Intelligent decision support. Handbook of applications and advances of the rough sets theory, Kluwer Academic Publishers, Dordrecht (1992)
27. Słowiński, R., Stefanowski, J.: 'RoughDAS' and 'RoughClass' software implementations of the rough set approach. In: Słowiński R. (ed.), Intelligent decision support. Handbook of applications and advances of the rough sets theory, Kluwer Academic Publishers, Dordrecht (1992) 445–456
28. Stefanowski J.: On rough set based approaches to induction of decision rules. (this book)
29. Stefanowski J., Słowiński K.: Rough sets s a tool for studying attribute dependencies in the urinary stones treatment **data** set. In: T.Y. Lin, N. Cercone (eds.), Rough sets and data mining, Kluwer Academic Publishers, Boston (1997) 177–198
30. Stefanowski J., Słowiński K.: Rough set theory and rule induction techniques for discovery of attribute dependencies in medical information systems. In Komorowski J., Zytkow J. (eds.), Principles of Knowledge Discovery. Proceedings of the First European Symposium (PKDD '97), Trondheim, Norway, June 1997. Springer Lecture Notes in AI **1263** Springer - Verlag (1997) 36–46
31. Stefanowski J., Vanderpooten D.: A general two stage approach to rule induction from examples. In: W. Ziarko (ed.): Rough Sets, Fuzzy Sets and Knowledge Discovery (RSKD'93). Workshops in Computing, Springer–Verlag & British Computer Society, London, Berlin (1994) 317–325
32. Wall A.J.: Peritoneal dialysis in treatment of severe acute pancreatitis. Medical Journal of Australia **52** (1965) 281–284
33. Ziarko W.: Review of basics of rough sets in the context of data mining. In: S. Tsumoto, S. Kobayashi, T. Yokomori, H. Tanaka, and A. Nakamura (eds.): Proceedings of the Fourth International Workshop on Rough Sets, Fuzzy Sets, and Machine Discovery (RSFD'96), The University of Tokyo, November 6–8 (1996) 447–457
34. Ziarko, W., Shan, N.: KDD-R: A comprehensive system for knowledge discovery in databases using rough sets. In: T.Y. Lin, A.M. Wildberger (eds.): Soft Computing: Rough Sets, Fuzzy Logic, Neural Networks, Uncertainty Management, Knowledge Discovery, Simulation Councils, Inc., San Diego, CA (1995) 298–301

Chapter 15

Reduction Methods for Medical Data

Hideo Tanaka[1] *and Yutaka Maeda*[1]

Department of Industrial Engineering, Osaka Prefecture University
1-1 Gakuen-cho, Sakai, Osaka 599-8531, JAPAN

1 Introduction

Pawlak [Pa1] has proposed the concept of approximate data analysis based on rough sets in 1982. Rough set theory has been developed to deal with many real-life problems. Basic concepts of rough set theory can be found in [Pa3] and [PG].

An application of rough sets to medical analysis for heart diseases has been studied by Pawlak [Pa2] where the inconsistency of the medical test data and expert's diagnoses have been clarified. Mrozek [Mr] constructed if -then rules using rough sets to control a rotary clinker kiln in a cement plant. This research was concerned with constructing an expert's inference mod el. Dubois et al. [DP] have extended the concept of the rough set by proposing twofold fuzzy sets. Tanaka et al. [TI] have proposed a new method of reducing information systems based on accuracy measures described in [Pa2].

Rough sets are defined by equivalence relations in an information system described as a database. A method of reducing attributes in the given information system has already been developed by equivalence relations with regard to attributes.

In this paper, we introduce first a reduction method of attributes using importance grades which is introduced in Pawlak [Pa2]. Here "ε- independent", "ε-dependent" and "ε-superfluous" are clearly defined and used to reduce some attributes. When "$\varepsilon = 0$, these definitions become conventional ones. Next, we propose a method for reducing divisions of attributes. To do so, the given data set is converted into the binary data set whose attribute value is 0 or 1. After transforming the integer data into the binary data, the information system with the binary data is reduced by the method of Tanaka et al. [TI]. As a result, we can also reduce the number of divisions of attributes. Thus, our proposed method is useful for discussing divisions in an attribute space. Finally, the proposed methods were applied to the medical data with good results.

As for divisions in an attribute space, Lenarcik and Piasta [LP] propos ed a similar binary representation to assign different data to different int ervals constructed by the Cartesian product. In our model, it is assumed that the divi-

vision of attributes is given by experts' knowledge. Shan et al [SH] have proposed discretization method that transforms continuous values to discrete ones.

2 Reduction of Information Systems

2.1 Basic Concepts of Rough Sets

Now, we describe the concept of rough sets by Pawlak [Pa2]. An approximation space A is defined as $A = (U, R)$, where U is the universal set and R is an equivalence relation. Equivalence classes of the relation R are called elementary sets in A. The empty set is assumed to also be an elementary set. Any finite union of elementary sets in A is called a definable set in A. Let $X \subseteq U$. The upper approximation of X in A denoted as $A^*(X)$ is defined by the least definable set in A, containing X. The lower approximation denoted as $A_*(X)$ is defined by the greatest definable set in A, contained in X. The accuracy measure of X in $A = (U, R)$ is defined as

$$\alpha_A(X) = \frac{Card(A_*(X))}{Card(A^*(X))} \tag{1}$$

where $Card(B)$ is the cardinality of the set B. Let $F = \{X_1, \cdots, X_n\}$ be a classification of U, i.e. $X_i \cap X_j = \emptyset$ for every $i \neq j$ and $\cup_{i=1}^n X_i = U$. Then, F is called a partition of U and X_i is called a class. The upper approximation and lower approximation of F can be written as

$$\begin{aligned} A^*(F) &= \{A^*(X_1), \cdots, A^*(X_n)\} \\ A_*(F) &= \{A_*(X_1), \cdots, A_*(X_n)\}. \end{aligned} \tag{2}$$

The accuracy measure of F in A is defined as

$$\beta_A(F) = \frac{Card\left(\bigcup_{i=1}^{n} A_*(X_i)\right)}{Card(U)}, \tag{3}$$

which is known as the quality of approximation.

Theorem 1. *Given a classification F, it follows for the subset $P' \subset P$ that*

$$\beta_A(\tilde{P'}) \leq \beta_A(\tilde{P}) \tag{4}$$

where P' and P are subsets of Q and $\beta_A(\tilde{P})$ denotes the accuracy measure of F in an approximation space induced by $\tilde{P}$ which is the equivalence relation with regard to the subset P of attributes.

2.2 Reduction Method

In this section, we introduce the method for reducing information systems p roposed by Tanaka et al. [TI]. Let $S = (U, Q, V, \phi, F)$ be an information system, where U is the universe of S, elements of U are called objects , Q is a set of attributes, $V = \cup_{q \in Q} V_q$ is a set of values of attributes, $\phi : U \times Q \rightarrow V$ is a description function and F is a classification of U given by experts' knowledge.

Definition 2. i) Let P be a subset of Q. A subset P is said to be independent in an information system S if and only if

$$\beta_A(\tilde{P'}) < \beta_A(\tilde{P}) \quad \text{for all} \quad P' \subset P. \tag{5}$$

Also, P is said to be dependent in S if and only if there is $P' \subset P$ such that

$$\beta_A(\tilde{P'}) = \beta_A(\tilde{P}). \tag{6}$$

ii) Let $P' \subset P$ and $P'' = P - P'$. A subset P' is said to be superfluous in P if and only if

$$\beta_A(\tilde{P''}) = \beta_A(\tilde{P}). \tag{7}$$

Theorem 3. *If P' is superfluous in P and $\{p_i\}$ is superfluous in $P - P'$, then $P' \cup \{p_i\}$ is superfluous in P.*

The upper approximation of X in the approximation space induced by Q is denoted as $Q^*(X)$ and the lower approximation of X in the approximation space induced by Q is denoted as $Q_*(X)$. The accuracy measure of X in the approximation space induced by Q is defined as

$$\alpha^Q(X) = \frac{Card(Q_*(X))}{Card(Q^*(X))}. \tag{8}$$

It is assumed that an information system is given in the form of Table 1 where importance grades of X_i, $i = 1, 2, 3$ are written as $1 - \varepsilon_i$. If $\varepsilon_i = 0$, then X_i belongs to the important group and if $\varepsilon_i > 0$ then X_i belongs to the other group. Suppose that importance grades are given by experts' knowledge.

Definition 4. i) Let P be a subset of Q. A subset P is said to be ε-independent in an information system S if and only if for any $P' \subset P$

$$\alpha^P(X_i) \geq \alpha^{P'}(X_i) + \varepsilon_i, \quad i = 1, \ldots, n, \tag{9}$$

and for any $P' \subset P$, there exists some k

$$\alpha^P(X_k) > \alpha^{P'}(X_k) + \varepsilon_k, \quad k \in \{1, \ldots, n\}. \tag{10}$$

Also, P is said to be ε-dependent in S if and only if there is $P' \subset P$ such that there exists some k such that

$$\alpha^P(X_k) < \alpha^{P'}(X_k) + \varepsilon_k, \quad k \in \{1, \ldots, n\}. \tag{11}$$

ii) Let $P' \subset P$ and $P'' = P - P'$. A subset P' is said to be ε-superfluous in P if and only if it holds that

$$\alpha^P(X_i) \leq \alpha^{P''}(X_i) + \varepsilon_i, \quad i = 1, \ldots, n, \tag{12}$$

or there exists some k such that

$$\alpha^P(X_k) < \alpha^{P''}(X_k) + \varepsilon_k, \quad k \in \{1, \ldots, n\}. \tag{13}$$

It should be noted that for any $P' \subset P$,

$$\alpha^{P'}(X_i) \leq \alpha^P(X_i), \quad i = 1, \ldots, n.$$

If $\varepsilon_i = 0$ for all i, then the ε-independence coincides with independence introduced by Definition 2. It is assumed that the importance grades are given as intuitive values by experts' knowledge. The discussion of ε-independence falls into a general discussion of the notion of independence.

Table 1. An example of an information system

F	U	q_1	q_2	q_3	$Card$	Importance grade
	x_1	1	1	1	16	
X_1	x_2	1	1	3	9	1.0 (ε_1=0.0)
	x_3	1	2	2	8	
	x_4	1	2	2	11	
X_2	x_5	2	2	2	20	0.8 (ε_1=0.2)
	x_6	2	1	1	4	
	x_7	2	1	3	8	
X_3	x_8	1	3	2	11	0.5 (ε_1=0.5)
	x_9	1	3	3	13	

Theorem 5. *"ε-independent" and "ε-dependent" are exclusive.*

This theorem can be proved from the fact that the negation of "ε-independent" is the same as "ε-dependent".

Definition 6. A subset $P \subset Q$ is called an ε-reduct of Q in S if and only if $Q - P$ is ε-superfluous and P is ε-independent in S. The corresponding system $S' = (U, P, V', \phi', F)$ is called the ε-reduced system where ϕ' is the reduction of ϕ to the set $U \times P$ and V' is the corresponding restriction of V.

The algorithm for obtaining an ε-reduct of Q from Theorem 3 and Definition 6 can be described as follows.

Algorithm

Step 0: Set $P = Q$.
Step 1: Find an ε-superfluous attribute, say p_i, in P. If there is not such a p_i, go to Step 4.
Step 2: Set $P = P - \{p_i\}$.
Step 3: If any p_i in P is not ε-superfluous in P, go to Step 4. Otherwise, go to Step 1.
Step 4: End. P is the ε-reduct of the given attributes.

If we reduce attributes by the above algorithm, the obtained accuracy measure might be worse than before because of $\varepsilon_i > 0$ for some i. On the other hand, in case of $\varepsilon_i = 0$ for all i, the accuracy measure is not changed after the reducing attributes by the above algorithm.

Let us consider the information system shown in Table 1 to illustrate the above algorithm. First, let us take $Q = \{q_1, q_2, q_3\}$ and calculate the accuracy measures of X_i, $i = 1, 2, 3$. Then, we have

$$\alpha^Q(X_1) = 25/44, \quad \alpha^Q(X_2) = 24/43, \quad \alpha^Q(X_3) = 32/32.$$

Next, let us examine whether q_i is superfluous or not. Removing the attribute q_1 and setting $P_1 = \{q_2, q_3\}$, we have

$$\alpha^{P_1}(X_1) = 0/76 < \alpha^Q(X_1)$$

which means that q_1 is not superfluous. Setting $P_2 = \{q_1, q_3\}$ and $P_3 = \{q_1, q_2\}$, we have

$$\alpha^{P_2}(X_1) = 16/68 < \alpha^Q(X_1), \quad \alpha^{P_3}(X_1) = 25/44 = \alpha^Q(X_1)$$

which mean that q_2 is not superfluous, but q_3 has the possibility of being ε-superfluous. Then, we obtain

$$\alpha^{P_3}(X_2) = 20/51 < \alpha^Q(X_2), \quad \alpha^{P_3}(X_3) = 24/36 < \alpha^Q(X_3).$$

From Definition 4, we need to calculate the following accuracy measures:

$$\begin{aligned} \alpha^Q(X_2) - \alpha^{P_3}(X_2) &= 24/43 - 20/51 (= 0.165\cdots) < 0.2 \\ \alpha^Q(X_3) - \alpha^{P_3}(X_3) &= 32/32 - 24/36 (= 0.333\cdots) < 0.5. \end{aligned}$$

It can be concluded that q_3 is ε-superfluous. Thus, the ε-reduct of Q is $P_3 = \{q_1, q_2\}$. In other words, we can remove the attribute q_3 to reduce the information system. Table 2 shows the ε-reduced information system of Table 1. It should be noted that we can not remove any attribute when $\varepsilon_i = 0$, $i = 1, 2, 3$.

Let us consider the case where predictive rules are constructed from the given information system. In the statistical inference model, we have dealt with errors of the first and the second kinds. Let an observed object be x_o which has $q_1(x_o) = 1$ and $q_2(x_o) = 2$ in the information system shown in Table 2. It is assumed that there is no information about q_3. Let us consider the problem of assigning x_o to either X_1 or X_2. The importance grades for classes yield an order relation, i.e. $X_1 \succ X_2 \succ X_3$. This relation ($\succ$) means that X_1 (X_2) is more important than X_2 (X_3). Thus, if x_o belongs to X_1, we have to avoid the error that x_o is assigned to X_2. Conversely, it might be acceptable that x_o is a-ssigned to X_1 even if x_o belongs to X_2.

Table 2. The ε-reduced information system

F	U	q_1	q_2	$Card$	Importance grade
	x_1	1	1	16	
X_1	x_2	1	1	9	1.0 (ε_1=0.0)
	x_3	1	2	8	
	x_4	1	2	11	
X_2	x_5	2	2	20	0.8 (ε_1=0.2)
	x_6	2	1	4	
	x_7	2	1	8	
X_3	x_8	1	3	11	0.5 (ε_1=0.5)
	x_9	1	3	13	

With the above in view, the given database will be modified. It can be seen from Table 2 that x_3 and x_4 are assigned to X_1 and X_2 respectively in spite of the fact that the attribute values of x_3 are the same as those of x_4. Since $X_1 \succ X_2$, x_4 should be moved into X_1. This modification ensures to avoid a serious error in constructing predictive rules from the given database. Similarly, for the case x_6 and x_7, x_7 should be moved into X_2. Then we have Table 3. This modification technique is useful for deriving predictive rules for classification from an information system.

Table 3. The reformed information system for constructing predictive rules

F	U	q_1	q_2	$Card$	Importance grade
	x_1	1	1	16	
X_1	x_2	1	1	9	1.0 (ε_1=0.0)
	x_3	1	2	8	
	x_4	1	2	11	
	x_5	2	2	20	
	x_6	2	1	4	0.8 (ε_1=0.2)
X_2	x_7	2	1	8	
	x_8	1	3	11	
X_3	x_9	1	3	13	0.5 (ε_1=0.5)

3 Reduction Method for Divisions of Attributes

Now, we discuss a reduction method for divisions of attributes. In doing so, we try to convert given data into binary data which have only two values, 0 and 1. There are many transformations of integer data into binary data. For example, we can use categorical data by which $V_q = \{1,2,3\}$ is represented as {(0,0,1), (0,1,0), (1,0,0)} shown in Table 4 where z_i is regarded as an attribute. This transformation needs n-dimensional vectors for representing n values of an attribute. Even if z_1 can be removed by the reduction method in Section 2, $V_q = \{1,2,3\}$ is represented as {(0,1), (1,0), (0,0)} whose vectors are all different from one another. Therefore, this transformation is redundant.

With the above in view, we represent elements of V_q as vectors which have all different numbers of values 1. The vector representing an element of V_q has the property that if the jth term of the vector is 1, then the ith term of the vector has to be 1 for any $i > j$.

Table 4. A categorical representation of $V_q = \{1,2,3\}$

V_q	z_1	z_2	z_3
1	0	0	1
2	0	1	0
3	1	0	0

For example, $V_q = \{1,2,3\}$ can be represented as {(0,0), (0,1), (1,1)}. By this transformation, the attribute q is replaced with $\{z_1, z_2\}$ as shown in Table 5. It can be seen that the attribute z_1 distinguishes between $\{1,2\}$ and $\{3\}$ and z_2 distinguishes between $\{1\}$ and $\{2,3\}$. Similarly, $V_q = \{1,2,3,4\}$ is represented as {(0,0,0), (0,0,1), (0,1 ,1), (1,1,1)} so that the attribute q is replaced with $\{z_1, z_2, z_3\}$ as shown in Table 6. It can also be seen that the attribute z_1 distinguis hes between {1,2,3} and {4},the attribute z_2 distinguishes between {1,2} and {3,4}, and the attribute z_3 distinguishes between {1} and {2,3,4}.By this transformation, the ith value of an attribute is converted into the vector with $(i-1)$ elements of values 1. Therefore, this transformation needs $n-1$ dimensions of vectors for representing n integers as attribute values.

Table 5. A binary representation of $V_q = \{1,2,3\}$

V_q	z_1	z_2
1	0	0
2	0	1
3	1	1

Table 6. A binary representation of $V_q = \{1,2,3,4\}$

V_q	z_1	z_2	z_3
1	0	0	0
2	0	0	1
3	0	1	1
4	1	1	1

We have arrived at this binary representation from the idea that the given divisions of attributes have to be reduced as much as possible. From another point of view, Lenarcik and Piasta [LP] have obtained the same binary representation.

Example 1. In order to illustrate our proposed method for divisions, let us consider the information system of Table 7 where

$$U = \{x_1, \cdots, x_6\},\ Q = \{q_1, \cdots, q_4\},\ V_{q_1} = V_{q_4} = \{1,2\}$$

$$V_{q_2} = V_{q_3} = \{1,2,3\},\ F = \{X_1\},\ X_1 = \{x_1, \cdots, x_6\}.$$

First, we obtained the reduct of Q as $\{q_1, q_2, q_3\}$ by using the algorithm in Section 2 because q_4 is a superfluous attribute. Next, by the proposed transformation, the attributes q_2 and q_3 were changed to $\{z_2, z_3\}$ and $\{z_4, z_5\}$ and $V_{q_1} = V_{q_4} = \{1,2\}$ was changed to $\{0,1\}$ as shown in Table 8. Applying the algorithm to the binary data shown in Table 8, we obtained the reduct of $Z = \{z_1, \cdots, z_6\}$ as $\{z_1, z_2, z_5\}$ because $\{z_3, z_4, z_6\}$ is superfluous . The elimination of z_3 means that there is no distinction between 1 and 2 in V_{q_2} and the elimination of z_4 means that there is no distinction between 2 and 3 in V_{q_3}. The elimination of z_6 is equal to the elimination of q_4. As a result, we obtained Table 9. Thus, we conclude that we can reduce attributes themselves and divisions of attributes by converting integer data into binary data.

Table 7. An example of information system

F	U	q_1	q_2	q_3	q_4
	x_1	1	3	2	1
	x_2	1	2	3	2
X_1	x_3	2	1	2	1
	x_4	2	1	2	1
	x_5	2	3	2	1
	x_6	2	3	1	1

Table 8. A binary representation of Table 7

F	U	z_1	z_2	z_3	z_4	z_5	z_6
	x_1	0	1	1	0	1	0
	x_2	0	0	1	1	1	1
X_1	x_3	1	0	0	0	1	0
	x_4	1	0	0	0	1	0
	x_5	1	1	1	0	1	0
	x_6	1	1	1	0	0	0

Table 9. The reduction for divisions in Table 7

F	U	q_1	q_2	q_3
	x_1	1	3	2,3
	x_2	1	1,2	2,3
X_1	x_3	2	1,2	2,3
	x_4	2	1,2	2,3
	x_5	2	3	2,3
	x_6	2	3	1

4 Application

In order to show that this reduction method in Section 3 is useful, we applied our method to medical data for hepatic diseases. A part of the database in the information system is presented in Table 10. These data consist of 5 classes (Healthy person, Hepatoma, Acute hepatitis, Chronic hepatitis, and Liver cirrhosis). The number of medical inspections is 20. Table 11 shows the reduced attributes obtained by Algorithm in Section 2.2 where we set $\varepsilon_i = 0$ for all i so that all attributes are fully important. The discretization of continuous valued attributes is shown in Table 11. A default value is represented as 0 in the data. The given data from the Kawasaki Medical College are as follows:

$$\begin{array}{ll} U = \{x_i\},\ \ i = 1,\ldots,468 & (468 \text{ samples}) \\ Q = \{q_j\},\ \ j = 1,\ldots,20 & (20 \text{ medical inspects}) \\ F = \{X_k\},\ k = 1,\ldots,5 & (5 \text{ classes}). \end{array}$$

The accuracy measure of the information system (3) was obtained as

$$\beta_A(F) = 433/437 = 0.991. \tag{14}$$

Because of $\varepsilon_i = 0$ for all i, the accuracy measure is not changed after reducing attributes. The way of reducing the number of attributes and the number of divisions of attributes at the same time will take a lot of time because of the large number of attributes and divisions. Thus, we will take two steps where first we reduce only the number of attributes by our re duction method and next the reduced database are transformed into binary data to reduce the number of divisions of attributes.

According to the above view, we propose the following two-step procedure to reduce the number of attributes and divisions of attributes.

I)**First step** : Apply our reduction method to integer data and then obtain the reduced information system described as integers.

II)**Second step** : Transform the integer data obtained in the first step into binary data whose codes are shown in Table 6. Then, apply our method to binary data to reduce the number of divisions of attributes.

The two-step procedure was applied to the data of hepatic diseases to obtain the following results. In the first step, we obtained the reduct of Q as $\{q_1, q_2, q_9, q_{10}, q_{16}, q_{19}, q_{20}\}$ shown in Table 11. It follows for Tables 10 and 11 that the number of attributes was reduced from 20 to 7 by our method. In the second step, the binary codes for the reduced attributes are shown in Table 12 where q_2, q_{16} and q_{19} have 4 divisions, q_1 and q_{20} have 5 divisions, and q_9 and q_{10} have 6 divisions. Transforming integer data into binary data by the binary codes in Table 12, we applied our reduction method to the binary data. Then we obtained the reduced divisions shown in Table 13 where the sets denoted as $\{\}$, e.g. $\{1,2\}$, were integrated into one division. It can be seen from Table 13 that in the first step we obtained 7 attributes with 34 divisions, but in the second step the total number of divisions was reduced to 25 by the proposed reduction method. It should be noted that a default value is assigned to the integer 1 which is a normal value of each inspection. A default value of some inspection means that the medical doctor did not pay attention to the inspection. This is the reason why we assigned a default value to a normal value.

Table 10. Information system of hepatic disease

		q_1	q_2	q_3	q_4	q_5	q_6	q_7	q_8	q_9	q_{10}	q_{11}	q_{12}	q_{13}	q_{14}	q_{15}	q_{16}	q_{17}	q_{18}	q_{19}	q_{20}
X_1	x_1	3	2	1	1	1	1	1	4	5	1	1	2	2	0	5	2	2	2	2	1
	x_2	3	2	1	1	1	1	1	4	5	1	1	2	2	0	5	3	2	3	1	1
	x_3	3	2	1	1	1	1	1	4	5	1	1	2	2	0	5	2	2	2	1	1
	x_4	3	2	1	1	2	1	1	4	5	1	1	2	2	0	4	3	2	3	2	1
	x_5	3	2	1	2	1	1	1	4	5	1	1	2	2	0	5	2	2	2	1	1
	⋮	⋮	⋮	⋮	⋮	⋮	⋮	⋮	⋮	⋮	⋮	⋮	⋮	⋮	⋮	⋮	⋮	⋮	⋮	⋮	⋮
X_2	x_{87}	1	3	1	2	1	1	1	2	1	1	1	2	1	1	4	2	2	2	2	1
	⋮	⋮	⋮	⋮	⋮	⋮	⋮	⋮	⋮	⋮	⋮	⋮	⋮	⋮	⋮	⋮	⋮	⋮	⋮	⋮	⋮
⋮	⋮	⋮	⋮	⋮	⋮	⋮	⋮	⋮	⋮	⋮	⋮	⋮	⋮	⋮	⋮	⋮	⋮	⋮	⋮	⋮	⋮
X_5	x_{349}	1	1	1	1	1	1	2	2	3	1	1	3	2	1	5	1	2	2	3	1
	⋮	⋮	⋮	⋮	⋮	⋮	⋮	⋮	⋮	⋮	⋮	⋮	⋮	⋮	⋮	⋮	⋮	⋮	⋮	⋮	⋮

Table 11. Divisions of medical test data for the reduced aattributes

	Medical inspection	1	2	3	4	5	6
q_1	SP	~ 5.5	$5.6 \sim 6.5$	$6.6 \sim 7.5$	7.6 sim8.5	$8.6 \sim$	
q_2	II	~ 4	$5 \sim 6$	$7 \sim 9$	$10 \sim$		
q_9	ChE	~ 100	$101 \sim 150$	$151 \sim 200$	201 sim250	$251 \sim 500$	$501 \sim$
q_{19}	GPR	~ 25	$26 \sim 100$	$101 \sim 200$	201 sim500	$501 \sim 1000$	$1001 \sim$
q_{16}	Lympho	~ 20.0	$20.1 \sim 40.0$	$40.1 \sim 60.0$	$60.1 \sim$		
q_{19}	A1-%	~ 2.5	$2.6 \sim 3.7$	$3.8 \sim 5.0$	5.1 sim		
q_{20}	AFP	~ 20	$21 \sim 100$	$101 \sim 200$	201 sim1000	$1001 \sim$	

Table 12. Binary representation of 7 attributes

Division	q_2, q_{16}, q_{19}	q_1, q_{20}	q_9, q_{10}
hline 0	0 0 0	0 0 0 0	0 0 0 0 0
1	0 0 0	0 0 0 0	0 0 0 0 0
2	0 0 1	0 0 0 1	0 0 0 0 1
3	0 1 1	0 0 1 1	0 0 0 1 1
4	1 1 1	0 1 1 1	0 0 1 1 1
5		1 1 1 1	0 1 1 1 1
6			1 1 1 1 1

5 Conclusions

In this paper, we propose a new method of reducing information systems by binary data representation. Using our proposed method, not only can we reduce the number of attributes, but also the number of divisions of some attibutes. We applied our proposed method to medical diagnosis system and obtained a good result. In real applications, if all attribute values are changed into binary data, it may be happened that computational complexity increases greatly for of large database. Thus, we adopted the two-step procedure provided in Section 4. By this two-step procedure, we can reduce computational complexity. We can see that the number of attribute divisions obtained from medical experts, 34,

Table 13. The obtained reduction of divisions

Step 1	20 attributes $\Rightarrow$		7 attributes
Step 2	7 attributes 34 divisions $\Rightarrow$		7 attributes 25 divisions
	Attribute 1	:	{1,2}, {3}, {4}, {5}
	Attribute 2	:	{1}, {2}, {3,4}
	Attribute 9	:	{1}, {2}, {3}, {4,5,6}
	Attribute 10	:	{1}, {2}, {3,4}, {5,6}
	Attribute 16	:	{1}, {2}, {3}, {4}
	Attribute 19	:	{1}, {2}, {3,4}
	Attribute 20	:	{1}, {2}, {3,4,5}

reduced to 25. Thus, it is emphasized that reasonable divisions of attributes can be obtained by our proposed method.

References

[DP] Dubois, D. and Prade, H.: Twofold fuzzy sets and rough sets-some issues in knowledge representation. Int. J. of Fuzzy Sets and Systems **23** (1987) 3–18

[LP] Lenarcik, A. and Piasta, Z.: Deterministic rough classifiers. In: T.Y. Lin (ed.): Proceedings of the Third International Workshop on Rough Sets and Soft Computing (RSSC'94), San Jose State University, San Jose, California, USA, November 10–12, (1994) 434–441

[Mr] Mrozek, A.: Rough sets and dependency analysis among attributes in computer implementat ions of expert's inference models. Int. J. of Man-Machine Studies **30** (1989) 457–473

[Pa1] Pawlak, Z.: Rough sets. Int. J. of Information and Computer Sciences **11** (1982) 341–356

[Pa2] Pawlak, Z.: Rough classification. Int. J. of Man - Machine Studies **20** (1984) 469–485

[Pa3] Pawlak, Z.: Rough sets: theoretical aspects of data analysis, Kluwer Academic Publishers, Dordrecht (1991)

[PG] Pawlak, Z., Grzymala, J. W., Slowinski, R. and Ziarko, W.: Rough sets. Communication of the ACM **38** (1995) 88–95

[TI] Tanaka, H., Ishibuchi, H. and Matsuda, N.: Fuzzy expert system based on rough sets and its application to medical diagnosis. Int. J. of General Systems **21** (1992) 83–97

[SH] Shan, N., Hamilton, H. J., Ziarko, W. and Cercone N.: Discretization of continuous valued attributes in classification systems. In: S. Tsumoto, S. Kobayashi, T. Yokomori, H. Tanaka, and A. Nakamura (eds.): Proceedings of the Fourth International Workshop on Rough Sets, Fuzzy Sets, and Machine Discovery (RSFD'96), The University of Tokyo, November 6–8 (1996) 74–81

Chapter 16

Formalization and Induction of Medical Expert System Rules Based on Rough Set Theory

Shusaku Tsumoto

Department of Information Medicine, Medical Research Institute,
Tokyo Medical and Dental University,
1-5-45 Yushima, Bunkyo-city Tokyo 113 Japan.
E-mail: tsumoto@computer.org

1 Introduction

One of the most important problems in developing expert systems is knowledge acquisition from experts[BS1]. In order to automate this problem, many inductive learning methods, such as induction of decision trees[BF1, QU1], rule induction methods[MI1, MI2, QU1] and rough set theory[PA1, ZI1], are introduced and applied to extract knowledge from databases, and the results show that these methods are appropriate.

However, most of the approaches focus only on inducing classification rules, although medical experts also learn other information important for medical diagnostic procedures. Focusing on their learning procedures, Matsumura et al. propose a diagnostic model, which consists of three reasoning processes, and develop an expert system, called RHINOS(Rule-based Headache and facial pain INformation Organizing System[MM1]).

Since these processes are found to be based on the concept of set theory, as shown in [MM1], it is expected that a set-theoretic approach describes this model and the procedures of knowledge acquisition.

In order to characterize these procedures, the concepts of rough set theory are introduced, which is developed to describe how to classify a certain set (denoted as a "class") by intersection or union of several sets which satisfy one equivalence relation. By the use of this theory, a system PRIMEROSE-REX (Probabilistic Rule Induction Method based on Rough Sets and Resampling methods for Expert systems), is developed which extracts rules for an expert system from clinical databases, and applies resampling methods to estimate certainty factors of derived rules.[1]

This system is evaluated on three datasets of medical domain. The results show that the proposed method induces RHINOS-type rules correctly from

[1] This system is an extension of PRIMEROSE, which induces classification rules from databases, based on rough sets and resampling methods[TT2].

databases and that resampling methods estimate the performance of these rules and certainty factors.

The paper is organized as follows: Section 2 discusses RHINOS diagnostic model. Section 3 shows rough set theory and representation of RHINOS rules based on this theory. Section 4 presents an algorithm for induction of RHINOS-type rules. Section 5 gives experimental results. Section 6 and 7 discusses the problems of PRIMEROSE-REX and related work, respectively. Finally, Section 8 concludes this paper.

2 RHINOS

RHINOS is an expert system which diagnoses clinical cases on headache or facial pain from manifestations. In this system, a diagnostic model proposed by Matsumura[MM1] is applied to the domain, which consists of the following three kinds of reasoning processes: exclusive reasoning, inclusive reasoning, and reasoning about complications.

First, exclusive reasoning excludes a disease from candidates when a patient does not have a symptom which is necessary to diagnose that disease. Secondly, inclusive reasoning suspects a disease in the output of the exclusive process when a patient has symptoms specific to a disease. Finally, reasoning about complications suspects complications of other diseases when some symptoms which cannot be explained by the diagnostic conclusion are obtained.

Each reasoning is rule-based and all the rules needed for diagnostic processes are acquired from medical experts in the following way.

(1)Exclusive Rules These rule correspond to exclusive reasoning. In other words, the premise of this rule is equivalent to the necessity condition of a diagnostic conclusion. ¿From the discussion with medical experts, the following six basic attributes are selected which are minimally indispensable for defining the necessity condition: *1. Age, 2. Pain location, 3. Nature of the pain, 4. Severity of the pain, 5. History since onset, 6. Existence of jolt headache.* For example, the exclusive rule of common migraine is defined as:

```
In order to suspect common migraine,
the following symptoms are required:
pain location: not eyes,
nature :throbbing or persistent or radiating,
history: paroxysmal or sudden and
jolt headache: positive.
```

One of the reasons why the six attributes are selected is to solve an interface problem of expert systems: if all attributes are considered, all the symptoms should be input, including symptoms which are not needed for diagnosis. To make exclusive reasoning compact, we chose the minimal requirements only. It is notable that this kind of selection can be viewed as the ordering of given attributes, which is expected to be induced from databases. This issue is discussed later in Section 6.

(2)Inclusive Rules The premises of inclusive rules are composed of a set of manifestations specific to a disease to be included. If a patient satisfies one set, this disease should be suspected with some probability. This rule is derived by asking the medical experts about the following items for each disease: *1. a set of manifestations by which we strongly suspect a disease. 2. the probability that a patient has the disease with this set of manifestations:SI(Satisfactory Index) 3. the ratio of the patients who satisfy the set to all the patients of this disease:CI(Covering Index) 4. If the total sum of the derived CI(tCI) is equal to 1.0 then end. Otherwise, goto 5. 5. For the patients with this disease who do not satisfy all the collected set of manifestations, goto 1.* Therefore a positive rule is described by a set of manifestations, its satisfactory index (SI), which corresponds to *accuracy measure*, and its covering index (CI), which corresponds to *total positive rate.* Note that SI and CI are given empirically by medical experts.

For example, one of three positive rules for common migraine is given as follows.

```
If history: paroxysmal, jolt headache: yes,
nature: throbbing or persistent,
prodrome: no, intermittent symptom: no,
persistent time: more than 6 hours,
and location: not eye,
then common migraine is suspected with
accuracy 0.9 (SI=0.9) and this rule covers
60 percent of the total cases (CI=0.6).
```

(3)Disease Image This rule is used to detect complications of multiple diseases, acquired by all the possible manifestations of the disease. By the use of this rule, the manifestations which cannot be explained by the conclusions will be checked, which suggest complications of other diseases. For example, the disease image of common migraine is:

```
The following symptoms can be explained by
common migraine: pain location: any or
depressing: not or jolt headache: yes or ..
```

Therefore, when a patient who suffers from common migraine is depressing, it is suspected that he or she may also have other disease.

As shown above, three kinds of rules are straightforward, and an inducing algorithm is expected to be implemented on computers easily. Thus, we introduce rough set theory in order to describe these algorithms as shown in the next section.

3 Formalization of Rules

3.1 Probabilistic Rules

In this section, a probabilistic rule, which is a basis for describing three kinds of diagnostic rules, is defined by the use of the following three notations of rough

Table 1. A Small Database

	age	loc	nat	prod	nau	M1	class
1	50-59	occ	per	0	0	1	m.c.h.
2	40-49	who	per	0	0	1	m.c.h.
3	40-49	lat	thr	1	1	0	migra
4	40-40	who	thr	1	1	0	migra
5	40-49	who	rad	0	0	1	m.c.h.
6	50-59	who	per	0	1	1	m.c.h.

DEFINITIONS: loc: location, nat: nature, prod: prodrome, nau: nausea, M1: tenderness of M1, who: whole, occ: occular, lat: lateral, per: persistent, thr: throbbing, rad: radiating, m.c.h.: muscle contraction headache, migra: migraine, 1: Yes, 0: No.

set theory[PA1].

First, a combination of attribute-value pairs, corresponding to a complex in AQ terminology[MI1], is denoted by a formula R. For example, $[age = 50 - 59]\&[loc = occular]$ will be one formula, denoted by $R = [age = 50 - 59]\&[loc = occular]$.

Secondly, a set of samples which satisfy R is denoted by $[x]_R$, corresponding to a star in AQ terminology. For example, when $\{2,3,4,5\}$ is a set of samples which satisfy $[age = 40 - 49]$, $[x]_{[age=40-49]}$ is equal to $\{2,3,4,5\}$. [2]

Finally, U, which stands for "Universe", denotes all training samples.

According to these notations, a probabilistic rule is defined as follows:

Definition 1 (Probabilistic Rules). Let R be a formula (conjunction of attribute-value pairs), D denote a set whose elements belong to a class d, or positive examples in all training samples (the universe), U. Finally, let $|D|$ denote the cardinality of D. A probabilistic rule of D is defined as a quadruple, $< R \stackrel{\alpha,\kappa}{\rightarrow} d, \alpha_R(D), \kappa_R(D) >$, where $R \stackrel{\alpha,\kappa}{\rightarrow} d$ satisfies the following conditions: [3]

$$(1) \qquad [x]_R \bigcap D \neq \phi,$$

$$(2) \qquad \alpha_R(D) = \frac{|[x]_R \bigcap D)|}{|[x]_R|},$$

$$(3) \qquad \kappa_R(D) = \frac{|[x]_R \bigcap D)|}{|D|}.$$

In the above definition, α corresponds to the accuracy measure: if α of a rule is equal to 0.9, then the accuracy is also equal to 0.9. On the other hand, κ is

[2] In this notation, "n" denotes the nth sample in a dataset (Table 1).

[3] It is notable that this rule is a kind of probabilistic proposition with two statistical measures, which is one kind of an extension of Ziarko's variable precision model(VPRS) [ZI1].

a statistical measure of what proportion of D is covered by this rule, that is, a coverage or a true positive rate: when κ is equal to 0.5, half of the members of a class belong to the set whose members satisfy that formula.

For example, let us consider a case of a rule $[age = 40-49] \rightarrow m.c.h.$ Since $[x]_{[age=40-49]} = \{2,3,4,5\}$ and $D = \{1,2,5,6\}$, accuracy and coverage are obtained as: $\alpha_{[age=40-49]}(D) = |\{2,5\}|/|\{2,3,4,5\}| = 0.5$ and $\kappa_{[age=40-49]}(D) = |\{2,5\}|/|\{1,2,5,6\}| = 0.5$. Thus, if a patient, who complains of a headache, is 40 to 49 years old, then m.c.h. is suspected, whose accuracy and coverage are equal to 0.5.

3.2 RHINOS Diagnostic Rules

By the use of these notations, RHINOS diagnostic rules are described in the following way.

(1) Exclusive rules: $R \overset{\alpha,\kappa}{\rightarrow} d$ *s.t.* $R = \wedge_i R_i = \wedge_i \vee_j \vee_k [a_j = v_k]$, *and* $\kappa_{R_i}(D) = 1.0$.

In the above example, the formula R for "migraine" is described as: $[age = 40-49] \wedge ([location = lateral] \vee [location = whole]) \wedge [nature = throbbing] \wedge ([history = paroxysmal] \vee [history = persistent]) \wedge [jolt = yes] \wedge [prod = yes] \wedge [nau = yes] \wedge [M1 = no] \wedge [M2 = no]$. Strictly speaking, this proposition should be written as: $d \rightarrow R$. However, for comparison with other two types of rules, we choose this notation.

(2) Inclusive rules: $R \overset{\alpha,\kappa}{\rightarrow} d$ *s.t.* $R = \vee_i R_i = \vee_i \wedge_j \vee_k [a_j = v_k]$, $\alpha_{R_i}(D) > \delta_\alpha$, *and* $\kappa_{R_i}(D) > \delta_\kappa$.

In the above example, the simplest relation R for "migraine", is described as: $[nature = throbbing] \vee [history = paroxysmal] \vee [jolt = yes] \vee [M1 = yes]$. However, induction of inclusive rules gives us two problems. First, accuracy and coverage are overfitted to the training samples. Secondly, many rules will be induced from the above training samples if the thresholds for accuracy and coverage are not suitably chosen. Therefore some of them should be selected from primary induced rules under some preference criterion. These problems will be discussed in the next section.

(3) Disease Image: $R \overset{\alpha,\kappa}{\rightarrow} d$ *s.t.* $R = \vee_j \vee_k [a_j = v_k]$, *and* $\alpha_{R_i}(D) > 0 \, (\kappa_{R_i}(D) > 0)$.

In the above example, the relation R for "migraine" is described as: $[age = 40-49] \vee [location = lateral] \vee [location = whole] \vee [nature = throbbing] \vee [severity = strong] \vee [severity = weak] \vee [history = paroxysmal] \vee [nausea = yes] \vee [jolt = yes] \vee [M1 = no] \vee [M2 = no]$.

It is notable that a coverage $\kappa_R(D)$ plays an important role in the definition of these rules.

4 Induction of Rules

An induction algorithm of RHINOS rules consists of two procedures. One is an exhaustive search procedure to induce the exclusive rule and the disease image through all the attribute-value pairs, corresponding to *selectors* in AQ [MI1], and the other is a postprocessing procedure to induce inclusive rules through the combinations of all the attribute-value pairs, which corresponds to *complexes* in AQ.

4.1 Exhaustive Search

Let D denote training samples for the target class *d*, or *positive examples.* This search procedure is defined as shown in Figure 1. In the above example in Table

[t]

procedure *Exhaustive Search*;
  var
    L : *List*; /* A list of elementary relations */
  begin
    $L := P_0$; /* P_0: A list of elementary relations */
    while $(L \neq \{\})$ **do**
      begin
        Select one pair $[a_i = v_j]$ from L;
        if $([x]_{[a_i=v_j]]} \cap D \neq \phi)$ **then do** /* D: a set of positive examples */
          begin
            $R_{di} := R_{di} \vee [a_i = v_j]$; /* Disease Image */
            if $(\kappa_{[a_i=v_j]}(D) > \delta_\kappa)$
              then Append $[a_i = v_j]$ to L_{ir}; /* Candidates for Inclusive Rules */
            if $(\kappa_{[a_i=v_j]}(D) = 1.0)$
              then $R_{er} := R_{er} \wedge [a_i = v_j]$; /* Exclusive Rule */
          end
        Delete $[a_i = v_j]$ from L;
      end
  end {*Exhaustive Search*};

Fig. 1. An Algorithm for Exhaustive Search

1, let d be "migra", and $[age = 40 - 49]$ be selected as $[a_i = v_j]$. Since the intersection $[x]_{[age=40-49]} \cap D(= \{3, 4\})$ is not equal to ϕ, this pair is included in the disease image. However, since $\alpha_{[age=40-49]}(D) = 0.5$, this pair is not included in the inclusive rule. Finally, since $D \subset [x]_{[age=40-49]}(= \{2, 3, 4, 5\})$, this pair is also included in the exclusive rule.

Next, the other attribute-value pair for age, $[age = 50 - 59]$ is selected. However, this pair will be abandoned since the intersection of $[x]_{[age=50-59]}$ and D is empty, or $[x]_{[age=50-59]} \cap D = \phi$.

When all the attribute-value pairs are examined, not only the exclusive rule and disease image shown in the above section, but also the candidates for inclusive rules are also derived. The latter ones are used as inputs to the second procedure.

4.2 Postprocessing Procedure

Because the definition of inclusive rules is a little weak, many inclusive rules can be obtained. In the above example, a formula $[nau = 1]$ satisfies $D \cap [x]_{[nau=1]} \neq \phi$, so it is also a candidate of the inclusive rules of "m.c.h.", although the accuracy of that rule is equal to 1/3. In order to suppress induction of such rules, which have low classificatory power, only formulas whose the accuracy is larger than the threshold should be selected. For example, since the above relation $[age = 40-49]$ is less than this precision, it is eliminated from the candidates for inclusive rules. This procedure is described as shown in Figure 2. In the above example in

[t]

procedure *Postprocessing Procedure*;
  var
    i : *integer*; M, L_i : *List*;
  begin
    $L_1 := L_{ir}$; /* Candidates for Inclusive Rules */
    $M := \{\}$;
    for $i := 1$ **to** n **do** /* n: Total number of attributes */
      begin
        while ($L_i \neq \{\}$) **do**
          begin
            Select one formula R from L_i;
            $L_i := L_i - \{R\}$;
            if $(\alpha_R(D) > \delta_\alpha$ and $\kappa_R(D) > \delta_\kappa)$
              then do $S_{ir} := S_{ir} + \{R\}$; /* Include R as Inclusive Rule */
            else $M := M + \{R\}$;
          end
        L_{i+1} := (A list of all possible conjunctions of two-element subsets from M);
      end
  end {*Postprocessing Procedure* };

Fig. 2. An Algorithm for Postprocessing Procedure

Table 1, the coverage of an attribute-value pair $[prod = 0]$ for "m.c.h" takes the maximum value. Furthermore, since the accuracy $\alpha_{[prod=0]}(D)$ is equal to 1.0, it is included in inclusive rules of "m.c.h". The next maximum one is $[M1 = 1]$, whose coverage is equal to 1.0. The accuracy of this relation is also equal to 1.0, so it is also included in inclusive rules. At this point, the following two inclusive rules are induced: $< [prod = 0] \rightarrow m.c.h., 1.0, 1.0 >$, and $< [M1 =$

$1] \rightarrow m.c.h., 1.0, 1.0>$. By repeating these procedures, all the inclusive rules are acquired.

4.3 Estimation of Statistical Measures

The above definition of statistical measures shows that small training samples may be overestimated. In the above example, both of the measures are equal to 1.0. This means that this rule correctly diagnoses and covers all the cases of the disease "migraine". However, in general, these meanings hold only in the world of the small training samples. In this sense, accuracy and coverage are biased. So these biases should be corrected by introducing other estimating methods, since the biases cannot be detected by the induced method.

Note that this problem is similar to that of error rates of discriminant function in multivariate analysis [EF1], the field in which resampling methods are reported to be useful for the estimation.

Hence the resampling methods are applied to estimation of accuracy and coverage, as shown in the following subsection.

4.4 Cross-Validation and the Bootstrap method

Cross-validation method for error estimation is performed as following: first, the whole list of training samples $\mathcal{L}$ is split into V blocks: $\{\mathcal{L}_1, \mathcal{L}_2, \cdots, \mathcal{L}_V\}$. Secondly, we repeat V times the procedure in which rules are induced from the training samples $\mathcal{L} - \mathcal{L}_i (i = 1, \cdots, V)$ and examine the error rate err_i of the rules using $\mathcal{L}_i$ as test samples. Finally, the total error rate err is derived by averaging err_i over i, that is, $err = \sum_{i=1}^{V} err_i / V$ (this method is called V-fold cross-validation). Therefore this method for estimation of CI and SI can be used by replacing the calculation of err by that of CI and SI, and by regarding test samples as unobserved cases.

On the other hand, the Bootstrap method is executed as follows: first, empirical probabilistic distribution(F_n) is generated from the original training samples [EF1]. Secondly, the Monte-Carlo method is applied and training samples are randomly taken by using F_n. Thirdly, rules are induced by using new training samples. Finally, these results are tested by the original training samples and statistical measures, such as error rate are calculated. These four steps are iterated for finite times. Empirically, it is shown that about 200 times' repetition is sufficient for estimation [EF1].

Interestingly, Efron shows that estimators by two-fold cross-validation are asymptotically equal to predictive estimators for completely new pattern of data, and that Bootstrap estimators are asymptotically equal to maximum likelihood estimators and are a little overfitted to training samples [EF1]. Hence, the former estimators can be used as the lower bounds of the both measures, and the latter as their upper bounds.

Furthermore, in order to reduce the high variance of estimators by cross validation, repeated cross validation method is introduced [WO1]. In this method, cross validation methods are executed repeatedly (safely, 100 times)[TT2], and estimates are averaged over all the trials. In summary, since our strategy is to avoid the overestimation and the high variabilities, combination of repeated two-fold cross-validation and the Bootstrap method is adopted in this paper.

5 Experimental Results

PRIMEROSE-REX is evaluated on the following three medical datasets: differiential diagnosis of headache, RHINOS domain, whose training samples consist of 1477 samples, 10 classes, and 20 attributes, cerebulovasular diseases, whose training samples consist of 620 samples, 15 classes, and 25 attributes, and meningitis, whose training samples consists of 213 samples, 3 classes, and 27 attributes. In these experiments, δ_α and δ_κ is set to 0.75 and 0.5, respectively. [4] The experiments are performed by the following four procedures. First, these samples are randomly split into half (new training samples) and half (new test samples). For example, 1477 samples are split into 738 training samples and 739 training samples. Secondly, PRIMEROSE-REX, AQ15 and CART are applied to the new training samples. Thirdly, the repeated cross validation method and the bootstrap method are applied to the new training samples in order to estimate accuracy and coverage of PRIMEROSE-REX. Finally, the induced results are tested by the new test samples. These procedures are repeated for 100 times and average all the estimators over 100 trials.

Experimental results on the performance of this system are summarized in Table 2 to 4. Exclusive rule accuracy(ER-A) means how many training samples that do not belong to a class are excluded correctly from the candidates. Inclusive rule accuracy(IR-A) is equivalent to the averaged classification accuracy. Finally, disease image accuracy(DI-A) shows how many symptoms, which cannot be explained by diagnostic conclusions, are detected by the disease image. The first row is the results obtained by using PRIMEROSE-REX, and the second one is the results derived from medical experts. Next, classification accuracies of inclusive rules are compared with those of CART and AQ-15, which is shown in the third and fourth row. Finally, in the fifth and sixth row, the results of estimation by repeated cross-validation method (R-CV) and the bootstrap method (BS) are presented. These results can be summarized in the following three points. First, the induced rules perform a little worse than those of medical experts. Secondly, our method performs a little better than classical empirical learning methods, CART and AQ15. Finally, thirdly, R-CV estimator and BS estimator can be regarded as the lower boundary and the upper boundary of each rule accuracy. Hence the interval of these two estimators can be used as the estimator of performance of each rule.

---

[4] These values are given by medical experts as good thresholds for rules in these three domains.

Table 2. Experimental Results (Headache)

Method	ER-A	IR-A	DI-A
PRIMEROSE-REX	95.0%	88.3%	93.2%
Experts	98.0%	95.0%	97.4%
CART	–	85.8%	–
AQ15	–	86.2%	–
R-CV	72.9%	78.7%	83.8%
BS	98.4%	91.6%	95.6%

DEFINITIONS. ER-A: Exclusive Rule Accuracy,
IR-A: Inclusive Rule Accuracy,
DI-A: Disease Image Accuracy

Table 3. Experimental Results (Cerebulovasculuar Diseases)

Method	ER-A	IR-A	DI-A
PRIMEROSE-REX	91.0%	84.3%	94.3%
Experts	97.5%	92.9%	93.6%
CART	–	79.7%	–
AQ15	–	78.9%	–
R-CV	72.9%	78.7%	83.8%
BS	93.4%	92.5%	95.9%

6 Discussion

6.1 Induced Rules and Experts' Rules

Table 5 shows comparison between induced rules and medical experts' rules with respect to the number of attribute-value pairs used to describe. The most important difference is that medical experts' rules are longer than induced rules for diseases of high prevalence. For example, the induced rule for muscle contraction headache is described by three attribute-value pairs in the following way:

Table 4. Experimental Results (Meningitis)

Method	ER-A	IR-A	DI-A
PRIMEROSE-REX	88.9%	82.5%	92.6%
Experts	95.4%	93.2%	96.7%
CART	–	81.4%	–
AQ15	–	82.5%	–
R-CV	64.3%	61.3%	73.8%
BS	89.5%	93.2%	98.2%

```
[location=whole] & [Jolt Headache=no]
                  & [Tenderness of M1=yes]
                   => muscle contraction headache.
```

On the other hand, the corresponding medical experts' rule is represented by nine attributes as follows:

```
[Jolt Headache=no] & [Tenderness of M1=yes]
       & [Tenderness of B1=no] & [Tenderness of B2=no]
       & [Tenderness of B3=no]
       & [Tenderness of C1=no] & [Tenderness of C2=no]
       & [Tenderness of C3=no] & [Tenderness of C4=no]
                    => muscle contraction headache.
```

Thus, the most significant difference between these rules is that the former rule does not include negative information.

Table 5. Comparision of Rule Length between Induced Rules and Medical Experts' Rules

Disease	Samples	PR-REX	RHINOS
Muscle Contraction Headache	923	3.00	9.00
Disease of Cervical Spine	163	5.50	3.50
Common Migraine	112	4.00	7.50
Psychological Headache	79	6.67	3.67
Tension Vascular Headache	79	11.00	10.50
Classical Migraine	49	4.50	9.00
Teeth Disease	21	3.25	6.00
Costen Syndrome	19	4.00	3.00
Sinusitus	11	4.50	5.00
Neuritis of Occipital Nerves	5	10.00	14.00
Ear Disease	5	8.50	7.00
Intracranial Mass Lesion	2	2.75	3.75
Intracranial Aneurysm	2	4.00	2.00
Autonomic Disturbance	1	5.25	3.50
Trigeminus Neuralgia	1	5.25	3.50
Inflammation of Eyes	1	6.00	8.00
Arteriosclerotic Headache	1	9.50	11.00
Herpes Zoster	1	3.00	1.00
Tolosa-Hunt syndrome	1	6.00	4.00
Ramsey-Hunt syndrome	1	3.00	7.00
Total	1477		

DEFINITIONS. PR-REX: PRIMEROSE-REX.

Those characteristics of medical experts' rules are fully examined not by comparing between those rules for the same class, but by comparing experts' rules with those for another class. For example, a classification rule for muscle contraction headache is given by:

```
[Jolt Headache=no]
    & ([Tenderness of M0=yes] or [Tenderness of M1=yes] or
          [Tenderness of M2=yes])
    & [Tenderness of B1=no] & [Tenderness of B2=no] &
          [Tenderness of B3=no]
    & [Tenderness of C1=no] & [Tenderness of C2=no]
    & [Tenderness of C3=no] & [Tenderness of C4=no]
                        =>  muscle contraction headache.
```

This rule is very similar to the following classification rule for disease of cervical spine:

```
[Jolt Headache=no]
     & ([Tenderness of M0=yes] or [Tenderness of M1=yes] or
           [Tenderness of M2=yes])
     & ([Tenderness of B1=yes] or [Tenderness of B2=yes] or
         [Tenderness of B3=yes] or
         [Tenderness of C1=yes] or [Tenderness of C2=yes] or
         [Tenderness of C3=yes] or [Tenderness of C4=yes])
                       => disease of cervical spine.
```

The differences between these two rules are attribute-value pairs, from tenderness of B1 to C4. Thus, these two rules can be simplified into the following form:

$$a_1 \& A_2 \& \neg A_3 \rightarrow \textit{muscle contraction headache}$$
$$a_1 \& A_2 \& A_3 \rightarrow \textit{disease of cervical spine}$$

The first two terms and the third one represent different reasoning. The first and second term a1 and A2 are used to differentiate muscle contraction headache and disease of cervical spine from other diseases. The third term A3 are used to make a differential diagnosis between these two diseases. Thus, medical experts firstly selects several diagnostic candidates, which are very similar to each other, from many diseases and then make a final diagnosis from those candidates. Especially, negative information is very important for the final diagnosis. However, conventional rule induction methods do not incorporate such decisions, which will be an important future direction for research on rule induction.

6.2 Exclusive Rules and Diagnostic Model

As discussed in Section 3, the whole given attribute set is used to induce exclusive rules, although the original exclusive rules are described by the six basic questions. Therefore induced exclusive rules have the maximum number of attributes whose conjunction R also satisfies $\kappa_R(D) = 1.0$. If this maximum combination includes the six basic attributes as a subset, then this selection of basic attributes is one of possible good choices of attributes, although redundant. Otherwise, the given six attributes may be redundant or the induced results may be insufficient. For the above example shown in Table 1, the maximum combination of attributes {age, loc, nat, jolt, prod, nau, M1 } is included in both exclusive rules.

On the contrary, in the database for the above experiments, the maximum combination is 13 attributes, derived as follows: Age, Pain location, Nature of the pain, Severity of the pain, History since onset, Existence of jolt headache, Tendency of depression, and Tenderness of M1 to M6, which is a superset of the six basic attributes. Thus, this selection can be a good choice.

In this way, the induction of maximum combination can be also used as a "rough" check of induced results or our diagnosing model on exclusive rules, which can be formulated as below. [5]

Let A and E denote a set of the induced attributes for exclusive rules and a set of attributes acquired from domain experts. Thus, the following four relations can be considered. First, if $A \subset E$, then either A is insufficient or E is redundant. Secondly, if $A = E$, then both sets are sufficient to represent diagnosing model in an applied domain. Thirdly, if $A \supset E$, then either A is redundant or E is insufficient. Finally, fourth, if intersection of A and E is not empty ($A \cap E \neq \phi$), then either or both sets are insufficient.

The reader may say that the above relations are weak and indeterminate. However, the above indefinite parts should be constrained by information on domain knowledge. For example, let us consider the case when $A \subset E$. When E is validated by experts, A is insufficient in the first relation. However, in general, E can be viewed as A obtained by large samples, and $A \supset E$ should hold, which shows that a given database is problematic. Moreover, the constraint on exclusive rules, $\kappa_R(D) = 1.0$, suggests that there exist a class which does not appear in the database, because the already given classes cannot support $\kappa_R(D) = 1.0$, that is, $[x]_R \cap D \neq D$ will hold in the future.

On the other hand, when E is not well given by experts and A is induced from sufficiently large samples, E will be redundant, which means that the proposed model for E does not fit to this database or this domain.

This kind of knowledge is important, because we sometimes need to know whether samples are enough to induce knowledge and whether an applied inducing model is useful to analyze databases.

Thus, the above four relations give simple examinations to check the characteristics of samples and the applicability of a given diagnosing model. It is

[5] This discussion assumes that the whole attributes are sufficient to classify the present and the future cases into given classes.

our future work to develop more precise checking methodology for automated knowledge acquisition.

6.3 Precision for Inclusive Rules

In the above experiments, the thresholds δ_α and δ_κ for selection of inclusive rules are set to 0.75 and 0.5, respectively. Although this precision contributes to the reduction of computational complexity, this methodology, which gives a threshold in a static way, cause a serious problem. For example, there exists a case when the accuracy for the first, the second, and the third candidate is 0.5, 0.49, and 0.01, whereas accuracy for other classes is almost equal to 0. Formally, provided an attribute-value pair, R, the following equations hold: $\alpha_R(D_1) = 0.5, \alpha_R(D_2) = 0.49, \alpha_R(D_3) = 0.01$, and $\alpha_R(D_i) \approx 0 (i = 4, \cdots, 10)$. Then, both of the first and the second candidate should be suspected because those accuracies are very close, compared with the accuracy for the third and other classes. However, if a threshold is statically set to 0.5, then this pair is not included in positive rules for D_2. In this way, a threshold should be determined dynamically for each attribute-value pair. In the above example, an attribute-value pair should be included in positive rules of D_1 and D_2.

¿From discussion with domain experts, it is found that this type of reasoning is very natural, which may contribute to the differences between induced rules and ones acquired from medical experts. Thus, even in a learning algorithm, comparison between the whole given classes should be included in order to realize more plausible reasoning strategy.

Unfortunately, since the proposed algorithm runs for each disease independently, the above type of reasoning cannot be incorporated in a natural manner, which causes computational complexity to be higher. It is also our future work to develop such interacting process in the learning algorithm.

7 Related Work

7.1 AQ family

AQ is a rule induction system, which is based on STAR algorithm[MI1]. This algorithm selects one "seed" from positive examples and starts from one "selector" (attribute-value pair) contained in this "seed" example. It adds selectors incrementally until the "complexes" (conjunction of attributes) explain only positive examples, called a **bounded star**. Since many complexes can satisfy these positive examples, AQ finds the most preferred ones, according to a flexible extra-logical criterion.

It would be worth noting that the positive examples which support the complexes correspond to the lower approximation, or the positive region in rough set theory. That is, the rules induced by AQ are equivalent to consistent rules defined by Pawlak when neither constructive generalization[MI1, WM1] nor truncation[MI2] are used, and when the length of STAR is not restricted. As a matter of fact, AQ's star algorithm without constructive generalization can be reformulated by the concepts of rough sets. For example, a bounded star denoted by $G(e|U - D, m_0)$ in Michalski's notation is equal to $G = \{R_i | [x]_{R_i} = D_j\}$, such that $|G| = m_0$ where $|G|$ denotes the cardinality of G. [6] This star is composed of many complexes, each of which is ordered by the value of LEF_i, lexicographic evaluation functional, defined as the following pair: $< (-negcov, \tau_1), (poscov, \tau_2) >$ where *negcov* and *poscov* are numbers of negative and positive examples, respectively, covered by an expression in the star, and where τ_1 and τ_2 are tolerance threshold for criterion *poscov*, *negcov* ($\tau \in [0..100\%]$). This algorithm shows that AQ method is a kind of the greedy algorithm which finds independent variables using selectors which are equivalent to equivalence relations in terms of rough sets.

Thus, our postprocessing method is very similar to AQ method, while our method uses statistical measures, rather than LEF criterion, which implicitly includes the notions of accuracy and coverage. The difference between our postprocessing procedure and AQ method is that PRIMEROSE-REX explicitly uses accuracy and coverage and that it only uses elementary attribute-value pairs selected by the exhaustive search procedure, according to the characteristics of coverage, although AQ implicitly uses the criteria for both measures. The main reason why our system PRIMEROSE-REX uses statistical measures is that discussion about the statistical characteristics of both measures is easier and that the definition of probabilistic rules is much clearer. As shown in Section 4, three kinds of rules are easily classified into three categories with respect to accuracy and coverage. Especially, since coverage plays an important role in the classification of rules, it is very easy to implement an induction algorithm of exclusive rules and disease image. Thus, PRIMEROSE-REX can be viewed as a combination of AQ algorithm and the exhaustive search method.

7.2 Discovery of Association Rules

Mannila et al.[MT1] report a new algorithm for discovery of association rules, which is one class of regularities, introduced by Agrawal et al.[AI1]. Their method is very similar to ours with respect to the following two points.

(1) Association Rules: The concept of association rules is similar to our induced rules. Actually, association rules can be described in the rough set framework.

That is, we say that an association rule over r (training samples) satisfies $W \Rightarrow B$ with respect to γ and σ, if

$$|[x]_W \cap B| \geq \sigma n, \tag{1}$$

and

$$\frac{|[x]_W \cap B|}{|[x]_W|} \geq \gamma, \tag{2}$$

[6] AQ's INDUCE method uses m_0 in order to suppress the exponential growth of the search space G. Thus, strictly, AQ is a modified version of the greedy algorithm. However, in the subsequent sections, we first assume that m_0 is not given *a priori*: that is, the length of STAR is not restricted.

where n, γ, and σ denote the size of training samples, confidence threshold, and support threshold, respectively. Also, W and B denote a formula and a set whose members belong to a target class, respectively. Furthermore, we also say that W is *covering*, if

$$|[x]_W| \geq \sigma n. \tag{3}$$

It is notable that the left side of the above formulae (1) and (3) correspond to the formula for κ, coverage, and the left side of the formula (2) corresponds to the formula for α, accuracy. The only difference is that we classify rules, corresponding to association rules, into three categories: exclusive rules, inclusive rules, and disease image.

The reason why we classify these rules is that this classification reflects the diagnostic model of medical experts, by which the computational speed of diagnostic reasoning is higher.

(2) Mannila's Algorithm: Mannila introduces an algorithm to find association rules based on Agrawal's algorithm [MT1]. The main points of their algorithm are the following two procedures: database pass and candidate generation. Database pass produces a set of attributes L_s as the collection of all covering sets of size s in C_s. Then, candidate generation calculates C_{s+1}, which denotes the collection of all the sets of attributes of size s, from L_s. Then, again, database pass is repeated to produce L_{s+1}. The effectiveness of this algorithm is guaranteed by the fact that all subsets of a covering set are covering.

The main difference between Mannila's algorithm and PRIMEROSE-REX is that Mannila uses the check algorithm for covering to obtain association rules, whereas we use both accuracy and coverage to compute and classify rules.

In the discovery of association rules, all the combinations of attribute-value pairs in C_s have the property of covering. On the other hand, our algorithm does not focus on the above property of covering. It removes an attribute-value pair which has both high accuracy and high coverage. That is, PRIMEROSE-REX does not search for regularities which satisfy covering, but search for regularities important for classification.

Thus, interestingly, when many attribute-value pairs have the covering property, or covers many training samples, Mannila's algorithm will be slow, although PRIMEROSE-REX algorithm will be fast in this case. When few pairs cover many training samples, Mannila's algorithm will be fast, and our system will not be faster.

References

[AI1] Agrawal, R., Imielinski, T., and Swami, A.: Mining association rules between sets of items in large databases. In: Proceedings of the 1993 International Conference on Management of Data (SIGMOD 93) (1993) 207–216

[BF1] Breiman, L., Freidman, J., Olshen, R., and Stone, C.: Classification and regression trees. Wadsworth International Group (1984)

[BS1] Buchanan, B. G., Shortliffe, E. H.(eds.): Rule-based expert systems. Addison-Wesley, Reading MA (1984)
[EF1] Efron, B.: The jackknife, the bootstrap and other resampling plans. SIAM (1982)
[MT1] Mannila, H., Toivonen, H., Verkamo, A.I.: Efficient algorithms for discovering association rules. In: Proceedings of the AAAI Workshop on Knowledge Discovery in Databases (KDD-94), AAAI Press (1984) 181–192
[MM1] Matsumura, Y., et al.: Consultation system for diagnoses of headache and facial pain: RHINOS. Medical Informatics **11** (1988) 145–157
[MI1] Michalski, R. S.: A theory and methodology of Machine Learning. In: Michalski, R.S., Carbonell, J.G. and Mitchell, T.M. (eds.), Machine Learning - an Artificial Intelligence approach, Morgan Kaufmann, Palo Alto (1983)
[MI2] Michalski, R. S., Mozetic, I., Hong, J. and Lavrac, N.: The multi-purpose incremental learning system AQ15 and its testing application to three medical domains. In: Proceedings of the Fifth National Conference on Artificial Intelligence, AAAI Press (1986) 1041–1045
[PA1] Pawlak, Z.: Rough sets. Kluwer Academic Publishers, Dordrecht (1991)
[QU1] Quinlan, J.R.: C4.5 - programs for Machine Learning, Morgan Kaufmann, San Mateo CA (1993)
[TT1] Tsumoto, S. and Tanaka, H.: Induction of medical expert system rules based on rough sets and resampling methods. In: Proceedings of the 18th Symposium on Computer Applications on Medical Care, Washington, D.C., Hanley & Belfus, Philadelphia (1994) 1066–1070
[TT2] Tsumoto, S., Tanaka, H.: PRIMEROSE: Probabilistic Rule Induction MEthod based on ROugh SEts and resampling methods. Computational Intelligence **11** (1995) 389–405
[WO1] Walker, M. G., Olshen, R. A.: Probability estimation for biomedical classification problems. In: Proceedings of the Sixteenth Symposium on Computer Applications in Medical Care, McGraw Hill, New York (1992)
[WM1] Wnek, J., Michalski, R.Z.: Hypothesis-driven constructive induction in AQ17-HCI: a method and experiments. Machine Learning **14** (1994) 139–168
[ZI1] Ziarko, W.: Variable precision rough set model. Journal of Computer and System Sciences **46** (1993) 39–59

Chapter 17

Rough Sets for Database Marketing

Dirk Van den Poel

Department of Applied Economic Sciences, Catholic University Leuven,
Naamsestraat 69, B-3000 Leuven, Belgium

Abstract. This chapter describes how rough sets can be used for response modeling in database marketing. We use real-world data from one of the largest European mail-order companies. Past transaction data of customers, personal characteristics and their response behavior are used to determine whether these clients are good mailing prospects during the next period.

We provide a comparison of statistical techniques, machine learning, mathematical programming, rough sets and neural networks in a classification task, and show that rough sets can also be successfully used for response modeling in database marketing.

The performance of alternative techniques is judged on the percentage of correct classifications in the validation sample, and on gains chart analysis. The results indicate that on a dataset with only categorical information, the predictive performance of statistical techniques, machine learning techniques and neural networks on a validation dataset is very similar. Still the observed differences are significant.
Keywords. Database marketing, response modeling, classification techniques.

1 Introduction

Database marketing can be defined as a method of analyzing customer data to look for patters among existing customer preferences and to use these patterns for more targeted selection of customers [FP1]. A Business Week article [Be1] clearly illustrated the importance of the concept to current business practice.

Database marketing is characterized by enormous amounts of data at the level of the individual consumer. However, these data have to be turned into information in order to become useful. To this end, several different problem specifications can be investigated. These include cross-selling [Va1] and response modeling. The latter problem formulation tries to predict, based on all available data, whether a customer will purchase during the next mailing period. The response variable in the specification which we will investigate is binary (0/1). The information at the level of the individual customer is then used to construct a response score, which is a reflection of the probability of purchase. Current practice in most mail-order companies is to rank the available customers on the basis of the response score. Based on a break-even analysis and the available budget, a catalog company decides on a cut-off point. Customers below this critical point are deemed to be "inferior" prospects for the next mailing campaign and are suppressed from the mailing list. The key issue in response modeling is to find a good way of obtaining a response score on which to base the customer ranking [RB1].

Several techniques can be used to solve the classification problem at hand. Michie (see[M1]) provides a comparative study of some classification techniques. In database marketing, however, we find very few studies which cover most techniques, which can be used to derive good response models. Even though several techniques can cope with unequal costs of misclassification and unequal prior probabilities of classes, we investigate the techniques with equal costs of misclassification and equal prior probabilities.

This chapter contains a comparison of statistical, machine learning, mathematical programming, rough set, and neural network techniques in the evaluation of current customers. As statistical techniques we use discriminant analysis and logistic regression, which have a long record of application in mail-order response modeling [RB1], as well as CHAID and CART, which are two non-parametric techniques. CHAID has been introduced to the database marketing community by Magidson (see[Ma1]). Machine learning techniques such as C4.5, mathematical programming and the methodology of rough sets are very new to the mail-order industry. Neural networks have always been seen as a separate category because of the decreased interpretability of the results. Nevertheless, there is some evidence of the strong predictive performance of this black box technique [Fu1].

The substantive relevance for this topic comes from the fact that response models in database marketing clearly show significant profit increases [Th1]. A response lift of 1 % on just one mailing can result in a profit increase of 100.000 USD for a large mail-order company. Given a tendency of rising mailing costs and increasing competition (which may cause average revenue per customer to drop), we see an increasing importance for response modeling.

The rest of this chapter is organized as follows: first, we present the available dataset. Then we give a brief theoretical review of the classification methods that will be used in the empirical study. In the next section we discuss the results of the analysis. Finally, some conclusions and guidelines for further research are given.

2 Dataset

We obtained data from an anonymous European mail-order company. A random sample from the mail-order company database containing 6.800 observations was taken in such a way that 50 % of the sample responded to the offers during a 6 month period (i.e., the dependent variable) and 50 % did not respond to the offer. This sample was randomly split in half to obtain a "learning sample" and a "validation sample". All models were built on the basis of the learning sample and test on the validation sample i.e., the predictive performance was judged on the basis of observations which the techniques had not used during the estimation or learning phase.

Direct marketing techniques such as direct mail or electronic commerce (over the world wide web) enable companies to establish a one-to-one relationship with its customers. This leads to the availability of data at the level of the individual customer in terms of:

1. very detailed past transaction information;
2. customer characteristics.

However, an important consequence of this way of doing business is that competition is unaware of the breadth of which and how many customer segments are targeted, and its effect in terms of responses or purchases. This implies that two sources of information are not available for database marketing modeling (1) competitive purchase data (cf. panel data) and (2) competitive mailing action data, which are usually included in sales response models [HP1].

Among the many variables that could be constructed based on past transaction data, three variables have been identified by Cullinan already in the 1920's (see [PB1]) to be of particular importance in database marketing modeling: recency, frequency and monetary value. Several instances of these RFM-variables are included in this study as shown in table 1.

All variables were already categorized and were provided by the mail-order company at the level of the individual customer. A description of the variables used is shown in table 1.

One specific characteristic of the data is that all variables are categorical. This is current practice in some mail-order companies because of the lower storage requirements. A side benefit of this limitation is that it improves the comparability of the results of different techniques, since some of them only operate on categorical variables, such as CHAID.

3 Classification Methods

Four broad classes of classification models are considered in this study. Both discriminant analysis and logistic regression can be categorized as "classical" statistical techniques. CHAID and CART are usually identified as non-parametric advanced tree-structured statistical techniques, which were specifically developed to uncover important interaction effects among variables. Neural networks are well-known for their ability to uncover very complex relationships between variables. LP classification implements the mathematical programming approach to the classification problem. C4.5 represents the machine learning algorithms, and two types of rough set classifiers are included.

Table 1. Description of the variables in the dataset

Name	Type	Description
Buy_t-1	0/1	did the customer buy during the previous 6 months?
Buy_t-2	0/1	did the customer buy in the period: 1 year ago - 6 months ago?
Buy_t-3	0/1	did the customer buy during the period: 1.5 years - 1 year ago?
Buy_t-4	0/1	did the customer buy during the period 2 years- 1.5 years ago?
Customer	6 cat.	for how long is this person a customer?
LastFreq	9 cat.	what was the purchasing frequency during the last 6 months?
LastSales	5 cat.	sales generated by the customer during the last 6 months?
LastProfit	10 cat.	profit generated by the customer during the last 6 months?
Unimulti	3 cat.	does the customer live in a stand-alone home or an appartment
Socclass	6 cat.	social class of the customer
VAT	0/1	is the person self-employed?
Household	4 cat.	type of household the customer belongs to
Family	4 cat.	number of families living at the address
Natclass	6 cat.	nationality distribution in the street of the customer
State	9 cat.	province of Belgium the customer lives in

3.1 Discriminant Analysis

Discriminant analysis is a well-known statistical classification method which allows the researcher to study differences between groups of objects (in this case: responders versus non-responders) with respect to several variables simultaneously [Mc1]. Discriminant analysis is a technique which relates one nominal (dependent) variable to several interval-level variables. Two important assumptions [Kl1] are: 1. that each group is drawn from a population which has a multivariate normal distribution; and 2. that the population covariance matrices are equal for each group. Although the use of discriminant analysis on the basis of dummy variables is controversial on theoretical grounds [Kl1], it is often used in database marketing. For the purpose of this comparison, a quadratic discriminant function is used.

3.2 Logistic Regression

Logistic regression has been developed as a way to resolve the problems of "traditional" linear regression with a dependent variable that is bounded. In the case of response modeling the specific structure of the dependent variable is binary: purchase or non-purchase [AN1]. This parametric statistical method is particularly suited for use in response modeling given the asymptotic properties of the estimation method (i.e., maximum likelihood estimation) and the availability of large samples in database marketing. The main assumption of logistic regression is that the exact relationship between the dependent variable and the independent variables follows the logistic curve.

3.3 CHAID

Chi-squared Automatic Interaction Detector (CHAID) is a non-parametric tree-structure technique, which derives mutually exclusive and exhaustive segments based on a categorical dependent variable [Ma1]. Both dependent and independent variables have to be categorical. It uses an iterative procedure that builds a tree top-down using the chi-squared test of independence as a criterion to choose among predictors. Disadvantages of this technique are the requirement to categorize variables before the CHAID analysis is performed; and the fact that a tree is built in one direction until a stopping criterion is satisfied (unidirectionality).

3.4 CART

Breiman (see[BF1]) introduced classification and regression trees (CART) as an advanced non-parametric tree-structure technique. It builds a tree in a top-down way until all elements are partitioned into a separate leaf. Then a pruning process takes place based on cross-validation, which determines the optimal depth of the tree. Another key difference between CART and other tree-building techniques is its ability to handle continuous variables. This capability makes a discretization process before starting the procedure unnecessary and undesirable because this process may results in a loss of information.

3.5 Neural Networks

Artificial neural networks (ANNs) are not a statistical technique, but a development from artificial intelligence [Fu1]. Some of the supervised learning algorithms can be used to represent very general response functions. A key feature of these techniques is the fact that they are not limited by distributional assumptions, functional forms, and interaction effects. Therefore, neural networks can also be considered as a generalization of (logistic) regression.

We implement a multi-layer perceptron using the backpropagation learning algorithm. Because building neural networks involves the specification of many network design parameters, the development of a network is as much an art as a science. We followed the guidelines of Burgess (see[Bu1]) to obtain a response model using neural networks.

3.6 C4.5

C4.5 is a well known example of a classification tree algorithm. This type of algorithm [Qu1] tries to fit a tree to a training sample using recursive partitioning. This means that the training set is split into increasingly homogeneous subsets until the leaf nodes contain only cases from a single class. An important problem in learning classification trees is overfitting on the training example. To this end, pruning strategies can be adopted, whereby the classification tree is simplified by discarding one or more subtrees and replacing them with leaves.

Although a classification tree can be extremely accurate, in realistic cases, however, this tree is too complex to be understood by the expert. Therefore, it has to be transformed in a formalism which is more understandable by the expert. In C4.5 the classification tree is reexpressed as a set of rules.

3.7 Rough Sets

Rough set theory, introduced by Pawlak (see[Pa1, PG1]) is a technique to deal with vagueness and uncertainty. Rough sets have been used in many artificial intelligence applications. In this chapter, we will focus on the ability of rough sets to acquire rules from data (i.e., its data mining capability). In this chapter we include results from using two rough set algorithms:

1. the system LERS (Learning from Examples based on Rough Sets) developed at the University of Kansas, Grzymala-Busse (see[Gr1]). LERS induces a set of certain and possible rules from the data set. In this case the 'all rules' option was used.
2. ProbRough introduced by Piasta (see[PL1]) and Lenarcik (see[LP1]).

3.8 LP Classification

Mathematical programming techniques have been proposed to the classification problem to cope with serious violations of the assumptions underlying statistical models [RS1]. The basic idea behind these techniques is to identify a hyperplane which can be used to distinguish between observations belonging to two different groups. Gochet (see[GS1]) introduced an interesting multi-group extension to these techniques, which is implemented as a linear programming problem.

4 Results

The performance of all techniques is judged on the basis of two criteria:

1. percentage correctly classified in the validation sample;
2. gains chart analysis.

The gains chart criterion is widely used in comparing alternative techniques as shown in Furness (see[Fu1]). It is in fact an application of the Lorenz curve of incremental expenditure to the database marketing setting [Th1]. The one-fold stratified 50/50 cross-validation results in table 2 show that all models are capable of producing substantial increases over the "no model" situation in the percentage of correctly classified both for the learning and validation sample. CHAID performs best on the validation sample, but the difference between the best technique and the worst one is rather small. The ProbRough rough set implementation scores second, and is characterized by only a small drop-off between the learning and estimation sample.

Because the validation sample consists of cases that were not shown during training or estimation, all predictive results are worse for the validation sample,

Table 2. Classification percentages

Technique	% correctly classified on the "learning" sample	% correctly classified on the "validation" sample
CHAID	75.68	74.62
ProbRough	75.50	74.35
LP classification	75.65	73.88
CART	75.24	73.68
Logit	75.91	73.24
Neural network	73.16	73.12
C4.5	78.50	72.88
Discriminant	69.41	70.85
Rough sets	92.22	68.32
No model	50.00	50.00

with the exception of discriminant analysis. The differences between the results for the two samples are lowest for neural networks. The higher drop-off between learning and validation sample for C4.5 and 'all rules' rough sets is remarkable. The latter effect illustrates that selecting all rules on noisy data is not the most appropriate strategy. Some more advanced strategies for extracting strong rules should be chosen. The drop-off for the other techniques is rather low, which may be an indication of the external validity of the relationships that were modeled.

We follow Kohavi's (see[Ko1]) recommendation to use a ten-fold stratified cross-validation for model selection. These results are shown in table 3, and lead to the conclusion that confidence intervals based on these results show an important overlap. Both statistical techniques (discriminant analysis and logistic regression) have the smallest standard deviation, followed by the backpropagation neural network. Tree structure techniques like CHAID and CART both have higher mean accuracy and standard deviations. ProbRough offers interesting results because its solution is very similar to CART (in terms of the number of rules generated and in terms of the variables in the rules). Moreover, the ProbRough rough sets technique generated rules, which turned out to be identical for all ten cross-validation samples.

Under normal conditions a mail-order company will try to cut off between 10 % and 40 % of its "unattractive" part of the mailing list. This means that the most important part of the gains chart lies between a mailing depth of 60 % and 90 %. When looking at the figures 1-3, we observe the largest differences at this part of the graph, which leads to the conclusion that although the performance of most techniques is relatively equivalent, the difference in the gains chart at the relevant range is important. Assume that the break-even point is at 25 %. From table 4, which contains the results for the different techniques of a vertical crossection at 75 %, we learn that the statistical techniques perform best at this mailing depth. When the mail-order company decides to mail to 75 % of its mailing list, it can expect to tap almost 92 % of its buying potential when using a logistic regression model, compared to 87 % when using CART.

Table 3. Ten-fold stratified cross-validation

Technique	Mean accuracy	Standard deviation
CHAID	75.74	1.43
CART	75.46	1.41
C4.5	75.03	1.04
ProbRough	75.03	1.24
LP classification	74.93	1.40
Neural network	73.25	0.95
Logit	73.20	0.91
Discriminant	73.03	0.94

Table 4. Cum. response % at a mailing depth of 75 %

Technique	% cumulative response
Logit	91.82
Discriminant analysis	91.06
CHAID	91.00
C4.5	89.94
Rough sets	89.00
Neural network	88.47
CART	87.06
LP classification	86.82
ProbRough	85.41
No model	75.00

Now, our discussion will focus on the gains chart analysis in figures 1-3. All charts include the "no model" and logistic regression results for purposes of comparison with respectively the worst and the best alternative. Figure 1 shows that there are virtually no differences in predictive ability between logistic regression and discriminant analysis. The gains chart of neural networks is very similar to the statistical techniques up till a mailing list depth of 50 %. However, for larger depths, neural networks performance on the validation sample is inferior to both statistical techniques.

The results in figure 2 reveal very good predictive performance of CHAID, which is very close to the statistical logistic regression. CART can only compete with CHAID and logistic regression for mailing depths between 30 and 54 %.

The machine learning algorithm C4.5 (cf. figure 3) beats logistic regression for the range of mailing depths from 45 to 59 %. However, for lower mailing depths its performance is the lowest of the group of techniques. Rough sets reveal a more stable performance over the full range of mailing depths when compared to C4.5.

When comparing the three graphs, we observe that the gains chart results of both C4.5 and CART are very similar. Both techniques only perform comparably

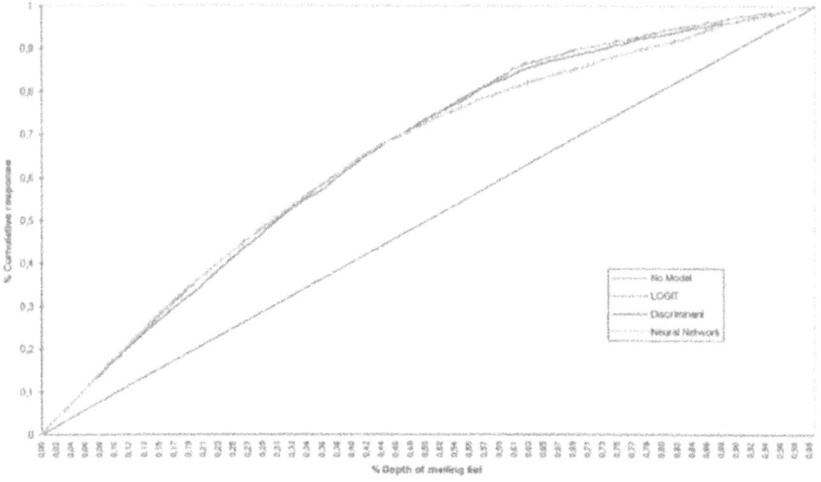

Fig. 1. Gains chart including statistical techniques and neural networks

to the other techniques for the mid-range (40 - 50 %) of mailing depths. The gains chart is inferior for both the upper and lower ranges of mailing depth.

Both rough set techniques have distinctly different gains charts. The 'all rules' results, generated by LERS, offers good predictive capability at the end of the chart, whereas ProbRough only shows top performance at low mailing depths.

5 Conclusions and Further Research

The results of this comparison reveal that classical statistical parametric techniques, logistic regression and discriminant analysis, perform very well for the relevant range of the gains chart. The use of CHAID gives the best outcome on the percentage classified criterion, and it nearly equals the best score for the gains chart criterion. The conclusion with respect to CART is dependent to the criterion used. It scores very well on the percentage correctly classified; on the gains chart, however, it scores poorly. Furthermore, this example clearly shows that neural networks are not always superior to traditional techniques in terms of predictive performance. Finally, the machine learning algorithm C4.5 performs reasonably well on this example. Although some notable differences from the other techniques can be observed: 1. the drop-off between learning sample and validation sample is higher than for the other techniques. 2. the shape of the gains chart for C4.5 is especially interesting; the obtained result that C4.5 performs better at mid-range mailing depths and worse for lower and higher ranges needs further research. Overall, we can conclude that techniques new to database marketing such as machine learning, rough sets and mathematical programming can also be used successfully as techniques for response modeling. However, given

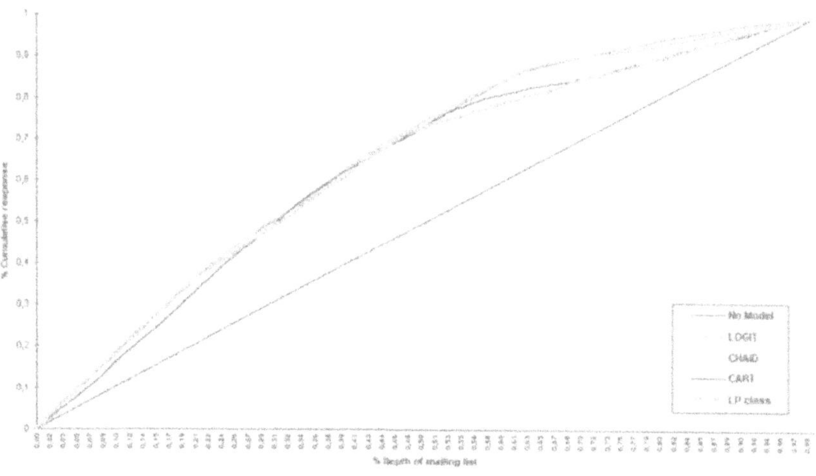

Fig. 2. Gains chart including non-parametric tree-structure techniques and LP

noisy marketing data, some rule selection for extracting strong rules should be used to avoid a drop-off between the learning and validation sample.

Even though the gains chart analysis shows little difference among the various techniques, a 5 may decide between success and failure of a whole campaign.

Important issues for further research are:

- to determine whether the nature of the data (only categorical versus mixed categorical and continuous) has an influence on the ranking of the predictive performance of the different techniques. This can be determined by applying the same techniques to mixed variable data. We may assume that techniques like CART and neural networks will increase their performance versus the other statistical and machine learning algorithms.
- the performance of all techniques was compared under the assumption of equal costs of misclassification and equal prior probabilities of classes. Further studies may look into relaxing both assumptions.

Acknowledgements

We thank Koncept bvba for the use of the SPSS/PC+ CHAID 5.0 software, Software Development Service bvba for the use of NeuralWorks Professional II+, W. Gochet and Y. Goegebeur for the use of the LP classification software, J. Grzymala-Busse for the use of the LERS software, and Z. Piasta for the use of the ProbRough algorithm.

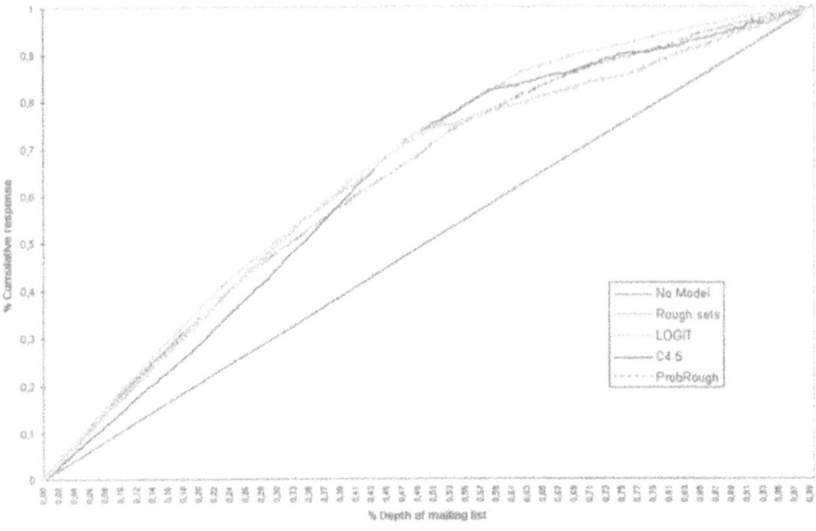

Fig. 3. Gains chart including rough sets and machine learning techniques

References

[AN1] Aldrich, J. H., Nelson, F. D.: Linear probability, logit, and probit models. Sage Publications, Beverly Hills CA (1991)

[Be1] Berry J.: Database marketing. Business Week, September 5 (1994) 56–62

[BF1] Brieman, L., Friedman, J. H., Olshen, R. A., Stone, C. J.: Classification and regression trees. Wadsworth & Brooks, Monterey CA (1984)

[Bu1] Burgess, N.: How neural networks can improve database marketing. Journal of Database Marketing **2/4** (1995) 312–327

[FP1] Fayyad, U. M., Piatetsky-Shapiro, G., Smyth, P.: From data mining to knowledge discovery: an overview. In: Advances in knowledge discovery and data mining, AAAI Press (1996)

[Fu1] Furness, P.: New pattern analysis methods for database marketing. Journal of Database Marketing **1/3** (1994) 220–232

[Gs1] Gochet, W., Stam, A., Chen, S., Srinivasan, V.: Multi-group discriminant analysis using linear programming. Operations Research **45/2** (1997) 213–225

[Gr1] Grzymala-Busse, J. W.: Managing uncertainty in machine learning from examples. In: Proceedings of Workshop Intelligent Information Systems III, Wigry, Poland, June 6-10 (1994) 70–84

[HP1] Hanssens, D. M., Parsons, L. J., Schultz, R. L.: Market response models: econometric and time series analysis. Kluwer Academic Publishers, Boston (1992)

[Kl1] Klecka, W. R.: Discriminant analysis. Sage Publications, Beverly Hills CA (1990)

[Ko1] Kohavi, R.: A study of cross-validation and bootstrap for accuracy estimation and model selection (working paper). Computer Science Department, Stanford University (1995)

[LP1] Lenarcik, A., Piasta, Z.: An invariant method of rough classifier construction. Proceedings of the poster session of ISMIS '96, Oak Ridge Laboratory (1996) 146–156

[Ma1] Magidson, J.: Improved statistical techniques for response modeling. Journal of Direct Marketing **2/4** (1988) 6–18

[Mc1] McLachlan, G. J.: Discriminant analysis and statistical pattern recognition. John Wiley, New York (1992)

[MS1] Michie, D., Spiegelhalter, D. J., Taylor C. C.: Machine learning, neural and statistical classification. Ellis Horwood series in artificial intelligence. Prentice Hall, Englewood Cliffs NJ (1994)

[Pa1] Pawlak, Z.: Rough sets. International Journal of Information and Computer Science **11** (1982) 341–356

[PG1] Pawlak, Z., Grzymala-Busse, J. et al.: Rough sets. Communications of the ACM **38** (1995) 89–95

[PB1] Petrison, L. A., Blattberg, R. C., Wang P.: Database marketing: past, present, and future. Journal of Direct Marketing **7** (1993) 27–43

[PL1] Piasta, Z., Lenarcik, A.: Rule induction with probabilistic rough classifiers. ICS Research Report 24/96, Institute of Computer Science, Warsaw University of Technology (1996)

[Qu1] Quinlan, J. R.: C4.5 programs for machine learning. Morgan Kaufmann, San Mateo CA (1993)

[RS1] Ragsdale, C. T., Stam, A.: Mathematical programming formulations for the discriminant problem: an old dog does new tricks. Decision Sciences **22** (1991) 296–306

[RB1] Roberts, M. L., Berger P. D.: Direct marketing management. Prentice Hall, Englewood Cliffs NJ (1989)

[Th1] Thompson, J.: Targeting for response value and profit. Journal of Targeting, Measurement and Analysis for Marketing **3** (1994) 133–146

[Va1] Van den Poel, D.: Cross-selling with neural nets. Proceedings of the NCDM'96 conference (1996) 831–840

Chapter 18

A New Halftoning Method Based on Error Diffusion with Rough Set Filtering

Huanglin Zeng[1] *and R. Swiniarski*[2]

[1] Sichuan Institute of Light Industry and Chemical Technology 643033, P.R. China
[2] Department of Mathematical and Computer Sciences, San Diego State University, San Diego, CA 92182, USA

Abstract. A new technique is proposed for converting a continuous tone image into a halftone image using the combined error diffusion with rough set (Pawlak, 1991; Skowron, Stepaniuk, 1994; Polkowski, Skowron, Zytkow, 1995; Swiniarski, 1993; Lin, 1997) filtering. The rough set filtering uses the concepts of tolerance relation and (Skowron, Stepaniuk, 1994, 1996; Polkowski, Skowron, Zytkow, 1995) and approximation spaces to define a tolerance class of neighboring pixels in a processing mask, then utilizes the statistical mean of the tolerance classes to replace the gray levels of the central pixel in a processing mask. The error diffusion uses the correction factor which is composed with the weighted errors for pixels (prior to addition of the pixel to be processed to diffuse error over the neighboring pixels in a continuous tone image). A system implementation as well as an algorithm of halftoning on error diffusion with rough sets are introduced in the paper. A specific example of halftoning is conducted to evaluate the efficient performances of the new halftoning system proposed in comparison with that of an adaptive error diffusion strategy.

1 Introduction

Since there are many applications that deal with storage, display and transmission of huge data such as texts, graphics and images, the techniques of compression and reproduction with low loss of information have been the focus of extensive research. Among the methods commonly used to deal with image processing, the electronic techniques are widely used to transform continuous tone and pictorial images into spatially encoded representations compatible with binary output processes since a large percentage of the electronic devices utilize a binary mode of operation. Moreover, a halftone image have a great compression rate.

Halftoning is a process of converting a continuous tone image into a halftone image whose pixels are either white or black, and a halftone image appears to have multiple gray level due to the microstructure varying the average of covered

area (Javvis, et al., 1976a, 1976b; Mohamed, 1995; Stuck, 1981; Stevenson, Acce, 1985; Ulichney, 1987; Weszka, 1978; Shu, 1995; Ullman, 1974). Many halftoning algorithms and techniques have been developed. The basic idea in these techniques is the comparison of the gray level for an input sample from a continuous tone image with a kind of a threshold value. If the gray level is above such a value, then the halftoning output result will be assumed to be black, otherwise it is white. The following major halftoning methods has been developed: ***globally fixed level thresholding*** (Weszka, 1978), ***locally adaptive thresholding*** (Ullman, 1974), ***constrained average thresholding*** (Javvis, 1976a), ***pseudorandom thresholding (order dither)*** (Javvis, 1976b), ***error diffusion*** (Ochi, et al., 1987; Stuck, et al, 1981; Stevenson, Arce, 1985; Ulichney, 1987; Shu, 1995), and so on (Mohamed, 1995; Stuck, et al., 1981). Among them, the error diffusion approach has been received considerable attention, since the error of the resulting binary outputs are diffused over the weighted neighboring pixels by the technique of error diffusion .
However, there are still some problems, such as the existence of false textures in uniform areas, and presence of visible low spatial frequency artifacts in a halftone image.

We propose a new approach of halftoning which combines the techniques of error diffusion with rough set filtering. The proposed new approach, which is based on rough set concept of set approximation, has shown many of improvements on the quality of halftoning and the complexity of computation. The paper describes a new halftoning system based on error diffusion with rough set filtering. A resulting new halftoning algorithm as well as its implementation and applications are presented. Finally, a few pertinent remarks related to proposed halftoning are given.

2 Halftoning based on error diffusion with rough set filtering

It is well known that continuous tone image is the class of imagery containing multiple gray levels with no perceptible quantization to them. The original gray level values of a pixel at coordinate (i,j) can be expressed by $f(i,j)$ as an element of a matrix. We may denote a pixel at the location (i,j) as a pair $((i,j), f(i,j))$. A halftone imagery is the class of imagery containing ideally of only two gray levels, 0 (white) and 255 (black). In halftoning the resulting binary output value of a pixel (i,j) can be expressed by $O(i,j) \in \{0, 255\}$.

Now we propose a system implementation of halftoning combining the techniques of error diffusion with rough set filtering. At first, we introduce the concepts of rough set filtering in a halftoning before describing the process of the error diffusion.
Rough sets (Pawlak, 1991; Skowron, Stepaniuk, 1994, 1996; Polkowski, Skowron,

Zytkow, 1995) are defined on an image approximation space composed of an image I (defined by f) and a tolerance relation R included in $I \times I$. A rough set approximating a set V included in an image I is a pair of subsets $\underline{R}V$ and $\overline{R}V$, where $\underline{R}V$ and $\overline{R}V$ are respectively defined as follows

$$\underline{R}V = \{v \in I : [v]_R \subseteq V\} \qquad (2.1a)$$

$$\overline{R}V = \{v \in I : [V]_R \cap V \neq 0\} \qquad (2.1b)$$

Here $V \in I$ is a subimage, and $[v]_R = \{v' : vRv'\}$ is a tolerance class defined by v. $\underline{R}V$ represents the lower approximation of V by R. From the above definition we can see that the lower approximation of v with respect to the tolerance relation R is the union of all tolerance classes of R which are entirely included in V. $\overline{R}V$ represents the upper approximation of V by R. We see the the upper approximation of V with respect to the tolerance relation R is the union of all tolerance classes R with at least one pixel from V. The upper approximation of a singleton $\{v\}$ is equal to the tolerance class defined by v.

The rough filter of a set $V \in I$ is the family of all upper approximations of elements from V, more formally the set of pairs $\{(v, tolerance\ class\ defined\ by\ v) : v \in V\}$.

Now we define a processing mask to be a movable window W composed of $(M \times M - 1)$ neighbors and a pixel to be processed. The $(M \times M - 1)$ neighbors are considered for a central pixel at coordinates (i, j) as its horizontal, vertical and at the diagonal neighbors such that they are symmetrically located about (i, j), and each of the first layer of surrounding pixel is at the unit of distance from (i, j), similarly, each of the second layer surrounding pixel is at the unit of distance from the first layer surrounding pixels, and so on. For example, a 3×3 window $W(i, j)$ composed of an 8-neighbors of the central pixel at coordinate (i, j) can be expressed by

$$\begin{matrix} f(i-1,j-1) & f(i-1,j) & f(i-1,j+1) \\ f(i,j-1) & f(i,j) & f(i,j+1) \\ f(i+1,j-1) & f(i+1,j) & f(i+1,j+1) \end{matrix} \qquad (2.2)$$

We define an approximation space of a processing mask to be a pair $(W(i,j), R)$, where the universe $W(i,j)$ is the set of neighboring pixels in a movable window. The tolerance relation $R_{f,W}$ defined by the the window $W(i,j)$ is

$$((i,j), f(i,j)) \ R_{f,W} \ ((x+i, y+j), f(x+i, y+j)) \quad iff$$

$$|f(i,j) - f(x+i,y+j)| \leq D, \ for\ any\ (i,j)\ and\ f(x+i,y+j) \in W(i,j) \qquad (2.3)$$

where $f(i,j)$ is a gray level of the central pixel (i,j) and $f(x+i,y+j)$ is a gray level of a neighboring pixel $(x+i, y+j)$ in a window $W(i,j)$. D is a positive

constant denoting a tolerance error of a tolerance class.
It is obvious that the tolerance class

$$[(i,j)]_{R_{f,W}} = \{(x+i, y+j) : ((i,j), f(i,j)) \; R_{f,W} \; ((x+i, y+j), f(x+i, y+j)) \text{ and } f(x+i, y+j) \in W(i,j)\}$$

consists of all pixels which have the similar gray levels with the pixel $((i,j), f(i,j))$ in a window (i.e., an upper approximation of the central pixel $((i,j), f(i,j))$). Based on the tolerance classes (pixels) in a window, a statistical mean $F(i,j)$ of the neighbors, which belong to the upper approximation of (i,j) with respect to $R_{f,W}$, can be calculated as follows

$$F(i,j) = \frac{1}{K} \sum_{K} f(m,n) \qquad (2.4)$$

Here, $f(m,n)$ represents the gray level of the pixel belonging to the tolerance class of the central pixel $f(i,j)$ in a window, and K is the number of the pixel belonging to the tolerance class $((i,j), f(i,j))$ with respect to $R_{f,W}$.
Let us assume that a new gray level $F(i,j)$ of the central pixel $f(i,j)$ has been computed according to the equations (2,3) and (2,4). Moving a processing mask over the whole image, then passing all pixels of the image through the rough set filter, we can get new gray level values.
The process of the error diffusion is performed as follows: to the new value $F(i,j)$ a correction factor $C(i,j)$ is added, and then this value is compared with the determined threshold T to produce the binary output of the pixel to be processed

$$O(i,j) = 128 \times [1 + sign(F(i,j) + C(i,j) - T)] \qquad (2.5)$$

The correction factor $C(i,j)$ is obtained on the basis of the error for those pixels prior to addition of the gray level for $F(i,j)$. It can be expressed as follows

$$C(i,j) = \mathbf{e} * E \qquad (2.6)$$

where $\mathbf{e}$ denotes the computed errors matrix for those pixels prior to addition of the gray level for $F(i,j)$, * denotes a kind of product operation of these errors and the corresponding elements of an error diffusion filter, and E denotes a kind of error diffusion filter (designed experimentally).
For example, for scanning direction from left to right and up to down, a 9 neighboring pixel error diffusion filter for the rectangular grid (Ulichney, 1987) can be expressed by

$$\begin{matrix} 3/16 & 5/16 & 1/16 \\ 7/16 & 0 & 0 \\ 0 & 0 & 0 \end{matrix} \qquad (2.7)$$

An element $e(i,j)$ of the error $\mathbf{e}$ is computed by comparing the binary output $O(x,y)$ with the new gray level value $F(i,j)$ and adding a correction factor $C(i,j)$

$$e(i,j) = F(i,j) + C(i,j) - O(i,j) \qquad (2.8)$$

The error signal $e(i,j)$, with the errors for those pixels prior to addition of gray level for the next input pixel, is passed through an error filter to produce a correction factor to be added to the new value of the next input pixel. For example, based on an error filter shown as (2.7), the factor $C(i,j)$ can be computed as follows

$$C(i,j) = [3e(i-1,j-1)+5e(i-1,j)+1e(i-1,j+1)+7e(i,j-1)]/16 \quad (2.9)$$

The next input pixel is passed through the rough set filter to obtain its new gray level, then the correction factor $C(i,j)$ is added to compare with the threshold value to yield its binary output $O(i,j)$, and so on. ¿From i=1 to N and j=1 to N, an $N \times N$ continuous tone image will be converted into a halftone image in which errors, of past pixel, are diffused over the weighted neighboring pixels.

3 Practical considerations of an algorithm of implementation of the system

Based on the scheme proposed above, system implementation and an algorithm for the new halftoning system can be suggested as follows:

1. Begin at the pixel at coordinate (1,1) in a matrix composed of image elements. Apply a scanning direction from left to right and up to down. Define a processing mask to be a movable window containing $(M \times M - 1)$ neighboring pixels. Here M is an odd number, and neighboring pixels are symmetrically located around the central pixel to be processed. For example, a 3×3 window is given by the equation (2.2). It is also noted that if (i,j) is on the border of the image, then some of the neighbors of the central pixel will be outside of an image. In this case, the outside pixels are assumed to be zero gray level, i.e., if $i < 1$ or $y < 1$, and $x > N$ or $y > N$ then $f(i,j) = 0$.
2. Find out all of the neighboring pixels belonging to the upper approximation of pixels in a window based on the relation defined by the equation (2.3).
3. Applying equation (2.4) calculate the statistical mean $F(i,j)$ of the pixel belonging to the tolerance class in a window.
4. Applying a selected error filter with using the errors for those pixels prior to addition of gray level for $f(i,j)$, calculate a correction factor $C(i,j)$. Notice that we assume that $e(i,j) = 0$, if $x < 1$ or $y < 1$, and $x > N$ or $y > N$.
5. Based on the equation (2.5) calculate the resulting binary output $O(i,j)$ of the continuous tone pixel $f(i,j)$.
6. Based on equation (2.8), calculate the error signal $e(i,j)$ of the pixel $f(i,j)$ for the next input pixel.
7. From i=1 to N and j=1 to N, repeat step (2) through step (6) until all of the pixels of a continuous tone image has been converted into the halftone pixels.

4 Simulation results and summaries

In order to evaluate the efficient performance of the new proposed halftoning system combining an error diffusion with rough set filtering, we converted a continuous tone image into a halftone image applying the techniques proposed above. We provided a comparison of our technique with that of an adaptive error diffusion (AED) method proposed in (Shu, 1995)
An original image consisted of 128 pixels with continuous tone gray levels. We selected a 3×3 movable window to process the image, and we applied the basis error filter defined by the equation (2.8). Based on the approach that we suggested (with Matlab program implementation) the resulting binary images can be obtained in 1.05×10^6 floating point operations. Comparatively, the resulting binary image obtained using the method J. Shu requires 3.144×10^6 floating point operations. It is obvious that the quality of halftoning with error diffusion shows many of improvements as compared with the method of fixed level threshold. The quality of halftoning by method we proposed is almost the same as that obtained with the application of the method proposed by J. Shu. However, the computational time of halftoning of an image by the method that we proposed is only 1/3 of the computational time required by the latter method.

It is shown that the technique proposed has the following merits:

1. The halftoning has a large compression rate. For color halftoning, 24 bit/pixel continuous tone image may by converted into 3 or 4 bit/pixel for CMY or CMYK colors (1bit/pixel per color).
2. A new rough set mean filter gas been added at the front end of a general error diffusion in order to replace an order dither procedure. As a result, if we assume that the original image pixel and local neighborhood having similar gray level constraints, the technique proposed here not only has improved the quality of halftoning, but has also eliminated the some random noises in a continuous tone image.
3. The error diffusion effect is easily adjusted by selecting the different extent value D of the tolerance class in the rough sets universe. The technique suggested here is easily implemented by software as well as by hardware adequate for the real-time image processing.

References

1. Javvis, J. F., et al. (1976a). "A new technique for displaying continuous tone images on a bilevel display", IEEE Trans on Comm., Vol. Com-24, 891-89.
2. Javvis, J. F. et al. (1976b). "A survey of techniques for the display of continuous tone images on a bilevel display", Comput. Graphics, Image Processing, Vol. 5, 13-40.
3. Mohamed, S. A. (1995). "Binary image compression using efficient partitioning into rectangular regions", IEEE Trans on Comm. Vol.43, 1888-1893.

4. Lin, T. Y. (1997). "Neighborhood systems - information granulation". In: P.P. Wang (ed.), Joint Conference of Information Sciences, March 1-5, Duke University, Vol. **3** (1997) 161–164
5. Ochi, H. et al., (1987). "A new halftone reproduction and transmission method using standard black and white facsimile code, IEEE Trans on Comm., Vol. COM-35, 466-470.
6. Pawlak, Z. (1991). *Rough Sets.* Kluwer Academic Publishers.
7. Polkowski, L., Skowron, A., and Zytkow, J., (1995), "Tolerance based rough sets", in: T.Y. Lin and A. Wildberger (eds.), *Soft Computing: Rough Sets, Fuzzy Logic Neural Networks, Uncertainty Management, Knowledge Discovery,* Simulation Councils, Inc. San Diego CA, 55–58.
8. Shu, J. (1995). "Adaptive Filtering for Error Diffusion Quality Improvement", SID'95 DIGEST, 833-836.
9. Skowron, A., and Stepaniuk, J., (1994), "Generalized approximation spaces", in: T.Y. Lin and A.M. Wildberger (eds.), *The Third International Workshop on Rough Sets and Soft Computing Proceeding (RSSC'94),* San Jose State University, San Jose, California, USA, November 1-12, 156–163.
10. Skowron, A., and Stepaniuk, J., (1996), "Tolerance approximation spaces", *Fundamenta Informaticae,* 27, 245–253.
11. Skowron, A., (1994), "Data filtration: a rough set approach", in: W. Ziarko (ed.), *Rough Sets, Fuzzy Sets and Knowledge Discovery,* Workshops in Computing, Springer-Verlag & British Computer Society, London, Berlin, 18–118.
12. Skowron, A., (1995), "Synthesis of adaptive decision systems from experimental data", in: A. Aamadt and J. Komorowski (eds.), *Proc. of the Fifth Scandinavian Conference on Artificial Intelligence SCAI-95,* Fundamenta Informaticae, Amsterdam, 220–238.
13. Stevenson R. L., and G. R. Arce. (1985). "Binary display of hexagonally sampled continuous tone images", J. Opt. Soc. Am. A. Vol.2, 1009-1013.
14. P. Stuck, P. et al. (1981). "A multiple error correcting computation algorithm for bilevel image hardcopy reproduction", RZ1060, IBM Research Lab. Switzerland.
15. Swiniarski, R. (1993). Introduction to Rough Sets". Materials of The International Short Course Neural Networks. Fuzzy and Rough Systems."
16. Tentush, I., (1995), "On minimal absorbent sets for some types of tolerance relations", *Bull. Polish Acad. Sci. Tech.,* 43/1, 79–88.
17. Ulichney,R. (1987). *Digital halftoning,* MIT Press, Cambridge.
18. Ullman, J. R. (1974). Binarization using associative addressing, Pattern Recognition, Soc. Vol. 6.
19. Vakarelov, D., (1991a), "Logical approach of positive and negative similarity relations in property systems", *Processing of the First World Conference on the Fundamentals of AI, WOCFAI'91,* Paris, July 1-5,
20. Weszka, J. S. (1978). "A survey of threshold selection techniques", Comput. Graphics, Image Processing, Vol.7, PP.259-265,1978.
21. Yao, Y.Y., (1997), "Binary relation based neighborhood operators", in: P.P. Wang (ed.), *Joint Conference of Information Sciences,* March 1-5, Duke University, Vol. 3, 169–172.

PART 3:

HYBRID APPROACHES

Chapter 19

IRIS Revisited: A Comparison of Discriminant and Enhanced Rough Set Data Analysis

Ciarán Browne[1*], *Ivo Düntsch*[1*] *and Günther Gediga*[2*]

[1] School of Information and Software Engineering, University of Ulster, Newtownabbey, BT 37 0QB, N.Ireland. E-mail: {C. Browne,I.Duentsch}@ulst.ac.uk

[2] FB Psychologie / Methodenlehre, Universität Osnabrück, 49069 Osnabrück, Germany. E-mail: ggediga@luce.psycho.Uni-Osnabrueck.DE

1 Introduction

Rough set data analysis (RSDA) was introduced to Computer Science in the early 1980s by Z. Pawlak [Paw82] and has since come into focus as an alternative to the more widely used methods of machine learning and statistical data analysis. A good overview of the state of the art are *Fundamenta Informaticae*, Vol. 27 (1996), and [LC97].

Just like other new approaches, RSDA needs to show that its methods are as good as or even superior to commonly used – mainly statistical – data analysis strategies. Even though singular attempts have been made to compare RSDA to other approaches, e.g. [WZY86, TB92, KBSS92, KSS92], a systematic comparison is as yet missing.

In this paper, we use the IRIS data set to compare the ROUGHIAN extension of RSDA developed by two of the authors [DG97c] with Fisher's discriminant analysis method, and exhibit some general principles regarding the power of the two approaches. This need of further comparison arises, because the methods of [DG97c] enable the researcher to treat quantitative attributes in an "RSDA compatible" way, which could not be done in the previous comparison studies.

The structure of this paper is as follows: To make the paper self contained, we first briefly describe Fisher's discriminant analysis and its application to the IRIS data set, and then proceed to highlight the main points of the ROUGHIAN method.

Section 4 gives an RSDA analysis of the IRIS data set, and comments on earlier comparisons. In Sect. 5 we present the ROUGHIAN analysis of the IRIS data, as well as validation and testing procedures of prediction.

---

* Equal authorship implied

2 IRIS Data: The Historical Perspective

2.1 Fisher's Discriminant Analysis

Suppose that we have a situation where we have cases or subjects divided into groups, and quantitative attributes which should predict the group membership; it was Fisher [Fis36] who discovered ***discriminant analysis*** (DA), which enables the researcher to find linear combinations of the predicting attributes – called ***canonical discriminant functions*** (CDF) – which best characterize the differences between the groups. Once one has found these characterizations, one can compute the differences between any object and every centroid of the group means in terms of the canonical classification functions; one is able to assign every object – and even new objects – to the group whose centroid is nearest to the coordinates of the object. Other assignment procedures are also possible: For example, if we assume that the prediction attributes can be described by the same multivariate normal density within any class of the decision attribute, the assignment can be done by choosing the group which maximizes the likelihood $f(object = i|group = j)$.

Nowadays – more than 60 years later – discriminant analysis has turned into a class of methods using the same spirit and some ideas of the original Fisherian one. In order to compare RSDA results with results of "the" discriminant analysis, we have to specify what kind of discriminant analysis we shall use. Our idea is that we take a ***modal type analysis***, which uses the following underpinnings:

- The predicting attributes are quantitative variables and no data transformation is done before entering the discriminant analysis process.
- It is assumed that the within-group covariance matrices of the predicting attributes are identical. Although this assumption puts severe restrictions on the data, the "modal" DA is run with this restriction.
- We use the simple centroid classification rule to (re)classify objects to classes.

2.2 Fisher's IRIS Data

The data used by Fisher to demonstrate his discriminant analysis consists of 50 specimen of each of the iris species ***Setosa, Versicolor,*** and ***Virginica***, measured by the features given in Tab. 1.

Table 1. IRIS Data

No	Attribute	Range in mm	No	Attribute	Range in mm
A1	Sepal length	$43 \le x \le 79$	**A3**	Petal length	$10 \le x \le 69$
A2	Sepal width	$22 \le x \le 44$	**A4**	Petal width	$1 \le x \le 25$

Applying DA to the data, it turns out that there are two canonical discriminant functions necessary to describe the differences between the groups. It is well known that petal length is the most prominent variable to constitute the first CDF, which is indicated by the highest pooled-within-groups correlations between petal length and the first CDF (Tab. 2). Petal width and sepal width turned out to be equally important, whereas the sepal length has no remarkable impact on the CDF.

Table 2. Pooled-within-groups Correlations between Discriminating Variables and Canonical Discriminant Functions

	CDF 1	CDF 2
Petal length	.73 (.91)	.19 (-.41)
Petal width	.65 (.81)	.72 (.58)
Sepal length	.24	.34
Sepal width	-.13	.87

In order to be compatible with the results of the RSDA, we choose the pair *(petal length, petal width)* as attributes for further analysis. Reclassification using these two variables works very well, as the results of Tab. 3 indicate. A geometrical interpretation of the DA can be given by plotting each case as a point in the space built by the axes of the two CDFs. Figure 1 shows the data projected into the space of the two CDFs based on petal length and petal width.

Table 3. Classification Results Using Bayesian Reclassifier

	IRIS species		
Predicted classes	Setosa	Versicolor	Virginica
Setosa	1.000	0.000	0.000
Versicolor	0.000	0.960	0.080
Virginica	0.000	0.040	0.920

3 ROUGHIAN – Rough Information Analysis

[DG97c] have developed a ***rough information analysis*** (ROUGHIAN) which enhances traditional rough set data analysis by three additional procedures, namely,

- Significance testing,
- Data filtering
- Uncertainty measuring.

In this section we shall describe these features as well as our notation of RSDA. To make this chapter more self contained, some of the material of this section was taken from [DG96] and [DG97c]. Further applications of the ROUGHIAN model can be found in [Bro97] and [DGR97]. All computations were done using the rough set engine Grobian [DG97b].

Fig. 1. The Space of Two CDFs

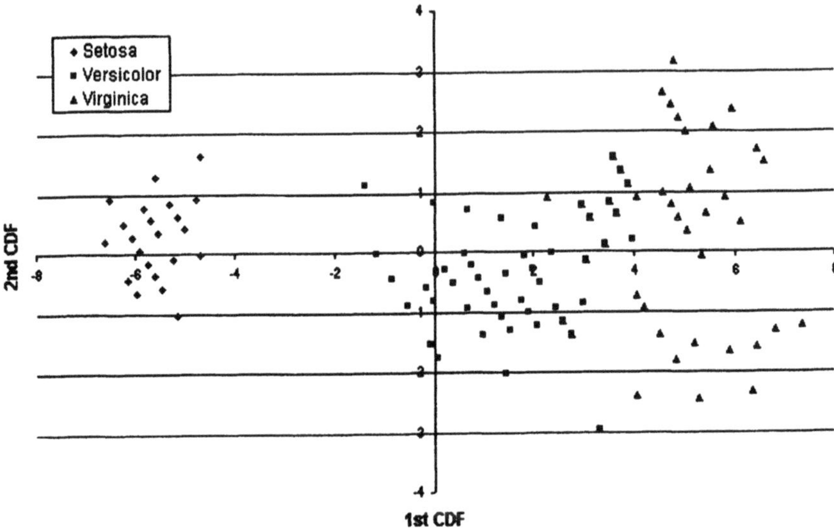

3.1 Basics

We assume that the reader is familiar with the philosophy and the basic terms of RSDA, so that we will just outline our notation and definitions.

An *information system*

$$\mathcal{I} = \langle U, \Omega, V_q, f_q \rangle_{q \in \Omega}$$

consists of

1. A finite set U of objects,
2. A finite set Ω of attributes,
3. For each $q \in \Omega$
   (a) A set V_q of attribute values,
   (b) An information function $f_q : U \to V_q$,

We extend the information functions f_q to functions f_Q, $Q \subseteq \Omega$ in the canonical way.

The subsets Q of Ω can be used to define the indiscernibility relations θ_Q by

$$x \theta_Q y \overset{\text{def}}{\iff} (\forall q \in Q)(f_q(x) = f_q(y)).$$

If $x \in X$, then the class of x with respect to θ_Q is written as $Q[x]$, and the set of classes of θ_Q is denoted by K_Q.

If $P, Q \subseteq \Omega$ we call a class X of θ_Q P– *deterministic* (or just *deterministic* if P is understood), if it is contained in a class of θ_P. Each such class induces a rule of the form

$$f_Q(x) = \bar{t} \Rightarrow f_P(x) = \bar{s},$$

where $\bar{t}$ and $\bar{s}$ are the feature vectors of x determined by Q, resp. P.

If $X \in K_Q$ intersects $Y_0, \dots, Y_k \in K_P$, $k > 0$, then we obtain an indeterministic rule

$$f_Q(x) = \bar{t} \Rightarrow f_P(x) = \bar{s}_0 \vee \cdots \vee f_P(x) = \bar{s}_k.$$

We write $Q \to P$ for the conjunction of all deterministic and indeterministic rules obtained this way, and – with some abuse of language – call $Q \to P$ a rule as well. Strictly speaking, we should consider equivalence classes of rules, but we will not do this, as it is clear what we mean.

3.2 Rough Sets and Statistics

While RSDA is a non–numeric method of data analysis, it implicitly makes statistical assumptions which we want to explore in this section. We first review briefly some properties of finite general statistics. A ***probability space*** is a triple $\langle U, B, p\rangle$, where U is a finite non–empty set, B a Boolean subalgebra of $\langle \mathfrak{P}(U), \cap, \cup, -, \emptyset, U\rangle$, and p a probability measure on B, i.e. a function $p : B \to [0, 1]$ which satisfies the Kolmogorov axioms

1. $p(\emptyset) = \emptyset$,
2. $p(U) = 1$,
3. $p\left(\bigcup_{i \in I} X_i\right) = \sum_{i \in I} p(X_i)$, if each $X_i \in B$, and the sets X_i are pairwise disjoint.

If B is a proper subalgebra of $\mathfrak{P}(U)$, then the function p is not defined on all of $\mathfrak{P}(U)$; there are two standard ways to extend p over all of $\mathfrak{P}(U)$, see e.g. [HF92]:

$$p_*(Y) = \sup\{p(X) : X \subseteq Y,\ X \in \mathcal{P}\}, \qquad \text{(Inner measure)} \qquad (1)$$

$$p^*(Y) = \inf\{p(X) : X \supseteq Y,\ X \in \mathcal{P}\}. \qquad \text{(Outer measure)} \qquad (2)$$

Suppose that $\langle U, \theta\rangle$ is an approximation space (i.e. U is a nonempty set and θ an equivalence relation on U), and that $\mathcal{P}$ is the partition associated with θ. The *lower*, resp. *upper approximation* of X by θ is defined by

$$\underline{X}_\theta \stackrel{def}{=} \bigcup\{Y \in \mathcal{P} : Y \subseteq X\},$$

resp.

$$\overline{X}^\theta \stackrel{def}{=} \bigcup\{Y \in \mathcal{P} : Y \cap X \neq \emptyset\}.$$

The metrics of $\langle U, \theta\rangle$ are the two "approximation functions"

$$\gamma_\theta(X) \stackrel{def}{=} \frac{|\underline{X}_\theta| + |\underline{-X}_\theta|}{|U|}, \tag{3}$$

$$\alpha_\theta(X) \stackrel{def}{=} \frac{|\underline{X}_\theta|}{|\overline{X}^\theta|} \text{ (for } X \neq \emptyset), \tag{4}$$

see [Paw91], p. 16ff. If θ is understood, we shall usually omit the subscripts.

Usually, one interprets $\gamma(X)$ as the percentage of objects of U which can be correctly classified with the knowledge given by θ as being in X or not, while $\alpha(X)$ expresses the degree of completeness of our knowledge of X.

We define two associated statistics for $\langle U, \theta \rangle$ by

$$\mu_*(X) \stackrel{def}{=} \frac{|\underline{X}|}{|U|}, \qquad \mu^*(X) \stackrel{def}{=} \frac{|\overline{X}|}{|U|}.$$

It is easy to see that $\mu^*(X) = 1 - \mu_*(-X)$, and

$$\gamma(X) = \mu_*(X) + \mu_*(-X), \qquad \alpha(X) = \frac{\mu_*(X)}{\mu^*(X)},$$

so that we can regard μ_* as the basic measure of RSDA.

For each equivalence θ on U we let B_θ be the subalgebra of $\langle \mathfrak{P}(U), \cap, \cup, -, \emptyset, U \rangle$ whose atoms are the classes of θ. Now, the restriction $\mu_* \upharpoonright B_\theta$ is a probability measure on B whose inner measure is just μ_*, and the measurable sets of $\langle U, B_\theta, \mu_* \upharpoonright B \rangle$ are just the θ–definable sets. Following [HF92], we say that a probability measure p on B_θ is *compatible with* θ, if

$$\mu_*(X) \leq p(X) \leq \mu^*(X),$$

for all $X \in B_\theta$. It is easy to see that the only probability measure on $\mathfrak{P}(U)$ which is compatible to all functions μ_* is given by

$$p(X) = \frac{|X|}{|U|}, \tag{5}$$

so that $p(x) = \frac{1}{|U|}$ for all $x \in U$. In other words, rough set theory assumes the ***random world model*** described in [BGHK94], also called the ***principle of indifference***, where in the absence of further knowledge all basic events are assumed to be equally likely.

Thus, the statistical interpretation of the rough set approach is quite simple:

- *Rough set analysis neglects the underlying joint distributions of the attributes and the reported statistics μ_*, resp. γ, are sufficient only if the joint distributions of the attributes are constant as in* (5).

This sounds like a drawback, but one should note that rough set analysis is applied (and applicable!) in a "few – objects – many – attributes" situation which is very different to the situations usually encountered in statistical modeling. In the field of applied regression analysis it was shown that in comparable situations the assumption "simple is better" – e.g. using 0–1 regression weights – results in more stable estimates than using an approach with many parameters [Coh90].

As a measure of the *quality of an approximation* of a partition $\mathcal{P}$ by a set Q of attributes we define the function $\gamma_Q : Part(U) \to [0,1]$ by

$$\gamma(Q, \mathcal{P}) = \frac{\sum_{X \in \mathcal{P}} |\underline{X}_{\theta_Q}|}{|U|}, \tag{6}$$

thus generalizing γ_θ of (3) to include partitions with more than two classes. In case $\mathcal{P}$ is induced by θ_P for some $P \subseteq \Omega$, we will write $\gamma(Q \to P)$ instead of $\gamma(Q, \mathcal{P})$ to indicate that γ measures the approximation quality of the rule $Q \to P$. It is not hard to see that

$$\gamma(Q \to P) = \frac{|\bigcup\{M \in K_Q : M \text{ is } P \text{ - deterministic}\}|}{|U|}$$

If $\gamma(Q \to P) = 1$, we call P *dependent on* Q, and write $Q \Rightarrow P$. This is the case exactly when $\theta_Q \subseteq \theta_P$.

3.3 Significance Testing

We can use the approximation quality defined in (6) as an internal index of a rule $Q \to P$. If $Q \Rightarrow P$, then the prediction is perfect, otherwise, $\gamma(Q \to P) < 1$. However, a perfect or high approximation quality is not a guarantee that the rule is valid. If, for example, the rough set method discovers a rule $Q \to P$ which is based on only a few observations – which one might call a *casual rule* – the approximation quality of the rule may be due to chance. Thus, the validity of inference rules for prediction must be validated by statistical techniques – otherwise, application beyond attribute reduction in the concrete situation might as well be done by throwing bones into the air and observing their pattern. We are certainly not the first to observe this phenomenon:

> "Consider a dataset in which there is a nominal attribute that uniquely identifies each example ... Using this attribute one can build a 1 – rule that classifies a given training set 100% correctly: needless to say, the rule will not perform well on an independent test set" [Hol93].

Thus, although rough set theory uses a only few parameters which need simple statistical estimation procedures (e.g. the cardinalities of equivalence classes and the associated probability function on its partition), the validity of obtained rules should be controlled using statistical testing procedures, in particular, when they are used for modeling and prediction of events.

[DG97e] have developed two simple procedures, both based on randomization techniques, which evaluate the validity of a rule based on the approximation quality of attributes. These procedures seem to be particularly suitable for the soft computing approach of RSDA since they do not require information from outside the data under consideration; in particular, it is not assumed that the information system under discussion is a representative sample. The reader is invited to consult [Edg87] or [Man91] for the background and justification of randomization techniques in these situations.

Let Σ be the set of all permutations of U, $\sigma \in \Sigma$, and suppose that we want to test the significance of $Q \to P$. We define new information functions $f_r^{\sigma(P)}$ by

$$f_r^{\sigma(P)}(x) \stackrel{def}{=} \begin{cases} f_r(\sigma(x)), & \text{if } r \in P, \\ f_r(x), & \text{otherwise.} \end{cases}$$

The resulting information system $\mathcal{I}_\sigma$ permutes the P–columns according to σ, while leaving the Q–columns constant. We now use the permutation distribution $\{\gamma(Q \to \sigma(P)) : \sigma \in \Sigma\}$ to evaluate the strength of the prediction $Q \to P$. The value $p(\gamma(Q \to P)|H_0)$ measures the extremeness of the observed approximation quality and it is defined by

$$p(\gamma(Q \to P)|H_0) := \frac{|\{\sigma \in \Sigma : \gamma(Q \to \sigma(P)) \geq \gamma(Q \to P)\}|}{|U|!} \tag{7}$$

If $\alpha = p(\gamma(Q \to P)|H_0)$ is low, traditionally below 5%, then the rule $Q \to P$ is deemed significant, and the (statistical) hypothesis "$Q \to P$ is due to chance" can be rejected.

One can see that the procedure is computationally expensive, and that it is not always feasible (or, indeed, possible) to exactly compute α. However, a randomly chosen set of permutations will usually be sufficient: It is known [Dwa57] that the significance level of a randomization test is in a sense exact even when the randomization distribution is only sampled.

In rough set analysis, the decline of the approximation quality when omitting one attribute is normally used to determine whether an attribute within a reduct is of high value for the prediction. However, this view does not take into account that the decline of approximation quality may be due to chance. This observation leads to the following definition: We call an attribute $q \in Q$ *conditional casual*, if there are only a few observations in which the attribute q is needed to predict P. More precisely, the statistical approach is to compare the actual $\gamma(Q \to P)$ with the results of a random system: For each permutation σ of U and each $q \in Q$ we obtain a new information function $f^{\sigma,q}$ by setting

$$f^{\sigma,r}(x) \stackrel{def}{=} \begin{cases} f_r(\sigma(x)), & \text{if } r = q, \\ f_r(x), & \text{otherwise.} \end{cases}$$

The resulting approximation quality of P by Q is denoted by $\gamma(Q, \sigma(q) \to P)$, and we define $p(\gamma(Q, q \to P)|H_0)$ in analogy to (7) and call it the *relative significance* of q within Q.

As above, if $p(\gamma(Q, q \to P)|H_0)$ is below 5%, the assumption of (random) conditional casualness can be rejected, otherwise we will call the attribute *conditional casual within* Q, or just *conditional casual*, if Q is understood.

3.4 Data Filtering

As we seen in the previous section, if the granularity of an information system is high, it may lead to rules which are based on a few observations only, and thus, their validity is doubtful. In this case, the α value will be high, and the rule may be due to chance. Thus, rough set analysis as a conditional method needs a preprocessing step in which unnecessary granularity is removed, but in which no essential (dependency) information is lost. One way to increase the significance is to reduce the granularity of information by using appropriate data filters on the sets V_q, which may reduce the number of classes of θ_Q while at the same time keeping the dependency information.

[DG97d] develop a simple data filtering procedure which is compatible with the rough set approach and which may result in an improved significance of rules.

The main tool are 'binary information systems'. These are those systems, in which every attribute has exactly two values. Roughly speaking, we obtain a binary system $\mathcal{I}^B$ from an information system $\mathcal{I}$ by replacing a non–binary attribute q with a set of attributes, each corresponding to an attribute value of q; the associated information functions have value 1 if and only if x has this value under f_q. In the process of binarization no information is lost; indeed, information is shifted from the columns to the rows.

Strictly speaking, we should distinguish between "symmetric" and "asymmetric" binary attributes, but we shall omit this here for reasons of brevity.

Let us consider $Q \to d$, and choose some $m \in Q$; suppose that m leads to the binary attributes $m_0, \dots, m_r$. For each $t \in \{f_d(x) : x \in U\}$ do the following:

1. Find the binary attributes m_i for which
$$(\forall x \in U)(f_{m_i}(x) = 1 \to f_d(x) = t).$$
If there is no such m_i, go to step 3.
2. Build their union within m in the following sense: If, for example $m_{i_0}, \dots, m_{i_k}$ satisfy the condition above, then we define a new binary attribute $m_{i_0 \dots i_k}$ by
$$f_{m_{i_0 \dots i_k}}(x) = 1 \overset{\text{def}}{\Longleftrightarrow} \max_{j \in \{i_0, \dots, i_k\}} f_{m_j}(x) = 1,$$
and simultaneously replace $m_{i_0}, \dots, m_{i_k}$ by $m_{i_0 \dots i_k}$.
3. Collect the resulting binary attributes in m to arrive at the filtered attribute.

Step 3 aggregates all classes of θ_m (i.e. attribute values) which are totally contained in a class of θ_d.

The main result shows that filtering preserves the dependency structure and may improve the statistical significance of the rule:

Proposition 1. *Let $Q \to P$ be a rule of $\mathcal{I}$ and $Q' \to P$ its filtered version. Then,*

1. $\gamma(Q \to P) = \gamma(Q' \to P)$.
2. $p(\gamma(Q \to P)|H_0) \geq p(\gamma(Q' \to P)|H_0)$.

Details and applications, as well as a proof of Proposition 1, can be found in [DG97d].

It may be worth to point out that this type of filtering is applicable to any type of attribute, and that it does not use any metric information from within the attribute domains. If one is willing to take these into account and also use e.g. genetic algorithms, there are more sophisticated methods available, for example, [SN95], [NNS96], [SP96], or [DG97a] for a purely data driven approach.

3.5 Uncertainty Measures

To compare different rules and/or compare different measures of uncertainty one needs a general framework in which to perform the comparisons. To define an unconditional measure of prediction success one can use the idea of combining program complexity (i.e. to find a deterministic rule) and statistical uncertainty (i.e. a measure of uncertainty within the indeterministic rules) to a global measure of prediction success. The broad idea behind this is the well known approach of *constructive probability* or *Kolmogorov complexity*; we invite the reader to consult [LV93] for a detailed exposition of the theory.

The tool which we use is (information theoretic) entropy: If $\{p_i : i \leq n\}$ is a probability distribution, then its entropy is given by

$$H(p_0, \ldots, p_n) = \sum_{i \leq n} p_i \cdot \log_2 \frac{1}{p_i}.$$

The entropy measures three things [McE77]:

- The amount of information provided by an observation E,
- The uncertainty about E,
- The randomness of E.

The appeal of this approach is that information of uncertainty described by a probability distribution is mapped into a dimension which has its own meaning in terms of size of a computer program, and which has the consequence that

- Effort of the coding the "knowledge" in terms of optimal coding of given rules and
- Consequences of "guessing" in terms of optimal number of decisions to classify a random chosen observation

can be aggregated in the same dimension.

There are several possibilities to describe what is meant by "quality of non–deterministic prediction" in RSDA, and [DG97f] present three different approaches to handle uncertainty of a rule $Q \to P$. Within each approach it has to be made explicit how deterministic rules and guessing should work together to predict a class of θ_P; different models M how to predict such a class, given θ_Q, are then mapped to an entropy value $H_M(Q \to P)$.

Entropy has been discussed in the RSDA context before, e.g. by [WZY86] or [TB92]. However, the class of models studied there is very narrow, which prohibits its use as a general method; furthermore, [DG97e] have shown that the main theoretical result of [WZY86] is incorrect.

In this paper we shall concentrate on the approach closest to the philosophy of RSDA. Let us suppose that U is our set of objects with cardinality n, and let $\mathcal{P}$ be a partition of U with classes $X_i, i \leq k$, each having cardinality r_i. In compliance with the statistical assumption of the rough set model (see Sect. 3.2) we assume that the elements of U are uniformly distributed within the classes of $\mathcal{P}$, so that the probability of an element x being in class X_i is just $\frac{r_i}{n}$. We now define the *entropy* of $\mathcal{P}$ by

$$H(\mathcal{P}) \stackrel{def}{=} \sum_{i=0}^{k} \frac{r_i}{n} \cdot \log_2(\frac{n}{r_i}).$$

If θ is an equivalence relation on U and $\mathcal{P}$ its induced partition, we will also write $H(\theta)$ instead of $H(\mathcal{P})$.

The entropy estimates the mean number of comparisons minimally necessary to retrieve the equivalence class information of a randomly chosen element $x \in U$; we can also think of the entropy of $\mathcal{P}$ as a measure of granularity of the partition.

Suppose that the classes of θ_Q are $X_0, \ldots, X_m$, and that the probability distribution of the classes is given by $\hat{\pi}_i = \frac{|X_i|}{n}$; let $X_0, \ldots X_c$ be the deterministic classes with respect to P, and V be their union.

The approach is based on the pure rough set assumption that we know the world only up to the equivalence classes of θ_Q, and that we admit complete ignorance about what happens "inside" these classes.

Consequently, given a class Y of θ_P, any observation y in the set $Y \setminus V$ is the result of a random process whose characteristics are totally unknown to the researcher; according to the principle of indifference, any element of $U \setminus V$ must be viewed as a realization of a probability distribution with uncertainty $\frac{1}{n}\log_2(n)$. Hence, we use only those classes of θ_Q which are contained in V, and put each $x \in U \setminus V$ is in its own class. In other words, we assume the maximum entropy principle, and look at the equivalence relation θ_Q^+ defined by

$$x \equiv_{\theta_Q^+} y \stackrel{\text{def}}{\Longleftrightarrow} x = y \text{ or there exists some } i \leq c \text{ such that } x, y \in X_i.$$

Its associated probability distribution is given by $\{\hat{\psi}_i : i \leq c + |U \setminus V|\}$ with

$$\hat{\psi}_i \stackrel{def}{=} \begin{cases} \hat{\pi}_i, & \text{if } i \leq c, \\ \frac{1}{n}, & \text{otherwise.} \end{cases} \tag{8}$$

We now define the *entropy of rough prediction* (with respect to $Q \to P$) as

$$H_{\text{rough}}(Q \to P) \stackrel{def}{=} H(\theta_Q^+) = \sum_i \hat{\psi}_i \cdot \log_2(\frac{1}{\hat{\psi}_i}).$$

We choose this type of entropy because of our basic aim to use as few assumptions outside the data as possible:

> "Although there may be many measures μ that are consistent with what we know, the *principle of maximum entropy* suggests that we adopt that μ^* which has the largest entropy among all the possibilities. Using the appropriate definitions, it can be shown that there is a sense in which this μ^* incorporates the 'least' additional information [Jay57]".

We invite the reader to consult [GHK94] (from which the quote above is taken) for more details of the interplay of the principle of indifference and the maximum entropy principle.

There are other possibilities, for example, taking into account the distribution of elements in $Y \setminus V$. It would be outside the scope of this paper to discuss these approaches in detail, and we refer the interested reader to [DG97f].

The entropy of the combined information $Q \cup P$

$$H_{\text{total}}(Q \to P) \stackrel{def}{=} H(Q \cup P).$$

– more traditionally written as $H(Q, P)$ – measures the uncertainty of the overall system. The boundary of both entropy measures is given by

$$H(P) \leq H_{\text{rough}}(Q \to P), H_{\text{total}}(Q \to P) \leq \log_2(|U|).$$

A measure $H_{\text{rough}}(Q \to P)$ near $H(P)$ is favourable, since little or no additional information is needed to code the prediction attributes Q. If $H_{\text{rough}}(Q \to P)$ is close to $\log_2(|U|)$, the worst case in terms of entropy is met.

In order to normalize the outcome of the uncertainty estimation we transform the measures to *normalized overall information* (NOI) and *normalized rough information* (NRI) by the functions

$$\text{NOI}(Q \to P) \stackrel{def}{=} 1 - \frac{H_{\text{total}}(Q \to P) - H(P)}{\log_2(|U|) - H(P)},$$

$$\text{NRI}(Q \to P) \stackrel{def}{=} 1 - \frac{H_{\text{rough}}(Q \to P) - H(P)}{\log_2(|U|) - H(P)}.$$

If both normalized measures have a value near 1, the chosen attribute combination is favourable, whereas a value near 0 indicates casualness. Note, that the normalization does not use moving standards as long as we do not change the decision attribute P. Therefore, any comparison of NOI or NRI values between different predicting attribute sets given a fixed set of decision attributes is feasible. The normalized rough information is always smaller than the normalized overall information. Big differences between both indicate that the local structure within Q determines indeterministically much of the local structure within P.

A discussion of where the approximation quality γ can be located within this context can be found in [DG97f].

4 Rough Set Analysis of IRIS Data

Several earlier studies compare statistical techniques such as discriminant analysis with RSDA [KBSS92, KSS92, TB92]. Their result can be summarized to the claim that RSDA and statistical techniques offer similar approaches. If so, RSDA would be the method of choice, because RSDA is a "soft" data analysis method, which does not assume structural information outside the data.

One may have reservations about this claim:

- An attribute with continuous values usually cannot be used by RSDA in its pure original form, whereas discriminant analysis is based on the interpretation of metric information within the data. Therefore, discriminant analysis uses more details within the data for the price of using a "hard" dimensional data representation as an underpinning.
- RSDA needs a fixed number of equivalence classes within any attribute. If we use data with continuous metric information, the number of equivalence classes of the raw data may be as high as the number of objects under study. Hence, if we like to result in statistically stable rules, a preprocessing stage (which we call *filtering*) has to be performed before data can be analysed. Although a filter procedure is a precondition to perform a reliable RSDA using continuous metric attributes, a "dependency preserving" filtering procedure was not included in the previous studies.

In the next subsections we will show how the IRIS data are processed by the traditional RSDA approach, and discuss the filtering of the IRIS data used in [TB92].

4.1 Pure RSDA Description of IRIS Data

RSDA starts by finding (global) dependency information, i.e. computation of reducts and core, as well as the rules of the information system under review. The ranges and the number of classes of each attribute are given in Tab. 4

The full IRIS data set has each three element set of attributes as a reduct, and thus, it has an empty core. This indicates a high substitution rate among the attributes. The approximation qualities of the nonempty attribute sets are given in Tab. 5. We see that petal length (A3) has a high classification quality, followed by petal width (A4). Together, they can account for 98% of all cases.

Using all four dependent attributes, Grobian has found a total of 243 rules. We give the 58 deterministic rules for single petal attributes in Tab. 6.

Table 4. IRIS - Unfiltered Data

Attribute	Interval	No of classes
Sepal length:	[43,79]	35
Sepal width:	[20,44]	23
Petal length:	[10,69]	43
Petal width:	[1,25]	22

Table 5. Approximation Qualities

Attributes	γ	Attributes	γ
A1, A2, A3	1.00	A2, A3	0.97
A1, A2, A4	1.00	A2, A4	0.94
A1, A3, A4	1.00	A3, A4	0.98
A2, A3, A4	1.00	A1	0.21
A1, A2	0.85	A2	0.13
A1, A3	0.97	A3	0.82
A1, A4	0.94	A4	0.73

4.2 A Previous RSDA Analysis of IRIS Data

In the rough set context, the IRIS data have been explored by [TB92] with a data filtering displayed in Tab. 7. The resulting system does not explain the data, since $\gamma(\{A1, A2, A3, A4\} \rightarrow \text{D}) = 0.77$. If we compare this result with the 96% reclassification success of discriminant analysis using two attributes only (Tab. 3), the result does not look favorable for RSDA, if this is the best such data analysis can offer. The original unfiltered data show that $\gamma(\{A3, A4\} \rightarrow D) = 0.98$, so that the low approximation quality is only due to the filtering.

The attribute sets $\{A3, A4\}$ and $\{A1, A2, A4\}$ have an approximation quality of $\gamma = 0.75$, resp. $\gamma = 0.72$; thus, it seems that these sets should have been considered in the data analysis as well. If one is prepared to accept an approximation quality of $\gamma = 0.77$ with four features, it is surely acceptable to eliminate two of these in return for a drop in the approximation quality of only 0.02.

In order to show that the attribute set $\{A3, A4\}$ is the optimal combination, we can compare the uncertainty measures of the attribute sets

$$\{A1, A2, A3, A4\}, \{A1, A2, A4\}, \{A3, A4\},$$

see Tab. 8. The results show that the petal attributes are by far preferred, and that in terms of uncertainty measure the complete set of attributes is the worst.

[TB92] offer, among others, the following conclusions to their work:

"The three main advantages of rough sets theory are

- its very clear interpretation for the user,
- its independence to any statistical assumptions,
- its efficiency and its rapidity."

Table 6. IRIS Rules, Petal Attributes (Unfiltered Full Set)

Rule	Instances	Rule	Instances	Rule	Instances
A3=14 ⇒ D=1	13	A3=37 ⇒ D=2	1	A3=69 ⇒ D=3	1
A3=10 ⇒ D=1	1	A3=43 ⇒ D=2	2	A3=63 ⇒ D=3	1
A3=17 ⇒ D=1	4	A3=30 ⇒ D=2	1	A4=2 ⇒ D=1	29
A3=13 ⇒ D=1	7	A3=36 ⇒ D=2	1	A4=3 ⇒ D=1	7
A3=16 ⇒ D=1	7	A3=50 ⇒ D=3	4	A4=5 ⇒ D=1	1
A3=19 ⇒ D=1	2	A3=56 ⇒ D=3	6	A4=1 ⇒ D=1	5
A3=12 ⇒ D=1	2	A3=52 ⇒ D=3	2	A4=6 ⇒ D=1	1
A3=11 ⇒ D=1	1	A3=55 ⇒ D=3	3	A4=4 ⇒ D=1	7
A3=15 ⇒ D=1	13	A3=59 ⇒ D=3	2	A4=11 ⇒ D=2	3
A3=46 ⇒ D=2	3	A3=54 ⇒ D=3	2	A4=13 ⇒ D=2	13
A3=48 ⇒ D=2	2	A3=67 ⇒ D=3	2	A4=12 ⇒ D=2	5
A3=39 ⇒ D=2	3	A3=57 ⇒ D=3	3	A4=10 ⇒ D=2	7
A3=47 ⇒ D=2	5	A3=66 ⇒ D=3	1	A4=17 ⇒ D=3	2
A3=40 ⇒ D=2	5	A3=53 ⇒ D=3	1	A4=22 ⇒ D=3	3
A3=38 ⇒ D=2	1	A3=64 ⇒ D=3	1	A4=24 ⇒ D=3	3
A3=44 ⇒ D=2	4	A3=60 ⇒ D=3	2	A4=23 ⇒ D=3	8
A3=33 ⇒ D=2	2	A3=48 ⇒ D=3	2	A4=20 ⇒ D=3	6
A3=41 ⇒ D=2	3	A3=61 ⇒ D=3	3	A4=25 ⇒ D=3	3
A3=35 ⇒ D=2	2	A3=58 ⇒ D=3	3	A4=21 ⇒ D=3	6
A3=42 ⇒ D=2	4				

Table 7. Data Filtering of [TB92]

	Very small (1)	Small (2)	Large (3)	Very large (4)
Sepal length	$x < 50$	$50 \leq x < 60$	$60 \leq x < 70$	$70 \leq x$
Sepal width	$x < 24$	$24 \leq x < 31$	$31 \leq x < 38$	$38 \leq x$
Petal length	$x < 30$	$30 \leq x < 40$	$40 \leq x < 55$	$55 \leq x$
Petal width	$x < 10$	$10 \leq x < 14$	$14 \leq x < 21$	$21 \leq x$

We are somewhat more skeptical. Even though the basis of RSDA consists of a very simple mathematical model which is clearly understandable, the interpretation of results is not always all that clear; we believe that e.g. the considerations of Sect. 3.3 regarding the statistical validation of rough set rules show that care has to be taken when interpreting the results of a rough set data analysis, and that the results are by no means always clear and straightforward.

The rough set model is not independent of any statistical assumptions. Even

Table 8. Entropy Values

Q	$H(Q)$	$H(Q,D)$	NOI	NRI
$\{A1, A2, A3, A4\}$	4.416	4.621	0.462	0.362
$\{A1, A2, A4\}$	4.023	4.290	0.520	0.392
$\{A3, A4\}$	2.520	2.763	0.791	0.607

though it requires no (exterior) prior probabilities it has an underlying statistical model as shown in Sect. 3.2.

In view of the fact that for example minimal reduct search is NP hard, it seems hardly justified to claim efficiency and rapidity for RSDA except for very small databases. Having said this, one should mention that heuristic tools for reduct finding have been developed, for example [Wro95] or [BK97]. On the other hand, these methods need assumptions outside the data at hand, which we are trying to avoid.

5 Rough Information Analysis of IRIS Data

5.1 Data Filtering

We have used the procedure outlined in Sect. 3.4 to obtain the data conversions given in Tab. 9; there, the choice of a value is irrelevant. We also list the resulting number of classes, and in brackets as a reminder the number of classes of the unfiltered data. Observe the dramatic fall in the number of classes of the petal attributes. We shall use this filtering for all subsequent computations, unless indicated otherwise.

Table 9. Rough Filtering

Attribute	Filter	No of classes
Sepal length:	43–48, 53 → 46	22 (35)
	66,70 → 70	
	71–79 → 77	
Sepal width:	35, 37, 39–44 → 35	16 (23)
	20, 24 → 24	
Petal length:	10–19 → 14	8 (43)
	30–44,46,47 → 46	
	50, 52, 54–69 → 50	
Petal width:	1–6 → 2	8 (22)
	10–13 → 11	
	17, 20–25 → 17	

5.2 Significance

We found that no attribute set $\emptyset \neq Q \subseteq \{A1, A2, A3, A4\}$ was casual with respect to D. The values of relative significances is given in Tab. 10. The results clearly indicate that the combination (A3, A4) is the best choice to describe the IRIS data in terms of rules. Whereas any other combination of attributes contains at most one attribute which is not conditional casual, A3 and A4 show significant (0.004), resp. marginally significant (0.063) test results of the hypothesis of conditional casualness.

Table 10. Relative Significance

Attributes	A1	A2	A3	A4
A1, A2, A3, A4	1.00	1.00	1.00	1.00
A1, A2, A3	0.901	0.862	0.604	
A1, A2, A4	0.843	0.710		0.336
A1, A3, A4	0.944		0.857	0.857
A2, A3, A4		0.860	0.843	0.790
A1, A2	0.127	0.213		
A1, A3	0.874		0.001	
A1, A4	0.727			0.213
A2,A3		0.814	0.001	
A2,A4		0.884		0.001
A3, A4			0.004	0.063

5.3 Uncertainty Measures

The entropy values are given in Tab. 11. Observe that in case $Q \Rightarrow D$, we have of course $H(Q) = H(Q, D)$, since there is no unexplained information, and also NOI = NRI.

Table 11. Entropy Values (Filtered)

Q	$H(Q)$	$H(Q,D)$	NOI	NRI
Reducts				
$\{A2, A3, A4\}$	5.683	5.683	0.274	0.274
$\{A1, A3, A4\}$	5.657	5.657	0.279	0.279
$\{A1, A2, A3\}$	6.683	6.683	0.097	0.097
$\{A1, A2, A4\}$	6.724	6.724	0.090	0.090
Non − reducts				
$\{A1, A2\}$	6.500	6.644	0.104	0.094
$\{A1, A3\}$	5.310	5.337	0.335	0.335
$\{A1, A4\}$	5.492	5.550	0.297	0.294
$\{A2, A3\}$	5.340	5.371	0.329	0.326
$\{A2, A4\}$	5.400	5.459	0.314	0.311
$\{A3, A4\}$	3.285	3.303	0.696	0.693
$\{A1\}$	4.314	5.020	0.391	0.139
$\{A2\}$	3.759	4.818	0.427	0.694
$\{A3\}$	2.358	2.488	0.840	0.780
$\{A4\}$	2.562	2.722	0.799	0.674

The remarks above concerning significance are reflected in the results of the entropy values of Tab. 11. Large values for NOI and NRI are recorded for attribute sets $\{A3\}$, $\{A4\}$, and $\{A3, A4\}$, with corresponding low values for H(Q) and H(Q,D).

Attribute A2 records a high value for NOI, with corresponding values for H(Q) and H(Q,D) being about average. Perhaps this indicates A2's rank in ability to distinguish between the species, i.e., not as good as A3 or A4 but better than A1. It is interesting to note that the reducts of the full information system perform badly on both entropy results and relative significance.

To summarize the NOI/NRI analysis, both unconditional measures vote for $A3$ – and if we want to predict more objects for the price of a small decrease in information – the prediction set $\{A3, A4\}$. Any other combination of two or more attributes is by far too crude in terms of NOI/NRI.

5.4 Rules

Rough filtering not only reduces the number of classes and increases the significance of rules, it also reduces the number of rules. Using all four independent attributes, Grobian has found 118 deterministic rules. The 6 deterministic rules for the petal attributes alone are given in Tab. 12, as well as some other rules which make make up the whole data set.

Table 12. Some IRIS Rules (Filtered Full Set)

Rule	Instances
A3=14 ⇒ D=1	50
A4=2 ⇒ D=1	50
A3=46 ⇒ D=2	37
A4=11 ⇒ D=2	28
A3=45, A4=15 ⇒ D=2	5
A1=60, A4=16 ⇒ D=2	2
A2=32, A3=48 ⇒ D=2	1
A3=49, A4=15 ⇒ D=2	2
A3=53, A4=19 ⇒ D=2	1
A1=68, A4=14 ⇒ D=2	1
A3=50 ⇒ D=3	36
A4=17 ⇒ D=3	31
A3=51, A4=15 ⇒ D=3	1
A3=51, A4=19 ⇒ D=3	2
A2=30, A4=18 ⇒ D=3	4
A3=49, A4=18 ⇒ D=3	2
A1=62, A4=18 ⇒ D=3	2

The class *Setosa* needs only one prediction rule (A3 = 14 or A4 = 2), and it is obvious that it is rather different from the other two. The class *Virginica* is fairly well explained: The (filtered) values A3 = 50 or A4 = 17 explain 42 instances of *Virginica*. There is only one object which needs an A1-based rule, and there are only four objects that need an A2-based rule.

The class *Versicolor* causes difficulties. The rules "(A3 = 53, A4 = 19) $\Rightarrow$ D = 2", and "(A3 = 51, A4 = 19) $\Rightarrow$ D = 3" have no frame of interpretation because of their "closeness". Observe that none of the occurring values is filtered.

5.5 ROUGHIAN Prediction of IRIS Data

In machine learning, a common procedure to test the accuracy of the prediction value of a rule set is done in the following way:

1. Split the data into a *training set* and a *testing set.*
2. Learn a rule set in the training set.
3. Measure the accuracy of the rule set (in the given theoretical system) in the testing set.

Repeat this procedure about twenty times and find the mean and standard deviation of the obtained values.

We have followed this procedure to find out the prediction quality of the filtered data set for certain attribute sets. To this end, we have generated twenty random partitions of the whole data set into two equally sized classes of 75 specimen each. We then have filtered the training set and, with this filtering, computed the approximation quality of the attribute sets

$$\{A3, A4\}, \{A1, A3, A4\}, \{A2, A3, A4\}$$

on the testing set, and the α–value of (4) for each species. We have also tested on the whole data set whether the random partition is conditional casual for the attribute set under consideration, i.e. whether we can assume that the partition is really random. The mean and the standard deviation of the resulting sequences of values can be found in Tab. 13. The results show that the filter derived from

Table 13. Means and Standard Deviations of the 20 IRIS Files for γ, α for Each Species, and the Relative Significance of the Random Variable

	γ		α, Setosa		α, Versicolor		α, Virginica		Rel. signif.	
Attributes	Mean	Std.dev.	Mean	Std.dev.	Mean	Std.dev.	Mean	Std.dev.	Mean	Std.dev.
A1,A3,A4	0.972	0.028	1	0	0.791	0.130	0.797	0.157	0.685	0.347
A2,A3,A4	0.992	0.014	1	0	0.818	0.119	0.780	0.151	0.863	0.275
A3,A4	0.896	0.088	1	0	0.613	0.138	0.602	0.167	0.329	0.358

the first half of the data can be used in principle in the second half of the data set. The prediction quality is about as high as in the overall data analysis (see Table 5). A further check of the admissibility of the filter procedure is presented in the last two columns of Table 13: The training set / testing set coding should have no influence on the prediction in the overall system given the filter of the training set; hence, the random variable should be conditional casual. As the last two columns of Table 13 indicate, we cannot observe a significant influence of the random variable to the overall prediction success.

RSDA faces a problem which is common to every structural data analysis: There may be observations within the testing set which cannot be expressed by a rule extracted from the training set, simply because this rule does not occur in the training situation. To solve this problem, [SS92] adopt metric information about the data in their 'ROUGHCLASS' approach to compute the best 'nearby' rule(s) which can be used for prediction. Although this approach is not in line with the original soft computing aims of the RSDA (since one has to enter external assumptions about the data), we are forced to use a similar approach, because – up to now – no non–invasive data analysis counterpart for the classification problem is at hand.

Our validation using the "training - testing - set" paradigm runs as follows:

- Initialize 9 counters $N(P|D)$, where D is true value of the specimen in the testing set, and P is the predicted value of the specimen from rules of the training set.
- For each of the 20 training sets do
    - Compute the filter rules based on the 4 predicting attributes and the specimen decision attribute.
    - Compute the rules based on petal length and petal width within the training set based on the respective filter.
    - Apply the filter derived from the training set to the testing set objects.
    - For every object of the testing set do
        * Compute those rules which have the same *minimal* Euclidean distance to the current (petal length, petal width) combination.
        * Choose one of these rules with minimal distance randomly, and use the value of the decision attribute of the chosen rule as the prediction P for the testing object under study.
        * Increase the counter $N(P|D)$ by 1.
- Normalize each counter $N(P|D)$ by $N(.|D) = N(1|D) + N(2|D) + N(3|D)$ resulting in $\hat{p}(P|D) = \frac{N(P|D)}{N(.|D)}$.

Table 14 shows the result of the RSDA validation procedure. Whereas Setosa is captured perfectly, the error rates of the classification of Versicolor and Virginica in the testing set are between are 8% and 9%.

Table 14. Mean Prediction Quality Using Rough Analysis (Half Sample Prediction)

Predicted class	Classes in the testing set		
	Setosa	Versicolor	Virginica
Setosa	1.000	0.000	0.000
Versicolor	0.000	0.914	0.080
Virginica	0.000	0.086	0.920

With the same simulation procedure, but using discriminant analysis instead, we see in Table 15 that discriminant analysis outperforms RSDA by about additional 2% correct predictions.

Table 15. Mean Prediction Quality Using Discriminant Analysis

Predicted class	Classes in the testing set		
	Setosa	Versicolor	Virginica
Setosa	1.000	0.000	0.000
Versicolor	0.000	0.940	0.069
Virginica	0.000	0.060	0.931

It should be noted that the jack–knife ("leave-one-out") validation results in more optimistic estimations of prediction success (Tab. 16), and these probabilities are comparable to those of the discriminant analysis. [KBSS92] use a

Table 16. Mean Prediction Quality Using Rough Analysis (Jack-knife Validation)

Predicted class	Classes given in data		
	Setosa	Versicolor	Virginica
Setosa	1.000	0.000	0.000
Versicolor	0.000	0.939	0.071
Virginica	0.000	0.061	0.929

jack–knife procedure for validation, and thus, the goodness of the RSDA classification compared to DA may be overestimated and should be taken with care. Furthermore, all their attributes are conditional casual, which indicates a large inhomogencity of the data, and one could conclude that the sample size is too small to allow a reliable prediction.

The dependency of the prediction success on the chosen validation method seems to be a disadvantage of the RSDA. If we compare the jack-knife approach with the half sample prediction, we observe that the number of rules generated by RSDA tends to be smaller in case of the half sample prediction. Because sometimes essential rules may be missing, a misclassification will occur, and the prediction quality will decrease. In case of discriminant analysis, a smaller number of subjects will only decrease the precision of estimators, and will not decrease the number of structural parameters as in case of RSDA.

6 Conclusion

We have performed a traditional RSDA analysis of Fisher's IRIS data, and supplemented it with the ROUGHIAN procedures *data filtering, significance testing, and uncertainty measures.*

Given a measurement situation like in the case of the IRIS data, which is a standard one for performing discriminant analysis, there is a need for reducing the granularity of the predicting attributes. Categorization by researchers may be suboptimal in terms of approximation quality of the filtered attributes, as e.g. the results of [TB92] indicate. The data filtering procedure offers a method to reduce the granularity of the data, which does not change the prediction success of the attribute under study.

Significance testing is necessary for a decision whether the rules derived from an information system are more than just rules generated by a random process (casualness) or whether part of the rules can be explained by chance (conditional casualness) respectively. Classical approaches of RSDA usually overfit the data by using either casual systems or an abundance of conditional casual attributes. It turns out that the increase in rule significance obtained by our filtering procedure makes ROUGHIAN a viable data description method even in those cases where DA seems to be the method of choice. We argue that this result could not have been obtained by RSDA alone since the γ statistics as a measure of "determinacy" does not generally suffice to evaluate the quality of rules. For example, in the unfiltered system, the relative significance of $A3$ and $A4$ in $\{A3, A4\}$ with 1000 simulations is 0.621, resp. 0.516 – thus, both attributes are conditional casual – , but in the filtered system only 0.004, resp. 0.063.

We have shown that the combination of filtering and significance testing achieved the same combination of variables in which the DA resulted, with about the same coverage in terms of posterior probabilities.

Using the significance and entropy procedures as additional information providers significantly simplifies model selection within RSDA, and justifies the appropriate choice.

Using the IRIS data set, we have shown that prediction using the ROUGHIAN model is nearly as good as that of discriminant analysis, even though

- ROUGHIAN does not use the metric information of the data set, except that rules "nearby" have to be evaluated,
- ROUGHIAN does not assume an underlying linear model within the data,
- ROUGHIAN does not make any homogeneity or spatial distributional assumption,

in contrast to the discriminant analysis.

However, the problem of the dependency of the prediction success on the choice of the validation method is a problem which should not be underestimated, and should be investigated further.

References

[BGHK94] F. Bacchus, A. J. Grove, J. Y. Halpern, and D. Koller: From statistical knowledge bases to degrees of belief. Technical report 9855, IBM (1994)

[BK97] Anders Torvill Bjorvand and Jan Komorowski: Practical applications of genetic algorithms for efficient reduct computation. Proc. 15th IMACS World Congress, Berlin (1997) (to appear)

[Bro97] Ciarán Browne: Enhanced rough set data analysis of the Pima Indian diabetes data. Proc. 8th Ireland Conference on Artificial Intelligence (1997) (to appear)

[Coh90] Jacob Cohen: Things I have learned (so far). American Psychologist **45** (1990) 1304–1312

[DG96] Ivo Düntsch, Günther Gediga: The rough set model for data analysis – introduction and overview (preprint). `http://www.infj.ulst.ac.uk/~cccz23/papers/roughmod.html`(August 1996)

[DG97a] Ivo Düntsch, Günther Gediga: Relation restricted prediction analysis. Proc. 15th IMACS World Congress , Berlin (1997)(to appear) `http://www.infj.ulst.ac.uk/~cccz23/papers/ordg.html`

[DG97b] Ivo Düntsch, Günther Gediga: The rough set engine GROBIAN. Proc. 15th IMACS World Congress, Berlin (August 1997)(to appear) `http://www.infj.ulst.ac.uk/~cccz23/papers/grobian.html`

[DG97c] Ivo Düntsch, Günther Gediga: Roughian – Rough information analysis, an introduction. Technical report, University of Ulster, `http://www.infj.ulst.ac.uk/~cccz23/papers/roughian.html`(1997) Extended abstract to appear in: Proc. 15th IMACS World Congress, Berlin

[DG97d] Ivo Düntsch, Günther Gediga: Simple data filtering in rough set systems. International Journal of Approximate Reasoning (1997) (to appear) `http://www.infj.ulst.ac.uk/~cccz23/papers/bininf.html`

[DG97e] Ivo Düntsch, Günther Gediga: Statistical evaluation of rough set dependency analysis. International Journal of Human–Computer Studies **46** (1997) 589–604 `http://www.infj.ulst.ac.uk/~cccz23/papers/rougheva.html`

[DG97f] Ivo Düntsch, Günther Gediga: Uncertainty measures of rough set prediction (manuscript) (1997) `http://www.infj.ulst.ac.uk/~cccz23/papers/rmml.html`

[DGR97] Ivo Düntsch, Günther Gediga and Joseph Rogner: Archetypal psychiatric patients: an application of rough information analysis. Preprint, Fachbereich Psychologie, Universität Osnabrück (1997)

[Dwa57] M. Dwass: Modified randomization tests for non-parametric hypothesis. Annals of Mathematical Statistics **28** (1957) 181–187

[Edg87] Eugene S. Edgington: Randomization tests, statistics. Textbooks and Monographs **31** Marcel Dekker, New York and Basel 1987

[Fis36] R. A. Fisher: The use of multiple measurements in taxonomic problems. Ann. Eugen. **7** (1936) 179–188

[GHK94] A. J. Grove, J. Y. Halpern and D. Koller: Random worlds and maximum entropy. Journal of AI Research **2** (1994) 33–88

[HF92] Joseph Y. Halpern and Ronald Fagin: Two views of belief: belief as generalized probability and belief as evidence. Artificial Intelligence **54** (1992) 275–317

[Hol93] Robert C. Holte: Very simple classification rules perform well on most commonly used datasets. Machine Learning **11** (1993) 63–91

[Jay57] E.T. Jaynes: Information theory and statistical mechanics. Physical Review bf106 (1957) 620–630

[KBSS92] E. Krusińska, Ankica Babic, Roman Słowiński, and J. Stefanowski: Comparison of the rough sets approach and probabilistic data analysis techniques on a common set of medical data. In: Intelligent decision support: Handbook of applications and advances of rough set theory [Sło92] 251–265

[KSS92] E. Krusińska, Roman Słowiński, and J. Stefanowski: Discriminant versus rough set approach to vague data. Appl. Stochastic Models and Data Analysis bf8 (1992) 43–56

[LC97] T. Y. Lin, N. Cercone (eds.): Rough sets and data mining, Kluwer Academic Publishers, Boston (1997)

[LV93] Ming Li and Paul Vitányi: An introduction to Kolmogorov complexity and its applications. Springer–Verlag, Berlin (1993)

[Man91] B. F. J. Manly: Randomization and Monte Carlo methods in Biology. Chapman and Hall, London (1991)

[McE77] Robert J. McEliece: The theory of information and coding. Encyclopedia of Mathematics and its Applications **3** Addison–Wesley, Reading (1977)

[NNS96] H. S Nguyen, S. H. Nguyen and A. Skowron: Searching for features defined by hyperplanes. Preprint, Institute of Mathematics, Warsaw University (1996)

[Paw82] Zdzisław Pawlak: Rough sets. Internat. J. Comput. Inform. Sci. bf11 (1982) 341–356

[Paw91] Zdzisław Pawlak: Rough sets: theoretical aspects of reasoning about data. Kluwer Academic Publishers, Dordrecht (1991)

[Sło92] Roman Słowiński: Intelligent decision support: Handbook of applications and advances of rough set theory. Kluwer Academic Publishers, Dordrecht (1992)

[SN95] A. Skowron and H. S. Nguyen: Quantization of real value attributes. Proc. of the Second Joint Annual Conference on Information Sciences, North Carolina (September 1995) 34–37

[SP96] Andrzej Skowron and Lech Polkowski: Analytic morphology: Mathematical morphology of decision tables. Fund. Inform. **27** (1996) 255–271

[SS92] Roman Słowiński and Jerzy Stefanowski: ROUGHDAS and ROUGHCLASS software implementations of the rough sets approach. In: Intelligent decision support: Handbook of applications and advances of rough set theory, [Sło92] 445–456

[TB92] Jacques Teghem and Mohammed Benjelloun: Some experiments to compare rough sets theory and ordinal statistical methods, In: Intelligent decision support: Handbook of applications and advances of rough set theory, [Sło92] 267–284

[Wro95] Jakub Wroblewski: Finding minimal reducts using genetic algorithms. ICS Research Report 16, Warsaw University of Technology (1995)

[WZY86] S. K. M. Wong, Wojciech Ziarko and R. Li Ye: Comparison of rough–set and statistical methods in inductive learning. Internat. J. Man–Mach. Stud. **24** (1986) 53–72

Chapter 20

Applications of Rough Patterns

Pawan Lingras

Algoma University College
Sault Ste. Marie, Ontario, P6A 2G4, Canada

Abstract. This paper discusses the notion of rough patterns and its potential applications. Rough patterns consist of a sequence of rough values. A rough value is defined using an upper and a lower bound. Rough values can be used to effectively represent a range or a set of values of variables. This paper summarizes three different experiments that demonstrate the use of rough patterns in neurocomputing. Fuzzy values are also shown to provide potentially useful complement to the rough values.

1 Introduction

Many decisions in real life are based on projected upper and lower bounds of values of certain important parameters. Some of the examples include: daily high and low temperatures; range of rain fall; high and low traffic volumes; high and low values of stocks or stock market indices. Interval calculus provides an ability to deal with an interval of numbers. A rough value can be used to represent an interval or a set of values, where only the upper and lower bounds of the values are used in the computations. Many of the mathematical operations on rough values are borrowed from interval calculus. The scope of interval calculus is broader than rough values which form the focus of this study. A rough pattern consisting of rough values has several semantic and computational advantages in many analytical applications.

Any computation done using rough values can also be rewritten in the form of conventional numbers. However, the use of rough values provide a better semantic interpretation of results in terms of upper and lower bounds. Moreover, some of the numeric computations cannot be conceptualized without explicitly discussing the upper and lower bound framework. This is analogous to many other techniques in computer science. For example, a heap sort can be written simply in terms of array manipulations. However, it is difficult to understand heap sort without discussing the concept of binary tree and its special case called heap. It would have been even more difficult to derive the heap sort algorithm by limiting visualization exclusively to array operations. Object oriented programming is another example which shows importance of appropriate semantics. Any object oriented program can also be written in a procedural programming language. But object oriented technology makes it easier to design, implement and analyze programs.

This paper describes three different experiments [Li1, Li2, Li3] which demonstrate the advantages of rough computations. The experiments are limited to neuro-computing. The neural networks used in this study consist of rough and neofuzzy neurons in addition to conventional neurons. Rough neurons provide an ability to use rough patterns. Each rough neuron stores the upper and lower bounds of the input and output values. Depending upon the nature of the application, two rough neurons in the network can be connected to each other using either two or four connections. A rough neuron can also be connected to a conventional neuron using two connections. Neofuzzy neurons transform crisp input to fuzzy membership functions which are then forwarded to conventional neurons for further processing. A neofuzzy neuron essentially classifies a given input into various categories and also provides fuzzy membership for each category. Addition of such fuzzy semantics has been shown to improve the performance of a conventional neural network [NGL].

The first experiment uses rough Kohonen neural networks for classification of rough patterns. The classification obtained using rough patterns is more meaningful than average patterns. The rough Kohonen networks can be reformulated using conventional Kohonen networks. However, rough patterns are helpful in the design of the network and the analysis of the results. The next experiment illustrates the estimation of an important highway traffic parameter using rough neural networks. As the rough neural networks become increasingly complex, one can see the advantages of using rough computing over the conventional computing in the design of the neural networks. The final experiment uses a combination of rough and neofuzzy neurons in the time series analysis of highway traffic volumes.

The purpose of the experiments described in this study is not to propose better methods for solving these particular problems. Even though in all cases rough computing provided better results over the conventional computing, the models used in the experiments were too simplistic to make any concrete recommendations. Instead the paper argues the semantic advantages of using rough values in the design of analytical models. The variety of experiments can also be seen as an evidence of the breadth of possible applications of rough values. The combination of rough and fuzzy values used in the study also provides further support for continued study of rough values.

Section 2 introduces the notions of rough and neofuzzy neurons used in the experiments which are described in subsequent sections. Section 3 illustrates the use of rough patterns in classification. Section 4 uses rough patterns for predictions based on rough neurons. Combination of rough and neofuzzy neurons for the time series analysis is described in section 5. Section 6 contains a discussion on other possible applications of rough patterns. Summary and conclusions appear in section 7.

2 Neural Networks with Rough and Neofuzzy Extensions

In its most general form, an artificial neural network is a collection of neurons connected to each other. The nature of connections and data exchange through the connections depend upon the application. Researchers have introduced different semantic interpretations that assist in the design of an artificial neural network [He1]. This section describes two complementary types of neurons, namely, rough neurons [Li1] and neo-fuzzy neurons [NGL]. A combination of conventional, rough and neofuzzy can be used to introduce semantic structures in a neural network.

2.1 Rough Neurons

In a rough pattern, the value of each variable is specified using the upper and lower bound for the value. A conventional pattern can be easily represented as a rough pattern by specifying both upper and lower bounds to be equal to the value of the variable. The rough values can be added as:

$x + y = (\overline{x} + \overline{y}, \underline{x} + \underline{y})$,

where x and y are rough values given by pairs $(\overline{x}, \underline{x})$ and $(\overline{y}, \underline{y})$, respectively. A rough value x can be multiplied by a number c as:

$c \times y = (c \times \overline{x}, c \times \underline{x})$.

Note that these operations are borrowed from the conventional interval calculus. As mentioned before, a rough value is used to represent an interval or a set of values, where only the upper and lower bounds are considered relevant in the computation.

A rough neuron r can be viewed as a pair of neurons, one for the upper bound called *upper neuron* ($\overline{r}$) and the other for the lower bound called *lower neuron* ($\underline{r}$). A rough neuron is connected to another rough neuron through two or four connections. Fig. 1 depicts three types of connections between rough neurons. The overlap between the upper and lower neurons indicates that upper and lower neurons exchange information. Two rough neurons in Fig. 1(a) are *fully connected.* A rough neuron r is said to be *fully connected* to another rough neuron s, if $\overline{r}$ and $\underline{r}$ are connected to both $\overline{s}$ and $\underline{s}$. If a rough neuron r is fully connected to s, then there are four connections from r to s. In Fig. 1(b) and Fig. 1(c), there are only two connections from r to s. If the rough neuron r *excites* the activity of s (i.e. increase in the output of r will result in the increase in the output of s), then r will be connected to s as shown in Fig. 1(b). On the other hand, if r *inhibits* the activity of s (i.e. increase in the output of r corresponds to the decrease in the output of s), then r will be connected to s as shown in Fig. 1(c).

The input and output of rough neurons depend upon the application. Only restriction on the output of the rough neuron is that the output of the upper neuron will be consistently larger than the lower neuron. The input of a conventional, lower, or upper neuron is calculated using the weighted sum as:

$$input_i = \sum_{\text{there is a connection from j to i}} w_{ji} \times output_j \qquad (1)$$

Fig. 1. Connections between rough neurons

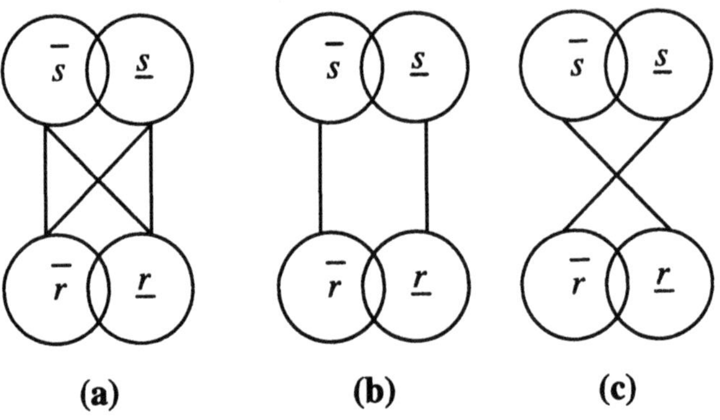

Fig. 2. A neofuzzy neuron

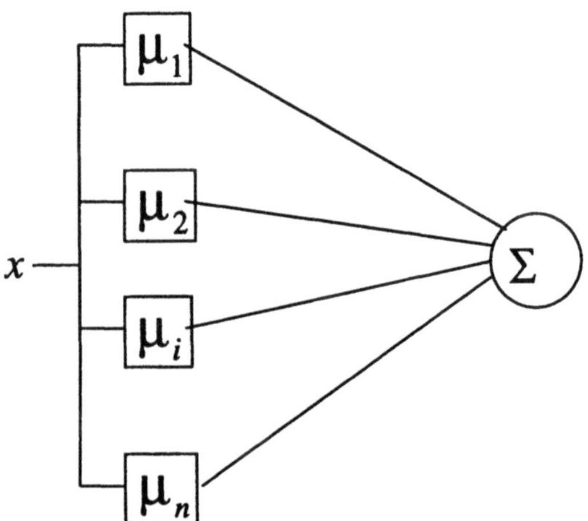

where i and j are either the conventional neurons or upper/lower neurons of a rough neuron. The outputs of a rough neuron r are calculated using a transfer function, t, as:

$$output_{\overline{r}} = max(t(input_{\overline{r}}), t(input_{\underline{r}})) \quad (2)$$

$$output_{\underline{r}} = min(t(input_{\overline{r}}), t(input_{\underline{r}})) \quad (3)$$

If two rough neurons are partially connected, then the excitatory or inhibitory nature of the connection is determined dynamically by polling the connection weights. The network designer can make initial assumptions about the excitatory or inhibitory nature of the connections. If a partial connection from a rough neuron r to another rough neuron s is assumed to be excitatory and weights of both the connections are negative, then the connection from r to s is changed from excitatory to inhibitory. On the other hand, if r is assumed to have an inhibitory partial connection to s and weights of both the connections are positive, then the connection from r to s is changed from inhibitory to excitatory.

2.2 Neofuzzy Neurons

The structure of a neofuzzy neuron [NGL] is depicted in Fig. 2. A crisp input x is partitioned into n fuzzy segments using membership functions $\mu_1, \ldots, \mu_n$. The membership functions are then used to calculate the defuzzified weighted sum. A neofuzzy neuron can be added to a conventional neural network. The weights $w_1, \ldots, w_n$ are modified using a conventional learning rule such as the generalized delta rule. The fuzzy segments in neofuzzy neurons are based on semantic interpretations of the input and can generally be used only in the input layer. Neofuzzy neurons can be easily implemented by preprocessing the input pattern to add fuzzy segments as additional input values. The modified input pattern can then be used with a conventional neural network.

3 Classification using rough patterns

Many of the existing classification methods represent an object with a single precise pattern. However, some of the objects in real life are more complex, and hence, do not lend themselves well to such a simple abstract representation. These complex objects may in general be represented by multiple types of patterns. Moreover, there may be several instances of a given type of pattern.

An example of such an object is a highway section. It is necessary to classify highway sections into different types of categories to establish guidelines regarding their upgrading and maintenance. Highways need to be classified on the basis of trip purpose and trip length into classes such as commuter, business, long distance, and recreational. Traffic volume patterns are used as surrogates for the trip purpose and trip length characteristics. Some of the important traffic patterns include hourly, daily, and monthly traffic patterns

For the purpose of classification, each highway section needs to be represented using three different types of patterns mentioned above. Moreover, for each highway section there are several patterns of each type. For example, if one year data is used for classification, there will be one monthly pattern, 52 daily patterns, and 365 hourly patterns for a given highway section.

This section describes rough Kohonen neural network classifiers [Li2] for the classification of complex objects represented by rough patterns. Similar to the Kohonen neural networks, the rough Kohonen neural networks use unsupervised learning during the classification process. In unsupervised learning, the desired output from the neurons is not known. The network attempts to classify patterns from the training set into different groups. Rough Kohonen neural networks use rough neurons in the input layers.

Traffic volume data used in the study consist of five year traffic volumes collected at various permanent traffic counter (PTC) sites in the province of Alberta, Canada. The objective of the experiment is to classify highway sections based on daily volume patterns over a week in the months of July and December. Months of July and December are chosen because these two months generally have significantly different travel patterns.

The Kohonen networks used in this study consist of two layers. The first layer is called the input layer and the second layer is called the Kohonen layer. If an input pattern belongs to the ith group, then i^{th} neuron in the Kohonen layer has a output value of one and other Kohonen layer neurons have output values of zero.

The conventional model has seven input neurons and five output neurons. Neurons in the input layer are fully connected to neurons in the output layer. The input to the conventional neural network model consists of average weekly pattern, i.e. average daily volumes on Sundays, Mondays, Tuesdays, ..., Saturdays for an object. The output is the class in which the object would be classified.

The rough neural network model has seven rough input neurons and five output neurons. Rough neurons in the input layer are fully connected to conventional neurons in the output layer. The input to the rough neural network model consists of rough weekly pattern, i.e. upper and lower bounds of daily volumes on Sundays, Mondays, Tuesdays, ..., Saturdays for an object. The output is the class in which the object would be classified. Since the output is a unique value, the output layer used conventional neurons.

Each connection is assigned a weight g_i. Weights of all the connections to a Kohonen layer neuron make up a k-dimensional weight vector $\mathbf{g}$. The weight vector $\mathbf{g}$ for a Kohonen layer neuron is the vector representation of the group corresponding to that neuron. For any input vector $\mathbf{z}$, the network compares the input with the weight vector for a group using the measure $E(\mathbf{g}, \mathbf{z})$ given by:

$$E(\mathbf{g}, \mathbf{z}) = \frac{\sum_{j=1}^{k} distance(g_j, z_j)}{k}, \tag{4}$$

where g_j and z_j are j^{th} components of the vectors $\mathbf{g}$ and $\mathbf{z}$, respectively. The function *distance* provides the distance between two values of the jth component of the two vectors as:

$$distance(g_j, z_j) = (g_j - z_j)^2 \tag{5}$$

The pattern $\mathbf{z}$ belongs to the group with minimum value for $E(\mathbf{g}, \mathbf{z})$. The Kohonen neural network generates the groups through a learning process as follows. Initially, the network connections are assigned somewhat arbitrary weights. The training set of input vectors is presented to the network several times. For each iteration the group weight vector $\mathbf{g}$ that is closest to the pattern $\mathbf{z}$ is modified using the equation:

$$\mathbf{g}_{new} = \mathbf{g}_{old} + \alpha(t) \times \mathbf{z}, \tag{6}$$

where $\alpha(t)$ is a learning factor which starts with a high value at the beginning of the training process and is gradually reduced as a function of time.

Fig. 3 shows patterns for the five groups obtained from the conventional Kohonen neural network. Fig. 4 shows rough patterns obtained from the Kohonen neural network with rough neurons. The group labels in both classifications are adjusted for comparison. Highway sections in groups obtained from rough and conventional patterns are somewhat different. The conventional grouping uses only the day to day variation of traffic volume, while the rough pattern classification takes into account the daily and seasonal variations. The rough pattern classification provides more meaningful characterization of classes. For example, the first group in Fig. 4 has high weekend traffic and high seasonal variation. This corresponds to recreational use of the road. The second group, on the other hand, has low weekend traffic and low seasonal variation indicating predominant work related or commuter traffic. Group 5 has average daily pattern similar to group 1 but low seasonal variation as shown by the rough patterns. This distinction between group 1 and group 5 is not obvious with the average traffic patterns. Group 3 and group 4 both have similar average daily patterns. The rough patterns indicate that group 4 has more seasonal variation on Sunday suggesting optional Sunday trips depending upon the season. Again, the use of rough patterns enable us to see the distinction between group 3 and group 4. The rough traffic patterns seem to provide a reasonable solution for accommodating two different types of temporal variations. In this experiment, the rough Kohonen neural network successfully used two different types of variations, namely the daily and the seasonal traffic variations. A more detailed study of the results from a traffic analyst's point of view is necessary.

4 Predicting parameters using rough patterns

The neural networks have shown to be more effective than the existing methods for estimation of traffic parameters such as the Design Hourly Volume (DHV) for a highway section [LA1]. This section outlines the rough and conventional neural network models used in the study to predict the DHV. The hourly traffic volumes for the entire year were sorted and the thirtieth highest hourly volume was used as the DHV. For all the highway sections in the experiment, the DHV is known.

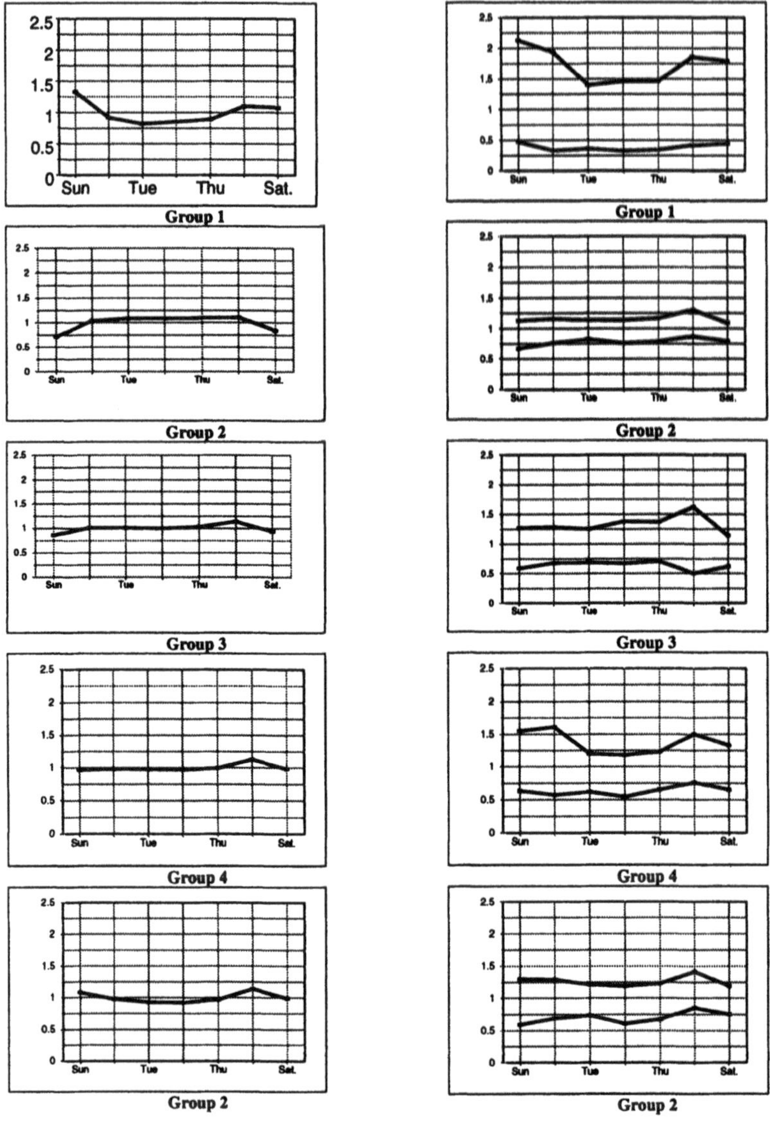

Fig. 3. Average Group Patterns

Fig. 4. Rough Group Patterns

The objective of the experiment is to estimate the DHV based on daily volume patterns over a week in the months of July and December. These predictions are useful for estimating DHV from short term traffic volume counts [LA1]. Months of July and December were chosen because these two months generally have significantly different travel patterns.

Fig. 5 shows the conventional neural network model used for the estimation. The conventional model has seven input neurons, four hidden layer neurons and one output neuron. Neurons in the input layer are fully connected to neurons in the hidden layer. Neurons in the hidden layer are fully connected to the neuron in the output layer. The input to the conventional neural network model consists of average weekly pattern, i.e. average daily volumes on Sundays, Mondays, Tuesdays, ..., Saturdays for an object. The output is the DHV for the object. The first rough neural network model shown in Fig. 6 has seven rough input neurons, eight hidden layer conventional neurons, and one output neuron. Rough neurons in the input layer are fully connected to conventional neurons in the hidden layer. Conventional neurons in the hidden layer are fully connected to the conventional neuron in the output layer. Since the hidden and output layer neurons are conventional neurons, this network can be easily implemented using existing neural network packages such as Stuttgart Neural Network Simulator (SNNS) [Ze1].

The second rough neural network model shown in Fig. 7 has seven rough input neurons, and four hidden layer rough neurons and one output neuron. Rough neurons in the input layer are fully connected to rough neurons in the hidden layer. Rough neurons in the hidden layer are fully connected to the conventional neuron in the output layer. The rough network shown in Fig. 7 can also be implemented using SNNS. However it was necessary to add two activation functions to implement eq. (2) and eq. (3). The input to both the rough neural network models consists of rough weekly pattern, i.e. upper and lower bounds of daily volumes on Sundays, Mondays, Tuesdays, ..., Saturdays for an object. The output is the DHV for the object. Since the output is a unique value, the output layer for both the models used a conventional neuron.

Fig. 8 shows reduction of errors during the training process for all the three networks. The reduction in errors is more dramatic for rough neural networks than the conventional network. The first rough neural network with conventional neurons in the hidden layer results in somewhat higher errors than the second rough neural network which uses rough neurons in the hidden layer. This indicates that the use of rough neurons in place of conventional neurons wherever possible may improve the performance of the neural network.

5 Time series analysis using rough values

The modeling of traffic volume time series is important for prediction of traffic volumes in the immediate future. Such predictions will have applications in Intelligent Vehicle Highway Systems (IVHS). The main objective of the experiment in this section is to demonstrate the semantic structures that can be introduced

Fig. 5. Conventional neural network model for estimation of DHV

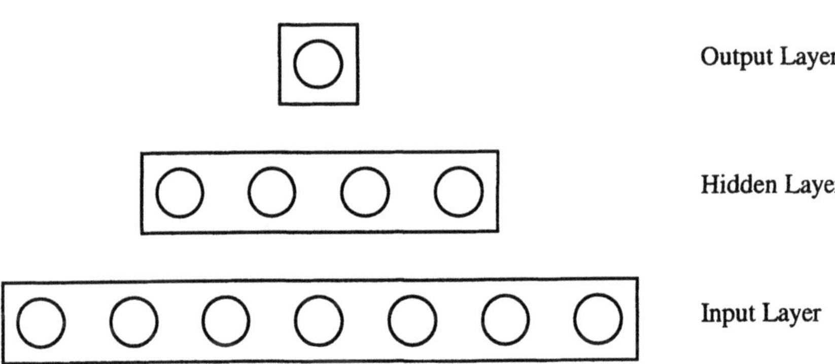

Fig. 6. Rough neural network model with conventional neurons in the hidden layer for estimation of DHV

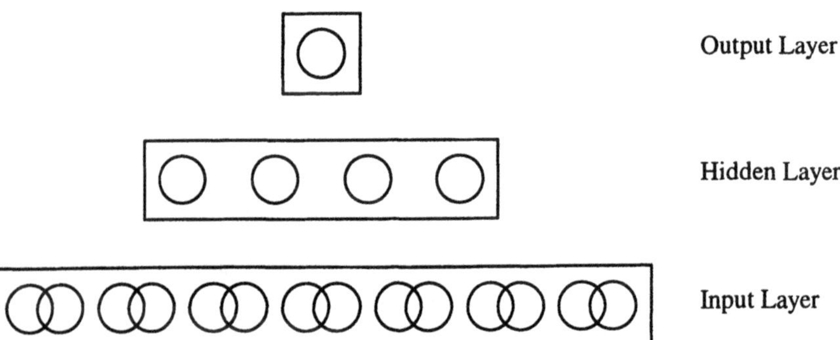

Fig. 7. Rough neural network model with rough neurons in hidden layer for estimation of DHV

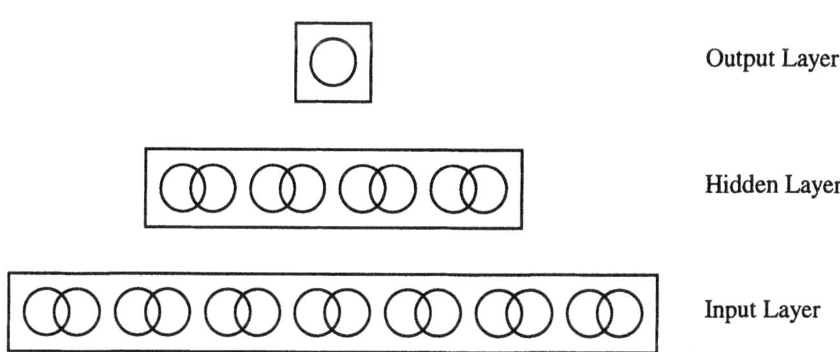

Fig. 8. Reduction of errors during training for estimation of DHV

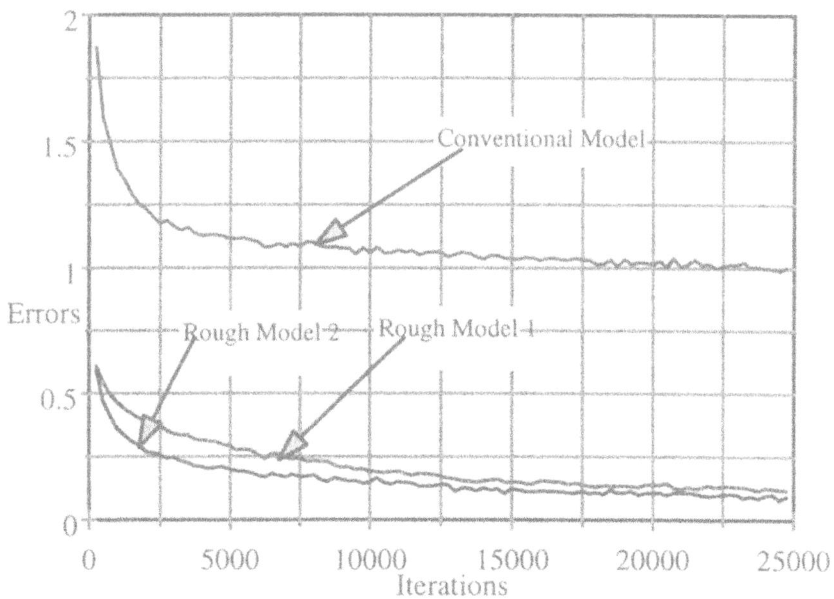

by rough and neofuzzy neurons. This section outlines the three different neural network models used in the experiment.

Traffic volume data used in the study consisted of five year traffic volumes collected at a permanent traffic counter (PTC) site on a urban highway section north of Calgary, Alberta, Canada. The PTC site collects data for every hour in a given year. Modeling of hourly traffic volumes can be useful for the prediction of the future demand in intelligent vehicle highway systems. However, such a modeling is computationally expensive. Recently, Lingras and Osborne [LO1] used daily traffic volumes for studying the characteristics of traffic flow time series. This study uses the same time series for the illustration of rough and neofuzzy computing. Based on Lingras and Osborne's experiments, previous thirteen daily traffic volumes were used as input to predict the current daily traffic volume.

The conventional neural network model, shown in Fig. 9, has thirteen input neurons, seven hidden layer neurons and one output neuron. Neurons in the input layer are fully connected to neurons in the hidden layer. Neurons in the hidden layer are fully connected to the neuron in the output layer. The conventional model is modified by the introduction of a rough neuron. Weekly variations in the traffic volume are affected by seasons as well as special events such as holidays. Such effects should be explicitly taken into account during the modeling process. This study used an additional rough neuron in an intermediate layer between input and hidden layer as shown in Fig. 10. The rough neuron r accepts all the inputs from the input layer. The upper neuron $\overline{r}$ sends out the maximum value of the inputs. The minimum value of the inputs is the output of the lower neuron $\underline{r}$. The outputs from upper and lower neurons are sent to a conventional neuron c. The output of the conventional neuron is a function of the output from the rough neuron:

$$output_c = \frac{output_{\overline{r}} - output_{\underline{r}}}{average(output_{\overline{r}}, output_{\underline{r}})} \tag{7}$$

The above function uses the difference between outputs of upper and lower neurons and normalizes it by the average of the outputs of upper and lower neurons. Such a function may provide a reasonable indication of the fluctuation between the daily volumes in previous two weeks. In addition to the output from the input layer neurons, $output_c$ is sent to the hidden layer. In the third model the crisp value $output_c$ is sent as input to the neofuzzy extension as shown in Fig. 11. The crisp value is partitioned into 3 fuzzy segments called *high fluctuation*, *medium fluctuation* and *low fluctuation* using the membership functions shown in Fig. 12. The output in the form of membership values from the fuzzy segments is sent to the hidden layer along with the output from the input layer neurons. Fig. 13 shows reduction of errors during the training process for all the three networks. The error goes down with the progressive additions of rough and fuzzy components. It should perhaps be emphasized that this experiment demonstrates how rough and neofuzzy components can be used to add semantic structures. The enhanced model described here is not meant to be the final solution to the modeling of daily traffic volume time series.

Fig. 9. Conventional neural network model for traffic volume time series analysis

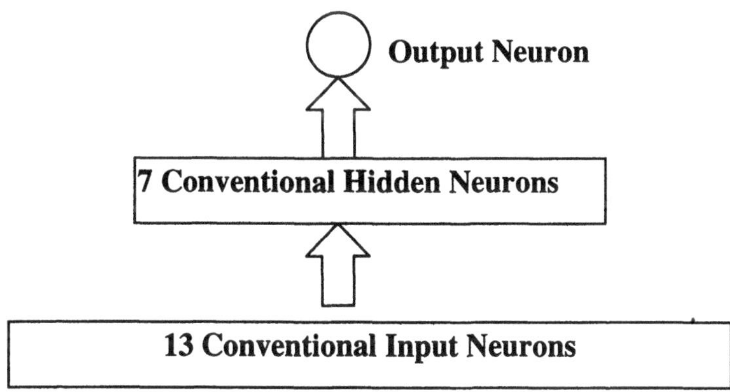

Fig. 10. Neural network model with a rough neuron for traffic volume time series analysis

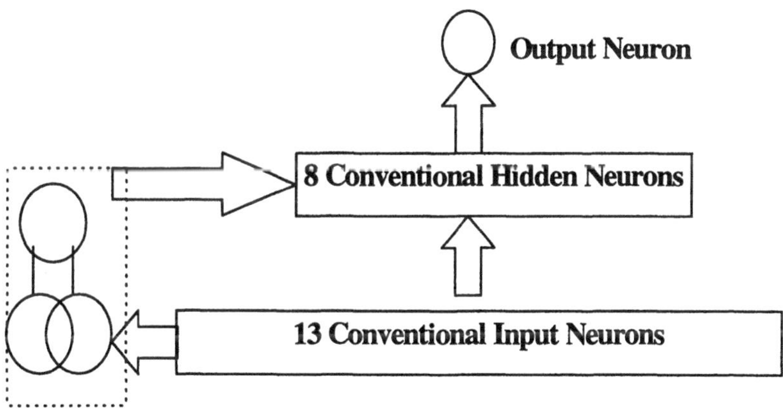

Fig. 11. Neural network model with a rough neuron and a neofuzzy neuron

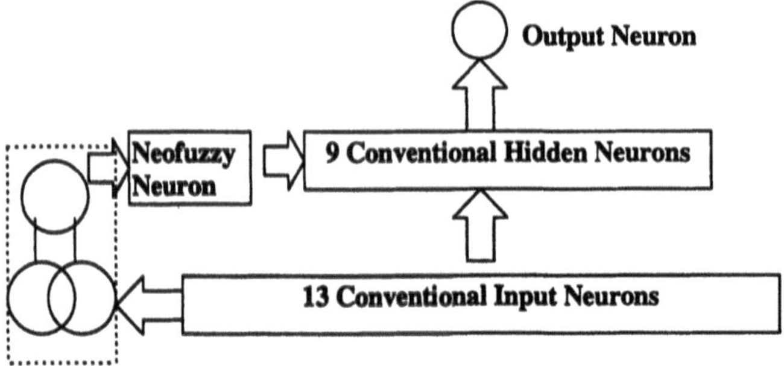

Fig. 12. Membership function for the neofuzzy neuron

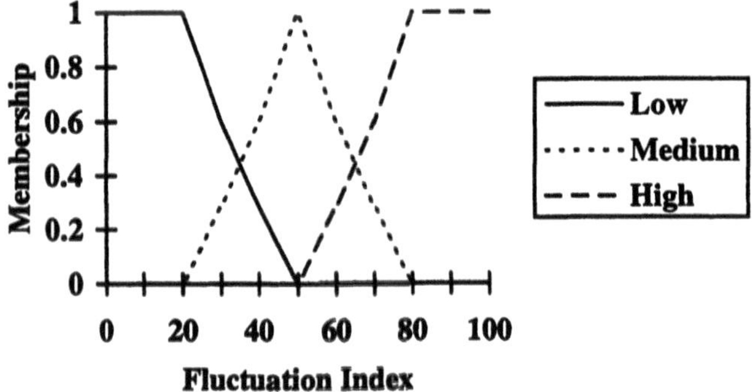

Fig. 13. Reduction of errors during the training for traffic volume time series analysis

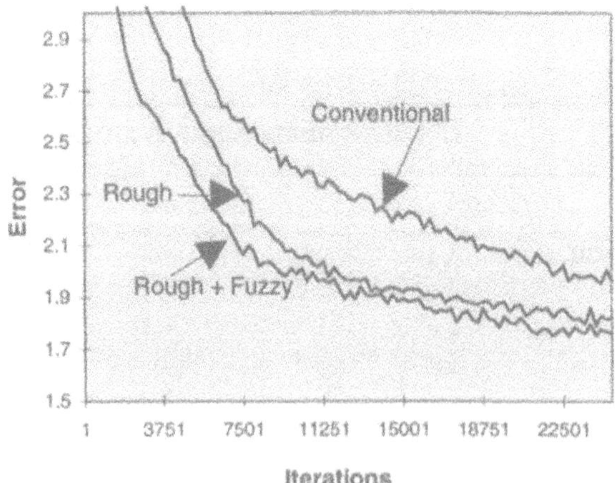

6 Discussion

Previous three sections illustrate usefulness of rough values in classification, prediction, and time series analysis. The experiments described in this study represent only a small portion of potential applications of rough values.

The classification of highway sections using rough patterns provides a mechanism for introducing a third dimension in the representation of a temporal series. The average weekly traffic pattern used in the study is essentially two dimensional and represents the weekly variations of traffic volumes. The rough pattern enables us to introduce the seasonal variation as a third dimension. Note that the actual implementation of the rough Kohonen classifier can be rewritten in terms of a conventional Kohonen classifier with twice as many variables, one for the upper bound and one for the lower bound. The use of rough patterns, however, makes it easy to visualize the design and analyze the results.

The prediction of design hourly volume (DHV) is used to illustrate the use of rough values instead of single precise values as inputs to a neural network. Similar to the rough Kohonen classifier, the first rough neural network can be simply implemented as a conventional neural network with twice as many input neurons. The advantage of using rough neural network is mainly in the design phase of the model. The second rough neural network for estimating DHV uses rough neurons in the hidden layer. This neural network model is significantly different from traditional neural networks. Its design cannot be easily justified or implemented based on conventional neural network terminology. If a neural network is going to use rough input and output variables, it seems natural to use rough neurons in the hidden layer. Such a network may have superior training performance, because the network always gets the higher value from an upper neuron and the smaller value from the corresponding lower neuron.

The last experiment showed how an existing model can be enhanced with the use of a rough neuron. The model was further extended using a neofuzzy neuron. The rough extension was used to explicitly consider the fluctuations in the value of a variable in the time series analysis. The neofuzzy enhancement was used to classify the fluctuations in different fuzzy segments. The rough and neofuzzy enhancements also demonstrate that these two concepts are complementary.

Financial and weather time series analyses are two other major areas of applications for rough and neofuzzy neuro computing. The range and fluctuations in the values are as important as the closing prices of stocks and stock market indices. The range of values can be accommodated using rough neurons while fluctuations can be incorporated using neofuzzy neurons. Similar comments can also be made about the weather data. Variables such as daily temperature cannot be represented using a single value. The normal practice is to represent daily temperatures by a rough value using upper and lower bounds, i.e. daily high's and low's. A fuzzy measure of difference between upper and lower bounds of the temperature can also play an important role in the prediction of next day's temperature.

The interval calculus provides a rich set of operations that can be beneficial to further development of rough computing. The concept of upper and lower bounds features in some of the statistical analysis, especially in financial applications. A comprehensive framework for rough and neofuzzy computations will enable systematic development of tools and techniques that can be used in a wide ranging applications.

7 Summary and Conclusions

This paper describes the notion of a rough value to represent an interval or a set of values. Three experiments presented in the paper demonstrate the versatility of the rough patterns in wide ranging areas of applications. Classification using rough patterns allows an analyst to use a third dimension in an object representation. Predictions using rough values incorporates more information in the estimation compared to the use of average values. Rough and neofuzzy extensions make it possible to consider fluctuations in the values of a variable during time series analysis. In some cases, rough computations result in significantly different design and implementation. But in all cases, rough patterns provide a better semantic view of the model design and analysis of results.

References

[He1] Hecht-Nielsen, R.: Neurocomputing. Addison-Wesley Publishing, Reading MA (1990)

[Li1] Lingras, P. J.: Rough neural networks. In: Proceedings of Sixth International Conference on Information Processing and Management of Uncertainty in Knowledge-Based Systems, Granada, Spain (1996) 1445–1450

[Li2] Lingras, P. J.: Unsupervised learning using rough Kohonen neural network classifiers. Proceedings of Symposium on Modelling, Analysis and Simulation, CESA'96 IMACS Multiconference, Lille, France, July 9-12 (1996) 753–757

[Li3] Lingras, P. J.: Comparison of neofuzzy and rough neural networks. Proceedings of the Fifth international Workshop on Rough Sets and Soft Computing (RSSC'97) in the Third Joint Conference on Information Sciences, Durham NC (March 1997)

[LA1] Lingras, P. J. and Adamo, M.: Average and peak traffic volumes: neural nets, regression, factor approaches. Journal of Computing in Civil Engineering, American Society of Civil Engineers. **10** (1996) 300–306

[LO1] Lingras, P.J., Osborne P. : Linearity in daily traffic volume time series. The Proceedings of Annual Conference of Canadian Society of Civil Engineers, Sherbrooke, Quebec (June 1995) (to appear)

[NGL] Nunes, W., Gomide F. and Loureiro, R.: Recurrent learning of neofuzzy neural models. Proceedings of the Sixth International Conference on Information Processing and Management of Uncertainty in Knowledge-Based Systems, Granada, Spain (1996) 1025–1030

[Ze1] Zell, et al.: Stuttgart neural network simulator. User Manual Version 4.0, University of Stuttgart, Institute of Parallel and Distributed High Performance Systems, Report **6/95** (1995)

Chapter 21

Time and Clock Information Systems: Concepts and Roughly Fuzzy Petri Net Models

James F. Peters III

Computational Intelligence Laboratory, Department of Electrical and Computer Engineering, University of Manitoba, Winnipeg, R3T 3E2, Canada

Abstract. Based on observations concerning time and its measurement, approximate time windows are introduced relative to vaguely known partitions of temporal intervals. Time window measurements are defined relative to durations between firings of transitions in Petri nets. The vagueness of the partitions of a time window stems from a lack of crisp knowledge of deadlines imposed on the activities (tasks) performed by agents.To model the construction of information system tables leading to approximate knowledge of observations extracted from time windows, a new class of fuzzy Petri nets is introduced, namely, roughly fuzzy Petri nets. In the context of approximate time windows for monitoring the time consumed by agents performing time-constrained tasks, roughly fuzzy Petri net models of clock representation systems are given. Several sample information system tables and approximations with rough sets are also given. A sample decision system is also constructed relative to fuzzy aggregations of observed durations. Our approach is based on the rough sets method of constructing decision systems and recent work on modeling clocks with fuzzy sets.
Keywords. Approximate, clock, discernibility, fuzzy sets, information system, Petri nets, rough sets, time.

1 Introduction

The rough sets approach to decision systems, especially in the context of real-time decision-making and the representation of decisions with Petri nets, has been investigated in [51, 57, 58]. There is some justification to revisit the issue of constructing decision tables for real-time decision-making due to the lack of crisp knowledge concerning time bounds imposed on tasks performed by agents. It is also obvious that there is considerable interest in modeling decision-making with Petri nets. It should be observed that the notion of a time window in measuring durations between firings of transitions of a Petri net has recently been introduced [29]. It therefore seems appropriate to consider a new form of time window with approximated partitions. Hence, approximate time windows are introduced. Rough set as well as fuzzy set views of durations taken from approximate time windows are considered. Decision-making tables can then be constructed relative to observations extracted from approximate time windows.

With the introduction of approximate time windows, the problem of modeling information processing systems based on fuzzy interpretations of durations needs to be considered. Fuzzy Petri nets have been introduced to process fuzzy data. Such nets have gained interest as models of computing with uncertainty. There are a number of generalizations of Petri nets documented in the literature. Many of these generalizations are geared toward knowledge representation and uncertainty processing [2]-[8], [12, 13, 18, 22, 31], [33]-[37], [47]-[49]. A rough sets approach to modeling real-time decision-making in the context of approximate time windows has led to the introduction of roughly fuzzy Petri nets. These nets combine rough sets and fuzzy sets in modeling processes designed to extract decisions based on observations from approximate time windows. Our approach is based on the rough sets approach to decision systems [2, 51, 52], [54]-[58] and recent work on reasoning about real-time systems [37]-[43]. The paper is structured as follows. In Section 2, the basic notions concerning time, clocks, time windows, and process modeling with Petri nets are introduced. A rough sets approach to time windows is explored in Section 3. Rough sets and fuzzy sets are combined in roughly fuzzy Petri nets in Section 4. The calibration of fuzzy Petri nets and a rough sets approach to extracting decision rules are also briefly covered in the context of clock representation systems in Section 4. Finally, roughly fuzzy Petri nets are extended in Section 5 to make it possible to model processes which compute rough fuzzy sets.

2 Time Windows

Time is commonly viewed as an interval between successive events or acts [24]. In this article, time is identified with the duration between firings of (not necessarily successive) transitions of a process. Knowledge concerning the duration between transitions in a process tends to be vague, imprecise. Clocks are commonly viewed as instruments for measuring time [24]. We are interested in measuring time consumed by an agent relative to a deadline (the maximum time allowed for an agent to complete a task). An agent is modeled as a discrete event system capable of communicating with other agents and its environment as in [20, 38]. Agents communicate with each other over hidden channels. The most precious resource which agents manage is time. Accordingly, every agent which is not atomic has at least one subagent which is a clock. In the context of state-transition systems used to model agents, time itself is viewed as the state of clocks [30]. Time consumption by an agent is measured with various forms of clocks. It is assumed that agent clocks measure local time and that time itself will vary depending on the interval being measured. This is in keeping with the view that time is a directly measurable quantity, which is closely related to the interval in which it is measured [23]. The time between events is identified with the time ticked off by a clock which passes through both events. This contrasts with the view that time is present equally everywhere and with all things [1].

In measuring time between transitions in a process, a clock is limited to measuring time relative to a what is known as a time window (see Fig. 1). To set up a time window, two articulations are necessary. First, the size of the time window must be articulated. Let $t0$, $t1$ be identified with the instants when transitions (with the same names) are observed to fire. Second, atomic judgments identifiable with readings relative to times between t_0 and t_1 boundaries of a time window must be articulated. Let t be a reading of a clock measuring the duration between t_0 and t_1.

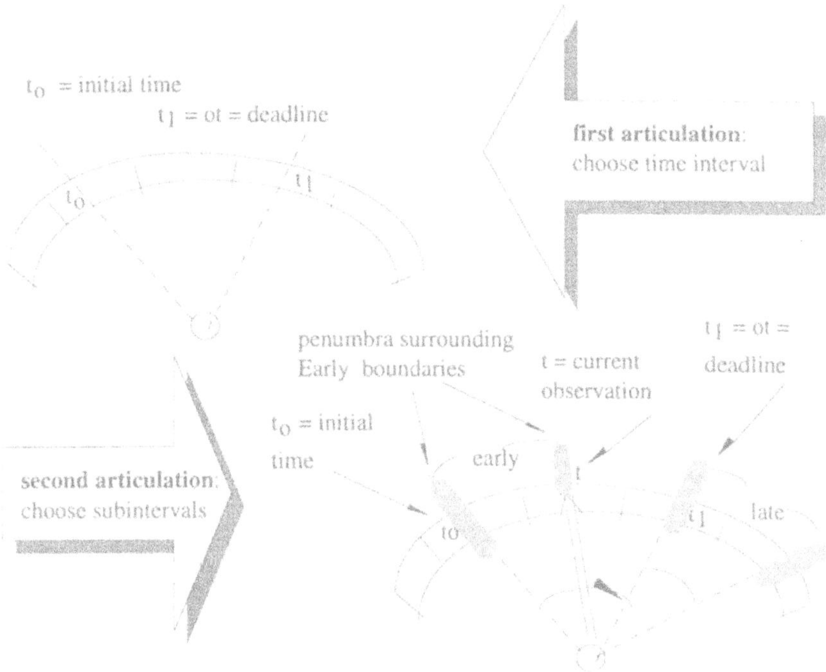

Fig. 1. Partition of time window

Axiom of Time Measurement [29]. Timings are a set of atomic judgments $= \{time\ t | t_0 < t < t_1\}$, where t_0 and t_1 belong to one articulation, and time t belongs to another articulation.

In addition, there is some motivation for partitioning time into subintervals. This partition is partly motivated by the perception of a process by an observer while waiting for an event. In the words of Heidegger, the 'until then' gets divided up by a number of 'from-then-till-thens' [14]. Let *ot* be a time limit (maximum allowed duration) for an agent to complete its task and be "on time". Durations in a time window can then be partitioned relative to deadline *ot*, namely, durations like ve, e, ot, l, and vl for very early, early, ontime, late, and very late, respectively (see Fig 1). In arriving at each of these partitions, there is vagueness (a certain "roughness") concerning the boundaries of these partitions. This is due not so much to a subjective view of time expressed in observations like the perception of earliness in 'What early philosophic hours he keeps' (Cowper, 1781) or lateness in 'My late spring no bud or blossom shewth' (Milton, 1631). Rather, roughness of the boundaries in time window partitions stems from a lack of knowledge of exactly when an event will occur in the case where a designer of a time window estimates when an event will be early or on time or late. As a result, there is what might be described as a penumbra (shadow region, an overlapping) at the boundaries. Such a penumbra is associated with vagueness in our knowledge [45]. In other words, our knowledge near partition boundaries of a time window is not crisp. Hence the design of clocks which take into account the vagueness of knowledge about the temporal performance of agents is aided by approximations provided by soft sets. A soft set is a non-crisp set such as a fuzzy set or rough set used in characterizing approximate knowledge of objects in a universe of discourse. The term soft set was introduced by Pawlak [25]. Membership of an element in a soft set is measured by a characteristic function which returns a value in the interval $[0, 1]$. By contrast, in a crisp set (from set theory introduced by G. Cantor in 1874) an element either belongs or does not belong to the set. The characteristic function for a crisp set returns a value in $\{0, 1\}$. The structure in Fig. 1 can be described as an approximate time window, since measurements of time derived from these windows are approximate rather than crisp. In addition, our knowledge of these measurements can be assessed with soft sets.

2.1 Process Modeling with Petri Nets

Petri nets were introduced in 1962 by Petri to describe and analyze the structure and information flow in systems containing concurrent processes [21, 28]. A Petri Net is a structure (P, T, I, O, F, W, M_o) where P is a finite set of places; T, a finite set of transitions; mapping $I : T \rightarrow P$ to a collection of input places; mapping $O : T \rightarrow P$ to a collection of output places; arcs $F \subseteq (P \times T) \cup (T \times P)$; weight function $W : F \rightarrow \{1, 2, \ldots\}$; and initial marking $M_o : P \rightarrow \{0, 1, 2, \ldots\}$. A marking is an assignment of tokens to places of a net. A token represents a typeless fragment of information. A black dot • symbolizes a single token. Tokens are used to define the execution of a Petri net. Places represent storage for input or for output. Transitions represent activities (transformations) which transform input into output. A sample Petri net is given in Fig. 2.

There are three transition firing rules for Petri nets. Petri nets are governed by transition firing rules:

- A transition is enabled if each of its input places is marked with at least $W(p, t)$ tokens, where the weight function $W(p, t)$ specifies the weight of the arc from input place p to transition t.

Fig. 2. Sample Petri Net

- A transition can only fire if it is enabled.
- Whenever a transition t fires, $W(p,t)$ tokens are removed from each input place p, and transition t adds $W(t,p)$ to each output place p, where $W(t,p)$ specifies the weight of the arc from transition t to output place p.

The significance of the first firing rule is that more than one transition can be enabled at the same time (concurrent processing is possible). Whenever transition t fires, it removes the token in place $p1$, and adds a token to place $p2$. In addition, $P \cap T = \emptyset$ and $P \cup T \neq \emptyset$. To facilitate formal specification and analysis of the structure, information flow, control and computation in systems, coloured Petri nets were introduced in 1988 by Jensen [15]-[16]. Formally, a *coloured Petri net* is a structure $(\Sigma, P, T, A, N, C, G, E, I)$ where P, T, A are the same as in a PN and

- Σ is a finite set of non-empty data types called color sets.
- N is a node function where $N : A \to (P \times T) \cup (T \times P)$.
- C is a color function where $C : P \to \Sigma$.
- G is a guard function where $G : T \to$ Boolean expressions.
- E is an arc expression function where $E : A \to$ expression $E(a)$ of type $C(p(a))$.
- I is an initialization function where $I : P \to$ closed expressions $p(a)$ of type $C(p)$.

A guard is a Boolean expression on a transition t which must be satisfied before t can fire. A CPN provides data typing (colour sets) and sets of values of a specified type for each place. The expression $E(p,t)$ is the name of a variable associated with the arc from input place p to transition t, and the expression $E(t,p)$ is associated with the transformation (activity) performed by transition t on its inputs to produce an output for place p. A guard $G(t)$ is an enabling condition associated with transition t. Each place in a CPN is associated with a data type. A sample CPN is given in Fig. 3, where place p1 supplies a value of x of type item to transition t, which outputs complement$(x) = 1 - x$ to place p2 whenever the token x in place p1 satisfies the guard $[x >= 0.45]$. The notation 1‘0.4 + 4‘0.3 specifies that a *multiset* contains 1 element with the value 0.5 and four elements with value 0.3. A multiset is a set which can have multiple appearances of the same element. The prefix 1 indicates the number of tokens in the multiset (in this case, one token in place $p1$), and the suffix indicates that x has been assigned an x-value. Whenever transition t fires, it augments the multiset associated with place p_2.

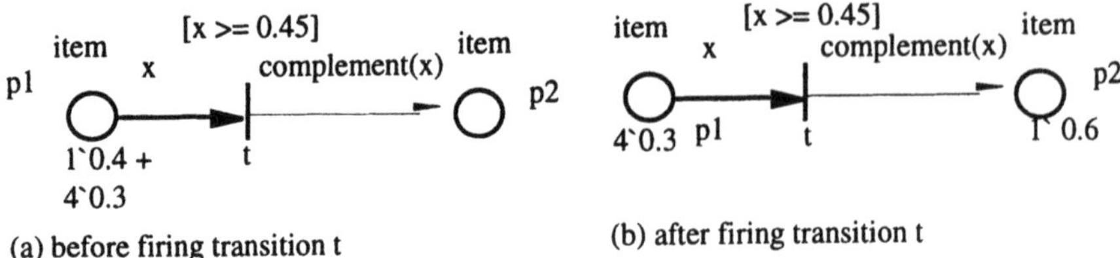

Fig. 3. Sample Coloured Petri Net

To simplify coloured Petri net models of complex, largescale systems, hierarchical Petri Nets (*hPNs*) with transitions representing subnets are introduced [17]. A basic *hPN* consists of a single input place p_j with an associated color named xtype, hierarchical transition t_i labeled x (also called an x transition), and output place p_k with a color type (see Fig. 4). The subnet which transition x represents is given in Fig. 5. Hierarchical Petri nets have been used to model the behavior of processes in real-time systems [38, 39, 41, 42].

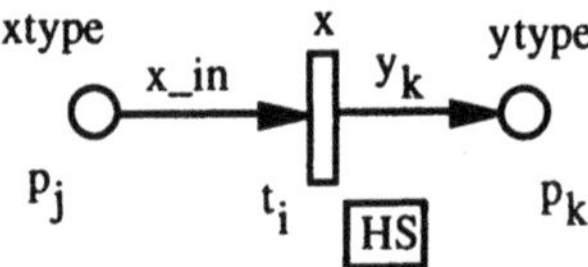

Fig. 4. hFPN

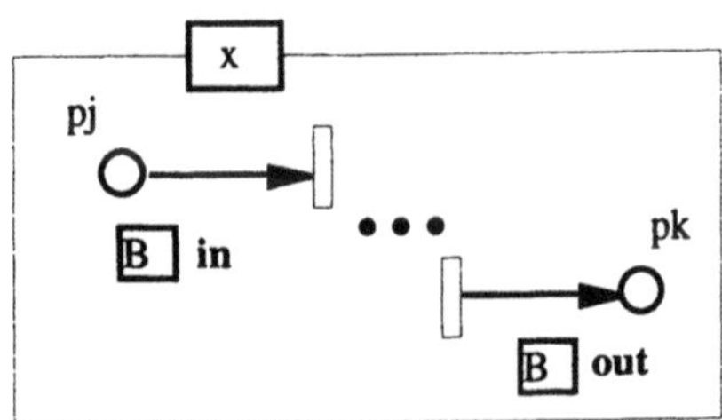

Fig. 5. Subnet for hFPN

2.2 Richter Clock Model

Coloured, hierarchical Petri nets can be used to describe the observable behavior of various clocks. In the context of time-constrained agents, clocks are designed relative to deadlines. In designing such clocks, a distinction is made between a time-originating mechanism (a pulse generator) and a clock, which consists of a time monitor, time interface (connections between monitor and monitor), and clock interface (connections supplying settings, deadlines, and display) as in [11, 44]. The time source (pulse generator) is separated from a clock because it may be shared by more than one clock (see Fig. 6). A simplified version of the basic Richter clock is used later as part of models of processes which construct clock representation systems (see Fig. 7).

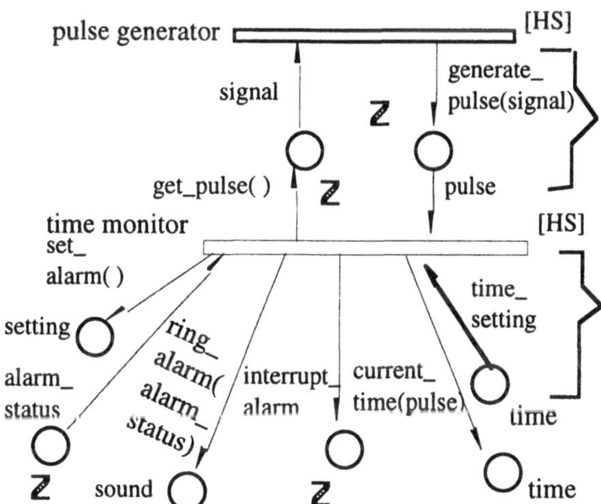

Fig. 6. Alarm Clock Model

The pulse generator and time monitor transitions in Figures 6 and 7 are hierarchical. The details of how pulses are generated, how pulse-frequency is controlled, and how time is monitored are hidden. The basic monitoring mechanism in both clocks is incrementing a sum-of-pulses variable (a local variable hidden inside the time monitor). This mechanism is represented with the following pseudocode:

sum-of-pulses : = sum-of-pulses + 1;
current_time(pulse) : = sum-of-pulses;

The current_time(pulse) outputs the value of sum_of_pulses each time a pulse is received from the pulse generator. The main drawback to a Richter clock

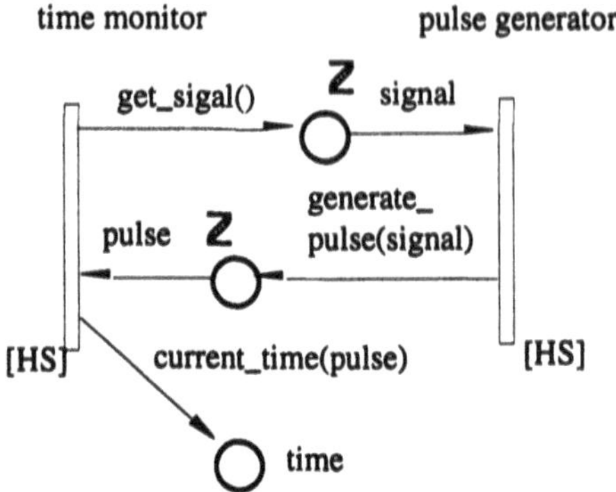

Fig. 7. Simplified Clock

is that it has no provision for partitions of a time window, and no response mechanism whenever an event occurs either earlier or later than anticipated. In more sophisticated clocks considered in this article, the Richter time monitor is subsumed in an information system providing the basis for decisions about time-constrained agents. The pulse generator-time monitor combination (without the other features in a Richter clock) is useful in constructing more sophisticated clocks. The simplified clock model in Fig. 7 captures this combination, and is used as a building block in constructing clocks for monitoring agents in real-time systems.

3 Rough View of Time

Rough sets make it possible to cope with the problem of making judgments about the timings of agents. Rough sets offer a means of approximating a set by other sets [26].

3.1 Basic Concepts

To begin, let $S = (U, A)$ be an information system with set U (universe of objects) and set A (attributes). Then let R be a relation defined on U. For $x, y \in U$, let xRy indicate that x has relation R to y. R is a tolerance relation, if xRx (reflexivity) for $x \in U$ and for all $x, y \in U$, if xRy, then yRx (symmetry). In the case where transitivity also holds, R is an equivalence relation over U. The notation U/R (known as the quotient set) denotes the family of equivalence classes of R. For $x \in U$, the notation $[x]_R$ identifies an equivalence class in U/R. The equivalence class $[x]_R$ is called an elementary category or concept of R [26]. A subset X in U is called a reference set, which can be approximated with two other sets in (1) and (2).

$$\underline{R}X = \{x \in U | [x]_R \subseteq X\}, \textit{ lower approximation} \tag{1}$$

$$\overline{R}X = \{x \in U | [x]_R \cap X \neq \emptyset\}, \textit{ upper approximation} \tag{2}$$

The pair $\underline{R}X, \overline{R}X$ is a rough set with reference set X. The vagueness of a set stems from its borderline region. A measure of the accuracy of a set $X \subseteq U$ is computed using $\alpha_R(X)$ (see (3)).

$$\alpha_R(X) = \frac{|\underline{R}X|}{|\overline{R}X|}, \textit{ accuracy measure} \tag{3}$$

The accuracy measure $\alpha_R(X)$ captures the degree of completeness of our knowledge represented by X [26]. The degree of incompleteness of our knowledge represented by a set X (its roughness) is computed using $\rho_R(x)$ given in (4).

$$\rho_R(X) = 1 - \alpha_R(X), R- \textit{ roughness of } X \tag{4}$$

Similarity among members of an equivalence class provides the basis for what is known as the indiscernibility relation. Let B be a subset of the set of attributes A, and let $Ind(B)$ be the set of all elements of X that match each other relative to B (see (5)).

$$Ind(B) = \{(x, y) | \forall a \in B, a(x) = a(y)\} \tag{5}$$

The $Ind(B)$ relation simplifies the investigation of a particular information system, where the representatives of $U/Ind(B)$ are studied. Knowledge reduction is possible using the method shown in [26]. A minimal subset $B \subseteq A$ such that $Ind(B) = Ind(A)$ is called a reduct of A (denoted $RED(A)$). Any set of attributes has one or more reducts [50]. Let $a \in P$ in A. The attribute a is indispensable in P if $Ind(P) \neq Ind(P - \{a\})$. The set of all indispensable attributes in P is called the core of P (denoted $CORE(P)$), which can be considered the most important part of knowledge [26]. For an information system S, the set of all reducts in S is denoted $RED(S)$ [57].

In deriving decision system rules, the discernibility matrix and discernibiliy function are essential [53]. Given an information system $S = (U, A)$, the $n \times n$ matrix (c_{ij}) is called the discernibility matrix of S (denoted $M(S)$) defined in (6).

$$c_{ij} = \{a \in A : a(x_i) \neq a(x_j)\}, \text{ for } i, j = 1, \ldots, n. \tag{6}$$

A discernibility function $f_{M(S)}$ for information S is a boolean function of m boolean variables corresponding to attributes $a_1^*, \ldots, a_m^*$ respectively, and defined in (7).

$$f_{M(S)}(a_1^*, \ldots, a_m^*) =_{df} \wedge\{\vee c_{ij}^* | 1 \leq j < i \leq n, c_{ij} \neq \emptyset\}, c_{ij}^* = \{a^* | a \in c_{ij}\} \tag{7}$$

3.2 Rough Sets Approach to Time Windows

To begin this approach, it is first necessary to design an information system (selection of universe of objects and selection of attributes) based on time windows. This design is accomplished by (a) selecting a universe consisting objects which are observations of durations derived from a time window and (b) instrumenting a time window with sensors used in making judgments relative to observed durations. The sensors are identified with attributes in an information system. The selection of the "mechanism" which defines the operation of a sensor is a non-trivial task, and depends on engineering skills, intuition, and an understanding of the behavior of agents in accomplishing their tasks in a particular hard, real-time system. By *hard real-time system*, we mean a system which enforces deadlines imposed on agent tasks. It is our knowledge of the "usual" distribution of task completion times which underlies design choices concerning sensors. This knowledge is imprecise, and possibly faulty. In addition, the domains of sensors are chosen so that they overlap. This overlap provides a degree of fault-tolerance in physical implementations of sensors, since it makes it possible for time-monitoring to continue adequately (although less precisely) despite the failure of a sensor. To see this, let a_{i-1}, a_i, a_{i+1} be sensors with overlapping domains. Let $x_1 \leq \ldots \leq x_k \leq \ldots x_m \leq \ldots \leq x_n$ be real numbers in neighboring intervals $[x_1, x_k]$, $[(x_k - x_1)/2, x_m]$, $[(x_m - (x_k - x_1)/2)/2, x_n]$ representing the domains of sensors a_{i-1}, a_i, a_{i+1}, respectively. In the case where sensor a_i fails, for example, observations of completion times in the interval $[(x_k - x_1)/2, x_m]$will still be recorded by either sensor a_{i-1} or a_{i+1}. Initially, the roughness of our knowledge of certain aspects of time (degree of being early or ontime or late) will be assessed. Later, the study of time window-based information systems will lead to rules useful in assessing the design of time windows.

To begin, a time window is subsumed in a what is known as a clock representation system (U_{time_window}, A), where universe U_{time_window} consists of durations (readings from a time window) and A is a set of attributes mapping durations in U_{time_window} to values V_a, i.e., $a : U_{time\_window} \rightarrow V_a$ for $a \in A$. The set A are the sensors of the information system, interpreting each observation x in U_{time_window} in terms of the mathematical model for a particular sensor. A sample clock representation system (U_{time_window}, A) is constructed by partitioning a time window relative to deadline $t1$, observation x, and boolean valued sensors VE, E, OT, L, VL defined relative to overlapping intervals [0, 45], [25, 75], [55, 150], [135, 200], and [185, 300], respectively. In each case, a sensor returns 1 if an observation belongs to the time window partition associated with the sensor. Otherwise, the sensor returns 0. For example, VE is defined in (8).

$$VE(x) = \begin{cases} 1, & x \in [0, 45] \\ 0, & \text{otherwise} \end{cases} \tag{8}$$

The system (U_{time_window}, A) is represented in Table 1 in terms of $x_1, \ldots, x_{16}$ observed durations in U_{time_window}. When it is clear from the context, U_{time_window} is replaced by U. Given the set of attributes $A = \{VE, E, OT, L, VL\}$, *Ind*(A) partitions the set of objects X from Table 1 into the equivalence classes in (9).

$$\begin{aligned} X_1 = [44]_A &= \{x_1, x_2, x_7, x_{13}, x_{14}\} = \{44, 35, 26, 30\} \\ X_2 = [72]_A &= \{x_3, x_6, x_{15}\} = \{72, 56\} \\ X_3 = [190]_A &= \{x_4, x_9\} = \{190, 192\} \\ X_4 = [49]_A &= \{x_5\} = \{49\} \\ X_5 = [127]_A &= \{x_8, x_{12}\} = \{127, 90\} \end{aligned} \tag{9}$$

Duration x (of task)		VE: $x \to \{0,1\}$ $x \in [0,45]$	E: $x \to \{0,1\}$ $x \in [25,75]$	Attribute OT: $x \to \{0,1\}$ $x \in [55,150]$	L: $x \to \{0,1\}$ $x \in [135,200]$	VL: $x \to \{0,1\}$ $x \in [185,300]$
x_1	44	1	1	0	0	0
x_2	35	1	1	0	0	0
x_3	72	0	1	1	0	0
x_4	190	0	0	0	1	1
x_5	49	0	1	0	0	0
x_6	72	0	1	1	0	0
x_7	26	1	1	0	0	0
x_8	127	0	0	1	0	0
x_9	192	0	0	0	1	1
x_{10}	145	0	0	1	1	0
x_{11}	159	0	0	0	1	0
x_{12}	90	0	0	1	0	0
x_{13}	30	1	1	0	0	0
x_{14}	44	1	1	0	0	0
x_{15}	56	0	1	1	0	0
x_{16}	201	0	0	0	0	1

Table 1. Duration Information Table

$$X_6 = [145]_A = \{x_{10}\} = \{145\}$$
$$X_7 = [159]_A = \{x_{11}\} = \{159\}$$
$$X_8 = [201]_A = \{x_{16}\} = \{201\}$$

In making judgments about the performance of an agent over time, we can classify the elements of X relative to a subset of the sensors, namely, $B = \{E, OT, L\}$. The subset B is of interest because two of its members "surround" the sensor OT which measures the timeliness of an observation. The relation $Ind(B)$ partitions X into the equivalence classes in (10).

$$\begin{aligned} C_1 &= [44]_B = \{x_1, x_2, x_5, x_7, x_{13}, x_{14}\} = \{44, 35, 49, 26, 30\} \\ C_2 &= [72]_B = \{x_3, x_6, x_{15}\} = \{72, 56\} \\ C_3 &= [190]_B = \{x_4, x_9, x_{11}, x_{16}\} = \{190, 192, 159\} \\ C_4 &= [127]_B = \{x_8, x_{12}\} = \{127, 90\} \\ C_5 &= [145]_B = \{x_{10}\} = \{145\} \end{aligned} \tag{10}$$

The roughness of our knowledge of the equivalence classes $X_1, \ldots, X_8$ is computed in Table 2. This Table indicates that the timing information represented by X_i is rough in the extreme cases where a duration has overlapping interpretations (except in the case where the overlap includes $OT(x_i) = 1$ for $i = 3, 6, 8, 10, 12, 15$). After constructing the discernibility matrix derived

Equivalence Classes	Lower Approx. $\underline{B}X_i$	Upper Approx. $\overline{B}X_i$	Accuracy Measure $\alpha B(X_i)$	Measure of roughness of information $\rho B(X_i)$
$X_1 = \{x_1, x_2, x_7, x_{13}, x_{14}\}$	$\underline{B}X_1 = \{\}$	$\overline{B}X_1 = \{x_2 \; x_5, x_{13}, x_{14}\}$	0	1
$X_2 = \{x_3, x_6, x_{15}\}$	$\underline{B}X_2 = \{x_3, x_6, x_{15}\}$	$\overline{B} = \{x_3, x_6, x_{15}\}$	1	0
$X_3 = \{x_4, x_9\}$	$\underline{B}X_3 = \{\}$	$\overline{B}X_3 = \{x_4, x_9, x_{11}, x_{16}\}$	0	1
$X_4 = \{x_5\}$	$\underline{B}X_4 = \{\}$	$\overline{B}X_1 = \{x_1, x_2, x_5, x_7, x_{13}, x_{14}\}$	0	1
$X_5 = \{x_8, x_{12}\}$	$\underline{B}X_5 = \{x_8, x_{12}\}$	$\overline{B}X_5 = \{x_8, x_{12}\}$	1	0
$X_6 = \{x_{10}\}$	$\underline{B}X_6 = \{\}$	$\overline{B}X_6 = \{x_{10}\}$	1	0
$X_7 = \{x_{11}\}$	$\underline{B}X_7 = \{\}$	$\overline{B}X_7 = \{x_4, x_9, x_{11}, x_{16}\}$	0	1
$X_8 = \{x_{16}\}$	$\underline{B}X_8 = \{\}$	$\overline{B}X_8 = \{x_4, x_9, x_{11}, x_{16}\}$	0	1

Table 2. Approximations and Measures of Clock Outputs

form $Ind(A)$, it is easily shown that the discernibility function $f_{M(S)}(A) = VE \wedge E \wedge OT \wedge L \wedge VL$. The reducts and core of A are given in (11).

$$RED(S) = \{CORE(S)\} \text{ and } CORE(S) = \{VE, E, OT, L, VL\} \tag{11}$$

4 Fuzzy Sets View of Time

It has been observed that the rough sets approach overlaps with the fuzzy sets in dealing with vagueness [27]. In this section, rough sets are combined with fuzzy sets in developing clock representation systems.

4.1 Fuzzy Sets: Basic Concepts

The characteristic function for a set X returns a value indicating the degree of membership of an element x in X. For a crisp set, the characteristic function returns a value in $\{0, 1\}$. A fuzzy set is non-crisp, and was introduced by Zadeh [60]. By contrast with a crisp set, the characteristic function for a fuzzy set returns a value in $[0, 1]$. Let $U, X, \tilde{A}, x$ be a universe of objects, subset of U, fuzzy set in U, and an individual object, respectively. For a set $X, \mu_{\tilde{A}} : X \to [0, 1]$ is a function which determines the degree of membership an object x in U. A fuzzy set $\tilde{A}$ is then defined to be a set of ordered pairs as in (12).

$$\tilde{A} = \{(x, \mu_{\tilde{A}}(x)) | x \in X\} \tag{12}$$

The set X is called the reference set. The counter-parts of intersection and union (crisp sets) are the t-norm and s-norm operators in fuzzy set theory. For the intersection of fuzzy sets, the min operator was suggested by Zadeh [60], and belongs to a class of intersection operators (min, product, bold intersection) known as triangular or t-norms. A t-norm is a mapping $t : [0,1]^2 \to [0,1]$ satisfying some additional properties (see [31]). The algebraic sum (also called probabilistic sum) is commonly used for the union of fuzzy sets [60] as in (13). The probabilistic sum belongs to a class of union operators called triangular co-norms (or s-norms). An s-norm is a mapping $s : [0,1]^2 \to [0,1]$ satisfying some additional conditions (see [31]). For example, let x, y belong to a fuzzy set $\tilde{A}$, and compute the s-norm relative to x and y as in (14)

$$\mu_{\tilde{A}}(x) s \mu_{\tilde{A}}(y) = \mu_{\tilde{A}}(x) + \mu_{\tilde{A}}(y) - \mu_{\tilde{A}}(x)\mu_{\tilde{A}}(y) \tag{13}$$

4.2 Fuzzy Petri Nets

Generalized fuzzy Petri nets were introduced to model processes in reasoning systems and, in particular, logic processing where computations are performed in the context of fuzzy sets [33]. Fuzzy Petri nets offer a concise means of modeling and analyzing the structure of approximate time windows used to construct information systems. In addition, this approach to modeling time windows makes it possible to check safety, boundedness, liveness, and reachability properties of a particular fuzzy Petri net model. A particularly important benefit of fuzzy Petri nets is that they can be extended with rough sets to provide an approach to modeling approximate reasoning. The result is a new form of process modeling technology known as roughly fuzzy Petri nets. This form of Petri net is a natural outcome of the concurrency inherent in every information system table. That is, the individual elements of each row of an information system table are derived by the concurrent operation of sensors as well as concurrent computations performed in the context of rough sets theory. Also notice that by allowing transitions in a roughly fuzzy Petri net to be hierarchical, it is possible to model multi-agent systems where one information system table being constructed by a particular agent (e.g., a coordinator agent) results from input from concurrent computations performed by agents constructing local information systems tables. By extending fuzzy Petri nets to include operations from rough sets theory, it then becomes possible to model decision-making systems and, in particular, to model rules extracted from information systems constructed relative to time windows. A generalized Fuzzy Petri Net (FPN) is a structure $(\Sigma, P, T, A, N, C, E, I, R, W, Z, \varrho, \rho)$ where $\Sigma, P, T, A, N, C, E, I$ are as in a CPN [37]. Strengths of connections (chosen from a finite set of weights W) are determined by $\rho : A \to W$, and reference points (chosen from the finite set R) are determined by $\varrho : A \to R$. A *strength of connection* $w_i \in W$ specifies the relative importance of input, and guarantees a certain magnitude of input to a transition. A *reference point* $r_i \in R$ is also known as a modulator, which prescribes a certain magnitude of level of marking of place which must be maintained. Weights and modulators are restricted to values in the interval [0, 1]. The arc expression function E has been specialized relative to a finite set Z such that $E : A \rightarrow Z$. The expressions in Z make it possible to compute degrees of membership of values in a universe of discourse in fuzzy sets, to perform aggregations, and any other necessary operations for the functioning of a particular system. Minimally, Z has four operations consisting of what are known as a dominance AND {OR} as well as conjunctive {disjunctive} ways of aggregating weighted inputs to a transition (see 14).

$$\begin{aligned} Z = \{ & \mathop{T}_{n=1}^{n} ((r_i \rightarrow) s\, w_i) && \text{–dominance AND operation,} \\ & \mathop{S}_{n=1}^{n} ((r_i \rightarrow x_i) t\, w_i) && \text{–dominance OR operation,} \\ & \mathop{S}_{n=1}^{n} (x_i\, t\, w_i) && \text{–OR operation,} \\ & \mathop{T}_{n=1}^{n} (x_i\, s\, w_i) && \text{–AND operation } \} \end{aligned} \tag{14}$$

The operations in Z employ triangular norms s, t, as well as the implication operator $\rightarrow$ where r_i specifies a threshhold level which modulates the strength of firing coming from the ith input place. Depending on the marking of the input places, a transition can fire. In contrast to two-valued Petri nets, the generalized version studied here includes a gradual firing (strength of firing) of transitions together with level of marking of places. First, let us discuss a generic model of a transition, Fig.8. An elementary FPN has a single multivalued (fuzzy) transition z_i with inputs x_i (input signal), r_i (reference point), w_i (weight), and single output place out_k (see Fig. 8a). Each input x_i is a fuzzy number (i.e., the result of applying a membership function to an element of a universe of discourse which consists of real numbers). The results $out_1, \ldots, out_n$ of elementary FPNs are aggregated by transition Z in Fig. 8b. The level of firing of transition Z in Fig. 8b is determined by (15).

$$Z = \mathop{T}_{n=1}^{n} [(r_i \rightarrow x_i\, s\, w_i] \tag{15}$$

For the computation (15) associated with transition Z, the limit "n" denotes the number of input places; x_i, a level of marking at the i-th place; r_i, a level of modulation of the input; and w_i, an associated degree of contribution of the x_i to the overall firing of the transition. Here "s" and "T" (or t) denote s- and t-norms. Similarly, "$\rightarrow$" denotes a multivalued implication operation. Many forms of implication are possible (cf. [31]).

For simplicity, it is assumed that $r_i \rightarrow x_i = min(1, \frac{x_i}{r_i})$. Let us consider a special case by specifying $w_i = 0.0$ and $r_i = 1.0$ for all i, $i = 1, 2, \ldots, n$. This reduces the original model of the transition Z to its two-valued counterpart. From (15), we immediately derive that $Z = 1$ when $x_i = 1$, for all i. The role of the parameters in this structure is also self-explanatory (see Table 3).

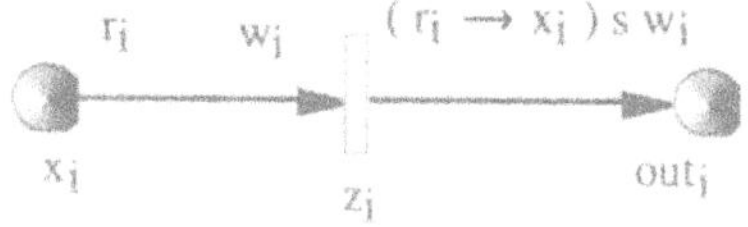

Fig 8. a. Elementary fuzzy Petri net

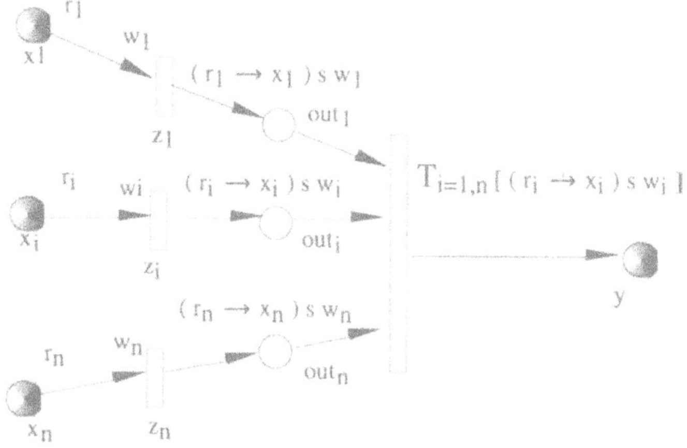

Fig. 8. b. Fuzzy Petri net with aggregated inputs

Parameter	Role
connection w_i	• Contribution of input x_i to the overall process of firing increases as $w_i \to 0$ • Impact of a particular input is totally masked and does not make any contribution to the overall level of firing, if $w_i = 1$.
modulator r_i	• Contribution of input x_i to the level of firing of transition z becomes lower as $r_i \to 1$. • In the limit, $r_i \to x_i = x_i$ for $r_i = 1$ no matter which model of implication operation has been implemented.

Table 3. Role of FPN parameters

The expression in (15) defines a dominance neuron; this allows us to rewrite Z as shown in (16).

$$Z = DOM(\mathrm{x}; \mathbf{r}, \mathbf{w}) \tag{16}$$

In (16), $\mathbf{r}$ and $\mathbf{w}$ are vectors of the parameters of the neuron. Usually, $\mathbf{r}$ is referred to as a reference point (or a modulator) while $\mathbf{w}$ collects the connections of the neuron. Fuzzy Petri nets are ideally suited for modeling clocks where there is vagueness in our knowledge of deadlines and speed of processing in achieving a goal which are not crisply known.

4.3 Roughly Fuzzy Petri Nets

By augmenting the set Z of operations in an FPN with operations derived from rough set theory, a new class of fuzzy Petri nets can be identified. This is the class of roughly fuzzy Petri Nets (rfPNs). The introduction of rfPNs is motivated by the need to develop mathematical models of decision-making information system such that the models are capable of learning, and are designed to react to dynamic changes in the reduct set for different samples of decision tables [2]. Let $S = (U, A)$ be an information system and let R be an equivalence relation which forms the quotient set X/R, where $R \subseteq A$ and $X \subseteq U$. The set $POS_R(X) = \underline{R}X$ is the set of all elements of U which can be classified as elements of X. Similarly, the set $NEG_R(X) = U - \overline{R}X$ is the set of those elements of U which can be classified as elements of $U - X$ [26]. Let the set $\mathbb{Q}$ contain

$$\sigma_{X/R}, \rho_{POS_R(X)}, \rho_{NEG_R(X)}$$

which are distinguished operations used to construct the quotient set X/R, the set $POS_R(X)$ and the set $NEG_R(X)$, respectively. A roughly fuzzy Petri Net (rfPN) is a structure given in (17)

$$(\Sigma, P, T, A, N, C, E, I, R, W, Z \cup \mathbb{Q}, \varrho, \rho) \tag{17}$$

where $\Sigma, P, T, A, N, C, E, I, R, W, Z \cup \mathbb{Q}, \varrho, \rho$ are as in a generalized fuzzy Petri net.
The set Z is augmented with operations in $\mathbb{Q}$ to construct the quotient set, as well as upper and lower approximations for the equivalence classes of X/R. In effect, an rfPN is an extension of the generalized fuzzy Petri net model, which provides a concise means of modeling decisions systems constructed with objects which are fuzzy sets.

Let $\mu_L : X \to [0, 1], L \in \{VE, E, OT, L, VL\}$ be a function which determines the degree of membership of $x \in X$ in the fuzzy set L. Next we consider an information system $S = (U_{time\_window}, A \cup \{\gamma\} \cup \{d\})$, which contains a distinguished attribute d called a decision. The elements of A are called conditions [51]. Each sensor a_i of A is defined by a membership function μ_L relative to its own modulator r_i and strength of connection (weight) w_i. The sensor γ is a closeness measure (negation of relative error) in comparing an observation with deadline ot (see (18)).

$$\gamma(x_i) = 1 - \frac{|x_i - ot|}{ot} \tag{18}$$

We also introduce a sensor $d(x_i)$ for a particular x_i of X in S as a measure of the degree of acceptance of an observed duration, which is computed in terms of the level of firing of one or more sensors. This form of a sensor has been introduced to measure the interaction of the nearness sensor with other sensors considered extremely important in monitoring performance of an agent relative to hard deadlines. For example, we can define $d(x_i)$ in terms of attributes $a1, a2, a3$ (representing VE, E, OT, respectively), and nearness measure γ in (19).

$$d(x_i) = min(a_1(x_i),\ a_2(x_i,\ a_3(x_i), (x_i)) \tag{19}$$

The table for S is obtained by repeated firing of the hierarchical transition Z in the net in Fig. 9. Transition Z decomposes into a subnet which collects the outputs of transitions $z_1, ldots, z_n$, and computes the measure of nearness $\gamma(x_i)$ as well as $d(x_i)$ (degree of acceptance of an observed duration x_i). The output of transition Z is a vector y with entries shown in (20).

$$y = (x_i, [(r_i \rightarrow \mu_{VE}(xi))s\, w_i], \ldots, [(r_i \rightarrow \mu_{VL}(x_i))s\, w_i], \gamma(x_i), d(x_i)) \tag{20}$$

Each output y is collected in the input place for transition t_0. This collection process continues until an external process interrupts the data collection (an interrupt coincides with setting the guard $\lambda = 1$ on transition t_o). The accumulated information system table is read by transition t_0 whenever the guard $\lambda = 1$ (an indication that the observed agent has completed its task). Once transition t_o fires, the hierarchical transitions labelled $sigma_{X/Ind(B)}()$ and $\sigma_{Ind/C}()$ partition the table into equivalence classes $X_1, \ldots, X_m$ and $C_1, \ldots, C_n$, respectively. Then transitions $t_{11}, t_{12}, \ldots, t_{n1}, t_{n2}$ compute $NEG(X_1)$, $POS(X_1), \ldots, NEG(X_n)$, $POS(X_n)$.

4.4 Calibration of Fuzzy Petri Nets

It has been shown that fuzzy Petri nets can be calibrated [31]-[34], [36]. In the case where an rfPN has subnets which are generalized fuzzy Petri nets, the modulators and weights of these subnets can be adjusted during supervised learning. This feature of rfPNs is helpful in discovering reducts in the case where rules for decision systems are derived from changing environments. We mention briefly how this is done. The learning scheme exploits a standard mode of supervised learning where the marking of the input places and output places is given. More formally, denote the collection of these pairs in (21).

$$\{\mathbf{x}(k), \mathbf{target}(k)\} \tag{21}$$

where $k = 1, 2, \ldots, N$. The objective is to modify the parameters of the fuzzy Petri net (connections of the corresponding neurons) in such a way that the markings $y(1), \ldots, y(k)$ of the output places are made as close as possible to the required target (see Fig. 10).

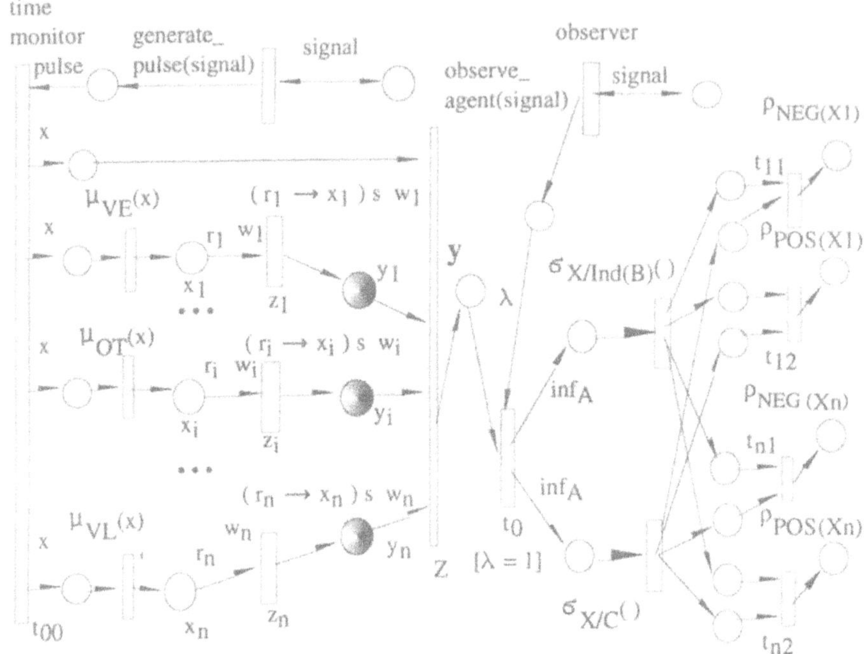

Fig. 9. Fuzzy Petri net to construct Table for (U, A)

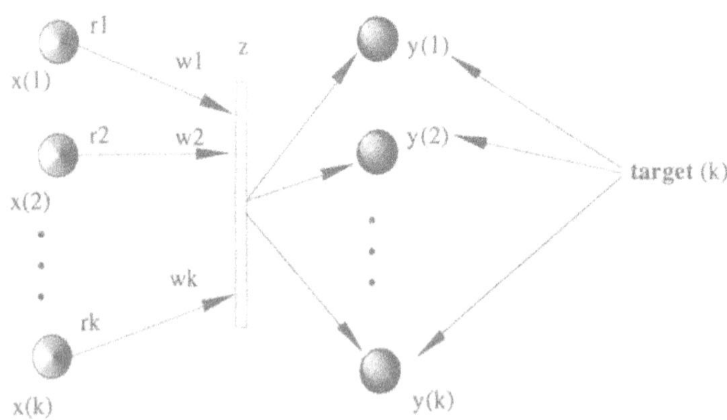

Fig. 10. Gradient – based learning in a fuzzy Petri net

Let $\mathbf{x}(k)$, $\mathbf{r}$, $\mathbf{w}$ denote input places, vector $\mathbf{r}$ (modulators), and vector $\mathbf{w}$ (connections), respectively. (Usually the objective function (performance index) Q is defined as the sum of squared errors (see (22)).

$$Q = \sum_{k=1}^{N} [target(k) - y(\mathbf{x}(k), \mathbf{r}, \ \mathbf{w})]^2 \tag{22}$$

The gradient – based optimization method is driven by the increments in the parameter space (23).

$$-\frac{\partial Q}{\partial \, \mathbf{param}} \tag{23}$$

where the gradient is taken over the connections (here denoted as param) of the neurons forming the Petri net. Thus the formula reads as given in (24).

$$\mathbf{param}(new) = \text{param} - \alpha \frac{\partial Q}{\partial \mathbf{param}} \tag{24}$$

Coefficient $a > 0$ in (24) is the learning rate. The detailed expressions can be easily derived once we confine ourselves to some specific forms of the triangular norms. Let $z(k) = y(\mathbf{x}(k); \mathbf{r}, \mathbf{w})$. Omitting the intermediate steps which can be found in [31], we subsequently derive (25) and (26).

$$\frac{\partial z(k)}{\partial w_i} = \frac{\partial}{\partial w_i}[\, \mathop{T}_{j=1}^{n} [(r_j \to x_j) s \, w_j]\,] \tag{25}$$

$$\frac{\partial z(k)}{\partial r_i} = \frac{\partial}{\partial r_i}[\, \mathop{T}_{j=1}^{n} [(r_j \to x_j) s \, w_j\,]\,] \tag{26}$$

Let $r_j \to w_j$ denote the implication operator defined in (27).

$$r_j \to x_j = min\left(1, \frac{x_j}{r_j}\right), x_j \in [0,1], r_j \in (0,1] \tag{27}$$

In addition, let A be defined in (28).

$$A = \mathop{T}_{j \neq 1}^{n} [(r_j \to x_j) s \, w_j] \tag{28}$$

and assume that the triangular norm s is given as the probabilistic sum (i.e., BsC is rewritten as $B + C - B * C$). Then from (26) we derive the formula for the connections in (29).

$$\frac{\partial z(k)}{\partial w_i} = \frac{\partial}{\partial w_i}[A\,[(r_i \to x_i)\, s\, w_i]] = A\,[1 - (r_i \to x_i)] \tag{29}$$

A similar formula can also derived from (27). The appeal of the result in (29) is that its implementation is straightforward. As a result, the "front end" of a process model (i.e., a subnet like the one starting with transition t_{00} and ending with transition Z in Fig. 9) for a rough information system can be calibrated before the information system table and subsequent approximations as well as the extraction of rules $RED(S)$ are computed.

4.5 Sample Clock Information System

At this point, the issue of appropriateness of the design of a clock information system can be examined in the context of roughness and discernibility. The construction of a discernibility matrix will lead to the extraction of rules, which can be used to assess the design. The observations $x_1, \ldots, x_{16}$ in Table 1 are now studied in the context of fuzzy sets. Processing these observations in the manner shown in **y** in line (20) produces Table 4. The clock information system in Table 4 can be analyzed with rough sets. For conciseness, we only consider the case where $B = \{a_2, a_3, a_4\} = \{E, OT, L\}$, and do not consider the impact of a_1, a_5, and γ. Considering only B, we obtain the quotient set $X/Ind(B)$ having equivalence classes $X_1, \ldots, X_{10}$ given in (30).

$$\begin{aligned}
X_1 &= [44]_B = \{x_1, x_{14}\} = \{44\} \\
X_2 &= [35]_B = \{x_2\} = \{35\} \\
X_3 &= [72]_B = \{x_3, x_6, x_{12}\} = \{72, 90\} \\
X_4 &= [190]_B = \{x_4, x_9\} = \{190, 192\} \\
X_5 &= [49]_B = \{x_5\} = \{49\} \\
X_6 &= [26]_B = \{x_7, x_{13}\} = \{26, 30\} \\
X_7 &= [127]_B = \{x_8\} = \{127\} \\
X_8 &= [145]_B = \{x_{10}, x_{11}\} = \{145, 159\} \\
X_9 &= [56]_B = \{x_{15}\} = \{56\} \\
X_{10} &= [201]_B = \{x_{16}\} = \{201\}
\end{aligned} \tag{30}$$

Let $C = \{a_3\} \subset B$, which is a judicious choice, since we are interested in measuring the roughness of the information in $X/Ind(B)$ in terms of the "on-timeness" of an observation. Then $X/Ind(C)$ has equivalence classes $C_1, \ldots, C_4$ given in (31).

$$\begin{aligned}
C_1 &= [44]_C = \{x_1, x_2, x_3, x_5, x_6, x_7, x_{12}, x_{13}, x_{14}, x_{15}, x_{16}\} \\
C_2 &= [190]_C = \{x_4, x_9\} \\
C_3 &= [127]_C = \{x_8\} \\
C_4 &= [145]_C = \{x_{10}, x_{11}\}
\end{aligned} \tag{31}$$

The partitions of X in (30) and (31) make it possible to derive the approximations and measures in Table 5. Let the set of attributes in Table 4 be represented by A, where $A = \{a_1, a_2, a_3, a_4, a_5, a_6, a_7\}$, $a_6 = \gamma$, and $a_7 = d$. The redundant rows derived from inputs x_6 and x_{14} in Table 4 are dropped, and the information system S = (U, A) is represented by Table 6. The discernibility matrix M(S) in Table 7 is derived from the information system in Table 6 relative to A. To simplify table entries, let $a_1, \ldots, a_6, a_7$ be represented by $a, \ldots, f, g$, respectively. In addition, the column for x_{16} has no entries, and has been omitted.

Duration x (of task)	Attribute $a_1(x)$ m =40, s =200, r=0.5 w=0.6	$a_2(x)$ m = 75, s=500, r=0.5 w=0.8	$a_3(x)$ m = 150, s=400, r=0.5 w=0.85	$a_4(x)$ m=200 s=400, r=0.5 w=0.9	$a_5(x)$ m=300 s=1500, r=0.5 w=0.95	nearness measure $a_6(x) = \gamma(x)$	degree of accept-ancel $a_7(x) = d(x)$
x_1 44	1.00	0.86	0.85	0.90	0.95	0.30	0.30
x_2 35	1.00	0.82	0.85	0.90	0.95	0.30	0.20
x_3 72	0.60	1.00	0.85	0.90	0.95	0.50	0.50
x_4 190	0.60	0.80	0.86	1.00	0.95	0.70	0.70
x_5 49	1.00	0.90	0.85	0.90	0.95	0.33	0.33
x_6 72	0.60	1.00	0.85	0.90	0.95	0.50	0.50
x_7 26	0.90	0.80	0.85	0.90	0.95	0.20	0.20
x_8 127	0.60	0.80	0.93	0.90	0.95	0.80	0.80
x_9 192	0.60	0.80	0.86	1.00	0.95	0.70	0.70
x_{10} 145	0.60	0.80	1.00	0.90	0.95	0.96	0.80
x_{11} 159	0.60	0.80	1.00	0.90	0.95	0.94	0.80
x_{12} 90	0.60	1.00	0.85	0.90	0.95	0.60	0.60
x_{13} 30	1.00	0.81	0.85	0.90	0.95	0.20	0.20
x_{14} 44	1.00	0.86	0.85	0.90	0.95	0.30	0.30
x_{15} 56	0.82	0.99	0.85	0.90	0.95	0.40	0.40
x_{16} 201	0.60	0.80	0.85	1.00	0.95	0.70	0.70

Table 4. Clock Information System

After simplification, the discernibility function (derived from Table 7) is

$$\begin{aligned} f_{M(S)}(A) &= (b \vee g) \wedge f \wedge (a \vee b) = (a \wedge b \wedge f) \vee (a \wedge g \wedge f) \\ &\quad \vee (b \wedge f) \vee (b \wedge g \wedge f) \\ &= (a_1 \wedge a_2 \wedge a_6) \vee (a_1 \wedge a_7 \wedge a_6) \vee (a_2 \wedge a_6) \vee (a_2 \wedge a_7 \wedge a_6) \end{aligned}$$

with $RED(S) = \{\{a, b, f\}, \{a, g, f\}, \{b, f\}, \{b, g, f\}\}$ and $CORE(S) = \{f\}$.

4.6 Decision Rules

Precise conditions for decision rules can be extracted from a discernibility matrix as in [51]. For the information system $S = (U, A)$, let $B \subseteq A$ and let $P(V_a)$ denote the powerset of V_a. For every $d \in A - B$, a decision function $d_d^B : U \rightarrow P(V_a)$ is defined in (32).

$$d_d^B(u) = \{v \in V_d | \exists u' \in U, (u', u) \in Ind_B.d(u') = v\} \tag{32}$$

In other words, $d_d^B(u)$ is the set of all elements of the decision column of S such that the corresponding object is a member of the same equivalence class as argument u. The next step is to determine a decision rule with a minimal number

Equivalence Classes	Lower Approximation	Upper Approximation	accuracy $\alpha_C(X)$	Roughness $\rho_C(X)$
$X_1 = [44]_B = \{x_1, x_{14}\}$	$\underline{C}X_1 = \{\}$	$\overline{C}X_1 = \{x_1, x_2, x_3, x_5, x_6, x_7, x_{12}, x_{13}, x_{14}, x_{15}, x_{16}\}$	0	1
$X_2 = [35]_B = \{x_2\}$	$\underline{C}X_2 = \{\}$	$\overline{C}X_2 = \{x_1, x_2, x_3, x_5, x_6, x_7, x_{12}, x_{13}, x_{14}, x_{15}, x_{16}\}$	0	1
$X_3 = [72]_B = \{x_3, x_6, x_{12}\}$	$\underline{C}X_3 = \{\}$	$\overline{C}X_3 = \{x_1, x_2, x_3, x_5, x_6, x_7, x_{12}, x_{13}, x_{14}, x_{15}, x_{16}\}$	0	1
$X_4 = [190]_B = \{x_4, x_9\} = \{190, 192\}$	$\underline{C}X_4 = \{x_4, x_9\}$	$\overline{C}X_4 = \{x_4, x_9\}$	1	0
$X_5 = [49]_B = \{x_5\}$	$\underline{C}X_5 = \{\}$	$\overline{C}X_5 = \{x_1, x_2, x_3, x_5, x_6, x_7, x_{12}, x_{13}, x_{14}, x_{15}, x_{16}\}$	0	1
$X_6 = [26]_B = \{x_7, x_{13}\}$	$\underline{C}X_6 = \{\}$	$\overline{C}X_5 = \{x_1, x_2, x_3, x_5, x_6, x_7, x_{12}, x_{13}, x_{14}, x_{15}, x_{16}\}$	0	1
$X_7 = [127]_B = \{x_8\}$	$\underline{C}X_7 = \{x_8\}$	$\overline{C}X_5 = \{x_8\}$	1	0
$X_8 = [145]_B = \{x_{10}, x_{11}\}$	$\underline{C}X_8 = \{x_{10}, x_{11}\}$	$\overline{C}X_8 = \{x_{10}, x_{11}\}$	1	0
$X_9 = [56]_B = \{x_{15}\}$	$\underline{C}X_9 = \{\}$	$\overline{C}X_9 = \{x_1, x_2, x_3, x_5, x_6, x_7, x_{12}, x_{13}, x_{14}, x_{15}, x_{16}\}$	0	1
$X_{10} = [201]_B = \{x_{16}\}$	$\underline{C}X_{10} = \{\}$	$\overline{C}X_{10} = \{x_1, x_2, x_3, x_5, x_6, x_7, x_{12}, x_{13}, x_{14}, x_{15}, x_{16}\}$	0	1

Table 5. Roughness Measures Table

of descriptors on the left-hand side. A decision rule over the set of attributes A and values V is an expression of the form given in (33).

$$a_{i_1}(u_i) = v_{i_1} \wedge \ldots \wedge a_{i_j}(u_i) = v_{i_j} \wedge \ldots \wedge a_{i_r}(u_i) = v_{i_r} \Rightarrow_S d(u_i) = v \tag{33}$$

where $u_i \in U$, $v_{i_j} \in V_{a_{i_j}}$, $v \in V_d$, $j = 1, \ldots, r$ and $r \leq |A|$. Let $||\tau||_S$ denote the meaning of the term τ. A rule is true in system S if (34) holds.

$$||(a_{i_1} = v_{i_1}) \wedge \ldots \wedge (a_{i_r} = v_{ir})|| \subseteq ||(a_p = v_p)|| \tag{34}$$

The fact that a rule is true is indicated by writing it in the form given in (35).

$$(a_{i_1} = v_{i_1}) \wedge \ldots \wedge (a_{i_r} = v_{ir}) \Rightarrow_S (a_p = v_p) \tag{35}$$

$U\backslash A$4 $\{d\}$	$a_1(=a)$	$a_2(=b)$	$a_3(=c)$	$a_4(=d)$	$a_5(=d)$	$a_6(=d)$	$d(=g)$
x_1 : 44	1.00	0.86	0.85	0.90	0.95	0.30	0.30
x_2 : 35	1.00	0.82	0.85	0.90	0.95	0.30	0.20
x_3 : 72	0.60	1.00	0.85	0.90	0.95	0.50	0.50
x_4 : 190	0.60	0.80	0.86	1.00	0.95	0.70	0.60
x_5 : 49	1.00	0.90	0.85	0.90	0.95	0.33	0.33
x_7 : 26	0.90	0.80	0.85	0.90	0.95	0.20	0.20
x_8 : 127	0.60	0.80	0.93	0.90	0.95	0.80	0.60
x_9 : 192	0.60	0.80	0.86	1.00	0.95	0.70	0.60
x_{10} : 145	0.60	0.80	1.00	0.90	0.95	0.96	0.60
x_{11} : 159	0.60	0.80	1.00	0.90	0.95	0.94	0.60
x_{12} : 90	0.60	1.00	0.85	0.90	0.95	0.60	0.60
x_{13} : 30	1.00	0.81	0.85	0.90	0.95	0.20	0.20
x_{15} : 56	0.82	0.99	0.85	0.90	0.95	0.40	0.40
x_{16} : 201	0.60	0.80	0.85	1.00	0.95	0.66	0.60

Table 6. Information System Table (without redundant rows)

	x_1	x_2	x_3	x_4	x_5	x_7	x_8	x_9	x_{10}	x_{11}	x_{12}	x_{13}	x_{15}
x_1													
x_2	bg												
x_3	abf g	abf g											
x_4	abc dfg	abc dfg	bcd fg										
x_5	bfg	bfg	abf g	abc dfg									
x_7	abf g	abf	abf g	acd fg	abf g								
x_8	abc fg	abc fg	bcf g	cdf	abc fg	acf g							
x_9	abc dfg	abc dfg	bcd fg		abc dfg	abc fg	cdf						
x_{10}	abc fg	abc fg	bcf g	cdf	abc fg	abf g	cf	cdf					
x_{11}	abc fg	abc fg	bcf g	cdf	abc fg	acf g	cf	cdf	f				
x_{12}	abf g	abf g	fg	bcd f	abf g	abf g	bcf g	bcd fg	bcf	bcf			
x_{13}	bfg	bf	abf g	abc dfg	bfg	ab	abc fg	abc dfg	abc fg	abc fg	abf g		
x_{15}	abf g	abf g	abf g	abc dfg	abf g	abf g	abc fg	abc dfg	abc fg	abc fg	abf g	abf g	
x_{16}	abd fg	abd fg	bdf g	cf	abd fg	adf g	df	cf	cdf	cdf	bdf	abd fg	abd fg

Table 7. Discernibility Matrix M(S)

Let $B = \{a_2, a_6\}$ (a reduct derived from Table 7), then we know that

$$\{b, f\} \rightarrow \{a, c, d, e, g\}$$

which leads to the elementary dependencies

$$\{b, f\} \rightarrow \{a\}, \{b, f\} \rightarrow \{c\}, \{b, f\} \rightarrow \{d\}, \{b, f\} \rightarrow \{e\}, \{b, f\} \rightarrow \{g\}.$$

We consider only the last of these dependencies, namely, $\{b, f\} \rightarrow \{g\}$, and consider $S = (U, B \cup g)$ from Table 6, which is represented in Table 8.

$U \backslash B$	$a_2(=b)$	$a_6(=f)$	$d(=g)$	d_d^B
x_1	0.86	0.30	0.30	{0.30}
x_2	0.82	0.30	0.20	{0.20}
x_3	1.00	0.50	0.50	{0.50}
x_4	0.80	0.70	0.60	{0.60}
x_5	0.90	0.33	0.33	{0.33}
x_7	0.80	0.20	0.20	{0.20}
x_8	0.80	0.80	0.60	{0.60}
x_9	0.80	0.70	0.60	{0.60}
x_{10}	0.80	0.96	0.60	{0.60}
x_{11}	0.80	0.94	0.60	{0.60}
x_{12}	1.00	0.60	0.60	{0.60}
x_{13}	0.81	0.20	0.20	{0.20}
x_{15}	0.99	0.40	0.40	{0.40}
x_{16}	0.80	0.66	0.60	{0.60}

Table 8. $S = (U, B \cup \{g\})$

For Tables 6, the discernibility matrix with respect to B is given in Table 9 (the column representing x_{16} has no entries, and has been omitted).

The discernibility functions corresponding to the values of the function d_d^B given in the last column of Table 8 ($b = a_2, f = a_6$) are as follows:

These rules provide an explanation of the design of the system (choices of w, r, and the method used to compute degree of acceptance). In general, it can be observed that whenever the nearness measure (a_6) is low, acceptance of the performance of a system represented by time window readings is also low. That is, the values computed by sensor a_2 (measure of Earliness) will be ignored if it exceeds the value of a_6 (nearness). For example, Rule 6 says that even though the completion of a task by an agent is nearly perfectly early ($a_2 = 0.99$), we deduce a value of 0.4 computed by a_6. Also, notice that in the case where the nearness sensor values vary (e.g., Rule R4), it is the lowest value computed by a_6 that appears in the conclusion of the rule. In effect, these rules tell us that this particular clock information system has been designed conservatively, letting values computed by the nearness measure dominate.

	x_1	x_2	x_3	x_4	x_5	x_7	x_8	x_9	x_{10}	x_{11}	x_{12}	x_{13}	x_{15}
x_1													
x_2	b												
x_3	bf	bf											
x_4	bf	bf	bf										
x_5	bf	bf	bf	bf									
x_7	bf	bf	bf	f	bf								
x_8	bf	bf	bf	f	bf	f							
x_9	bf	bf	bf		bf	bf	f						
x_{10}	bf	bf	bf	f	bf	bf	f	f					
x_{11}	bf	bf	bf	f	bf	f	f	f	f				
x_{12}	bf	bf	f	bf	bf	bf	bf	bf	bf	bf			
x_{13}	bf	bf	bf	bf	bf	b	bf	bf	bf	bf	bf		
x_{15}	bf	bf	bf	bf	bf	bf	bf	bf	bf	bf	bf	bf	
x_{16}	bf	bf	bf	f	f	f	f	f	f	f	bf	bf	bf

Table 9. Discernibility Matrix

Case 1. $d_d^B(X_1) = \{0.3\} : a_2$
Case 2. $d_d^B(X_2) = \{0.2\} : a_2$
Case 3. $d_d^B(X_3) = \{0.5\} : a_6$
Case 4. $d_d^B(X_4) = \{0.6\} : a_6$
Case 5. $d_d^B(X_5) = \{0.33\} : a_6$
Case 6. $d_d^B(X_7) = \{0.2\} : a_2 \wedge a_6$
Case 7. $d_d^B(X_8) = \{0.6\} : a_6$
Case 8. $d_d^B(X_9) = \{0.6\} : a_6$
Case 9. $d_d^B(X_{10}) = \{0.6\} : a_6$
Case 10. $d_d^B(X_{11}) = \{0.6\} : a_6$
Case 11. $d_d^B(X_{12}) = \{0.6\} : a_6$
Case 12. $d_d^B(X_{13}) = \{0.2\} : a_2$
Case 13. $d_d^B(X_{15}) = \{0.4\} : a_2 \vee a_6$
Case 14. $d_d^B(X_{16}) = \{0.6\} : a_6$

Based on the above cases, the following decision rules can be extracted:

$R1 : (a_2 = 0.86) \Rightarrow_S (d = 0.3)$
$R2 : (a_2 = 0.82) \vee (a_2 = 0.80 \wedge a_6 = 0.20) \vee (a_2 = 0.81) \Rightarrow_S (d = 0.2)$
$R3 : (a_6 = 0.50) \Rightarrow_S (d = 0.5)$
$R4 : (a_6 = 0.70) \vee (a_6 = 0.80) \vee (a_6 = 0.96) \vee (a_6 = 0.94) \vee$
$(a_6 = 0.60) \vee (a_6 = 0.66) \Rightarrow_S (d = 0.6)$
$R5 : (a_6 = 0.33) \Rightarrow_S (d = 0.33)$
$R6 : (a_2 = 0.99 \vee a_6 = 0.40) \Rightarrow_S (d = 0.4)$

4.7 Extended Roughly Fuzzy Petri Nets

Roughly fuzzy Petri nets can be extended to include operations needed to model decision system processes. The definition of an rfPN can be enriched to include operations ρ_M, ρ_{RED}, ρ_{fM}, ρ_{OPT}, which construct a discernibility matrix, the set of reducts of S, the disjunctive normal form of discernibility function f_M, and the set OPT(S) of all decision rules of the form in (35), respectively. The refinement of the structure of a roughly fuzzy Petri net is given in (36).

$$\begin{aligned}&(\Sigma, P, T, A, N, C, E, I, R, W,\\&Z \cup \{\sigma_{X/R}, \rho_{POSR(X)}, \rho_{NEGR(X)}, \rho_{M(S)}, \rho_{RED(S)}, \rho_{fM(S)}\}, \varrho, \rho)\end{aligned} \tag{36}$$

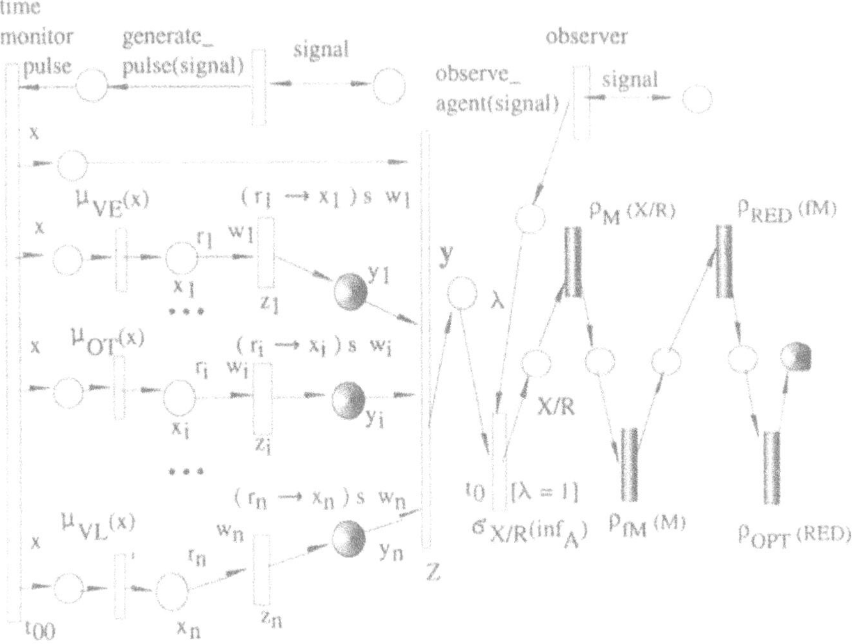

Fig. 11. Process to Derive Clock Information System with Decisions

where $\Sigma, P, T, A, N, C, E, I, R, W, Z, \varrho, \rho$ are as in a roughly fuzzy Petri net. The set Z is augmented with the operations ρ_M, ρ_{RED}, ρ_{fM}, ρ_{OPT}. This form of an rfPN makes it possible to model at a sufficiently high level the basic features of a process which derives OPT(S) from an information system having objects which are fuzzy sets (see Fig. 11). Each of the shaded transitions in Fig. 11 is hierarchical (i.e., they are decomposable into subnets for particular computations). For example, the transition labeled rOPT(S) represents a subnet which constructs the set of decision rules for S. The algorithm to construct OPT(S) is given in [55]. In a chaotic environment, it is necessary to tune the sensors of an information system to derive satisfactory rules. To construct a set of decision rules from a table derived from objects which are fuzzy sets, it is enough to implement the following procedure written in pseudocode with a syntax close to Occam to facilitate implementation (see Fig. 12). Notice that transition t_0 in Fig. 11 is hierarchical and is decomposable into a subnet designed to calibrate the sensors so that table entries satisfy a performance index Q for the fuzzy Petri net. The procedure in Fig. 12 calls build_table( ) and calibrate( ), procedures to build an information system table and calibrate an information system table according to performance index Q. These procedures are left hidden, since they are well-understood.

```
PROC tune( [ ] object_type x,
               [ ] sensor_type a, [ ] decision_type d,
               [ ] real w, [ ] real r, [ ] real target, real tolerance,
               [ ] [ ] table_type M,
               string fM,
               set of string RED, OPT) =
VAL real Q, λ :
    int i, j :
    [n] [m] table_type table :
```

$$Q = \sum_{k=1}^{N} [targer(k) - y(\mathbf{x}(k), \mathbf{r},\ \mathbf{w})]^2$$

```
initialize i, j,
WHILE true
  SEQ
  build_table(x[i], a[j], r[j], w[j], d[i]; table )   –construct table (by transition Z)
WHILE Q > tolerance
  calibrate(table, tolerance, Q)                       –adjust r, w (also by transition Z)
ρ_M(table; M)                                           –construct discernibility matrix
ρ_fM(M; fM)                                             –construct discernibility function
ρ_RED(fM; RED)                                          –construct set of reducts
ρ_OPT(RED; OPT)                                         –construct set of rules
:
```

Fig. 12. Procedure to construct a set of rules

5 Approximate Fuzzy Petri Nets

The basic definition of a roughly fuzzy Petri net requires a straightforward modification to make it possible to model processes which compute rough fuzzy sets.

5.1 Rough Fuzzy Sets

A fuzzy set F (also called a reference set) can be described succinctly by a pair of fuzzy sets in an approximation space [9, 10, 59]. That is, the fuzzy set F is characterized as lying "between" two other fuzzy sets, namely, the upper approximation (37) and lower approximation (38).

$$\mu_{\overline{R}F}(x) = \sup\{\mu_F(y)|y \in [x]_R\},\ \textit{upper approximation} \tag{37}$$

$$\mu_{\underline{R}F}(x) = \inf\{\mu_F(y)|y \in [x]_R\},\ \textit{lower approximation} \tag{38}$$

The membership value x belonging to the upper approximation is the maximum value in the equivalence class $[x]_R$ containing x. Similarly, x in the lower approximation is the minimum value in $[x]_R$. In effect, the three fuzzy sets

$\mu_{\overline{R}F}(x),\ \mu_{\underline{R}F}(x)$

and reference set F characterize a rough fuzzy set. The pair

$$(\mu_{\overline{R}F}(x),\ \mu_{\underline{R}F}(x))$$

is called a rough fuzzy set with the reference set F. Approaches to defining equivalence relations on fuzzy sets are covered in [9]. The characterization of fuzzy sets is useful in cases where the objects in an information system are fuzzy sets.

5.2 Approximate Fuzzy Petri Nets

Let F in U be a fuzzy set defined by membership function μ_F, and let R be an equivalence relation which forms F/R, where $[x]_R \subseteq F$. It is in the context of the quotient set X/R that we introduce roughly fuzzy Petri nets. Such nets are extensions of fuzzy Petri nets, and provide concise means of modeling decisions systems relative to fuzzy sets. An approximate fuzzy Petri Net ($apr_R fPN$) is a structure given in (39)

$$(\Sigma, P, T, A, N, C, E, I, R, W, Z \cup \{\mu_{\underline{R}F}\} \cup \{\mu_{\overline{R}F}\}, \varrho, \rho) \tag{39}$$

where $\Sigma, P, T, A, N, C, E, I, R, W, Z, \varrho, \rho$ are as in a roughly fuzzy Petri net. The set Z of a roughly fuzzy Petri net is augmented with the operations to compute the upper and lower approximations for the equivalence classes of F/R. The motivation for introducing the $apr_R fPN$ class of fuzzy Petri nets derives from the fact they make it possible to model the approximation of fuzzy sets contained in selected classes of information systems. These nets are useful, since they can be calibrated to optimize their outputs relative to predetermined targets. Examples of the simplest forms of $apr_R fPNs$ are given in Table 10.

(i) rfPN computes upper approximation of an equivalence class $[x_i]_R$ for x_i in F/R.	(ii) rfPN computes lower approximation of an equivalence class $[x_i]_R$ for x_i in F/R.
$[x_i]_R$ $\mu_{\overline{R}F}(x_i)$ y z	$[x_i]_R$ $\mu_{\underline{R}F}(x_i)$ y z

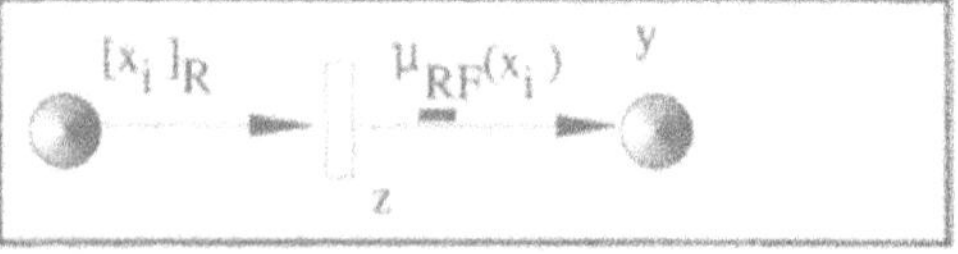

Table 10. Elementary rfPNs

The input to transition z in Part (i) of Table 10 is an equivalence class $[x_i]_R$ in F/R. In the net in (i), transition z computes upper approximation (i.e., $\sup\{\mu_F(y) | y \in [x_i]_R\}$). The output y of the net in (i) is a value in [0, 1]. Similarly, the net in Part (ii) computes an upper approximation of a fuzzy set.

5.3 Application of Approximate Fuzzy Petri Nets

Approximate fuzzy Petri nets make it possible to model the extraction of rough fuzzy sets from information systems having objects which are fuzzy sets. The $apr_R fPN$ model of a process which constructs a rough fuzzy clock information system $S = (U, A)$ and computes the rough fuzzy sets for S is given in Fig. 13.

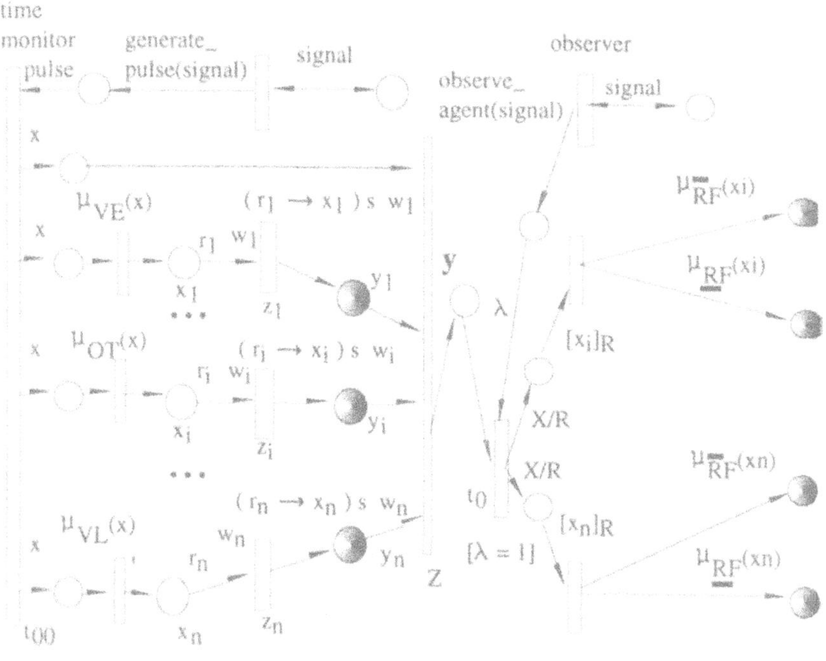

Fig. 13. $apr_R fPN$ model to compute rough fuzzy sets

6 Conclusion

Time is viewed as a duration between firings of transitions in a process. Time is measured by clocks through various time windows. An ordinary time window is structured in terms of three observations: beginning time t_0, current time t, and ending time t_1 where t is some instant between t_0 and t_1. In the context of real-time systems where the activities of an agents are monitored relative to some deadline *delta*, the interval between t_0 and t_1 in a time window is partitioned into subintervals representing durations before and after δ. Knowledge about the lengths of the subintervals of a time window structured in terms of a deadline δ tends to be vague, uncertain, imprecise rather than crisp, certain, and precise. To deal with this problem, approximate time windows are introduced and measurements of time are approximated using rough sets as well as fuzzy sets.

The modeling of processes which construct clock information systems derived from observations of durations extracted from approximate time windows motivates the introduction of new forms of generalized fuzzy Petri nets. Such nets were introduced to model logic processing. These nets can be calibrated to produce desired outputs. By augmenting the set of operations performed by such nets with operations derived from rough set theory, a new class of nets called roughly fuzzy Petri nets is introduced. This form of fuzzy Petri net makes it possible to combine fuzzy sets and rough sets in processes designed to construct sets of decision rules useful in assessing and managing time-constrained agents.

There are a number of issues considered outside the scope of this paper, which are currently being investigated. First, the properties of roughly fuzzy Petri nets provide a rich harvest of information for designers of processes used to develop real-time decision systems. Fortunately, rfPNs inherit properties from generalized fuzzy Petri nets. These properties which have been studied in terms of generalized fuzzy Petri nets are liveness of transitions, boundedness, and reachability. It remains to be proved that these properties can also be found in rfPNs. It should also be observed that a new class of roughly fuzzy Petri nets can be introduced in the context of rough mereology [52]. Second, a complete theory of approximate time windows needs to be established. In addition, the use of rfPNs in modeling the production of real-time decision rules in the presence of dynamically changing reducts needs to be investigated. This theory will include the investigation of additional axioms, propositions and properties for such time windows. There is some reason for believing that rough mereology is applicable in theorizing about the sets associated with the partitions of approximate time windows. In the context of real-time systems, there is also the issue of approximate time windows "belonging" to mobile agents and how readings of these windows would influence coordination in multi-agent systems. It is possible to apply evolutionary computing techniques in managing a population of approximate time windows. Third, the calibration of rfPNs needs to be investigated thoroughly. Experiments demonstrating the effects of calibration need to be performed relative to a variety of approximate time windows. Finally, the possible application of clock information systems like the ones described in this paper needs to be investigated.

Acknowledgement

First, I want to thank Prof. Andrzej Skowron for providing me with a wealth of information, published papers and research reports related to this research. I also thank Prof. Skowron for the invitation to write this paper, for his insights, suggestions and comments concerning concerning the paper, and for the discussions we have had concerning this research. I wish to thank Prof. Witold Pedrycz for introducing me to the calibration algorithm for fuzzy Petri nets, and for the discussions we have had concerning fuzzy sets, fuzzy Petri nets, and many other topics. I also wish to thank Zbigniew Suraj, Institute of Mathematics, Rzeszow and members of the Institute of Mathematics at Warsaw University, Dario Maravall and Luis Baumela, Facultad de Informatica at the University of Madrid, and William Hankley, Department of Computing and Information Sciences at Kansas State University for discussions we have had concerning this research.

References

1. Aristotle, Physics **IV**, 218^b14. In: J. Barnes, (ed.), The Complete Works of Aristotle, I, NJ, Princeton University Press (1984)
2. Bazan, J. G., Skowron, A., Synak, P.: Discovery of decision rules from experimental data. In: T.Y. Lin (ed.): Proceedings of the Third International Workshop on Rough Sets and Soft Computing (RSSC'94), San Jose State University, San Jose, California, USA, November 10–12, (1994) 526–533
3. Bugarin, A.J., Barro, S.: Fuzzy reasoning supported by Petri nets. IEEE Trans. on Fuzzy Systems **2/2** (1994) 135–150
4. Barro, S., Bugarin, A., Carinena, P.Felix, P., Fraga, S.: Petri nets for fuzzy reasoning on dynamic systems. In: Proc. of Seventh Int. Fuzzy Systems Association World Congress (IFSA'97) **III** (1997) 279–284
5. Cao, T.: Variable reasoning and analysis about uncertainty with fuzzy Petri nets. In: M. A. Marson, (ed.), Lecture Notes in Computer Science, Springer–Verlag, Berlin **691** (1993) 126–145
6. Chen, S.-M., Ke, J.-S., Chang, J.-F.: Knowledge representation using fuzzy Petri nets. IEEE Trans. on Knowledge and Data Engineering **2/3** (1990) 311–319
7. Cardoso, J., Valette, R., Dubois, D.: Petri nets with uncertain markings. In: G. Rozenberg, (ed.), Advances in Petri Nets, Lecture Notes in Computer Science, Springer–Verlag, Berlin **483** (1990) 65–78
8. Sandri, S., Cardoso, J.: Management of incomplete information in the processing of safe Petri nets with fuzzy durations. In: Proc. of Seventh Int. Fuzzy Systems Association World Congress (IFSA'97) **III** (1997) 300–305
9. Dubois, D., Prade, H.: Rough fuzzy sets and fuzzy rough sets. Int. J. General Systems **17** (1990) 191–209
10. Dubois, D., Prade, H.: Putting rough sets and fuzzy sets together. Intelligent Decision Support: Handbook of Applications and Advances of the Rough Sets Theory, R. Słowiński, (ed.), Academic Publishers, Dordrecht (1992) 203–222
11. Dedic, M., Richter, G.: Time & clocks & task management. In: Proc. of Int. Workshop on Timed Petri Nets, Torino, Italy (1985) 116–125
12. Fay, A., Schnieder, E.: Knowledge representation and reasoning with fuzzy Petri nets for expert system design and application. In: Proc. of Seventh Int. Fuzzy Systems Association World Congress (IFSA'97) **III** (1997) 288–293
13. Garg, M. L., Ahson, S. I., Gupta, P. V.: (1991) A fuzzy Petri net for knowledge representation and reasoning. Information Processing Letters **39** (1991) 165–171
14. Heidegger, M.: Sein und Zeit. Tbingen, Max Niemeyer Verlag (1957)
15. Jensen, K.: (1986) Coloured Petri nets. Advances in Petri Nets **254** (1986) 288–299
16. Jensen, K.: Coloured Petri nets–basic concepts, analysis methods and practical use 1. Springer–Verlag, Berlin (1992)

17. Huber, P., Jensen, K., Shapiro, R. M.: Hierarchies in coloured Petri nets. Proc. Int. Conf. Science on Application and Theory of Petri Nets. In: G. Rozenberg, (ed.), Lecture Notes in Computer **483** (1986) 261–292
18. Lipp, H. P., Gunther, R.: A fuzzy Petri net concept for complex decision making processes in production control. In: Proc. First European Congress on Fuzzy and Intelligent Technology (EUFIT'93), Aachen, Germany **I** (1993) 290–294
19. Looney, C. G.: Fuzzy Petri nets for rule-based decision making. IEEE Trans. on Systems, Man, and Cybernetics **18/1** (1988) 178–183
20. Milner, R.: Communication and concurrency. Prentice-Hall, NJ (1989)
21. Murata, T.: Petri nets: properties, analysis and applications. In: Proceedings of the IEEE **77/4** (1989) 541–580
22. Murata, T.: Temporal uncertainty and fuzzy-timing high-level Petri nets. In: Proc. 17th Int. Conf. Applications of Theory of Petri Nets, Osaka, Japan (1996) 10–28
23. Naber, G. L.: Spacetime and singularities: An introduction. UK, Cambridge University Press (1988)
24. Oxford English Dictionary, H. W. Fowler, F. G. Fowler, J. B. Sykes, (eds.), Oxford, Oxford University Press (1982)
25. Pawlak, Z.: Hard sets and soft sets. Bull. Pol. Sci. Tech. **36** (1988) 119–123
26. Pawlak, Z.: Rough sets: present state and future prospects. ICS Research Report **32/95**, Institute of Computer Science, Warsaw Institute of Technology (1995)
27. Pawlak, Z.: Rough sets: Theoretical aspects of reasoning about data. Kluwer Academic Publishers, Dordrecht (1991)
28. Petri, C. A.: Kommunikation mit Automaten. Schriften des IIM Nr. 3, Institut fur Instrumentelle Mathematik, Bonn, West Germany. See, also, Communication with Automata (in English). Griffiss Air Force Base, New York Technical Report RADC-Tr-65-377, **1**, Suppl. 1 (1962)
29. Petri, C. A.: Nets, time and space. Theoretical Computer Science **153** (1996) 3–48
30. Petri, C. A.: 'Forgotten topics' of net theory. Lecture Notes in Computer Science **255** 500–514, Berlin, Springer-Verlag (1987)
31. Pedrycz, W.: Fuzzy sets engineering. Boca Raton, FL, CRC Press (1995)
32. Pedrycz, W., Peters, J.F., Ramanna, S., Furuhashi, T.: From data to fuzzy Petri nets: generalized model and calibration abilities. In: Proc. of Seventh Int. Fuzzy Systems Association World Congress (IFSA'97) **III** (1997) 294-299
33. Pedrycz, W., Gomide, F.: A generalized fuzzy Petri net model. IEEE Trans. on Fuzzy Systems **2/4** (1994) 295-301
34. Pedrycz, W., Peters, J. F.: Learning in fuzzy Petri nets. In: J. Cardoso, S. Sandri (eds.), Fuzzy Petri Nets, Physica Verlag, Heidelberg (1997)
35. Pedrycz, W., Peters, J. F.: Information granularity uncertainty principle: Contingency tables and petri net representations. Proc. NAFIPS'97 (to appear)
36. Pedrycz, W., Peters, J. F. Baumela, L.: Family of fuzzy Petri nets: concepts and realizations. IEEE Trans. on Fuzzy Systems (submitted) (1997)
37. Pedrycz, W., Peters, J. F. Ramman, S.: Software quality assessment: Neuro-fuzzy approach. In: Proc. AOWSM'97, Couer d'Alene, Idaho (1997) 11–12
38. Peters, J. F.: Mechanization of real-time linear CSP with higher order logic. Fundamenta Informatica **29/1-2** (1997) 135–164
39. Peters, J. F.: Real-time linear logic. Methods of Logic **1** (1994) 379–412
40. Peters, J. F.: Reasoning about real-time systems. Australian Computer Journal **24/4** (1993) 135–147

41. Peters, J. F. Ramanna, S.: Synchronizing and optimizing multimedia communication with fuzzy clocks. In: Proc. IEEE Canadian Conference on Electrical and Computer Engineering, St. John's, Newfoundland (1997) 229–232
42. Peters, J. F., Sohi, N.: Coordination of multiagent systems with fuzzy clocks. Concurrent Engineering: Research and Applications **4/1** (1996) 73–88
43. Peters, J. F., Zhou, G.: Fuzzy clocks in monitoring the settling times of control systems. Proc. IEEE WESCANEX (1997) 296–301
44. Richter, G.: Clocks and their use for time modeling. Information Systems: Theoretical and Formal Aspects (1985) 49–66
45. Russell, B.: Vagueness". Australian J. of Philosophy **1** (1923) 84–92
46. Scrinivan, P., Gracarin, D.: Approximate reasoning with fuzzy Petri nets. Proc. IEEE Int. Conf. on Fuzzy Systems, San Francisco, CA (1993) 396–401
47. Scarpelli, H., Gomide, F.: Relational calculus in designing fuzzy Petri nets. In: W. Pedrycz, (ed.), Fuzzy Modelling: Paradigms and Practice, Kluwer Academic Publishers, Boston, MA (1996) 70–89
48. Scarpelli, H., Gomide, F.: Fuzzy reasoning and high level fuzzy Petri nets. Proc. First European Congress on Fuzzy and Intelligent Technologies, Aachen, Germany (1993) 600–605
49. Scarpelli, H., Gomide, F. Yager, R.: A reasoning algorithm for high-level fuzzy Petri nets. IEEE Trans. on Fuzzy Systems **4/3** (1996) 282–295
50. Sienkiewicz, J.: Rough sets for boolean functions minimization. Research Report, Warsaw Institute of Technology (1995)
51. Skowron, A.: Extracting laws from decision tables: a rough set approach. Computational Intelligence **11/2** (1995) 371–388
52. Polkowski, L., Skowron, A.: Rough mereology: A new paradigm for approximate reasoning. *Journ. of Approximate Reasoning* **15**(4) (1996) 333–365
53. Skowron, A., Rauszer, C.: The discernibility matrices and functions in information systems. In: R. Słowiński, (ed.), Intelligent Decision Support, Handbook of Applications and Advances of the Rough Sets Theory, Kluwer Academic Publishers, Dordrecht (1992) 331–362
54. Skowron, A., Suraj, Z.: A rough set approach to real-time state identification. Bulletin EATCS **50** (1993) 264–275
55. Skowron, A., Suraj, Z.: Synthesis of concurrent systems specified by Information systems. ICS Research Report 39/94, Institute of Computer Science, Warsaw Institute of Technology (1994)
56. Skowron, A., Suraj, Z.: Discovery of concurrent data models from experimental data tables: a rough set approach. Institute of Computer Science Research Report 15/95, Warsaw Institute of Technology (1995)
57. Skowron, A., Suraj, Z.: A parallel algorithm for real-time decision making: a rough set approach. J. of Intelligent Systems **7** (1996) 5–28
58. Skowron, A., Suraj, Z.: A rough set approach to real-time state identification for decision making. Institute of Computer Science Research Report 18/93, Warsaw University of Technology (1993)
59. Yao, Y. Y.: Combination of rough and fuzzy sets based on a-level sets. In: T.Y. Lin, N. Cercone (eds.), Rough Sets and Data Mining: Analysis of Imprecise Data, Kluwer Academic Publishers, Boston (1997) 301–322
60. Zadeh, L.: Fuzzy sets. Information and Control **8** (1965) 338–353

Chapter 22

The Synthesis Problem of Concurrent Systems Specified by Dynamic Information Systems

Zbigniew Suraj

Institute of Mathematics
Pedagogical University
Rejtana 16A, 35-310 Rzeszów, Poland
e-mail: zsuraj@univ.rzeszow.pl

Abstract. We discuss the synthesis problem of concurrent systems from observations or specification encoded in data table (information system) [Pawlak,1991]. In the paper we first introduce a new notion of a so-called dynamic information system, and then we apply this notion as a tool for specification of concurrent systems behaviour [Pawlak,1992], [Pawlak,1997]. Finally, we present two methods of construction from any dynamic information system DS with its underlying system S, and transition system TS describing the behaviour of DS, a concurrent model in the form of an elementary net system $\boldsymbol{N}$ [Thiagarajan,1987] with the following property: a given transition system TS is isomorphic to the transition system associated with the constructed net system $\boldsymbol{N}$. In the first method we assume that the data table representing a given dynamic information system DS contains the whole knowledge about the observed or specified behaviour of the system. For this setting, we adopt a method of construction a solution of the synthesis problem of concurrent system models suggested by [Desel and Reisig,1996]. A solution of the synthesis problem is any net which is constructed using the concept of regions of transition systems, introduced in [Ehrenfeucht and Rozenberg,1990]. The second method presented in the paper is based on approach that a given data table consists of only partial knowledge about the system behaviour. Thus, we at first compute an extension DS' of the dynamic information system DS, i.e. the system in which the set of all global states of DS' is consistent with all rules true in the underlying information system S of DS, and the set of all global states of DS' represents the largest extension of S consistent with the knowledge represented by S. Next, for finding a solution of the synthesis problem considered here we use the first method. This approach is based on rough set theory [Pawlak,1991] and Boolean reasoning [Brown,1990]. We have implemented program on IBM PC generating a net model from a dynamic information system.

In our approach we also use a modification of the process independence definition presented in [Pawlak,1992]. This paper is an attempt to present a new approach to concurrency based on the rough set philosophy.

We illustrate our ideas by an intuitive example of traffic signal control [Pawlak,1997].

We assume that the reader is familiar with the basic ideas of concurrent systems [Milner,1989], Petri nets [Murata,1989], [Reisig,1985] and information systems [Pawlak,1991].

Our results seem to have some significance for methods of explanation of the system behaviour. Besides, the proposed approach can be seen as basis for a certain class of control system design [Pawlak,1997], and it could be also used for software specification [Hurley,1983].

Key words: information systems, rough sets, concurrent systems, Petri nets.

1 Introduction

The synthesis problem of concurrent systems is the problem of synthesizing a concurrent system model from observations or specification of certain processes. This problem has been discussed for various formalisms, among others: parallel programs [Lengauer and Hehner,1982], COSY-expressions [Janicki,1985], Petri nets [Krieg,1977], [Ehrenfeucht and Rozenberg,1990], [Nielsen, Rozenberg, and Thiagarajan,1992], [Mukund,1992], [Bernadinello,1993], [Desel and Reisig,1996].

In the paper we consider the synthesis problem of concurrent systems specified by a so-called dynamic information systems and denoted by DS. The synthesis problem informally can be formulated as follows.

Synthesis problem. Let $A = \{a_1, ..., a_m\}$ be a non-empty finite set of processes. With every process $a \in A$ we associate a finite set V_a of *its local states.* We assume that the behaviour of such a process system is presented by a designer in a form of two integrated subtables denoted by S and TS, respectively. Each row in the first subtable includes the record of local states of processes from A, and each record is labelled by an element from the set U of *global states of the system,* whereas the second subtable represents a transition system. Columns of the second subtable are labeled by events, rows, analogously as for the underlying system, by objects of interest and entries of the subtable for a given row (state) are follower states of that state. The first row in the first subtable represents the initial state of a given transition system.

The problem is: For a given dynamic information system DS with its transition system TS, find a concurrent model in the form of an elementary net system N [Thiagarajan,1987] with the property: the transition system TS is isomorphic to the transition system associated with the constructed elementary net system N.

Two approaches here are possible. In the first case we assume that the table representing a given dynamic information system contains all possible state combinations, i.e. the table contains the whole knowledge about the observed behaviour of the system. In the second one only a part of possible observations is contained in the table, i.e. they contain partial knowledge about the system behaviour only. In the paper we discuss both approaches.

Some relationships of information systems and rough set theory with the synthesis problem have been recently discussed in [Pawlak,1992], [Pawlak,1997].

Our considerations are based on the notion of processes independence. We apply the definition of the total independence of processes which is a modification of the independence definition used in [Pawlak,1992]. The main idea of the total independence of two sets B and C of processes can be explained as follows: two sets B and C of processes are totally independent in a given information system S if and only if in S the set of local states of processes from B (from C) does not uniquely determine the set of local states of processes from C (from B). This property can be formulated by applying the partial dependency and rule notions [Pawlak,1991]. The total independency of processes allows us to obtain our main result, i.e. a method for constructing from a given dynamic information system DS its concurrent model in the form of an elementary net system N with the following property: a given transition system TS is isomorphic to the transition system associated with the constructed net system N. The set of all global states of DS is consistent with all rules true in the underlying information system S of DS. The set of all global states of DS represents the largest extension of S consistent with the knowledge represented by S.

Our method for constructing a Petri net model consists of two phases. In the first phase, all dependencies between processes in the system are extracted from the given set of global states, the extension of the system is computed and, if necessary, a modification of the given transition system is done. In the second phase, an elementary net system corresponding to the computed extension of the given dynamic information system is built by employing a method solving the synthesis problem of Petri nets presented in [Desel and Reisig,1996].

This paper is an attempt to present a new approach to concurrency based on the rough set philosophy.

A designer of concurrent systems can draw Petri nets directly from a specification in a natural language. We propose a method which allows automatically to generate an appropriate Petri net from a specification given by a dynamic information system and/or rules. This kind of specification can be more convenient for the designers of concurrent systems than drawing directly nets especially when they are large. The designer of concurrent systems applying our method is concentrated on a specification of local processes dependencies in global states. These dependencies are represented by an information system [Pawlak,1991], [Pawlak and Skowron,1993], [Skowron,1993a,b], [Skowron and Suraj,1993b,c,d]. The computing process of the solution is iterative. In a successive step the constructed so far net is automatically redesigned when some new dependencies are discovered and added to a specification. The nets produced automatically by application of our method can be simplified by an application of some reduction procedures. This problem is out of scope of this paper. We expect that our method can be applied as a convenient tool for the synthesis of larger systems [Baar,Cohen, and Feigenbaum,1989], [Shapiro and Eckroth,1987].

We illustrate our ideas by an example of traffic signal control [Pawlak,1997].

The idea of concurrent system representation by information systems is due to Professor Z. Pawlak [1992].

It is still worth to mention that discovering relations between observed data is the main objective of the machine discovery area (cf. [Żytkow,1991]). Our main result can be interpreted as a construction method of all global states consistent with knowledge represented by the underlying system S of DS (i.e. with all rules true in S). For example, checking if a given global state is consistent with S is equivalent to checking if this state is reachable from the initial state of the net system N representing DS. It seems that our approach can be applied for synthesis and analysis of knowledge structure by means of its concurrent models.

We assume that the reader is familiar with the basic ideas of concurrent systems [Milner,1989], Petri nets [Murata,1989], [Reisig,1985] and information systems [Pawlak,1991].

The text is organized as follows. In Section 2 we recall some basic notions of rough set theory [Pawlak,1991]. Section 3 describes how to compute a concurrent data models from information systems. The relationships between dependencies in information systems and partially (totally) independent sets of processes are discussed in Subsection 3.1. In Subsection 3.2 we explain the role of reducts as maximal partially independent sets of processes. In particular, we show that methods for reducts computing can be applied for computing maximal partially independent sets of processes. Subsection 3.3 deals with maximal totally independent sets of processes. Section 4 contains a method for generating rules in minimal form, i.e. with a minimal number of descriptors on its the left hand side. The method is based on the idea of Boolean reasoning [Brown,1990] applied to discernibility matrices defined in [Skowron and Rauszer,1992] and modified here for our purposes. This section realizes the first step in the construction of a concurrent model of knowledge embedded in a given information system. Section 5 and 6 contain basic definitions and notation from transition systems and net theory. In section 7 we define the notion of a dynamic information system and we state the synthesis problem formally. Section 8 contains the solution of the synthesis problem based on synthesis of rules describing transition relation of a given dynamic information system. In the conclusions we suggest some directions for further research related to the representation of information systems by concurrent models.

2 Preliminaries of Rough Set Theory

In this section we recall basic notions of rough set theory. Among them are those of information systems, indiscernibility relations, discernibility matrices, functions, reducts and rules.

2.1 Information Systems

Information systems (sometimes called data tables, attribute-value systems, condition-action tables, knowledge representation systems etc.) are used for representing knowledge. The notion of an information system presented here is due to Z. Pawlak and was investigated by several authors (see e.g. the bibliography in [Pawlak,1991]). Among research topics related to information systems are: rough set theory, problems of knowledge representation, problems of knowledge reduction, dependencies in knowledge bases. Rough sets have been introduced [Pawlak,1991] as a tool to deal with inexact, uncertain or vague knowledge in artificial intelligence applications.

This subsection contains basic notions related to information systems that will be necessary in order to understand our results.

An *information system* is a pair $S = (U, A)$, where U - is a non-empty, finite set called the *universe*, A - is a non-empty, finite set of *attributes*, i.e. $a : U \rightarrow V_a$ for $a \in A$, where V_a is called the *value set* of a.

Elements of U are called *objects* and interpreted as e.g. cases, states, patients, observations. Attributes are interpreted as features, variables, processes, characteristic conditions etc.

In the paper attributes are meant to denote the processes of the system, the values of attributes are understood as local states of processes and objects are interpreted as global states of the system.

The set $V = \bigcup_{a \in A} V_a$ is said to be the *domain* of A.

For $S = (U, A)$, a system $S' = (U', A')$ such that $U \subseteq U'$, $A' = \{a' : a \in A\}$, $a'(u) = a(u)$ for $u \in U$ and $V_a = V_{a'}$ for $a \in A$ will be called a $U'-$*extension* of S (or an extension of S, in short). S is then called a *restriction* of S'. If $S = (U, A)$ then $S' = (U, B)$ such that $A \subseteq B$ will be referred to as a $B-$*extension* of S.

Example 1 [Pawlak,1997]. Let us consider an information system $S = (U, A)$ such that $U = \{u_1, u_2, u_3\}, A = \{a, b, c\}$ and the values of the attributes are defined as in Table 1.

U/A	a	b	c
u_1	1	1	0
u_2	0	2	0
u_3	0	0	2

Table 1. An example of an information system

This information system we can treat as a specification of system behaviour concerning distributed traffic signals control presented in Figure 1.

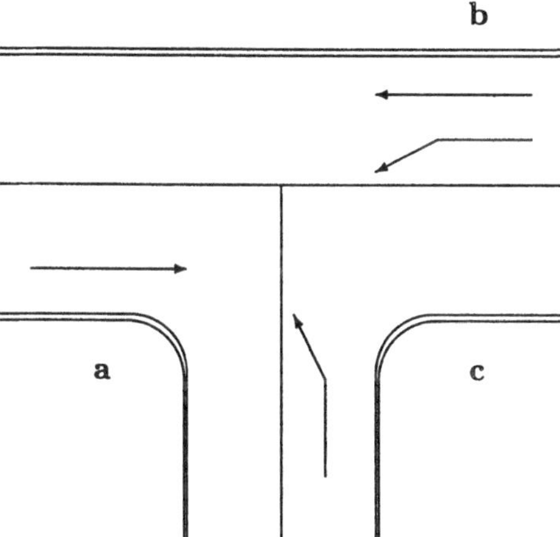

Figure 1. T-intersection

In this case we assume that attributes a, b, and c denote the traffic signals, objects labeled by u_1, u_2, u_3 denote the possible states of the observed system, whereas entries of the table 0, 1 and 2 denote colours of the traffic lights, red, green and green arrow, respectively.

In a given information system, in general, we are not able to distinguish all single objects (using attributes of the system). Namely, different objects can have the same values on considered attributes. Hence, any set of attributes divides the universe U into some classes which establish a partition [Pawlak,1991] of the set of all objects U. It is defined in the following way.

Let $S = (U, A)$ be an information system. With any subset of attributes $B \subseteq A$ we associate a binary relation $ind(B)$, called an *indiscernibility relation,* which is defined by: $ind(B) = \{(u, u') \in U \times U$ for every $a \in B, a(u) = a(u')\}$.

Notice that $ind(B)$ is an equivalence relation and $ind(B) = \bigcap_{a \in B} ind(a)$, where $ind(a)$ means $ind(\{a\})$.

If $u \; ind(B) \; u'$, then we say that the objects u and u' are indiscernible with respect to attributes from B. In other words, we cannot distinguish u from u' in terms of attributes in B.

Any information system $S = (U, A)$ determines an *information function*

$$Inf_A : U \to P(A \times V)$$

defined by $Inf_A(u) = \{(a, a(u)) : a \in A\}$, where

$V = \bigcup_{a \in A} V_a$ and $P(X)$ denotes the powerset of X. The set $\{Inf_A(u) : u \in U\}$ is denoted by INF(S).

Hence, $u \; ind(A) \; u'$ if and only if $Inf_A(u) = Inf_A(u')$.

The values of an information function will be sometimes represented by vectors of the form $(v_1, ..., v_m), v_i \in V_a$, for $i = 1, ..., m$, where $m = \text{card}(A)$. Such vectors are called *information vectors* (over V and A).

Let $S = (U, A)$ be an information system, where $A = \{a_1, ..., a_m\}$. Pairs (a, v) with $a \in A, v \in V$ are called *descriptors*. Instead of (a, v) we also write $a = v$ or a_v.

The set of *terms* over A and V is the least set containing descriptors (over A and V) and closed with respect to the classical propositional connectives: $\neg$ (negation), $\vee$ (disjunction), and $\wedge$ (conjunction), i.e. if τ, τ' are terms over A and V then $\neg\tau, (\tau \vee \tau'), (\tau \wedge \tau')$ are terms over A and V.

The meaning $\| \tau \|_S$ (or in short $\| \tau \|$) of a term τ in S is defined inductively as follows:

$$\| (a, v) \| = \{u \in U : a(u) = v\} \text{ for } a \in A \text{ and } v \in V_a;$$

$$\| \tau \vee \tau' \| = \| \tau \| \cup \| \tau' \|;$$

$$\| \tau \wedge \tau' \| = \| \tau \| \cap \| \tau' \|;$$

$$\| \neg\tau \| = U - \| \tau \| .$$

Two terms τ and τ' are equivalent, $\tau \Leftrightarrow \tau'$, if and only if $\| \tau \| = \| \tau' \|$. In particular we have: $\neg(a = v) \Leftrightarrow \bigvee\{a = v' : v' \neq v \text{ and } v' \in V_a\}$.

2.2 Rules in Information Systems

Rules express some of the relationships between values of the attributes described in the information systems. This subsection contains the definition of rules as well as other related concepts.

Let $S = (U, A)$ be an information system and let $B \subset A$. For every $a \notin B$) we define a function $d_a^B : U \to P(V_a)$ such that

$d_a^B(u) = \{v \in V_a : \text{there exists } u' \in U \; u' \; ind(B) \; u \text{ and } a(u') = v\}$,

where $P(V_a)$ denotes the powerset of V_a.

Hence, $d_a^B(u)$ is the set of all the values of the attribute a on objects indiscernible with u by attributes from B. If the set $d_a^B(u)$ has only one element, this means that the value $a(u)$ is uniquely defined by the values of attributes from B on u.

Let $S = (U, A)$ be an information system and let $B, C \subseteq A$. We say that the *set* C *depends* on B in S in *degree* k $(0 \leq k \leq 1)$, symbolically $B \xrightarrow[S,k]{} C$, if $k = \frac{card(POS_B(C))}{card(U)}$, where $POS_B(C)$ is the *B-positive region of* C in S [Pawlak,1991].

If $k = 1$ we write $B \xrightarrow[S]{} C$ instead of $B \xrightarrow[S,k]{} C$. In this case $B \xrightarrow[S]{} C$ means that $ind(B) \subseteq ind(C)$. If the right hand side of a dependency consists of one attribute only, we say the dependency is *elementary*.

It is easy to see that a simple property given below is true.

Proposition 1. *Let S=(U,A) be an information system and let* $B, C, D \subseteq A$. If $B \xrightarrow[S]{} C$ and $B \xrightarrow[S]{} D$ then $B \xrightarrow[S]{} C \cup D$.

A *rule* over A and V is any expression of the following form:

$$(1)\quad a_{i_1} = v_{i_1} \vee ... \vee a_{i_r} = v_{i_r} \Rightarrow a_p = v_p$$

where $a_p, a_{i_j} \in A, v_p, v_{i_j} \in V_{a_{i_j}}$ for $j = 1, ..., r$.

A rule of the form (1) is called *trivial* if $a_p = v_p$ appears also on the left hand side of the rule. The rule (1) is *true in* S (or in short: is *true*) if

$$\emptyset \neq \| a_{i_1} = v_{i_1} \wedge ... \wedge a_{i_r} = v_{i_r} \| \subseteq \| a_p = v_p \|$$

The fact that the rule (1) is true in S is denoted in the following way:

$$(2)\quad a_{i_1} = v_{i_1} \wedge ... \wedge a_{i_r} = v_{i_r} \underset{S}{\Longrightarrow} a_p = v_p.$$

In the case (2) we also shall say that the values (local states) $v_{i_1}, ..., v_{i_r}$ of processes $a_{i_1}, ..., a_{i_r}$ can *coexist* in S.

By $D(S)$ we denote the set of all rules true in S.

Let $R \subseteq D(S)$. An information vector $\mathbf{v} = (\mathbf{v_1}, ..., \mathbf{v_m})$ is *consistent* with R if and only if for any rule $a_{i_1} = v_{i_1} \wedge ... \wedge a_{i_r} = v_{i_r} \underset{S}{\Longrightarrow} a_p = v_p$ in R if $\mathbf{v}_{i_j} = v_{i_j}$ for $j = 1, ..., r$ then $v_p = \mathbf{v_p}$. The set of all information vectors consistent with R is denoted by CON(R).

Let $S' = (U', A')$ be a U'-extension of $S = (U, A)$. We say that S' is a *consistent extension* of S if and only if $D(S) \subseteq D(S')$. S' is a *maximal* consistent extension of S if and only if S' is a consistent extension of S and any consistent extension S'' of S is a restriction of S.

We apply here the Boolean reasoning approach to the rule generation [Skowron,1993a].

The Boolean reasoning approach [Brown,1990], due to G. Boole, is a general problem solving method consisting of the following steps: (i) construction of a Boolean function corresponding to a given problem; (ii) computation of prime implicants of the Boolean function; (iii) interpretation of prime implicants leading to the solution of the problem.

It turns out that this method can be also applied to the generation of rules with certainty coefficients [Skowron,1993b]. Using this approach one can also generate the rule sets being outputs from some algorithms known in machine learning, like AQ-algorithms [Michalski,Carbonell,and Mitchell,1983], [Skowron and Stepaniuk,1994].

2.3 Reduction of Attributes

Let $S = (U, A)$ be an information system. Any minimal subset $B \subseteq A$ such that $ind(B) = ind(A)$ is called a *reduct* in the information system S [Pawlak,1991]. The set of all reducts in S is denoted by RED(S).

Now we recall two basic notions, namely those of *discernibility matrix* and *discernibility function* [Skowron and Rauszer,1992]], which will help to compute minimal forms of rules with respect to the number of attributes on the left hand side of the rules.

Let $S = (U, A)$ be an information system, and let us assume that $U = \{u_1, ..., u_n\}$, and $A = \{a_1, ..., a_m\}$. By $M(S)$ we denote an $n \times n$ matrix (c_{ij}), called the *discernibility matrix* of S, such that $c_{ij} = \{a \in A : a(u_i) \neq a(u_j)\}$ for $i, j = 1, ..., n$.

Intuitively an entry c_{ij} consists of all the attributes which discern objects u_i and u_j. Since $M(S)$ is symmetric and $c_{ii} = \emptyset$ for $i = 1, ..., n, M(S)$ can be represented using only elements in the lower triangular part of $M(S)$, i.e. for $1 \leq j < i \leq n$.

With every discernibility matrix $M(S)$ we can uniquely associate a *discernibility function* $f_{M(S)}$, defined in the following way:

A *discernibility function* $f_{M(S)}$ for an information system S is a Boolean function of m propositional variables $a_1^*, ..., a_m^*$ (where $a_i \in A$ for $i = 1, ..., m$) defined as the conjunction of all expressions $\bigvee c_{ij}^*$, where $\bigvee c_{ij}^*$ is the disjunction of all elements of $c_{ij}^* = \{a^* : a \in c_{ij}\}$, where $1 \leq j < i \leq n$ and $c_{ij} \neq \emptyset$. In the sequel we write a instead of a^*.

Proposition 2 gives an important property which enables us to compute all reducts of S.

Proposition 2. [Skowron and Rauszer,1992]. *Let $S = (U, A)$ be an information system, and let $f_{M(S)}$ be a discernibility function for S. Then the set of all prime implicants* [Wegener,1987] *of the function $f_{M(S)}$ determines the set* RED*(S) of all reducts of S, i.e. $a_{i_1} \wedge ... \wedge a_{i_k}$ is a prime implicant of $f_{M(S)}$ if and only if* $\{a_{i_1}, ..., a_{i_k}\} \in$RED$(S)$.

In the following propositions [Pawlak,1991] the important relationships between the reducts and the dependencies are given.

Proposition 3. *Let S=(U, A)be an information system and let B* $\in$RED(S). If $A - B \neq \emptyset$ *then* $B \underset{S}{\rightarrow} A - B$.

Proposition 4. *If $B \underset{S}{\rightarrow} C$ then $B \underset{S}{\rightarrow} C'$, for every $\emptyset \neq C' \subseteq C$. In particular, $B \underset{S}{\rightarrow} C$ implies $B \underset{S}{\rightarrow} \{a\}$, for every $a \in C$.*

Proposition 5. *Let B* $\in$RED(S). *Then attributes in the reduct B are pairwise independent, i.e. neither $\{a\} \underset{S}{\rightarrow} \{a'\}$ nor $\{a'\} \underset{S}{\rightarrow} \{a\}$ holds, for any a, $a' \in B, a \neq a'$.*

Below we present a procedure for computing reducts [Skowron and Rauszer,1992].

PROCEDURE for computing RED(S):

Input: An information system S.
Output: The set of all reducts in S.

Step 1. Compute the discernibility matrix for the system S.
Step 2. Compute the discernibility function $f_{M(S)}$ associated with the discernibility matrix $M(S)$.
Step 3. Compute the minimal disjunctive normal form of the discernibility function $f_{M(S)}$ (The normal form of the function yields all the reducts).

One can show that the problem of finding a minimal (with respect to cardinality) reduct is NP-hard [Skowron and Rauszer,1992]. In general the number of reducts of a given information system can be exponential with respect to the number of attributes (i.e. any information system S has at most m over $[m/2]$ reducts, where m=card(A)). Nevertheless, existing procedures for reduct computation are efficient in many applications and for more complex cases one can apply some efficient heuristics (see e.g. [Bazan,Skowron, and Synak,1994b], [Nguyen and Skowron,1995], [Skowron,1995], [Skowron,Polkowski, and Komorowski,1996], [Nguyen,1997]).

Example 2. Applying the above procedure for the information system S from Example 1, we obtain the following discernibility matrix $M(S)$ presented in Table 2 and discernibility function $f_{M(S)}$ presented below:

U	u_1	u_2	u_3
u_1			
u_2	a, b		
u_3	a, b, c	b, c	

Table 2. The discernibility matrix $M(S)$ for the information system S from Example 1

$$f_{M(S)}(a, b, c) = (a \vee b) \wedge (a \vee b \vee c) \wedge (b \vee c).$$

We consider non-empty entries of the table (see Table 2), i.e. $a, b; b, c$ and a, b, c; next a, b, c are treated as Boolean variables and the disjunctions $a \vee b$; $b \vee c$ and $a \vee b \vee c$ are constructed from these entries; finally, we take the conjuction of all the computed disjunctions to obtain the discernibility function corresponding to $M(S)$.

After reduction (using the absorption laws) we get the following minimal disjunctive normal form of the discernibility function $f_{M(S)}(a, b, c) = (a \wedge c) \vee b$.

There are two reducts: $R_1 = \{a, c\}$ and $R_2 = \{b\}$ of the system. Thus $\text{RED}(S) = \{R_1, R_2\}$.

Example 3 illustrates how to find all dependencies among attributes using Propositions 3 and 4.

Example 3. Let us consider again the information system S from Example 1. By Proposition 3 we have for the system S the dependencies:

$$\{a, c\} \underset{S}{\rightarrow} \{b\} \text{ and } \{b\} \underset{S}{\rightarrow} \{a, c\}.$$

Next, by Proposition 4 we get the following elementary dependencies:

$$\{a, c\} \underset{S}{\rightarrow} \{b\}, \{b\} \underset{S}{\rightarrow} \{a\}, \{b\} \underset{S}{\rightarrow} \{c\}.$$

3 Computing Concurrent Data Models from Information Systems

We base our considerations about independency of processes on the notions of dependency and partial dependency of sets of attributes in an information system S. The set of attributes C depends in S on the set of attributes B in S if one can compute the values of attributes from C knowing the values of attributes from B. The set of attributes C depends in S partially in degree k $(0 \leq k < 1)$ on the set of attributes B in S if the B-positive region of C in S consists of k % of global states in S.

A set of processes $B \subseteq A$ in a given information system $S = (U, A)$ is called *partially independent* in S if there is no partition of B into sets C and D such that D is dependent on C in S. We show that maximal partially independent sets in S are exactly reducts in S. In this way we have a method for computing maximal partially independent sets (in S) based on methods of reducts computing [Skowron and Rauszer,1992].

We say that a set $B \subseteq A$ is a ***totally independent set of processes in*** $S=(U, A)$ if there is no partition of B into C and D such that D depends on C in S in the degree $0 < k \leq 1$.

In the following we show a method for computing maximal totally independent sets of processes in $S = (U, A)$. These are all totally independent maximal subsets of reducts in S.

3.1 Dependencies in Information System and Independence of Processes

In this section we present two basic notions related to independency of processes.

Let $S = (U, A)$ be an information system (of processes) and let $\emptyset \neq B \subseteq A$. The set B of processes is called ***totally independent*** in S if and only if $\mathrm{card}(B) = 1$ or there is no partition of B into C, D such that $C \underset{S,k}{\rightarrow} D$, where $k > 0$.

Let $S = (U, A)$ be an information system (of processes) and let $\emptyset \neq B \subseteq A$. The set B of processes is called ***partially independent*** in S if and only if $\mathrm{card}(B) = 1$ or there is no partition of B into C, D such that $C \underset{S}{\rightarrow} D$.

One can prove from the above definitions the following properties.

Proposition 6. *If B is a totally independent set of processes in S and $\emptyset \neq B' \subseteq B$ then B' is also totally independent set of processes in S.*

Proposition 7. *B is a totally independent set of processes in S if and only if* card(B)*=1 or $B - \{a\} \underset{S,0}{\rightarrow} \{a\}$ for any $a \in B$.*

Proposition 8. *B is a partially independent set of processes in S if and only if* card(B)*=1 or B consists of B-indispensable* [Pawlak,1991] *attributes in S only.*

3.2 Reducts as Maximal Partially Independent Sets of Processes

We have the following relationship between the partially independent sets of processes and reducts:

Proposition 9. *B is a maximal partially independent set of processes in S if and only if $B \in$RED(S), where* RED(S) *denotes the set of all reducts in S.*

In order to compute the partially independent parts of a given information system, first we have to execute the presented above procedure generating reducts (see Section 2).

3.3 Maximal Totally Independent Sets of Processes

In the previous section we have discussed the problem of construction of the family of partially independent sets of processes and a relationship between these sets and reducts. Now we are interested in a construction of all maximal totally independent sets of processes.

From the definition of totally independent sets of processes in a given information system S it follows that for an arbitrary totally independent set B in S there is a reduct $C \in \mathrm{RED}(S)$ such that $B \subseteq C$. Hence to find all maximal totally independent sets of processes it is enough to find for every $C \in \mathrm{RED}(S)$ all maximal independent subsets of C.

To find all maximal totally independent sets of processes in $S = (U, A)$ it is enough to perform the following steps:

Step 1. $\mathbf{T}$:= RED(S); $\mathbf{I}$:= $\{\{a_1\}, ..., \{a_m\}\}$;
Step 2. if ($\mathbf{T}$ is empty) then goto Step 4
else begin
CHOOSE_ A_ SET $B \in \mathbf{T}$;
$\mathbf{T}$:= $\mathbf{T} - \{B\}$
end;
Step 3. if card$(B) \leq 1$ then goto Step 2;
$L := 0$;
for every $a \in B$ do
if $B - \{a\} \overrightarrow{_{\mathrm{S,k}}} \{a\}$ for some $k > 0$ then $\mathbf{T} := \mathbf{T} \cup \{B - \{a\}\}$
else $L := L + 1$;
if $L = \mathrm{card}(B)$ then $\mathbf{I} := \mathbf{I} \cup \{B\}$;
goto Step 2;
Step 4. The maximal sets in $\mathbf{I}$ (with respect to the inclusion $\subseteq$) are maximal totally independent sets in S.

Let OPT(S) be the set of all rules of the form (1) $a_{i_1} = v_{i_1} \wedge ... \wedge a_{i_r} = v_{i_r} \underset{\mathrm{S}}{\Rightarrow} a = v$, with the left hand side in minimal form (see Section 4). If γ is in the form (1) then by $L(\gamma)$ we denote the set $\{a_{i_1}, ..., a_{i_r}\}$. It is easy to see that one can take in the first line of Step 1 the instruction $\mathbf{T} := \{L(\gamma) : \gamma \in \mathrm{OPT}(S)\}$ instead of $\mathbf{T}$:= RED(S). In this way we obtain more efficient version of the presented method. The time and space complexity of the discussed problem is, in general, exponential because of the complexity of RED(S) computing. Nevertheless, existing procedures and heuristics help us to compute all maximal independent sets for many practical applications.

At the end let us note the following characterization of reducts being maximal totally independent set of processes:

Proposition 10. Let $S = (U, A)$ be an information system and let $C \in$RED(S) with card$(C) > 1$. C is a maximal totally independent set of processes in S if and only if for every $u \in U$ and $a \in C$ card$(d_a^C(u)) > 1$.

4 Minimal Rules in Information Systems

In this section we present a method for generating the minimal form of rules (i.e. rules with a minimal number of descriptors on the left hand side).

Let $S = (U, A \cup \{a^*\})$ be an information system and $a^* \notin A$. We are looking for all minimal rules in S of the form: $a_{i_1} = v_{i_1} \wedge ... \wedge a_{i_r} = v_{i_r} \underset{S}{\Rightarrow} a = v$, where $a \in A \cup \{a^*\}, v \in V_a, a_{i_j} \in A$ and $v_{i_j} \in V_{a_{i_j}}$ for $j = 1, ..., r$.

The above rules express functional dependencies between the values of the attributes of S. These rules are computed from systems of the form $S' = (U, B \cup \{a\})$ where $B \subset A$ and $a \in A - B$ or $a = a^*$.

First, for every $v \in V_a, u_l \in U$ such that $d_a^B(u_l) = \{v\}$ a modification $M(S'; a, v, u_l)$ of the discernibility matrix is computed from $M(S')$.
By $M(S'; a, v, u_l) = (c_{ij}^*)$ (or M, in short) we denote the matrix obtained from $M(S')$ in the following way:

IF $i \neq l$ **THEN** $c_{ij}^* = \emptyset$;
IF $c_{lj} = \emptyset$ and $d_a^B(u_j) \neq \{v\}$ **THEN** $c_{lj}^* = c_{lj} \cap B$ **ELSE** $c_{lj}^* = \emptyset$.

Next, we compute the discernibility function f_M and the prime implicants [Wegener,1987] of f_M taking into account the non-empty entries of the matrix M (when all entries c_{ij}^* are empty we assume f_M to be always true).

Finally, every prime implicant $a_{i_1} \wedge ... \wedge a_{i_r}$ of f_M determines a rule $a_{i_1} = v_{i_1} \wedge ... \wedge a_{i_r} = v_{i_r} \underset{S}{\Rightarrow} a = v$, where $a_{i_j}(u_l) = v_{i_j}$ for $j = 1, ..., r$, $a(u_l) = v$.

Let $S = (U, A)$ be an information system. In the following we shall apply the above method for every $R \in$RED(S). First we construct all rules corresponding to nontrivial dependencies between the values of attributes from R and $A - R$ and next all rules corresponding to nontrivial dependencies between the values of attributes within a reduct R. These two steps are realized as follows.

(i) For every reduct $R \in$RED(S), $R \subset A$ and for every $a \in A - R$ we consider the system $S' = (U, R \cup \{a\})$. For every $v \in V_a$, $u_l \in U$ such that $d_a^R(u_l) = \{v\}$ we construct the discernibility matrix $M(S'; a, v, u_l)$, next the discernibility function f_M and the set of all rules corresponding to prime implicants of f_M.

(ii) For every reduct $R \in$RED(S) with card$(R) > 1$ and for every $a \in R$ we consider the system $S'' = (U, B \cup \{a\})$, where $B = R - \{a\}$. For every $v \in V_a, u_l \in U$ such that $d_a^B(u_l) = \{v\}$ we construct the discernibility matrix $M(S''; a, v, u_l)$, then the discernibility function f_M and the set of all rules corresponding to prime implicants of f_M.

The set of all rules constructed in this way for a given $R \in$RED(S) is denoted by OPT(S, R).

We put OPT$(S) = \bigcup\{$ OPT$(S, R) : R \in$RED$(S)\}$.

Let us observe that if $a_{i_1} = v_{i_1} \wedge ... \wedge a_{i_r} = v_{i_r} \overset{\Rightarrow}{S} a_p = v_p$ is a rule from OPT(S), then $U \cap \| a_{i_1} = v_{i_1} \wedge ... \wedge a_{i_r} = v_{i_r} \|_S \neq \emptyset$.

Proposition 11 [Pawlak,1992]. *Let S=(U, A) be an information system, $R \in$RED(S), and $R \subset A$. Let $f_{M(S')}$ be a relative discernibility function for the system $S' = (U, R \cup \{a^*\})$ where $a^* \in A - R$. Then all prime implicants of the function $f_{M(S')}$ correspond to all $\{a^*\}$ - reducts of S'.*

Now we are ready to present a very simple procedure for computing an extension S' of a given information system S. Let OPT(S) be the set of all rules constructed as described above.

PROCEDURE for computing an extension S' of S:

Input: An information system $S = (U, A)$ and the set OPT(S) of rules.

Output: An extension S' of S.

Step 1. Compute all admissible global states of S, i.e. the cartesian product of the value sets for all attributes a from A.

Step 2. Verify using the set OPT(S) of rules which admissible global states of S are consistent with rules true in S.

The next example illustrates how to find all nontrivial dependencies between the values of attributes in a given information system. At the end of example we give information about an extension of the information system.

Example 4. Let us consider the information system S from Example 1 and the discernibility function for S presented in Table 2. We compute the set of rules corresponding to nontrivial dependencies between the values of attributes from the reduct R_1 of S with b (i.e. those outside of this reduct) as well as the set of rules corresponding to nontrivial dependencies between the values of attributes within the reduct of that system. In both cases we apply the method presented above.

Let us start by computing the rules corresponding to nontrivial dependencies between the values of attributes from the reduct $R_1 = \{a, c\}$ of S with b.

We have the following subsystem $S_1 = (U, B \cup \{b\})$, where $B = R_1$, from which we compute the rules mentioned above:

U/B	a	c	b	d_b^B
u_1	1	0	1	$\{1\}$
u_2	0	0	2	$\{2\}$
u_3	0	2	0	$\{0\}$

Table 3. The subsystem $S_1 = (U, B \cup \{b\}$ with the function d_b^B, where $B = \{a, c\}$

In the table the values of the function d_b^B are also given. The discernibility matrix $\boldsymbol{M}$ $(S_1; b, v, u_l)$ where $v \in V_b$, $u_l \in U$, $l = 1, 2, 3$, obtained from $M(S_1)$ in the above way is presented in Table 4.

U	u_1	u_2	u_3
u_1		a	a, c
u_2	a		c
u_3	a, c	c	

Table 4. The discernibility matrix $\boldsymbol{M}(S_1; b, v, u_l)$ for the matrix $M(S_1)$

The discernibility functions corresponding to the values of the function d_b^B are the following:

Case 1. For $d_b^B(u_1) = \{1\} : a \wedge (a \vee c) = a$.

We consider non-empty entries of the column labelled by u_1 (see Table 4), i.e. a and a, c; next a, c are treated as Boolean variables and the disjunctions a and $a \vee c$ are constructed from these entries; finally, we take the conjuction of all the computed disjunctions to obtain the discernibility function corresponding to $\boldsymbol{M}(S_1; b, v, u_l)$.

Case 2. For $d_b^B(u_2) = \{2\} : a \wedge c$.

Case 3. For $d_b^B(u_3) = \{0\} : (a \vee c) \wedge c = c$.

Hence we obtain the following rules: $a_1 \underset{S}{\Rightarrow} b_1$, $a_0 \wedge c_0 \underset{S}{\Rightarrow} b_2$, $c_2 \underset{S}{\Rightarrow} b_0$.

Now we compute the rules corresponding to all nontrivial dependencies between the values of attributes within the reduct R_1.

We have the following two subsystems $(U, C \cup \{c\})$, $(U, D \cup \{a\})$ of S, where $C = \{a\}$, and $D = \{c\}$, from which we compute the rules mentioned above:

U/C	a	c	d_c^C
u_1	1	0	$\{0\}$
u_2	0	0	$\{0,2\}$
u_3	0	2	$\{0,2\}$

Table 5. The subsystem $(U, C \cup \{c\})$ with the function d_c^C, where $C = \{a\}$

U/D	c	a	d_a^D
u_1	0	1	$\{0,1\}$
u_2	0	0	$\{0,1\}$
u_3	2	0	$\{0\}$

Table 6. The subsystem $(U, D \cup \{a\})$ with the function d_a^D, where $D = \{c\}$

In the tables the values of the functions d_c^C, and d_a^D are also given.

The discernibility functions corresponding to the values of these functions are the following:

Table 5. For $d_c^C(u_1) = \{0\}$: a.

Table 6. For $d_a^D(u_3) = \{0\}$: c.

Hence we obtain the following rules:

From Table 5: $a_1 \underset{S}{\Rightarrow} c_0$.

From Table 6: $c_2 \underset{S}{\Rightarrow} a_0$.

Finally, the set of rules corresponding to all nontrivial dependencies between the values of attributes within the reduct R_1 has the form: $a_1 \underset{S}{\Rightarrow} c_0$, $c_2 \underset{S}{\Rightarrow} a_0$.

Eventually, we obtain the set $\mathrm{OPT}(S, R_1)$ of rules corresponding to all nontrivial dependencies for the reduct R_1 in the considered information system S:

$a_1 \underset{S}{\Rightarrow} b_1$, $a_0 \wedge c_0 \underset{S}{\Rightarrow} b_2$, $c_2 \underset{S}{\Rightarrow} b_0$, $a_1 \underset{S}{\Rightarrow} c_0$, $c_2 \underset{S}{\Rightarrow} a_0$.

In a similar way one can compute the set $\mathrm{OPT}(S, R_2)$ of rules corresponding to all nontrivial dependencies for the reduct R_2 in the system S. This set consists of one kind of rules, i.e. the rules corresponding to all nontrivial dependencies between the values of attributes from R_2 with a, c of the form: $b_1 \underset{S}{\Rightarrow} a_1$, $b_0 \vee b_2 \underset{S}{\Rightarrow} a_0$, $b_1 \vee b_2 \underset{S}{\Rightarrow} c_0$, $b_0 \underset{S}{\Rightarrow} c_2$, whereas the second set of rules corresponding to all nontrivial dependencies between the values of attributes within the reduct R_2 is empty, because this reduct has only one element.

The set $\mathrm{OPT}(S)$ of all rules constructed in this way for the information system S of Example 1 is the union of sets $\mathrm{OPT}(S, R_1)$ and $\mathrm{OPT}(S, R_2)$.

It is easy to verify that in this case the extension S' of the system S computed by using our procedure presented above is the same as the original one.

Remark 1. The above rules explain behaviour of the system from Figure 1.

Remark 2. Our approach to rule generation is based on procedures for the computation of reduct sets. It is known that in general the reduct set can be of exponential complexity with respect to the number of attributes. Nevertheless, there are several methodologies allowing to deal with this problem in practical applications. Among them are the feature extraction techniques or clustering methods known in pattern recognition [Nadler and Smith,1993] and machine learning [Michalski, Carbonell, and Mitchell,1983], allowing to reduce the number of attributes or objects so that the rules can be efficiently generated from them. Another approach is suggested in [Bazan Skowron, and Synak,1994a]. It leads to the computation of only so called the most stable reducts from the reduct set in a sampling process of a given decision table (i.e. a special case of an information system, see [Pawlak,1991]). The rules are produced from these stable reducts only. This last technique can be treated as relevant feature extraction from a given set of features. The result of the above techniques applied to a given information system is estimated as successful if rules can be efficiently generated from the resulting compressed information system by the Boolean reasoning method and if the quality of the classification of unseen objects by these rules is sufficiently high. We assume that the information systems which create inputs for our procedures satisfy those conditions.

5 Transition Systems

Transition systems create a simple and powerful formalism for explaining the operational behaviour of models of concurrency. This section contains basic notions and notations connected with transition systems that will be necessary for understanding of our main result.

A *transition system* is a quadruple $TS = (S, E, T, s_0)$, where S is a nonempty set of *states*, E is a set of *events*, $T \subseteq S \times E \times S$ is the *transition relation*, $s_0 \in S$ is the *initial state*.

A transition system can be pictorially represented as a rooted edge-labelled directed graph. Its nodes and its directed arcs represent states and state transition, respectively. As different state transitions may be caused by equal events, different arcs may be labelled by equal symbols. If $(s, e, s') \in T$ then a transition system TS can go from s to s' as a result of the event e occurring at s.

Example 5. In Figure 2 a transition system is shown, where the initial state is indicated by an extra arrow without source and label.

An isomorphism between transition systems is defined in the following way:

Let $TS = (S, E, T, s_0)$ and $TS' = (S', E', T', s'_0)$ be two transition systems. A bijection $f : S \to S'$ is an *isomorphism* from TS to TS' (denoted $f : TS \to TS'$) if and only if the following two conditions are satisfied:

(i) $f(s_0) = s'_0$

(ii) $(s, e, s') \in T$ if and only if $(f(s), e, f(s')) \in T'$.

Two transition systems TS and TS' are called *isomorphic* (denoted $TS \simeq TS'$) if and only if there exists an isomorphism $f : TS \to TS'$.

It is worth to observe that we demand that the set of events of E from a transition system TS coincides with the set of events of E' from TS'.

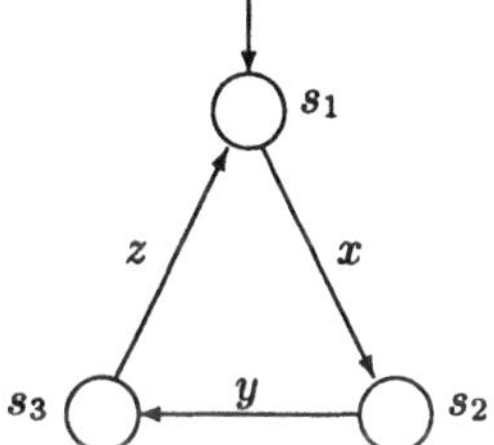

Figure 2. An example of a transition system

Let $TS = (S, E, T, s_0)$ be a transition system. We say that the event e has *concession in* the state s (is *enabled at* s) if there exists a state s' such that $(s, e, s') \in T$.

The notion of regions, introduced in [Ehrenfeucht and Rozenberg,1990] is important for this paper.

Let $TS = (S, E, T, s_0)$ be a transition system. A set R of states of TS is a *region* of TS if and only if for equally labelled arcs (s, e, s') and (s_1, e, s_1') holds:

if $s \in R$ and $s' \notin R$ then $s_1 \in R$ and $s_1' \notin R$, and

if $s \notin R$ and $s' \in R$ then $s_1 \notin R$ and $s_1' \in R$.

$\emptyset$ and S are called *trivial regions* of TS. By R_{TS} we denote the set of all non-trivial regions of TS.

Let $TS = (S, E, T, s_0)$ be a transition system.

For $e \in E$,

$$^\bullet e = \{R \in R_{TS} : \text{there exists } (s, e, s') \in T \ s \in R \text{ and } s' \notin R\}$$

is called the *pre* $-$ *region* of e,

$$e^\bullet = \{R \in R_{TS} : \text{there exists } (s, e, s') \in T \ s \notin R \text{ and } s' \in R\}$$

is called the *post* $-$ *region* of e.

Example 6. For the transition system shown in Figure 2, $X = \{s_1\}, Y = \{s_2\}$ and $Z = \{s_3\}$ are regions, and $^\bullet x = \{X\}, y^\bullet = \{Z\}$.

6 Elementary net systems

In this section we recall basic notions connected with the basic system model of net theory, called *elementary net system* [Thiagarajan,1987].

In net theory, models of concurrent systems are based on objects called nets which specify the local states and local transitions and the relationships between them.

A triple $N = (S, T, F)$ is called a *net* if and only if

(i) S and T are disjoint sets (the elements of S are called $S-$*elements*, the elements of T are called $T-$*elements*).

(ii) $F \subseteq (S \times T) \cup (T \times S)$ is a binary relation, called the *flow relation.*

(iii) For each $x \in S \cup T$ there exists $y \in S \cup T$ such that $(x, y) \in F$ or $(y, x) \in F$.

In the following the S-elements will be called *conditions* and the T-elements will be called *events*. Moreover, we use B to denote the set of conditions and E to denote the set of events; consequently a net will be denoted as the triple (B, E, F).

Let $N = (B, E, F)$ be a net. For $x \in B \cup E, {}^\bullet x = \{y : (y, x) \in F\}$ is called the *preset* of x, $x^\bullet = \{y : (x, y) \in F\}$ is called the *postset* of x.

The element $x \in B \cup E$ is called isolated if and only if ${}^\bullet x \cup x^\bullet = \emptyset$.

It is worth to observe that the condition (iii) in the net definition states that we do not permit isolated elements in considered nets.

The net $N = (B, E, F)$ is called ***simple*** if and only if distinct elements do not have the same pre- and postset, i.e. for each $x \in B \cup E$ the following condition is satisfied:

if ${}^\bullet x = {}^\bullet y$ and $x^\bullet = y^\bullet$ then $x = y$.

A quadruple $\mathbf{N} = (B, E, F, c_0)$ is called an *elementary net system* if and only if

(i) $N = (B, E, F)$ is a simple net without isolated elements, called the *underlying net* of $\mathbf{N}$ and denoted by $N_{\mathbf{N}}$,

(ii) $c_0 \subseteq B$ is the ***initial state.***

In diagrams the conditions will be drawn as circles, the events as boxes and elements of the flow relations as directed arcs. The initial state will be indicated by marking (with small black dots) the elements of the initial state.

Example 7. An elementary net system shown in Figure 3 has three conditions X, Y, Z, and three events x, y, z. Its initial state is $\{X\}$. The preset of x is equal to $\{X\}$, and the postset of y is $\{Z\}$.

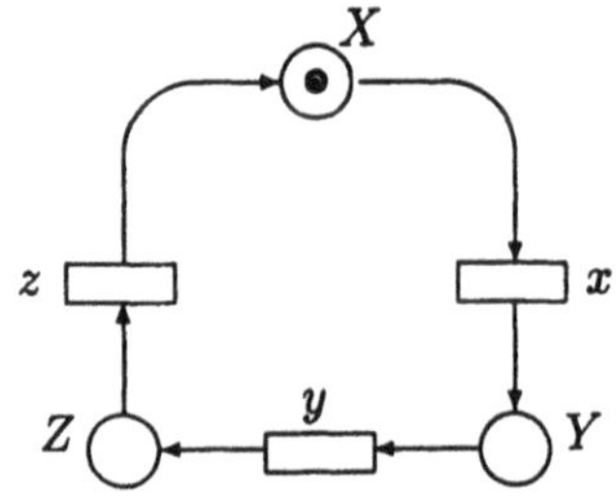

Figure 3. An elementary net system

From now on we will often refer to elementary net systems as just net systems. The dynamics of a net system are straightforward. The states of a net system consists of a set of conditions that hold concurrently. The system can go from a state to a state through the occurrence of an event. An event can occur at a case if and only if all its pre-conditions (i.e. conditions in its preset) hold and none of its post-conditions (i.e. conditions in its postset) hold at the state. When an event occurs then all its pre-conditions cease to hold and all its post-conditions begin to hold. Formally, the dynamics of a net system is described by the so-called the *transition relation* of that net system.

Let $N = (B, E, F)$ be a net. Then $tr_N \subseteq P(B) \times E \times P(B)$ is the *transition relation* of N defined as follows: $(c, e, c') \in tr_N$ if and only if $c - c' = {}^{\bullet}e$ and $c' - c = e^{\bullet}$.

Let $\boldsymbol{N} = (B, E, F, c_0)$ be a net system.

(i) $C_{\boldsymbol{N}}$ is the *state space* of $\boldsymbol{N}$ and it is the smalest subset of $P(B)$ containing c_0 which satisfies the condition: if $(c, e, c') \in tr_{N_N}$ and $c \in C_N$ then $c' \in C_N$.

(ii) $tr_{\boldsymbol{N}}$ is the *transition relation* of $\boldsymbol{N}$ and it is tr_{N_N} restricted to $C_N \times E \times C_N$.

(iii) $E_{\boldsymbol{N}}$ is the set of active events of $\boldsymbol{N}$ and it is the subset of E given by $E_{\boldsymbol{N}} = \{e : \text{there exists } (c, e, c') \in tr_{\boldsymbol{N}}\}$.

It is possible to associate a transition system with a net system to explain its operational behaviour.

Let $\boldsymbol{N} = (B, E, F, c_0)$ be a net system. Then the transition system $TS_{\boldsymbol{N}} = (C_{\boldsymbol{N}}, E_{\boldsymbol{N}}, tr_{\boldsymbol{N}}, c_0)$ is called the *transition system associated with* $\boldsymbol{N}$.

A transition system TS is an *abstract transition system* if and only if there exists a net system $\boldsymbol{N}$ such that $TS \simeq TS_{\boldsymbol{N}}$.

Example 8. The state space of the net system presented in Figure 3 is $\{\{X\}, \{Y\}, \{Z\}\}$. It is easy to verify that the transition system associated with the net system of Figure 3 is isomorphic with the transition system shown in Figure 2.

7 Dynamic Information Systems

Now we introduce the notion of a *dynamic information system* which plays a central role in this paper.

A *dynamic information system* is a quintuple $DS = (U, A, E, T, u_0)$ where

(i) $S = (U, A)$ is an information system called the *underlying system* of DS,

(ii) $TS = (U, E, T, u_0)$ is a transition system.

Dynamic information systems will be presented in the form of two integrated subtables. The first subtable represents the underlying system, wheras the second one the transition system. Columns of the second subtable are labeled by events, rows, analogously as for the underlying system, by objects of interest and entries of the subtable for a given row (state) are follower states of that state. The first row in the first subtable represents the initial state of a given transition system. We will both subtables have the same number of rows, but the number of columns is different.

Example 9. In Table 7 is shown an example of a dynamic information system $DS = (U, A, E, T, u_0)$ such that its underlying system is represented by Table 1, whereas the transition system is represented by the graph in Figure 2. In this case the initial state of the system is represented by u_1. We show also that, for instance in the state u_2 the event y has concesion and when it occurs then a new state u_3 of DS appears.

U/A	a	b	c	U/E	x	y	z
u_1	1	1	0		u_2		
u_2	0	2	0			u_3	
u_3	0	0	2				u_1

Table 7. *A* dynamic information system

Now we are ready to formulate the synthesis problem of concurrent systems specified by dynamic information systems.

The synthesis problem:

Let $DS = (U, A, E, T, u_0)$ be a dynamic information system. Is a given transition system $TS = (U, E, T, u_0)$ an abstract transition system? If yes, construct a net system N satisfying $TS \simeq TS_N$.

8 The solution of the synthesis problem

In this section we present a solution of the synthesis problem stated in this paper.

8.1 The first approach

A solution method of the problem is based on the approach proposed in [Desel and Reisig,1996]. Now we describe shortly their approach connected with a procedure to decide whether or not a given transition system TS is an abstract transition system. In the positive case, the procedure provides a net system whose transition system is isomorphic to TS.

Since every condition corresponds to a region and every region generates a potential condition we can construct a net system from a transition system, using only generated conditions.

Let $DS = (U, A, E, T, u_0)$ be a dynamic information system, let $TS = (U, E, T, u_0)$ be the transition system of DS, and let m be a set of regions of TS. Then the *m-generated net system* is $N_m^{TS} = (m, E, F, c_0)$ where for each region $R \in m$ and each event $e \in E$ the following conditions are satisfied:
(i) $(R, e) \in F$ if and only if $R \in {}^\bullet e$,
(ii) $(e, R) \in F$ if and only if $R \in e^\bullet$,
(iii) $R \in c_0$ if and only if $u_0 \in R$.

Example 10. The transition system from Example 5 with the regions X, Y, Z of Example 6 generates the net system shown in Figure 3.

We can now formulate the synthesis problem in the following way: Given a transition system TS, construct the net system generated by the regions of TS. If the transition system associated with this net system is isomorphic to TS, then the net system is a basic solution to the synthesis problem and the procedure is finished. In the oposite case, there exists no a net system which corresponds to TS and so TS is no abstract transition system. This fact follows from the following

Theorem [Desel and Reisig,1996]. A transition system TS is an abstract transition system if and only if $TS \simeq TS_{N_m^{TS}}$, where m denotes the set of all regions of TS.

Example 11. The transition system TS from Example 5 is an abstract transition system. The transition system associated with the net system from Figure 3 is shown in Figure 4. It is isomorphic to TS.

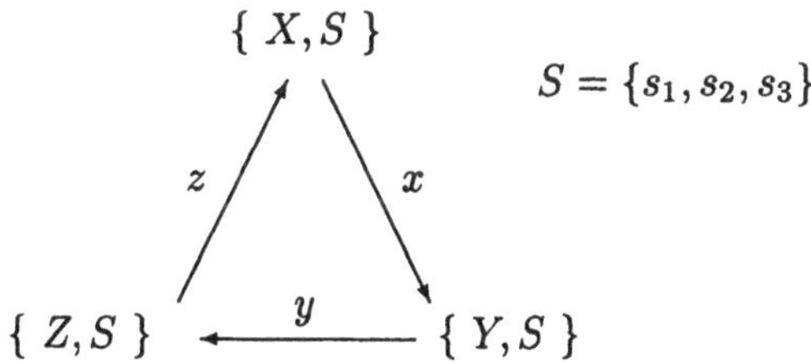

Figure 4. The transition system associated with the net system from Figure 3

Remark 3. To decide if two graphs are isomorphic is in general a nontrivial problem. Fortunately, the procedure proposed above, decides this problem very easily since there exists at most one isomorphism transforming a given transition system TS onto a transition system associated with a net system generated by the regions of TS. It follows from the following proposition, which is reformulated to our formalism:

Proposition 12 [Desel and Reisig,1996]. Let $DS = (U, A, E, T, u_0)$ be a dynamic information system, let $TS = (U, E, T, u_0)$ be its transition system, and let m denotes the set of all regions of TS. Then there is exactly one isomorphism f from TS to $TS_{N_m^{TS}}$, where N_m^{TS} denotes the *m-generated net system* which is defined as follows: $f(s) = \{R \in m : s \in R\}$.

8.2 The second approach

Now we describe shortly a solution of the synthesis problem stated in the paper based on the second approach, i.e. we assume that a given data table DS consists of only partial knowledge about the system behaviour. Thus, we at first compute an extension DS' of the data table DS, i.e. the system in which the set of global states of DS' is consistent with all rules true in the underlying information system S of DS as well as the set of global states of DS' represents the largest extension of S consistent with the knowledge represented by S. Next, for finding a solution of the synthesis problem in the form of a net system we use the method described in the previous section. The idea of our method is presented by example and a very simple procedure given below.

At first, we give one more definition from rough set theory.

A *decision table* is any information system of the form $S = (U, A \cup \{d\})$, where $d \notin A$ is a distinguished attribute called *decision*. The elements of A are called *conditional attributes (conditions)*.

Example 12. Let us consider an example of a decision table $S = (U, A \cup \{d\})$ defined by the data table presented in Table 8.

In the example we have $U = \{u_1, u_2, ..., u_9\}$, $A = \{a, b, c, a', b', c'\}$. The decision is denoted by d. The possible values of attributes (conditions and the decision) from $A \cup \{d\}$ are equal to 0, 1 or 2. This data table has been constructed on the basis of the dynamic information system $DS = (U, A, E, T, u_0)$ from Example 9. Table 8 contains all possible pairs of global states from the underlying system of DS. The value of decision d is equal to 1 if and only if there exists an event $e \in E$ such that $(u, e, u') \in T$. Thus, this decision table we can treat as a description of the characteristic function of the transition relation T. For the decision table S we obtain the following discernibility matrix $M(S)$ presented in Table 9.

U/A	a	b	c	a'	b'	c'	d
u_1	1	1	0	0	2	0	1
u_2	1	1	0	1	1	0	0
u_3	1	1	0	0	0	2	0
u_4	0	2	0	0	0	2	1
u_5	0	2	0	0	2	0	0
u_6	0	2	0	1	1	0	0
u_7	0	0	2	1	1	0	1
u_8	0	0	2	0	0	2	0
u_9	0	0	2	0	2	0	0

Table 8. An example of a decision table

U	u_1	u_2	u_3	u_4	u_5	u_6	u_7	u_8	u_9
u_1									
u_2	a',b',d								
u_3	b',c',d	a',b',c'							
u_4	a,b,b',c'	a,b,a',b',c',d	a,b,d						
u_5	a,b,d	a,b,a',b'	a,b,b',c'	b',c',d					
u_6	a,b,a',b',d	a,b	a,b,a',b',c'	a',b',c',d	a',b'				
u_7	a,b,c,a',b'	a,b,c,d	a,b,c,a',b',c',d	b,c,a',b',c'	b,c,a',b',d	b,c,d			
u_8	a,b,c,b',c',d	a,b,c,a',b',c'	a,b,c	b,c,d	b,c,b',c'	b,c,a',b',c'	a',b',c',d		
u_9	a,b,c,d	a,b,c,b',c'	a,b,c,b',c'	b,c,b',c',d	b,c	b,c,a',b'	a',b',d	b',c'	

Table 9. The discernibility matrix $M(S)$ for the decision table S

U/A	a	b	c	a'	b'	c'	d	d_d^A
u_1	1	1	0	0	2	0	1	$\{1\}$
u_2	1	1	0	1	1	0	0	$\{0\}$
u_3	1	1	0	0	0	2	0	$\{0\}$
u_4	0	2	0	0	0	2	1	$\{1\}$
u_5	0	2	0	0	2	0	0	$\{0\}$
u_6	0	2	0	1	1	0	0	$\{0\}$
u_7	0	0	2	1	1	0	1	$\{1\}$
u_8	0	0	2	0	0	2	0	$\{0\}$
u_9	0	0	2	0	2	0	0	$\{0\}$

Table 10. The decision table S with the function d_d^A

Now we compute the set of rules corresponding to nontrivial dependencies between the values of conditions and the decision values. In this case we also apply the method for generating the minimal form of rules presented in the Section 4. Let us start by computing the decision rules corresponding to the conditions $A = \{a, b, c, a', b', c'\}$ and the decision d. We have the decision table

$S = (U, A \cup \{d\})$ from which we compute the decision rules mentioned below.

In the table the values of the function d_d^A are also given. The discernibility matrix $\boldsymbol{M}(S; d, v, u_l)$ where $v \in V_d$, $u_l \in U$, $l = 1, 2, ..., 9$, obtained from $M(S)$ in the above way is presented in Table 11.

U	u_1	u_2	u_3	u_4	u_5	u_6	u_7	u_8	u_9
u_1									
u_2	a', b'								
u_3	b', c'								
u_4		a, b, a', b', c'	a, b						
u_5	a, b			b', c'					
u_6	a, b, a', b'			a', b', c'					
u_7		a, b, c	a, b, c, a', b', c'		b, c, a', b'	b, c			
u_8	a, b, c, b', c'			b, c			a', b', c'		
u_9	$a, b, c,$			b, c, b', c'			$a', b',$		

Table 11. The discernibility matrix $\boldsymbol{M}(S; d, v, u_l)$ for the $M(S)$

The discernibility functions corresponding to the values of the function d_d^A after reduction (using the absorption laws) are the following:

Case 1. For $d_d^A(u_1) = \{1\}: \ a \wedge a' \wedge c' \vee b \wedge a' \wedge c' \vee a \wedge b' \vee b \wedge b'$.
Case 2. For $d_d^A(u_2) = \{0\}: \ a \wedge a' \vee b \wedge a' \vee c \wedge a' \vee a \wedge b' \vee b \wedge b' \vee c \wedge b'$.
Case 3. For $d_d^A(u_3) = \{0\}: \ a \wedge b' \vee a \wedge c' \vee b \wedge b' \vee b \wedge c'$.
Case 4. For $d_d^A(u_4) = \{1\}: \ b \wedge c' \vee b \wedge b' \vee a \wedge c \wedge b' \vee a \wedge c \wedge c'$.
Case 5. For $d_d^A(u_5) = \{0\}: \ a \wedge b' \vee b \wedge b' \vee b \wedge c' \vee a \wedge c \wedge c' \vee a \wedge a' \wedge c'$.
Case 6. For $d_d^A(u_6) = \{0\}: \ b \wedge a' \vee b \wedge b' \vee b \wedge c' \vee c \wedge b' \vee c \wedge a' \vee a \wedge c \wedge c'$.
Case 7. For $d_d^A(u_7) = \{1\}: \ b \wedge a' \vee b \wedge b' \vee c \wedge a' \vee c \wedge b'$.
Case 8. For $d_d^A(u_8) = \{0\}: \ b \wedge a' \vee b \wedge b' \vee b \wedge c' \vee c \wedge a' \vee c \wedge b' \vee c \wedge c'$.
Case 9. For $d_d^A(u_9) = \{0\}: \ b \wedge a' \vee c \wedge a' \vee a \wedge b' \vee a \wedge a' \wedge c' \vee b \wedge b' \vee c \wedge b'$.

Hence we obtain the following decision rules:

$$a_1 \wedge a_0' \wedge c_0' \vee b_1 \wedge a_0' \wedge c_0' \vee a_1 \wedge b_2' \vee b_1 \wedge b_2' \underset{S}{\Rightarrow} d_1,$$
$$b_2 \wedge c_2' \vee b_2 \wedge b_0' \vee a_0 \wedge c_0 \wedge b_0' \vee a_0 \wedge c_0 \wedge c_2' \underset{S}{\Rightarrow} d_1,$$

$$b_0 \wedge a_1' \vee b_0 \wedge b_1' \vee c_2 \wedge a_1' \vee c_2 \wedge b_1' \underset{S}{\Rightarrow} d_1,$$
$$a_1 \wedge a_1' \vee b_1 \wedge a_1' \vee c_0 \wedge a_1' \vee a_1 \wedge b_1' \vee b_1 \wedge b_1' \vee c_0 \wedge b_1' \underset{S}{\Rightarrow} d_0,$$
$$a_1 \wedge b_0' \vee a_1 \wedge c_2' \vee b_1 \wedge b_0' \vee b_1 \wedge c_2' \underset{S}{\Rightarrow} d_0,$$
$$a_0 \wedge b_2' \vee b_2 \wedge b_2' \vee b_2 \wedge c_0' \vee a_0 \wedge c_0 \wedge c_0' \vee a_0 \wedge a_0' \wedge c_0' \underset{S}{\Rightarrow} d_0,$$
$$b_2 \wedge a_1' \vee b_2 \wedge b_1' \vee b_2 \wedge c_0' \vee c_0 \wedge b_1' \vee c_0 \wedge a_1' \vee a_0 \wedge c_0 \wedge c_0' \underset{S}{\Rightarrow} d_0,$$
$$b_0 \wedge a_0' \vee b_0 \wedge b_0' \vee b_0 \wedge c_2' \vee c_2 \wedge a_0' \vee c_2 \wedge b_0' \vee c_2 \wedge c_2' \underset{S}{\Rightarrow} d_0,$$
$$b_0 \wedge a_0' \vee c_2 \wedge a_0' \vee a_0 \wedge b_2' \vee a_0 \wedge a_0' \wedge c_0' \vee b_0 \wedge b_2' \vee c_2 \wedge b_2' \underset{S}{\Rightarrow} d_0,$$

These decision rules allow us to verify which global states of the dynamic information system DS from Example 9 are in the transition relation T of DS.

Let $DS = (U, A, E, T, u_0)$ be a dynamic information system and $S = (U, A)$ its underlying system. Sometimes, it is possible that an extension of the underlying system S of DS contains new global states consistent with the knowledge represented by S, i.e. with the all rules from the set OPT(S). The extension of the system S we can obtain applying the procedure for computing an extension S' of S described in Section 4. Thus, the method of finding the decision rules in a given dynamic information system presented in the above example allows us to extend the transition relation T of DS to a new transition relation T'. In consequence, we obtain a new dynamic information system $DS' = (U', A, E', T', u_0)$ called an *extension of the dynamic information system DS*, where $S' = (U', A)$ is an extension of S, E', is a set of events, $E \subset E'$, and T' is the extension of the transition relation T, $T' \subseteq U' \times E' \times U'$. Further, for constructing from a dynamic information system DS' with its transition system $TS' = (U', E', T', u_0)$ describing the behaviour of DS' a concurrent model in the form of an elementary net system we can proceed analogously to the method presented in Subsection 8.1.

Now we are ready to present a very simple procedure for computing an extension $DS' = (U', A, E', T', u_0)$ of a given dynamic information system $DS = (U, A, E, T, u_0)$.

PROCEDURE for computing an extension DS' of DS:

Input: A dynamic information system $DS = (U, A, E, T, u_0)$ with its underlying system $S = (U, A)$.

Output: An extension DS' of the system DS.

Step 1. Construct the decision table $S' = (U', A \cup \{d\})$ with the function d_d^A in the way described in Section 4.

Step 2. Compute the discernibility matrix $M(S')$.

Step 3. Compute the discernibility matrix $M(S'; d, v, u_l)$ where $v \in V_d$, $u_l \in U'$, $l = 1, 2, \ldots, \text{card}(U')$ for the $M(S')$.

Step 4. Compute the discernibility functions corresponding to the values of the function d_d^A in the way described in Section 4.

Step 5. Compute the decision rules true in S', i.e. the set $D'(S')$ of rules corresponding to nontrivial functional dependencies between the values of conditions and the decision values from the decision table S'.

Step 6. Compute an extension $S'' = (U', A)$ of the underlying system S of DS using procedure described in Section 4.

Step 7. Compute an extension T' of the transition relation T using the decision rules obtained in Step 5 in the followig way:

(i) construct all possible pairs of global states of S, i.e. a set $U \times U$,

(ii) verify using the set of decision rules obtained in Step 5 which pairs of global states of S are consistent with these rules, i.e. execute instructions

1. $T' := \emptyset$; $E' := \emptyset$.

2. For every pair $(u, u') \in U \times U$ do

if $(u, u') \in U \times U$ and an information vector v corresponding to a pair (u, u') is consistent with $D'(S')$ then add (u, e, u') to T' and e to E'.

Step 8. Construct the extension $DS' = (U', A, E', T', u_0)$.

It is easy to verify that the extension DS' of the dynamic information system DS from Example 9 computed by using our procedure presented above is the same as the system DS (see Example 4 and Example 12). Thus, the net system for the extension DS' is identical as for the system DS (see Figure 3).

9 Conclusions

We have formulated a method of the synthesis problem of concurrent systems specified by dynamic information systems. Our solution is based on a construction of a solution of the synthesis problem of Petri nets discussed in [Desel and Reisig,1996]. We have proposed a solution of the synthesis problem of a net system from a dynamic information system. It is also possible to solve this problem for finite place/transition Petri nets, since finite self-loop-free place/transition nets are equivalent to vector addition systems, introduced by Karp and Miller [1969]. The solution of our problem for place/transitions Petri nets is also simple to obtain.

The paper is concerned with some approach to concurrency based on rough set theory. Petri nets have been chosen as a model for concurrency. The application of Petri nets to represent a given information system and a modified definition of these systems enables:

- to discover in a simple way new dependencies between local states of processes being in the system,

- to represent in an elegant and visual way the dependencies between local states of processes in the system,

- to observe concurrent and sequential subsystems of the system.

On the basis of Petri net approach it was possible to understand better the structure and dynamics of a given information system.

Moreover, to some extent, it is a matter of taste which of the modelling method of concurrent systems to use. Drawing Petri nets by hand one can produce very compact solutions for problems solved rather by small nets. For large models some automatic methods could be accepted even if the produced by them nets are not so compact or small. Comparing the presented examples it is possible to see that our method can also produce solutions close to those obtained by designers.

The method presented in the paper allows to generate automatically from an arbitrary dynamic information system its concurrent model in the form of a net system. We have implemented a program on IBM PC generating a net model of the system specified by a dynamic information system. The resulting net can be analyzed by the PN-tools system for computer aided design and analysis of concurrent models [Suraj,1995].

It seems for us that the presented in the paper results as well as the further investigations of relationships between Petri net theory and rough set theory will stimulate the theoretical research related to them and new practical applications of both of them, e.g. in the area of knowledge discovery systems, control system design, decomposition of information systems as well as for real-time state identification.

Moreover, we would like to investigate to what extent our method could be applied for automatic synthesis of parallel programs from examples [Shapiro and Eckroth,1987], [Smith,1984].

Acknowledgement. I am grateful to Professor A. Skowron for stimulating discussions and interesting suggestions about this work. This work was partially supported by the grant #8T 11C 01011 from the State Committee for Scientific Research (KBN) in Poland and by the ESPRIT project 20288 CRIT-2.

References

1. Baar, A., Cohen, P.R,. Feigenbaum, E.A.: The handbook of artificial intelligence **4** Addison Wesley (1989)
2. Bazan, J., Skowron, A., Synak, P.: Dynamic reducts as a tool for extracting laws from decision tables. In: Z. W. Ras, M. Zemankova (eds.), Proceedings of the Eighth Symposium on Methodologies for Intelligent Systems, Charlotte, NC, October 16-19, Lecture Notes in Artificial Intelligence **869**, Springer-Verlag (1994) 346–355
3. Bazan, J., Skowron, A., Synak, P.: Discovery of decision rules from experimental data. In: T.Y. Lin (ed.), Proc. of the Third International Workshop on Rough Sets and Soft Computing, San Jose CA, November 10-12 (1994) 526–533
4. Bernadinello, L.: Synthesis of net systems. In: Proc. of the Application and Theory of Petri Nets. Lecture Notes in Comput. Sci. **691**, Springer-Verlag, Berlin (1993) 89–105
5. Brown E.M.: Boolean reasoning. Kluwer Academic Publishers, Dordrecht (1990)
6. Desel, J., Reisig, W.: The synthesis problem of Petri nets. Acta Inf. **33/4** (1996) 297–315
7. Ehrenfeucht, A., Rozenberg, G.: Partial 2-structures Part II. State space of concurrent systems. Acta Inf. **27** (1990) 348–368
8. Hack, M.: Decidability questions for Petri nets. Ph.D thesis. Department of Electrical Engineering, Massachusetts Institute of Technology, Cambridge MA (1975)
9. Hurley, R.B.: Decision tables in software engineering. Van Nostrad Reinhold Company, New York (1983)

10. Janicki, R.: Transforming sequential systems into concurrent systems. Theoretical Comp. Sci. **36** (1985) 27–58
11. Karp, R.M., and Miller, R.E.: Parallel program schemata. Journal of Computer and System Science **3/4** (1969) 167–195
12. Kodratoff, Y., Michalski, R. (eds.): Machine learning **3** Morgan Kaufmann Publishers, San Mateo CA (1990)
13. Krieg, B.: Petrinetze und Zustandsgraphen. IFI-Bericht **B-29/77** Institut für Informatik, Universität Hamburg (1977)
14. Lengauer, C., Hehner, E.C.R.: A methodology for programming with concurrency: an informal presentation. Sci. Comp. Progr. **2** (1982) 1–18
15. Michalski, R., Carbonell, J.G., Mitchell, T.M. (eds.): Machine learning: an artificial intelligence approach **1** Tioga/Morgan Kaufmann Publishers, Los Altos CA (1983)
16. Michalski, R., Carbonell, J.G., Mitchell, T.M. (eds.): Machine learning: an artificial intelligence approach **2** Morgan Publishers, Los Altos CA (1986)
17. Michalski, R.S., Kerschberg, L., Kaufman, K.A., and Ribeiro, J.S.: Mining for knowledge in databases: The INLEN architecture, initial implementation and first results. Intelligent Information Systems: Integrating Artificial Intelligence and Database Technologies **1/1** (1992) 85–113
18. Milner,R.: Communication and concurrency. Prentice-Hall, Englewood Cliffs, NJ (1989)
19. Mukund, M.: Petri nets and step transition systems. Int. Journal of Foundations of Computer Science **3/4** (1992) 443–478
20. Murata, T.: Petri nets: properties, analysis and applications. In: Proc. of the IEEE **77/4** (1989) 541–580
21. Nadler, M., Smith, E.P: Pattern recognition engineering. John Wiley and Sons, New York (1993)
22. Nguyen, H. Son, Skowron, A.: Quantization of real value attributes. In: P.P. Wang (ed.), Second Annual Joint Conference on Information Sciences (JCIS'95), September 28 – October 1, Wrightsville Beach, North Carolina, USA (1995) 34–37
23. Nguyen, H. Son: Discretization of real value attributes: Boolean reasoning approach. Ph.D thesis, Warsaw University, Warsaw (1997) 1–90
24. Nielsen, M., Rozenberg, G., Thiagarajan, P.S.: Elementary transition systems. Theoretical Comp. Sci. **96/1** (1992) 3–33
25. Pawlak, Z.: Rough sets – Theoretical aspects of reasoning about data. Kluwer Academic Publishers, Dordrecht (1991)
26. Pawlak, Z.: Concurrent versus sequential: The rough sets perspective. Bulletin of the EATCS **48** (1992) 178–190
27. Pawlak, Z, and Skowron, A.: A rough set approach for decision rules generation. In: Proceedings of the Workshop W12: The Management of Uncertainty in AI at 13th IJCAI, Chambery Savoie, France, August 30, see also: ICS Research Report **23/93** Warsaw University of Technology (1993) 1–19
28. Pawlak, Z.: Some remarks on explanation of data and specification of concurrent processes. Bulletin of International Rough Set Society **1/1** (1996) 1–4
29. Petri, C.A.: Kommunikation mit Automaten. Bonn: Inst. Instrum.Math., Schr. IIM **3** (1962). Also in English: Communication with automata, Griffith Air Force Base. Tech. Rep. RADC-Tr-65-377 **1** Suppl. 1 (1966)
30. Reisig,W.: Petri nets. An introduction. Springer-Verlag, Berlin (1985)
31. Shapiro, S.C., Eckroth, D.: Encyclopedia of artificial intelligence **1** Wiley, New York (1987) 18–35

32. Skowron, A.: Boolean reasoning for decision rules generation. In: J. Komorowski, Z.W. Ras (eds.), Proceedings of of the Seventh International Symposium on Methodologies for Intelligent Systems (ISMIS'93), Trondheim, Norway, June 15–18, 1993, Lecture Notes in Computer Science **689** (1993) 295–305
33. Skowron, A.: A synthesis of decision rules: applications of discernibility matrix properties. In: Proc. of the Conference Intelligent Information Systems, Augustów, Poland, June 7-11 (1993)
34. Skowron, A: Synthesis of adaptive decision systems from experimental data (invited talk). In: A. Aamodt, J. Komorowski (eds.), Proceedings of the Fifth Scandinavian Conference on Artificial Intelligence (SCAI'95), May 29–31, 1995, Trondheim, Norway, IOS Press, Amsterdam (1995) 220–238
35. Skowron, A., Polkowski, L., Komorowski, J.: Learning tolerance relations by Boolean descriptors: automatic feature extraction from data tables. In: S. Tsumoto, S. Kobayashi, T. Yokomori, H. Tanaka, and A. Nakamura (eds.): Proceedings of the Fourth International Workshop on Rough Sets, Fuzzy Sets, and Machine Discovery (RSFD'96), The University of Tokyo, November 6–8 (1996) 11–17
36. Skowron, A., and Rauszer, C.: The discernibility matrices and functions in information systems. In: R. Słowiński (ed.), Intelligent decision support – Handbook of applications and advances of the rough sets theory. Kluwer Academic Publishers, Dordrecht (1992) 331–362
37. Skowron, A., and Stepaniuk, J.: Decision rules based on discernibility matrices and decision matrices. In: T.Y. Lin (ed.), Proc. of The Third International Workshop on Rough Sets and Soft Computing, San Jose CA, November 10-12 (1994) 156–163
38. Skowron, A., and Suraj, Z.: A rough set approach to the real-time state identification. Bulletin of the EATCS **50** (1993) 264–275
39. Skowron, A., and Suraj, Z.: Rough sets and concurrency. Bull. Polish Acad. Sci., Ser. Sci. Tech. **41/3** (1993) 237–254
40. Skowron, A., and Suraj, Z.: Synthesis of concurrent systems specified by information systems Part 1. Institute of Computer Science Report **4/93**, Warsaw University of Technology (1993)
41. Skowron, A., and Suraj, Z.: Synthesis of concurrent systems specified by information systems Part 2. Examples of synthesis. Institute of Computer Science Report **38/93**, Warsaw University of Technology (1993)
42. Skowron, A., and Suraj, Z.: Synthesis of concurrent systems specified by information systems. Institute of Computer Science Report **39/94**, Warsaw University of Technology (1994)
43. Skowron, A., and Suraj, Z.: Discovery of concurrent data models from experimental tables: a rough set approach. In: U.M. Fayyad, R. Uthurusamy (eds.), Proceedings of the First International Conference on Knowledge Discovery and Data Mining (KDD'95), August 20-21, 1995, Montreal, AAAI Press, Menlo Park CA (1995) 288–293
44. Skowron, A., and Suraj, Z.: A Parallel algorithm for real-time decision making: A rough set approach. Journal of Intelligent Information Systems **7** (1996) 5–28
45. Smith, D.R.: The synthesis of LISP programs from examples: a survey. In: A. Bierman, G. Guiho, Y. Kodratoff (eds.), Automatic program construction techniques, Macmillan, New York (1984) 307–324
46. Słowiński, R. (ed.): Intelligent decision support – Handbook of applications and advances of the rough sets theory. Kluwer Academic Publishers, Dordrecht (1992)

47. Suraj, Z.: Tools for generating and analyzing concurrent models specified by information systems. In: T.Y. Lin (ed.): Proceedings of the Third International Workshop on Rough Sets and Soft Computing (RSSC'94), San Jose State University, San Jose CA, November 10–12 (1994) 610–617
48. Suraj, Z.: PN-tools: environment for the design and analysis of Petri nets. Control and Cybernetics (published by Systems Research Institute of Polish Academy of Sciences) **24/2** (1995) 199–222
49. Suraj, Z.: An application of rough set methods to cooperative information systems re-engineering. In: S. Tsumoto, S. Kobayashi, T. Yokomori, H. Tanaka, and A. Nakamura (eds.): Proceedings of the Fourth International Workshop on Rough Sets, Fuzzy Sets, and Machine Discovery (RSFD'96), The University of Tokyo, November 6–8 (1996) 364–371
50. Thiagarajan, P.S.: Elementary net systems. Advances in Petri nets 1986 Part I. Lecture Notes in Computer Science **254** Springer-Verlag, Berlin (1987) 26–59
51. Wegener, I.: The complexity of Boolean functions. Wiley and B.G. Teubner, Stuttgart (1987)
52. Ziarko, W., and Shan, N.: An incremental learning algorithm for constructing decision rules. In: W. Ziarko (ed.): Proceedings of the Second International Workshop on Rough Sets and Knowledge Discovery (RSKD'93), Banff, Alberta, Canada, October 12–15 (1993) 335–346
53. Żytkow, J.: Interactive mining of regularities in databases. In: G. Piatetsky-Shapiro and W. Frawley (eds.), Knowledge Discovery in Databases, The AAAI Press, Menlo Park CA (1991)

Chapter 23

Rough Sets and Artificial Neural Networks

Marcin S. Szczuka

Institute of Mathematics, Warsaw University
Banacha 2, 02-097 Warsaw, Poland
e-mail: szczuka@mimuw.edu.pl

1 Introduction

This work is an attempt to summarize several approaches aimed at connecting Rough Set Theory with Artificial Neural Networks. Both methodologies have their place among intelligent classification and decision support methods. Artificial Neural Networks belong to most commonly used techniques in applications of Artificial Intelligence. During the last twenty years of its development numerous theoretical and applied works have been done in that field. Rough Set Theory which emerged about fifteen years ago is nowadays rapidly developing branch of AI and Soft Computing.

At the first glance the two methodologies we talk about have not too much in common. Basic rough sets deal with symbolic representation of data, they construct representation of knowledge in terms of attributes, semantic decision rules etc. On the contrary, neural networks in their basic form do not consider the detail meaning of knowledge gained in the process of model construction and learning. But, in spite of those differences it is interesting to try to incorporate both approaches into some combined system. The challenge is to get as much as possible from this association.

This work presents several approaches to the task of incorporating rough set and neural network methods into one system for decision (classification) support. Different results of attempts to preprocess data for a neural network with rough set methods, to construct a the network using knowledge from rough set calculations or to refine rough set results using network are described.

The work is organized as follows:

First section introduces the formalism necessary to describe basic notions of rough sets and neural networks.

Second section presents, using several examples of applications, the attempts to use rough set based methods as a data preprocessor. In those examples data are treated by rough set reduction and then a network is constructed over simplified dataset. Possible advantages and threads of such a way of creating decision support system are briefly discussed.

In the third section we present the concept of incorporating rough sets methods into construction of the neural net by using so called *rough neurons.*

Last section discusses usage of rough set methods and knowledge gained from them in the process of establishing the architecture and initial state of a neural network for a given problem. It touches numerous problems of dealing with continuously-valued features, continuous decision and others.

2 Basic notions

2.1 Rough set preliminaries

The basic notions of rough sets theory are: information system, decision table, reduct and others. We will introduce them now step by step. In order to represent the sets of data we use information systems.

An *information system* is defined by a pair $\mathbf{A} = (U, A)$, where U is a non-empty, finite set of *objects* (rows, records, samples, cases) called universe, $A = \{a_1, \ldots, a_{n_A}\}$ is a non-empty, finite set of *attributes,* i.e. $a_i : U \to V_{a_i}$ for $i \in \{1, ..., n_A\}$, where V_{a_i} is called *the domain of the attribute* a_i.

In case of real-valued attributes, where for each $i \leq n_A$ $a_i : U \to \Re$ is a real function on the universe U, its elements can be characterized as points:

$$P_u = (a_1(u), a_2(u), ..., a_{n_A}(u))$$

in n_A-dimensional affine space $\Re^{n_A}$.

To deal with tasks formulated as decision making or classification problems we will use the notion of a *decision table.* A decision table is generally an information system with distinguished decision. Formally, decision table is a pair $\mathbf{A} = (U, A \cup \{d\})$, $d \notin A$ where d is called *decision attribute* or *decision.* The elements of A are called *conditions.* We assume that the set V_d of values of the decision d is equal to $\{v_1, \ldots, v_{n_d}\}$ for some positive integer n_d called *the range of d.*The *decision classes* are defined by

$$C_i = \{x \in U : d(x) = v_i\}, \text{ for } i = 1, 2, ..., n_d.$$

They determine the partition $\{C_1, ..., C_{n_d}\}$ of the universe U.

For any information system we can define a relation between objects using their attribute values. For a given attribute a, the objects x, y are *a-indiscernible* if they have the *same value* on a, i.e. $a(x) = a(y)$. In these terms we call two objects indiscernible if one cannot distinguish between them using only the knowledge available in the decision table. This definition can be extended to any subset $B \subseteq A$ by

$$xIND(B)y \Leftrightarrow \forall_{a \in B}\, a(x) = a(y)$$

$IND(B)$ denotes the relation determined on the subset $B \subseteq A$.

Obviously, $IND(B)$ is an equivalence relation . Objects x, y satisfying the relation $IND(B)$ are *indiscernible* by attributes from B. We denote by

$$[x]_{IND(B)} = \{y : \langle x, y \rangle \in IND(B)\}$$

the equivalence class defined by the object $x \in U$.

The notions of an indiscernibility relation and an indiscernible object allow us to introduce key concepts in rough set theory: the *reduct* and the *core*.

A subset B of attribute set A is a *reduct* for A iff

$$IND(B) = IND(A) \text{ and } \forall_{b \in A} IND(B - \{b\}) \neq IND(A)$$

In other words, a reduct is a subset of attributes such that it is enough to consider only the features that belong to this subset and still have the same amount of information. Moreover the reduct have the property of minimality i.e. it cannot be reduced any more without loss in quality of information. There can be of course a lot of reducts for a given information system (decision table), in extreme cases as much as $\binom{n}{\lfloor \frac{n}{2} \rfloor}$. Those reducts can intersect or be disjoint. By $RED(A)$ we denote the family of all reducts of a given information system. Reducts with the least possible number of attributes are called *minimal reducts* of A.

With an information system we may also connect the notion of the *core*:

$$CORE(A) = \bigcap RED(A)$$

The core corresponds to this part of information which cannot be removed from the system without loss in knowledge that can be derived from it. The core can be empty if there exist some disjoint reducts of A.

An information space of A is defined by $INF_A = \prod_{a \in A} V_a$. We define the information function $Inf_A : U \to INF_A$ by

$$\mathrm{Inf}_A (x) = (a_1 (u), \ldots, a_{n_A} (u)), \text{for any } u \in U.$$

Any object $u \in U$ is represented by its *information vector* $Inf(u)$.

Every information system $\mathbf{A} = (U, A)$ and a non-empty set $B \subseteq A$ define a *B-information function* by $Inf_B(u) = (a_i(u) : a_i \in B)$ for $u \in U$ and some linear order $A = \{a_1, ..., a_{n_A}\}$. The set $\{Inf_{Bd}(u) : u \in U\}$ is called the *B-information set* and it is denoted by V_B.

We may define indiscernibility relation in other terms using information functions as:

$$IND(B) = \{(u, u') \in U \times U : Inf_B(u) = Inf_B(u')\}$$

The equivalence relation $IND(B)$ is also a useful tool to approximate subsets of the universe U. For any $X \subseteq U$ one can define the lower approximation and the upper approximation of X by:

$$\underline{X} = \{x \in U : [x]_{IND(B)} \subseteq X\} \text{ lower approximation}$$
$$\overline{X} = \{x \in U : [x]_{IND(B)} \bigcap X \neq \emptyset\} \text{ upper approximation .}$$

The pair $(\underline{X}, \overline{X})$ is referred to as the rough set of X.

The *boundary region* of $X \subseteq U$ is defined by $Bd(X) = \overline{X} - \underline{X}$.

For many of applications presented in this work the key feature of decision table is its *consistency*. We will say that decision table is *consistent* if there are no two objects in the table which have the same values of conditional attributes and different decision value. In case the decision table is consistent we have clear decomposition of attribute-value space into decision classes. In the opposite case we have to introduce some fault tolerance measurement to deal with cases that cause inconsistency.

A *decision rule* is a formula of the form:

$$((a_{i_1} = v_1) \wedge (a_{i_2} = v_2) \wedge ... \wedge (a_{i_k} = v_k)) \Rightarrow d = v_d$$

where $a_{i_1}, ..., a_{i_k} \in A$, $v_j \in V_{i_j}$ for $1 \leq j \leq k$, $v_d \in V_d$, $i_1, ..., i_k \in \{1, ..., n_A\}$ and $i_j \neq i_i$ for $i \neq j$. This kind of formula tells us that if the values of conditional attributes are as specified in the left part of the rule then the decision is as given inthe right part (i.e. v_d).

2.2 Neural networks

Artificial neural networks are described in detail in many publications. Here we will not provide detailed definition for all network paradigms to be used. We only briefly outline the main facts about networks that will be further discussed. In most of the applications presented in this work the classical multilayer feed-forward network as described in [2] or [5] is utilized. The most commonly used learning algorithm is backpropagation. By a *sigmoidal excitation function* for a neuron we will understand a mapping of the form:

$$f(x) = \frac{1}{1 + e^{-\beta x}}$$

where x represents weighted sum of inputs for a given neuron and β is the coefficient called *gain*, which determines the slope of our function.

3 Pre-processing with rough sets

One method of combining those two approaches is to use rough sets as the preprocessing tool for neural networks. This idea was investigated by several researchers and turned out to be effective for some applications. Herein some of them are presented together with the results of experiments that had been performed on different datasets. More detailed description can be found in papers referred to below.

First of all, we need to understand the basic idea at the basis of our proposed approach. We know that rough set methods allow us to reduce the size of dataset by removing some of the attributes while preserving information included in basic system. We may consider the possibility of reducing the dataset and then performing construction and learning of the neural net.

Obviously, one has to consider several measurements that determine usefulness of methods proposed. Here the ones that matter are:

- Change in the quality of classification before and after using rough set methods for data preprocessing.
- Change in network size measured in number of processing units (neurons) and weights.
- Change in learning effectiveness measured in time (number of steps) necessary to accomplish learning with desired effect.
- Flexibility of trained network (ability to recognize unseen objects).

The main thing that has to be done is to find the connection between the way we make reductions with rough sets and the characteristic of network constructed after these reductions. We should possess some guidelines to avoid considering all possible combinations. The attempts to that task were made and we will look into some of them.

The straightforward approach to this task is based on the following procedure:

1. Take the learning part of the decision table and calculate the set of possibly shortest (preferably minimal) reducts and the core.
2. Reduce the table using some reduct or sum of several calculated reducts i.e. remove from the table attributes not belonging to the reducts chosen.
3. Construct the neural network over the reduced set of data.
4. Perform network learning.
5. Do steps 3-4 until there is no chance for significantly better results of classification with this network.
6. Do steps 2-5 until satisfiable quality is obtained.

This procedure although very simple turned out to be effective for some datasets.

Below the results of experiments with data are presented. We will briefly describe the nature of datasets used for those experiments, outlining also differences between the technique described above and approaches used in particular cases.

Before we will discuss experimental results some fact have to be realized. First of all we have to understand the constraints of the process of reduction. The generic problem of finding a minimal reduct for a given decision table belong to the NP-hard class. It is, in general, equivalent to the problem of minimal prime implicant construction for a given boolean function (see [18]). Therefore, it is necessary to use different approximating techniques in order to obtain the set of minimal or sub-minimal reducts for a table. Among them are heuristic methods as well as genetic algorithms.

In this work we deal with connections between neural networks and rough sets, so it is proper to mention here that an attempt to use neural network for finding minimal reducts has been made. In [17] the method for constructing a Boltzmann machine which searches for a minimal reduct is described. It uses the technique of Simulated Annealing as the engine of optimization process.

Another constraint is the size of attribute value sets. If an attribute describes some continuous measurement then it can posses very large sert of possible values. For the rough set approach this situation is unwanted because in such cases there are many objects that differ on this attribute. Sometimes such a difference is negligible from the point of view of considered real world process, but still, due to equivalence condition in indiscernibility relation rough sets methods treat them as separate cases. Such a property of rough set methods leads to modified approaches that claim to resolve the mentioned problem. One of possible solutions is to use some preprocessing techniques to reduce the size of attribute value sets. Another way of solving such a problem is to introduce somehow weakened indiscernibility relation. We will discuss some of these methods further.

Now let us look at some applications of rough set reduction.

Example 1 Lymphography. This set of data is described in detail in [11]. It contains 148 objects. Each object is described by 18 attributes. Objects belong to 4 decision classes and the distribution among classes is 2,4,61,81. The table is consistent. This example is taken from [3].

Example 2 Picture. This dataset was created from microscopic histological pictures. From every picture 155 binary features were extracted. Data table consists of 216 such objects that are divided into 7 classes corresponding to different types of brain cancer. Table is consistent. Detailed description of this example can be found in [4].

Example 3 Election. This example comes from [3]. The table contains 444 objects. There are 30 conditional attributes. Objects belong to 2 decision classes and the distribution among classes is 211 to 233. The table is consistent.

Example 4 Digits. This data table was created using some feature extraction techniques from the set of 32×32 pixel images. Those images are part of NIST database of handwritten digits. After extraction each of 1000 objects has 80 binary descriptors. There are 10 decision classes representing digits from 0 to 9. Distribution between classes is almost uniform. The table is consistent. This case came from [20] and [21].

Example 5 Onko. This data table describes effects of some oncological examinations. It contains 267 cases representing 12 decision classes. Each case is described by 28 conditional attributes. The table is consistent. This example is described in [3].

Example 6 Volleyball. The important features were extracted from video-recorded games of USA Men's Olympic Volleyball Team in 1993. The 144 cases with 13 conditional attributes and binary decision were examined. The table and results are taken from [22].

Example 7 Buses. This dataset collected at the Mechanical Department, Technical University of Poznań consists of 76 objects. There are 8 attributes and 2 decision classes with 30 and 46 objects respectively. Example came from [3].

Example 8 Production. This data table consist of some characteristics of automated production process. The goal is to foresee the level of possible breakdown in production circuit. Every sample is described by 28 attributes. There are 5 possible decisions. The table used for calculation was consistent but it may change with possible new cases as the modeled situation is time-changing. This example was published in [23] and [24].

Example 9 Breast Cancer. This dataset originally collected at the University Medical Centre, Institute of Oncology, Ljubljana was taken from the well known Machine Learning Database at the University of California, Irvine [10]. 285 cases are described by 8 conditional attributes. There are two possible decisions. This dataset contains some inconsistency. The example came from [3].

The table below summarizes some results of experiments over presented decision tables.

Name	*Input before*	*Input after*	*Net size before*	*Net size after*	*Result after*
Lymphography	35	18	40	24	-2.02%
Picture	155	17	192	53	-1.96%
Election	32	5	26	17	+3.38%
Digits	80	58	189	134	+1.4%
Onko	159	62	72	55	+6.37%
Volleyball	13	6	20	13	-0.6%
Buses	8	5	15	10	-5.27%
Production	28	6	35	13	better
Breast Cancer	14	13	24	24	+0.7%

The results shown in the table require some comments. First of all we have to explain the meaning of particular columns:

- *Input before* corresponds to the number of inputs to the network before rough set reduction.
- *Input after* corresponds to the number of inputs to the network after attribute reduction.
- *Net size before* corresponds to the size of the network before reduction measured in number of neurons. Sometimes also the number of weights is given in braces.
- *Net size after* corresponds to the size of the network after reduction measured in number of neurons. Sometimes also the number of weights is given in braces.
- *Results after.* This column summarizes change in quality of network answers after reduction. As the examples come from different sources, it is in fact impossible to find the common format for representing results.The most common measurement is the change in percentage of misclassified objects. This will be explained separately.

We have to make one more important remark before we step to result explanation. Cautious reader will notice for sure that in some of the examples the number of network inputs (***Input before***) does not match the number of attributes in decision table as described above. This situation occurs for following datasets: ***Lymphography, Election, Breast Cancer, Onko***. It is the result of applying encoding procedure to some of the attributes.

Authors in [3] distinguish among others those attributes which have symbolic unordered values. It means that it is impossible to arrange values of particular attribute along some axis of significance. This kind of attributes is very inconvenient for neural network. To resolve possible problems the *one-from-n* encoding is applied. This encoding creates a binary vector whose elements correspond to network inputs. When an attribute takes a particular value, the corresponding vector element is equal to 1, while others to 0. Usage of such encoding allowed to perform extended reduction. If some attributes are encoded using the presented method, then we can take the decision table extended in such way and reduce it (calculate reducts and core). In this case, in fact, we make not only attribute reduction but also attribute domain reduction.

Now we can discuss the results of experiments.

In case of ***Lymphography, Election, Breast Cancer, Onko*** and ***Buses*** several experiments using reduction of attributes as well as reduction of attribute domains were performed. In the table the change in the missclassification rate over whole dataset is presented. In order to give better understanding we provide the table below with more detailed description of those cases.

	Election	*Breast Cancer*	*Buses*	*Lymphography*	*Onko*
Change in neurons(%)	-34.6	-12.5	-33.3	-42.8	-23.6
Change in weights(%)	-83.2	-20	-59.6	-82.4	-77.4
Error before(%)	7.21	28.77	6.58	19.59	3.74
Change in error(%)	+3.38	+0.70	-5.26	-2.02	+6.37

Change in neurons in table below is calculated using $(\frac{n_{old}}{n_{new}} \cdot 100) - 100$ where n_{old}, n_{new} represent number of neurons in network before and after reduction respectively. In the same manner **change in weights** is calculated using $(\frac{w_{old}}{w_{new}} \cdot 100) - 100$ where w_{old}, w_{new} represent number of adjustable weights in network before and after reduction respectively.

Error before represents percentage of missclassified samples for network before reduction.

Change in error correspond to the difference in percentage of misclassified cases after and before reduction. We can easily see that in those cases presented in our table significant reduction of network size was achieved. Although the classification error was sometimes bigger for reduced network, the network itself was far more manageable from computational point of view.

In case of *Picture* decision table authors constructed non-reduced neural network and performed some tests using the cross-validation technique. The average quality of reclassification over 10 repeats was 86.15%. After reduction the size of network decreased rapidly. The reduced set of attributes was almost 10 times smaller than original. It allowed to perform more attempts to construct a network. The best one had two hidden layers and achieved 88.07 % accuracy of reclassification on whole set of examples.

The *Digits* example differs slightly from others in method of reduction. For construction of reduced data set several reducts were used. The shortest reduct had 24 attributes. But experiments showed that it would be extremally difficult to construct the network in case only one reduct is used. Therefore reduction was done using the union of several reducts. After several experiments reduction from 80 to 58 attributes turned to be optimal. The loss of quality measured over several cross-validation tests dropped by 1.4% on whole data (1.9% on testing set) and was equal to 93.6% (85.6% respectively). But size of the network was significantly smaller. Moreover the number of learning steps necessary to achieve good classification dropped from 8000 to 4000. Stronger reduction gave better improvement in computational aspects but loss of classification quality was significant.

In the *Volleyball* example the reduction of attributes was compared with other prediction techniques, in particular, with basic rough set approach i.e. calculation of reducts and decision rules. The combination of rough set reduction and neural network produced best classifier among considered. The error rate dropped from 13.73% to 12.67% on the training set. On the testing set, the quality was worse that for non-reduced network by less than 1%. So, overall performance was better but the reduced network lost some ability to recognize unseen objects.

The *Production* data is an example of making time prediction using neural network. In this particular case the goal was not the quality of classification for separate objects, but the degree of similarity between actual curve representing dynamics of production (and possible breaks in circuit) and the one approximated using neural predictor. According to the detailed explanation presented in [23], [24] the neural network based on reduced set of attributes behaved better as it showed better stability. As the unimportant features have been removed, the reduced network reacted only slightly to noisy information.

Summarizing the outcome of presented examples we may say that rough set reduction of network input data turned to be effective especially if we could not overcome the computational problems related to the size of the neural network. It is understandable that for some application we have to accept the trade-off between quality and computational ability.

We mentioned earlier that for some data, especially in case of continuously-valued attributes, rough set methods face some problems. As we will return to this topic further here we would like to provide simple example in order to illustrate the hard part.

Let us consider the well-known simple dataset *Iris* of iris classification. It was first published in 50's by R.A.Fisher and now is available in [10]. The decision table consists of 150 objects, each described by four conditional attributes and one decision attribute. The conditional attributes have numerical values, the decision takes one of three possible states. The simple calculation shows that any three-element subset of the set of attributes is a reduct. Such a situation is easy to predict as the conditions have many different values (large attribute domains). Several computational experiments have been made in attempt to use rough set reduction in this case. But results of experiments clearly showed that removal of any of the attributes causes rapid decrease of network classification quality. In non-reduced case simple network of 14 neurons with two hidden layers gave almost 100% accuracy for learning, testing sets being halves of the whole table. After reduction the best network gave only 75% accuracy on the whole table (as few as 55% on the testing set) even for a network significantly larger than the original, non-reduced one. The only possible conclusion is that rough set methods should be applied to the cases when attributes have large domains together with other methods that allow to preserve the important part of information which is redundant in straightforward rough set approach.

4 Rough set neurons and networks

We have already seen the definition of upper and lower approximations for a given set X of objects in the information system (decision table). To get some intuition about those approximations, it is convenient to think about the upper approximation as the set of object that are ***possibly (plausibly)*** similar to those in X according to the knowledge taken from decision table. The lower approximation of X is a set of objects that are ***with certainty*** similar only to the elements of X. The elements that belong to the boundary region are treated as those which may or may not belong to our set.

Driven by the idea of decomposing the set of all objects into three parts: the lower approximation, the boundary region and the outside area with respect to given X, Lingras ([8],[9]) introduced the idea of a rough neuron. Following his definitions we will now show the idea of rough neural network and present some application.

A rough neural network consists of both conventional and *rough* neurons. They form the classical multilayer structure with connections coming from layer to layer.

A ***rough neuron*** r may be understand as a pair of usual neurons. One of those two is referred as the ***upper bound*** denoted as $\overline{r}$, the other is called *lower bound* and denoted $\underline{r}$. The upper and lower bounds for a given rough neuron r "overlap" i.e. those two neurons exchange information.

The connections between classical and rough neurons are made as in usual case. While connecting rough neuron with classical one, we connect $\underline{r}$ and $\overline{r}$ separately. The situation starts to be more interesting when we want to connect two rough neurons. As each of rough neurons r, s is in fact a pair $\underline{r}, \overline{r}$ and $\overline{s}, \underline{s}$ respectively, we will distinguish three kinds of possible connections between them. The *full connectionism* occurs iff each of the components of r is connected both to $\overline{s}$ and $\underline{s}$. So in the situation of full connectionism we have together four connections between r and s.Two more possible ways of connecting such neurons are called *excitatory* and *inhibitory*. If the rough neuron r *excites* the activity of rough neuron s (i.e. increase in the output of r will result in the increase of the output of s) then we connect only $\overline{s}$ with $\overline{r}$ and $\underline{s}$ with $\underline{r}$. In the opposite situation, if r *inhibits* the activity of s (i.e. increase in the output of r corresponds to the decrease in the output of s) we connect only $\underline{s}$ with $\overline{r}$ and $\overline{s}$ with $\underline{r}$.

The classical neurons in our rough set network behave as usual. For calculation of their output we use sigmoidal function taken over a weighted sum of incoming signals. In case of the rough neuron we calculate outputs of upper and lower bound neurons using:

$$output_{\overline{r}} = \max\left(f\left(input_{\overline{r}}\right), f\left(input_{\underline{r}}\right)\right)$$

$$output_{\underline{r}} = \min\left(f\left(input_{\overline{r}}\right), f\left(input_{\underline{r}}\right)\right)$$

where f stands for a sigmoidal function and $input_{\overline{r}}, input_{\underline{r}}$ denote collected weighted input i.e.

$$input_i = \sum_{j:\ j \text{ connected with } i} w_{ij} \cdot output_j$$

for a neuron i.

If two rough neurons are partially connected then the excitatory or inhibitory nature of such connection is determined dynamically by polling the connection weights. At the beginning, we can make some assumptions about initial character (excitatory or inhibitory) of the connections. If we have assumed that the partial connection from rough neuron r to another rough neuron s is excitatory and $w_{\overline{r}\overline{s}} < 0$ and $w_{\underline{r}\underline{s}} < 0$, then the connection from rough neuron r to s is changed from excitatory to inhibitory by assigning $w_{\underline{r}\overline{s}} = w_{\underline{r}\underline{s}}$ and $w_{\overline{r}\underline{s}} = w_{\overline{r}\overline{s}}$. The links $(\overline{s}, \overline{r})$ and $(\underline{s}, \underline{r})$ are disabled while links $(\underline{s}, \overline{r})$ and $(\overline{s}, \underline{r})$ are enabled. On the other hand if neuron r is assumed to have an inhibitory partial connection to s and $w_{\underline{r}\overline{s}} > 0$ and $w_{\overline{r}\underline{s}} > 0$ then the connection between rough neurons r and s is changed from inhibitory to excitatory by assigning $w_{\underline{r}\underline{s}} = w_{\underline{r}\overline{s}}$ and $w_{\overline{r}\overline{s}} = w_{\overline{r}\underline{s}}$. The links $(\underline{s}, \overline{r})$ and $(\overline{s}, \underline{r})$ are disabled while links $(\overline{s}, \overline{r})$ and $(\underline{s}, \underline{r})$ are enabled.

The learning process for the network introduced above is based on the classical backpropagation paradigm. We tend to decrease the rate of error over the part of available examples that form the training set. As we perform the supervised learning and the desired values of network outputs over training samples are known, calculation of error is not a problem. In most cases this error is just a difference between expected and received network output. As all the neurons, both classical and rough in our network, use sigmoidal excitation function, the backpropagation step in learning process is also relatively easy to perform. Weights in the network are adjusted according to the simple backpropagation scheme (no momentum, no cumulative effects) using the equation:

$$w_{ji}^{new} = w_{ji}^{old} + \alpha \cdot err_i \cdot f'(input_i)$$

where f' is the derivative of sigmoidal function, α is the learning coefficient and err_i is an error for i-th neuron. Due to the properties of sigmoidal function, calculation of $f'(x) = f(x) \cdot (1 - f(x))$ is also easy. We perform learning by checking if trained network gives the required result for cases from testing set that were not presented to the network during training.

Having in mind the above construction of rough neurons let us look how this idea was utilized in some practical application. In [8] the dataset containing information about traffic parameters called DHV is described. The task is to predict the volume of traffic using data about this volume from the last week.

The classical neural network (Conventional) constructed for this task has seven input neurons corresponding to the values in particular days of previous week, four neurons in hidden layer and one output neuron. The neurons in this typical network are fully connected.

Two different networks to solve this problem were constructed using the idea of rough neuron. First of them (Rough 1) had rough neurons only in input layer. This network had seven input rough neurons, eight hidden conventional neurons and one output conventional neuron. In fact this particular network was only an extension of the normal model because it contained no connections between rough neurons. The second rough network model (Rough 2) had seven input neurons, four hidden rough neurons and one output classical neuron. The important difference in rough network approach is that they take as the inputs the upper and lower bounds for attributes. So in fact this network has twice the number of inputs as compared to the conventional one.

The table below presents results obtained for the traffic data using three described networks.

Network model	*Training set Max. Error*	*Training set Avg. Error*	*Testing set Max. error*	*Testing set Avg. error*
Conventional	46.2%	9.6%	28.1%	9.7%
Rough1	17.5%	5.5%	24.9%	8.1%
Rough2	13.7%	5.8%	23.0%	8.0%

5 Rough sets and discretization in network construction

So far, we have seen utilization of some simple rough set concepts in creation of neural networks. Now we would like to deal with a little bit more complicated task. Rough set methods give us the possibility to search for classifiers defined in terms of decision rules, reducts, discernibility etc. It is natural that equipped with such a knowledge we should be able to construct the neural network with better initial architecture than the one constructed without such guidelines. We are eager to reduce the exhausting stage of designing proper network architecture by applying some automated technique which utilizes knowledge about data that we already have. Secondly, the network itself does not provide us with clear interpretation of knowledge it contains ([19]). Fortunately, rough set methods ([15],[18]) can help to construct initial network in terms of such parameters like the numbers of scaling conditions, minimal decision rules and decision classes in discrete case.

As mentioned above the classical rough set approach faces difficulties when confronted with continuously valued attributes. Therefore we will present some discretization (quantization) techniques that allow to produce attributes with small, discrete sets of values preserving information included in original, real-valued decision table. The presented approach comes from [16].

5.1 Hyperplane discretization

The main problem of such discretization is how to approximate decision classes $\{C_1, ..., C_{n_d}\}$ by possibly small and regular family of subsets $\tau_k \subseteq \Re^{n_A}$, where any k points to some decision value $v_{l(k)}$ e.g. in terms of its high frequency of occurrence for objects in τ_k.

In [14] searching for such decision rules was performed by defining hyperplanes over $\Re^n$. Any hyperplane

$$H = \{(x_1, x_2, ..., x_n) \in \Re^{n_A} : \alpha_0 + \alpha_1 x_1 + \cdots + \alpha_{n_A} x_{n_A} = 0\}$$
$$\text{where } \alpha_0, \alpha_1, \alpha_2, \ldots, \alpha_{n_A} \in \Re$$

splits C_l into two subclasses defined by:

$$C_l^{U,H} = \{u \in C_l : H(u) \geq 0\}$$

$$C_l^{L,H} = \{u \in C_l : H(u) < 0\}$$

where, for a given hyperplane, the function

$$H : U \rightarrow \Re$$

is defined by

$$H(u) = H(Inf_A(u))$$

Let us propose some measures estimating the quality of hyperplanes with respect to the decision classes $C_1, C_2, ..., C_{n_d}$. Consider the function $award(H) =$

$$\sum_{l1 \neq l2} card\left(C_{l1}^{U,H}\right) \cdot card\left(C_{l2}^{L,H}\right) \tag{1}$$

If $award(H) > award(H')$ for some hyperplanes H, H', then the number of discernible pairs of objects from different decision classes by H is greater than the corresponding number defined by H'. Thus, this is H which should be considered while building decision rules.

In view of large complexity of searching for fixed number of hyperplanes simultaneously, the following sequential algorithm was implemented.

1. Find optimal hyperplane H_1 with respect to *award*.

2. Find hyperplane H_2 by maximizing function $award(H/H_1) =$

$$\sum_{case=L,U}\sum_{l1\neq l2} card\left(C_{l1}^{U,H}\cap C_{l1}^{case,H_1}\right)\cdot card\left(C_{l2}^{L,H}\cap C_{l1}^{case,H_1}\right)$$

3. Repeat the above step considering function $award(H/H_1,...,H_j)$ constructed for hyperplanes found step by step, until obtaining satisfactory degree of decision classes' approximation for some number n_h of hyperplanes.

Remark. Function (1) can be combined with parameters like e.g.

$$penalty(H)=\sum_{l=1}^{n_d} card\left(C_l^{U,H}\right)\cdot card\left(C_l^{L,H}\right)$$

or replaced by others, with respect to requirements.

Remark. The number of decision rules, equal to 2^{n_h} due to all possible combinations of position of objects with respect to n_h hyperplanes, can be reduced to the number $n_r\leq 2^{n_h}$ of minimal decision of the form $\tau_k\Rightarrow d=v_{l(k)}$, where no component τ_{kj} corresponding to hyperplane H_j can be rejected without decrease in given degree of approximation.

A method for generating hyperplanes, its advantages and limitations is also described in detail in one of the chapters in this book, namely the one authored by Nguyen Hung Son.

5.2 Hyperplane-based network

Once the hyperplanes and decision rules are constructed for a given $\mathbf{A}$, we may put them into the neural network.

Proposition 1. *Given a decision table* $\mathbf{A}=(U,A\cup\{d\})$ *and the set of* n_h *hyperplanes inducing* n_r *decision rules, one can construct four-layer neural network with* n_A+1 *inputs,* n_h *and* n_r *neurons in hidden layers respectively, and with* n_d *outputs, such that it recognizes objects in* U *just like in the case of corresponding hyperplane decision tree.*

Proof. The network has n_A inputs corresponding to conditional attributes. There is also one additional constant input called bias. Every input neuron sends its signal to all neurons in hidden layer. For each hyperplane H we construct one neuron in hidden layer. This neuron has weights equal to coefficients describing corresponding hyperplane.

For all neurons in the first hidden layer the threshold functions have the same form

$$h_j(x)=\begin{cases}1\ for\ x\geq 0\\ -1\ for\ x<0\end{cases}$$

This is also the case for thresholds in the second hidden layer, which are given as

$$r_k(x) = \begin{cases} 1 \; for \; x \geq 1 \\ 0 \; for \; x < 1 \end{cases}$$

Neurons in this layer correspond to binary hyperplane decision rules. The weights connecting these two layers correspond to the way of occurrence of hyperplane attributes in rules. For instance, let the 5-th minimal decision rule τ_5 be of the form

$$(H_2(u) < 0) \; \& \; (H_4(u) \geq 0) \; \& \; (H_7(u) < 0) \Rightarrow d(u) = v_4 \tag{2}$$

Then the corresponding weights leading to the 5-th neuron in the second hidden layer take the following values:

$$w_{j5} = \begin{cases} \frac{1}{3} \; for \; j = 4 \\ -\frac{1}{3} \; for \; j = 2 \; or \; 7 \\ 0 \; otherwise \end{cases} \tag{3}$$

Thus, according to the above example, the 5-th neuron in the second hidden layer will be active (its threshold function will reach 1) for some $u \in U$ iff u satisfies conditions of the above decision rule.

For every decision value we construct one neuron in output layer, so together n_d outputs from the network. The l-th output is supposed to be active iff given object put into the network belongs to corresponding decision class C_l. To achieve such a behavior we link every decision rule neuron only with the output neuron corresponding to decision value indicated by decision rule. Thus, in case of our example, the weights between the 5-th neuron in the second hidden layer and the output layer are as follows:

$$w_{5l} = \begin{cases} 1 \; for \; l = 4 \\ 0 \; otherwise \end{cases}$$

All neurons in the output layer receive threshold functions

$$out_l(x) = \begin{cases} 1 \; for \; x \geq 1 \\ 0 \; for \; x < 1 \end{cases}$$

To give some intuition how this method of network construction works, let us take a brief look at the iris classification example presented above. As decision in this case has three possible values, our universe should be decomposed into three decision classes. For Iris data, decision classes are linearly separable except for two objects. But there exists a single hyperplane distinguishing one of decision classes from the others. The remaining two classes can be distinguished using simple hyperplane if we allow two mentioned objects to be missclassified or else we have to use more than one hyperplane. In case we want 100% accuracy the network constructed using technique from above will have 4 inputs, 4 neurons in first hidden layer (as 4 hyperplanes are necessary to completely decompose universe), 5 neurons in second hidden layer corresponding to decision rules and finally 3 output neurons corresponding to the decision.

5.3 Modifications of the weights

The above neural network, although clear and valid in its construction, does not express as much yet as it could. First of all, it does not deal with non-deterministic decision rules which are often the only way to derive any information from data. Let us go back to the example of decision rule (2) and assume that it was stated with some degree of approximation not less than 0.9, where the value

$$P\left(d = v_4 \mid H_2 < 0, H_4 \geq 0, H_7 < 0\right) = 0.9$$

corresponds to the frequency of occurrence of v_4 as a decision value for the subspace

$$C_4^{L,H_2} \cap C_4^{U,H_4} \cap C_4^{L,H_7}$$

corresponding to conditions of decision rule. In this case we propose to replace previous output functions by

$$out_l\left(x\right) = x$$

and link output neurons with weights w_{kl} corresponding to frequency of decision value v_l conditioned by decision rule τ_k. Then, answering with a decision value with the highest value of the output function, we obtain the same classification as in case of decision rules. Additional information about degrees of approximation for applied rules can be derived as well.

One should realize that in case of non-deterministic rules frequencies of decision values may be often similar under given conditions. In fact, to evaluate degrees of approximation for non-deterministic decision rules, we need a measure not corresponding to concrete decision values, like e.g.

$$Q\left(\tau_k\right) = \sum_{v_l \in V_d} \left(P\left(d = v_l | \tau_k\right)\right)^q \tag{4}$$

where $q > 1$, τ_k decision rule. Now, one can express the meaning of particular hyperplanes with respect to the given decision rule by computing the change of Q caused by rejecting particular hyperplane conditions. Let us denote by ρ_{kj} decision rule τ_k without the j-th component τ_{kj}. Then, for any $j = 1, .., n_h$ and $k = 1, .., n_r$ we would like to put

$$w_{jk} = \pm \frac{1}{N_k} \cdot \left(Q\left(\tau_k\right) - Q\left(\rho_{kj}\right)\right)$$

Remark. If one regards function (4) as the degree of approximation of decision classes, then the factor $1/N_k$ is due to normalize weights coming into the neuron corresponding to the k-th decision rule. Due to remark 5.1, each decision rule is minimal in the sense that Q may only decrease after rejecting any hyperplane condition. Thus, the sign $\pm$ is adjusted just for denoting the position of points in τ_k with respect to the j-th hyperplane (compare with (3)).

5.4 Interpretation of neuron functions

To improve flexibility of learning, replacing original threshold functions with continuous ones should be performed. In fact, such a change enables to encode more information within our network model. Let us consider the class of (rescaled) bipolar sigmoidal functions of the form

$$h_j(x) = \frac{2}{1+e^{-\alpha_j x}} - 1$$

for hyperplane layer. Parameters α_j express degrees of vagueness for particular hyperplanes. Parallel nature of computations along the neural network justifies searching for such parameters locally for each H_j with respect to other hyperplanes, by applying adequate statistical or entropy-based methods (compare with [6],[25]).

Degrees of vagueness, proportional to the risk of basing on corresponding hyperplane cuts, find very simple interpretation. Let us weaken decision rule thresholds by replacing the initial function r_k by

$$r_k(x) = \begin{cases} 1 \; for \; x \geq 1-\varepsilon_k \\ 0 \; for \; x < 1-\varepsilon_k \end{cases}$$

where parameter ε_k expresses the degree of belief in decision rule supported by τ_k or, more precisely, in the quality of hyperplanes which generate it. Then, for fixed ε_k, increasing α_j for some H_j occurring in τ_k implies that for objects which are "uncertain" with respect to the j-th cut function r_k equals to 0 and no classification is obtained.

If one wants to modify functions in the second hidden layer similarly as in the first, the idea of extracting initial weights from the degrees of precision for reasoning with given hyperplanes as conditions should be followed. We claim that formulas for the decision rule functions should be derived from the shapes of functions in the previous layer. Thus, for function

$$r_k(x) = \frac{1}{1+e^{-\beta_k x}}$$

corresponding to the decision rule τ_k, the quantity of β_k is given by formula

$$\beta_k = \sum_{j=1}^{h} \alpha_j \cdot |w_{jk}|$$

5.5 Tuning of conditional hyperplanes

Modifications introduced for initial model of hyperplane-based neural network enable to include necessary information for improvement of decision classification. Obviously, described changes may cause that our network becomes inconsistent with decision rules for some part of training objects. It means that, e.g. for majority frequency rules, the output corresponding to a decision value pointed by some rule may not be the one with the highest value of the output function.

Such inconsistency, however, is justified by computing all weights and neuron functions from decision table itself. Moreover, we have still possibility of tuning the network by the wide range of learning techniques.

In classical backpropagation networks ([2],[5]) update of weights is based on gradient descent technique. The backpropagation method allows us to perform learning by minimizing any differentiable error function δ. The update for any weight w in the network is given by:

$$\Delta w = -\eta \frac{\partial \delta}{\partial w}$$

where η is a learning coefficient.

To be in agreement with the way of computing initial weights in the learning process, we consider error functions of the form

$$\delta(u) = \frac{1}{q} \sum_{1 \leq l \leq n_d} (out_l(u) - in_l(u))^q$$

where $out_l(u) =$

$$\sum_{1 \leq k \leq n_r} w_{kl} \left(1 + \exp\left(-\beta_k \sum_{1 \leq j \leq n_h} w_{jk} \left(\frac{2}{1 + \exp(-\alpha_j H_j(u))} - 1\right)\right)\right)^{-1}$$

and

$$in_l(u) = \begin{cases} 1 \; for \; d(u) = v_l \\ 0 \; otherwise \end{cases}$$

We can also use the cumulative error given by $\delta(U) =$

$$\frac{1}{q \cdot card(U)} \sum_{u \in U} \sum_{1 \leq l \leq n_d} (out_l(u) - in_l(u))^q$$

In this case we back-propagate the global error from the whole set of objects.

Once more we would like to stress that error functions given above correspond to the quality measure Q introduced before. Thus, if one would like to consider hyperplane decision rules minimal in sense of another criterion, the way of measuring classification error should be verified properly.

In classical neural network learning we may manipulate with some coefficients to control the learning process ([2],[5]). In presented approach we may use this ability in order to introduce some meaning for such operations. Change of weights in the first hidden layer corresponds to the change of elevation of hyperplanes. Hence, by setting constraints for value of learning coefficients we may induce the learning in case we e.g. do not want the hyperplanes to change too rapidly. The standard heuristics in the area of network learning, like momentum factor ([5]), can also be used, although they do not have explicit interpretation in terms of hyperplanes and decision trees.

During the learning process we should still remember about the interpretation of weights and functions. Starting from the initial structure obtained from data by the sequential algorithm for finding hyperplanes, we begin to modify weights due to given learning method. Then, however, for possibly improved classification we cannot determine how the decision rules behave over data actually. Another point is to keep decision rules minimal for foregoing hyperplane weights to make the whole process more clear. Thus, it turns out to be very important to preserve the balance between what is derived from the learning process and what is obtained from described construction.

5.6 Searching for optimal decision scaling

From the very beginning of this section we considered decision tables with real-valued conditions and discrete decision with n_d possible values. Such a case, occurring in many classification problems, becomes much more complicated when decision attribute d is real-valued as well. Obviously, one can assume some initial scaling over d and perform the decision process just like before. However, although sometimes such a scaling is given, in many applications we do not need to scale properly but also reason with real values after obtaining decision rules.

Objectives of proper decision scaling create wide range of often contradictive requirements. One of possible methods is to scale decision attribute to obtain a small number of hyperplane-based decision rules. In such a case, however, derived rules may be not precise or safe enough to apply in real-life situation. One solution is to scale decision attribute uniformly under some assumed degree of scaling precision expressed by n_d and to construct hyperplane-based neural network for n_d outputs. Then, we obtain some kind of parallel fuzzy inference model with continuous excitation functions corresponding to the states of binary fuzzy variables ([7],[19]).

Now, there are two methods of obtaining the proper decision system for a given data table. The first one is to synthesize a corresponding neural network by methods described previously, where the new error function is defined by

$$\delta(u) = \frac{1}{q}\left(\frac{\sum_{1 \le l \le n_d} v_l \cdot (out_l(u) - in_l(u))}{\sum_{1 \le l \le n_d} out_l(u)}\right)^q \tag{5}$$

The main disadvantage of such an approach is, however, the lack of information about the quality of initial decision scaling. Thus, although we can obtain quite effective model for reasoning, it is a black box because our knowledge about dependencies within data becomes unclear.

Another possibility is to use the network constructed and tuned for the scaled decision attribute to improve the scaling itself. In this case we tune the values v_l corresponding to particular outputs to minimize function (5). As such a optimization process is very complex, we propose to use some heuristics like e.g. genetic algorithm ([12]), where each chromosome in any evolution step corresponds to some scaling of decision attribute. The length of chromosomes is due to initially assumed exactness of scaling and the fitness of any individual is oppositely proportional to the quantity (5) computed from the network.

Remark. During the evolution process the weights of the neural network remain constant as expressing linguistic rules ([19]) corresponding to such a fuzzy-neural inference. However, parameters of excitation functions may be sometimes modified according to the changes of the scaled decision values for the points in $\Re^{n_A}$. Another solution is to optimize these parameters in parallel with decision scaling. It leads, however, to considering longer chromosomes in population steps.

The presented above methodology is still in the process of development and it does require thorough experimental verification. There are some other recent results of application of rough set methods in design of fuzzy MLP's (Multi Layer Perceptrons), but they do not touch the problem of real-valued attributes and decisions. For reference see [1].

Acknowledgement First of all I want to thank professor Andrzej Skowron for the invitation to write this text. I want to thank the authors of papers I cite in this work. They really did me a favor by providing the information about their previous and current research. Many thanks to my colleagues Nguyen Hung Son and Dominik Ślęzak who contributed a lot to my work.
This work was partially supported by the grant No 08T11C01011 from National Committee for Scientific Research and by the ESPRIT project 20288 CRIT-2.

References

1. Banerjee, M., Mitra, S., Pal, S.K. Rough fuzzy MLP: Knowledge encoding and classification. IEEE Transactions on Neural Networks(1997) (submitted)
2. Hecht-Nielsen, R.: Neurocomputing. Addison-Wesley, New York (1990)
3. Jelonek, J., Krawiec, K., Słowiński, R.: Rough set reduction of attributes and their domains for neural networks, Computational Intelligence **11/2** (1995) 339–347
4. Jelonek, J., Krawiec, K., Słowiński, R., Stefanowski, J., Szymaś, J.: Rough sets as an intelligent front-end for the neural network. In: Proceedings of First National Conference "Neural Networks and their Applications", April 12-15, Kule (1994) 268–273
5. Karayiannis, N.B., Venetsanopoulos, A.N.: Artificial neural networks: Learning algorithms, performance evaluation and applications. Kluwer, Dortrecht (1993)
6. Kohavi, R., Sahami, M.: Error–based and entropy–based discretization of continuous features. In: E. Simoudis, J. Han, and U.M. Fayyad (eds.): Proc. of the Second International Conference on Knowledge Discovery & Data Mining. Portland, Oregon (1996) 114–119
7. Kruse, R., Gebhardt, J., Klawonn F.: Foundations of fuzzy systems. Wiley, Chichester (1994)
8. Lingras, P.: Rough neural networks. In: Proceedings of the Sixth International Conference, Information Procesing and Management of Uncertainty in Knowledge-Based Systems (IPMU'96), July 1-5, Granada, Spain (1996) **3** 1445–1450
9. Lingras, P.: Comparison of neofuzzy and rough neural networks. In: P.P. Wang (ed.): Proceedings of the Fifth International Workshop on Rough Sets and Soft Computing (RSSC'97) at Third Annual Joint Conference on Information Sciences (JCIS'97), Duke University, Durham, NC, USA, Rough Set & Computer Science **3**, March 1–5 (1997) 259–262

10. Machine learning databases, University of California, Irvine. ftp://ics.uci.edu/machine-learning-databases
11. Michalski, R.S., Mozetic, I., Hong, J., Lavrac, N.: The multi-purpose incremental learning system AQ15 and its testing applications to three medical domains. In: Proc. of 5 National Conference on Artificial Intelligence, Philadelphia, Morgan-Kaufman, (1986) 1041-1045
12. Michalewicz, Z.: Genetic algorithms + data structures = evolution programs. Springer-Verlag, Berlin (1992)
13. Nguyen, H.Son, Nguyen, S. Hoa: From optimal hyperplanes to optimal decision tree. In: S. Tsumoto, S. Kobayashi, T. Yokomori, H. Tanaka, and A. Nakamura (eds.): Proceedings of the Fourth International Workshop on Rough Sets, Fuzzy Sets, and Machine Discovery (RSFD'96), The University of Tokyo, November 6-8 (1996) 82-88
14. Nguyen, H. Son., Nguyen, S. Hoa, Skowron, A.: Searching for features defined by hyperplanes. In: In: Z.W. Ras, M. Michalewicz (eds.), Ninth International Symposium on Methodologies for Intelligent Systems. Zakopane, Poland, June 9-13, Lecture Notes in Artificial Intelligence (ISMIS'96) **1079**, Springer-Verlag, Berlin (1996) 366-375
15. Nguyen, H.Son, Skowron, A.: Quantization of real-valued attributes. Rough Set and Boolean Reasoning Approaches. In: P.P. Wang (ed.): Second Annual Joint Conference on Information Sciences (JCIS'95), Wrightsville Beach, North Carolina, 28 September - 1 October (1995) 34-37
16. Nguyen, H. Son, Szczuka, M., Ślęzak, D.: Neural networks design: Rough set approach to real-valued data. In: J. Komorowski, J. Zytkow, (eds.), The First European Symposium on Principle of Data Mining and Knowledge Discovery (PKDD'97), June 25-27, Trondheim, Norway, Lecture Notes in Artificial Intelligence **1263**, Springer-Verlag, Berlin (1997) 359-366
17. Sapiecha, P.: An approximation algorithm for certain class of NP-hard problems. In: ICS Research Report **21/92** Warsaw University of Technology (1992)
18. Skowron, A., Rauszer, C.: The discernibility matrices and functions in information systems. In: R. Słowiński (ed.): Intelligent Decision Support - Handbook of Applications and Advances of the Rough Sets Theory, Kluwer Academic Publishers, Dordrecht (1992) 331-362
19. Szczuka, M., Ślęzak, D.: Hyperplane-based neural networks for real-valued decision tables. In: P.P. Wang (ed.): Proceedings of the Fifth International Workshop on Rough Sets and Soft Computing (RSSC'97) at Third Annual Joint Conference on Information Sciences (JCIS'97), Duke University, Durham, NC, USA, Rough Set & Computer Science **3**, March 1-5 (1997) 265-268
20. Szczuka, M.: Aproksymacja funkcji za pomocą sieci neuronowych z wykorzystaniem metod zbiorów przybliżonych. Master Thesis, Faculty of Mathematics, Informatics and Mechanics, The University of Warsaw (1995)
21. Szczuka, M.: Rough set methods for constructing artificial neural networks. In: B.D. Czejdo, I.I. Est, B. Shirazi, B. Trousse (eds.), Proceedings of the Third Biennial European Joint Conference on Engineering Systems Design and Analysis **7**, July 1-4, Montpellier, France (1996) 9-14
22. Świniarski, R., Berzins, A.: Rouh sets expert system for on-line prediction of volleyball game progress. In: B.D. Czejdo, I.I. Est, B. Shirazi, B. Trousse (eds.), Proceedings of the Third Biennial European Joint Conference on Engineering Systems Design and Analysis **7**, July 1-4, Montpellier, France (1996) 3-8

23. Świniarski, R., Hunt, F., Chalvet, D., Pearson, D.: Prediction system based on neural networks and rough sets in a highly automated production process. In: Proceedings of the 12th System Science Conference, Wrocław, Poland (1995)
24. Świniarski, R., Hunt, F., Chalvet, D., Pearson, D.: Intelligent data processing and dynamic process discovery using rough sets, statistical reasoning and neural networks in a highly automated production systems. In: Proceedings of the First European Conference on Application of Neural Networks in Industry, Helsinki, Finland (1995)
25. Vapnik, V.N.: The nature of statistical learning theory. Springer–Verlag, New York (1995)

Chapter 24

Genetic Algorithms in Decomposition and Classification Problems

Jakub Wróblewski

Institute of Mathematics,
Warsaw University
02-097, Banacha Str. 2, Warsaw Poland
e-mail: jakubw@alfa.mimuw.edu.pl

1 Introduction

Some combinatorical problems concerned with using rough set theory in knowledge discovery (KD) and data analysis can be successfully solved using genetic algorithms (GA) - a sophisticated, adaptive search method based on the Darwinian principle of natural selection (see [4], [6]). These problems are frequently NP-hard, as in case of reducts or templates finding (see [12]), and there is no fast and reliable way to solve them in deterministic way.

Genetic algorithms are flexible and universal - they can be used in various situations. On the other hand, approximate but fast heuristics are known for many of considered tasks. They are designed and tuned up especially for a problem, and often are more efficient than simple genetic algorithm. Unfortunately, they are often suboptimal and cannot avoid local optima. Moreover, if they are deterministic, there is no hope for improvement even if one can spend more time on computations.

The advantages of both genetic and heuristic algorithms can be exploited by hybrid algorithms - nondeterministic, problem-oriented heuristics controlled by genetic algorithm. In this work some examples of hybrid systems are presented, as well as the theory of order-based genetic algorithms being used in these systems.

In the second section of this work an idea and general scheme of hybrid algorithms is discussed in details.

In the third section a theory of order-based genetic algorithms is presented, as well as an overview of order-based genetic operators used in various situations.

The next section involves two examples of application of hybrid algorithms supporting rough set methods in knowledge discovery: a system for short reducts generation and a method of templates finding (see [12] for comparison with another methods).

In the last section ordinal-based genetic algorithms are presented. This is a new, promising technique which can be used in hybrid algorithms in some problems, when order-based GA are not appropriate. An NP-hard problem of matrix covering is presented as an example of application.

2 Hybrid algorithms

In a case of *classical genetic algorithms* (see [4], [6]) we are given a state space S (finite, but large) and a function: $f : S \rightarrow R_+$. Our goal is to find x_o: $f(x_o) = max\{f(x): x \in S\}$. Elements of set S are "*individuals*". The main idea of classical genetic algorithms is based on the Darwinian principle of natural selection. We treat a value of the function f as ability to survive in the environment ("*fitness*"), and we simulate the process of evolution as follows:

1. We choose the representation scheme (and change "individuals" to "chromosomes" - usually bit strings).
2. We randomly choose the set of chromosomes as an initial population.
3. We calculate "fitness" $F(c)$ of each chromosome c as a value of $f(s(c))$, where $s(c)$ is the individual encoded by c. Then we create a new population, replacing the chromosomes with low fitness by those with higher fitness.
4. We randomly affect the new population by *genetic operators*, e.g. *mutation* (small, random modifications of chromosomes) and *crossing-over* (exchange of "genetic material" between some pairs of chromosomes).
5. We repeat 3-4 with the new population, until a stopping criterion is satisfied.

The result of evolution is the best individual x_{max} which is usually nearly as good as the global optimum x_o.

The scheme presented above is general and domain-independent. In a case of real application we have to answer to a few questions - some of them are crucial for efficiency of our algorithm. We have do choose a method of individuals' representation (a genetic code), a method of selection, genetic operators, a stopping criterion, other parameters (e.g. population size, probabilities of mutation and crossing-over). Theory and practice of genetic algorithms give us some suggestions how to design the genetic system [4]; detailed solutions are usually domain-dependent.

A class of *heuristic algorithms* is hard to characterise. Roughly speaking, these are approximate deterministic algorithms, often based on intuitions, using problem-dependent mechanisms and tricks. They are often based on a *greedy* paradigm: construct a result step by step, in each of them achieve as much as possible. We usually get a good, but not necessarily optimal solution, depending on an initial state or parameters of algorithm.

A nice example of using a kind of heuristic algorithm in an NP-hard problem is one described in [3]. A method of solving the graph coloring problem, which is one of the classical NP-hard problems [5], is presented there.

A version of the graph coloring problem considered in [3] can be formulated as follows: given a graph with weights assigned to nodes and n colors, assign colors to nodes in such way that no adjacent nodes have the same color; if it is not possible to color all the graph, maximize the sum of weights of colored nodes. A greedy algorithm for this problem acts as follows: sort nodes in ascending order using weights, then for each node assign the lowest possible color number. This strategy produces good, but often suboptimal solutions. As the next step, an order-based genetic algorithm was used to produce a permutation of nodes. This permutation was used as control sequence in the greedy algorithm: now nodes are considered in the order generated by this permutation. Results obtained by this hybrid algorithm were significantly better than these obtained by the greedy algorithm as well as by the greedy algorithm controlled by random permutations.

The hybridisation strategy described in [3] represents more general approach to combinatorical optimisation problems. The general scheme of *hybrid algorithm* is as follows:

1. Find a strategy (heuristic algorithm) which gives an approximate result.
2. Modify (parametrise) the strategy using a control sequence, so that the result depends on this sequence (recipe).
3. Encode the control sequence to a chromosome.
4. Use a genetic algorithm to produce control sequences. Proceed with the heuristic algorithm controlled by the sequence. Evaluate an object generated by the algorithm and use its quality measure as a fitness of the control sequence.
5. A result of evolution is the best control sequence, i.e. the sequence producing the best object. Send this object to the output of the hybrid algorithm.

When a new hybrid algorithm is designed, we should remember about two following conditions:

1. All control sequences generated by our genetic algorithm should be properly recognised and used by a heuristic algorithm.
2. All potential solutions should be accessible using our algorithm, i.e. there should exist a control sequence which produces it.

The first condition can be omitted: if the heuristic algorithm encounters an unintelligible control sequence, it simply skips it and assigns zero as a fitness value. The second condition is necessary.

A well-constructed hybrid algorithm has many advantages over both a simple genetic algorithm (with literal encoding of search space), and heuristic strategies:

- Since control sequences are generated by a nondeterministic genetic algorithm, the more time we spend on computations, the better result we obtain. There is no such an advantage in case of deterministic heuristics: we get just one suboptimal solution.
- A genetic algorithm produces a number of different suboptimal solutions of good quality.
- A simple genetic algorithm (or another search technique) with literal encoding of state space evaluates many very bad solutions. A hybrid algorithm actually searches only a part of state space - a class of good, but not optimal, solutions. Every evaluation (via a heuristic algorithm) generates quite good solution. Therefore we can terminate evolution process even after the first step, and we will get a good solution; this feature can be important in some real-time applications.

- Because of its modular structure, hybrid algorithms should be easy designed and reused in other, similar applications. As on Figure 1, we can use one, universal genetic library to support many heuristic algorithms. An example of a situation, when one order-based genetic algorithm controls two different tasks in knowledge discovery system, is described in one of the next sections.

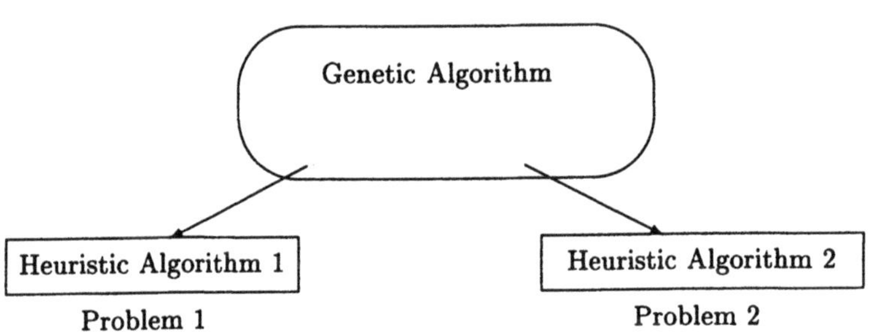

Fig. 1. A hybrid system.

An order-based genetic algorithm is one of the most widely used component of various hybrid systems. Theoretical foundations and practical construction of this algorithm are presented in the next section. Another type of genetic algorithm, an ordinal one, can be easily used as a generator of control sequences. This promising technique is described in the last section of this work.

3 Order-based genetic algorithms

3.1 An overview of algorithm

In the *order-based genetic algorithms* a chromosome is an n-element permutation σ, represented by a sequence of numbers: $\sigma(1)\ \sigma(2)\ \sigma(3)\ \ldots\ \sigma(\mathrm{n})$. The evolution proceeds as follows:

1. Initial population of M individuals is generated randomly.
2. The population is affected by genetic operators of mutation and recombination.
3. Fitness function of every individual is calculated. In the case of a hybrid algorithm a heuristic part is launched under control of individual; a fitness value depends on the result of heuristic algorithm. See the next section for details.

4. New population is generated using "roulette wheel" algorithm: the fitness value of every individual is normalised and treated as probability distribution on population; then randomly choose M new individuals using this distribution.
5. Repeat from step 2. Stop after obtaining good results.

Mutation of order-based individual means one random transposition of its genes:

$$\mathbf{1\,2}\,3\,6\,5\,4 \xrightarrow{Mutation} \mathbf{2\,1}\,3\,6\,5\,4$$

There are various methods of recombination (*crossing-over*) considered in literature. In [4] such methods as PMX (Partially Matched Crossover), CX (Cycle Crossover) and OX (Order Crossover) are described.

The PMX operator was used in the Traveling Salesman Problem [4], where a state space of possible paths of a salesman through a set of cities was literally encoded in the form of permutations (an order of visiting the cities). In the PMX method a matching section is set for both parents as a part of chromosome with a random beginning and end. Then, the adjacent genes from matching sections of both parents are combined into pairs. Finally, these pairs are treated as transpositions; both parents are altered due to these transpositions. E.g.:

$$\begin{array}{c|c|c} 1\,2\,3 & 4\,5 & 6 \\ 2\,1\,4 & 6\,3 & 5 \end{array} \xrightarrow{PMX} \begin{array}{c} 1\,2\,5\,6\,3\,4 \\ 2\,1\,6\,4\,5\,3 \end{array}$$

Vertical lines indicate matching section.

Other type of crossover operator, UOX (Uniform Order-based Crossover) was used in the hybrid algorithm described in [3].

We will use another type of crossing-over operator for further analysis: MOX (Modified Order Crossover), [22]. This recombination operator affects two parent chromosomes and replaces them by two children. First, we choose one gene in first parent's chromosome at random. This gene will be the end of a matching section, starting at the beginning of chromosome. Identical matching section is marked on second parent's chromosome. Then, we leave the matching sections unchanged, but the rest of genes of the first chromosome is set in the order of appearance in the second chromosome. We perform the same operation on the second parent. For example:

$$\begin{array}{c|c} 1\,2\,3 & 4\,5\,6 \\ 4\,2\,1 & 3\,6\,5 \end{array} \xrightarrow{MOX} \begin{array}{c|c} 1\,2\,3 & 4\,6\,5 \\ 4\,2\,1 & 3\,5\,6 \end{array}$$

Vertical line indicates the end of matching section.

3.2 Theoretical foundations

One of the most important results concerned with a theoretical foundations of classical genetic algorithm is a notion of schema and schema theorem [6], [4]. This approach is focused on *schemata* - subsets of the state space described by a certain combination of genes' values. Due to this theory, an efficiency of genetic algorithms is concerned with the "implicit parallelism": the algorithm favores better (in average) schemata; each individual is a realisation of many different schemata, so the algorithm works with much more schemata than individuals. One must believe, that the optimal solution is possible to reach by combining "good" schemata; this approach is called "building block hypotesis". The *schema theorem* formulates an estimation of a number of schema representatives after one step of evolution - this estimation shows, that the average number of good (in a sense of average fitness) schemata will grow expotentially.

The notion of schema can be generalised into the case of order-based genetic algorithms. Some of these generalisations are described in [4]. The notion of schema (or *o-schema*, for "order-based") can be defined in different ways, but useful definitions should obey some principles (formulated in [17]) binding schemata and operators of crossing-over. On the other hand, a reasonable schema definition should refer to an internal structure of state space. In the case of hybrid algorithms, a notion of *rd-schemata* (relative dispersed) is shown [22] to be more adequate than those presented in [4].

Definition: Relative dispersed schema $rd^n(\ a_1\ a_2\ \ldots\ a_k\ )$ expands to the set of all individuals of length n with genes $a_1 \ldots a_k$ located in this order (not necessarily sequentially). The *order* $o(\cdot)$ of an rd-schema is defined to be equal to the number k.

This kind of o-schemata was used in [3] and described in details in [22]. The modified order crossover (MOX) operator is concerned with the rd-schemata. An analogy of the classical schema theorem can be formulated for a given relative dispersed schemata S and MOX operator:

$$E\left(N_{t+1}\right) \geq N_t \frac{f}{\overline{f}}\left(1 - p_{cross} \cdot Pc \cdot \left(1 - \frac{N_t}{M}\right) - p_{mut} \cdot Pm\right)$$

where:
N_t - a number of representatives of S in the t-th population,
f - an average value of fitness function in population,
$\overline{f}$ - an average value of fitness function of individuals matching S,
p_{cross} - a probability of crossing-over,
p_{mut} - a probability of mutation of individual,
M - a number of individuals in population,
Pm - a probability of disruption of schema S by a mutation,
Pc - a probability of disruption of schema S by the MOX operation.
The values of Pc and Pm was calculated in [22] as:

$$Pc \leq \frac{1}{n+1} \sum_{k=0}^{n} \frac{\binom{n}{l} - \binom{k}{l}}{\binom{n}{l}} \cdot \frac{\binom{n}{l} - \binom{n-k}{l}}{\binom{n}{l}}$$

$$Pm = \frac{l}{n^2 - n} \left(l - 1 + \frac{2 \cdot (n-l)}{n \cdot (n-1)} \sum_{k=1}^{n-2} 2\,(n-k-1) \frac{\binom{n-2}{k} - \binom{n-l-1}{k}}{\binom{n-2}{k}} \right)$$

where:
n - a number of genes in chromosome,
l - an order $o(S)$ of scheme S.

The main result is nearly identical with the classical case. Therefore we may use classical results like the building block hypothesis, the analogy with k-armed bandit, theory of deceptiveness in the order-based genetic algorithms.

There are other approaches to the problem of genetic algorithms convergence and efficiency. Many of them are based on Markov chain as a tool for modelling behaviour of GA. Some interesting results are presented in [15], [20].

In [15] authors model a simple genetic algorithm using a Markov chain with N states - each of it corresponds to one possible population. In case of order-based GA, number N can be calculated by:

$$N = \binom{M + n! - 1}{n! - 1}$$

where M is the number of individuals in population, n - size of chromosome (permutation). The size of transition matrix Q of the chain is $N \times N$, so it is too large to perform direct analysis.

Some of the results concerned with the classical case are recalculated in [22] for the order-based genetic algorithms. Particularly, the Markov chain describing order-based GA was shown to be ergodic (as in [15]) and the convergence rate was estimated (as in [20]). Moreover, an optimal mutation probability was calculated (unfortunately, this result is practically useless, because it assumes complete knowledge about the fitness function, including its extrema etc.).

Results presented in [22] suggests, that the order-based genetic algorithms used in hybrid systems are based on as reliable theoretical foundations as the classical GAs are. On the other hand, these foundations are still not satisfactory from the practical point of view - in both classical and order-based case.

4 Applications

4.1 Short reduct finding using genetic algorithm

The notion of a reduct is one of the main notions of rough set theory [16].

Suppose we have an *information system* (see [12]): a set of m object $\{o_1, ...o_m\}$ $= U$, each described by n attributes $\{a_1, ...a_n\} = A$. We have a decision value d assigned to each object. Suppose that every two objects with different decision values have different values of at least one attribute.

Definition: Let a *(relative) reduct* $R \subseteq A$ of an information system be a minimal (with respect to inclusion) subset of attributes satisfying the following property:

$$\forall k, l\ \forall a_i \in R : a_i(o_k) = a_i(o_l) \Longrightarrow d(o_k) = d(o_l)$$

The problem of finding a globally minimal reduct for a given information system is NP-hard (see [19]). On the other hand, short reducts are often used to build effective decision algorithms: if a subset of attributes is known as a reduct, we are able to predict $d(x)$ using only this subset of data. The decision rules generated from this subset should be (if the reduct is short enough) simple and easy to find.

4.1.1 Classical genetic algorithm One can use classical, binary genetic algorithm [21] to generate reducts: every binary individual encodes one subset of attributes - a potential reduct. For example:

$$1001001100 \longleftrightarrow \{a_1, a_4, a_7, a_8\}$$

A classical binary mutation and crossover operators [4] and the "roulette wheel" selection algorithm are used. The fitness function of a subset R has a form:

$$F(R) = \frac{n - L_R}{n} + \frac{2C_R}{m^2 - m}$$

where L_R denotes a number of "1" in the subset R, and C_R denotes the number of object pairs (with different decision values) discerned by the attribute subset R.

The process of calculating C_R is the most time-consuming operation; to make it faster an additional structure called a ***distinction table*** is generated for an information system. This is a binary matrix of size $(n+1) \times (m^2 - m)/2$. Each column of the matrix corresponds to one attribute, each row corresponds to one pair of different objects. Value "1" means, that an attribute has different value on the pair of objects. To find a reduct means to find a column covering of the matrix.

The results of this experiment are described in [21]. However, these results were still not satisfactory, because there was no sure, that an obtained subset is a reduct (not a superreduct), and the second method of generating of short reducts was introduced: a hybrid algorithm.

4.1.2 Hybrid algorithm In the hybrid algorithm [21] a simple, deterministic method was used for reduct generation:

1. Let R be a set of all attributes and let $(b_1 \ldots b_n) = \tau(a_1 \ldots a_n)$ be an ordered list of attributes - the order is represented by a permutation τ.
2. For $i = 1$ to n repeat steps 3 and 4:
3. Let $R \longleftarrow R - b_i$.
4. If R does not satisfies a condition from the definition of reduct, undo step 3.

The result of the algorithm will always be a reduct. Every reduct can be found using this algorithm, the result depends on the order of attributes (proof: see [21]). The genetic algorithm is used to generate the proper order. To calculate the function of fitness for a given permutation (order of attributes) we have to perform one run of the deterministic algorithm and calculate the length of the reduct found. The function of fitness depends only on this length:

$$F(\tau) = \frac{1}{L_\tau}$$

Another fitness formula was considered also in [14]:

$$F(\tau) = n - L_\tau + 1$$

and the results improved. Linear scaling [4] was used in both cases.

The hybrid algorithm described above performs much slower that the classical one. On the other hand, the reducts obtained by this algorithm are usually shorter. Moreover, the hybrid algorithm generates from 50 to 500 different reducts in comparison with 5 to 50 reducts generated by the classical GA at the same time.

In [14] an improvement of the hybrid algorithm is presented. General scheme is the same as described above, but a procedure of testing whether a subset is a reduct, was improved. Now the algorithm acts as follows:

1. We have to determine, whether a subset s is a reduct or superreduct (a superset of a reduct). First, we search a list of known reducts. If there exists a reduct r such that $r \subset s$, the answer is YES.
2. We search for s in a treelike structure of known subreducts. If we find s, the answer is NO.
3. If both of pervious steps fail, we are looking in our data for a pair of objects with equal values on attributes from s, but with the different decisions. We are inserting all objects from the table into a binary tree - this is equivalent to sorting the data by the attribute values on s. Now the pair is easy to find - if one exists. If such a pair is found, we can reorder objects and bring the pair to the beginning (it can save up to 25% of time).
4. If we find such a pair, the answer is NO and we can add s to the tree of subreducts.
5. If there is no such a pair, the answer is YES and we can add s to the list of (super)reducts, removing all its supersets.

This new procedure is not only faster, than a method based on the distinction table (see above), but also occupies much less space. The results of computation time for some data tables are presented in Figure 2. A set of up to 30 short reducts was generated in each case. All computations were performed on a Pentium-100 machine.

Table size obj × attr	Comp. time sec
4,495 × 37	63
30,000 × 10	61
471 × 33	6.2
225 × 490	69
15,534 × 16	3

Fig. 2. Computation time for various data sets.

In [22] the average efficiency (the average length of obtained reducts) using three recombination operators: PMX, OX and MOX is compared. The results obtained using MOX were better than those obtained using OX, and were significantly better than those obtained using PMX operator (based on absolute positions of attributes). This suggests, that rd-schemata (concerned with the MOX operator) create a good tool for analysing this hybrid algorithm.

4.1.3 Optimisation based on the number of rules Both algorithms described above generate possibly shortest reducts, i.e. the reducts with as few attributes as possible. On the other hand, our goal is not to calculate reducts, but to construct an efficient system for classification or decision making. The set of decision rules generated from the set of short reducts should be general enough to deal with a new object. This assumption creates a foundation of decision systems described in [1], [9], [11], [14].

Another approach is to select a reduct due to the number of rules it generates rather than to its length. Every reduct generates an indiscernibility relation (see [12]) on the universe and in most cases it identifies some pairs of objects. Therefore the number of rules generated by a reduct is less than the number of objects. If a reduct generates less rules, it means, that the rules are more general and they should better recognise new objects.

The number of rules can be easily computed due to the improvement of the reduct generation system described in [14] (see pervious section). When the program determines whether a subset is a reduct, it constructs a tree of all objects. The number of nodes in this tree is equal to the number of rules generated by the reduct. So the number of rules can be computed with nearly no additional time. The hybrid algorithm described in the pervious section can be used to find reducts generating the minimal number of rules. All we have to do is to change the fitness formula:

$$F(\tau) = m - R_\tau + \frac{n - L_\tau + 1}{n}$$

where R_τ denotes the number of rules generated by the reduct. Now the primary criterion of optimisation is the number of rules, the secondary is the reduct length.

Some data sets were used in experiments to compare the classification efficiency of systems basing on the shortest reducts and the smallest sets of rules. The results are presented on Figure 3, where m_1 is a number of objects in training set, m_2 - a number of objects in test set, n - a number of attributes, R - a reduction rate of rule set. The results involve a training time (Pentium-100) and a number of correct classifications of test objects, basing on rule set generated by the best 30 reducts found using either the old algorithm or the new one.

m_1	m_2	n	Time sec.	Minimal no. of rules	Minimal red. length	R
357	154	41	18	44.1%	33.1%	5.7%
24000	6000	10	52	97.1%	97.1%	2.3%
4435	2000	37	284	27.1%	26.7%	0.1%
800	200	81	397	76.4%	76.6%	5.0%
16000	4000	17	138	44.2%	43.3%	0.6%

Fig. 3. Results of classification.

We can conclude, that the classification system based on the reducts optimised due to the number of rules performs better (or not worse) than the short reduct based one. Moreover, due to the rule set reduction, it occupies less memory and classifies new objects faster.

4.2 Finding templates using genetic algorithm

In the article [12] in this book the problem of template generation is presented in details, including some heuristic methods of template generation. We are interested in good templates, i.e. templates with many fixed positions and matching many objects. Some versions of the problem of finding the best (in this sense) template is proven to be NP-hard. Another method for template generation, a hybrid algorithm (as in [10], [14]), is presented below.

Note that every template can be represented by a binary string of length n (indicating which attributes are fixed) and any object matching it (called a base object). This representation will be the most natural in problems as follows: "Find the largest template matching the object x_0". There are also other questions, like: "Find the globally best template in this information system", that can be reformulated in terms of finding the best template matching one specific object. In fact, the heuristic algorithm described below finds a good template for a given base object:

1. Get an object x_0 as a base object.
2. Let σ be an order of attributes.
3. Consider a set of templates of the form: $T_1 = (a_{\sigma_1} = v_{\sigma_1})$, $T_2 = (a_{\sigma_1} = v_{\sigma_1}) \wedge (a_{\sigma_2} = v_{\sigma_2})$, etc., where v_i denotes a value of i-th attribute on x_0.
4. Choose the best template among T_1,...,T_n. This is a result generated by permutation σ.

Every locally maximal template can be found using this algorithm - the result depends on the order of attributes. The time complexity of this algorithm is bounded by $O(n^2m)$. The algorithm described above can be optimised in many ways: for example, objects that do not match the base object in any position can be deleted from database (a pre-processing). Our goal is to find the proper order of attributes and we use genetic algorithms to do this job. Our chromosome will be a permutation of length n, and its fitness value depends on a quality of a template T found by the heuristic algorithm.

The value of the fitness function, $F(T)$, depends on two parameters viz. the number O_T of objects in the data table matching the given template (base object excluded) and the number A_T of fixed positions:

$$F(T) = O_T \cdot A_T$$

Calculating $F(T)$ is the most time-consuming operation, but some techniques can be used to make it faster. For example, we can store fitness values in memory and try to recall them instead of calculating them again.

The "roulette wheel" algorithm was used as a selection strategy. The results were slightly better in the case when the elitist strategy was used as an additional technique. The best individual was copied to the new population without changes.

Crossing-over affects chromosomes selected to reproduction with the probability of $P_c = 0.7$. We use PMX [4] and MOX [22] method.

There is no simple and fast way to generate globally good templates by this algorithm - generating the best template for any object is rather unacceptable for large databases. On the other hand, a globally good template means that it matches many objects from the database (in examples presented below - up to 60%). Note, that if we choose any of them as our base object, we find global optimum. So, we can simply choose randomly as many objects as possible and calculate the templates - the largest of them will probably be a global optimum.

See [12] for experimental results in comparison with other algorithms.

Note, that the genetic algorithm used in the hybrid system described above is identical (except of fitness function) with that used to produce short reducts (see pervious section). Actually, in our real knowledge discovery system [7] with both these hybrid algorithms implemented, control sequences generates one genetic algorithm.

The same hybrid algorithm can be used to produce decision templates. We have only to change the fitness formula:

$$F(T) = c_1 \left(\frac{O_+}{O_+ + O_-} \right)^3 + c_2 \left(\frac{O_+}{O_+ + O_{used}} \right)^3 + \frac{O_+}{O_{class}}$$

where:

O_+ = the number of objects matching the template and belonging to the decision class;

O_- = the number of objects matching the template and not belonging to the decision class;

O_{used} = the number of objects matching the template and belonging to the decision class, but already covered by the previously generated templates.

O_{class} = the number of objects belonging to the decision class;

c_1, c_2 - parameters.

Using this fitness function, we can cover whole decision class with templates. We start with a random object in the class as a base object, then the obtained template is stored in the memory. The next base object is chosen randomly from the class, but we do not take into account objects covered by the already produced templates.

Observe that a high value of c_1 forces the templates chosen not to cover any object outside the class, but the templates are shorter and we have to use more of them. If the value of c_2 is high then obtained templates are separated. We can use the conjunction of obtained templates as our approximate definition of the decision class.

The results of experiments presented in [10] show, that in real cases we have to be very careful in choosing value of c_1. If the value is too high, then we obtain too many templates; if the value is too low, the obtained decision algorithm is useless: it cannot recognise properly too many objects. On the other hand, there are many templates covering only 1 or 2 objects. These "exceptions" can be omitted if we are interested in short and general rules.

5 Ordinal-based genetic algorithms

The flexibility and universality of order-based genetic algorithms cannot assure efficiency of all possible hybrid applications. Thus, there is a need for other types of genetic algorithms able to control various heuristic procedures. An example of such a genetic algorithm is an ordinal-based one.

In the *ordinal-based genetic algorithm* an individual has the following form:

$$\{ x_1 \; x_2 \; x_3 \; x_4 \; \cdots \; x_n \}$$

where n is a chromosome length, $x_i \in [1, ..., b]$ and b is a given (usually small) integer.

Mutation operator affects a single random gene in individual increasing it (with probability P_+) or decreasing by one. E.g.:

$$\{1\,1\,2\,1\,3\} \overset{Mutation}{\longrightarrow} \{1\,1\,3\,1\,3\}$$

Decreasing of value 1 is ignored.

Crossing-over operator is very similar to the classical one [4]. A matching section is chosen randomly, then the values of genes in matching sections of parents are exchanged. E.g.:

$$\begin{array}{c|c} 1\,2\,1 & 1\,4 \\ 2\,3\,1 & 2\,2 \end{array} \longrightarrow \begin{array}{c|c} 2\,3\,1 & 1\,4 \\ 1\,2\,1 & 2\,2 \end{array}$$

Vertical line indicates the end of matching section.

This type of genetic algorithm can be used in hybrid system solving the matrix covering problem [2], [5]. We have a binary matrix of size $n \times n$. Our goal is to find a covering, i.e. a subset of columns, such that in each row there exists at least one "1" in one of the columns from the covering (if possible). The problem of finding the smallest covering is one of the classical NP-hard problems. On the other hand, some NP-hard problems concerned with the rough set theory (e.g. short reducts finding) can be formulated in terms of minimal covering of a matrix.

Let us consider a simple "greedy" heuristic for this problem:

1. Find a column covering the most rows in the matrix.
2. Choose this column to our covering. Remove covered rows from matrix.
3. Repeat from step 1 until the matrix is covered.

This algorithm gives good, but suboptimal solutions. We will transform it to a hybrid version:

1. Let $i = 1$. Let $\{x_1, ...x_n\}$ be an ordinal-based individual.
2. Sort columns in descending order with respect to the number of covered rows.
3. Choose x_i-th column for our covering. Remove the covered rows from matrix.
4. Let $i = i + 1$.
5. Repeat from step 2 until the matrix is covered.

For example, if our individual has a form $\{1, 2, 1, ...\}$, we choose the best column in the first step, the second column in the second step, the best column in the third step etc... Now the algorithm can find every possible covering, including the optimal one. The formula of fitness function depends on the size of covering found.

6 Conclusions

A hybrid algorithm is a system where a genetic algorithm controls behaviour of a simple heuristic search method. These algorithms can be successfully used in NP-hard problems related to the rough set methods in KD and data mining. Application of hybrid methods in such problems like short reducts finding or template finding was described in this work.

There are two methods of short reducts finding presented in this work: a classical genetic algorithm with binary chromosomes, and a hybrid system based on the order-based genetic algorithm. Both these methods produce good results in relatively short time. The classical method is faster, but the hybrid one gives more different reducts in one pass. Moreover, the reducts obtained by hybrid algorithm are shorter; the classical method sometimes produces superreducts.

The hybrid algorithm can be easily modified to produce reducts generating the smallest number of rules. These reducts are shown to be better in classification algorithms than the shortest ones.

The order-based genetic algorithm is used also in the hybrid system which generates large templates. There are some heuristic algorithms to large templates finding as good as a hybrid system is. On the other hand, the hybrid algorithm described in this work can be easily adopted to a problem of decision templates finding, where other methods fail.

An order-based genetic algorithm was used as the driving force of hybrid systems described in this work. An overview of order-based genetic operators and the theoretical foundations was presented in section 3.

An ordinal-based genetic algorithm presented in section 5 is a new, promising technique, which can be used in hybrid algorithms. A method of usage the ordinal-based GA in rough set methods in KD, as well as its theoretical foundations, needs more researches.

Acknowledgements

This work has been supported by the grant #8T11C01011 from Polish National Committee for Scientific Research (Komitet Badań Naukowych) and by the ESPRIT project 20288 CRIT-2.

References

1. Bazan, J., Skowron, A., Synak, P.: Dynamic reducts as a tool for extracting laws from decision tables. In: Z. W. Ras, M. Zemankova (eds.), Proceedings of the Eighth Symposium on Methodologies for Intelligent Systems, Charlotte, NC, October 16-19, Lecture Notes in Artificial Intelligence **869**, Springer-Verlag (1994) 346–355
2. Cormen, T.H., Leiserson, C.E., Rivest, R.L.: Introduction to algorithms. The MIT Press, Cambridge (1992) 974–978
3. Davis, L. (ed.): Handbook of genetic algorithms. New York, Van Nostrand Reinhold (1991)

4. Goldberg, D.E.: GA in search, optimisation, and machine learning. Addison-Wesley (1989)
5. Garey, M.R., Johnson, D.S.: Computers and intractability. A guide to the theory of NP-completeness. W.H. Freeman and Company, New York (1979)
6. Holland, J.H.: Adaptation in natural and artificial systems. The MIT Press, Cambridge (1992)
7. Komorowski, J., Ohrn A.: ROSETTA - a rough set toolkit for analysis of data. In: P.P. Wang (ed.): Proceedings of the Fifth International Workshop on Rough Sets and Soft Computing (RSSC'97) at Third Annual Joint Conference on Information Sciences (JCIS'97), Duke University, Durham, NC, USA, Rough Set & Computer Science **3**, March 1–5 (1997) 403–407
8. Michalewicz, Z.: Genetic algorithms + data structures = evolution programs. Springer-Verlag (1994)
9. Nguyen, H. Son, Nguyen, T. Trung, Skowron, A., Synak, P.: Knowledge discovery by rough set methods. In: Proceedings of The International Conference On Information Systems Analysis and Synthesis, July 22–26, 1996, Orlando, USA (1996) 26–33
10. Nguyen, S. Hoa, Polkowski, L., Skowron, A., Synak, P., Wróblewski, J.: Searching for approximate description of decision classes. In: S. Tsumoto, S. Kobayashi, T. Yokomori, H. Tanaka, and A. Nakamura (eds.): Proceedings of the Fourth International Workshop on Rough Sets, Fuzzy Sets, and Machine Discovery (RSFD'96), The University of Tokyo, November 6–8 (1996) 153–161
11. Nguyen, H. Son, Skowron, A., Synak, P.: Rough sets in data mining: approximate description of decision classes. In: Proceedings of The fourth European Congress on Intelligent Techniques and Soft Computing, Aachen, Germany, September 2–5 (1996) 149–153
12. Nguyen, S. Hoa, Skowron, A., Synak, P.: Discovery of data patterns with applications to decomposition and classification problem. (in this book)
13. Nguyen, S. Hoa, Nguyen, H. Son: Some efficient algorithms for rough set methods. In: Proceedings of the Sixth International Conference, Information Procesing and Management of Uncertainty in Knowledge- Based Systems (IPMU'96), July 1-5, Granada, Spain (1996) 1451–1456
14. Nguyen, S. Hoa, Skowron, A., Synak, P., Wróblewski, J.: Knowledge discovery in databases: rough set approach. In: Proceedings of The Seventh International Fuzzy Systems Association World Congress **2** IFSA'97, Prague, Czech Republic (1997) 204–209
15. Nix, A., Vose, M.D.: Modelling genetic algorithms with Markov chains. Annals of Mathematics and Artificial Intelligence (1991)
16. Pawlak, Z.: Rough sets. Theoretical aspects of reasoning about data. Kluwer Academic Publishers, Dordrecht (1991)
17. Radcliffe, N.J.: Forma analysis and random respectful recombination. In: Proceedings of the Fourth International Conference on Genetic Algorithms, Morgan Kaufmann Publishers (1991) 222–229
18. Skowron, A., Polkowski, L.: Rough mereological foundations for analysis, synthesis, design and control in distributive system. In: Proceedings of the Second Annual Joint Conference on Information Sciences, Sept. 28 – Oct. 1, 1995, Wrightsville Beach, NC (1995) 346–349
19. Skowron, A., Rauszer, C.: The discernibility matrices and functions in information systems. In: R. Slowiński (ed.), Intelligent Decision Support. Handbook of

Applications and Advances of the Rough Sets Theory. Kluwer, Dordrecht (1992) 331–362
20. Suzuki, J.: A Markov chain analysis on a genetic algorithm. In: Proceedings of the Fifth International Conference on Genetic Algorithms. Morgan Kaufmann Publishers (1993) 146–153
21. Wróblewski, J.: Finding minimal reducts using genetic algorithms. In: Proceedings of the Second Annual Join Conference on Information Sciences, September 28 – October 1, 1995, Wrightsville Beach, NC (1995) 186–189
22. Wróblewski, J.: Theoretical foundations of Order–Based Genetic Algorithms. In: Fundamenta Informaticae **28/3-4** (1996) 423–430

APPENDIX 1:

ROUGH SET BIBLIOGRAPHY

Selected Bibliography on Rough Sets

The bibliography starts with a list of books, proceedings, and special issues of journals dedicated to rough set theory and applications. In the bibliography we refer to them by using abbreviations specified below.

RS Pawlak, Z.: Rough Sets – Theoretical Aspects of Reasoning about Data. Kluwer Academic Publishers, Dordrecht (1991)

RS'92 R. Słowiński, J. Stefanowski (eds.): Proceedings of the First International Workshop on Rough Sets: State of the Art and Perspectives. Kiekrz – Poznań, Poland September 2–4 (1992)

IDS R. Słowiński (ed.): Intelligent Decision Support – Handbook of Applications and Advances of the Rough Sets Theory. Kluwer Academic Publishers, Dordrecht (1992)

FCDS'93 R. Słowiński, J. Stefanowski (eds.), Foundations of Computing and Decision Sciences **18/3–4** (1993) 155–396 (special issue)

RSKD'93a W. Ziarko (ed.): Proceedings of the Second International Workshop on Rough Sets and Knowledge Discovery (RSKD'93). Banff, Alberta, Canada, October 12–15 (1993)

RSKD'93b W. Ziarko (ed.): Rough Sets, Fuzzy Sets and Knowledge Discovery (RSKD'93). Workshops in Computing, Springer–Verlag & British Computer Society, London, Berlin (1994)

RSSC'94 T.Y. Lin (ed.): Proceedings of the Third International Workshop on Rough Sets and Soft Computing (RSSC'94). San Jose State University, San Jose, California, USA, November 10–12 (1994)

SC T.Y. Lin, A.M. Wildberger (eds.): Soft Computing: Rough Sets, Fuzzy Logic, Neural Networks, Uncertainty Management, Knowledge Discovery. Simulation Councils, Inc., San Diego, CA (1995)

CI W. Ziarko (ed.): Computational Intelligence: An International Journal **11/2** (1995) (special issue)

RSSC'95 P.P. Wang (ed.): Proceedings of the International Workshop on Rough Sets and Soft Computing at Second Annual Joint Conference on Information Sciences (JCIS'95), Wrightsville Beach, North Carolina, 28 September - 1 October (1995)

DM T.Y. Lin (ed.): Proceedings of the Workshop on Rough Sets and Data Mining at 23rd Annual Computer Science Conference. Nashville, Tenessee, March 2 (1995)

RSFD'96 S. Tsumoto, S. Kobayashi, T. Yokomori, H. Tanaka, and A. Nakamura (eds.): Proceedings of the Fourth International Workshop on Rough Sets, Fuzzy Sets, and Machine Discovery (RSFD'96). The University of Tokyo, November 6–8 (1996)

IA T.Y. Lin (ed.): Journal of the Intelligent Automation and Soft Computing **2/2** (1996) (special issue)

AR T.Y. Lin (ed.): International Journal of Approximate Reasoning **15/4** (1996) (special issue)

FI W. Ziarko (ed.): Fundamenta Informaticae **27/2–3** (1996) (special issue)

BUL1 S. Tsumoto (ed.): Bulletin of International Rough Set Society **1/1** (1996)

BUL2 S. Tsumoto (ed.): Bulletin of International Rough Set Society **1/2** (1997)

RSSC'97 P.P. Wang (ed.): Proceedings of the Fifth International Workshop on Rough Sets and Soft Computing (RSSC'97) at Third Annual Joint Conference on Information Sciences (JCIS'97). Duke University, Durham, NC, USA, Rough Set & Computer Science **3**, March 1–5 (1997)

RSDM T.Y. Lin, N. Cercone (eds.): Rough Sets and Data Mining. Analysis of Imprecise Data. Kluwer Academic Publishers, Boston, Dordrecht (1997)

II E. Orłowska (ed.): Incomplete information: Rough set analysis. Physica–Verlag, Heidelberg (1997)

FSRS S.K. Pal, A. Skowron (eds.): Fuzzy Sets, Rough Sets and Decision Making Processes. Springer–Verlag, Singapore (in preparation)

Selected Papers on Rough Sets

1. Aasheim, Oe. T., Solheim, H. G.: Rough sets as a framework for data mining. Technical Report (project), Knowledge Systems Group, The Norwegian University of Science and Technology, Trondheim, Norway (1996)
2. Albaraan, M.: Weak controllability in a parallel flow model of computation and its relationship with rough sets. In: P.P. Wang (ed.): Proceedings of the International Workshop on Rough Sets and Soft Computing at Second Annual Joint Conference on Information Sciences (JCIS'95), Wrightsville Beach, North Carolina, 28 September - 1 October (1995) 205–208
3. An, A., Chan, C., Shan, N., Cercone, N., Ziarko, W.: Applying knowledge discovery to predict water-supply consumption. IEEE Expert **12/4** (1997) 72–78
4. An, A., Shan, N., Chan, C., Cercone, N.: ELEM: A novel method for inducing rules from examples. In: 7th IEEE International Conference on Tools with Artificial Intelligence, Washington, D.C (1995)
5. An, A., Shan, N., Chan, C., Cercone, N., Ziarko, W.: Discovering rules from data for water demand prediction. In: Proceedings of the Workshop on Machine Learning in Engineering (IJCAI'95), Montreal (1995) 187–202; see also: Journal of Intelligent Real-Time Automation: Engineering Applications of Artificial Intelligence **9/6** (1996) 645–654
6. Archangelsky, D.A., Tajtslin, M.A.: A logic for information systems. Studia Logica **58/1** (1997) 3–16
7. Arciszewski, T., Hoda, S., Khasnabis, T., Ziarko, W.: Machine learning in transportation engineering: A feasibility study. Journal of Applied Artificial Intelligence **8/1** (1994) 109–124
8. Arciszewski, T., Mustafa, M., Ziarko, W.: A methodology of design knowledge acquisition for use in learning expert systems. Journal of Man–Machine Studies **27** (1987) 23–32
9. Arciszewski, T., Ziarko, W.: Adaptive expert system for preliminary engineering design. In: Proceedings of the Sixth International Workshop on Expert Systems and their Applications, Avignon, France (1986) 695–712; see also: Revue Internationale de CFAO et D'Infographie **2/1** (1987) 26–39
10. Arciszewski, T., Ziarko, W.: Verification of morphological table based on probabilistic rough set approach. In: Proceedings of the 18th Annual Meeting of Fine Particle Society, Boston (1987); see also: Particulate Science and Technology: An International Journal **6/2** (1988) 193–205
11. Arciszewski, T., Ziarko, W.: Adaptive expert system for preliminary design of wind–bracings in steel skeleton structures. In: Second Century of Skyscraper, Van Norstrand (1987) 847–855
12. Arciszewski, T., Ziarko, W.: Inductive learning in civil engineering: Rough sets approach. Microcomputers and Civil Engineering **5/1** (1990)
13. Arciszewski, T., Ziarko, W.: Structural optimization: Case-based approach. Computing in Civil Engineering, Journal of American Society of Civil Engineers **5/2** (1991) 159–174

14. Arciszewski, T., Ziarko, W.: Machine learning and knowledge acquisition in civil engineering. In: T. Arciszewski (ed.), Knowledge Acquisition in Civil Engineering, American Society of Civil Engineers (1992) 50–69
15. Arciszewski, T., Ziarko, W., Hajdo, P., Aktan, H.: Inductive shallow approach for generation of engineering models. In: Proceedings of the Ninth European Meeting on Cybernetics and Systems Research, Vienna, Austria (1988) 933–940
16. Arciszewski, T., Ziarko, W., Khan, T.L.: Learning conceptual design rules: A rough sets approach. In: [RSKD'93b] 444–449
17. Baker, J., Miller III, W.T., Ruciński, A.: Rough sets as a front end for neural computing. In: [RS'92] 1–6
18. Balbiani, P.: Axiomatization of logics based on Kripke models with relative accessibility relations. In: [II] 553-578
19. Balbiani, P., Orłowska, E.: A hierarchy of modal logics with relative accessibility relations. Journal of Applied Non-Classical Logics (to appear)
20. Baltzersen, J.K.: Quinlan's algorithms and the rough set approach. (Project in Technical Report), Knowledge Systems Group, The Norwegian University of Science and Technology, Trondheim, Norway (1995)
21. Baltzersen, J.K.: An attempt to predict stock market data: A rough sets approach. Master Thesis, supervisor J. Komorowski. Knowledge Systems Group, The Norwegian University of Science and Technology, Trondheim, Norway (1995)
22. Banerjee, M.: A cathegorical approach to the algebra and logic of the indiscernible. Ph.D dissertation, Department of Pure Mathematics, University of Calcutta, India (1994)
23. Banerjee, M.: Rough sets and 3-valued Lukasiewicz logic. Fundamenta Informaticae (1997) **32/1** 213–220
24. Banerjee, M., Chakraborty, M.K.: A category for rough sets. In: [RS'92] 7–9; see also: [FCDS'93] 167–180
25. Banerjee, M., Chakraborty, M.K.: Logic of rough sets. In: V. Alagar, S. Bergler, and F.Q. Dong (eds.), Incompleteness and Uncertainty in Information Systems, Proceedings of SOFTEKS Workshop on Incompleteness and Uncertainty in Information Systems, Concordia University, Montreal, Canada 1993, Workshops in Computing, Springer–Verlàg & British Computer Society, London, Berlin (1994) 223–233
26. Banerjee, M., Chakraborty, M.K.: Rough consequence and rough algebra. In: [RS-KD' 93b] 196–207
27. Banerjee, M., Chakraborty, M.K.: Rough sets through algebraic logic. Fundamenta Informaticae **3/4** (1996) 211–221
28. Banerjee, M., Chakraborty, M.K.: Rough logics: A survey with further directions. In: [II] 579-600
29. Banerjee, M., Mitra, S., Pal, S.K.: Rough fuzzy MLP: Knowledge encoding and classification. Preprint (1996)
30. Banerjee, M., Pal, S.K.: Roughness of a fuzzy set. Information Sciences (Informatics and Comp. Sc.) **93/3-4** (1996) 235–246
31. Bazan, J.: Dynamic reducts and statistical inference. In: Proceedings of the Sixth International Conference, Information Processing and Management of Uncertainty in Knowledge–Based Systems (IPMU'96), July 1-5, Granada, Spain (1996) **3** 1147–1152
32. Bazan, J., Nguyen, H. Son, Nguyen, T. Trung, Skowron, A., Stepaniuk, J.: Some logic and rough set applications for classifying objects. Institute of Computer Science, Warsaw University of Technology, ICS Research Report **38/94** (1994)

33. Bazan, J., Nguyen Son, H., Nguyen Trung, T., Skowron, A., Stepaniuk, J.: Application of modal logics and rough sets for classifying objects. In: M. De Glas, Z. Pawlak (eds.), Proceedings of the Second World Conference on Fundamentals of Artificial Intelligence (WOCFAI'95), Paris, July 3-7, Angkor, Paris (1995) 15–26
34. Bazan, J. G., Nguyen Son, H., Nguyen Trung, T., Skowron, A., Stepaniuk, J.: Synthesis of decision rules for object classification. In: [II] 23–57
35. Bazan, J., Skowron, A., Synak, P.: Market data analysis. Institute of Computer Science, Warsaw University of Technology, ICS Research Report **6/94** (1994)
36. Bazan, J., Skowron, A., Synak, P.: Dynamic reducts as a tool for extracting laws from decision tables. In: Z.W. Ras, M. Zemankova (eds.), Proceedings of the Eighth Symposium on Methodologies for Intelligent Systems, Charlotte, NC, October 16-19, Lecture Notes in Artificial Intelligence **869**, Springer-Verlag (1994) 346–355; see also: Institute of Computer Science, Warsaw University of Technology, ICS Research Report **43/94** (1994)
37. Bazan, J., Skowron, A., Synak, P.: Discovery of decision rules from experimental data. In: [RSSC'94] 526–533; [SC] 276–279
38. Beaubouef, T., Petry, F.E.: A rough set model for relational databases. In: [RSKD' 93b] 100–107
39. Beaubouef, T., Petry, F.E.: Rough querying of crisp data in relational databases. In: [SC] 85–88
40. Beaubouef, T., Petry, F.E.: Fuzzy set quantification of roughness in rough relational database model. In: Proceedings of the Third International Conference on Fuzzy Systems, Orlando, Florida (1994) 172–177
41. Beaubouef, T., Petry, F.E., Arora, G.: Information–theoretic measures of uncertainty for rough sets and rough relational databases. In: [RSSC'97] 336–339
42. Beaubouef, T., Petry, F.E., Arora, G.: Information measures for rough and fuzzy sets and applications to uncertainty in relational databases. In: [FSRS]
43. Beaubouef, T., Petry, F.E., Buckles, B.P.: Extension of the relational database and its algebra with rough set techniques. In: [CI] 233–245
44. Bjorvand, A.T.: Time series and rough sets. Master Thesis, supervisor J. Komorowski, Knowledge Systems Group, The Norwegian University of Science and Technology, Trondheim, Norway (1995)
45. Bjorvand, A.T.: Mining time series using rough sets - A case study. In: J. Komorowski, J. Żytkow, (eds.), The First European Symposium on Principles of Data Mining and Knowledge Discovery (PKDD'97), June 25–27, Trondheim, Norway, Lecture Notes in Artificial Intelligence **1263**, Springer-Verlag, Berlin (1997) 351–358
46. Bodjanova, S.: Approximation of fuzzy concepts in decision making. Fuzzy Sets and Systems **85** (1997) 23–29
47. Bonikowski, Z.: A certain conception of the calculus of rough sets. Notre Dame Journal of Formal Logic **33** (1992) 412–421
48. Bonikowski, Z.: Algebraic structures of rough sets. In: [RSKD'93b] 242–247
49. Bonikowski, Z.: Sets approximated by representations (in Polish). Ph.D. Dissertation, supervisor U. Wybraniec-Skardowska, Institute of Computer Science, Polish Academy of Sciences, Warsaw (1996)
50. Bonikowski, Z., Bryniarski, E., Wybraniec–Skardowska, U.: Extensions and intensions in the rough set theory. In: [RSSC'97] 65–68
51. Boryczka, M.: Algorithms for approximate data analysis (in Polish). Podstawy Sterowania **16** (1986) 249–254

52. Boryczka, M.: Applications of rough set theory to analysis of multi–criteria decision problems (in Polish). Archiwum Automatyki i Telemechaniki **33** (1988) 355–366
53. Boryczka, M.: Rough sets in multicriteria decision problems. Bull. Polish Acad. Sci. Tech. **36/3-4** (1988) 251–260
54. Boryczka, M.: Optimizing decision tables using rough sets. Bull. Polish Acad. Sci. Tech. **37** (1989) 309–319
55. Brindle, D.: Speaker-independent speech recognition by rough sets analysis. In: [RSSC'94] 376–383; [SC] 101–106
56. Browne, C.: Enhanced rough set data analysis of the Pima Indian diabetes data. In: Proceedings of the Eighth Ireland Conference on Artificial Intelligence, Derry (1997) 32–39
57. Bryniarski, E.: A calculus of rough sets of the first order. Bull. Polish Acad. Sci. Math. **37** (1989) 71–78
58. Bryniarski, E.: Formal description of rough sets (in Polish). Ph. D. Dissertation, supervisor U. Wybraniec–Skardowska, University of Wrocław (1993); see also: [RSKD'93a] 269–283; [RSKD'93b] 208–216; Institute of Computer Science, Warsaw University of Technology, ICS Research Report **21/94** (1994); [FI] 109–136
59. Bryniarski, E.: Principles of correct approximate object description (in Polish). In: Proceedings of the 39-th Conference on History of Logic, November 9–10, 1993, Cracow, Ruch Filozoficzny **LI/3-4** (1994) 315–320
60. Bryniarski, E.: Object revolution and description of rough sets (in Polish). In: In: Proceedings of the 40-th Conference on History of Logic, November 16–17, 1994, Cracow, Ruch Filozoficzny **LII/3-4** (1995) 443–447
61. Bryniarski, E., Wybraniec-Skardowska, U.: On a generalization of rough sets. Institute of Computer Science, Warsaw University of Technology, ICS Research Report **63/94** (1994)
62. Bryniarski, E., Wybraniec-Skardowska, U.: Generalized rough sets in contextual spaces. Institute of Computer Science, Warsaw University of Technology, ICS Research Report **40/95** (1995); see also: [RSDM] 339–354
63. Bryniarski, E., Wybraniec-Skardowska, U.: Calculus of contextual rough sets in contextual spaces. Institute of Computer Science, Warsaw University of Technology, ICS Research Report **63/95** (1995); see also: Journal of Applied Non-Classical Logics (special issue) (1996)
64. Bryniarski, E., Wybraniec-Skardowska, U.: On a generalization of rough sets. In: [DM] 185–190
65. Bryniarski, E., Wybraniec–Skardowska, U.: Formal and ontological aspects of names. Acta Universitatis Wratislaviensis **1890** (1997) 71–82
66. Bryniarski, E., Wybraniec–Skardowska, U., Bonikowski, Z.: Extensions and intensions in the rough set theory. In: [RSSC'97] 65–68
67. Budihardjo, A., Grzymała–Busse, J.W.: An overview of the learning program LERS–LB 2.5. Department of Computer Science, University of Kansas TR **90/4** (1990) 1–9
68. Budihardjo, A., Grzymała–Busse, J.W., Woolery, L.: Program LERS–LB 2.5 as a tool for knowledge acquisition in nursing. In: Proceedings of the Fourth International Conference on Industrial and Engineering Applications of Artificial Intelligence and Expert Systems, Koloa, Kauai, Hawaii, June 2–5, (1991) 735–740
69. Buszkowski, W., Orłowska, E.: Indiscernibility–based formalisation of dependencies in information systems. In: [II] 293–315
70. Cattaneo, G.: Local Boolean manifolds from knowledge representation systems. Mathware & Soft Computing, **3** (1996) 113–123

71. Cattaneo, G.: A unified algebraic approach to fuzzy algebras and rough approximations. In: R. Trappl (ed.), Proceedings of the 13th European Meeting on Cybernetics and Systems Research (CSR'96), April 9–12, The University of Vienna (1996) **1** 352–357
72. Cattaneo, G.: Abstract rough approximation spaces (Bridging the gap between fuzziness and roughness). In: Proceedings of the Fifth IEEE International Conference on Fuzzy Systems (FUZZ-IEEE'96), September 8–11, New Orleans, Louisiana (1996) **2** 1129–1134
73. Cattaneo, G.: Mathematical foundations of roughness and fuzziness. In: [RSFD'96] 241–247
74. Cattaneo, G.: Generalized rough sets (Preclusivity fuzzy-intuitionistic BZ lattices). Studia Logica **58/1** (1997) 47–77
75. Cattaneo, G., Dalla Chiara, M., Giuntini, R.: Some algebraic structures for many-valued logics, In: Tatra Mountains Math. Pub. (1997)
76. Cattaneo, G., Giuntini, R., Pilla, R.: MVBZ algebras and their substructures. The abstract approach to roughness and fuzziness. In: M. Mares, R. Meisar, V. Novak, and J. Ramik (eds.), Proceedings of the Seventh International Fuzzy Systems Assotiation World Congress (IFSA'97), June 25–29, Academia, Prague, (1997) **1** 155–161
77. Cattaneo, G., Giuntini, R., Pilla, R.: MVBZ^{dM} and Stonian algebras (Applications to fuzzy sets and rough approximations). In: Fuzzy Sets and Systems (1997)
78. Cercone, N.: Human-computer interfaces: DBLEARN and SystemX. In: [RSKD'-93a] 27–28
79. Cercone, N., Hamilton, H., Hu, X., Shan, N.: Data mining using attribute oriented generalization and information reduction. In: [RSDM] 199–227
80. Cercone, N., Hamilton, H., Shan, N.: Learning stronger rules with RIAC system. In: [RSSC'97] 348–349
81. Chakraborty, M.K., Banerjee, M.: Rough consequence. Bull. Polish Acad. Sci. Math. **41/4** (1993) 299–304
82. Chakraborty, M.K., Banerjee, M.: In search of a common foundation for rough sets and fuzzy sets. In: Proceedings of the Fifth European Congress on Intelligent Techniques and Soft Computing (EUFIT'97), Aachen, Germany, Verlag Mainz (1997) **1** 218–220
83. Chakraborty, M.K., Biswas, R., Nanda, S.: On rough relations. Research Report, Indian Institute of Technology, Kharagpur (1997)
84. Chan, C.-C.: Incremental learning of certain and possible rules from examples. In: [DM] 122–123
85. Chan, C.-C.: A rough set approach to attribute generalization in data mining. In: [RSSC'97] 391–394
86. Chan, C.-C., Grzymała-Busse, J.W.: Rough–set boundaries as a tool for learning rules from examples. In: Z.W. Ras (ed.), Proceedings of the Fourth International Symposium on Methodologies for Intelligent Systems (ISMIS'89), Charlotte, North Carolina, October 12–14, North Holland (1989) 281–288
87. Chan, C.-C., Grzymała-Busse, J.W.: On the lower boundaries in learning rules from examples. Department of Computer Science, University of Kansas, TR **91/13** (1991) 1–15; see also: [II] 58–74
88. Chan, C.-C., Grzymała-Busse, J. W.: On the attribute redundancy and the learning programs ID3, PRISM, and LEM2. Department of Computer Science, University of Kansas, TR **91/14** (1991) 1–20

89. Chan, C.-C., Grzymała-Busse, J. W.: On the two local inductive algorithms: PRISM and LEM2. Foundations of Computing and Decision Sciences **19** (1994) 185–203
90. Chen, K., Grzymała-Busse, J. W.: An overview of the learning programs LEM1.1 and LERS1.1. Department of Computer Science, University of Kansas, TR **89/9** (1989) 1–11
91. Chen, J.-G., Tan, S., Watson, C., de Korvin, A. Webster, L.: Validation of authentic reasoning expert systems. In: [RSSC'97] 309–312
92. Chen, K., Pettorossi, A., Ras, Z.W., Skowron, A.: Attributes and rough properties in information systems. In: Proceedings of Conference on Information Sciences and Systems, March 14–16, Princeton University Press, Princeton (1984) 362–366; see also: International Journal of Approximate Reasoning **2/4** (1988) 365–376
93. Chen, R., Lin, T.Y.: Supporting rough set theory in very large databases using Oracle RDBMS. In: Y.-Y. Chen, K. Hirota, and J.-Y. Yen (eds.), Proceedings of Asian Fuzzy Systems Symposium - Soft Computing in Intelligent Systems and Information Processing, December 11–14, Kenting, Taiwan, ROC. (1996) 332–337
94. Chiu, T., Lin, T.Y.: Tuning rough controllers by genetic algorithms. In: Y.-Y. Chen, K. Hirota, and J.-Y. Yen (eds.), Proceedings of Asian Fuzzy Systems Symposium – Soft Computing in Intelligent Systems and Information Processing, December 11–14, Kenting, Taiwan, ROC. (1996) 326–331
95. Chmielewski, M., Grzymała–Busse, J.W.: Global discretization of continuous attributes as preprocessing for inductive learning. Department of Computer Science, University of Kansas, TR **92/7** (1989) 1–28; see also: [RSSC'94] 474–480; [SC] 294–297
96. Chmielewski, M., Grzymała–Busse, J.W.: Global discretization of continuous attributes as preprocessing for machine learning. In: [AR] 319–332
97. Chmielewski, M. R., Grzymała–Busse, J.W., Peterson, N., Than, S.: The rule induction system LERS - A version for personal computers. In: [FCDS'93] 181–212
98. Choubey, S.K., Deougun, J.S., Raghavan, V.V., Sever, H.: A comparison of feature selection algorithm in the context of rough classifiers. In: Proceedings of the Fifth IEEE International Conference on Fuzzy Systems (FUZZ-IEEE'96), September 8–11, New Orleans, Louisiana (1996) 1122–1128
99. Chuchro, M.: A certain conception of rough sets in topological Boolean algebras. Bulletin of the Section of Logic **22/1**, (1993) 9–12
100. Chuchro, M.: On rough sets in topological Boolean algebras. In: [RSKD'93a] 153–158; [RSKD'93b] 157–160
101. Comer, S.: An algebraic approach to the approximation of information. Fundamenta Informaticae **14** (1991) 492–502
102. Comer, S.: On connections between information systems, rough sets and algebraic logic. Algebraic Methods in Logic and Computer Science. Banach Center Publications **28** (1993)
103. Cykier, A.: Prime implicants of boolean functions: Computing methods and applications. Master Thesis, supervisor A. Skowron, Institute of Mathematics, Warsaw University (1997)
104. Czogała, E., Mrózek, A., Pawlak, Z.: The idea of rough-fuzzy controller. Fuzzy Sets and Systems **72** (1995) 61–63
105. Czyżewski, A.: New learning algorithms for the processing of old audio recordings. In: 99th Convention of the Audio Engineering Society, October 6–9, New York, USA, preprint **4078** (1995)
106. Czyżewski, A.: Managing noisy data in the AI-based processing of old audio recordings. In: Proceedings of Conference of the Intelligent Data Analysis (IDA'95), Au-

gust 17–19, Baden–Baden, Germany, The International Institute for Advanced Studies in Systems Research and Cybernetics (1995) **1** 38–42

107. Czyżewski, A.: Some methods for detection and interpolation of impulsive distortions in old audio recordings. In: IEEE ASSP Workshop on Applications of Signal Processing to Audio and Acoustics Proceedings, October 15-18, New York, USA (1995)
108. Czyżewski, A.: Speaker–independent recognition of digits – Experiments with neural networks, fuzzy logic and rough sets. In: [IA] 133–146
109. Czyżewski, A.: Speaker-independent recognition of digits based on soft computing methods. Bull. Polish Acad. Sci. Tech. **44/3** (1996) 357–377
110. Czyżewski, A.: Mining knowledge in noisy audio data. In: E. Simoudis, J. Han, and U. Fayyad (eds.), Proceedings of the Second International Conference on Knowledge Discovery and Data Mining (KDD'96), August 2–4, Portland, Oregon, USA, AAAI Press, Menlo Park (1996) 220–225
111. Czyżewski, A.: Learning algorithms for audio signal enhancement – Part I: Neural network implementation for the removal of impulse distortions. Journal of the Audio Engineering Society **45/10** (1997) 815–831
112. Czyżewski, A.: Learning algorithms for audio signal enhancement - Part II: Rough set method implementation for the removal of hiss. Journal of the Audio Engineering Society **45/11** (1997) 931–943
113. Czyżewski, A., Kaczmarek, A.: Multilayer knowledge based system for speaker-independent recognition of isolated words. In: [RSKD'93b] 387–394
114. Czyżewski, A., Kaczmarek, A.: Speaker-independent recognition of isolated words using rough sets. In: P.P. Wang (ed.): Proceedings of the International Workshop on Rough Sets and Soft Computing at Second Annual Joint Conference on Information Sciences (JCIS'95), Wrightsville Beach, North Carolina, 28 September - 1 October (1995) 397–400
115. Czyżewski, A., Kaczmarek, A.: Speech recognition systems based on rough sets and neural networks. In: [SC] 97–100
116. Czyżewski, A., Kostek, B.: Rough set-based filtration of sound applicable to hearing prostheses. In: [RSFD'96] 168–175
117. Czyżewski, A., Kostek, B.: Restoration of old records employing artificial intelligence methods. Proceedings of IASTED International Conference – Artificial Intelligence, Expert Systems and Neural Networks, August 19–21, Honolulu, Hawaii, USA (1996) 372–375
118. Czyżewski, A., Królikowski, R.: New methods of intelligent filtration and coding of audio. In: 102nd Convention of the Audio Engineering Society, March 22–25, preprint **4482**, Munich, Germany (1997)
119. Czyżewski, A., Królikowski, R.: Perceptual noise reduction based on artificial neural networks. In: Proceedings of the Symposium on Computer Science and Engineering Cybernetics, August 18–23, Baden–Baden, Germany, The International Institute for Advanced Studies in Systems Research and Cybernetics (1995)
120. Czyżewski, A., Królikowski, R.: Applications of fuzzy logic and rough sets to audio signal enhancement. In: [FSRS]
121. Czyżewski, A., Królikowski, R., Skórka, P.: Automatic detection of speech disorders. In: Proceedings of the Fourth European Congress on Intelligent Techniques and Soft Computing (EUFIT'96), September 2–5, Aachen, Germany, Verlag Mainz (1996) **1** 183–187
122. Das–Gupta, P.: Rough sets and information retrieval. In: Proceedings of the Eleventh Annual International ACM SIGIR Conference on Research and Development

in Information Retrieval (1988) 567–582
123. Dean, J.S., Grzymała-Busse, J.W.: An overview of the learning from examples module LEM1. Department of Computer Science, University of Kansas, TR **88/2** (1988) 1–13
124. Deja, R.: Conflict analysis based on distance function. Institute of Computer Science, Institute of Computer Science, Warsaw University of Technology, ICS Research Report **18/95** (1995)
125. Deja, R.: Negotiations in the conflict analysis model. Institute of Computer Science, Warsaw University of Technology, ICS Research Report **43/95** (1995)
126. Deja, R.: Conflict model with negotiations. Institute of Computer Science, Warsaw University of Technology, ICS Research Report **51/95** (1995); see also: Bull. Polish Acad. Sci. Tech. (to appear)
127. Deja, R.: Conflict analysis. In: [RSFD'96] 118–124
128. Demri, S.: The validity problem for the logic DALLA is decidable. Bull. Polish Acad. Sci. Tech. **44/1** (1996) 79–86
129. Demri, S.: A class of information logics with a decidable validity problem. In: Lecture Notes in Computer Science **1113**, Springer-Verlag (1996) 291–302
130. Demri, S.: Finite model property for a logic for data analysis. In: Proceedings of the Sixth International Conference, Information Processing and Management of Uncertainty in Knowledge–Based Systems (IPMU'96), July 1–5, Granada, Spain (1996) **2** 871–876
131. Demri, S.: A completeness proof for a logic with an alternative necessity operator. Studia Logica **58/1** (1997) 99–112
132. Demri, S.: Extensions of modal logic S5 preserving NP-completeness. Bulletin of the Section of Logic **26** (1997) 73–84
133. Demri, S.: A class of decidable information logics. Theoretical Computer Science (to appear)
134. Demri, S., Orłowska, E.: Logical analysis of indiscernibility. Institute of Computer Science, Warsaw University of Technology, ICS Research Report **11/96** (1996); see also: [II] 347–380
135. Demri, S., Orłowska, E.: A class of modal logics with a finite model property with respect to the set of $\Diamond$-formulae. Bulletin of the Section of Logic **26/1** (1997) 39–49
136. Deogun, J., Raghavan, V., Sarkar, A., Sever, H.: Exploiting upper approximation in the rough set methodology. In: U.M. Fayyad, R. Uthurusamy (eds.), Proceedings of the First International Conference on Knowledge Discovery and Data Mining (KDD'95), August 20-21, 1995, Montreal, AAAI Press, Menlo Park CA (1995) 69–74
137. Deogun, J., Raghavan, V., Sarkar, A., Sever, H.: Data mining: Trends in research and development. In: [RSDM] 9–45
138. Deogun, J., Raghavan, V., Sever, H.: Revised rough classifiers. In: Proceedings of the Fourth European Congress on Intelligent Techniques and Soft Computing (EUFIT'96), September 2–5, Aachen, Germany, Verlag Mainz (1996) **1** 219
139. Dubois, D., Prade, H.: Twofold fuzzy sets and rough sets – Some issues in knowledge representation. Fuzzy Sets and Systems **23** (1987) 3–18
140. Dubois, D., Prade, H.: Rough fuzzy sets and fuzzy rough sets. International J. General Systems **17** (1990) 191–209
141. Dubois, D., Prade, H.: Putting rough sets and fuzzy sets together. In: [IDS] 203–232
142. Dubois, D., Prade, H.: Graded indiscernibility, fuzzy rough sets and modal logics. In: Proceedings of the Fifth International Fuzzy Systems Association Congress (IFSA), July, 1993, Seoul, Korea (1993)

143. Dubois, D., Prade, H.: Similarity versus preference in fuzzy set–based logics. In: [II] 441–461
144. Düntsch, I.: Rough relation algebras. Fundamenta Informaticae **21** (1994) 321–331
145. Düntsch, I.: A logic for rough sets. Theoretical Computer Science **179/1-2** (1997) 427–436
146. Düntsch, I.: Rough sets and algebras of relations. In: [II] 95–108
147. Düntsch, I., Gediga, G.: Rough set dependency analysis in evaluation studies: An application in the study of repeated heart attacks. University of Ulster, Informatics Research Reports **10** (1995) 25–30
148. Düntsch, I., Gediga, G.: Algebraic aspects of attribute dependencies in information systems. Fundamenta Informaticae **29** (1997) 119–133
149. Düntsch, I., Gediga, G.: ROUGHIAN – Rough information analysis an introduction (extended abstract). In: A. Sydow (ed.), Proceedings of the 15th IMACS World Congress IMACS97, August, Berlin Wissenschaft und Technik Verlag, Berlin (1997) **4** 631–636
150. Düntsch, I., Gediga, G.: Relation restricted prediction. (Extended abstract). In: A. Sydow (ed.), Proceedings of the 15th IMACS World Congress IMACS97, August, Berlin Wissenschaft und Technik Verlag Berlin (1997) **4** 619–624
151. Düntsch, I., Gediga, G.: Simple data filtering in rough set systems. University of Ulster (1997); see also: International Journal of Approximate Reasoning (to appear)
152. Düntsch, I., Gediga, G.: Uncertainty measures of rough set prediction. University of Ulster (1997) (submitted)
153. Düntsch, I., Gediga, G.: The rough set engine GROBIAN. In: A. Sydow (ed.), Proceedings of the 15th IMACS World Congress IMACS97, Berlin Wissenschaft und Technik Verlag **4** (1997) 613–618
154. Düntsch, I., Gediga, G.: Non–invasive data analysis. Proceedings of the Eighth Ireland Conference on Artificial Intelligence, Derry (1997) 24–31
155. Düntsch, I., Gediga, G.: Statistical evaluation of rough set dependency analysis. International Journal of Human-Computer Studies **46** (1997) 589–604
156. Düntsch, I., Gediga, G., Juetting, A.: GROBIAN – An engine for rough set data analysis. Proceedings of the First International Conference on Practical Aspects of Knowledge Management, October, Basel (1996)
157. Eiben, A.E., Euverman, T.J., Kowalczyk, W., Slisser, F.: Modelling customer retention with statistical techniques, rough data models, and genetic programming. In: [FSRS]
158. Farinas del Cerro, L., Orłowska, E.: DAL–A logic for data analysis. Theoretical Computer Science **36** (1985) 251–264; see also: Corrigendum: ibidem **47** (1986) 345
159. Farinas del Cerro, L., Prade, H.: Rough sets, twofold fuzzy sets and modal logic – Fuzziness in indiscernibility and partial information. In: A. Di Nola, A.G.S. Ventre (eds.), The Mathematics of Fuzzy Systems, Verlag TUV Rheinland, Koeln (1986) 103–120
160. Fedrizzi, M., Kacprzyk, J., Nurmi, H.: How different are social choice functions: A rough sets approach. Quality & Quantity **30**, Kluwer Academic Publishers, the Netherlands (1996) 87–99
161. Fernandes–Baizan, M.C., Menasalvas Ruiz, E., Castano, M.: Integrating RDMS and data mining capabilities using rough sets. In: Proceedings of the Sixth International Conference, Information Processing and Management of Uncertainty in

Knowledge-Based Systems (IPMU'96), July 1-5, Granada, Spain (1996) **2** 1439–1445
162. Fernandes-Baizan, M. C., Menasalvas, E., Pena, J.M., Castano, M.: A new approach for the efficient calculation of reducts in large databases. In: [RSSC'97] 340–343
163. Fernandes-Baizan, M.C., Menasalvas, E., Pena, J.M., Castano, D., Santos, E., Portaencasa, R., Perez, C.: Integrating RDMS and data mining capabilities to a RDMS. In: Proceedings of IMACS Multiconference: Computational Engineering in Systems Applications (CESA '96) July 9–12, Lille, France (1996) **3/4** 764–768
164. Fernandes-Baizan, M. C., Menasalvas Ruiz, E., Pena, J.M., Santos, E.: Using RDMS to mine microbiological data. In: Nagib C. Callaos (ed.), Proceedings of the International Conference on Information Systems Analysis and Synthesis (ISAS'96), July 22–26, Orlando, USA (1996) 551–554
165. Fibak, J., Pawlak, Z., Słowiński, K., Słowiński, R.: Rough sets based decision algorithm for treatment of duodenal ulcer by HSV. Bull. Polish Acad. Sci., Biological Sci. **34/10-12** (1986) 227–246
166. Fibak, J., Słowiński, K., Słowiński, R.: The application of rough sets theory to the verification of treatment of duodenal ulcer by HSV. In: Proceedings of the Sixth International Workshop on Expert Systems and their Applications, Agence de l'Informatique, Paris (1986) 587–599
167. Funakoshi, K., Ho, T.B.: Information retrieval by rough tolerance relation. In: [RSFD'96] 31–35
168. Furuta, H., Hirokane, M., Tanaka, S., Mikumo, Y., Kobayashi, T.: A color determination method of bridge beam by using 'rough sets' and 'fuzzy theory'. In: [RSFD'96] 276–283
169. Garcia, A., Shasa, D.: Using rough sets to order questions leading to database queries. In: Nagib C. Callaos (ed.), Proceedings of the International Conference on Information Systems Analysis and Synthesis (ISAS'96), July 22–26, Orlando, USA (1996) 555–560
170. Golan, R.: The rough approach to knowledge marts with data warehouses. In: [RSFD'96] 360–363
171. Golan, R., Edwards, D.: Temporal rules discovery using datalogic/R+ with stock market data. In: [RSKD'93b] 74–81
172. Golan, R., Ziarko, W.: A methodology for stock market analysis utilizing rough set theory. In: Proceedings of IEEE/IAFE Conference on Computational Intelligence for Financial Engineering, New York City (1995) 32–40
173. Gonzalez, G., Grzymała-Busse, J.W.: On the comparison of the LEM1 and LEM2 algorithms. Department of Computer Science, University of Kansas, TR **91/15** (1991) 1–13; see also: [RS'92] 10–12
174. Greco, S., Matarazzo, B., Słowiński, R.: Rough approximation of a preference information by dominance relations. In: [RSFD'96] 125–130
175. Greco, S., Matarazzo, B., Słowiński, R.: L'approccio dei rough sets ai problemi di scelta. Atti del Ventesimo Convegno Annuale A. M. A. S. E. S., Urbino (1996) 357–375
176. Greco, S., Matarazzo, B., Słowiński, R.: A new rough set approach to evaluation of bankruptcy risk. In: C. Zopounidis (ed.), New Operational Tools in the Management of Financial Risks, Kluwer Academic Publishers, Dordrecht (to appear)
177. Greco, S., Matarazzo, B., Słowiński, R.: Rough set approach to multi-attribute choice and ranking problems. Institute of Computer Science, Warsaw University of Technology, ICS Research Report **38/95** (1995); see also: G. Fandel, T. Gal (eds.),

Multiple Criteria Decision Making: Proceedings of 12th International Conference in Hagen, Springer–Verlag, Berlin (1997) 318–329
178. Greco, S., Matarazzo, B., Słowiński, R., Tsoukias, A.: Exploitation of a rough approximation of the outranking relation. In: T. Stewart, R. van den Honert (eds.), Proceedings of 13th International Conference on Multiple Criteria Decision Making, Cape Town, January 6–10, Springer-Verlag, Berlin (1997) (to appear)
179. Green, J., Horne, N., Orłowska, E., Siemers, P.: A rough set model of information retrieval. Institute of Computer Science, Warsaw University of Technology, ICS Research Report **9/94** (1994); see also: Fundamenta Informaticae **28** (1996) 273–296
180. Grysa, K., Lenarcik, A., Piasta, Z., Ramocka, E., Sekalski, M.: Questionnaire analysis by decision algorithm generation. In: W.W. Koczkodaj, P.E. Laurer, and A.A. Toptsis (eds.), Proceedings of the Fourth International Conference on Computing and Information (ICCI'92), Toronto, Canada, May 28-30, IEEE Computer Society Press, Los Alamitos (1992) 216–219
181. Grzymała–Busse, D.M., Grzymała–Busse, J.W.: Comparison of machine learning and knowledge acquisition methods of rule induction based on rough sets. In: [RSKD'93b] 282–288
182. Grzymała–Busse, D.M., Grzymała–Busse, J.W.: Evaluation of machine learning approach to knowledge acquisition. In: Proceedings of the 14th International Avignon Conference, May 30–June 3, Paris (1994) 183–192
183. Grzymała-Busse, D.M., and Grzymała-Busse, J.W.: The usefulness of machine learning approach to knowledge acquisition. [CI] 268–279
184. Grzymała-Busse, J.W.: Algebraic properties of knowledge representation systems. In: Z.W. Ras, M. Zemankova (eds.), Proceedings of the ACM SIGART International Symposium on Methodologies for Intelligent Systems (ISMIS'86), Knoxville, Tennessee, October 22–24, ACM Special Interest Group on Artificial Intelligence (1986) 432–440
185. Grzymała-Busse, J.W.: Learning from examples based on rough multisets. In: Z.W. Ras, M. Zemankova (eds.), Proceedings of the Second International Symposium on Methodologies for Intelligent Systems (ISMIS'87), October 14–17, Charlotte, North Carolina, North Holland (1987) 325–332
186. Grzymała-Busse, J.W.: Knowledge acquisition under uncertainty – A rough set approach. Journal of Intelligent & Robotic Systems **1/1** (1988) 3–16
187. Grzymała-Busse, J.W.: On the learning of minimal discriminant rules from examples. Department of Computer Science, University of Kansas, TR **89/3** (1989) 1–18
188. Grzymała-Busse, J.W.: Learning minimal discriminant rules from examples with inconsistencies – A rough set approach. Department of Computer Science, University of Kansas, TR **89/4** (1989) 1–17
189. Grzymała-Busse, J.W.: An overview of the LERS1 learning system. In: Proceedings of the Second International Conference on Industrial and Engineering Applications of Artificial Intelligence and Expert Systems, June 6–9, Tullahoma, TN (1989) 838–844
190. Grzymała-Busse, J.W.: On the reduction of instance space in learning from examples. In: Z.W. Ras, M. Zemankova, and M.L. Emrich (eds.) Proceedings of the Fifth International Symposium on Methodologies for Intelligent Systems (ISMIS'90), Knoxville, TN, October 25-27, North Holland (1990) 388–395
191. Grzymała-Busse, J.W.: The LERS family of learning systems based on rough sets. In: Proceedings of the Third Midwest Artificial Intelligence and Cognitive Science

Society Conference, April 12–14, Carbondale, IL (1991) 103–107
192. Grzymała-Busse J.W.: Managing uncertainty in expert systems. Kluwer Academic Publishers, Dordrecht (1991)
193. Grzymała-Busse, J.W.: On the unknown attribute values in learning from examples. In: Z.W. Ras, M. Zemankova (eds.), Proceedings of the Sixth International Symposium on Methodologies for Intelligent Systems (ISMIS'91), Charlotte, NC, October 16–19, 1991, Lecture Notes in Artificial Intelligence **542**, Springer–Verlag (1991) 368–377
194. Grzymała–Busse, J.W.: LERS – A system for learning from examples based on rough sets. In: [IDS] 3–18
195. Grzymała–Busse, J.W.: ESEP: An expert system for environmental protection. In: [RSKD'93b] 466–474
196. Grzymała–Busse, J.W.: Selected algorithms of machine learning from examples. Fundamenta Informaticae **18** (1993) 193–207
197. Grzymała-Busse, J.W.: Managing uncertainty in machine learning from examples. In: M. Dąbrowski, M. Michalewicz, and Z.W. Ras (eds.), Proceedings of the Third International Workshop on Intelligent Information Systems, Wigry, Poland, June 6-10, 1994, Institute of Computer Science, Polish Academy of Sciences, Warsaw (1994) 70–84
198. Grzymała-Busse, J.W.: Rough sets. Advances in Imaging and Electrons Physics **94** (1995)
199. Grzymała-Busse, J.W.: On the reduction of knowledge representation systems. In: Proceedings of the Sixth International Workshop on Expert Systems & Their Applications, April 28–30, Avignon, France, (1995) 463–478
200. Grzymała-Busse, J.W.: LERS: A system of knowledge discovery based on rough sets. In: [RSFD'96] 443–444
201. Grzymała-Busse, J.W.: Classification of unseen examples under uncertainty. Fundamenta Informaticae **30** (1997) 255–267
202. Grzymała-Busse, J.W.: A new version of the rule induction system LERS. Fundamenta Informaticae **31** (1997) 27–39
203. Grzymała-Busse, J.W., Goodwin, L.K.: Predicting preterm birth risk using machine learning from data with missing values. In: [BUL1] 17–21
204. Grzymała-Busse, J.W., Goodwin, L.K.: A comparison of less specific versus more specific rules for preterm birth prediction. In: Proceedings of the First Online Workshop on Soft Computing WSC1 on the Internet, served by Nagoya University, Japan, August 19–30 (1996) 129–133
205. Grzymała-Busse, J.W., Gunn, J.D.: Global temperature analysis based on the rule induction system LERS. In: Proceedings of the Fourth International Workshop on Intelligent Information Systems, Augustów, Poland, June 5–9, 1995, Institute od Computer Science, Polish Academy of Sciences, Warsaw (1995) 148–158
206. Grzymała-Busse, J.W., Lakshmanan, A.: LEM2 with interval extension: An induction algorithm for numerical attributes. In: [RSFD'96] 67–73
207. Grzymała-Busse, J.W., Mithal, S.: A comparison of four tests for attribute dependency in the LEM and LERS systems for learning from examples. Department of Computer Science, University of Kansas, TR **89/5** (1989) 1–15; see also: Proceedings of the the Third International Conference on Industrial and Engineering Applications of Artificial Intelligence and Expert Systems, July 16–18, Charleston, SC (1990) 949–958
208. Grzymała-Busse, J.W., Mithal, S.: On the choice of the best test for attribute

dependency in programs for learning from examples. International Journal of Software Engineering and Knowledge Engineering **1** (1991) 413–438

209. Grzymała-Busse, J.W., Noordeen, M.: CRS – A program for clustering based on rough set theory. Department of Computer Science, University of Kansas, TR **88/3** (1988) 1–13
210. Grzymała-Busse, J.W., Old, L.J.: A machine learning experiment to determine part of speach from word-endings. In: Z.W. Ras, A. Skowron (eds.), Proceedings of the Tenth International Symposium on Methodologies for Intelligent Systems, Foundations of Intelligent Systems (ISMIS'97), October 15-18, Charlotte, NC, USA, Lecture Notes in Artificial Intelligence **1325**, Springer-Verlag, Berlin (1997) 497–506
211. Grzymała–Busse, J.W., Sedelow, S.Y., Sedelow, W.A.Jr.: Machine learning & knowledge acquisition, rough sets, and the English semantic code. In: [DM] 86–104; also in [RSDM] 91–107
212. Grzymała-Busse, J.W., Sedelow, W.A.Jr.: On rough sets and information system homomorphisms. Bull. Polish Acad. Sci. Tech. **36** (1988) 233–239
213. Grzymała-Busse, J.W., Sikora, D.J.: LERS1 – A system for learning from examples based on rough sets. Department of Computer Science, University of Kansas, TR **88/5** (1988) 1–16
214. Grzymała-Busse, J.W., Stefanowski, J., Ziarko, W.: Rough sets: Facts versus misconceptions. Institute of Computer Science, Warsaw University of Technology, ICS Research Report **61/95** (1995); see also: Informatica **20** (1996) 455–465
215. Grzymała-Busse, J.W., Than, S.: On the compression of data in learning from examples. In: [RS'92] 13–15
216. Grzymała-Busse, J.W., Than, S.: On the compression of instance space in inductive learning. In: Proceedings of the Fourth Midwest Artificial Intelligence and Cognitive Science Society Conference, May 3–4, Utica, IL (1992) 92–96
217. Grzymała-Busse, J.W., Than, S.: Reduction of instance space in machine learning from examples. In: Proceedings of the Fifth International Symposium on Artificial Intelligence, December 7–11, Cancun, Mexico (1992) 303–309
218. Grzymała-Busse, J.W., Than, S.: Data compression in machine learning applied to natural language. Behavior Research Methods, Instruments, & Computers **25** (1993) 318– 321
219. Grzymała-Busse, J.W., Than, S.: An algorithm to compress data in learning from examples. In: [RSSC'94] 294–301; see also: [SC] 294–297
220. Grzymała-Busse, J.W., Than, S.: An algorithm for data reduction in learning from examples. In: [IA] 161–167
221. Grzymała-Busse, J.W., Than, S.: Partition triples: A tool for reduction of data sets. Journal of Computer and System Sciences **53** (1996), 575–582
222. Grzymała-Busse, J.W., Wang, A.Y.: Modified algorithms LEM1 and LEM2 for rule induction from data with missing attribute values. In: [RSSC'97] 69–72
223. Grzymała-Busse, J.W., Wang, C.P.B.: Classification and rule induction based on rough sets. In: Proceedings of the Fifth IEEE International Conference on Fuzzy Systems (FUZZ-IEEE'96), September 8–11, New Orleans, Louisiana (1996) 744–747
224. Grzymała-Busse, J.W., Wang, C.P.B.: Classification methods in rule induction. In: Proceedings of the Fifth Workshop on Intelligent Information Systems, June 2–5, 1996, Dęblin, Poland, Institute of Computer Science, Polish Academy of Sciences (1996) 120–126

225. Grzymała-Busse, J.W., Werbrouck, P.: On the best search method in the LEM and LEM2 algorithms. Department of Computer Science, University of Kansas, TR **91/16** (1991) 1–26; see also: [II] 75–91
226. Grzymała-Busse, J.W., Woolerly, L.: Improving prediction of preterm birth using a new classification scheme and rule induction. In: Proceedings of the 18th Annual Symposium on Computer Applications in Medical Care (SCAMC), November 5-9, Washington D. C. (1994) 730–734
227. Grzymała-Busse, J.W., Yang, C.H.: LERS-LB – An implementation of lower boundaries for learning rules from examples. Department of Computer Science, University of Kansas, TR **89/10** (1989) 1–8
228. Grzymała-Busse, J.W., Yue, L.: The machine learning programs LEM2 and LERS-LB2 based on single coverings and blocks. Department of Computer Science, University of Kansas, TR **90/3**, (1990) 1–15
229. Gunn, J.D., Grzymała-Busse, J.W.: Global temperature stability by rule induction: An interdisciplinary bridge. Human Ecology **22** (1994) 59–81
230. Hadjimichael, M.: A model for generalization. In: [RSSC'97] 177–180
231. Hadjimichael, M., Wasilewska, A.: Rough sets-based study of voter preference in 1988 USA presidential election. In: [IDS] 137–152
232. Hadjimichael, M., Wong, S.K.M.: Fuzzy repersentations in rough set approximations. In: [RSKD'93b] 349–356
233. Haines, S.: The practical application of rough sets to semantics and simulation. In: [SC] 85–88
234. Haines, S., Longshaw, T., Magee, G.: The practical application of rough sets to sementics and simulation. In: [RSSC'94] 392–398
235. Haines, S., Longshaw, T., Magee, G.: Rough sets and event stream analysis. In: P.P. Wang (ed.): Proceedings of the International Workshop on Rough Sets and Soft Computing at Second Annual Joint Conference on Information Sciences (JCIS'95), Wrightsville Beach, North Carolina, 28 September – 1 October (1995) 42–45
236. Hamilton, H., Shan, N., Ziarko, W.: Machine learning of credible classifications. In: Proceedings of the Tenth Australian Conference on Artificial Intelligence, Perth, Australia (to appear)
237. Hashemi, R., Pearce, B., Arani, R., Hinson, W., Paule, M.: A fusion of rough sets, modified rough sets, and genetic algorithms for hybrid diagnostic systems. In: [RSDM] 149–175
238. Herment, M., Orłowska, E.: Handling information logics in a graphical proof editor. In: [CI] 297–322
239. Ho, T.B., Nguyen, T.D.: A rough sets based measure for attribute selection in decision tree induction. In: [RSFD'96] 339–343
240. Ho, T.B., Funakoshi, K.: Information retrieval using rough sets (submitted to Journal of Japanese Society for Artificial Intelligence)
241. Hou, Y., Ziarko, W.: A rough sets approach to handwriting classification. In: [RSFD'96] 372–382
242. Hu, X., Cercone, N.: Discovery of decision rules from databases: A rough set approach. In: Proceedings of the Third International Conference on Information and Knowledge Management Systems (CIKM'94), (1994) 392–400
243. Hu, X., Cercone, N.: Mining knowledge rules from databases: A rough set approach. In: Proceedings of the 12th International Conference on Data Engineering, New Orleans (1995) 96–105
244. Hu, X., Cercone, N.: Learning in relational databases: A rough set approach. In: [CI] 323–338

245. Hu, X., Cercone, N.: Rough sets similarity–based learning from databases. In: U.M. Fayyad, R. Uthurusamy (eds.), Proceedings of the First International Conference on Knowledge Discovery and Data Mining (KDD'95), August 20–21, 1995, Montreal, AAAI Press, Menlo Park CA (1995) 162–167
246. Hu, X., Cercone, N.: Learning maximal generalized decision rules via discretization, generalization, and rough set feature selection. In: Proceedings of the Ninth IEEE International Conference on Tools with Artificial Intelligence, Newport Beach, Ca. (1997) 548–557
247. Hu, X., Cercone, N., Han, J.: An attribute–oriented rough set approach for knowledge discovery in databases. In: [RSKD'93b] 90–99
248. Hu, X., Cercone, N., Shan, N.: A rough set approach to compute all the maximal generalized rules from databases, Journal of Computing and Information (special issue from Sixth International Conference on Computing and Information – ICCI'94) **1/1** (1995) 1078–1089
249. Hu, X., Cercone, N., Xie, J.: Learning data trend regularities from databases in a dynamic environment. In: Knowledge Discovery in Databases (KDD'94), Seattle (1994) 323–334
250. Hu, X., Cercone, N., Ziarko, W.: Generation of multiple knowledge from databases based on rough set theory. In: [RSDM] 109–121
251. Hu, X., Cercone, N., Ziarko, W.: GRS: A generalized rough sets model for data mining applications. In: [RSSC'97] 181–186
252. Hu, X., Shan, N., Cercone, N., Ziarko, W.: DBROUGH: A rough set based knowledge discovery system. In: Z.W. Ras, M. Zemankova (eds.), Proceedings of the Eighth International Symposium on Methodologies for Intelligent Systems (ISMIS'94), Charlotte, NC, October 16–19, 1994, Lecture Notes in Artificial Intelligence **869**, Springer-Verlag (1994) 386–395
253. Inuiguchi, M., Sakawa, M.: Possibility and necessity of roughly defined ill–known sets. In: [RSFD'96] 248–254
254. Iwiński, T.: Algebraic approach to rough sets. Bull. Polish Acad. Sci. Math. **35** (1987) 673–683
255. Iwiński, T.: Rough order and rough concepts. Bull. Polish Acad. Sci. Math. (1988) 187–192
256. Iwiński, T.: Ordinal information systems. Bull. Polish Acad. Sci. Math. **36** (1988) 446–476
257. Jackson, A.G., Leclair, S.R., Ohmer, M.C., Ziarko, W., Al-Kamhawi, H.: Rough sets applied to material data. Acta Metallurgica et Materialia (1996) 44–75
258. Jackson, A.G., Ohmer, M., Al–Kamhawi, H.: Rough sets analysis of chalcopyrite semiconductor band gap data. In: [RSSC'94] 408–417
259. Järvinen, J.: A Representation of dependence spaces and some basic algorithms. Fundamenta Informaticae **29/4** (1997) 369–382
260. Järvinen, J.: Representations of information systems and dependence spaces, and some basic algorithms. Licentiate's Thesis, University of Turku, Finland (1997)
261. Jelonek, J., Krawiec, K., Słowiński, R.: Rough set reduction of attributes and their domains for neural networks. In: [CI] 339–347
262. Jelonek, J., Krawiec, K., Słowiński, R., Stefanowski, J., Szymas, J.: Neural networks and rough sets – Comparison and combination for classification of histological pictures. In: [RSKD'93b] 426–433
263. Jelonek, J., Krawiec, K., Słowinski, R., Stefanowski, J., Szymas, J.: Rough sets as an intelligent front–end for the neural network. In: Proceedings of the First

National Conference on Neural Networks and their Applications **2**, Częstochowa, Poland (1994) 116–122
264. Jelonek, J., Krawiec, K., Słowiński, R., Szymas, J.: Rough set reduction of features for picture–based reasoning. In: [RSSC'94] 418–425; see also: [SC] 89–92
265. Jelovsek, F.R., Hashemi, R.R.: Rough sets application to reduce combinatorial explosion of expert's rules. In: [DM] 63–69
266. Kandulski, M., Marciniec, J., Tukałło, K.: Infection of surgical wound – Rough sets approach. In: [RS'92] 16–17
267. Katzberg, J., Katzberg, P., Ziarko, W.: Variable precision rough sets approach to predicting factors affecting delay likelihoods. In: Proceedings of the Eighth International Conference on Industrial and Engineering Applications of Artificial Intelligence and Expert Systems, Melbourne, Australia (1995)
268. Katzberg, J., Ziarko, W.: Variable precision rough sets with asymmetric bounds. In: [RSKD'93b] 167–177
269. Katzberg, J., Ziarko, W.: Variable precision extension of rough sets. In: [FI] 155–168
270. Keen, D., Rajasekar, A.: Rough sets and data dependencies. In: V. Alagar, S. Bergler, and F.Q. Dong (eds.), Incompleteness and Uncertainty in Information Systems, Proceedings of SOFTEKS Workshop on Incompleteness and Uncertainty in Information Systems, Concordia University, Montreal, Canada 1993, Workshops in Computing, Springer–Verlag & British Computer Society, London, Berlin (1994) 87–102
271. Keiser, K., Szladow, A., Ziarko, W.: Rough sets theory applied to a large multispecies toxicity database. In: Proceedings of the Fifth International Workshop on QSAR in Environmental Toxicology, Duluth, Minnesota (1992)
272. Kent, R.E.: Rough concept analysis. In: [RSKD'93b] 248–255
273. Kent, R.E.: Rough concept analysis: A synthesis of rough sets and formal concept analysis. In: [FI] 169–181
274. Kent, R.E.: Soft concept analysis. In: [FSRS]
275. Khasnabis, S., Arciszewski, T., Hoda, S., Ziarko, W.: Urban rail corridor control through machine learning: An intelligent vehicle–highway system approach. Transportation Research Record **1453** (1994) 91–97
276. Kłopotek, S., Wierzchoń, S.: Qualitative versus quantitative interpretation of the mathematical theory of evidence. In: Z.W. Ras, A. Skowron (eds.), Proceedings of the Tenth International Symposium on Methodologies for Intelligent Systems, Foundations of Intelligent Systems (ISMIS'97), October 15–18, Charlotte, NC, USA, Lecture Notes in Artificial Intelligence **1325**, Springer–Verlag, Berlin (1997) 391–400
277. Kobayashi, S., Yokomori, T.: An extended rough set theory toward approximate learning of formal languages. In: [SC] 14–17
278. Kobayashi, S., Yokomori, T.: Approximately learning regular languages with respect to reversible languages: A rough set based analysis. In: [RSSC'97] 91–94
279. Kohavi, R.: A third dimension to rough sets. In: [SC] 316–319
280. Kohavi, R., Frasca, B.: Useful feature subsets and rough set reducts. In: [SC] 320–323
281. Komorowski, J., Polkowski, L., Skowron, A.: Towards a rough mereology–based logic for approximate solution synthesis Part 1. Studia Logica **58/1** (1997) 143–184
282. Komorowski, J., Polkowski, L., Skowron, A.: Rough sets for data mining and knowledge discovery (abstract of tutorial). In: J. Komorowski, J. Zytkow (eds.), First

European Symposium on Principles of Data Mining and Knowledge Discovery (PKDD'97), June 25–27, Trondheim, Norway, Lecture Notes in Artificial Intelligence **1263**, Springer–Verlag, Berlin (1997) 393–393
283. Konikowska, B.: A formal language for reasoning about indiscernibility. Bull. Polish Acad. Sci. Math. **35** (1997) 239–249
284. Konikowska, B.: A logic for reasoning about similarity. In: [II] 462–491
285. Konikowska, B.: A logic for reasoning about relative similarity. Studia Logica **58/1** (1997) 185–226
286. Kononenko, I.: On facts versus misconception about rough sets. Informatica **20** (1996) 465–468
287. Konrad, E., Orłowska, E., Pawlak, Z.: Knowledge representation systems. Polish Academy of Sciences, PAS Report **433** (1981)
288. Konrad, E., Orłowska, E., Pawlak, Z.: On approximate concept learning. In: Proceedings of the European Conference on AI, Orsay, France (1982)
289. Kos, J., Barton, R., Blass, K., Chadwick, W., Cooke, B., Hara, E., Katzberg, J., Mason, R., Ziarko, W., Menzies, R., Pawlak, Z., Skowron A.: A computer controlled, optimized hybrid engine. In: Proceedings of the 29th Intersociety Energy Conversion Conference, Monterey (1994) 955–960
290. Kostek, B.: Intelligent control system implementation to the pipe organ instrument. In: [RSKD'93b] 450–457
291. Kostek, B.: Application of learning algorithms to musical sound analysis. In: 97th Convention of the Audio Engineering Society, November 10–13, San Francisco, Calofornia, USA, preprint **3873** (1994)
292. Kostek, B.: Rough classification as a tool for acoustical analysis. In: [SC] 85–88
293. Kostek, B.: Computer based recognition of musical phrases using the rough set approach. In: P.P. Wang (ed.): Proceedings of the International Workshop on Rough Sets and Soft Computing at Second Annual Joint Conference on Information Sciences (JCIS'95), Wrightsville Beach, North Carolina, 28 September – 1 October (1995) 401–404
294. Kostek, B.: Statistical versus artificial intelligence based processing of subjective test results. In: 98th Convention of the Audio Engineering Society, Paris, February 25–28, Preprint **4018** (1995)
295. Kostek, B.: Rough set and fuzzy set methods applied to acoustical analyses. In: [IA] 147–160
296. Kostek, B.: Automatic reasoning about acoustic data - Problems with preprocessing, classification and decision uncertainty. In: Proceedings of the Conference on Intelligent Data Analysis (IDA'95), August 17–19, Baden–Baden, Germany, The International Institute for Advanced Studies in Systems Research and Cybernetics **1** (1995) 99–103
297. Kostek, B.: Intelligent analysis of musical databases. In: [RSFD'96] 300–306
298. Kostek, B.: Computer based recognition of musical phrases using the rough set approach. Journal of Information Sciences (to appear)
299. Kostek, B.: Soft set approach to the subjective assessment of sound quality. In: Proceedings of the Symposium on Computer Science and Engineering Cybernetics, August 18–23, 1997, Baden–Baden, Germany, The International Institute for Advanced Studies in Systems Research and Cybernetics (to appear)
300. Kostek, B.: Sound quality assessment based on the rough set classifier. In: Proceedings of the Fifth European Congress on Intelligent Techniques and Soft Computing (EUFIT'97), September 8–12, Aachen, Germany, Verlag Mainz (1997) 193–195

301. Kostek, B.: Assesment of concert hall acoustics using rough set and fuzzy approach, In: [FSRS]
302. Kostek, B., Czyżewski, A.: Automatic classification of musical timbres based on learning algorithms applicable to Cochlear implants. In: Proceedings of IASTED International Conference - Artificial Intelligence, Expert Systems and Neural Networks, August 19–21, Honolulu, Hawaii, USA (1996) 98–101
303. Kostek, B., Szczerba, M.: Rough set–based analysis of musical databases. In: Proceedings of the Fourth European Congress on Intelligent Techniques and Soft Computing, (EUFIT'96), September 2–5, Aachen, Germany, Verlag Mainz (1996) **1** 144–148
304. Kostek, B., Szczerba, M.: Parametric representation of musical phrases. In: 101st Convention of the Audio Engineering Society, November 8–11, Los Angeles, California, USA, preprint **4337** (1996)
305. Kostek, B., Szczerba, M., Czyżewski A.: Rough set based analysis of computer musical storage. In: Proceedings of the International Conference on Computing and Intelligent Multimedia Applications (ICCIMA'97), February 10–13, Brisbane, Australia (1997)
306. Kowalczyk, W.: TRANCE: A tool for rough data analysis, classification and clustering. In: [RSFD'96] 269–275
307. Kowalczyk, W.: Analyzing temporal patterns with rough sets. In: Proceedings of the Fourth European Congress on Intelligent Techniques and Soft Computing (EUFIT'96), September 2–5, Aachen, Germany, Verlag Mainz (1996) **1** 139–143
308. Kowalczyk, W., Piasta, Z.: Rough sets–inspired approach to knowledge discovery in business databases. In: The Second Pacific–Asian Conference on Knowledge Discovery and Data Mining, (PAKDD'98), Melbourne, Australia, April 15–17 (1998) (accepted)
309. Kowalczyk, W., Slisser, F.: Analyzing customer retention with rough data models. In: J. Komorowski, J. Żytkow (eds.), The First European Symposium on Principles of Data Mining and Knowledge Discovery (PKDD'97), June 25–27, Trondheim, Norway, Lecture Notes in Artificial Intelligence **1263**, Springer-Verlag, Berlin (1997) 4–13
310. Krawiec, K., Słowiński, R., Vanderpooten, D.: Construction of rough classifiers based on application of a similarity relation. In: [RSFD'96] 23–30
311. Krętowski, M., Polkowski, L., Skowron, A., Stepaniuk, J.: Data reduction based on rough set theory. In: Y. Kodratoff, G. Nakhaeizadeh, and Ch. Taylor (eds.), Proceedings of the Workshop on Statistics, Machine Learning and Knowledge Discovery in Data Bases, April 25–27, Crete, Greece (1995) 210–215; see also: Institute of Computer Science, Warsaw University of Technology, ICS Research Report **13/95** (1995)
312. Krętowski, M., Stepaniuk, J.: Selection of objects and attributes: A tolerance rough set approach. Institute of Computer Science, Warsaw University of Technology, ICS Research Report **54/95** (1995); see also: Proceedings of the Poster Session of the Ninth International Symposium on Methodologies for Intelligent Systems (ISMIS'96), Zakopane, Poland, June 9–13, Oak Ridge Laboratory (1996) 169–180
313. Królikowski, R., Czyżewski, A.: Application of intelligent decision systems to the perceptual noise reduction of audio signals. In: Proceedings of the Fifth European Congress on Intelligent Techniques and Soft Computing (EUFIT'97), September 8–12, Aachen, Germany, Verlag Mainz **1** 188–192
314. Krynicki, M.: A note on rough concepts logic. Fundamenta Informaticae **13/2** (1990) 227–235

315. Krynicki, M., Szczerba L.: On the logic with rough quantifier. In: [II] 601–613
316. Krysiński, J.: Rough set approach to the analysis of structure–activity relationship of quaternary imidazolium compounds. Arzneimittel Forschung / Drug Research **40/11** (1990) 795–799
317. Krysiński, J.: Grob Mengen Theorie in der Analyse der Struktur Wirkungs Beziehungen von quartaren Pyridiniumverbindungen. Pharmazie **46/12** (1992) 878–881
318. Krysiński, J.: Rough set approach to analysis of relationship between structure and activity of quaternary pyradinium compounds. In: [RS'92] 18–19
319. Krysiński, J.: Analysis of structure–activity relationships of quaternary ammonium compounds. In: [IDS] 119–136
320. Krysiński, J.: Application of the rough sets theory to the analysis of structure–activity relationships of antimicrobial pyridinium compounds. Die Pharmazie **50** (1995) 593–597
321. Krysiński, J.: Rough sets in the analysis of the structure–activity relationships of antifungal imidazolium compounds. Journal of Pharmaceutical Sciences **84/2** (1995) 243–247
322. Kryszkiewicz, M.: Rough set approach to incomplete information systems. In: P.P. Wang (ed.): Proceedings of the International Workshop on Rough Sets and Soft Computing at Second Annual Joint Conference on Information Sciences (JCIS'95), Wrightsville Beach, North Carolina, 28 September – 1 October (1995) 194–197
323. Kryszkiewicz, M.: Maintenance of reducts in the variable precision rough set model. In: [RSDM] 355–372
324. Kryszkiewicz, M.: Rules in incomplete information systems. In: [RSSC'97] 73–76
325. Kryszkiewicz, M.: Generation of rules from incomplete information systems. In: J. Komorowski, J. Żytkow (eds.), The First European Symposium on Principles of Data Mining and Knowledge Discovery (PKDD'97), June 25–27, Trondheim, Norway, Lecture Notes in Artificial Intelligence **1263**, Springer–Verlag, Berlin (1997) 156–166
326. Kryszkiewicz, M.: Generalized rules in incomplete information systems. In: Z.W. Ras, A. Skowron (eds.), Proceedings of the Tenth International Symposium on Methodologies for Intelligent Systems, Foundations of Intelligent Systems (ISMIS'97), October 15–18, Charlotte, NC, USA, Lecture Notes in Artificial Intelligence **1325**, Springer–Verlag, Berlin (1997) 421–430
327. Kryszkiewicz, M., Ras, Z.W.: Query rough-answering systems for CKBS. In: [RSFD'96] 162–167
328. Kryszkiewicz, M., Rybiński, H.: Finding reducts in composed information systems. In: [RSKD'93b] 261–273
329. Kryszkiewicz, M., Rybiński, H.: Computation of reducts of composed information systems. In: [FI] 183–195
330. Kryszkiewicz, M., Rybiński, H.: Attribute reduction versus property reduction. In: Proceedings of the Fourth European Congress on Intelligent Techniques and Soft Computing (EUFIT'96), September 2–5, Aachen, Germany, Verlag Mainz (1996) **1** 204–208
331. Kryszkiewicz, M., Rybiński, H.: Reducing information systems with uncertain real value attributes. In: Proceedings of the Sixth International Conference, Information Processing and Management of Uncertainty in Knowledge–Based Systems (IPMU'96), July 1–5, Granada, Spain (1996) **3** 1165–1168
332. Kryszkiewicz, M., Rybiński, H.: Mining in information systems with multivalued attributes. In: P. Borne, G. Dauphin–Tanguy, C. Sueur, and S. El Khattabi (eds.), Proceedings of IMACS Multiconference: Computational Engineering in Systems

Applications (CESA '96) July 9–12, Lille, France, Gerf EC Lille – Cite Scientifique (1996) **3/4** 958-963; see also: Nagib C. Callaos (ed.), Proceedings of the International Conference on Information Systems Analysis and Synthesis (ISAS'96), July 22–26, Orlando, USA (1996) 561–566

333. Kryszkiewicz, M., Rybiński, H.: Reducing information systems with uncertain attributes. In: Z.W. Ras, M. Michalewicz (eds.), Proceedings of the Ninth International Symposium on Methodologies for Intelligent Systems. Zakopane, Poland, June 9–13, Lecture Notes in Artificial Intelligence (ISMIS'96) **1079**, Springer–Verlag, Berlin (1996) 285–294
334. Krusińska, E., Babic, A., Słowiński, R., Stefanowski J.: Comparison of the rough sets approach and probabilistic data analysis techniques on a common set of medical data. In: [IDS] 251–265
335. Krusińska, E., Słowiński, R., Stefanowski, J.: Discriminant versus rough set approach to vague data analysis. Applied Stochastic Models and Data Analysis **8** (1992) 43–56
336. Krusińska, E., Stefanowski, J., Babic, A., Wigertz, O.: Rough sets and correspondence analysis as tools for knowledge discovery in studying data relationships. In: [RSKD'93a] 15–20
337. Krusińska, E., Stefanowski, J., Stromberg, J.E.: Comparability and usefulness of newer and classical data analysis techniques. Application in medical domain classification. In: E. Didey et al. (eds.), New Approaches in Classification and Data Analysis, Springer–Verlag, Studies in Classification, Data Analysis and Knowledge Organization (1993) 644–652
338. Kuroki, N.: Rough subgroup of a group. In: P.P. Wang (ed.): Proceedings of the International Workshop on Rough Sets and Soft Computing at Second Annual Joint Conference on Information Sciences (JCIS'95), Wrightsville Beach, North Carolina, 28 September – 1 October (1995) 46–47
339. Kuroki, N., Mordeson J.N., Chung, S.-Ch.: The upper approximation with respect to the least group congruence on B*–pure semigroups. In: [RSFD'96] 185–189
340. Lambert–Torres, G., Rossi, R., Alves da Silva, A.P., Jardini, J.A., Quintana, V.H.: Power system security analysis based on rough classification. In: [FSRS]
341. Larsen, V.: Comparative analysis of data mining tools. Master Thesis, supervisor J. Komorowski. Knowledge Systems Group, The Norwegian University of Science and Technology, Trondheim, Norway (1996)
342. Lasocki, R., Łuba, T.: On the optimal decision table decomposition. In: P.P. Wang (ed.): Proceedings of the International Workshop on Rough Sets and Soft Computing at Second Annual Joint Conference on Information Sciences (JCIS'95), Wrightsville Beach, North Carolina, 28 September – 1 October (1995) 38–41
343. Lau, S.S.Y.: Image segmentation based on the indiscernibility relation. In: [RSKD-'93b] 395–403
344. Lenarcik, A., Piasta, Z.: Discretization of condition attributes space. In: [IDS] 373–389
345. Lenarcik, A., Piasta, Z.: Probabilistic approach to decision algorithm generation in the case of continuous condition attributes. In: [FCDS'93] 213–223; see also: [RS'92] 20–22
346. Lenarcik, A., Piasta, Z.: Rough classifiers. In: [RSKD'93b] 298–316
347. Lenarcik, A., Piasta, Z.: Deterministic rough classifiers. In: [RSSC'94] 434–441
348. Lenarcik, A., Piasta, Z.: Minimizing the number of rules in deterministic rough classifiers. In: [SC] 32–35

349. Lenarcik, A., Piasta, Z.: An invariant method of rough classifier construction. In: Proceedings of the Poster Session of the Ninth International Symposium on Methodologies for Intelligent Systems, (ISMIS'96), Zakopane, Poland, June 9–13, Oak Ridge Laboratory (1996) 146–156
350. Lenarcik, A., Piasta, Z.: Probalilistic rough classifiers with mixture of discrete and continuous attributes. In: [RSDM] 373–383
351. Lenarcik, A., Piasta, Z., Masternak, M.: Probabilistic approach to attributes coding in the rough sets theory. In: W.W. Koczkodaj, P.E. Laurer, and A.A. Toptsis (eds.), Proceedings of the Fourth International Conference on Computing and Information (ICCI'92), Toronto, Canada, May 28–30, IEEE Computer Society Press, Los Alamitos (1992) 220–223
352. Liau Ch.-J.: On rough terminological logics. In: [RSFD'96] 47–54
353. Lin, T.Y.: Topological and fuzzy rough sets. In: [IDS] 287–304
354. Lin, T.Y.: Rough patterns in data – Rough sets and intrusion detection systems. In: [FCDS'93] 225–240
355. Lin, T.Y.: Fuzzy reasoning and rough sets. In: [RSKD'93b] 343–348
356. Lin, T.Y.: Rough–fuzzy controllers for complex systems. In: P.P. Wang (ed.): Proceedings of the International Workshop on Rough Sets and Soft Computing at Second Annual Joint Conference on Information Sciences (JCIS'95), Wrightsville Beach, North Carolina, 28 September – 1 October (1995) 18–21
357. Lin, T.Y.: Neighborhood systems – A qualitative theory for fuzzy and rough sets. In: [RSSC'95] 255–258 see also: P.P. Wang (ed.), Advances in Machine Intelligence and Soft Computing **4** (1996) 132–155
358. Lin, T.Y.: Rules in numerical databases. In: [DM] 38–39
359. Lin, T.Y.: Fuzzy controllers: An integrated approach based on fuzzy logic, rough sets, and evolutionary computing. In: [DM] 48–56; see also: [RSDM] 123–138
360. Lin, T.Y.: Rough set theory in very large databases. In: P. Borne, G. Dauphin–Tanguy. C. Sueur, and S. El Khattabi (eds.), Proceedings of IMACS Multiconference: Computational Engineering in Systems Applications (CESA'96) July 9–12, Lille, France, Gerf EC Lille – Cite Scientifique (1996) **3/4** 936–941
361. Lin, T.Y.: An overview of rough set theory from the point of view of relational databases. In: [BUL1] 23–30
362. Lin, T.Y.: Introduction to the special issue on rough sets. In: [AR] 287–290
363. Lin, T.Y.: A rough logic formalism for fuzzy controllers: A hard and soft computing view. In: [AR] 395–414
364. Lin, T.Y.: Neighborhood systems – Information granulation. In: [RSSC'97] 161–164
365. Lin, T.Y.: Granular computing: From rough sets and neighborhood systems to information granulation. In: Proceedings of the Fifth European Congress on Intelligent Techniques and Soft Computing (EUFIT'97), September 9–11, Aachen, Germany, Verlag Mainz (1997) 1602–1606
366. Lin, T.Y., Chen, R.: Finding reducts in very large databases. In: [RSSC'97] 350–352
367. Lin, T.Y., Hsiao, D.: Rough sets in AI as clustering in databases. In: [RS'92] 23–25
368. Lin, T.Y., Liau, J. C.: Probabilistics multivalued random variables – Belief functions and granular computing. In: Proceedings of the Fifth European Congress on Intelligent Techniques and Soft Computing, (EUFiT'97), September 8–12, Aachen, Germany, Verlag Mainz (1997) **1** 221–225
369. Lin, T.Y., Liau, J.C. : Belief functions based on probabilistic multivalued random variables. In: [RSSC'97] 269–272
370. Lin, T.Y., Liu, Q.: Rough approximate operators: Axiomatic rough set theory. In: [RSKD'93b] 256–260

371. Lin, T.Y., Liu, Q.: First-order rough logic I: Approximate reasoning via rough sets. Fundamenta Informaticae **27** (1996) 137–153
372. Lin, T.Y., Liu, Q., Zuo, X.: Models for first order rough logic applications to data mining. In: Y.-Y. Chen, K. Hirota, and J.-Y. Yen (eds.), Proceedings of 1996 ASIAN FUZZY SYSTEMS SYMPOSIUM – Soft Computing in Intelligent Systems and Information Processing, December 11–14, Kenting, Taiwan, ROC. (1996) 1–6
373. Lin, T.Y., Wildberger, M.: Algebra and geometry of rough logic controllers. In: [RSFD'96] 111–117
374. Lin, T.Y., Yao, Y.Y.: Mining soft rules using rough sets and neighborhoods. In: P. Borne, G. Dauphin–Tanguy. C. Sueur, and S. El Khattabi (eds.), Proceedings of IMACS Multiconference: Computational Engineering in Systems Applications (CESA'96) July 9–12, Lille, France, Gerf EC Lille - Cite Scientifique (1996) **3/4** 1095–1100
375. Lin, T.Y., Yao, Y.Y.: Neighborhoods systems: Measure, probability and belief functions. In: [RSFD'96] 202–208
376. Lin, T.Y., Yao, Y.Y.: Graded rough sets approximations based on nested neighborhood systems. In: Proceedings of the Fifth European Congress on Intelligent Techniques and Soft Computing (EUFIT'97), September 8–12, Aachen, Germany, Verlag Mainz (1997) **1** 196–200
377. Lingras, P.: Rough set theoretic operators and non–monotonic preference structures. In: [SC] 51–54
378. Lingras, P.: Rough neural networks. In: Proceedings of the Sixth International Conference, Information Processing and Management of Uncertainty in Knowledge–Based Systems (IPMU'96), July 1–5, Granada, Spain (1996) **2** 1445–1450
379. Lingras, P.: Learning using rough Kohonen neural networks classifiers. In: P. Borne, G. Dauphin–Tanguy, C. Sueur, and S. El Khattabi (eds.), Proceedings of IMACS Multiconference: Computational Engineering in Systems Applications (CESA'96) July 9–12, Lille, France, Gerf EC Lille - Cite Scientifique (1996) **3/4** 753–757
380. Lingras, P.: Comparison of neofuzzy and rough neural networks. In: [RSSC'97] 259–262
381. Lingras, P., Yao, Y.Y.: Belief functions in rough set models. In: P.P. Wang (ed.), Proceedings of the Second Annual Joint Conference on Information Sciences (JCIS-'95), Wrightsville Beach, North Carolina, 28 September – 1 October (1995) 190–193
382. Lissowska–Wójtowicz, A.: Some philosophical aspects of indiscernibility. In: [II] 381–398
383. Liu, Q.: Accuracy operator rough logic and its resolution reasoning. In: [RSFD'96] 55–59
384. Luxenburger, M.: Dependencies between many–valued attributes. In: [II] 316–343
385. Łuba, T., Rybnik, J.: Algorithmic approach to discernibility function with respect to attributes and objects reduction. In: [RS'92] 26–28; see also: [FCDS'93] 241–258
386. Łuba, T., Rybnik, J.: Rough sets and some aspects of logical synthesis. In: [IDS] 181–202
387. Maitan, J., Mrózek, A., Winiarczyk, R., Płonka, L.: Overview of the emerging control and communication algorithms suitable for embedding into smart sensors. In: Proceedings of the Second IEEE/NIST Workshop on Smart Sensor and Transducer Communication Standards, Cleveland, OH, September (1994)
388. Maitan, J., Ras, Z.W., Zemankova, M.: Query handling and learning in a distributed intelligent system. In: Z.W. Ras (ed.), Proceedings of the Fourth International Symposium on Methodologies for Intelligent Systems (ISMIS'89), Charlotte, NC, October 12–14, North Holland (1989) 118–127

389. Marek, W., Pawlak, Z.: Mathematical foundations of information storage and retrieval. Polish Academy of Sciences, CC PAS Reports **135–137** Warszawa (1973)
390. Marek, W., Pawlak, Z.: Information storage and retrieval system – Mathematical foundations. Theoretical Computer Science **1** (1976) 331–354
391. Marek, W., Pawlak, Z.: Rough sets and information systems. Fundamenta Informaticae **7/1** (1984) 105–115
392. Marcus, S.: Tolerance rough sets, Cech topologies, learning processes. Bull. Acad. Polish Sci. Tech. **42/3** (1994) 471–487
393. Maritz, P.: Pawlak and topological rough sets in terms of multifunctions. Glasnik Matematicki **31/51** (1996) 159–178
394. Marszał–Paszek, B.: Linking beta-approximation with evidence theory. In: Proceedings of the Sixth International Conference, Information Processing and Management of Uncertainty in Knowledge–Based Systems (IPMU'96), July 1–5, Granada, Spain (1996) **2** 1153–1158
395. Marszał–Paszek, B., Paszek, P., Wakulicz–Deja, A.: Applying rough sets to diagnose in children's neurology. Institute of Computer Science, Warsaw University of Technology, ICS Research Report **22/95** (1995)
396. Mazlack, L.: Understandable database mining and approximate reasoning. In: [RSSC'97] 363–366
397. Michael, J.B., Lin, T.Y.: Neighborhoods, rough sets, and query relaxation in collaborative computing. In: [DM] 173–176; [RSDM] 229–238
398. Mienko, R., Słowiński, R., Stefanowski, J.: Rough classifier based on valued closeness relation: RoughClass version 2.0. Institute of Computing Sciences, Poznań University of Technology, Report **RA 002/95** (1995)
399. Mienko, R., Słowiński, R., Stefanowski, J., Susmaga, R.: Rough Family – Software implementation of rough set based data analysis and rule discovery techniques. In: [RSFD'96] 437–440
400. Mienko, R., Stefanowski, J., Toumi, K., Vanderpooten, D.: Discovery–oriented induction of decision rules. Cahier du Lamsade **141**, Paris, Universite de Paris Dauphine (1996)
401. Millan, M., Machuca, F.: Using the rough set theory to exploit the data mining potential in relational databases systems. In: [RSSC'97] 344–347
402. Missaoui, R., Godin, R., Boujenoui, A.: Extracting exact and approximate rules from databases. In: V. Alagar, S. Bergler, and F.Q. Dong (eds.), Incompleteness and Uncertainty in Information Systems, Proceedings of SOFTEKS Workshop on Incompleteness and Uncertainty in Information Systems, Concordia University, Montreal, Canada 1993, Workshops in Computing, Springer–Verlag & British Computer Society, London, Berlin (1994) 209–222
403. Mitra, S., Banerjee, M.: Knowledge–based neural net with rough sets. In: T. Yamakawa et al. (eds.), Methodologies for the Conception, Design, and Application of Intelligent Systems, Proceedings of the Fourth International Conference on Soft Computing (IIZUKA'96), Iizuka, Japan 1996, World Scientific (1996) 213–216
404. Miyamoto, S.: Fuzzy multisets and application to rough approximation of fuzzy sets. In: [RSFD'96] 255–260
405. Modrzejewski, M.: Application of rough sets theory in testing combinational circuits. In: [RS'92] 29–31
406. Modrzejewski, M.: Feature selection using rough sets theory. In: Brazdil P.B., (ed.), Proceedings of the European Conference on Machine Learning (1993) 213–226
407. Mollestad, T.: Learning propositional default rules using rough set approach. In: A. Aamodt, J. Komorowski (eds.), Proceedings of the Fifth Scandinavian Conference

on Artificial Intelligence (SCAI'95), May 29–31, 1995, Trondheim, Norway, IOS Press, Amsterdam (1995) 208-219
408. Mollestad, T.: A rough set approach to data mining: Extracting a logic of default rules from data. Ph.D. Dissertation, supervisor J. Komorowski, Norwegian University of Science and Technology, Trondheim (1997)
409. Mollestad, T., Komorowski, J.: A rough set framework for propositional default rules data mining. In: [FSRS]
410. Mollestad, T., Skowron, A.: A rough set framework for data mining of propositional default rules. In: Z.W. Ras, M. Michalewicz (eds.), Proceedings of the Ninth International Symposium on Methodologies for Intelligent Systems (ISMIS'96), Zakopane, Poland, June 9–13, Lecture Notes in Artificial Intelligence **1079**, Springer–Verlag, Berlin (1996) 448–457
411. Moradi, H., Grzymała–Busse, J.W., Roberts, J.: Entropy of English text: Experiments with humans and machine learning system based on rough sets. In: P.P. Wang (ed.): Proceedings of the International Workshop on Rough Sets and Soft Computing at Second Annual Joint Conference on Information Sciences (JCIS'95), Wrightsville Beach, North Carolina, 28 September – 1 October (1995) 87–88
412. Moshkov, M.Ju.: Decision trees with quasilinear checks (in Russian). Trudy IM SO RAN **27** (1994) 108–141
413. Moshkov, M.Ju.: Optimization problems for decision trees. Fundamenta Informaticae **21** (1994) 391–401
414. Moshkov, M.Ju.: Decision trees. Theory and applications (in Russian). Nizhni Novgorod University Publishers, Nizhni Novgorod (1994)
415. Moshkov, M.Ju.: About the depth of decision trees computing Boolean functions. Fundamenta Informaticae **22** (1995) 203–215
416. Moshkov, M.Ju.: Two approaches to investigation of deterministic and non–deterministic decision tree complexity. In: M. De Glas, Z. Pawlak (eds.), Proceedings of the Second World Conference on Fundamentals of Artificial Intelligence (WOCFAI'91), Paris, July 3–7, Angkor, Paris (1995) 275–280
417. Moshkov, M.Ju.: Complexity of decision trees for regular language word recognition. In: Proceedings of the Second International Conference Developments in Language Theory, Magdeburg, Germany (1995)
418. Moshkov, M.Ju.: Complexity of deterministic and nondeterministic decision trees over information systems. In: [DM] 178–184
419. Moshkov, M.Ju.: Comparative analysis of deterministic and non–deterministic decision tree complexity. Global approach. Fundamenta Informaticae **25** (1996) 201–214
420. Moshkov, M.Ju.: Lower bounds on time complexity of deterministic conditional tests (in Russian). Diskretnaya Matematika **8/3** (1996) 98–110
421. Moshkov, M.Ju.: On the depth of decision trees over arbitrary check system (in Russian). In: Proceedings of the 11th International Conference on Problems of Theoretical Cybernetics, Uljanovsk, Russia (1996) 146–147
422. Moshkov, M.Ju.: On the depth of decision trees over infinite information systems. In: Proceedings of the Sixth International Conference, Information Processing and Management of Uncertainty in Knowledge–Based Systems (IPMU'96), July 1–5, Granada, Spain (1996) **2** 885–886
423. Moshkov, M.Ju.: On global Shannon functions of two–valued information systems. In: [RSFD'96] 142–143
424. Moshkov, M.Ju.: Diagnosis of constant faults of circuits. In: [RSFD'96] 325–327
425. Moshkov, M.Ju.: Some bounds on minimal decision tree depth. In: [FI] 197–203

426. Moshkov, M.Ju.: Unimprovable upper bounds on complexity of decision trees over information systems. Foundations of Computing and Decision Sciences **21/4** (1996) 219–231
427. Moshkov, M.Ju.: On complexity of decision trees over infinite information systems. In: [RSSC'97] 353–354
428. Moshkov, M.Ju.: Rough analysis for tree programs. In: Proceedings of the Fifth European Congress on Intelligent Techniques and Soft Computing (EUFIT'97), September 9–11, Aachen, Germany, Verlag Mainz (1997) 231–235
429. Moshkov, M.Ju.: Unimprovable upper bounds on time complexity of decision trees. Fundamenta Informaticae **31** (1997) 157–184
430. Moshkov, M.Ju.: Local approach to construction of decision trees. In: [FSRS]
431. Moshkov, M.Ju., Chikalov, I.V.: On the average depth of decision trees over information systems. In: Proceedings of the Fourth European Congress on Intelligent Techniques and Soft Computing (EUFIT'96), September 2–5, Aachen, Germany, Verlag Mainz (1996) 220–222
432. Moshkov, M.Ju., Chikalov, I.V.: Upper bound on average depth of decision trees over information systems. In: [RSFD'96] 139–141
433. Moshkov, M.Ju., Chikalov, I.V.: Bounds on average depth of decision trees. In: Proceedings of the Fifth European Congress on Intelligent Techniques and Soft Computing (EUFIT'97), September 9–11, Aachen, Germany, Verlag Mainz (1997) 226–230
434. Moshkov, M.Ju., Chikalov, I.V.: Bounds on average weighted depth of decision trees. Fundamenta Informaticae **31/1** (1997) 145–156
435. Moshkova, A., Moshkov, M.Ju.: Optimal bases for some closed classes of Boolean functions. In: Proceedings of the Fifth European Congress on Intelligent Techniques and Soft Computing (EUFIT'97), September 9–11, Aachen, Germany, Verlag Mainz (1997) 1643–1648
436. Mrózek, A.: Rough sets and some aspects of expert systems realization. In: Proceedings of the Seventh International Workshop on Expert Systems and their Applications, Avignon, France, May 13–15 (1987) 597–611
437. Mrózek, A.: Rough sets and dependency analysis among attributes in computer implementations of expert's inference models. Journal of Man–Machine Studies **30** (1989) 457–473
438. Mrózek, A.: Rough sets in identification, analysis and evaluation of experts' inference models. In: [RS'92] 32–34
439. Mrózek, A.: Rough sets in computer implementation of rule–based control of industrial processes. In: [IDS] 19–31
440. Mrózek, A.: A new method for discovering rules from examples in expert systems. Journal of Man–Machine Studies **36** (1992)
441. Mrózek, A., Płonka, L.: Rough sets in image analysis. In: [RS'92]; see also: [FC-DS'93] 259–273 (full version)
442. Mrózek, A., Płonka, L.: Knowledge representation in fuzzy and rough controllers. In: M. Dąbrowski, M. Michalewicz, and Z.W. Ras (eds.), Proceedings of the Third International Workshop on Intelligent Information Systems, Wigry, Poland, June 6–10, 1994, Institute of Computer Science Polish Academy of Sciences, Warsaw (1994) 324–337
443. Mrózek, A., Płonka, L.: Rough sets for controller synthesis. In: [RSSC'94]
444. Mrózek, A., Płonka, L., Kędziera, J.: The methodology of rough controller synthesis. In: Proceedings of the Fifth IEEE International Conference on Fuzzy Systems (FUZZ-IEEE'96), September 8–11, New Orleans, Louisiana (1996) 1135–1139

445. Mrózek, A., Płonka, L., Winiarczyk, R.: Rough sets for controller synthesis. In: [RSSC'94] 498–505
446. Munakata, T.: Commercial and industrial AI and a future perspective on rough sets. In: [SC] 219–222
447. Munakata, T.: Rough control: Basic ideas and applications. In: P.P. Wang (ed.), Proceedings of the Second Annual Joint Conference on Information Sciences (JC-IS'95), September 28 – October 1, Wrightsville Beach, North Carolina, USA (1995) 340–343
448. Munakata, T.: Rough control: A perspective. In: [RSDM] 77–88
449. Murai, T., Kanemitsu, H., Shimbo, M.: Fuzzy sets and binary–proximity–based rough sets. In: P.P. Wang (ed.): Proceedings of the International Workshop on Rough Sets and Soft Computing at Second Annual Joint Conference on Information Sciences (JCIS'95), Wrightsville Beach, North Carolina, 28 September – 1 October (1995) 259–262
450. Murai, T., Shimbo, M.: Vagueness and rough set theory, revisited. In: [RSFD'96] 97–104
451. Muraszkiewicz, M., Rybiński, H.: Basic rough sets operators by cellular arrays. In: [RS'92] 36–39
452. Muraszkiewicz, M., Rybiński, H.: Towards a parallel rough sets computer. In: [RSKD'93b] 434–443
453. Nakamura, A.: On a multi–modal fuzzy logic based on rough classifications. In: [RS'92] 40–42
454. Nakamura, A.: On a multi–modal logic based on the graded classifications. In: [FCDS'93] 275–292
455. Nakamura, A.: Fuzzy quantifiers and rough quantifiers. In: P.P. Wang (ed.), Advances in Fuzzy Theory and Technology **II** (1994) 111–131
456. Nakamura, A.: On a logic of information for reasoning about knowledge. In: [RS-KD'93b] 186–195
457. Nakamura, A.: Rough sets – Its theory and applications (in Japanese). J. of Japan Society for Fuzzy Theory and Systems **8** (1996) 594–603
458. Nakamura, A.: A rough logic based on incomplete information and its application. In: [AR] 367–378
459. Nakamura, A.: Conflict logic with degrees. In: [FSRS]
460. Nakamura, A., Tsumoto, S., Tanaka, H., Kobayashi, S.: Rough set theory and its application (in Japanese). J. of Japanese Society for Artificial Intelligence **11** (1996) 35–41
461. Nguyen, H. Son: A method of object classification based on modal logic. Institute of Computer Science, Warsaw University of Technology, ICS Research Report **2/93** (1993)
462. Nguyen, H. Son: Rule induction from continuous data. In: [RSSC'97] 81–84
463. Nguyen, H. Son: Discretization of real value attributes: Boolean reasoning approach. Ph.D. Dissertation, supervisor A. Skowron, Warsaw University (1997) 1–90
464. Nguyen, H. Son, Nguyen, S. Hoa: From optimal hyperplanes to optimal decision trees: Rough set and Boolean reasoning approach. In: [RSFD'96] 82–88
465. Nguyen, H. Son, Nguyen, S. Hoa: Discretization methods with back–tracking. In: Proceedings of the Fifth European Congress on Intelligent Techniques and Soft Computing (EUFIT'97), September 8–11, Aachen, Germany, Verlag Mainz (1997) 201–205

466. Nguyen, H. Son, Nguyen, S. Hoa, Skowron, A.: Searching for features defined by hyperplanes. In: Z.W. Ras, M. Michalewicz (eds.), Proceedings of the Ninth International Symposium on Methodologies for Intelligent Systems. Zakopane, Poland, June 9–13, Lecture Notes in Artificial Intelligence (ISMIS-96) **1079**, Springer-Verlag, Berlin (1996) 366–375
467. Nguyen, H. Son, Skowron, A.: Quantization of real value attributes. In: P.P. Wang (ed.): Proceedings of the International Workshop on Rough Sets and Soft Computing at Second Annual Joint Conference on Information Sciences (JCIS'95), Wrightsville Beach, North Carolina, 28 September - 1 October (1995) 34–37; see also: Institute of Computer Science, Warsaw University of Technology, ICS Research Report **11/95** (1995)
468. Nguyen, H. Son, Skowron, A.: Quantization of real value attributes: Rough set and boolean reasoning approach. In: [BUL1] 5–16
469. Nguyen, H. Son, Skowron, A.: Boolean reasoning for feature extraction problems. In: Z.W. Ras, A. Skowron (eds.), Proceedings of the Tenth International Symposium on Methodologies for Intelligent Systems, Foundations of Intelligent Systems (ISMIS'97), October 15-18, Charlotte, NC, USA, Lecture Notes in Artificial Intelligence **1325**, Springer–Verlag, Berlin (1997) 117–126
470. Nguyen, H. Son, Szczuka, M., Ślęzak, D.: Neural network design: Rough set approach to real–valued data. In: J. Komorowski, J. Żytkow, (eds.), The First European Symposium on Principles of Data Mining and Knowledge Discovery (PKDD'97), June 25–27, Trondheim, Norway, Lecture Notes in Artificial Intelligence **1263**, Springer–Verlag, Berlin (1997) 359–366
471. Nguyen, S. Hoa, Nguyen, H. Son: Discretization of real value attributes for control problems. In: Proceedings of the Fourth European Congress on Intelligent Techniques and Soft Computing, (EUFIT'96), September 2–5, Aachen, Germany, Verlag Mainz (1996) **1** 188–191
472. Nguyen, S. Hoa, Nguyen, H. Son: Some efficient algorithms for rough set methods. In: Proceedings of the Sixth International Conference, Information Processing and Management of Uncertainty in Knowledge–Based Systems (IPMU'96), July 1–5, Granada, Spain (1996) **2** 1451–1456
473. Nguyen, S. Hoa, Nguyen, T. Trung, Polkowski, L., Skowron, A., Synak, P., Wróblewski, J.: Decision rules for large data tables. In: P. Borne, G. Dauphin–Tanguy. C. Sueur, and S.El Khattabi (eds.), Proceedings of IMACS Multiconference: Computational Engineering in Systems Applications (CESA'96) July 9–12, Lille, France, Gerf EC Lille - Cite Scientifique (1996) **3/4** 942–947
474. Nguyen, S. Hoa, Nguyen, T. Trung, Skowron, A., Synak, P.: Knowledge discovery by rough set methods. In: Nagib C. Callaos (ed.), Proceedings of the International Conference on Information Systems Analysis and Synthesis (ISAS'96), July 22–26, Orlando, USA (1996) 26–33
475. Nguyen, S. Hoa, Polkowski, L., Skowron, A., Synak, P., Wróblewski, J.: Searching for approximate description of decision classes. In: [RSFD'96] 153–161
476. Nguyen, S. Hoa, Skowron, A.: Searching for relational patterns in data. In: J. Komorowski, J. Żytkow (eds.), Proceedings of the First European Symposium on Principles of Data Mining and Knowledge Discovery (PKDD'97). Trondheim, Norway, June 25–27, Lecture Notes in Artificial Intelligence **1263**, Springer–Verlag, Berlin (1997) 265–276
477. Nguyen, S. Hoa, Skowron, A., Synak, P.: Rough sets in data mining: Approximate description of decision classes. In: Proceedings of the Fourth European Congress on Intelligent Techniques and Soft Computing (EUFIT'96), September 2–5, Aachen,

Germany, Varlag Mainz (1996) 149–153
478. Nguyen, S. Hoa, Skowron, A., Synak, P., Wróblewski, J.: Knowledge discovery in data bases: Rough set approach. In: M. Mares, R. Meisar, V. Novak, and J. Ramik (eds.), Proceedings of the Seventh International Fuzzy Systems Association World Congress (IFSA'97), June 25–29, Academia, Prague, (1997) **2** 204–209
479. Nguyen, T. Trung, Nguyen, H. Son: An approach to the handwritten digit recognition problem based on modal logic. Master Thesis, supervisor A. Skowron, Institute of Mathematics, Warsaw University; see also: Institute of Computer Science, Warsaw University of Technology, ICS Research Report **44/93** (1993)
480. Nguyen, T., Swiniarski, R., Skowron, A., Bazan, J., Thagarajan, K.: Applications of rough sets, neural networks and maximum likelihood for texture classification based on singular value decomposition. In: [RSSC'94] 332–339; see also: [SC] 157–160
481. Nieminen, J.: Rough tolerance equality and tolerance black boxes. Fundamenta Informaticae **11** (1988) 289–296
482. Nieminen, J.: Rough sets, screens, roundings and relations. Bull. Polish Acad. Sci. Tech. **37** (1990) 351–358
483. Novotny, J., Novotny, M.: Notes on the algebraic approach to dependence in information systems. Fundamenta Informaticae **16** (1992) 263–273
484. Novotny, J., Novotny, M.: On dependence in Wille's contexts. Fundamenta Informaticae **19** (1993) 343–353
485. Novotny, M.: On sequents defined by means of information systems. Fundamenta Informaticae **4** (1981) 1041–1048
486. Novotny, M.: Remarks on sequents defined by means of information systems. Fundamenta Informaticae **6** (1983) 71–79
487. Novotny, M.: Dependence spaces of information systems. In: [II] 193–246
488. Novotny, M.: Applications of dependence spaces. In: [II] 247–289
489. Novotny, M., Pawlak, Z.: On a representation of rough sets by means of information systems. Fundamenta Informaticae **6/3–4** (1983) 289–296
490. Novotny, M., Pawlak, Z.: Characterization of rough top equalities and rough bottom equalities. Bull. Polish Acad. Sci. Math. **33/1–2** (1985) 91–97
491. Novotny, M., Pawlak, Z.: On rough equalities. Bull. Polish Acad. Sci. Math. **33/1–2** (1985) 99–104
492. Novotny, M., Pawlak, Z.: Black box analysis and rough top equalities. Bull. Polish Acad. Sci. Math. **33/1–2** (1985) 105–113
493. Novotny, M., Pawlak, Z.: Concept forming and black boxes. Bull. Polish Acad. Sci. Math. **35/1–2** (1987) 134–141
494. Novotny, M., Pawlak, Z.: Partial dependency of attributes. Bull. Polish Acad. Sci. Math. **36/7–8** (1988) 453–458
495. Novotny, M., Pawlak, Z.: Independence of attributes. Bull. Polish Acad. Sci. Math. **36/7–8** (1988) 459–465
496. Novotny, M., Pawlak, Z.: On superreducts. Bull. Polish Acad. Sci. Math. **38/1–2** (1990) 101–112
497. Novotny, M., Pawlak, Z.: Algebraic theory of independence in information systems. Fundamenta Informaticae **14** (1991) 454–476
498. Novotny, M., Pawlak, Z.: On problem concerning dependence space. Fundamenta Informaticae **16/3–4** (1992) 275–287
499. Nowicki, R., Słowiński R., Stefanowski, J.: Possibilities of applying the rough sets theory to technical diagnostics. In: Proceedings of the Ninth National Symposium

on Vibration Techniques and Vibroacoustics, Kraków, December 12–14, AGH University Press, Kraków (1990) 149–152

500. Nowicki, R., Słowiński, R., Stefanowski, J.: Rough sets analysis of diagnostic capacity of vibroacoustic symptoms. Journal of Computers and Mathematics with Applications **24** (1992) 109–123
501. Nowicki, R., Słowiński, R., Stefanowski, J.: Evaluation of vibroacoustic diagnostic symptoms by means of the rough sets theory. Journal of Computers in Industry **20** (1992) 141–152
502. Nowicki, R., Słowiński, R., Stefanowski, J.: Analysis of diagnostic symptoms in vibroacoustic diagnostics by means of the rough set theory. In: [IDS] 33–48
503. Nowicki, R., Stefanowski, J., Słowiński, R.: Rough sets approach to analysis of diagnostic symptoms in vibroacoustic technical diagnostics. In: [RS'92] 43–44
504. Nurmi, H., Kacprzyk, J., Fedrizzi, M.: Theory and methodology: Probabilistic, fuzzy and rough concepts in social choice. European Journal of Operational Research, Elsevier (1996) 264–277
505. Obtułowicz, A.: Rough sets and Heyting algebra valued sets. Bull. Polish Acad. Sci. Math. **35/9–10** (1988) 667–671
506. Øhrn, A.: Rough logic control. In: (Project), Technical Report, Knowledge Systems Group, Norwegian Institute of Technology, Trondheim, Norway (1993)
507. Øhrn, A., Komorowski, J.: Rosetta – A rough set toolkit for analysis of data. In: [RSSC'97] 403–407
508. Øhrn, A., Komorowski, J., Skowron, A., Synak, P.: Rosetta – Part I: System overview. Technical Report, Knowledge Systems Group, Norwegian University of Science and Technology, Trondheim, Norway (1997)
509. Øhrn, A., Komorowski, J., Skowron, A., Synak, P.: A software system for rough data analysis. In: [BUL2] 58–59
510. Øhrn, A., Vinterbo, S., Szymański, P., Komorowski, J.: Modelling cardiac patient set residuals using rough sets. In: Proceedings of AMIA Annual Fall Symposium (formerly SCAMC), Nashville, TN, USA, October 25–29 (1997) 203–207; see also: Technical Report, Knowledge Systems Group, Norwegian University of Science and Technology, Trondheim, Norway (1997) (extended version)
511. Oosthuizen, G.D.: Rough sets and concept lattices. In: [RSKD'93b] 24–31
512. Orłowska, E.: Dynamic information systems. Fundamenta Informaticae **5** (1982) 101–118
513. Orłowska, E.: Representation of temporal information. Polish Academy of Sciences, ICS PAS Reports **484** (1982); see also: International Journal of Computer and Information Sciences **11** (1982) 397–408
514. Orłowska, E.: Semantics of vague concepts. In: G. Dorn, P. Weingartner (eds.), Foundations of Logic and Linguistics. Problems and Solutions. Selected contributions to the Seventh International Congress of Logic, Methodology and Philosophy of Science, Salzburg, Plenum Press, London–New York (1983) 465–482
515. Orłowska, E.: Representation of nondeterministic information. Theoretical Computer Science **29** (1984) 27–39
516. Orłowska, E.: Modal logics in the theory of information systems. Zeitschrift fuer Mathematische Logik und Grundlagen der Mathematik **30** (1984) 213–222
517. Orłowska, E.: Logic approach to information systems. Fundamenta Informaticae **8** (1985) 359–378
518. Orłowska, E.: Logic of nondeterministic information. Studia Logica **44** (1985) 93–102; see also: Lecture Notes in Computer Science **208** (1985) 469–473
519. Orłowska, E.: Relative induction. Bull. Polish Acad. Sci. Math. **33** (1985) 469–473

520. Orłowska, E.: Semantical analysis of inductive reasoning. Theoretical Computer Science **43** (1986) 81–89
521. Orłowska, E.: Semantics of knowledge operators. Bull. Polish Acad. Sci. Math. **35** (1987) 255–263
522. Orłowska, E.: Representation of vague information. Information Systems **13** (1988) 167–174
523. Orłowska, E.: Kripke models with relative accessibility and their application to inferences from incomplete information. In: G. Mirkowska, H. Rasiowa (eds.), Mathematical Problems in Computation Theory, Banach Center Publications **21** (1988) 329–339
524. Orłowska, E.: Logical aspects of learning concepts. Journal of Approximate Reasoning **2** (1988) 349–364
525. Orłowska, E.: Logic for reasoning about knowledge. Zeitschrift fuer Mathematische Logik und Grundlagen der Mathematik **35** (1989) 559–572
526. Orłowska, E.: Kripke semantics for knowledge representation logics. Studia Logica **49** (1990) 255–272
527. Orłowska, E.: Verisimilitude based on concept analysis. Studia Logica **49** (1990) 307–320
528. Orłowska, E.: A rough set model of knowledge transfer in distributed systems. In: [RS'92] 45–47
529. Orłowska, E.: Rough sets semantics for non–classical logics. In: [RSKD'93b] 143–148
530. Orłowska, E.: Reasoning with incomplete information: Rough set based information logics. In: V. Alagar, S. Bergler, and F.Q. Dong (eds.), Incompleteness and Uncertainty in Information Systems, Proceedings of SOFTEKS Workshop on Incompleteness and Uncertainty in Information Systems, Concordia University, Montreal, Canada 1993, Workshops in Computing, Springer–Verlag & British Computer Society, London, Berlin (1994) 16–33
531. Orłowska, E.: Indiscernibility and orthogonality: Two paradigms of incompleteness. In: [SC] 64–71
532. Orłowska, E.: Information algebras. In: Proceedings of AMAST'95, Lecture Notes in Computer Science **639**, Montreal, Canada (1995) 50–65
533. Orłowska, E.: Studying incompleteness of information: A class of information logics. Institute of Computer Science, Warsaw University of Technology, ICS Research Report bf 27/96 (1996); see also: K. Kijania–Placek, J. Wolenski (eds.), The Lvov–Warsaw School and Contemporary Philosophy, Kluwer Academic Publishers, Dordrecht (to appear)
534. Orłowska, E.: Many–valuedness and uncertainty. In: Proceedings of the 27th International Symposium on Multiple Valued Logic, Antigonish, Canada (1997) 153–160
535. Orłowska, E.: A conceptual analysis of key distributions in cryptographic networks. In: Proceedings of the Fifth European Congress on Intelligent Techniques and Soft Computing (EUFIT'97), Aachen, Germany, Verlag Mainz (1997) 1597–1601
536. Orłowska, E.: Introduction: What you always wanted to know about rough sets. In: [II] 1–20
537. Orłowska, E., Orłowski, M.W.: Maintenance of knowledge in dynamic information systems. In: [IDS] 315–330
538. Orłowska, E., Pawlak, Z.: Measurement and indiscernibility. Bull. Polish Acad. Sci. Math. **32** (1984) 617–624
539. Orłowska, E., Pawlak, Z.: Logical foundations of knowledge representation. Polish Academy of Sciences, ICS PAS Reports **537** (1984) 1–106

540. Orłowska, E., Pawlak, Z.: Representation of nondeterministic information. Theoretical Computer Science **29** (1984) 27–39
541. Pagliani, P.: From concept lattices to approximation apaces: Algebraic structures of some spaces of partial objects. Fundamenta Informaticae **18/1** (1993) 1–25
542. Pagliani, P.: A pure logic–algebraic analysis of rough top and rough bottom equalities. In: [RSKD'93b] 227–236
543. Pagliani, P.: Towards a logic of rough set systems. In: [SC] 59–64
544. Pagliani, P.: Rough sets and Nelson algebras. In: [FI] 205–219
545. Pagliani, P.: A model relation algebra for generalized approximation spaces. In: [RSFD'96] 89–96
546. Pagliani, P.: Local and global logical behaviours: Re–visiting many valued logics through rough set systems. In: Proceedings of the Fifth European Congress on Intelligent Techniques and Soft Computing (EUFIT'97), Aachen, Germany, Verlag Mainz (1997) 1592–1596
547. Pagliani, P.: Rough set theory and logic–algebraic structures. In: [II] 109–190
548. Parsons, S., Kubat, M., Dohnal, M.: Rough sets for the analysis of complex systems. In: [RS'92] 48–50
549. Parsons, S., Kubat, M., Dohnal, M.: A rough logic for rule-based reasoning under uncertainty. In: M. Jamshidi, R. Lumis, J. Mullins, M. Shahinpoor (eds.), Robotics and Manufacturing; Recent Trends in Research, Education and Applications **4**, ASME Press, New York (1992)
550. Paszek, P., Wakulicz–Deja, A.: Optimalization diagnose in progressive encephalopathy applying the rough set theory. In: Proceedings of the Fourth European Congress on Intelligent Techniques and Soft Computing (EUFIT'96), September 2–5, Aachen, Germany, Verlag Mainz (1996) **1** 192–196
551. Paun, G., Polkowski, L., Skowron, A.: Rough–set–like approximations of context–free and regular languages. In: Proceedings of the Sixth International Conference, Information Processing and Management of Uncertainty in Knowledge–Based Systems (IPMU'96), July 1–5, Granada, Spain (1996) **2** 891–895
552. Paun, G., Polkowski, L., Skowron, A.: Parallel communicating grammar systems with negotiations. Fundamenta Informaticae **28/3-4** (1996) 315–330
553. Paun, G., Polkowski, L., Skowron, A.: Rough set approximations of languages. Fundamenta Informaticae **32/2** (1997) 149–162
554. Pawlak, Z.: Rough sets. International Journal of Computer and Information Sciences **11** (1982) 341–356
555. Pawlak, Z.: Rough classification. Journal of Man–Machine Studies **20** (1984) 469–483
556. Pawlak, Z.: Rough probability. Bull. Polish Acad. Sci. Math. **132/9–10** (1984) 607–612
557. Pawlak, Z.: Rough sets and fuzzy sets. J. of Fuzzy Sets and Systems **17** (1985) 99–102
558. Pawlak, Z.: Rough sets and multi expert systems. Bull. Polish Acad. Sci. Tech. **33/9–10** (1985) 499–504
559. Pawlak, Z.: Rough concept analysis. Bull. Polish Acad. Sci. Tech. **33/9–10** (1985) 495–498
560. Pawlak, Z.: On rough dependency of attributes in information systems. Bull. Polish Acad. Sci. Tech. **33/9–10** (1985) 481–485
561. Pawlak, Z.: Rough sets and decision tables. Lecture Notes, Springer–Verlag **208** (1986) 186–196
562. Pawlak, Z.: On rough relations. Bull. Polish Acad. Sci. Tech. (1986) 587–590

563. Pawlak, Z.: Decision table computer. Bull. Polish Acad. Sci. Tech. (1986) 591–595
564. Pawlak, Z.: Rough sets. International J. of Fuzzy Sets and Systems **19** (1986) 309–310
565. Pawlak, Z.: Rough functions. Bull. Polish Acad. Sci. Tech. **35/5–6** (1987) 249–251
566. Pawlak, Z.: Rough logic. Bull. Polish Acad. Sci. Tech. **35/5–6** (1987) 253–258
567. Pawlak, Z.: Learning from examples – The case of an imperfect teacher. Bull. Polish Acad. Sci. Tech. **35/5–6** (1987) 259–264
568. Pawlak, Z.: Decision tables – A rough set approach. Bulletin of the European Association for Theoretical Computer Science (EATCS) **33** (1987) 85–96
569. Pawlak, Z.: Knowledge, reasoning and classification – A rough set perspective. Bulletin of the European Association for Theoretical Computer Science (EATCS) **38** (1989) 199–210
570. Pawlak, Z.: Rough sets. Present state and the future. In: [RS'92] 51–53; [FCDS'93] 157–166
571. Pawlak, Z.: Rough sets: A new approach to vagueness. In: L. Zadeh, J. Kacprzyk (eds.), Fuzzy Logic for the Management of Uncertainty, John Wiley & Sons, Inc., New York (1992) 105–118
572. Pawlak, Z.: Hard and soft sets. In: [RSKD'93b] 130–135
573. Pawlak, Z.: Decision analysis using rough sets. International Trans. Opr. Res. **1/1** (1994) 107–114
574. Pawlak, Z.: Knowledge and uncertainty – A rough sets approach. In: V. Alagar, S. Bergler, and F.Q. Dong (eds.), Incompleteness and Uncertainty in Information Systems, Proceedings of SOFTEKS Workshop on Incompleteness and Uncertainty in Information Systems, Concordia University, Montreal, Canada 1993, Workshops in Computing, Springer–Verlag & British Computer Society, London, Berlin (1994) 34–42
575. Pawlak, Z.: An inquiry into vagueness and uncertainty. In: M. Dąbrowski, M. Michalewicz, and Z.W. Ras (eds.), Proceedings of the Third International Workshop on Intelligent Information Systems, Wigry, Poland, June 6–10, 1994, Institute of Computer Science, Polish Academy of Sciences, Warsaw (1994) 338–343
576. Pawlak, Z.: Rough sets: Present state and further prospects. In: [SC] 78–85
577. Pawlak, Z.: Rough sets and fuzzy sets. In: C. Jinshong (ed.), Proceedings of ACM, Computer Science Conference, February 28 – March 2, Nashville, Tennessee (1995) 262–264
578. Pawlak, Z.: Rough real functions and rough controllers. In: [DM] 57–62
579. Pawlak, Z.: Vagueness and uncertainty: A rough set perspective. [CI] 227–232
580. Pawlak, Z.: Rough sets, rough relations and rough functions. In; [FI] 103–108
581. Pawlak, Z.: Data versus logic – A rough set view. In: [RSFD'96] 1–8
582. Pawlak, Z.: Rough sets: Present state and perspectives. In: Proceedings of the Sixth International Conference, Information Processing and Management of Uncertainty in Knowledge–Based Systems (IPMU'96), July 1–5, Granada, Spain (1996) **2** 1137–1146
583. Pawlak, Z.: Some remarks on explanation of data and specifications of processes. In: [BUL1] 1–4
584. Pawlak, Z.: Why rough sets? In: Proceedings of the Fifth IEEE International Conference on Fuzzy Systems (FUZZ-IEEE'96), September 8–11, New Orleans, Louisiana (1996) 738–743
585. Pawlak, Z.: Rough sets and data analysis. In: Y.Y. Chen, K. Hirota, and J.Y. Yen (eds.), Proceedings of 1996 ASIAN FUZZY SYSTEMS SYMPOSIUM – Soft

Computing in Intelligent Systems and Information Processing, December 11–14, Kenting, Taiwan, ROC. (1996) 1–6
586. Pawlak, Z.: Rough set approach to knowledge–based decision support. European Journal of Operational Research **2933**, Elsevier (1997) 1–10
587. Pawlak, Z.: Rough sets. In: [RSDM] 3–8
588. Pawlak, Z.: Rough real functions and rough controllers. In: [RSDM] 139–147
589. Pawlak, Z.: Conflict analysis. In: Proceedings of the Fifth European Congress on Intelligent Techniques and Soft Computing (EUFIT'97), September 9–11, Aachen, Germany, Verlag Mainz (1997) 1589–1591
590. Pawlak, Z.: Rough sets, rough functions and rough calculus. In: [FSRS]
591. Pawlak, Z., Grzymała–Busse, J.W.: On some subsets of the partition set. Fundamenta Informaticae **7/4** (1984) 483–488
592. Pawlak, Z., Grzymała–Busse, J.W., Słowiński, R., Ziarko, W.: Rough sets. Communication of the ACM **38/11** (1995) 88–95
593. Pawlak, Z., Munakata, T.: Rough control: Application of rough set theory to control. In: Proceedings of the Fourth European Congress on Intelligent Techniques and Soft Computing (EUFIT'96), September 2–5, Germany, Verlag Mainz (1996) 1 209–218
594. Pawlak, Z., Rauszer, C.: Dependency of attributes in information systems. Bull. Polish Acad. Sci. Math. **33** (1985) 551–559
595. Pawlak, Z., Skowron, A.: A rough set approach for decision rules generation. In: Proceedings of the Workshop W12: The Management of Uncertainty in AI at 13th IJCAI, Chambery Savoie, France, August 30, see also: Institute of Computer Science, Warsaw University of Technology, ICS Research Report **23/93** (1993) 1–19
596. Pawlak, Z., Skowron, A.: Rough membership functions: A tool for reasoning with uncertainty. In: C. Rauszer (ed.), Algebraic Methods in Logic and Computer Science, Banach Center Publications **28**, Polish Academy of Sciences, Warsaw (1993) 135–150
597. Pawlak, Z., Skowron, A.: Rough membership functions. In: R.R. Yaeger, M. Fedrizzi, and J. Kacprzyk (eds.), Advances in the Dempster Shafer Theory of Evidence, John Wiley & Sons, Inc., New York (1994) 251–271
598. Pawlak, Z., Skowron, A.: Helena Rasiowa and Cecylia Rauszer research on logical foundations of computer science. In: A. Skowron (ed.), Logic, Algebra and Computer Science, Helena Rasiowa and Cecylia Rauszer in Memoriam, Bulletin of the Section of Logic **25/3–4** (1996) 174–184
599. Pawlak, Z., Słowiński, R.: Rough set approach to multi–attribute decision analysis. European Journal of Operational Research **72** (1994) 443–459 (Invited Review)
600. Pawlak, Z., Słowiński, K., Słowiński R.: Rough classification of patients after highly selected vagotomy for duodenal ulcer. Journal of Man–Machine Studies **24** (1986) 413–433
601. Pawlak, Z., Słowiński, R.: Decision analysis using rough sets. International Transactions in Operational Research **1/1** (1994) 107–114
602. Pawlak, Z., Wong, S.K.M., Ziarko, W.: Rough sets: Probabilistic versus deterministic approach. Journal of Man–Machine Studies **29** (1988) 81–85; see also: B. Gains, J. Boose (eds.), Machine Learning and Uncertain Reasoning **3**, Academic Press (1990) 227–242
603. Pedrycz, W.: Shadowed sets: Bridging fuzzy and rough sets. In: [FSRS]
604. Peters III, J.F., Ramanna, S.: A rough set approach to assessing software quality: Concepts and rough Petri net models. In: [FSRS]

605. Peterson, G.I.: Rough classification of pneumonia patients using a clinical database. In: [RSKD'93b] 412–419
606. Petry, E., Arora, G., Beaubouef, T.: Information–theoretic measures of uncertainty for rough set and rough relational databases. In: [RSSC'97] 336–339
607. Piasta, Z.: Diagnostic classification for brittle matrix composites assisted by pattern recognition and rough sets analysis. In: A.M. Brandt, I.H. Marshall (eds.), Brittle Matrix Composites **3**, Elsevier Applied Science, London, New York (1991) 258–268
608. Piasta, Z.: Statistical and logical classifiers: A comparative study. In: [RSKD'93a]
609. Piasta, Z.: An experimental study of relationships between the structure of an information system and classifiers' performance. In: [RSSC'94] 442–449
610. Piasta, Z.: Applications of rough sets and rough classifiers in marketing decision support. In: Proceedings of the 14th European Conference of Operations Research, EURO XIV, Jerusalem, Israel, July 3–6 (1995)
611. Piasta, Z.: A comparative analysis of classifiers' performance by using a simulation study. In: [SC] 65–68
612. Piasta, Z.: Rough classifiers in intelligent support of business decisions. In: Proceedings of the First Polish Conference on Theory and Applications of Artificial Intelligence (CAI'96), }Łódź, Poland (1996) 103–111
613. Piasta, Z.: Transforming data into engineering knowledge with rough classifiers. In: A.M. Brandt (ed.), Optimization Methods for Material Design of Cement–based Composites, Thomson Science & Professional, London (to appear)
614. Piasta, Z.: Data mining and knowledge discovery in marketing and financial databases with rough classifiers. Wydawnictwo Akademii Ekonomicznej we Wrocławiu, Wrocław (to appear, in Polish)
615. Piasta, Z., Lenarcik, A.: Rule induction with probabilistic rough classifiers. Machine Learning (to appear); see also: Institute of Computer Science, Warsaw University of Technology, ICS Research Report **24/96** (1996)
616. Piasta, Z., Lenarcik, A., Tsumoto, S.: Machine discovery in databases with probabilistic rough classifiers. In: [RSFD'96] 353–359; see also: [BUL2] 51–57
617. Płonka, L., Mrózek, A.: Rule–based stabilization of the inverted pendulum. In: [CI] 348–356
618. Płonka, L., Mrózek, A.: Requirements specification with decision tables and rough sets. Bull. Polish Acad. Sci. Tech. (to appear)
619. Płonka, L., Mrózek, A., Winiarczyk, R., Maitan, J.: Implementing rule–oriented knowledge bases on smart networks. In: Proceedings of the Fourth International Workshop on Intelligent Information Systems, Augustów, Poland, June 5–9, 1995, Institute od Computer Science, Polish Academy of Sciences, Warsaw (1995)
620. Polkowski, L.: On convergence of rough sets. In: [IDS] 305–311; see also: [RS'92] 54–56
621. Polkowski, L.: Mathematical morphology of rough sets. Bull. Polish Acad. Sci. Math. **41/3** (1993) 241–273
622. Polkowski, L.: Metric spaces of topological rough sets from countable knowledge bases. In: [FCDS'93] 293–306
623. Polkowski, L.: Concerning mathematical morphology of almost rough sets. Bull. Polish Acad. Sci. Tech. **42/1** (1994) 141–152
624. Polkowski, L.: Concerning mathematical morphology of rough sets. Bull. Polish Acad. Sci. Tech. **42/1** (1994) 125–140
625. Polkowski, L.,: Approximate mathematical morphology. Rough set approach. In: [FSRS]

626. Polkowski, L., Semeniuk–Polkowska, M.: On rough mereological constructibility. Anaphorically constructible many–object events. In: Gh. Paun, (ed.), Mathematical Aspects of Natural and Formal Languages, World Scientific Series in Computer Science **43**, World Scientific, Singapore (1995) 393–406
627. Polkowski, L., Skowron, A.: Rough mereology. In: Proceedings of the Symposium on Methodologies for Intelligent Systems, Charlotte, NC, October 16–19, Lecture Notes in Artificial Intelligence **869**, Springer–Verlag, Berlin (1994) 85–94; see also: Institute of Computer Science, Warsaw University of Technology, ICS Research Report **44/94** (1994)
628. Polkowski, L., Skowron, A.: Vagueness in the analysis and synthesis of complex objects: Rough set approach. Manuscript of a textbook prepared in TEMPUS JEP-1943 (1994) 1–312
629. Polkowski, L., Skowron, A.: Logic of rough inclusion, rough mereology, rough functions. Institute of Computer Science, Warsaw University of Technology, ICS Research Report **12/94** (1994)
630. Polkowski, L., Skowron, A.: Introducing rough mereological controllers. Rough quality control. In: [RSSC'94] 78–85; see also: [SC] 240–243
631. Polkowski, L., Skowron, A.: Rough mereology and analytical mereology: New developments in rough set theory. In: [DM] 144–158; see also: M. De Glas, Z. Pawlak (eds.), Proceedings of the Second World Conference on Fundamentals of Artificial Intelligence (WOCFAI'95), July 13–17, Angkor, Paris (1995) 343–354
632. Polkowski, L., Skowron, A.: Rough mereological approach to knowledge–based distributed AI. In: J.K. Lee, J. Liebowitz, and J.M. Chae (eds.), Critical Technology, Proceedings of the Third World Congress on Expert Systems, February 5–9, Seoul, Korea, Cognizant Communication Corporation, New York (1996) 774–781
633. Polkowski, L., Skowron, A.: Implementing fuzzy containment via rough inclusions: Rough mereological approach to distributed problem solving. In: Proceedings of the Fifth IEEE International Conference on Fuzzy Systems (FUZZ-IEEE'96), September 8–11, New Orleans, Louisiana (1996) 1147–1153
634. Polkowski, L., Skowron, A.: Rough mereology: A new paradigm for approximate reasoning. In: [AR] 333–365
635. Polkowski,L., Skowron, A.: Approximate reasoning in distributed systems. In: Proceedings of the Fifth European Congress on Intelligent Techniques and Soft Computing (EUFIT'97), September 9–11, Aachen, Germany, Verlag Mainz (1997) 1630–1633
636. Polkowski, L., Skowron, A.: Mereological foundations for approximate reasoning in distributed systems. In: Proceedings of the Second Polish Conference on Evolutionary Algorithms and Global Optimization, Rytro, September 15–19 (1997) 229–236 (plenary lecture)
637. Polkowski, L., Skowron, A.: Rough mereology and analytical morphology. In: [II] 399–437
638. Polkowski, L., Skowron, A.: Towards adaptive calculus of granules. In: Proceedings of the FUZZ-IEEE'98 International Conference, Anchorage, Alaska, USA, May 5–9 (1998) (to appear)
639. Polkowski, L., Skowron, A.: Grammar systems for distributed synthesis of approximate solutions extracted from experience. In: Gh. Paun, A. Salomaa (eds.), Gramatical Models of Multi–Agent Systems, Gordon and Breach Publ. Group, London (in print)
640. Polkowski, L., Skowron, A.: Approximate reasoning about complex objects in distributed systems: Rough mereological formalization. In: W. Pedrycz, J.F. Peters

III (eds.), Computational Intelligence and Software Engineering, World Scientific (to appear)

641. Polkowski, L., Skowron, A.: Adaptive calculus of granules in distributed systems. In: L.A. Zadeh, J. Kacprzyk (eds.), Computing with Words in Information/Intelligent Systems, Springer–Verlag Group (Physica–Verlag), Studies in Fuzziness and Soft Computing (in preparation)
642. Polkowski, L., Skowron, A., Komorowski, J.,: Approximate case–based reasoning: A rough mereological approach. In: H.D. Burkhard, M. Lenz (eds.), Fourth German Workshop on Case–Based Reasoning. System Development and Evaluation, Informatik Berichte **55**, Humboldt University, Berlin (1996) 144–151
643. Polkowski, L., Skowron, A., Żytkow, J.: Rough foundations for rough sets. In: [RSSC'94] 142–149; see also: Tolerance based rough sets in: [SC] 55–58
644. Pomykała, J., Pomykała, J.A.: The Stone algebra of rough sets. Bull. Polish Acad. Sci. Math. **36** (1988) 495–508
645. Pomykała, J.A.: Approximation operations in approximation space. Bull. Polish Acad. Sci. Math. **35** (1987) 653–662
646. Pomykała, J.A.: On definability of the nondeterministic information systems. Bull. Polish Acad. Sci. Math. **36** (1988) 193–220
647. Pomykała, J.A.: Approximation, similarity and rough construction. ILLC Prepublication Series, University of Amsterdam, **CT–93–07** (1993)
648. Pomykała, J.A., de Haas, E.: A note on categories of information systems. In: [RSKD'93a] 149–157; see also: [FI] 221–227
649. Prasad K.V.: Computer vision: Rough sets of inputs and soft rules of computing. In: [SC] 223–226
650. Przyłucki, K., Słupek, J.: System of decision tables analysis (in Polish). Master Thesis, supervisor A. Skowron, Institute of Mathematics, Warsaw University (1994)
651. Pułaczewski, J., Sienkiewicz, J.: A rough set approach to process control – Simulations and results. In: Proceedings of the Fourth European Congress on Intelligent Techniques and Soft Computing (EUFIT'96), September 2–5, Aachen, Germany, Verlag Mainz (1996) **1** 197–201
652. Quafafou, M.: Towards a transition from the crisp rough set theory to a fuzzy one. In: Proceedings of the Poster Session of the Ninth International Symposium on Methodologies for Intelligent Systems (ISMIS'96), Zakopane, Poland, June 9–13, Oak Ridge Laboratory (1996) 67–80
653. Quafafou, M.: α-RST: A generalization of rough set theory. In: [RSSC'97] 173–176
654. Quafafou, M.: Learning flexible concepts from uncertain data. In: Z.W. Ras, A. Skowron (eds.), Proceedings of the Tenth International Symposium on Methodologies for Intelligent Systems, Foundations of Intelligent Systems (ISMIS'97), October 15-18, Charlotte, NC, USA, Lecture Notes in Artificial Intelligence **1325**, Springer–Verlag, Berlin (1997) 507–518
655. Quafafou, M., Boussouf, M.: Induction of strong feature subsets. In: J. Komorowski, J. Żytkow (eds.), The First European Symposium on Principles of Data Mining and Knowledge Discovery (PKDD'97), June 25–27, Trondheim, Norway, Lecture Notes in Artificial Intelligence **1263**, Springer–Verlag, Berlin (1997) 384–392
656. Raghavan, V.V., Sever, H.: The state of rough sets for data mining applications. In: [DM] 1–11
657. Ras, Z.W.: On resolving rule conflicts in dictionaries of CKBS. In: M. Dąbrowski, M. Michalewicz, and Z.W. Ras (eds.), Proceedings of the Third International Workshop on Intelligent Information Systems, Wigry, Poland, June 6–10, 1994, Institute

of Computer Science Polish Academy of Sciences, Warsaw (1994) 235–246
658. Ras, Z.W.: Dictionaries in a distributed knowledge–based system. In: Proceedings of Concurrent Engineering: Research and Applications, Pittsburgh, Penn., USA, August 29–31, 1994, Concurrent Technologies Corporation, (1994) 383–390
659. Ras, Z.W.: Cooperative query answering. In: Proceedings of the Fourth International Workshop on Intelligent Information Systems, Augustów, Poland, June 5–9, 1995, Institute od Computer Science, Polish Academy of Sciences, Warsaw (1995) 32–41
660. Ras, Z.W.: Discovering rules in cooperative knowledge–based system. In: [DM] 12–13
661. Ras, Z.W.: Cooperative knowledge–based systems. In: [IA] 193–202
662. Ras, Z.W.: Collaboration control in distributed knowledge–based systems. Information Sciences Journal, Elsevier **96/3–4** (1997) 193–205
663. Ras, Z.W.: Resolving queries through cooperation in multi–agent systems. In: [RSDM] 239–258
664. Ras, Z.W.: Knowledge discovery for intelligent query answering. In: [RSSC'97] 367–370
665. Ras, Z.W., Chilumula, N.: Answering queries by cooperative knowledge–based system. In: [SC] 263–266
666. Ras, Z.W., Janikow, C.: Learning concepts in rough environment, an optimization procedure. In: Z.W. Ras, M. Zemankova (eds.), Proceedings of the Second International Symposium Methodologies for Intelligent Systems, October 14–17, Charlotte, North Carolina, North Holland (1987) 355–361
667. Ras, Z.W., Joshi, S.: Query answering system for an incomplete DKBS. In: Proceedings of the Fifth International Workshop on Intelligent Information Systems (WIS'96), Dęblin, Poland, June 2–5, 1996, Institute of Computer Science, Polish Academy of Sciences (1996) 81–94; see also: Fundamenta Informaticae **30/3–4** (1997) 313–324
668. Ras, Z.W., Koo, T.-M.: Knowledge discovery for intelligent query answering. In: [RSSC'97] 367–370
669. Ras, Z.W., Kudelska, A., Chilumula, N.: Can we simplify international physical performance test profile using rough set approach? In: P.P. Wang (ed.): Proceedings of the International Workshop on Rough Sets and Soft Computing at Second Annual Joint Conference on Information Sciences (JCIS'95), Wrightsville Beach, North Carolina, 28 September – 1 October (1995) 393–396
670. Ras, Z.W., Xiao, J.: A model of information sharing for fault–tolerant flexible manufacturing system. In: Z.W. Ras, M. Zemankova (eds.), Proceedings of the Sixth International Symposium on Methodologies for Intelligent Systems (ISMIS'91), Charlotte, NC, October 16–19, 1991, Lecture Notes in Artificial Intelligence **542**, Springer–Verlag (1991) 213–225
671. Rasiowa, H.: Rough concepts and multiple–valued logic. In: Proceedings of the 16th ISMVL'86, Blacksburg, VA, IEEE Computer Society Press (1986) 282–288
672. Rasiowa, H.: Logic approximating sequences of sets. In: Proceedings of Advanced Intern. School and Symp. on Math. Logic and its Applications, honorably dedicated to 80th anniversary of Kurt Gödel, Plenum Press, New York (1987) 167–186
673. Rasiowa, H.: An algebraic approach to some approximate reasonings. In: Proceedings of the 17th ISMVL'87, Boston, MA, May 24–26, IEEE Computer Society Press (1987) 342–347
674. Rasiowa, H.: Logic of approximation reasoning. In: Proceedings of the First Workshop on Computer Science Logic. Karlsruhe, Germany, 1987 Lecture Notes in Com-

puter Science **239**, Springer–Verlag, Berlin (1988) 188–210
675. Rasiowa, H.: On approximation logics: A survey. Jahrbuch 1990 Kurt Gödel Gessellschaft, Vienna (1990) 63–87
676. Rasiowa, H.: Mechanical proof systems for logic of reaching consensus by groups of intelligent agents. Intern. Journ. of Approximate Reasoning **5/4** (1991) 415–432
677. Rasiowa, H.: Axiomatization and completeness of uncountably valued approximation logic. Studia Logica **53/1** (1991) 137–160
678. Rasiowa, H., Epstein, G.: Approximation reasoning and Scott's information systems. In: Z. Ras, M. Zemankova (eds.), Proceedings of the Second International Symposium on Methodologies for Intelligent Systems, Charlotte, N.C., October 14–17, North Holland, Amsterdam (1987) 33–42
679. Rasiowa, H., Marek, W.: Approximating sets with equivalence relations. Theoret. Comput. Sci. **48** (1986) 145–152; see also: Z.W. Ras, M. Zemankova (eds.), Proceedings of the ACM SIGART International Symposium on Methodologies for Intelligent Systems (ISMIS'86), Knoxville, Tennessee, October 22–24, 1986, ACM Special Interest Group on Artificial Intelligence (1986) 19–28
680. Rasiowa, H., Marek, W.: Gradual approximating sets by means of equivalence relations. Bull. Polish Acad. Sci. Math. **35/3–4** (1987) 233–238
681. Rasiowa, H., Marek, W.: On reaching consensus by groups of intelligent agents. In: Z.W. Ras (ed.), Proceedings of the Fourth International Symposium on Methodologies for Intelligent Systems (ISMIS'89), North Holland, Amsterdam (1989) 234–243
682. Rasiowa, H., Marek, W.: Mechanical proof systems for logic II consensus programs and their processing. Journ. of Intelligent Information Systems **2/2** (1992) 149–164
683. Rasiowa, H., Skowron, A.: Rough concepts logic. In: A. Skowron (ed.), Computation Theory, Lecture Notes in Computer Science **208** (1985) 288–297
684. Rasiowa, H., Skowron, A.: Approximation logic. In: Proceedings of Mathematical Methods of Specification and Synthesis of Software Systems Conference, Akademie Verlag **31**, Berlin (1985) 123–139
685. Rasiowa, H., Skowron, A.: The first step towards an approximation logic. Meeting of The Association for Symbolic Logic, Chicago 1985, Journal of Symbolic Logic **51/2** (1986) 509
686. Rauszer, C.: Algebraic properties of functional dependencies. Bull. Polish Acad. Sci. Math. **33** (1985) 561–569
687. Rauszer, C.: An equivalence between theory of functional dependencies and a fragment of intuitionistic logic. Bull. Polish Acad. Sci. Math. **33** (1985) 571–579
688. Rauszer, C.: Remarks on logic for dependencies. Bull. Polish Acad. Sci. Math. **33** (1985) 249–252
689. Rauszer, C.: An equivalence between indiscernibility relations in information systems and a fragment of intuitionistic logic. In: A. Skowron (ed.), Proceedings of the Fifth Conference on Computation Theory, Zaborów, December 1984, Lecture Notes in Computer Science **208**, Springer–Verlag, Berlin (1985) 298–317
690. Rauszer, C.: An algebraic and logical approach to indiscernibility relations. Institute of Computer Science, Polish Academy of Sciences, Report **559** (1985)
691. Rauszer, C.: A logic for indiscernibility relations. In: Proceedings of the Conference on Information Sciences and Systems, Princeton University (1986) 834–837
692. Rauszer, C.: Reducts in information systems. Fundamenta Informaticae **15** (1991) 1–12
693. Rauszer, C.: Algebraic considerations of autoepistemic logic. Fundamenta Informaticae **15** (1991) 168–169

694. Rauszer, C.: Logic for information systems. Fundamenta Informaticae **16** (1992) 371–382
695. Rauszer, C.: Distributive knowledge representation systems. In: [RS'92] 57–58
696. Rauszer, C.: Dependencies in relational databases. Algebraic and logical approach. Fundamenta Informaticae **19** (1993) 235–274
697. Rauszer, C.: Distributive knowledge representation systems. In: [FCDS'93] 307–332
698. Rauszer, C.: Communication systems in distributed information systems. In: Proceedings of the International Workshop on Intelligent Information Systems, June 7–11, 1993, Augustów, Poland, Institute of Computer Science, Polish Academy of Sciences, Warsaw (1993) 15–29
699. Rauszer, C.: Approximation methods for knowledge representation systems. In: J. Komorowski, Z.W. Ras (eds.), Proceedings of the Seventh International Symposium on Methodologies for Intelligent Systems (ISMIS'93), Trondheim, Norway, June 15–18, 1993, Lecture Notes in Computer Science **689** (1993) 326–337
700. Rauszer, C.: Rough logic for multiagent systems. In: M. Masuch, L. Polos (eds.), Knowledge Representation and Reasoning under Uncertainty. Logic at Work, Lecture Notes in Artificial Intelligence **88** (1994) 161–181; see also: Institute of Computer Science, Warsaw University of Technology, ICS Research Report **27/93** (1993)
701. Rauszer, C.: Knowledge representation systems for groups of agents. In: J. Woleński (ed.), Philosophical Logic in Poland, Kluwer, Dordrecht (1994) 217–238
702. Rauszer, C., de Swart, H.: Different approaches to knowledge, common knowledge and Aumann's theorem. In: A. Laux, H. Wansing (eds.), Knowledge and Belief in Philosophy and Artificial Intelligence, Akademie Verlag, Berlin (1995) 87–12
703. Rauszer, C., Marek, W.: Query optimization in the database distributed by means of product of equivalence relations. In: Proceedings of the Workshop on Deductive Databases and Programming Languages, Washington (1986); see also: Fundamenta Informaticae **11** (1988) 241–286
704. Reinhard, A., Stawski, B., Weber, T., Wybraniec–Skardowska, U.: An application of rough set theory in the control conditions on a polder. In: [IDS] 331–362
705. Romański, S.: Operations on families of sets for exhaustive search given a monotonic function. In: Beeri, C., Smith, J.W., Dayal, U., (eds), Proceedings of the 3rd International Conference on Data and Knowledge Bases, Jerusalem, Israel (1988) 28–30
706. Rubin, S., Vanderpooten, S., Michałowski, W., Słowiński, R.: Developing an emergency room for diagnostic check list using rough sets – A case study of appendicitis. In: J. Anderson, M. Katzper (eds.), Simulation in the Medical Sciences, Proceedings of the Western Conference of the Society for Computer Simulation, Simulation Councils, Inc., San Diego, CA (1996) 19–24
707. Ruhe G.: Qualitative analysis of software engineering data using rough sets. In: [RSFD'96] 292–299
708. Ruhe G.: Knowledge discovery from software engineering data: Rough set analysis and its interaction with goal–oriented measurement. In: J. Komorowski, J. Żytkow (eds.), The First European Symposium on Principles of Data Mining and Knowledge Discovery (PKDD'97), June 25–27, Trondheim, Norway, Lecture Notes in Artificial Intelligence **1263**, Springer–Verlag, Berlin (1997) 167–177
709. Sapiecha, P.: An approximation algorithm for minimal reduct problem. In: [RS'92] 59–61
710. Sapiecha, P.: An approximation algorithm for a certain class of NP–hard problems. In: [FCDS'93] 333–342

711. Sapiecha, P.: A novel approach to minimal cover problem. In: [RSKD'93b] 227–236
712. Sapiecha, P., Perkowski, M., Łuba, T.: Decomposition of the information systems based on graph colouring heuristics. In: P. Borne, G. Dauphin–Tanguy, C. Sueur, and S. El Khattabi (eds.), Proceedings of IMACS Multiconference: Computational Engineering in Systems Applications (CESA '96) July 9–12, Lille, France, Gerf EC Lille – Cite Scientifique (1996) **3/4** 1101–1106
713. Sarkar, M., Yegnanarayana, B.: Fuzzy–rough sets and fuzzy integrals in modular neural networks. In: [FSRS]
714. Sedelow, W.A., Jr Sedelow, S.D.: Knowledge recognition, rough sets, and formal concept lattices. In: [RSKD'93b] 52–62
715. Semeniuk–Polkowska, M.: Rough sets in librarian science (in Polish). Chair of Formal Linguistics, Warsaw University (1996) 1–109
716. Sever, H., Raghavan, V., Deogun, J., Choubey, S.: Comparison of classification methods. In: [RSSC'97] 371–374
717. Shan, N., Hamilton, H.J., Cercone, N.: Induction of classification rules from imperfect data. In: Z.W. Ras, M. Michalewicz (eds.), Proceedings of the Ninth International Symposium on Methodologies for Intelligent Systems (ISMIS'96), Zakopane, Poland, June 9–13, Lecture Notes in Artificial Intelligence **1079**, Springer–Verlag, Berlin (1996) 118–127
718. Shan, N., Hamilton, H., Cercone, N.: GRG: Knowledge and discovery using information generalization, information reduction, and rule generation. International Journal of Artificial Intelligence Tools **5/1–2** (1996) 99–112 (special issue)
719. Shan, N., Hamilton, H., Cercone, N.: Parallel processing for learning decision rules. In: The Ninth Florida AI Research Symposium (FLAIRS'96), Key West, Florida (1996) 156–160
720. Shan, N., Hamilton, H., Cercone, N.: The GRG knowledge discovery system: design principles and architectural overview. In: The Ninth European Conference on Machine Learning (ECML'97), Prague (1997)
721. Shan, N., Hamilton, H.J., Ziarko, W., Cercone, N.: Discretization of continuous valued attributes in classification systems. In: [RSFD'96] 74–81
722. Shan, N., Hu, X., Ziarko, W., Cercone, N.: A generalized rough sets model. In: Proceedings of the Third Pacific Rim International Conference on Artificial Intelligence, Beijing, China (1994) 437–443
723. Shan, N., Zhang, C.N., Hamilton, H.J., Cercone, N.: Minimizing the rules of a fuzzy logic system by using rough sets. In: Pacific–Asian Conference on Expert Systems, Huangshan, China (1995) 198–204
724. Shan, N., Ziarko, W.: An incremental algorithm for constructing decision rules. In: [RSKD'93a] 335–346; see also: [RSKD'93b] 326–334
725. Shan, N., Ziarko, W.: Data–based acquisition and incremental modification of classification rules. In: [CI] 357–370
726. Shan, N, Ziarko, W.: Learning system for knowledge discovery. In: Florida AI Research Symposium (FLAIRS'95), Melbourne Beach (1995) 329–333
727. Shan, N., Ziarko, W., Hamilton, H., Cercone, N.: Using rough sets as tools for knowledge discovery. In: U.M. Fayyad, R. Uthurusamy (eds.), Proceedings of the First International Conference on Knowledge Discovery and Data Mining (KDD'-95), August 20–21, 1995, Montreal, AAAI Press, Menlo Park CA (1995) 263–268
728. Shan, N., Ziarko, W., Hamilton, H. Cercone, N.: Discovering classification knowledge in databases using rough sets. In: E. Simoudis, J. Han, and U. Fayyad (eds.), Proceedings of the Second International Conference on Knowledge Discovery and

Data Mining (KDD'96), August 2–4, Portland, Oregon, USA, AAAI Press, Menlo Park (1996) 271–274
729. Shenoi, S.: Rough sets in fuzzy databases. In: P.P. Wang (ed.): Proceedings of the International Workshop on Rough Sets and Soft Computing at Second Annual Joint Conference on Information Sciences (JCIS'95), Wrightsville Beach, North Carolina, 28 September – 1 October (1995) 263–264
730. Skowron, A.: On topology in information systems. Bull. Polish. Acad. Sci. Math. **36/7–8** (1989) 477–479
731. Skowron, A.: Rough decision problems in information systems. Bull. Polish. Acad. Sci. Tech. **37/1–2** (1989) 59–65
732. Skowron, A.: The relationship between the rough set theory and evidence theory. Bull. Polish Acad. Sci. Tech. **37/1–2** (1989) 87–90
733. Skowron, A.: The evidence theory and decision tables. Bulletin of the European Association for Theoretical Computer Science (EATCS) **39** (1989) 199–204
734. Skowron, A.: Recent and current research on reasoning with incomplete information. Bulletin of Applied Non–Classical Logics (1989) 2–4
735. Skowron, A.: The rough sets theory and evidence theory. Fundamenta Informaticae **13** (1990) 245–262
736. Skowron, A.: Boolean reasoning for decision rules generation. In: J. Komorowski, Z.W. Ras (eds.), Proceedings of the Seventh International Symposium on Methodologies for Intelligent Systems (ISMIS'93), Trondheim, Norway, June 15–18, 1993, Lecture Notes in Computer Science **689** (1993) 295–305
737. Skowron, A.: Data filtration: A rough set approach. In: [RSKD'93b] 108–118
738. Skowron, A.: Extracting laws from decision tables. In: [RSKD'93a] 101–104 (abstract of the invited lecture)
739. Skowron, A.: A synthesis of decision rules: Applications of discernibility matrix. In: Proceedings of the International Workshop on Intelligent Information Systems, Augustów, Poland, June 7–11, 1993, Institute of Computer Science, Polish Academy of Sciences, Warsaw (1993) 30–46 (invited lecture)
740. Skowron, A.: Management of uncertainty in AI – A rough set approach. In: Proceedings of the International Workshop on Incompleteness and Uncertainty in Information Systems, October 8–9, Montreal, Canada (1993) 36–62 (invited lecture); see also: V. Alagar, S. Bergler, and F.Q. Dong (eds.), Incompleteness and Uncertainty in Information Systems, Proceedings of SOFTEKS Workshop on Incompleteness and Uncertainty in Information Systems, Concordia University, Montreal, Canada 1993, Workshops in Computing, Springer–Verlag & British Computer Society, London, Berlin (1994) 69–86 (full version)
741. Skowron, A.: Data filtration: A rough set approach. In: [RSKD'93b] 108–118
742. Skowron, A.: Extracting laws from decision tables. In: [CI] 371–388
743. Skowron, A.: Synthesis of adaptive decision systems from experimental data. In: A. Aamodt, J. Komorowski (eds.), Proceedings of the Fifth Scandinavian Conference on Artificial Intelligence (SCAI'95), May 29–31, 1995, Trondheim, Norway, IOS Press, Amsterdam (1995) 220–238
744. Skowron, A.: Inductive concept learning: Applications of rough set methods. In: Proceedings of the Fourth International Workshop on Intelligent Information Systems, Augustów, Poland, June 5–9, 1995, Institute od Computer Science, Polish Academy of Sciences, Warsaw (1995)
745. Skowron, A.(ed.): Logic, algebra and computer science, Helena Rasiowa and Cecylia Rauszer in Memoriam. Bulletin of the Section of Logic **25/3–4** Warsaw, Poland (1996) 1–215

746. Skowron, A., Grzymała-Busse, J.W.: From rough set theory to evidence theory. In: R.R. Yaeger, M. Fedrizzi, and J. Kacprzyk (eds.), Advances in the Dempster Shafer Theory of Evidence, John Wiley & Sons, Inc., New York (1994) 193–236
747. Skowron, A., Nguyen, H. Son, Synak, P.: Rough sets in data mining: Towards approximate description of decision classes. In: Proceedings of the Fourth European Congress on Intelligent Techniques and Soft Computing (EUFIT'96), September 2–5, Aachen, Germany, Verlag Mainz (1996) **1** 149–154
748. Skowron, A., Polkowski, L.: Adaptive decision algorithms. In: M. Dąbrowski, M. Michalewicz, and Z.W. Ras (eds.), Proceedings of the Third International Workshop on Intelligent Information Systems, Wigry, Poland, June 6–10, 1994, Institute of Computer Science, Polish Academy of Sciences, Warsaw (1994) 103–120
749. Skowron, A., Polkowski, L.: Rough mereological foundations for design, analysis, synthesis, and control in distributive systems. In: P.P. Wang (ed.): Proceedings of the International Workshop on Rough Sets and Soft Computing at Second Annual Joint Conference on Information Sciences (JCIS'95), Wrightsville Beach, North Carolina, 28 September – 1 October (1995) 346–349; see also: Information Sciences International Journal (in print)
750. Skowron, A., Polkowski, L.: Vagueness in synthesis of complex systems. In: Third Polish-Spanish Conference on System Analysis and Computer Science, October 11–13, Barcelona (1995) (abstract of invited talk)
751. Skowron, A., Polkowski, L.: Analytical morphology: mathematical morphology of decision tables. In: [FI] 255–271
752. Skowron, A., Polkowski, L.: Learning synthesis schemes in intelligent systems. In: R.S. Michalski, J. Wnek (eds.), Proceedings of the Third International Workshop on Multistrategy Learning (MSL'96), Harpers Ferry, West Virginia, May 23–25, George Mason University and AAAI Press (1996) 57–68
753. Skowron, A., Polkowski, L.: Rough mereological controller. In: Proceedings of the Fourth European Congress on Intelligent Techniques and Soft Computing (EU-FIT'96), September 2–5, Aachen, Germany (1996) 223–227
754. Skowron, A., Polkowski, L.: Decision algorithms: A survey of rough set theoretic methods. Fundamenta Informaticae **30/3–4** (1997) 345–358
755. Skowron, A., Polkowski, L.: Synthesis of decision systems from data tables. In: [RSDM] 259–299
756. Skowron, A., Polkowski, L., Komorowski, J.: Learning tolerance relations by Boolean descriptors: Automatic feature extraction from data tables. In: [RSFD'96] 11–17
757. Skowron, A., Rauszer, C.: The discernibility matrices and functions in information systems. In: [IDS] 311–362
758. Skowron, A., Stepaniuk, J.: Towards an approximation theory of discrete problems. Fundamenta Informaticae **15/2** (1991) 187–208
759. Skowron, A., Stepaniuk, J.: Searching for classifiers. In: M. De Glas, D. Gabbay (eds.), Proceedings of the First World Conference on the Fundamentals of Artificial Intelligence (WOCFAI'91), 1–5 July, Angkor, Paris (1991) 447–460
760. Skowron, A., Stepaniuk, J.: Intelligent systems based on rough set approach. In: [RS'92] 62–64; see also: [FCDS'93] 343–360 (full version)
761. Skowron, A., Stepaniuk, J.: Variable precision rough sets. In: [RSKD'93a] 159–162
762. Skowron, A., Stepaniuk, J.: Approximation of relations. In: [RSKD'93b] 161–166; see also: Institute of Computer Science, Warsaw University of Technology, ICS Research Report **20/94** (1994)

763. Skowron, A., Stepaniuk, J.: Decision rules based on discernibility matrices and decision matrices. In: [RSSC'94] 602–609; see also: [SC] 6–9
764. Skowron, A., Stepaniuk, J.: Generalized approximation spaces. In: [RSSC'94] 156–163; [SC] 18–21; see also: Institute of Computer Science, Warsaw University of Technology, ICS Research Report **41/94** (1994)
765. Skowron, A., Stepaniuk, J.: Tolerance approximation spaces. In: [FI] 245–253
766. Skowron, A., Stepaniuk, J.: Information reduction based on constructive neighborhood systems. In: [RSSC'97] 158–160
767. Skowron, A., Stepaniuk, J.: Constructive information granules. In: Proceedings of the 15th IMACS World Congress on Scientific Computation, Modelling and Applied Mathematics, August 24–29, Berlin, Germany, Artificial Intelligence and Computer Science **4** (1997) 625–630
768. Skowron, A., Suraj, Z.: Synthesis of concurrent systems specified by information systems. Part 1. Institute of Computer Science, Warsaw University of Technology, ICS Research Report **4/93** (1993) 1–53
769. Skowron, A., Suraj, Z.: Synthesis of concurrent systems specified by information systems. Part 2: Examples of synthesis. Institute of Computer Science, Warsaw University of Technology, ICS Report **38/93** (1993) 1–34
770. Skowron, A., Suraj, Z.: Rough sets and concurrency. Bull. Polish Acad. Sci. Tech. **41/3** (1993) 237–254
771. Skowron, A., Suraj, Z.: A rough set approach to the real–time state identification. Bulletin of the European Association for Theoretical Computer Science (EATCS) **50** (1993) 264–275
772. Skowron, A., Suraj, Z.: Synthesis of concurrent systems specified by information systems. Institute of Computer Science, Warsaw University of Technology, ICS Research Report **39/94** (1994) 1–38
773. Skowron, A., Suraj, Z.: Discovery of concurrent data models from experimental data tables: A rough set approach. In: U.M. Fayyad, R. Uthurusamy (eds.), Proceedings of the First International Conference on Knowledge Discovery and Data Mining (KDD'95), Montreal, August, AAAI Press, Menlo Park, CA (1995) 288–293
774. Skowron, A., Suraj, Z.: A parallel algorithm for real–time decision making: A rough set approach. Journal of Intelligent Information Systems **7** (1996) 5–28
775. Ślęzak, D.: Certain methods of approximate reasoning (in Polish). Master Thesis, supervisor A. Skowron, Institute of Mathematics, Warsaw University (1996)
776. Ślęzak, D.: Approximate reducts in decision tables. Institute of Computer Science, Warsaw University of Technology, ICS Research Report **60/95** (1995); see also: Proceedings of the Sixth International Conference, Information Processing and Management of Uncertainty in Knowledge–Based Systems (IPMU'96), July 1–5, Granada, Spain (1996) **3** 1159–1164
777. Ślęzak, D.: Tolerance dependency model for decision rules generation. In: [RSFD'96] 131–138
778. Ślęzak, D.: Rough set reduct networks. In: [RSSC'97] 77–81
779. Ślęzak, D.: Attribute set decomposition of decision tables. In: Proceedings of the Fifth European Congress on Intelligent Techniques and Soft Computing (EUFIT'97), September 8–12, Aachen, Germany, Verlag Mainz **1** 236–240
780. Ślęzak, D.: Decision value decomposition of data tables. In: Z.W. Ras, A. Skowron (eds.), Proceedings of the Tenth International Symposium on Methodologies for Intelligent Systems, Foundations of Intelligent Systems (ISMIS'97), October 15–18, Charlotte, NC, USA, Lecture Notes in Artificial Intelligence **1325**, Springer–Verlag, Berlin (1997) 487–496

781. Ślęzak, D.: Decomposition and synthesis of decision tables with respect to generalized decision functions. In: [FSRS]
782. Ślęzak, D., Szczuka, M.: Hyperplane–based neural networks for real–valued decision tables. In: [RSSC'97] 265–268
783. Słowiński, K.: Rough classification of HSV patients. In: [IDS] 77–93
784. Słowiński, K., Sharif, E.S.: Rough sets analysis of experience in surgical practice. In: [RS'92] 65–67
785. Słowiński, K., Sharif, E.S.: Rough sets approach to analysis of data of diagnostic peritoneal lavage applied for multiple injuries patients. In: [RSKD'93b] 420–425
786. Słowiński, K., Słowiński, R.: Sensivity analysis of rough classification. Journal of Man–Machine Studies **32** (1990) 693–705
787. Słowiński, K., Słowiński, R.: Sensitivity of rough classification to changes in norms of attributes. In: [IDS] 363–372
788. Słowiński, K., Słowiński, R., Stefanowski, J.: Rough sets approach to analysis of data from peritoneal lavage in acute pancreatitis. Medical Informatics **13/3** (1988) 143–159
789. Słowiński, K., Stefanowski, J.: On limitations of using rough set approach to analyze non-trivial medical information systems. In: [RSFD'96] 176–184
790. Słowiński, K., Stefanowski, J.: Medical information systems – Problems with analysis and way of solutions. In: [FSRS]
791. Słowiński, K., Stefanowski, J., Antczak, A., Kwas, Z.: Rough sets approach to the verification of indications for treatment of urinary stones by extracorporeal shock wave lithotripsy (ESWL). In: [SC] 93–96
792. Słowiński, K., Stefanowski, J., Twardosz, W.: Rough set theory and rule induction techniques for discovery of attribute dependencies in experience with multiple injured patients. Institute of Computer Science, Warsaw University of Technology, ICS Research Report **6/97** (1997)
793. Słowiński, R.: Knowledge analysis using rough sets. Materiały IX. Szkoły "Diagnostics'90", Wydawnictwo Politechniki Poznańskiej, Poznań (1989) 111–122
794. Słowiński, R.: A generalization of the indiscernibility relation for rough sets analysis. In: [RS'92] 68–70
795. Słowiński, R.: A generalization of the indiscernibility relation for rough set analysis of quantitative information. Rivista di Matematica per le Scienze Economiche e Sociali **15/1** (1992) 65–78
796. Słowiński, R.: Rough sets with strict and weak indiscernibility relations. In: Proceedings of IEEE International Conference on Fuzzy Systems, IEEE **92CH3073-4**, San Diego, California (1992) 695–702
797. Słowiński, R.: Strict and weak indiscernibility of objects described by quantitative attributes with overlapping norms. In: [FCDS'93] 361–369
798. Słowiński, R.: Rough set learning of preferential attitude in multi–criteria decision making. In: J. Komorowski, Z.W. Ras (eds.), Proceedings of the Seventh International Symposium on Methodologies for Intelligent Systems (ISMIS'93), Trondheim, Norway, June 15–18, 1993, Lecture Notes in Computer Science **689** (1993) 642–651
799. Słowiński, R.: Rough set analysis of multi-attribute decision problems. In: [RSKD-'93b] 136–143
800. Słowiński, R.: Rough set approach to decision analysis. AI Expert **10** (1995) 18–25
801. Słowiński, R.: Rough set theory and its applications to decision aid. Belgian Journal of Operation Research, Francoro **35/3-4** (1995) 81–90 (special issue)
802. Słowiński, R.: Rough set processing of fuzzy information. In: [SC] 142–145

803. Słowiński, R., Słowiński, K.: An expert system for treatment of duodenal ulcer by highly selective vagotomy (in Polish). Pamiętnik 54. Jubil. Zjazdu Towarzystwa Chirurgów Polskich, Kraków 1989 **I** 223–228
804. Słowiński, R., Stefanowski, J.: Rough classification in incomplete information systems. Math. Comput. Modeling **12/10–11** (1989) 1347–1357
805. Słowiński, R., Stefanowski, J.: RoughDAS and roughClass' software implementations of the rough sets approach. In: [IDS] 445–456
806. Słowiński R., Stefanowski, J.: Rough classification with valued closeness relation. In: E. Diday, Y. Lechevallier, M. Schrader, P. Bertrand, and B. Burtschy (eds.), New Approaches in Classification and Data Analysis, Springer–Verlag, Berlin (1994) 482–488
807. Słowiński R., Stefanowski, J.: Handling various types of uncertainty in the rough set approach. In: [RSKD'93b] 366–376
808. Słowiński, R., Stefanowski, J.: Handling various types of uncertainty in the rough set approach. In: [RSKD'93b] 366–376
809. Słowiński, R., Stefanowski, J.: Managing uncertainty in the rough set approach. In: M. Dąbrowski, M. Michalewicz, and Z.W. Ras (eds.), Proceedings of the International Workshop on Intelligent Information Systems, Wigry, Poland, June 6–10, 1994, Institute of Computer Science, Polish Academy of Sciences, Warsaw (1994) 344–359
810. Słowiński, R., Stefanowski, J.: Rule–based system for classification support using a weighted proximity relation (in Polish). In: R. Kulikowski, L. Bogdan (red.), Wspomaganie Decyzji, Systemy Eksperckie, IBS PAN, Warszawa (1995) 420–429
811. Słowiński, R., Stefanowski, J.: Decision support based on rough set theory (in Polish). Materiały XI Konferencji SEP i WE PP nt. "Przetwarzanie i przesyłanie energii i informacji", Poznań (1995) 141–144
812. Słowiński, R., Stefanowski, J.: Using expert's knowledge in rule based classification of objects. In: Proceedings of the Fourth International Workshop on Intelligent Information Systems, Augustów, Poland, June 5–9, 1995, Institute od Computer Science, Polish Academy of Sciences, Warsaw (1995) 52–61
813. Słowiński, R., Stefanowski, J.: Rough–set reasoning about uncertain data. In: [FI] 229–243
814. Słowiński, R., Stefanowski, J., Susmaga, R.: Rough set analysis of attribute dependencies in technical diagnostics. In: [RSFD'96] 284–291
815. Słowiński, R., Vanderpooten, D.: Similarity relation as a basis for rough approximations. Institute of Computer Science, Warsaw University of Technology, ICS Research Report **53/95** (1995); see also: P.P. Wang (ed.), Advances in Machine Intelligence & Soft–Computing, Bookwrights, Raleigh, NC (1997) 17–33
816. Słowiński, R., Vanderpooten, D.: A generalized definition of rough approximations based on similarity. IEEE Transactions on Data and Knowledge Engineering (to appear)
817. Słowiński, R., Zopounidis, C.: Applications of the rough set approach to evaluation of bankruptcy risk. Working Paper **93–08**, Decision Support System Laboratory, Technical University of Crete, China, June (1993); see also: International J. Intelligent Systems in Accounting, Finance & Management, **4/1** (1995) 27–41
818. Słowiński, R., Zopounidis, C.: Rough set sorting of firms according to bankruptcy risk. In: M. Paruccini (ed.), Applying Multiple Criteria Aid for Decision to Environmental Management, Kluwer, Dordrecht, Netherlands, (1994) 339–357
819. Słowiński, R., Zopounidis, C.: Application of the rough set approach to evaluation of bankruptcy risk.

820. Słowiński, R., Zopounidis, C., Dimitras, A.I.: Prediction of company acquisition in Greece by means of the rough set approach. European Journal of Operational Research **100** (1997) 1–15
821. Srinivasan, P.: Approximations for information retrieval. In: Z. W. Ras, (ed.), Methodologies for Intelligent Systems **4**, Elsevier (1989) 128–136
822. Srinivasan, P.: Intelligent information retrieval using rough set approximations. Information Processing and Management **25** (1989) 347–361
823. Srinivasan, P.: The importance of rough approximations for information retrieval. Journal of Man–Machine Studies **34** (1991) 657-671
824. Stefanowski, J.: Classification and decision supporting based on rough sets theory. In: [RS'92] 71–73; see also: [FCDS'93] 371–380
825. Stefanowski, J.: Using valued closeness relation in classification support of new objects. In: [SC] 324–327
826. Stefanowski, J., Słowiński, K.: Rough sets as a tool for studying attribute dependencies in the urinary stones treatment data. In: [RSDM] 177–195
827. Stefanowski, J., Słowiński, K.: Rough set theory and rule induction techniques for discovery of attribute dependencies in medical information systems. In: Komorowski, J., Żytkow, J. (eds.), Proceedings of the First European Symposium on Principles of Data Mining and Knowledge Discovery (PKDD'97). Trondheim, Norway, June 25–27, 1997, Lecture Notes in Artificial Intelligence **1263**, Springer–Verlag, Berlin (1997) 36–47
828. Stefanowski J., Słowiński K., Słowiński R.: Supporting of therapeutic decisions based on the rough sets theory. In: Proceedings of the 16th Meeting of the EURO Working Group, Operational Research Applied to Health Services, and the First Polish National Conference on Operational Research Applied to Health Systems, Książ 30.07–4.08, Wydawnictwo Politechniki Wrocławskiej, Wrocław (1991) 249–255
829. Stefanowski J., Słowiński R., Nowicki, R.: The rough sets approach to knowledge analysis for classification support in technical diagnostics of mechanical objects. In: F. Belli, F.J. Radermacher (eds.), Industrial & Engineering Applications of Artificial Intelligence and Expert Systems. Lecture Notes in Economics and Mathematical Systems **604**, Springer-Verlag, Berlin (1992) 324–334
830. Stefanowski, J., Vanderpooten, D.: A general two–stage approach to inducing rules from examples. In: [RSKD'93b] 317–325
831. Stepaniuk, J.: Elementary approximation theory. Bull. Polish Acad. Sci. Tech. **38/1–12** (1990) 121–128
832. Stepaniuk, J.: Approximation logic of programs. Bull. Polish Acad. Sci. Tech. **38/1–12** (1990) 129–138
833. Stepaniuk, J.: Applications of finite models properties in approximation and algorithmic logics. Fundamenta Informaticae **14/1** (1991) 91–108
834. Stepaniuk, J.: Methods of approximate reasoning for discrete problems (in Polish). Ph.D. Dissertation, supervisor A. Skowron, Warsaw University (1992)
835. Stepaniuk, J.: Decision rules for consistent decision tables. In: Proceedings of the Polish–English Meeting on Information Systems, Bialystok, Poland, September 22 (1993) 76–86
836. Stepaniuk, J.: Reasoning under uncertainty using rough set methods (in Polish). In: VII Forum Informatyki Teoretycznej, Wrocław, Poland, December 3–4 (1993)
837. Stepaniuk, J.: Decision rules for decision tables. Bull. Polish Acad. Sci. Tech. **42/3** (1994) 457–469

838. Stepaniuk, J.: Approximation of binary relations (in Polish). In: VIII Forum Informatyki Teoretycznej, Gdańsk, Poland, December 2–3, (1994)
839. Stepaniuk, J.: Discernibility and decision matrices (in Polish). In: R. Kulikowski, L. Bogdan (eds.), Wspomaganie Decyzji, Systemy Eksperckie, Institute of System Analysis PAS, Warsaw, Poland (1995) 440–443
840. Stepaniuk, J.: Properties of rough relations. Institute of Computer Science, Warsaw University of Technology, ICS Research Report **48/95** (1995)
841. Stepaniuk, J.: Applications of rough sets and Boolean reasoning for decision rules generation (in Polish). In: XXIV Ogólnopolska Konferencja Naukowo–Szkoleniowa Zastosowań Matematyki, September 19–26, Zakopane–Kościelisko, Poland (1995)
842. Stepaniuk, J.: Modal logics and feature construction (in Polish). In: IX Forum Informatyki Teoretycznej, Kraków, December 1–2 (1995)
843. Stepaniuk, J.: Learning and similarity based rough set model. In: Proceedings of the Conference Circuits, System and Computers, Hellenic Naval Academy, July 1–17, Greece (1996) 597–601
844. Stepaniuk, J.: Rough sets, discretization of attributes and stock market data. In: Proceedings of the Fourth European Congress on Intelligent Techniques and Soft Computing, Proceedings (EUFIT'96), September 2–5, Aachen, Germany (1996) **1** 202–203
845. Stepaniuk, J.: Construction of new attributes using rough set methods (in Polish). In: XXV Ogólnopolska Konferencja Naukowo–Szkoleniowa Zastosowań Mate - matyki, 17–24 września, Zakopane–Kościelisko (1996)
846. Stepaniuk, J.: Similarity based rough sets and learning. In: [RSFD'96] 18–22
847. Stepaniuk, J.: Rough sets, first order logic and attribute construction. In: Proceedings of the Sixth International Conference, Information Processing and Management of Uncertainty in Knowledge–Based Systems (IPMU'96), July 1–5, Granada, Spain (1996) **2** 887–890
848. Stepaniuk, J.: Properties and applications of rough relations. In: Proceedings of the Fifth International Workshop on Intelligent Information Systems, June 2–5, 1996, Dęblin, Poland, Institute of Computer Science, Polish Academy of Sciences, Warsaw (1996) 136–141
849. Stepaniuk, J.: Rough sets and similarity relations. In: R. Bogacz, L. Bobrowski (eds.), Symulacja w badaniach i rozwoju, Trzecie Warsztaty Naukowe PTSK, Wigry, 26–28 września, 1996, Warszawa (1997) 405–413
850. Stepaniuk, J.: Searching for proper approximation space. In: [BUL2] 43–50; see also: Proceedings of the Sixth International Workshop on Intelligent Information Systems, June 9–13, 1997, Zakopane, Poland, Institute of Computer Science, Polish Academy of Sciences, Warsaw (1997)
851. Stepaniuk, J.: Similarity relations and rough set model. In: MENDEL'97 Proceedings, June 25–27, Brno, Czech Republic (1997)
852. Stepaniuk, J.: Attribute discovery and rough sets. In: J. Komorowski, J. Żytkow (eds.), Proceedings of the First European Symposium on Principles of Data Mining and Knowledge Discovery (PKDD'97). Trondheim, Norway, June 25–27, 1997, Lecture Notes in Artificial Intelligence **1263**, Springer–Verlag, Berlin (1997) 145–155
853. Stepaniuk, J.: Rough sets similarity based learning. In: Proceedings of the Fifth European Congress on Intelligent Techniques and Soft Computing, September 8–12, Aachen, Germany, Verlag Mainz (1997) 1634–1638
854. Stepaniuk, J.: Conflict analysis and groups of agents. In: Proceedings of the Poster

Session at Tenth International Symposium on Methodologies for Intelligent Systems (ISMIS'97), October 15–18, Charlotte, USA (1997) 174–185
855. Stepaniuk, J., Kretowski, M.: Decision system based on tolerance rough sets. Institute of Computer Science, Warsaw University of Technology, ICS Research Report **36/95** (1995); see also: Proceedings of the Fourth International Workshop on Intelligent Information Systems, Augustów, Poland, June 5–9, 1995, Institute od Computer Science, Polish Academy of Sciences, Warsaw (1995) 62–73
856. Stepaniuk, J., Tyszkiewicz, J.: Probabilistic properties of approximation problems. Bull. Polish Acad. Sci. Tech. **39/3** (1991) 535–555
857. Suraj, Z.: Tools for generating and analyzing concurrent models specified by information systems. In: [RSSC'94] 610– 617
858. Suraj, Z.: Tools for generating concurrent models specified by information systems. In: [SC] 107–110
859. Suraj, Z.: An application of rough set methods to cooperative information systems re–engineering. In: [RSFD'96] 364–714
860. Suraj, Z.: Discovery of concurrent data models from experimental tables: A rough set approach. Fundamenta Informaticae **28/3–4** (1996) 353–376
861. Suraj, Z.: Reconstruction of cooperative information systems under cost constraints: A rough set approach. In: [RSSC'97] 399–402
862. Swiniarski, R.: Introduction to rough sets. In: Materials of The International Short Course of Neural Networks, Fuzzy and Rough Systems, Theory and Applications, April 2, San Diego State University, USA (1993)
863. Swiniarski, R.: Rough sets expert system for on–line prediction of volleyball game progress for US Olympic team. In: B.D. Czejdo, I.I. Est, B. Shirazi, B. Trousse (eds.), Proceedings of the Third Biennial European Joint Conference on Engineering Systems Design and Analysis, July 1–4, Montpellier, France (1996) 15–20
864. Swiniarski, R.: Rough sets expert system for robust texture classification based on 2D fast Fourier transormation spectral features. In: [RSFD'96] 419–425
865. Swiniarski, R.: Rough sets and principal component analysis and their applications in feature extraction and selection, data model building and classification. In: [FSRS]
866. Swiniarski, R.: Design of nonlinear texture data model using localized principal components and rough sets. Application to texture classification. In: Proceedings of International Symposium on Nonlinear Theory and its Applications, Hawaii, USA, November 29 – December 3 (1997) (accepted)
867. Swiniarski, R.: Intelligent feature extraction: Rough sets and Zernike moments for data preprocessing and feature extraction in handwritten digits recognition. In: Proceedings of International Symposium on Engineering of Intelligent Systems, EIS98. University of Laguna, Tenerife, Spain, February 11–13 (1998) (accepted)
868. Swiniarski, R.: Texture recognition based on rough sets and 2D FFT feature extraction. In: Proceedings of World Automation Congress. Anchorage, Alaska, USA, May 9–14 (1998) (accepted)
869. Swiniarski, R.: Pattern recognition using Zernike moments, rough sets and neural networks. In: Proceedings of World Automation Congress. Anchorage, Alaska, USA, May 9–14 (1998) (accepted paper)
870. Swiniarski, R.: Texture feature extraction, reduction and recognition based on rough sets. In: Symposium on Object Recognition and Scene Classification from Multispectral and Multisensor Pixels. Columbus, Ohio, USA, July 6–10 (1998) (accepted paper)

871. Swiniarski, R., Berzins, A.: Rough sets for intelligent data mining, knowledge discovering and designing of an expert systems for on-line prediction of volleyball game progress. In: [RSFD'96] 413–418
872. Swiniarski, R., Hunt, F., Chalvet, D., Pearson, D.: Feature selection using rough sets and hidden layer expansion for rupture prediction in a highly automated production system. In: Proceedings of the 12th International Conference on Systems Science, September 12–15, Wroclaw, Poland (1995); see also: Systems Science **23/1** (1997)
873. Swiniarski, R., Hunt, F., Chalvet, D., Pearson, D.: Intelligent data processing and dynamic process discovery using rough sets, statistical reasoning and neural networks in a highly automated production systems. In: Proceedings of the First European Conference on Application of Neural Networks in Industry, August, Helsinki, Finland (1995)
874. Swiniarski, R., Hunt, F., Chalvet, D., Pearson, D.: Feature selection using rough sets and hidden layer expansion for rupture prediction in a highly automated production system.
875. Swiniarski, R., Nguyen, J.: Rough sets expert system for texture classification based on 2D spectral features. In: B.D. Czejdo, I.I. Est, B. Shirazi, B. Trousse (eds.), Proceedings of the Third Biennial European Joint Conference on Engineering Systems Design and Analysis, July 1-4, Montpellier, France (1996) 3–8
876. Swiniarski, R., Zeng, H.: Modeling of intelligent processing systems based on rough sets. In: Proceedings of the IEEE International Conference on Artificial Intelligence and Control, November, China, (1997); see also: IEEE First International Conference on Intelligent Processing Systems (IEEE ICIPS), October 20–24, China, (1997)
877. Swiniarski, R., Zeng, H.: A new approach to halftoning based on error diffusion with rough set filtering. In: Internal Rep. SDSU and Sichuan Inst. of Tech., China (1997)
878. Synak, P.: Methods of approximate reasoning in discovery of rough dependencies (in Polish). Master Thesis, supervisor A. Skowron, Institute of Mathematics, Warsaw University (1996)
879. Szczerba, L.W.: Rough quantifiers. Bull. Polish Acad. Sci. Math. **35** (1987) 251–254
880. Szczerba, L.W.: Rough quantifiers have Tarski property. Bull. Polish Acad. Sci. Math. **35** (1987) 663–666
881. Szczuka, M.: Applications of rough sets methods in neural network processing. Institute of Computer Science, Warsaw University of Technology, ICS Research Reports **43/93** (1993)
882. Szczuka, M.: Function approximation by neural networks and rough sets (in Polish). Master Thesis, supervisor A. Skowron, Institute of Masthematics, Warsaw University (1995)
883. Szczuka, M.: Rough set methods for constructing neural network. In: Proceedings of the Third Biennal Joint Conference On Engineering Systems Design and Analysis, Session on Expert Systems, Montpellier, France (1996) 9–14
884. Szczuka, M., Ślęzak, D., Tsumoto, S.: An application of reduct networks to medicine - Chaining decision rules. In: [RSSC'97] 395–398
885. Szladow, A.J.: Datalogic/R: Mining the knowledge in databases. PC AI **7/1** (1993) 40–41
886. Szladow, A.J., Ziarko, W.: Development of reaction engineering model by discovering rules from process data. In: Proceedings of the Workshop on Knowledge Discovery in Databases, AAAI National Conference on Artificial Intelligence, Anaheim

(1991)
887. Szladow, A.J., Ziarko, W.: Knowledge–based process control using rough sets. In: [IDS] 49–60 7
888. Szladow, A.J., Ziarko, W.: Rough sets: Working with imperfect data. AI Expert **7** (1993) 36–41
889. Szladow, A.J., Ziarko, W.: Adaptive process control using rough sets. In: Proceedings of the International Conference of Instrument Society of America, ISA/93, Chicago (1993) 1421–1430
890. Szladow, A.J., Ziarko, W.: Application of rough sets theory to process control. In: Proceedings of Calgary 93 Symposium of Instrument Society of America, Calgary (1993)
891. Tanaka, H., Furuta, S., Maeda, Y.: On reducing information systems by accuracy measures in rough sets. In: Y.-Y. Chen, K. Hirota, and J.-Y. Yen (eds.), Proceedings of 1996 ASIAN FUZZY SYSTEMS SYMPOSIUM – Soft Computing in Intelligent Systems and Information Processing, December 11–14, Kenting, Taiwan, ROC. (1996) 139–144
892. Tanaka, H., Ishibuchi, H., Shigenaga, T.: Fuzzy inference system based on rough sets and its application to medical diagnostic. In: [IDS] 111–117
893. Tanaka, H., Koyama, K., Maeda, Y.: Reduction method for divisions of attributes and its application to medical data. In: [RSFD'96] 61–66
894. Tanaka, H., Koyama, K., Maeda, Y.: A method for reducing information systems with binary data by rough sets. In: Proceedings of the Fifth IEEE International Conference on Fuzzy Systems (FUZZ-IEEE'96), September 8–11, New Orleans, Louisiana (1996) 755–760
895. Tanaka, H., Tsumoto, S.: Incremental learning of probabilistic rules from clinical databases based on rough set theory. In: [RSSC'97] 387–390
896. Tannhauser, F.: Reduct generation (in Polish). Master Thesis, supervisor A. Skowron, Institute of Mathematics, Warsaw University (1993)
897. Teghem, J., Benjelloun, M.: Some experiments to compare rough set theory and ordinal statistical methods. In: [IDS] 267–286
898. Teghem, J., Charlet J.-M.: Use of 'rough sets' method to draw premonitory factors for earthquakes by emphasing gas geochemistry: The case of a low seismic activity context in Belgium. In: [IDS] 165–180
899. Tentush, I.: On minimal absorbent sets for some types of tolerance relations. Bull. Polish Acad. Sci. Tech. **43/1** (1995) 79–88
900. Tentush, I.: On rough mereological Cech topologies. Bull. Polish Acad. Sci. Math. **43/1** (1995) 75–85
901. Tentush, I.: On minimal absorbents and closure properties of rough inclusions: New results in rough set theory. Ph.D. Dissertation, supervisor L. Polkowski, Institute of Foundations of Computer Science, Polish Academy of Sciences (1997)
902. Than, S.: Reduction of input data in learning from examples. In: [DM] 136–143
903. Thiele, H.: Fuzzy rough sets versus rough fuzzy sets – An interpretation and a comparative study using concepts of modal logics. In: Proceedings of the Fifth European Congress on Intelligent Techniques and Soft Computing (EUFIT'97), September 9–11, Aachen, Germany, Verlag Mainz (1997) 159–167
904. Tseng, H.Ch., Lin, T.Y., Chi, C.W.: Adaptive aggregation of modular control. In: Y.-Y. Chen, K. Hirota, and J.-Y. Yen (eds.), Proceedings of 1996 ASIAN FUZZY SYSTEMS SYMPOSIUM – Soft Computing in Intelligent Systems and Information Processing, December 11–14, Kenting, Taiwan, ROC. (1996) 506–508

905. Tsumoto, S.: Domain experts' interpretation of rules induced from clinical databases. In: Proceedings of the Fifth European Congress on Intelligent Techniques and Soft Computing (EUFIT'97), Aachen, Germany, Verlag Mainz (1997) **1** 1639–1642
906. Tsumoto, S.: Extraction of expert's decision process from clinical databases using rough set model. In: J. Komorowski, J. Żytkow, (eds.), The First European Symposium on Principles of Data Mining and Knowledge Discovery (PKDD'97), June 25–27, Trondheim, Norway, Lecture Notes in Artificial Intelligence **1263**, Springer–Verlag, Berlin (1997) 58–67
907. Tsumoto, S.: Induction of positive and negative deterministic rules based on rough set model. In: Z.W. Ras, A. Skowron (eds.), Proceedings of the Tenth International Symposium on Methodologies for Intelligent Systems, Foundations of Intelligent Systems (ISMIS'97), October 15–18, Charlotte, NC, USA, Lecture Notes in Artificial Intelligence **1325**, Springer–Verlag, Berlin (1997) 298–307
908. Tsumoto, S., Tanaka, H.: Induction of probabilistic rules based on rough set theory. In: Algorithmic Learning Theory, Lecture Notes in Artificial Intelligence **744** Springer–Verlag, Berlin (1993) 441–448
909. Tsumoto, S., Tanaka, H.: PRIMEROSE: Probabilistic rule induction method based on rough set theory. In: [RSKD'93b] 274–281
910. Tsumoto, S., Tanaka, H.: Characterization of structure of decision trees based on rough sets and greedoid theory. In: [RSSC'94] 450–461; see also: [SC] 271–275
911. Tsumoto, S., Tanaka, H.: AQ, rough sets and matroid theory. In: [RSKD'93b] 290–297
912. Tsumoto, S., Tanaka, H.: Induction of medical expert system rules based on rough sets and resampling methods. In: Proceedings of the 18th Annual Symposium on Computer Applications in Medical Care, Journal of the AMIA **1** (supplement) (1994) 1066–1070
913. Tsumoto, S., Tanaka, H.: PRIMEROSE: Probabilistic rule induction method based on rough set and resampling methods. In: [CI] 389–405
914. Tsumoto, S., Tanaka, H.: Automated selection of rule induction methods based on recursive iteration of resampling. In: U.M. Fayyad, R. Uthurusamy (eds.), Proceedings of the First International Conference on Knowledge Discovery and Data Mining (KDD'95), August 20–21, 1995, Montreal, AAAI Press, Menlo Park CA (1995) 312–317
915. Tsumoto, S., Tanaka, H.: Automated discovery of functional components of proteins from amino-acid sequences based on rough sets and change of representation. In: U.M. Fayyad, R. Uthurusamy (eds.), Proceedings of the First International Conference on Knowledge Discovery and Data Mining (KDD'95), August 20-21, 1995, Montreal, AAAI Press, Menlo Park CA (1995) 318–324
916. Tsumoto, S., Tanaka, H.: Extraction of expert system rules based on rough sets and resampling methods. In: Proceedings of MEDINFO'95, Part 1, IMIA, Geneva, (1995) 861–865
917. Tsumoto, S., Tanaka, H.: Algebraic formulation of machine learning methods based on rough sets, matroid theory, and combinatorial geometry. In: [DM] 105–121; see also: M. De Glas, Z. Pawlak (eds.), Proceedings of the Second World Conference on Fundamentals of Artificial Intelligence (WOCFAI'95), July 13–17, Angkor, Paris (1995) 393–404; see also: [RSDM] 385–410
918. Tsumoto, S., Tanaka, H.: Automated discovery of medical expert system rules from clinical databases based on rough sets. In: E. Simoudis, J. Han, and U. Fayyad (eds.), Proceedings of the Second International Conference on Knowledge Discovery and Data Mining (KDD'96), August 2–4, Portland, Oregon, USA, AAAI Press,

Menlo Park (1996) 63–69
919. Tsumoto, S., Tanaka, H.: A common algebraic framework of empirical learning methods based on rough sets and matroid theory. In: [FI] 273–288
920. Tsumoto, S., Tanaka, H.: Extraction of medical diagnostic knowledge based on rough set based model selection and rule induction. In: [RSFD'96] 426–436; see also: Y.-Y. Chen, K. Hirota, and J.-Y. Yen (eds.), Proceedings of 1996 ASIAN FUZZY SYSTEMS SYMPOSIUM – Soft Computing in Intelligent Systems and Information Processing, December 11–14, Kenting, Taiwan, ROC. (1996) 145–151
921. Tsumoto, S., Tanaka, H.: Automated induction of medical expert system rules from clinical databases based on rough sets. In: Proceedings of the Fourth European Congress on Intelligent Techniques and Soft Computing (EUFIT'96), September 2–5, Aachen, Germany, Verlag Mainz (1996) **1** 154–158
922. Tsumoto, S., Tanaka H.: Domain knowledge from clinical databases based on rough set model. In: P. Borne, G. Dauphin–Tanguy, C. Sueur, and S. El Khattabi (eds.), Proceedings of IMACS Multiconference: Computational Engineering in Systems Applications (CESA'96) **3/4** July 9–12, Lille, France, Gerf EC Lille – Cite Scientifique (1996) 742–747
923. Tsumoto, S., Tanaka, H.: Incremental learning of probabilistic rules from clinical databases. In: Proceedings of the Sixth International Conference, Information Processing and Management of Uncertainty in Knowledge–Based Systems (IPMU'96), July 1–5, Granada, Spain (1996) **2** 1457–1462
924. Tsumoto, S., Tanaka, H.: Induction of expert system rules from databases based on rough set theory and resampling methods. In: Z.W. Ras, M. Michalewicz (eds.), Proceedings of the Ninth International Symposium on Methodologies for Intelligent Systems. Zakopane, Poland, June 9–13, Lecture Notes in Artificial Intelligence (ISMIS'96) **1079**, Springer–Verlag, Berlin (1996) 128–138
925. Tsumoto, S., Tanaka, H.: Classification and rule induction based on rough sets. In: Proceedings of the Fifth IEEE International Conference on Fuzzy Systems (FUZZ-IEEE'96), September 8–11, New Orleans, Louisiana (1996) 748–754
926. Tsumoto, S., Tanaka, H.: Machine discovery of functional components of proteins from amino–acid sequences based on rough sets and change of representation. In: [IA] 169–180
927. Tsumoto, S., Tanaka, H.: PRIMEROSE3: Induction and estimation of probabilistic rules from medical databases based on rough sets and resampling methods. In: M. Witten (ed.), Computational Medicine, Public Health, and Biotechnology, Building a Man in the Machine **III**, World Scientific, Singapore (1996) 1173–1189
928. Tsumoto, S., Ziarko, W.: The application of rough sets–based data mining technique to differential diagnosis of meningoencephalitis. In: Z.W. Ras, M. Michalewicz (eds.), Proceedings of the Ninth International Symposium on Methodologies for Intelligent Systems. Zakopane, Poland, June 9–13, Lecture Notes in Artificial Intelligence (ISMIS'96) **1079**, Springer–Verlag, Berlin (1996) 438–447
929. Tsumoto, S., Ziarko, W., Shan, N., Tanaka, H.: Knowledge discovery in clinical databases based on variable precision rough sets model. In: Proceedings of the 19th Annual Symposium on Computer Applications in Medical Care, New Orleans, 1995, Journal of American Medical Informatics Association Supplement (1995) 270–274
930. Vakarelov, D.: Abstract characterization of some knowledge representation systems and the logic NIL of nondeterministic information. In: Ph. Jorrand, V. Sgurev (eds.), Artificial Intelligence II, Methodology, Systems, Applications, North Holland, Amsterdam (1987)

931. Vakarelov, D.: S4 and S5 together - S4+5. In: Proceedings of the Eighth International Congress of Logic, Methodology and Philosophy of Science (LMPS'87), 17–22 August 1987, Moscow, USSR (1987) **5/3** 271–274
932. Vakarelov, D.: Modal logics for knowledge representation systems. Lecture Notes in Computer Science **363** (1989) 257–277; see also: Theoretical Computer Science **90** (1991) 433–456
933. Vakarelov, D.: A modal logic for similarity relations in Pawlak knowledge representation systems. Fundamenta Informaticae **15** (1991) 61–79
934. Vakarelov, D.: Logical analysis of positive and negative similarity relations in property systems. In: M. De Glas, D. Gabbay (eds.), First World Conference on the Fundamentals of AI (WOCFAI'91), 1–5 July 1991, Paris, France, (1991), 491–499
935. Vakarelov, D.: Polyadic modal logics. Journal of Applied Non–Classical Logics **1/1** (1991) 9–35
936. Vakarelov, D.: Consequence relations and information systems. In: [IDS] 391–400
937. Vakarelov, D.: A duality between Pawlak's information systems and bi–consequence systems. In: M. De Glas, Z. Pawlak (eds.), Proceedings of the Second World Conference on Fundamentals of Artificial Intelligence (WOCFAI'95), July 13–7, Angkor, Paris (1995) 417–428; see also: Studia Logica **55/1** (1995) 205–228 (full version)
938. Vakarelov, D.: Many–dimensional arrow structures: Arrow logics II. In: M. Marx, L. Polos, and M. Masuch (eds.), Arrow Logic and Multi–Modal Logic, CSLI Publications (1996) 141–187
939. Vakarelov, D.: Hyper arrow structures. Arrow Logic III. In: Proceedings of the Workshop Advances in Modal Logic, Berlin, October 8–10, (1996) (invited lecture)
940. Vakarelov, D.: Information systems, similarity relations and modal logics. In: [II] 492–550
941. Van Dyne, M.M., Woolery, L.K., Grzymała–Busse, J., Tsatsoulis, C.: Using machine learning and expert systems to predict preterm delivery in pregnant women. In: Proceedings of the Tenth Conference on Artificial Intelligence Applications (1994) 344–350
942. Velasco, I., Teo, D., Lin, T.: Design optimization of rough–fuzzy controllers using a genetic algorithm. In: [RSSC'97] 313–317
943. Vigneron, L., Wasilewska, A.: On generalized rough sets. In: [RSSC'97] 165–169
944. Vigneron, L., Wasilewska, A.: Rough and modal algebras. In: P. Borne, G. Dauphin–Tanguy, C. Sueur, and S. El Khattabi (eds.), Proceedings of IMACS Multiconference: Computational Engineering in Systems Applications (CESA'96) July 9–12, Lille, France, Gerf EC Lille - Cite Scientifique (1996) **3/4** 1107–1113
945. Vinterbo, S., Øhrn, A.: A rough set approach to clustering. In: [RSSC'97] 383–386
946. Wakulicz–Deja, A.: Foundations of information retrieval systems. Method analysis (in Polish). Akademicka Oficyna Wydawnicza, Warszawa (1995)
947. Wakulicz–Deja, A., Paszek, P.: Optimization of decision problems on medical knowledge basis. In: Proceedings of the Fifth European Congress on Intelligent Techniques and Soft Computing (EUFIT'97), Aachen, Germany, Verlag Mainz (1997) **1** 1607–1610
948. Wakulicz–Deja, A., Paszek, P.: Diagnose progressive encephalopathy applying the rough set theory. International Journal of Medical Informatics **46** (1997) 119–127
949. Wakulicz–Deja, A., Paszek, P., Marszał–Paszek, B.: Optimization of decision making process (diagnosis) in medical databases (in Polish). In: Second National Conference on Medical Informatics, Jaszowiec, October 16–18 (1997) 279–286
950. Wakulicz–Deja, A., Paszek, P., Marszał–Paszek, B., Emrich, E.: Applying rough sets to diagnosis in children's neurology. In: Proceedings of the Sixth Interna-

tional Conference, Information Processing and Management of Uncertainty in Knowledge–Based Systems (IPMU'96), July 1–5, Granada, Spain (1996) **3** 1463–1468
951. Wang, J., Shi, Z.: Learning maximal length rules. In: [RSSC'97] 85–88
952. Wang, J., Shi, Z.: Variable attribute selection. In: [RSSC'97] 355–358
953. Wang, P.P. (ed.): Second Annual Joint Conference on Information Sciences (JCIS-'95), September 28 – October 1, Wrightsville Beach, North Carolina, USA (1995)
954. Wasilewska, A.: Automatic decisions in information systems. The Journal of Symbolic Logic **51/4**, Abstract of Association for Symbolic Logic National Meeting in Washington DC, USA (1986) 1090–1091
955. Wasilewska, A.: On normal term theorem. In: Proceedings of Logic and Computer Science Workshop, University of Kentucky, Lexington, Kentucky (1986) 60–69
956. Wasilewska, A.: Decision algorithms in decision logic. The Journal of Symbolic Logic **52/1**, Abstract of Association for Symbolic Logic European Meeting in Paris, France (1987) 348
957. Wasilewska, A.: On static learning. The Journal of Symbolic Logic **53/4** (Abstracts of Association for Symbolic Logic National Meeting in Conjunction with the Symposium on the Theory of Computation (STOC), Courant Institute, New York, 1987) (1988) 1271–1272; see also: In: Proceedings of the 20th International Congress Communication and Cognition, #CC20 Gant, Belgium (1988) 225–228
958. Wasilewska, A.: On linguistic definability. The Journal of Symbolic Logic **53/4**, (Abstracts of American Linguistic Association and Association for Symbolic Logic Meeting in Stanford, Cal. USA, 1987) (1988) 1281–1282
959. Wasilewska, A.: On correctness of decision algorithms in information systems. Fundamenta Informaticae **11** (1988) 219–240
960. Wasilewska, A.: Definable sets in knowledge representation systems. Bull. Polish Acad. Sci. Tech. **35/9–10** (1988) 629–636
961. Wasilewska, A.: Knowledge representation systems – Syntactic methods. In: Proceedings of IPMU'88 Conference, Lecture Notes in Computer Science **313**, Springer–Verlag (1988) 239–254
962. Wasilewska, A.: Approximate classification and static learning. The Journal for the Integrated Study of Artificial Intelligence, Cognitive Science and Applied Epistemology **6/1** (1989) 75–87
963. Wasilewska, A.: Linguistically definable concepts and dependencies. The Journal of Symbolic Logic **54/2** (1989) 671–672
964. Wasilewska, A.: Syntactic decision procedures in information systems. Journal of Man–Machine Studies **30** (1989) 273–285
965. Wasilewska, A.: On syntactic and linguistic definability. In: Computing and Information, Proceedings of the International Conference on Computing and Information (ICC'89), May 23–27, Toronto, Canada (1989) 427–432
966. Wasilewska, A.: Conditional knowledge representation systems – Model for an implementation. Bull. Polish Acad. Sci. **37/1–6** (1990) 63–69
967. Wasilewska, A.: On rough and LT–fuzzy sets. In: Y.-Y. Chen, K. Hirota, and J.-Y. Yen (eds.), Proceedings of 1996 ASIAN FUZZY SYSTEMS SYMPOSIUM – Soft Computing in Intelligent Systems and Information Processing, December 11–14, Kenting, Taiwan, ROC. (1996) 13–18
968. Wasilewska, A.: Topological rough algebras. In: [RSDM] 411–425
969. Wasilewska, A., Banerjee, M.: Rough sets and topological quasi–Boolean algebras. In: [DM] 159–164

970. Wasilewska, A., Hadjimichael, M.: Rules reduction for knowledge representation systems. Bull. Polish Acad. Sci. **38/1–12** (1990) 113–120
971. Wasilewska, A., Hadjimichael, M.: Conditional probabilistic learning algorithm – CPLA. In: Emrich et al. (eds.), Methodologies for Intelligent Systems: Selected Papers, ICAIT, Knoxville, TN (1990) 180–190
972. Wasilewska, A., Hadjimichael, M.: An inductive learning system. Bull. Polish Acad. Sci. Tech. **39/3** (1991)
973. Wasilewska, A., Hadjimichael, M.: Application of a rough set–based inductive learning system. Fundamenta Informaticae **18** (1993) 209–220
974. Wasilewska, A., Hadjimichael, M.: Interactive inductive learning. Journal of Man–Machine Studies **38** (1993) 147–167
975. Wasilewska, A., Hadjimichael, M.: A lattice–based model for information generalization. Naval Research Laboratory, CA (1997)
976. Wasilewska, A., Hadjimichael, M., Menasalvas, E.: Transformatiom and generalization operators in data mining. Naval Research Laboratory, CA (1997)
977. Wasilewska, A., Vigneron, L.: Rough equality algebras. In: P.P. Wang (ed.): Proceedings of the International Workshop on Rough Sets and Soft Computing at Second Annual Joint Conference on Information Sciences (JCIS'95), Wrightsville Beach, North Carolina, 28 September – 1 October (1995) 26–30
978. Wasilewska, A., Vigneron, L.: Rough R4 and R5 algebras. International Journal on Information Sciences (special issue, to appear)
979. Wiweger, A.: On topological rough sets. Bull. Polish Acad. Sci. Math. **37** (1988) 51–62
980. Wójcik, B., Wójcik, B.E.: Rough grammar for high performance management of processes on a distributed system. In: [IDS] 401–418
981. Wójcik, B., Wójcik, B.E.: Parallel shape recognition using rough sets with learning. In: P.P. Wang (ed.): Proceedings of the International Workshop on Rough Sets and Soft Computing at Second Annual Joint Conference on Information Sciences (JCIS'95), Wrightsville Beach, North Carolina, 28 September – 1 October (1995) 201–204
982. Wójcik, B., Wójcik, B.E.: Intelligence of rough sets inferences vs statistics, neural nets and fuzzy sets – Methodological viewpoint. In: P. Borne, G. Dauphin–Tanguy, C. Sueur, and S. El Khattabi (eds.), Proceedings of IMACS Multiconference: Computational Engineering in Systems Applications (CESA'96) July 9–12, Lille, France, Gerf EC Lille – Cite Scientifique (1996) **3/4** 954–957
983. Wójcik, B., Ziarko, W.: Rough sets approach to analysis of databases of women with breast cancer treated in the US military facilities. In: P. Borne, G. Dauphin–Tanguy, C. Sueur, and S. El Khattabi (eds.), Proceedings of IMACS Multiconference: Computational Engineering in Systems Applications (CESA'96) July 9–12, Lille, France, Gerf EC Lille – Cite Scientifique (1996) **3/4** 748–752
984. Wójcik, Z.M.: Intelligent image filtering using rough sets. In: [RSKD'93b] 377–386
985. Wójcik, Z.M.: Accurate edge detection using rough sets. In: [RSKD'93b] 403–411
986. Wójcik, Z.M., Wójcik, B.M.: Structural modeling using rough sets. In: Proceedings of the Fifth IEEE International Conference on Fuzzy Systems (FUZZ-IEEE'96), September 8–11, New Orleans, Louisiana (1996) 761–766
987. Wójcik, Z.M., Wójcik, B.M., Lawrence, P., Zalewski, J.: Rough grammar computer vs dataflow pipeline machine and MIMD computers. In: [DM] 70–85
988. Wong, S.K.M.: Interval structure – A qualitative measure of uncertainty. In: [SC] 22–27

989. Wong, S.K.M.: A rough–set model for reasoning about knowledge. In: [RSSC'97] 187–190
990. Wong, S.K.M., Lingras, P.: The compatibility view of Shafer–Dempster theory using the concept of rough set. In: Z.W. Ras (ed.), Proceedings of the Fourth International Symposium on Methodologies for Intelligent Systems (ISMIS'89), Charlotte, North Carolina, October 12–14, North Holland (1989) 33–42
991. Wong, S.K.M., Nie, X.: Rough sets: A special case of interval structures. In: [RSKD' 93b] 217–226
992. Wong, S.K.M., Wang, L.S., Yao, Y.Y.: On modeling uncertainty with interval structures. In: [CI] 406–426
993. Wong, S.K.M., Yao, Y.Y.: Roughness theory. In: Proceedings of the Sixth International Conference, Information Processing and Management of Uncertainty in Knowledge–Based Systems (IPMU'96), July 1–5, Granada, Spain (1996) **2** 877–884
994. Wong, S.K.M., Ziarko, W.: On optimal decision rules in decision tables. Bull. Polish Acad Sci. Tech. **33/11–12** (1985) 693–696
995. Wong, S.K.M., Ziarko, W.: Comparison of the probabilistic approximate classification and the fuzzy set model. Fuzzy Sets and Systems **21** (1986) 357–362
996. Wong, S.K.M., Ziarko, W.: On learning and evaluation of decision rules in the context of rough sets. In: Proceedings of the International Symposium on Methodologies for Intelligent Systems, Knoxville (1986) 308–224
997. Wong, S.K.M., Ziarko, W.: Algebraic versus probabilistic independence in decision theory. In: Proceedings of the International Symposium on Methodologies for Intelligent Systems, Knoxville (1986) 207–212
998. Wong, S.K.M., Ziarko, W.: INFER: An adaptive decision support system. In: Proceedings of the Sixth International Workshop on Expert Systems and Their Applications, Avignon, France (1986) 713–726
999. Wong, S.K.M., Ziarko, W.: A machine learning approach to information retrieval. In: Proceedings of the Ninth International Conference on Research and Development in Information Retrieval, Pisa, Italy (1986) 228–233
1000. Wong, S.K.M., Ziarko, W.: Algorithm for inductive learning. Bull. Polish Acad. Sci. Tech. **34/5** (1986) 271–276
1001. Wong, S.K.M., Ziarko, W.: Remarks on attribute selection criterion in inductive learning based on rough sets. Bull. Polish Acad. Sci. Tech. **34/5–6** (1986) 271–276
1002. Wong, S.K.M., Ziarko, W., Ye, L.W.: Comparision of rough set and statistical methods in inductive learning. Journal of Man–Machine Studies **24** (1986) 53–72
1003. Woolery, L.K., Grzymala–Busse, J.: Machine learning for an expert system to predict preterm birth risk. Journal of the American Medical Informatics Association **1** (1994) 439–446
1004. Woolery, L., Grzymała–Busse, J.W., Summers, S., Budihardjo, A.: The use of machine learning program LERS–LB 2.5 in knowledge acquisition for expert system development in nursing. Computers in Nursing **9** (1994) 227–234
1005. Woolery, L., Van Dyne, M., Grzymała–Busse, J.W., Tsatsoulis, C.: Machine learning for development of an expert system to support nurses' assessment of preterm birth risk. In: Nursing Informatics: An International Overview for Nursing in a Technological Era, Proceedings of the Fifth International Conference on Nursing Use of Computers and Information Sci., June 17–22, San Antonio, TX, Elsevier (1994) 357–361
1006. Wróblewski, J.: Approximate solution of some NP–hard problems using genetic algorithms: Theoretical foundations and applications (in Polish). Master Thesis, supervisor A. Skowron, Institute of Mathematics, Warsaw University (1996)

1007. Wróblewski, J.: Finding minimal reducts using genetic algorithm. Institute of Computer Science, Warsaw University of Technology, ICS Research Report **14/95** (1995); see also: P.P. Wang (ed.): Proceedings of the International Workshop on Rough Sets and Soft Computing at Second Annual Joint Conference on Information Sciences (JCIS'95), Wrightsville Beach, North Carolina, 28 September – 1 October (1995) 186–189
1008. Wróblewski, J.: Genetic approach to scalar quantization. In: Proceedings of the Fourth International Workshop on Intelligent Information Systems, Augustów, Poland, June 5–9, 1995, Institute od Computer Science, Polish Academy of Sciences, Warsaw (1995)
1009. Wu, B.H.: An intelligent tutoring system using a rough set approach. In: P.P. Wang (ed.): Proceedings of the International Workshop on Rough Sets and Soft Computing at Second Annual Joint Conference on Information Sciences (JCIS'95), Wrightsville Beach, North Carolina, 28 September – 1 October (1995) 409–412
1010. Wu, T.: Rough number structure and computation. In: [SC] 248–251
1011. Wu, T.: Real number, dyadic number, and rough number structures and computations. In: [RSSC'97] 318–319
1012. Wybraniec–Skardowska, U.: On a generalization of approximation space. Bull. Polish Acad. Sci. Math. **37** (1989) 51–62
1013. Wybraniec–Skardowska, U.: Unit operations. Zeszyty Naukowe Wyzszej Szkoly Pedagogicznej w Opolu, Matematyka **XXVIII**, Opole (1992) 113–129
1014. Wybraniec–Skardowska, U.: Status of rough information and the problem of vaguenness (in Polish). In: J. Pelc (ed.), Nauka i Język, Biblioteka Myśli Semiotycznej, Warszawa (1994) 409–431
1015. Wybraniec–Skardowska, U.: A Logical explication of incomplete and uncertain information. In: V. Alagar, S. Bergler, and F.Q. Dong (eds.), Incompleteness and Uncertainty in Information Systems, Proceedings of SOFTEKS Workshop on Incompleteness and Uncertainty in Information Systems, Concordia University, Montreal, Canada 1993, Workshops in Computing, Springer–Verlag & British Computer Society, London, Berlin (1994) 180–188
1016. Wybraniec–Skardowska, U.: On a conceptualization of vague knowledge (in Polish). Filozofia Nauki **3/15** (1996) 45–62
1017. Wybraniec–Skardowska, U.: Logic in view of imprecision information, semiotic around the word: Synthesis in diversity. In: I. Rauch (ed.), Proceedings of the Fifth Congress of the International Association for Semiotic Studies, Berkely 1994, Mouton de Gruyter, Berlin–New York, (1997) 817–881
1018. Xiang, Y., Wong, M., Cercone, N.: Quantifying uncertainty of knowledge discovered from databases. In: [RSKD'93b] 63–73; see also: Quantification of uncertainty in classification rules discovered from databases. In: [CI] 427–441
1019. Yang, A., Grzymała–Busse, J.W.: Modified algorithms LEM1 and LEM2 for rule induction from data with missing attribute values. In: [RSSC'97] 69–72
1020. Yao, Y.Y.: On combining rough and fuzzy sets. In: [DM] 165-172
1021. Yao, Y.Y.: Constructive and algebraic approaches for generalized rough set models. In: [BUL1] 22–29
1022. Yao, Y.Y.: Representations of rough set approximation operators. In: Y.-Y. Chen, K. Hirota, and J.-Y. Yen (eds.), Proceedings of 1996 ASIAN FUZZY SYSTEMS SYMPOSIUM – Soft Computing in Intelligent Systems and Information Processing, December 11–14, Kenting, Taiwan, ROC. (1996) 7–12
1023. Yao, Y.Y.: Two views on the theory of rough sets in finite universes. In: [AR] 291–318

1024. Yao, Y.Y.: Combination of rough and fuzzy sets based on alpha-level sets. In: [RSDM] 301-321
1025. Yao, Y.Y.: Binary relation based neighborhood operators. In: [RSSC'97] 169-172
1026. Yao, Y.Y., Chen, X.: Neighborhood based information systems. In: [RSSC'97] 154-157
1027. Yao, Y.Y., Li, X.: Uncertain reasoning with interval-set algebra. In: [RSKD'93b] 178-185
1028. Yao, Y.Y., Li, X.: Comparison of rough-set and interval-set models for uncertain reasoning. In: [FI] 289-298
1029. Yao, Y.Y., Wong, S.K.M.: Generalization of rough sets using relationships between attribute values. In: P.P. Wang (ed.): Proceedings of the International Workshop on Rough Sets and Soft Computing at Second Annual Joint Conference on Information Sciences (JCIS'95), Wrightsville Beach, North Carolina, 28 September - 1 October (1995) 30-33
1030. Yao, Y.Y., Wong, S.K.M.: Generalized probabilistic rough set models. In: Y.-Y. Chen, K. Hirota, and J.-Y. Yen (eds.), Proceedings of 1996 ASIAN FUZZY SYSTEMS SYMPOSIUM - Soft Computing in Intelligent Systems and Information Processing, December 11-14, Kenting, Taiwan, ROC. (1996) 158-163
1031. Yao, Y.Y., Wong, S.K.M.: Interval approaches for uncertain reasoning. In: Z.W. Ras, A. Skowron (eds.), Proceedings of the Tenth International Symposium on Methodologies for Intelligent Systems, Foundations of Intelligent Systems (ISMIS'97), October 15-18, Charlotte, NC, USA, Lecture Notes in Artificial Intelligence **1325**, Springer-Verlag, Berlin (1997) 381-390
1032. Yao, Y.Y., Wong, S.K.M., Lin, T.Y.: A review of rough set models. In: [RSDM] 47-75
1033. Yao, Y.Y., Wong, S.K.M., Lingras, P.: A decision-theoretic rough set model. In: Z.W. Ras, M. Zemankova, M.L. Emrich (eds.), Proceedings of the Fifth International Symposium on Methodologies for Intelligent Systems (ISMIS'90), Knoxville, TN, October 25-27, North Holland (1990) 17-24
1034. Yasdi, R.: Combining rough sets learning and neural learning method to deal with uncertain and imprecise information. Neurocomputing **7** (1995) 61-84
1035. Yasdi, R., Ziarko, W.: Conceptual schema design: A machine learning approach. In: Proceedings of the Second International Symposium on Methodologies for Intelligent Systems, Charlotte, North Holland (1987) 379-391
1036. Yasdi, R., Ziarko, W.: A learning expert system for conceptual schema design. In: Proceedings of the International Conference on Artificial Intelligence, San Sebastian, Spain (1987); see also: J. Cambell, J. Cuena (eds.), Perspectives in Artificial Intelligence, Ellis Horwood (1989) **2** 162-175
1037. Yasdi, R., Ziarko, W.: An expert system for conceptual schema design: A machine learning approach. International Journal of Man-Machine Studies **29** (1988) 351-376; see also: B. Gains, J. Boose (eds.), Machine Learning and Uncertain Reasoning **3** Academic Press (1990) 165-190
1038. Yokomori, T., Kobayashi, S.: Inductive learning of regular sets from examples: A rough set approach. In: [SC] 69-72
1039. Zadeh, L.: Information granulation, fuzzy logic and rough sets. In: [RSFD'96]
1040. Żak, J., Stefanowski, J.: Determining maintenance activities of motor vehicles using rough sets approach. In: Proceedings of Euromaintenance'94 Conference, Amsterdam (1994) 39-42
1041. Zhang, Q., Han, Z., Wen, F.: A new approach for fault diagnosis in power systems based on rough set theory. In: Proceedings of International Conference on Advances

in Power System Control, Operation and Management (APSCOM'97), Hong Kong, China, November 11–14, (1997)
1042. Zhang, X., Katzberg, J., Ziarko, W., Shan, N.: Automatic discovery of a decision list from experimental data. In: Proceedings of Pacific–Asian Conference on Expert Systems, Hefei, China (1995) 529–535
1043. Zhong, N., Dong, J., Ohsuga, S.: Soft techniques to rule discovery in data. In: Proceedings of the Fifth European Congress on Intelligent Techniques and Soft Computing (EUFIT'97), Aachen, Germany, Verlag Mainz (1997) **1** 212–216
1044. Ziarko, W.: On reduction of knowledge representation. In: Proceedings of the Second International Symposium on Methodologies for Intelligent Systems, Colloquia Series, Charlotte (1987) 89–99
1045. Ziarko, W.: Acquisition of design knowledge from examples. Mathematical and Computer Modelling **10/8** (1988) 551–554
1046. Ziarko, W.: Data analysis and case–based expert system development tool 'Rough'. In: Proceedings of Case–Based Reasoning Workshop, Morgan Kaufmann, Los Altos, CA (1989) 356–361
1047. Ziarko, W.: A technique for discovering and analysis of cause–effect relationships in empirical data. In: International Joint Conference on Artificial Intelligence, Proceedings of the Workshop on Knowledge Discovery in Databases, Detroit (1989) 390–396
1048. Ziarko, W.: Determination of locally optimal set of features for representation of implicit knowledge. In: Proceedings of International Conference on Computing and Information, Toronto, North Holland (1989) 433–438
1049. Ziarko, W.: The discovery, analysis and representation of data dependencies in databases. In: G. Piatetsky–Shapiro, W.J. Frawley (eds.), Knowledge Discovery in Databases, AAAI Press/MIT Press (1991) 177–195
1050. Ziarko, W.: Acquisition of control algorithms from operation data. In: [IDS] 61–75
1051. Ziarko, W.: Generation of control algorithms for computerized controllers by operator supervised training. In: Proceedings of the 11th IASTED International Conference on Modelling, Identification and Control, Innsbruck, Austria (1992) 510–513
1052. Ziarko, W.: Analysis of uncertain information in the framework of variable precision rough sets model. In: [RS'92] 74–77; see also: [FCDS'93] 381–396 (full version)
1053. Ziarko, W.: Variable precision rough set model. Journal of Computer and System Sciences **46/1** (1993) 39–59
1054. Ziarko, W.: The first international workshop on rough sets: State of the art and perspectives. AI Magazine **14/3** (1993) 29–31
1055. Ziarko, W.: Analysis of uncertain information in the framework of variable precision rough sets. In: [FCDS'93] 381–396
1056. Ziarko, W.: Variable precision rough sets model. Journal of Computer and Systems Sciences **46/1** (1993) 39–59
1057. Ziarko, W.: Rough sets and knowledge discovery: An overview. In: [RSKD'93b] 11–15
1058. Ziarko, W.: Introduction to the special issue on rough sets and knowledge discovery. In: [CI] 223–226
1059. Ziarko, W.: Review of the basics of rough sets in the context of data mining. In: [RSFD'96] 447–457
1060. Ziarko, W.: Rough sets and data mining. In: Proceedings of the Fifth European Congress on Intelligent Techniques and Soft Computing (EUFIT'97), Aachen, Germany, Verlag Mainz (1997) **1** 206–211

1061. Ziarko, W., Cercone, N., Hu, X.: Rule discovery from databases with decision matrices. In: Z.W. Ras, M. Michalewicz (eds.), Proceedings of the Ninth International Symposium on Methodologies for Intelligent Systems (ISMIS'96), Zakopane, Poland, June 9–13, Lecture Notes in Artificial Intelligence **1079**, Springer–Verlag, Berlin (1996) 653–662
1062. Ziarko, W., Golan, R., Edwards, D.: An application of DATALOGIC/R knowledge discovery tool to identify strong predictive rules in stock market data. In: Proceedings of AAAI Workshop on Knowledge Discovery in Databases, Washington, DC (1993) 89–101
1063. Ziarko, W., Katzberg, J.: Control algorithms acquisition, analysis and reduction: Machine learning approach. In: Knowledge–Based Systems Diagnosis, Supervision and Control, Plenum Press, Oxford (1989) 167–178
1064. Ziarko, W., Katzberg, J.: Rough sets approach to system modelling and control algorithm acquisition. In: Proceedings of IEEE WESCANEX 93 Conference, Saskatoon (1993) 154–163
1065. Ziarko, W., Shan, N.: Acquisition and analysis of decision logic from data. In: Proceedings of the Third Annual North Atlantic Test Workshop (NATW'94), Lowell, Massachusetts (1994)
1066. Ziarko, W., Shan, N.: A non–inductive incremental approximate learning from examples. In: Proceedings of the Third Pacific Rim International Conference on Artificial Intelligence, Beijng (1994) 395–400
1067. Ziarko, W., Shan, N.: Machine learning: Rough sets perspective. In: Proceedings of the Second International Conference on Expert Systems for Development, Bangkok, IEEE Computer Society Press (1994) 114–119
1068. Ziarko, W., Shan, N.: Knowledge discovery as a search for classifications. In: [DM] 23–29
1069. Ziarko, W., Shan, N.: KDD–R: A comprehensive system for knowledge discovery using rough sets. In: [RSSC'94] 164–173; see also: [SC] 298–301
1070. Ziarko, W., Shan, N.: Machine learning through data classification and reduction. In: M. Dąbrowski, M. Michalewicz, and Z.W. Ras (eds.), Proceedings of the International Workshop on Intelligent Information Systems, Wigry, Poland, June 6–10, 1994, Institute of Computer Science, Polish Acadamy of Sciences, Warsaw (1994) III 121–132
1071. Ziarko, W., Shan, N.: Discovering attribute relationships, dependencies and rules by using rough sets. In: Proceedings of the 28th Hawaii International Conference on Systems Sciences, IEEE Computer Society Press **3** (1995) 293–299
1072. Ziarko, W., Shan, N.: Mining strong data patterns with KDD–R system. In: P.P. Wang (ed.): Proceedings of the International Workshop on Rough Sets and Soft Computing at Second Annual Joint Conference on Information Sciences (JCIS'95), Wrightsville Beach, North Carolina, 28 September – 1 October (1995) 89–90
1073. Ziarko, W., Shan, N.: On discovery of attribute interactions and domain classifications. In: [IA] 211–218
1074. Ziarko, W., Shan, N.: Rough sets and knowledge discovery. Encyclopedia of Computer Science and Technology, Marcell Dekker Inc. **35**, supplement **20** (1996) 369–379
1075. Ziarko, W., Shan, N.: A method for computing all maximally general rules in attribute–value systems. In: [CI] 223–234
1076. Ziarko, W., Shan, N.: Machine learning through data classification and reduction. Fundamenta Informaticae **30** (1997) 373–382

1077. Żytkow, J.: Approximate knowledge of many agents and discovery systems. In: A. Skowron (ed.), Logic, Algebra and Computer Science, Helena Rasiowa and Cecylia Rauszer in Memoriam, Bulletin of the Section of Logic **25/3–4** (1996) 185–189

In addition some information on rough set research papers is available via

- List of some publications: *http://www.cs.uregina.ca/ roughset*
- Information about ICS Reports on rough sets: *bsk@ii.pw.edu.pl*
- List of some publications
  - *http://papcio.ii.pw.edu.pl/roughbib.html*
  - *ftp://ftp.ii.pw.edu.pl/pub/Rough/roughbib.ps*
  - *ftp://ftp.ii.pw.edu.pl/pub/Rough/roughbib.txt*

APPENDIX 2:

SOFTWARE SYSTEMS

GROBIAN

Ivo Düntsch[1] *and Günther Gediga*[2]

[1] School of Information and Software Engineering, University of Ulster, Newtownabbey, BT 37 0QB, N.Ireland. E-mail: I.Duentsch@ulst.ac.uk
[2] FB Psychologie / Methodenlehre, Universität Osnabrück, 49069 Osnabrück, Germany. E-mail: ggediga@luce.psycho.Uni-Osnabrueck.DE

Abstract. GROBIAN is an implementation of the rough information analysis ROUGHIAN described in [2]. The acronym GROBIAN comes from the German "GROBmengen Informations ANalyse", which is the same as "ROUGH set Information ANalysis - and the meaning of the German GROBIAN and the English ROUGHIAN is (roughly) the same. GROBIAN is bilingual (English / German). Beside the standard procedures of Rough Set Data Analysis, such as reduct analysis, γ and α – statistics and rule generation, GROBIAN has the following enhanced features:

- A randomization test for rule significance including a sequential testing procedure,
- A simple method for data filtering which may increase the significance of rules,
- Model selection based on information theoretic entropy,
- Jack–knife validation,
- Training/Testing validation.

A menu driven recoding and restriction procedure for data manipulation is an additional feature of GROBIAN.

Developers

1. Main developer: Günther Gediga, FB Psychologie and Institut für semantische Informationsverarbeitung, Universität Osnabrück, ggediga@Luce.psycho.uni-osnabrueck.de
2. Ivo Düntsch, Faculty of Informatics, University of Ulster, I.Duentsch@ulst.ac.uk

Publications

Publications about the system are [3] and [1].

History

V 0.01 – 0.06	Versions for internal use only.
V 0.07	First published GROBIAN version, including significance testing, rough filtering, rough entropy (July 1996).
V 0.08 – 0.13	Several minor changes and bug removal,
V 0.14	Removed the RSL-library from most parts of GROBIAN.
V 0.15	Added JACK–KNIFE validation procedure.
V 0.16	Added batch processing from a list of reducts.
V 0.17	Sequential Randomization Test is now available for significance testing. Added TRAINING SET - TESTING SET validation procedure.
V 0.18	Result windows can be handled as objects (Oct 1997).

Input

One table which may be portioned by data restrictions to enable many tables-applications. ASCII-files, RSL-SYS-files and specific GROBIAN files are possible input formats. There is no direct interaction with DBMS systems (except via ASCII export – import).

Output

The results of the chosen procedure on screen and as an ASCII file.

System requirements

- Processor: Intel 80386 or later,
- MS Windows family (3.1, Win95, NT),
- $\geq$ 12 mb RAM,
- $\geq$ 10 mb disk space.

Evaluation criteria applied by the system

- Approximation quality γ,
- Statistical significance of γ,
- Drop of γ,
- Statistical significance of drop of γ,
- Jack – knifed predicted success (lower bound and expectation),
- Training – testing set prediction success (lower bound and expectation),
- Information analysis (standard and rough information),
- Statistical significance of information measures,

Data Visualisation

None at present.

Differences to other systems

Emphasis on non – invasive data filtering and statistical validation of ϵ – reducts of information systems.

References

1. Düntsch, I., Gediga, G.: The rough set engine GROBIAN. In: A. Sydow (ed.), Proceedings 15th IMACS World Congress, Berlin, Wissenschaft und Technik Verlag, Berlin **4** (1997) 613–618, Abstract: `http://www. infj. ulst.ac.uk/~cccz23/papers/grobian.html`
2. Düntsch, I., Gediga, G.: ROUGHIAN – Rough information analysis, an introduction. Technical report, University of Ulster, `http://www. infj. ulst. ac.uk/~cccz23/papers/roughian.html`. Extended abstract in: Proceedings 15th IMACS World Congress **4** (1997) 631–636
3. Düntsch, I., Gediga, G., Jütting, A.: GROBIAN – An engine for rough set data analysis. In: Proceedings of the First International Conference on Practical Aspects of Knowledge Management, Basel (1996)

RSDM: Rough Sets Data Miner, A System to Add Data Mining Capabilities to RDBMS

Maria C. Fernandez-Baizán, Ernestina Menasalvas Ruiz, José M. Peña and Borja Pardo Pastrana*

Departamento de Lenguajes y Sistemas Informáticos e Ingenería del Software
Faculdad de Informática, Campus de Montegancedo, Madrid, Spain
e-mail: {cfbaizan, emenasalvas}@.fi.upm.es, {chema, borja}@orion.ls.fi.upm.es

Abstract. RSDM represents the architecture of a system that adds KDD capabilities to RDBMS. It also provides an API to easily add new Data Mining capabilities to the system in a way transparent to the final user. As a result, RSDM acts as a generic engine of Data Mining algorithms. Three main goals guided the design development of the system:

- Efficiency when dealing with extralarge volumes of data.
- Easy enhacement of the system.
- Independency from the underlying RDBMS.

Different techniques have been applied in order to get Data Mining capabilities, but Rough Set [?, ?] methodology has to be remarked as it has been applied to get most of the functionalities that are already working in the system.

Capabilities added by the system

As it has been already mentioned, RSDM keeps the power of the relational systems while adding Data Mining capabilities. Rough Set methodology, generalization and relational database techniques among others have been integrated to provide the following features:

- **Discretization possibilities:** When dealing with quantitative data, before applying any mining algorithm, the values have to be discretized.
- **Reduction of the set of attributes:** A reducing algorithm discovers dependencies among data and redundancies. This allows the system to eliminate some attributes before the execution of the mining algorithms. The algorithm is based on the ideas of [?].
- **The ability for extracting discriminant rules:** Given a concept, the discriminant procedure finds rules that discriminate objects belonging to it.
- **Extraction of characteristic rules:** The extraction of characteristic rules gives a set of rules that characterize elements in a set.

* This work is supported by Spanish Ministry of Education under project PB95-0301

Architecture

In order to get the functionalities just mentioned, the following architecture has been developed.

- **User Communication Module:** This module is the one attending queries from the user. It translates a communication grammar into a sequence of orders sent to *working area*. When the query has been solved this module returns the results to the user.
- **Working Area:** This one is the module that manages the data the system is working with in a particular moment. The data that are the target of the operators are stored in this module as well as their results. Then the above module takes the results to present them to the user.

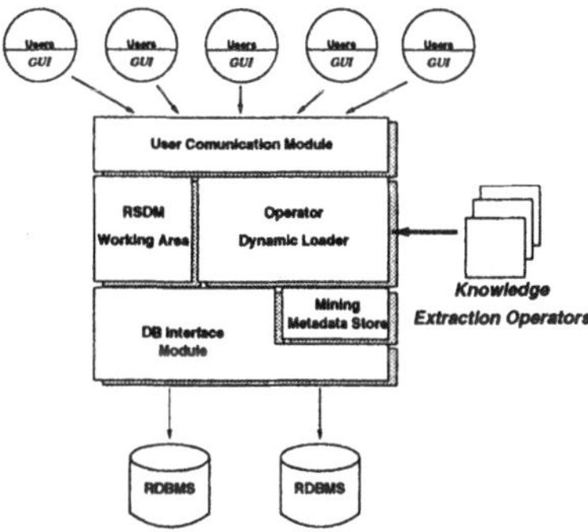

Fig. 1. System architecture

- **Operator Loader:** Queries from the user are sent by the *user communication module* to this one. Independently of the kind of algorithm, in order to gain effciency, every algorithm is going to be decomposed into atomic operations that will be executed in parallel. Each of these atomic units will be called an **'operator'**. In order for the query to be solved this module loads the needed operators in a dynamic way. The fact that algorithms are implemented in an independent way makes it possible to add new ones to the system without affecting its structure. In this way the architecture of RSDM gives support to new algorithms providing them the proper access, storage and communication methods needed to work properly.
- **Data Mining Catalog:** Some DM queries require prior to applying a process, to make calculations with the data. In order to gain efficiency, information about data that has to be repeatedly calculated when applying a particular algorithm, is precalculated and stored by this module. Some of the

information needed is already kept in the catalogue of relational database management systems. Storing information requires having available storage area, but the improvement in efficiency of the whole process justifies the cost.

- **Access to the Database:** The modules of the system will operate independently from the underlying RDBMS which will be transparent to them. Data needed by the system are asked to this module which in turn will translate the order to the particular database language. Thanks to the transparency supplied by this module, data from different platforms can be input to the system. To conclude, the independency from databases that RSDM provides, allows both to store and organize data in different databases as well as to use data from different platforms.

Implementation

The third of the goals of our design is to obtain an architecture that allows efficient management of extra large volumes of data to help companies to handle and analyse their data. Parallelism techniques have been used for the system to efficiently deal with extra large volumes of data.

In particular, *Light Weight Process* (LWP) technique has been used in the implementation of RSDM. The mentioned technique allows for the execution of different processes in a concurrent way, running in an environment of shared memory. Applying LWP makes it possible to execute the set of atomic operations in which each algorithm is structured in a parallel fashion. Each of these operators can be applied to different set of target data.

State of the art of the implementation

A prototype of the generic engine is already working. Algorithms for the calculation of positive region and reducts are also already working and it is possible to extract characteristic rules with the aid of them. Association rules algorithms are under development as well as a graphical user interface.

Comparison with other systems

RSDM has been conceived as an engine of KDD algorithms instead of a system that adds some particular capabilities. This approach has its advantages as well as disadvantages. On the one hand, the idea of building an engine of algorithms in contrast to all the existing Data Mining systems will allow to add new capabilities with the only task of building the module that will execute such capability, avoiding the complex process of codifying code for an integrated system in which you have to care not only for the coding of the algorithm but also for the communication, storing of intermediate results and so on. On the other hand, the process of construction of the architecture is more complex, and that is the reason why some Data Mining capabilities are not yet available such as the association rules, prediction, generalization tasks to name a few. However it has to be remarked once again that adding any of these capabilities is a straighforward task once the architecture has been finished.

Integration with RDBMS. RSDM provides an API to integrate different comercial and non-comercial database management systems. Up to the present moment the system interfaces **Postgres** and **Oracle**.

Methodologies that has been applied in the algorithms. Rough set theory as well as relational theory have been integrated by the discovery algorithms that have already been implemented in the system. Rough set operations have been translated first to relational algebra (when possible) and then to SQL in order to improve the efficiency. For a detailed description of the algorithms see [5].

Conclusions and future work

The architecture as well as the main properties of the system RSDM have been explained. Methodology used as well as advantages and disadvantages in comparison with other systems have been dicussed. We are currently working on the implementation and testing of tightly-coupled release of the algorithms as well as on the implementation of the association rules, extraction and discretization modules. The design of a proper *Data Warehouse* to help the mining tasks, is under development. As a result the data dictionary will be enhanced to support those data about the data that are neccesary for the efficient mining of the database.

Acknowledgements

We are very much indebted for inspiration to Dr. Ziarko, Dr. Pawlak and Dr. Skowron. Thanks are due to Dr. Wasilewska and Dr. Hadjimichael for several helpful comments.

References

1. Pawlak, Z.: Rough sets – Theoretical aspects of reasoning about data, Kluwer, Dordrecht (1991)
2. Skowron, A.: The discernibility matrices and functions in information systems. In: R. Słowiński (ed.), Decision Support by Experience, Kluwer Academic Publishers, Dordrecht (1992) 311–362
3. Ziarko, W.: Variable precision rough sets model. Journal of Computer and System Sciences **46** (1993) 39–59

LERS—A Knowledge Discovery System

Jerzy W. Grzymała-Busse

University of Kansas,
Lawrence, KS 66045, USA
e-mail: jerzy@eecs.ukans.edu

Abstract. LERS is a knowledge discovery system based on rough set theory. The system induces rules from databases. Rule induction is based on four different algorithms. Two algorithms are used for induction rules in the minimal discriminant form, remaining two are used for induction of all potential rules hidden in a database. Input data may be imperfect: data may contain errors, numerical attributes, missing attribute values and inconsistencies. LERS classifies new, unseen cases using principles similar to the bucket brigade algorithm. LERS is also equipped with a tool for multiple-fold cross validation. The system has been used in the medical area, nursing, global warming, environmental protection, natural language, and data transmission. LERS may process big datasets and frequently outperforms not only other rule induction systems but also human experts.

Introduction

The system LERS (Learning from Examples based on Rough Sets) was developed under the guidance of Jerzy Grzymala-Busse at the University of Kansas. The first implementation of the system was ready in 1988 [2, 8]. The full description of the LERS rule induction algorithms may be found in [3, 5]. The classification system of LERS was described in [6]. Some LERS applications were presented in [7].

Input data

Input data to LERS is any database in the format of text (i.e., saved as an ASCII file). The only modification is the addition of a header. The header contains two lists. The first list is a declaration of variables. It contains as many symbols as variables in the database, and two additional characters: "<" at he beginning of the list and ">" at the end of the list. Attributes are denoted by *a*s and decisions by *d*s. The first list may contain the letter x (corresponding variable and variable values will be ignored in all subsequent computations). The second line, starting from "[" and ending with "]", contains names of all variables. Missing values of attributes may be denoted by any special symbols, e.g., by question marks.

Output knowledge

LERS is based on rough set theory [9, 10], for inconsistent data it induces two sets of rules: *certain* rule set and *possible* rule set. The first set is computed from lower approximations of concepts, the second from upper approximations. Every rule is preceded by three numbers: specificity (the total number of attribute-value pairs on the left-hand side of the rule), strength (the total number of examples correctly classified by the rule during training), and the total number of training cases matching the left-hand side of the rule.

System Architecture

The first option available for the LERS user is using a tool for checking errors in the input data. Recognized errors are: numerical values out of the range, mixing symbolic values with numbers in the domain of the same attribute, and missing values (not denoted by special characters).

The next possibility of preprocessing is using one of several possible approaches to handling missing attribute values. For example, cases with missing attribute values may be ignored during rule induction, may be replaced by all existing attribute values for the attribute, or may be treated as special symbols.

If the input data have numerical attributes, one of many LERS tools for discretization should be used. LERS uses global approaches for discretization, i.e., all numerical attributes are discretized simultaneously. One may use a method based on cluster analysis, or global versions of methods based on equal interval width, equal frequency, or minimal entropy.

In general, LERS uses two different approaches to rule induction: one is used in machine learning, the other in knowledge acquisition [4]. In machine learning, or more specifically, in learning from examples, the usual task is to learn discriminant description, i.e., to learn the smallest set of minimal rules, describing the concept. To accomplish this goal LERS uses two algorithms: LEM1 and LEM2 (LEM1 and LEM2 stand for Learning from Examples Module, version 1 and 2, respectively). Both algorithms are described in [5]. The option LEM2 of LERS is most frequently used since—in most cases—it gives best results [1].

On the other hand, if the user wants to induce rules using an approach based on knowledge acquisition, two additional options of LERS are available. The first option computes global coverings of required size and then rules from all of these coverings using similar ideas as in LEM1. The other option is similar to LEM2 (both are local) [5, 6]. All rules in minimal form that can be derived from the input data are computed. In both options used algorithms are of exponential time complexity, with respect to the number of attributes.

A classification system uses the rule set to classify new cases. In general, the classification system classifies testing data using the rule set induced from training data. The new classification system of LERS is a modification of the bucket brigade algorithm [m]. The decision to which concept an example belongs is made on the basis of four factors: strength, specificity, matching factor, and support. Support is defined as the sum of scores of all matching rules from the concept. The concept C for which the support, i.e., the following expression

$$\sum_{\substack{\text{partially matching} \\ \text{rules } R \text{ describing } C}} Matching\_factor(R) * Strength(R) * Specificity(R)$$

is the largest is the winner and the example is classified as being a member of C.

LERS is fully automated. However, the user may have some input first by selecting options of the system, and in some cases, e.g., during error recognition or inducing rules from all global coverings, by a direct interaction with the system.

Using Rules

In LERS it is assumed that the rule set should be used automatically by a classification subsystem of LERS. Every new case is classified by this subsystem. On the other hand, induced rules are available and comprehensible by the user. Thus, it is possible to use rules manually, like in other systems.

Final Remarks

The performance of the LERS system is fully comparable with performance of AQ15 and C4.5 [6]. Advantages of the system are: a big family of discretization methods and many possible approaches for missing attribute values. Another advantage is a sound approach (based on rough set theory) to inconsistencies in input data. A disadvantage of the system is that—for time being—it is dispersed among a few programs. Moreover, the code was written having a specific platform: DEC Alpha ASP machines in mind.

References

1. Chan, C. C., Grzymała-Busse, J. W.: On the attribute redundancy and the learning programs ID3, PRISM, and LEM2. Department of Computer Science, University of Kansas, TR-91-14 (1991)
2. Dean, J. S., Grzymała-Busse, J. W.: An overview of the learning from examples module LEM1. Department of Computer Science, University of Kansas, TR-88-2 (1988) 1–13
3. Grzymała-Busse, J.W.: An overview of the LERS1 learning system. In: Proceedings of the 2nd Int. Conf. on Industrial and Engineering Applications of Artificial Intelligence and Expert Systems, Tullahoma, TN, June 6–9 (1989) 838–844
4. Grzymała-Busse, D. M., Grzymała-Busse, J. W.: The usefulness of machine learning approach to knowledge acquisition. Computational Intelligence **11** (1995) 268–279
5. Grzymała-Busse, J. W.: LERS—A system for learning from examples based on rough sets. In: Słowiński, R. (ed.), Intelligent Decision Support. Handbook of Applications and Advances of the Rough Sets Theory. Kluwer Academic Publishers, Dordrecht (1992) 3–18

6. Grzymała-Busse, J. W.: Managing uncertainty in machine learning from examples. In: Proceedings of the Third Intelligent Information Systems Workshop, Wigry, Poland, June 6–11 (1994) 70–84
7. Grzymała-Busse, J. W.: Applications of the rule induction system LERS. (in this book)
8. Grzymała-Busse, J.W., and Sikora, D.J.: LERS1—A system for learning from examples based on rough sets. Department of Computer Science, University of Kansas, TR-88-5 (1988) 1–16
9. Pawlak, Z.: Rough sets – Theoretical aspects of reasoning about data. Kluwer Academic Publishers, Dordrecht (1991)
10. Pawlak, Z., Grzymała-Busse, J.W., Słowiński, R., Ziarko, W.: Rough sets. Communications of the ACM **38** (1995) 88–95

TRANCE: A Tool for Rough Data Analysis, Classification, and Clustering

Wojciech Kowalczyk

Vrije Universiteit Amsterdam
De Boelelaan 1081A
1081 HV Amsterdam, The Netherlands
e-mail:wojtek@cs.vu.nl

Abstract. TRANCE is a system for generating rough models of data. A rough model consists of a partition of the data set into a number of clusters which are labelled with decisions. The system automatically searches for partitions which optimize a pre-defined performance measure. The conceptual simplicity of the underlying models makes their interpretation very simple. They are also used for extracting relevant rules. Low complexity of the involved algorithms allows for automatic (or semi-automatic) discovery of relevant attributes.

The system has been successfully applied in the field of marketing and finance to tasks such as: fraud detection, modelling customer behaviour, retention, attrition.

Introduction

- Developer(s) name(s), current affiliation(s), and addresses:
  dr. W. Kowalczyk
  Faculty of Mathematics and Computer Science
  Vrije Universiteit Amsterdam, De Boelelaan 1081A
  1081 HV Amsterdam, The Netherlands

- Date of first publication: November 1996.
- List of publications about the system:
  1. Kowalczyk, W.: TRANCE: A tool for rough data analysis, classification and clustering. In: S. Tsumoto, S. Kobayashi, T. Yokomori, H. Tanaka and A. Nakamura (eds.), Proceedings of the Fourth International Workshop on Rough Sets, Fuzzy Sets, and Machine Discovery (RSFD'96), Tokyo University (1996) 269–275
  2. Kowalczyk, W.: Analyzing temporal patterns with rough sets. In: Proceedings of the Fourth European Congress on Intelligent Techniques and Soft Computing (EUFIT'96), September 2–5, Aachen, Germany, Verlag Mainz, Aachen **1** (1996) 139–143
  3. Wilting, R.: Predicting card credit. A research on predictable behaviour of clients applying for card credit by means of Rough Data Models (in

Dutch). Master Thesis, Vrije Universiteit Amsterdam and Visa Card Services, March, 1997.

4. Kowalczyk, W. and Slisser, F.: Analyzing customer retention with rough data models. In: J. Komorowski, J. Zytkow, (eds.), The First European Symposium on Principle of Data Mining and Knowledge Discovery (PKDD'97), June 25–27, Trondheim, Norway, Lecture Notes in Artificial Intelligence **1263**, Springer–Verlag, Berlin (1997) 4–13

- History: The first prototype of the system was developed in 1996. In 1997 the system was extended by rule extraction procedures, improved search algorithms and a better user interface.

Input

The current version of TRANCE can handle only numerical data tables which are provided as text files.

Output knowledge

The system generates rough data models which are represented in the form of tables (lists of clusters), plots (various performance measures, e.g., gain and response curves), and lists of rules.

System architecture

TRANCE is a system that supports the process of constructing and evaluating rough data models. Basically, it can be used for processing numeric-valued data tables. It has been implemented in the MATLAB system–a general purpose system for matrix computations and visualization. TRANCE contains a number of modules that cover different stages of model construction process. The Data Pre-Processing Module contains numerous procedures (in MATLAB's terminology: m- files) that are useful for data pre-processing: procedures for removing outliers, for discretizing attributes, for statistical data analysis, for processing time series (rescaling, smoothing, aggregation), etc. The central part of the system is the Search Module. It is responsible for searching through the pre-defined space of models for an optimal one. Results of this module are passed to the Model Evaluation Module which contains procedures that calculate and plot various performance measures. Finally, the Rule Extraction Module generates rules from the best model. All modules are integrated by the MATLAB command interpreter which takes care of handling procedure calls and parameter passing. Small data sets can be processed interactively; bigger sets are processed in batch mode.

Search for knowledge

TRANCE tries to find partitions of the universe which optimize certain criterion. The objective function is usually expressed in terms of local properties of the resulting classification model (e.g., the highest classification rate of decision rules which cover at least 5% of all cases). The system uses either systematic or local search strategy. It makes no use of background knowledge.

User

The user of the system should know basic concepts of data mining and rough data models. Moreover, (s)he should be able to write simple scripts in MATLAB.

KDD process

TRANCE is suitable for processing huge data sets with millions of records. It has been successfully applied in the field of marketing and finance to tasks such as: fraud detection, modelling customer behaviour, retention, attrition. Due to the conceptual simplicity of the underlying models, results generated with TRANCE are easy to interpret. Low complexity of the involved algorithms allows for automatic (or semi-automatic) discovery of relevant attributes. On the other hand, models constructed with TRANCE are usually based on a few (3-5) attributes which may result in a poor accuracy. Another serious limitation of TRANCE is its inability of processing non-numerical data. Current research focuses on the elimination of these two drawbacks. The system and some of its applications are described in this book.

ProbRough — A System for Probabilistic Rough Classifiers Generation

Andrzej Lenarcik and Zdzisław Piasta

Kielce University of Technology
Mathematics Department
Al. 1000-lecia P.P. 5, 25-314 Kielce, Poland
e-mail: {zpiasta,lenarcik}@sabat.tu.kielce.pl

Abstract. ProbRough is a system for inducing decision rules from data. The rules enable us to predict values of a decision attribute for new objects on the basis of condition attribute values. Input data are given in the form of one decision table. Objects are characterized by any mixture of qualitative and quantitative condition attributes and one discrete decision attribute. The system accepts noisy and inconsistent data with missing attribute values. Background knowledge is used in the form of prior probabilities of decisions and different costs of misclassification. The domains of decision rules that compose the resultant rough classifiers are disjoint and fill up the space of all possible values of condition attributes. The set of domain rules forms a partition of this space. The ProbRough system searches through various partitions using a criterion based on minimizing the misclassification costs. ProbRough has demonstrated its usefulness on many real-world classification and knowledge discovery problems from the area of business, technology and medicine.

Introduction

The system ProbRough has been developed by A. Lenarcik and Z. Piasta at Kielce University of Technology. A description of the algorithm is presented in [5]. The extended versions of the system are described in [9] and [10].

An inspiration for developing the system was the problem of discretization of continuous attributes in a context of the rough set theory. A solution of this problem is proposed in [2]. In order to express the discovered knowledge in the form of a rule set a notion of a rough classifier was introduced ([3], [4], [9], [10]). Examples of successful applications of the ProbRough system may be found in [7], [8] and [1].

Input data

Input data to the ProbRough system is one decision table given as an ASCII file. Each condition attribute is characterized by its type: continuous, discrete ordered, or qualitative unordered. Continuous attributes are discretized by choosing elements from the sets of intermediate values. These sets are given in advance or can be obtained from the input decision table. Background knowledge is represented by prior probabilities that reflect the distribution of the decisions in the universe and a cost matrix that involves the unit costs of misclassification.

Output knowledge

For each number of iterations in the phase of partitioning the space of condition attribute values, not greater than the prespecified maximum number of iterations, the ProbRough system generates a family of equivalent decision rule sets (rough classifiers). The strength of each induced rule is expressed by the number of objects confirming the rule and by the average costs associated with the decisions.

System architecture and search strategy

ProbRough tries to find an optimal partition of the space of condition attribute values minimizing the average misclassification cost, and then induce the decision rules that describe the whole partition in a compact way. As a search strategy, ProbRough uses a beam search which is guided by the cost criterion. Each decision rule assigns a decision or a set of decisions to the subset of the space of values of condition attributes which is the domain of the rule. Each rule-domain has the form of a special Cartesian product which enables the presentation of the rule in a simple if—then logical form.

The system accepts missing attribute values. The objects with missing values are removed from the computations or a missing value is treated as an additional value of the attribute. The way of missing values treatment has to be given for each attribute. The minimum percentage of all learning objects that has to be used in computing the criterion value is given in advance. ProbRough accepts qualitative attributes with a great number of values. For each such value set all possible divisions into two disjoint subsets are considered in the phase of partitioning the space of condition attribute values. The number of divisions can not exceed the given upper bound.

Final remarks

Rule-sets generated by the ProbRough system are comparable or superior to many acknowledged classifiers, both in terms of predictive accuracy and capability to explain the learned knowledge. ProbRough does not require that input data is kept in the main memory. As a result, rough classfiers can be generated from large databases with practically unlimited numbers of objects and attributes. Any new object is covered by exactly one decision rule of the resultant classifier. The rough classifiers are not sensitive to outliers in the data. A disadvantage of ProbRough is that so far it is implemented on a PC DOS platform only (Unix and WindowsNT C versions are in preparation).

Acknowledgements

The ProbRough system is a result of work that was supported by the State Committee for Scientific Research in Poland (KBN) under grants #8 S503 033 06, #8 S503 021 06 and #8 T11C 010 12.

References

1. Kowalczyk, W., Piasta, Z.: Rough sets - inspired approach to knowledge discovery in business databases. In: The Second Pacific-Asia Conference on Knowledge Discovery and Data Mining (PAKDD-98), Melbourne, Australia, April 15-17, (1998), (submitted)
2. Lenarcik, A., Piasta, Z.: Discretization of condition attribute space. In: R. Słowiński (ed.), Intelligent Decision Support. Handbook of Applications and Advances of the Rough Sets Theory, Kluwer, Dordrecht (1992) 373–389
3. Lenarcik, A., Piasta, Z.: Rough classifiers. In: W. Ziarko (ed.), Rough Sets, Fuzzy Sets and Knowledge Discovery (RSKD'93). Workshops in Computing, Springer–Verlag & British Computer Society, London, Berlin (1994) 298–316
4. Lenarcik, A., Piasta, Z.: Deterministic rough classifiers. In: T.Y. Lin (ed.), The Third International Workshop on Rough Sets and Soft Computing Proceedings (RSSC'94), San Jose State University, San Jose, California, USA November 10-12,(1994) 434–441
5. Lenarcik, A., Piasta, Z.: An invariant method of rough classifier construction. In: Proceedings of the Poster Session of Ninth International Symposium on Methodologies for Intelligent Systems, Proceedings of the Poster Session, (ISMIS'96), Zakopane, Poland, June 9–13, Oak Ridge Laboratory (1996) 146–156
6. Lenarcik, A., Piasta, Z.: Probabilistic rough classifiers with mixtures of discrete and continuous condition attributes. In: T.Y. Lin, N. Cercone (eds.): Rough Sets and Data Mining. Analysis for Imprecise Data. Kluwer Academic Publishers, Dordrecht (1997) 373–383
7. Piasta, Z.: Rough classifiers in intelligent support of business decisions. In: Proceedings of the First Polish Conference on Theory and Applications of Artificial Intelligence (CAI'96), Łódź, Poland (1996) 103–111
8. Piasta, Z.: Transforming data into engineering knowledge with rough classifiers. In: A. M. Brandt (ed.), Optimization Methods for Material Design of Cement-based Composites, Thomson Science & Professional, London (to appear)
9. Piasta, Z., Lenarcik, A.: Rule induction with probabilistic rough classifiers. ICS Research Report **24/96** Warsaw University of Technology (1996), to appear in: Machine Learning
10. Piasta, Z., Lenarcik, A.: Learning rough classifiers from large databases with missing values (in this book)

The Rosetta Software System

Aleksander Øhrn[1], *Jan Komorowski*[1], *Andrzej Skowron*[2], *Piotr Synak*[3]

[1] Department of Computer and Information Science, Norwegian University of Science and Technology, 7034 Trondheim, Norway
[2] Institute of Mathematics, Warsaw University, 02-097 Warsaw, Banacha 2, Poland
[3] Polish-Japanese Institute of Computer Techniques, 02-018 Warsaw, Koszykowa 86, Poland

Abstract. ROSETTA is a software system for knowledge discovery and data mining within the framework of rough set theory. More than a flexible collection of algorithms, ROSETTA also offers a user-friendly GUI environment in which objects can be interactively manipulated and processed. The system is designed to support the overall knowledge discovery process – from initial browsing and preprocessing of the data, via reduct computation and rule generation, to validation and analysis of the extracted rules.

Introduction

As with all fields concerning themselves with empirical modelling, knowledge discovery and data mining have a high experimental content. The modelling process thus necessitates a set of tools that are both very flexible and user-friendly. Generally available software systems for this have been scarce, and rough set oriented ones even more so. In response to this, the ROSETTA [8, 9] system was developed. ROSETTA is a toolkit for knowledge discovery and data mining [2] within the framework of rough set theory [3]. Using tables with historical data, its basic purpose is to compute relevant feature subsets and generate classification rules. An extensive support environment is included around this – both in the form of a large base of algorithms, and by setting the tools in a highly intuitive GUI environment such that intermediate results can be viewed and analyzed, and decisions for further processing made. Intended users are people with some knowledge of rough set concepts, although the user-friendly GUI lowers this threshold. Also, the system can be configured to cater for less experienced users by allowing scripts to be run that partially automate the modelling process.

ROSETTA is not tied up to any particular application domain, but has already served as a research tool in different fields [6, 7, 10]. A restricted version of the system is made publicly available on the Internet [11] for non-commercial use. ROSETTA runs on 32-bit Windows platforms.

Input and output

As its basic input, ROSETTA takes flat data tables. Integration with a diverse range of data sources is possible, as ROSETTA can interface directly with such by means of ODBC. This means that tables and/or views in e.g. a spreadsheet or a relational DBMS may be analyzed directly.

Since a fundamental premise of rough set theory is that objects are perceived only through the information that is available about them, any background knowledge is assumed incorporated into the tables to analyze if such is to be used. In the current version ROSETTA does not support type hierarchies, although some simple metadata can be supplied.

Many structural objects are output from ROSETTA that are presented in the GUI, e.g. tables, reducts, rules, confusion matrices, partitions and set approximations. Also, very detailed output may be generated and output as ASCII log files and HTML documents.

Most structural objects are exportable to alien formats, e.g. to Prolog. This opens up a connection to other more advanced inference engines, where also any available domain theories can be utilized.

System features

ROSETTA was designed for extensibility, and the list of features given is likely to grow.

Knowledge discovery and data mining within the framework of rough sets covers several issues [3, 4], most of which are implemented in ROSETTA. Features currently offered by the computational kernel include algorithms for:

- Preprocessing of data tables with missing values.
- Discretization of numerical attributes.
- Computation of (approximate or absolute) reducts and rules.
- Filtering of reducts and rules according to specified evaluation criteria.
- Classification of new objects with synthesized rules using voting schemes.
- Computing rough set approximations.

Also, ROSETTA can execute command scripts, hence enabling automation of lengthy and repetitive user-specified command sequences without the use of the GUI. Examples of such are algorithmic pipelines and n-fold crossvalidation.

The ROSETTA GUI is a user-friendly environment for interactively manipulating data and triggering computations. With it, the user may control the flow of structures in the knowledge discovery pipeline; from selection of target data, preprocessing and transformation, through the actual data mining step, to interpretation and evaluation of the discovered patterns. Some of the features currently offered by the ROSETTA GUI include:

- Full Windows GUI conformance.
- Organization of project items in trees in order to retain data-navigational abilities.

- Viewing of all structures in intuitive grid environments using terms from the modelling domain.
- Context-sensitive pop-up menus and drag-and-drop functionality.
- Automatic generation of annotations that document the steps taken in a modelling session.

The tree organization of a project and the automatic generation of annotations facilitate experimenting with steps and parameter settings in the knowledge discovery process. For every step it is straightforward to create an alternative development, represented by a new branch in the tree. By allowing branching, more flexibility is offered than with a traditional line-oriented modelling paradigm.

In its present form, the ROSETTA GUI does not offer support for advanced graphical presentations and other visual techniques for knowledge discovery and data mining.

Search for knowledge

The space of rules considered by ROSETTA consists of if-then rules with a conjunctive antecedent and a disjunctive consequent. As a rule is trivially generated from a table once a suitable attribute (feature) subset is found, the major computational effort lies in calculating reducts, or approximations of such. A reduct is a minimal attribute (feature) subset that preserves an indiscernibility relation. Such a relation may be formulated either for the full system or relative to a particular class of objects.

Computing reducts is equivalent to computing prime implicants of a Boolean function, an NP-hard problem. An exhaustive search is thus not suitable for large tables. ROSETTA therefore offers heuristics for search and approximation based on both resampling techniques [1] and genetic algorithms [5]. Also, one may view discretization as a preprocessing step that may potentially significantly ease this search.

Discovered patterns should also be interesting and useful, and filtering of generated structures may be performed based on quantitites such as e.g. support counts, probabilities and user-supplied information about attribute costs.

Acknowledgements

The development of ROSETTA was supported in part by the European Union 4th Framework Telematics project CARDIASSIST, by the Human Capital and Mobility Norwegian Research Council (NFR) contract #101341/410, by NFR grant #74467/410, by NFR grant for Cooperation with Central Europe, by the National Committee for Scientific Research in Poland under grant #8T11C01011 and by the ESPRIT project 20288 CRIT-2.

References

1. Bazan, J., Skowron, A., Synak, P.: Dynamic reducts as a tool for extracting laws from decision tables. In: Z. W. Ras, M. Zemankova (eds.), Proceedings of the Eight

Symposium on Methodologies for Intelligent Systems, Charlotte, NC, October 16-19, Lecture Notes in Artificial Intelligence **869**, Springer-Verlag (1994) 346–355
2. Fayyad, U., Piatetsky-Shapiro, G., Smyth, P.: The KDD process for extracting useful knowledge from volumes of data. Comm. ACM **39/11** (1996) 27–34
3. Pawlak, P.: Rough sets – Theoretical aspects of reasoning about data, Kluwer Academic Publishers, Dordrecht (1991)
4. Skowron, A.: Synthesis of adaptive decision systems from experimental data. In: A. Aamodt and J. Komorowski (eds.), Proceedings of the Fifth Scandinavian Conference on Artificial Intelligence (SCAI-95), May 29–31, 1995, Trondheim, Norway, IOS Press, Amsterdam (1995) 220–238
5. Wróblewski, J.: Finding minimal reducts using genetic algorithms (extended version). In: P.P. Wang (ed.): Second Annual Joint Conference on Information Sciences (JCIS'95), Wrightsville Beach, North Carolina, 28 September - 1 October, (1995) 186–189
6. Zhang, Q., Han, Z., Wen, F.: A new approach for fault diagnosis in power systems based on rough set theory. In: Proceedings of the International Conference on Advances in Power System Control, Operation and Management (APSCOM-97), Hong Kong, China, November 11–14, (1997) 6 pages (to appear)
7. Zitner, D., Paterson, G. I., Fay, D. F.: Methods in health decision support systems: Methods for identifying pertinent and superfluous activity. In: J. Tan and S. Sheps (eds.), Health Decision Support Systems Aspen Publishers, Inc. (1997) (to appear)
8. Øhrn, A., Komorowski, J.: ROSETTA – A rough set toolkit for analysis of data. In: P.P. Wang (ed.), The Fifth International Workshop on Rough Sets and Soft Computing (RSSC'97) at Third Annual Joint Conference on Information Sciences (JCIS'97), Duke University, Duhram, NC, USA Rough Set & Computer Science **3**, March 1–5 (1997) 403–407
9. Øhrn, A., Komorowski, J., Skowron, A., Synak, P.: ROSETTA – Part I: System Overview. Technical report, Dept. of Computer and Information Science, Norwegian University of Science and Technology (NTNU), Trondheim, Norway (1997)
10. Øhrn, A., Vinterbo, S., Szymanski, P., Komorowski, J.: Modelling cardiac patient set residuals using rough sets. In: Proceedings AMIA Annual Fall Symposium (formerly SCAMC), Nashville, TN, USA, October 25–29, (1997) 203–207
11. *The* ROSETTA *WWW Homepage*, Available at URL `http://www.idi.ntnu.no/~aleks/rosetta/`.

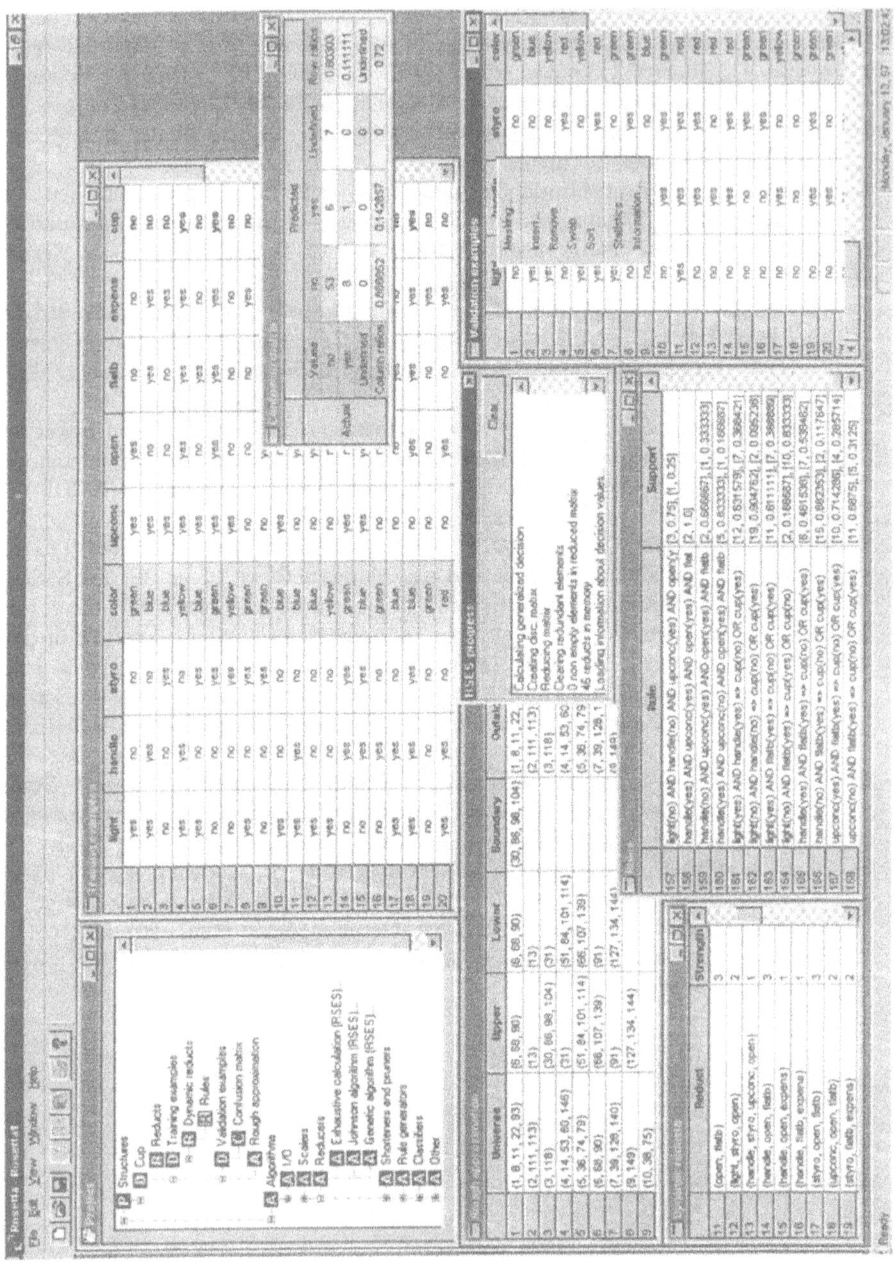

Fig. 1. Example ROSETTA workspace.

RSL – The Rough Set Library

Jacek Sienkiewicz

Institute of Computer Science Warsaw University of Technology
ul. Nowowiejska 15/19, 00 665 Warsaw, Poland

Introduction

The Rough Set Library (RSL) was created in 1993 by M. Gawryś and J. Sienkiewicz at the Institute of Computer Science of the Warsaw University of Technology. It was intended as a kernel for any academic or business application using rough set theory concepts [3], [4].

It is a C language routine library. It was written and tested in UNIX enviroment but it can easily be transformed and installed in MS–DOS or MS Windows [1], [2]. The library has been tested as a link-time library on a UNIX workstation and is available in the standard ANSI C source code. The only requirement for an application is that it includes the obligatory header file *rough.h.*

The source code of the library routines is contained in several files. Segmentation into the files corresponds to task segregation and, accordingly, to object segregation. For a detailed description of the source structure see [1], [2].

The RSL is available in the standard ANSI C source code. It has been designed on DPX–2000 computer. It is tested and used on IBM PC and HP Apollo 750. It has been successfully implemented for analysis of data from many different domains: geology, economy and phonetics. The RSL modules were used in a prototype speech recognition system.

General description

The RSL was meant as a tool for those wanting to build any application using rough set theory model, to do research on the theory itself or just to analyze their particular data. The library saves their time by providing a virtual rough set machine.

The first task of the library is a maintenance of the data structures for the information system. Since the simple attribute–value table is not the only solution, the library provides routines for keeping data in three different structures: the above mentioned attribute-value table [3], the discernibility matrix [4] and, proposed by the authors, the reduced discernibility matrix [1], [2]. The user can freely choose between them, use them seperately or simultaneously. The information system becomes a C language structure which can be declared, filed, read and stored on the disk by the use of the library routines.

The RSL answers all the basic questions that can be asked of the information system using the terminology of rough set theory, among them: approximations of sets, attribute dependencies, various coefficients, cores, etc.

The RSL solves the problem of algorithm optimization. There are three crucial tasks of high complexity that are solved by RSL: reduct finding, rule generation and new object classification. Each is implemented in a library module formed by many variations, different and optional versions. Some tool routines help to introduce user–defined strategies.

Computation time and construction of algorithms depends heavily on the information data structure. Since the library provides three different data structures, it also provides three, often totally different, routines leading to computation of the same answer. It leaves selection to the user. This makes it possible to compare the time and memory effectiveness of competing structures and algorithms. Effectiveness depends heavily on such system parameters as number of objects, number of attributes and size of attribute domains, and even on explicit attribute values.

During design and coding of library routines the authors developed a certain implementation philosophy. Knowledge of the underlying assumptions will certainly help in using the library.

First of all, the library has to be flexible, even at the price of an increased number of routines and an increased number of parameters. All the selection is left to users. The authors tried to anticipate all their expectations and nonstandard needs. This main assumption implies some of the following ones.

The library does not supply any INPUT/OUTPUT routines. Any interaction will require the design of a user interface.

Since the library was meant, among other uses, as a kernel for various systems using rough set concepts, speed was one of the most important criteria.

Another highly important requirement was to have a clear structure code. It was decided that only the lowest level functions should have a direct access to the system data. In consequence, the source code is easy to be analyzed, debugged and modified.

Architecture

The RSL can be used like any other C library, leaving the problem of input-output to the user, assuming he is also a C programmer. Any problem that takes rough sets as a model can be implemented. The RSL may also be of primary importance in testing the relative usefulness of the three different data structures proposed for the information system. The library allows the user to assess implied differences in memory consumption and computation time.

One of the main objectives of the RSL was to provide a kernel for an interactive system ready to be used by an inexperienced computer user. There are many possible forms of applications, yet we propose, as an example, to consider only two of them:

- **Interpreter of queries for the information system.** In this approach a programmer has to determine the type of input for the information system. It may be a full–screen editor of the attribute–value table. It can use the standard of file format provided by the RSL. The whole system takes the form of a pull–down menu calling the editor and calling the supplied functions of queries. This is generally very simple to program.
- **Expert system with knowledge acquisition module.** The architecture of an Inference Engine and an Explanatory Interface would not be determined by the use of the library. A Data Base should take the form of the information system and a Knowledge Base the form of rules deduced from this system. The library takes the role of a knowledge acquisition module. Routines from the classification module of RSL provide classification strategies but they can be reinforced with user-specified ones.

The library routines are grouped into four categories. Each category has a common method of placing parameters, returning results etc. Each one is implemented by one or more separate library modules.

System control – Routines from this category enable a wide range of operations on an information system descriptor: storing and retrieving it from a disk, writing, reading and generating its fields.

Data access – If a collection of queries supplied by the library is not satisfactory or, for any other reason, an application needs a direct access to data matrices (attribute–value table, discernibility matrix, reduced discernibility matrix), then such a facility is provided.

Set handling – Sets are parameters and results of most routines. Since a set is not any default C data type the library provides a data type definition and a collection of routines for set manipulating.

Queries – Functions from this category answer a wide range of queries one can ask about an information system using notions from rough set theory. Among them are: approximations, positive regions, core and reducts.

The Package contains also:

- the obligatory header file: *rough.h,*
- the header files of all library modules included by *rough.h,*
- some examples of information system data files of the special format,
- some examples of simple applications,
- converter of data files from some other formats (e.g. LERS format) to format accepted by RSL: *convert.c*

Software availability

The RSL (rsl.tar.Z) is available via FTP server:

ftp://ftp.ii.pw.edu.pl/pub/Rough/

References

1. Gawryś, M., Sienkiewicz, J.: RSL– The rough set library. Institute of Computer Science, Warsaw University of Technology, ICS Report **39/93** (1993) 1–15
2. Gawryś, M., Sienkiewicz, J.: Rough set library – User's manual (ver. 2.0, September 1993). Institute of Computer Science, Warsaw University of Technology, (1993) 1–50
3. Pawlak, Z.: Rough Sets – Theoretical aspects of reasoning about data. Kluwer Academic Publishers, Dordrecht (1991)
4. Skowron, A., Rauszer, C.: The discernibility matrices and functions in information systems. in: R. Słowiński (ed.), Intelligent Decision Support - Handbook of Applications and Advances of the Rough Sets Theory, Kluwer, Dordrecht (1992) 331–362

Rough Family - Software Implementation of the Rough Set Theory

Roman Słowiński and Jerzy Stefanowski

Institute of Computing Science,
Poznań University of Technology,
3A Piotrowo Street,
60-965 Poznań, Poland,
Roman.Slowinski@cs.put.poznan.pl
Jerzy.Stefanowski@cs.put.poznan.pl

Abstract. This note briefly describes main programs of the software package, called *Rough Family*, i.e. *ROSE* and *ProFIT*. They are interactive software systems designed for data analysis and knowledge discovery using the rough set approach.

Introduction

The *Rough Family* is a set of programs which are implementations of basic functions of the rough set approach and rule discovery techniques. These programs have been developed in the Institute of Computing Science, Poznań University of Technology under the supervision of Roman Słowiński and Jerzy Stefanowski. The main collaborators directly involved in the process of designing and programming are Robert Mieńko, Bartłomiej Prędki and Robert Susmaga.

Currently, the package has two following main components: *ROSE* and *ProFIT*. The *ROSE* system is a successor of the *RoughDAS* and *RoughClass* systems [8]. The *RoughDAS* program is historically one the first successful implementations of the rough set methodology. According to the literature, it is the rough set based software the most often used in real life applications (see, e.g., the list given in [4, 2, 7]). The *RoughClass* is an interactive system supporting classification of new coming objects based on decision rules discovered from examples. The *ProFIT* program is an implementation of the generalized rough set model that handles uncertain input data resulting from imprecise or inexact attribute values, missing values, or the attributes given in the form of real numbers and fuzzy linguistic qualifiers.

The aim of the *Rough Family* software is to enable the rough set based knowledge discovery process, i.e.: performing a rough set based analysis of the data (in particular, calculating approximations of decision classes, checking dependencies between attributes, looking for reduced subsets of attributes), extracting characteristic patterns from data, inducing decision rules from sets of learning examples, evaluating the discovered rules by means of different validations techniques, constructing decision support systems based on knowledge represented in the form of decision rules.

Both programs accept input data in a form of a table called an information system in which rows correspond to objects (cases, observations, etc.) and the columns correspond to attributes (features, characteristics, etc.). The attributes are divided into disjoint sets of condition attributes (e.g. results of particular tests or experiments) and decision attributes (expressing the partition of objects into decisions, i.e. their classification). The input data can be either introduced using an internal edit option or imported from text files. The input data files to all the programs are compatible with basic file formats used in the *ROSE* system and also with old formats introduced in the *RoughDAS* system, thanks to which the communication between the programs is possible.

Although *ROSE* and *ProFIT* systems have been created for MS-Windows environment running on PC compatible machines, their main computational modules (without GUI part) being implementations of the rough set approach are also available in versions running under Unix operating systems, e.g. on workstations or supercomputers.

The ROSE program

The program *ROSE* - **RO***ugh* **S***et Data* **E***xplorer* is an interactive software system running under 32 bit GUI operating systems (Windows 95/NT 4.0) on PC compatible machines.

Input data

The input data to the *ROSE* program is the information system/table which can be defined either by using an internal editor or can be imported from a file. The data are stored in a text file according to special syntax that, besides the description of objects by attributes, may contain additional information about the attributes, e.g. their type, definition of their domains, etc. The *ROSE* also accepts file formats coming from other systems, i.e. from its predecessor *RoughDAS*, input decision table used in Grzymala's *LERS* system, and formats of files containing learning examples for well-known C4.5 machine learning system.

Output data

Except visulatization in GUI, all results are also written to plain text files, so they are also readable outside the system, and can easily be converted to other required file formats.

Implemented methods

The *ROSE* offers currently the following functions:

- preprocessing of input data, e.g. detecting errors in the definition of input examples, handling missing values of attributes,
- discretization of real valued attributes by means of various techniques,
- qualitative estimation of the ability of the condition attributes to approximate the objects classification, using either standard rough set model or variable precision model extension; in both cases, it is possible to compute approximations of classes with their accuracies, calculate the quality of the approximation of the classification, check which objects belong to the given approximation; visualization of atoms and approximations is also available,

- finding the core of the attributes as well as looking for reducts in the information system (either all reducts or a given number of the best reducts according to an approximation algorithm),
- studying the significance of a given attribute for the classification of objects,
- reducing superfluous attributes and selecting the most significant attributes for the classification of objects; there are available several techniques that support the choice of the subsets of attributes ensuring a satisfactory quality of classification (e.g., the technique of adding the most discriminatory attributes to the core),
- inducing decision rules - certain or approximate on the basis of approximations of decision classes; decision rules can be induced by using either *LEM2* algorithm or *Explore* algorithm [3, 12],
- postprocessing of induced rules, e.g. pruning; looking for interesting rules according to the user's defined queries,
- applying the decision rules to classify new objects by means of various strategies, e.g. Valued Closeness Relation [6, 9],
- evaluation of the sets of decision rules by using k-fold cross validation techniques.

There are two groups of ROSE features that make this system unique and different than other rough set based software. The first group refers to GUI part while the other group is connected with particular methodological aspects. The graphical interface has been designed in such a way that working with the program is very easy and efficient. In particular, it refers to options of editing and preprocessing the information system and presentation of the rough set results as well as visualization of discovered rules. Moreover, the possibility of file transfer with other systems seems to be important for users and the practical applications. Methodologically, one should also notice that the *ROSE* offers all basic operations of the rough set approach necessary to perform the complete process of knowledge discovery. Particular attention has been paid to the selection of attributes. It does not include looking for all reducts only but is extended by several original approximation techniques that can be easily controlled by the user. The unique methodological features include also the possibility of choosing different techniques of rule induction, i.e.: the user can generate minimum set of rules, exhaustive set or satisfactory set of rules. The first technique is focused on describing input objects by the minimum number of necessary rules while the second approach tries to generate all allowed decision rules that can be discovered from the given information system. The third technique gives as a result the set of decision rules which satisfy given a priori user's requirements. For example, the user can prefer to discover all strong decision rules, i.e. supported by a relatively large number of input objects. The last approach is particularly useful for tasks of an interactive knowledge discovery. Lastly, the *ROSE* offers an original and efficient approach for using decision rules to create classification system. It is based on valued closeness relation and makes the system competitive to other well known machine learning and classification systems [2].

Moreover, the *ROSE* has a modular software construction that allows for its development in future and easy adaptation to various user's requirements and specificity of the given applications.

The ProFIT program

The program *ProFIT - Rough* **Pro***cessing of* **F***uzzy* **I***nformation* **T***ables* - is an implementation of the generalization of the rough set theory that handles uncertainty in the definition of the information system. Let us remind that in the standard rough set model it is assumed that each pair [object, attribute], must be defined in unique and precise way. In practice, however, these pairs may be neither unique nor precise, i.e. they can be uncertain. Here, the considered generalization allows to take into account the following situations: uncertain discretization of quantitative attributes, imprecise or inexact values of numerical attributes, multiple values possible for one pair [object, attribute] given, e.g. in a form of linguistic fuzzy qualifiers. A special way of modelling these three types of uncertainty [10, 11] uses fuzzy set theory, which boils them down to, so called, multiple fuzzy descriptors. Then, the generalization preserves all characteristic features of the rough set approach while enabling reasoning about uncertain data.

Part of operations offered by the program is the same as those of *ROSE*, but instead of producing standard rough set results, the *ProFIT* generates results specific to the generalized rough set theory, e.g. generalized accuracies of approximations or the generalized fuzzy decision rules.

The new features of the *ProFIT* program include, e.g.:

- accepting new representations of the input data, including new types of attributes, e.g. their single values can be replaced by sets of possible values; attribute values in the input table may be also given in the form of fuzzy numbers,
- discretizing the real valued attributes using various discretization algorithms; in particular, the user can choose fuzzy discretization instead of a crisp one,
- extended user-friendly edit option of GUI that enables to visualize and analyse different aspects of fuzzy set representation of the input information table,
- easy handling of degrees of possibility for objects in the fuzzy information systems necessary to obtain specific results of the generalized rough set theory,
- inducing fuzzy decision rules,
- classifying new objects with the fuzzy decision rules by means of fuzzy logic and valued closeness relation principles; it is also possible to evaluate the quality of decision rules with the help of standard cross-validation tests.

The *ProFIT* in its current version works in the MS-Windows ver. 3.1 (or higher) environment on PC compatible machines.

A survey of applications

The programs of the *Rough Family* and their predecessors *RoughDAS* and *Rough-Class* have been applied in many fields, e.g. medicine, pharmacy, technical diagnostics, finance and management, image and signal analysis, etc. The references to these applications are given, e.g. in [4, 2, 12, 5]. For example, the considered software has been successfully applied to analyse:

- the treatment of patients with duodenal ulcer after highly selected vagotomy,
- multi-stage therapeutic process for patients with peritoneal lavage in acute pancreatitis,
- attribute dependencies in the large data set concerning urinary stones treatment by ESWL technique,
- surgery experience concerning patients with multiple injuries,
- problems of fast diagnosing appendicitis at emergency units,
- chemical structures of pharmaceutical compounds (e.g. activity relationship of quaternary imidazolium or pyridinium compounds),
- processing of histological images,
- technical diagnostics of industrial machinery (e.g. rolling bearing, reducers),
- maintenance procedures in public transportation systems,
- financial data concerning evaluation of bankruptcy risk and loan assignment,
- multi-attribute decision problems,
- geological problems, i.e. with drawing premonitory factors for earthquakes by emphasing gas geochemistry in Belgium,
- software project evaluation.

References

1. Grzymała-Busse, J.W.: LERS - a system for learning from examples based on rough sets. In: R. Słowiński (ed.), Intelligent Decision Support – Handbook of Applications and Advances of the Rough Sets Theory, Kluwer Academic Publishers, Dordrecht (1992) 3–18
2. Grzymala-Busse, J.W., Stefanowski, J., Ziarko. W.: Rough sets: Facts versus misconceptions. Informatica **20** (1996) 455–464
3. Mienko,R., Stefanowski, J., Vanderpooten, D.: Discovery-oriented induction of decision rules. Cahier du Lamsade **141** Paris, Universite de Paris Dauphine, septembre 1996
4. Mienko, R., Słowiński, R., Stefanowski, J., Susmaga, R.: RoughFamily - software implementation of rough set based data analysis and rule discovery techniques. In: S.Tsumoto, S. Kobayashi, T. Yokomori, H. Tanaka, and A. Nakamura (eds.), Proceedings of the Fourth International Workshop on Rough Sets, Fuzzy Sets, and Machnine Discovery (RSFD'96), The University of Tokyo, November 6-8 (1996) 437-440
5. Pawlak, Z., Słowiński, R.: Rough set approach to multi- attribute decision analysis (Invited Review) In: European Journal of Operational Research **72** (1994) 443–459
6. Słowiński, R.: Rough set learning of preferential attitude in multi-criteria decision making. In: J. Komorowski and Z.W. Ras (eds.), Proceedings of the 7-th International Symposium on Methodologies for Intelligent Systems (ISMIS-93),

Trondheim, Norway, June 15–18, 1993, Lecture Notes in Computer Science **689** (1993) 642–651

7. Słowiński, R.: Rough set approach to decision analysis. AI Expert, March 1995, 19–25
8. Słowiński, R., Stefanowski. J.: 'RoughDAS' and 'RoughClass' software implementations of the rough set approach. In: R. Słowiński (ed.), Intelligent Decision Support. Handbook of Applications and Advances of the Rough Sets Theory, Kluwer Academic Publishers, Dordrecht (1992) 445–456
9. Słowiński, R., Stefanowski. J.: Rough classification with valued closeness relation. In: Didey E. et al. (eds.), New Approaches in Classification and Data Analysis, Springer - Verlag, Studies in Classification, Data Analysis and Knowledge Organization, Berlin (1993) 482–489
10. Słowiński, R., Stefanowski. J.: Handling various types of uncertainty in the rough set approach. In: W. Ziarko (ed.), Rough Sets, Fuzzy Sets and Knowledge Discovery (RSKD'93). Workshops in Computing, Springer–Verlag & British Computer Society, London, Berlin (1994) 366–376
11. Słowiński, R., Stefanowski. J.: Rough set reasoning about uncertain data. Fundamenta Informaticae **27/2-3** (1996) 229–244
12. Stefanowski, J.: On rough set based approaches to induction of decision rules. (in this book)

TAS: Tools for Analysis and Synthesis of Concurrent Processes using Rough Set Methods

Zbigniew Suraj

Institute of Mathematics
Pedagogical University
Rejtana 16A, 35-310 Rzeszów, Poland
e-mail: zsuraj@univ.rzeszow.pl

Abstract. *TAS* is a prototype system of programs for computer aided analysis and synthesis of concurrent models discovered from data tables. This system is based on rough set methods and Petri nets.

The main tasks of the system are:

- to discover concurrent models from data tables specified by information systems,

- to build parallel programs for decision making on the base of decision tables,

- to reconstruct a concurrent model when the specification for the system is changing.

TAS is running on IBM PC microcomputers under MS-DOS operating system with WINDOWS interface. The system is primarly intended for research goals.

Introduction

TAS is a window-based system for analysis and synthesis of concurrent processes. This system incorporates several of the newest research results obtained on the border of theory and application rough sets with Petri nets.

TAS is developed in the Institute of Mathematics, Pedagogical University of Rzeszów under the supervision of Zbigniew Suraj. The main collaborator directly involved in the process of designing and programming is Janusz Węgrzyn. Currently, the system consists of several separate programs described in Section 4.

The first version of the system was ready in 1994 [3, 5]. In the years 1995-97 *TAS* was extended by rule editing procedures, improved decomposition algorithms, new synthesis procedures and added a better user interface.

Input data

The current version of *TAS* can handle rule sets and data tables which are provided in the form of text. The format of rules consists of *if-then* rules with a conjunctive antecedent, and it is according to the syntax of rules generated by

ROSETTA (see the description of *ROSETTA* presented in this Appendix). *TAS* uses two kinds of rules:

- rules corresponding to all nontrivial dependencies between the values of attributes from the reduct of a given information system with those outside of that reduct,
- rules corresponding to all nontrivial dependencies between the values of attributes within the reduct of that system (see [1, 8, 10, 11, 12]).

The data tables used by *TAS* represent the decision tables in the standard form. The input data in the form of rules can be either introduced using an internal edit option or imported from text files. The data tables are imported from text files.

Output knowledge

TAS generates concurrent data models represented by Petri nets, and written in the form of a text table [3]. The system can also cooperate with the system *PN-tools* [7] for further comprehensive analysis of the obtained net model.

System architecture

The system *TAS* consists of three main and two auxiliary programs.

1. The program *CAI* can be used for:

1.1. Generating and editing rules in semi-automatic mode.

1.2. Generating in automatic mode from an arbitrary information system, represented by rules extracted from the system, its concurrent models in the form of a marked Petri net with the following property: the reachability set of the net corresponds exactly to the set of global states (objects) consistent with all rules true in the given information system. The reachability set of the net represents the largest extension of the given information system consistent with the knowledge represented by this system.

1.3. Generating parallel algorithms (represented by Petri nets) from the given decision tables, which allow us to take the proper decision related to the identified global states (new objects).

For more information see [1, 8].

2. The program *RSC* can be used for:

2.1. Automatic discovery of data models represented by concurrent systems from experimental data tables (information systems). The basic step of the construction consists of decomposition of any information system (with respect to any of its reduct) into components linked by some connections which allow to preserve some constraints. Any component represents in a sense the strongest functional module of the system. The connections between components represent constraints which must be satisfied when these functional modules coexist in the system. The components together with the connections define a covering of the system. Coverings of the system are used in construction of its concurrent model in the form of a marked Petri net with the analogical property as defined above for the result net obtained by the program *CAI* described above. For more information see [6, 10].

2.2. Supporting the process of reconstructing of the synthesized concurrent system when the specification for the system is changing e.g. by adding new requirements (new objects, attributes or values of attributes). This program produces a plan of reconstruction of a given system by specifying which parts (components and/or connections) can remain unchanged and which must be changed to satisfy new requirements. It can make comparisons between the results obtained from different components and/or coverings. In case the cost of components and connections can be estimated the system computes also the cost of reconstruction.

2.3. Classification of new objects with synthetized components of a system using voting scheme.

For more information see [9, 11].

3. The program *DIS* can be used for synthesis of concurrent models from observations or specification encoded in data table representing a dynamic information system. For more information see [12].

In *TAS* are also available two auxiliary programs for optimization of a set of rules by removing redundant rules, i.e. rules subsumed by other rules and for computing an extension of a given information system (see [1]).

User

The system *TAS* is primarly intended for research goals.

Final remarks

TAS is a prototype system for discovery and analysis of concurrent models. This system is now being extended by adding new methods and being improved by providing it with a better user interface.

Acknowledgements

I am grateful to Professor A. Skowron for stimulating discussions and interesting suggestions about this work. This research reported in this paper was partially supported by the National Committee for Scientific Research in Poland under grant # 8T 11C 01 011 and by the ESPRIT project 20288 CRIT-2.

References

1. Skowron, A., Suraj, Z.: Rough sets and concurrency. Bulletin of the Polish Academy of Sciences, Technical Sciences **41/3** (1993) 237–254
2. Skowron, A., Suraj, Z.: A rough set approach to real–time state identification. Bulletin of the European Association for Theoretical Computer Science **50** (June 1993) 264–275

3. Skowron, A., Suraj, Z.: Synthesis of concurrent systems specified by information systems. Part 2. Examples of synthesis. In: Institute of Computer Science Report **38/93** Warsaw University of Technology (1993)
4. Suraj, Z.: Tools for generating and analyzing concurrent models specified by information systems. In: T.Y. Lin (ed.): Proceedings of the Third International Workshop on Rough Sets and Soft Computing (RSSC'94), San Jose State University, San Jose, California, USA, November 10–12, (1994) 610–617
5. Suraj, Z.: Tools for generating concurrent models specified by information systems. In: T.Y. Lin, A.M. Wildberger (eds.): Soft Computing: Rough Sets, Fuzzy Logic, Neural Networks, Uncertainty Management, Knowledge Discovery, Simulation Councils, Inc., San Diego, CA (1995) 107–110
6. Skowron, A., Suraj, Z.: Discovery of concurrent data models from experimental tables: A rough set approach. In: U.M. Fayyad, R. Uthurusamy (eds.), Proceedings of the First International Conference on Knowledge Discovery and Data Mining (KDD'95), Montreal, August, AAAI Press, Menlo Park, CA (1995) 288–293
7. Suraj, Z.: PN-tools: Environment for the design and analysis of Petri nets. Control and Cybernetics **24/2** (1995) 199–222
8. Skowron, A., Suraj, Z.: A parallel algorithm for real-time decision making: A rough set approach. Journal of Intelligent Information Systems **7** (1996) 5–28
9. Suraj, Z.: An application of rough set methods to cooperative information systems re-engineering. In: S. Tsumoto, S. Kobayashi, T. Yokomori, H. Tanaka, and A. Nakamura (eds.): Proceedings of the Fourth International Workshop on Rough Sets, Fuzzy Sets, and Machine Discovery (RSFD'96), The University of Tokyo, November 6–8 (1996) 364–371
10. Suraj, Z.: Discovery of concurrent data models from experimental tables: A rough set approach. Fundamenta Informaticae (1996) **28/3-4** 353–376
11. Suraj, Z.: Reconstruction of cooperative information systems under cost constraints. In: P.P. Wang (ed.): Proceedings of the Fifth International Workshop on Rough Sets and Soft Computing (RSSC'97) at Third Annual Joint Conference on Information Sciences (JCIS'97), Duke University, Durham, NC, USA, Rough Set & Computer Science **3**, March 1–5 (1997) 399–402
12. Suraj, Z.: The synthesis problem of concurrent systems specified by dynamic information systems. (submitted)

RoughFuzzyLab - a System for Data Mining and Rough and Fuzzy Sets Based Classification

Roman W. Swiniarski

San Diego State University, San Diego, California 92182-7720, U.S.A.

Abstract. RoughFuzzyLab is a data mining, knowledge discovery software system based on rough and fuzzy sets theory. The system is specially predisposed to process databases containing images and decision tables. The system has been used for image recognition, hand-writen character recognition, prediction of time-series, and in the medical area of breast cancer detection.

Introduction

The RoughFuzzyLab software system was developed in 1995 in Roman Swiniarski scientific group at San Diego State University. The system was designed, based on rough sets theory (Pawlak, 1991; Skowron, 1990) and fuzzy sets (Zadeh, 1965), for data mining and knowledge discovery. Two of major functions of the system are: extraction of important features and design and classifiers from a given data set. RoughFuzzyLab provides two different approaches in a design of classification rules from data. First technique uses rough sets based rule design rule design (with an idea of minimum concept description). Second technique provides fuzzy sets methodology for rule design (using features selected by rough sets). System is specially effective for image recognition.

Input data

Input data to RoughFuzzyLab can be an ASCI data set containing

- Images.
- An information system.
- Decision table.

Output knowledge

The system allows to extract important features from images applicable for compression and recognition. For decision tables and classification task, system allows to find strongly relevant attribute set called core. Additionally, RoughFuzzyLab provides finding sets of weakly relevant attributes called reducts. A reduct is a minimal set of attributes describing all concept in a decision table. Eventually system finds rough sets and fuzzy sets based classification rules.

System Architecture

The software system was designed to be user friendly, effective, and efficient. The graphical user interface provided by the system is the PC Windows interface which is very friendly and easy for the user. Results can be shown graphically and statistically. A decision table is designed in the form of spreadsheet, so the user can understand and modify data quickly.

There are five main functions provided in the system:

1. **Data** editing and basic preprocessing (including **Image** functions)
2. **Feature extraction** function
3. **Rough sets** function
4. **Fuzzy sets** function

Each major operation generates related resulting files.

Data editing and basic preprocessing provides variety of operations on data sets including powerful **Image** processing functions. Images can be preprocessed, displayed, extensively edited, including noise adding, thinning, etc.

For the input data having continuous attributes (real-valued), RoughFuzzyLab provides several methods for attribute discretization including cluster analysis and statistical methods.

The major **Feature extraction** function relates to extraction of invariant features from images based on theory of complex Zernike moments (Swiniarski, 1993). This function also provides feature editing, pattern forming, and labeling patterns by classes.

Basic **Rough sets** functions are provided by the system for discovering: dependencies, set approximations, classification accuracy, feature importance, etc. (Swiniarski, 1995). Rough sets based classifier design and testing is also implemented in this main function. A user can build a rough sets classification rule base by **Build Rough Rules**. Then the user can load a test data file to do the classification by either **Classify Current Case** or **Classify All Cases**. **Fuzzy Sets** function provides users with a fuzzy recognition system. To build a fuzzy recognition system, a user builds a fuzzy rule base and membership functions with **Build Fuzzy Rule** which will generate a fuzzy sets file. It is important to note that a fuzzy rule base would be built based on a chosen reduct set in a decision table. Therefore, a user must select a reduct set to build a fuzzy rule base. Membership functions are automatically created by to provided methods. Fuzzy rules can be shown by **Show Rules** and membership functions can be shown by **Show Membership Functions**. Besides, fuzzy rules can be shown graphically by **Graph of Rules and Classification**. This function can also show the degree of membership functions when an object is classified.

The software system was written in the "ANSI C" programming language and consists of a Windows interface and several "engine" programs as well as several include files. The interface and programs were complied with Borland

C++ 3.1 (or Microsoft C/C++ 7.0) and run on PCs with a Microsoft Windows 3.1 operating system. Although RoughFuzzyLab is a fully interactive system with advanced graphical user interface, some batch processing possibilities are also available.

Using Rules

In RoughFuzzyLab it is assumed that the classification rules should be used automatically. Every new input object can be classified by this system. The constructed rules are also available in comprehensible form for the user.

Final Remarks

Advantages of the system are: a family of image preprocessing functions, discretization methods, and invariant feature extraction from images. Another advantage is a merging rough sets and fuzzy sets functionalities in a classifier design. A disadvantage of this version of the system is lack of tools for preprocessing of raw time-series. An extensive interactive graphical user interface is also an advantage of the system. The RoughFuzzyLab was used in variety of applications (Swiniarski, 1996a, 1996b): including image recognition, handwritten character recognition, breast cancer detection, prediction, etc.

References

1. Pawlak, Z.: Rough sets – Theoretical aspects of reasoning about data. Kluwer Academic Publishers, Dordrecht (1991)
2. Pawlak, Z., Grzymała-Busse, J.W., Słowiński, R., and Ziarko, W.: Rough sets. *Communications of the ACM* **38** (1995) 88–95
3. Skowron, A.: The rough sets theory and evidence theory. Fundamenta Informaticae **13** (1990) 245–262
4. Swiniarski, R.: Zernike moments and their application for image recognition. Internal report of San Diego State University, Department of Mathematical and Computer Sciences (1993)
5. Swiniarski, R.: "RoughFuzzyLab." A software package developed at San Diego State University, Department of Mathematical and Computer Sciences (1995)
6. Swiniarski, R.: (1996a), "Rough sets for intelligent data mining, knowledge discovering and designing of an expert systems for on-line prediction of volleyball game progress", in: S. Tsumoto, S. Kobayashi, T. Yokomori, H. Tanaka and A. Nakamura (eds.), The Fourth International Workshop on Rough Sets, Fuzzy Sets, and Machine Discovery (RS96FD), November 6-8, The University of Tokyo (1996a) 413–418
7. Swiniarski, R.: Rough sets expert system for robust texture classification based on 2D fast Fourier transformation spectral features. In: S. Tsumoto, S. Kobayashi, T. Yokomori, H. Tanaka and A. Nakamura (eds.), The Fourth International Workshop on Rough Sets, Fuzzy Sets, and Machine Discovery (RS96FD), November 6-8, The University of Tokyo (1996b) 419–425
8. Zadeh, L.: Fuzzy sets. Inf. Control **8** (1965) 338-353

PRIMEROSE

Shusaku Tsumoto

Medical Research Institute,
Tokyo Medical and Dental University
1-5-45 Yushima, Bunkyo-ku Tokyo 113 Japan
E-mail: tsumoto@computer.org

Abstract. PRIMEROSE (Probabilistic Rule Induction Methods based on Rough Sets) generates probabilistic rules from databases. This system includes induction of rules with conditional probabilities, called accuracy and coverage, or with test statistics, for example, χ^2-statistics, estimation of conditional probabilities or test statistics by using resampling methods (cross-validation and bootstrap method), and calculation of statistics of induced rules. This system also allows concept hierarchy and applies attribute-oriented generalization technique to rule induction. The main target domain of this system is medicine and this system succeeds in automated acquistion of medical expert systems and medical knowledge discovery.

Introduction

PRIMEROSE (Probabilistic Rule Induction Methods based on Rough Sets) is developed by Shusaku Tsumoto[1], which is firstly introduced in 1993. This system is first introduced to discover probabilistic rules from medical databases based on Ziarko's VPRS model and estimate the reliability of induced rules by using resampling methods[1, 2, 3, 4, 6, 8]. Next, in order to apply this system to genome sequence analysis, PRIMEROSE is extended with calculation of test statistics, transformation of attributes based on attribute-oriented generalization[5, 7]. Finally, this system is extended with calculation of statistics of rules, similarities between rules and automatic comparison between domain experts' knowledge[9].

Input

PRIMEROSE induces rules from one table, which includes condition and decision attributes. Although this system can induce rules without background knowledge, in order to control the number of rules, it requires the following

[1] Correspondence: Department of Information Medicine, Medical Research Institute, Tokyo Medical and Dental University 1-5-45 Yushima, Bunkyo-ku Tokyo 113 Japan E-mail: tsumoto@computer.org

parameters: (1) thresholds for accuracy ($p(R|D)$) and coverage($p(D|R)$), (2) selection of resampling methods, and (3) selection of rule statistics. Additionally, PRIMEROSE allows (4) concept hierarchy of attributes and (5) domain experts' knowledge for further analysis. PRIMEROSE can also control search for rules using background knowledge, which is described by first-order predicate logic.

Output

PRIMEROSE outputs induced rules, whose conditional parts are represented by DNF, with probabilities or statistics calculated from training samples, estimation of probabilities and statistics, and statistics of rules (the number of induced rules for each decision class, the averaged rule length, similarity between induced rules, and so on.) Furthermore, PRIMEROSE can output the following knowledge: (1) if concept hierarchy of attributes is given, then PRIMEROSE applies transformation of attributes and induces rules using this hierarchy. (2) if domain experts' knowledge is given, then PRIMEROSE compares induced rules with it and outputs the difference between induced and given knowledge.

System architecture

PRIMEROSE consists of four modules, data transformation module, resampling module, rule induction module, and output interface module, and runs as follows: First, this system induces rules from raw databases without evoking resampling modules. Second, it estimates probabilities and induces rules using resampling modules. Thirdly, it applies data transformation to raw databases and repeats the first and second procedures. Finally, PRIMEROSE outputs rules both in natural language form and in PROLOG predicates using output interface module.

Users only have to input tables and background knowledge including parameters. Induced knowledge are stored as PROLOG predicates and users can compare between rules induced with different parameters.

Search for knowledge

PRIMEROSE generates rules whose conditional parts are represented as DNF form, using a kind of heuristic search. As evaluation functions, it uses conditional probabilities and test statistics. Then, for estimation of probabilities and test statistics, cross-validation and/or the bootstrap method are/is applied.

User

This system is intended not only for analyst but also domain users.

KDD process

The main target domain is medicine and genome sequence analysis. Induced knowledge is presented as rules understandable for domain experts, with numeric information, such as probabilities and test statistics. Furthermore, statistics of rules is also presented as a summarized table.

The system has the following advantages: (1) PRIMEROSE allows multiple choices for evaluation functions and can make comparisons between induced results obtained by different evaluation functions. (2) this systems can compare induced rules with domain experts' knowledge and detect the differences between them. (3) PRIMEROSE allows domain knowledge represented by first-order predicate logic. On the other hand, the disadvantage of this system is that PRIMEROSE is rather slower than other systems because it is written by PROLOG.

In biomedical domain, PRIMEROSE obtains the following nice results on automated knowledge acquisition and has made several new discoveries in biomedical databases: (1) PRIMEROSE induces probabilistic rules, which matches domain experts' knowledge[2, 4, 6, 9]. (2) Introduced resampling methods correctly estimate (predictive) conditional probabilities[2, 8]. (3) PRIMEROSE discovers several new knowledge from genome sequence databases, which is partially validated by biochemical experiments[7].

References

1. Tsumoto, S., Tanaka, H.: Induction of probabilistic rules based on rough set theory. In: Algorithmic Learning Theory - 93, Lecture Notes in Artificial Intelligence **744** Springer-Verlag, Berlin (1993) 441–448
2. Tsumoto, S., Tanaka, H.: PRIMEROSE: Probabilistic rule induction method based on rough sets. In: W. Ziarko (ed.), Rough Sets, Fuzzy Sets and Knowledge Discovery (RSKD'93). Workshops in Computing, Springer–Verlag & British Computer Society, London, Berlin (1994) 274–281
3. Tsumoto, S., Tanaka, H.: Induction of medical expert system rules based on rough sets and resampling methods. In: Proceedings of the Eighteenth Annual Symposium on Computer Applications in Medical Care, Journal of the AMIA **1** (supplement) (1994) 1066–1070
4. Tsumoto, S., Tanaka, H.: PRIMEROSE: Probabilistic rule induction method based on rough sets and resampling methods. Computational Intelligence **11** (1995) 389–405
5. Tsumoto, S., Tanaka, H.: Automated discovery of functional components of proteins from amino-acid sequences based on rough sets and change of representation. In: U.M. Fayyad, R. Uthurusamy (eds.), Proc. of the First International Conference on Knowledge Discovery and Data Mining (KDD'95), August 20-21, 1995, Montreal, AAAI Press, Menlo Park CA (1995) 318-324
6. Tsumoto, S., Tanaka, H.: Extraction of expert system rules based on rough sets and resampling methods. In: Proceedings of MEDINFO'95, Part 1, IMIA, Geneva, (1995) 861–865

7. Tsumoto, S., Tanaka, H.: Machine discovery of functional components of proteins from amino-acid sequences based on rough sets and change of representation. Journal of Intelligent Automation and Soft Computing **2/2** (1996) 169–180
8. Tsumoto, S., Tanaka, H.: PRIMEROSE3: Induction and estimation of probabilistic rules from medical databases based on rough sets and resampling methods. In: Witten, M. (ed), Computational Medicine, Public Health, and Biotechnology. Buildng a Man in the Machine (Part III), World Scientific, Singapore (1996) 1173–1189
9. Tsumoto, S., Tanaka, H.: Automated discovery of medical expert system rules from clinical databases based on rough sets. In: E. Simoudis, J. Han, and U. Fayyad (eds.), Second International Conference on Knowledge Discovery and Data Mining, Proceedings (KDD'96), August 2–4, Portland, Oregon, USA, AAAI Press, Menlo Park (1996) 63–69

KDD-R: Rough Sets-Based Data Mining System

Wojciech Ziarko

Computer Science Department
University of Regina, Regina
Saskatchewan, S4S-0A2, Canada
e-mail: ziarko@cs.uregina.ca

Abstract. KDD-R is a comprehensive set of tools for rough sets-based data mining. This is a prototype system which incorporates many of the newest research results obtained in the area of rough sets. It is developed around variable precision rough sets model. The main discovery task of the system is the computation of probabilistic rules satisfying predefined rule length (number of rule conditions), strength (number of supporting cases) and rule predictive probability constraints from a flat table containing data in attribute-value format. The rules can be computed from real, integer or categorical data, or a mix of them. The results of the analysis are presented in three forms: a tabular form, ASCII text in the format IF (conditions) THEN (decision) with probability P and strength N, and in the histogram form. In the current version KDD-R is UNIX-based with X-Windows interface. The main application area for the system is market research. Other potential applications, are banking, insurance, stock market prediction, medical data analysis, sensor data analysis for control, or questionaire analysis.

Introduction

This note presents system KDD-R (Knowledge Discovery in Data using Rough sets) developed at the University of Regina. KDD-R is a successor of two earlier commercial systems for rough sets-based data analysis designed by the author and implemented by his students, systems DataQuest and DataLogic [5]. The basic underlying methodology behind KDD-R is the theory of rough sets [1-3], and in particular its extension called variable precision model of rough sets [4]. The inner workings of the system have been described in more detail in [6]. KDD-R is a prototype system which incorporates many of the research results obtained in the area of rough sets. In the current version KDD-R is UNIX-based with X-Windows interface.

Input

The system accepts input in the form of a single ASCII table with columns separated by at least one space. The original table must be associated with a format description prepared by the user in which each data column is given attribute name, value type and each attribute name must be designated as condition or decision ("independent" or "dependent" variable). System utility program exists to help in preparation of the format description. The system permits presence of one symbol representing "unknown" data value. The rules are subsequently computed with respect to selected values of decision attribute. When preparing format description the user is supposed to provide discretization definition for numeric attributes. This can be done based on his/her understanding of the problem domain, or system-supplied utility program can be used in selecting discretization points. In the current version the KDD-R system is not integrated with any particular DBMS.

Output knowledge

The main discovery task of the system is the computation of probabilistic rules satisfying predefined rule length (number of attributes), strength (number of supporting cases) and rule predictive probability constraints from a flat table containing data in attribute-value format. The rules can be computed from real, integer or categorical data, or a mix of them. The results of the analysis are presented in three forms: a tabular form, ASCII text in the format IF (conditions) THEN (decision) with probability P and strength N, or in histogram form. The system produces two rule sets: 1. all rules satisfying predefined constraints and 2. only maximal rules, that is rules which are not subsumed by other rules.

System architecture

The system consists of the following major components:

- data preprocessing component which is responsible for creation of the format description, discretization of the numeric data and selection of discretized attributes for inclusion in the computed rules;
- the rule search component which utilizes user supplied rule strength and rule predictive probability constraints to identify all rules meeting these constraints with respect to selected value of the decision (target) attribute and selected discretized condition attributes. During rules search process, the original data are reclassified number of times creating different "approximation spaces" which are then used to identify elementary sets (corresponding to rules) of "lower approximations" of the target decision [1-4]. The rule search process can handle "unknown" values in data without replacing them with assumed values.
- The postprocessing component responsible for:
  1. translation of rules from table format into text format;
  2. optimization of rules by removing redundant rules (rules subsumed by other rules).
  3. visualisation of rules in the histogram form.

Search for knowledge

The system is using a form of "branch-and-bound" technique for exhaustive search for rules satisfying predefined criteria. Since valuable and "credible" from application perspective rules are relatively short, strong and have relatively high predictive probability, the bounded search process is typically quite effective at significantly reducing the search space. The user background knowledge used in limiting the search space is expressed implicitly through the following user's decisions:

- selection of discretization definition;
- selection of the minimal acceptable rule strength;
- selection of the minimal predictive probability of the rule.

User

The system is primarily intended for trained domain users. The operation of the system is simple and minimal background is required to master the concepts behind the system's principles and operation. No knowledge of rough sets theory is required to effectively use the system.

Knowledge discovery process

The system have been used primarly for market-oriented research serving data tables of up to 700000 customer records. These applications involved analysis of customer demographic and other characteristics in relationship to his/her ability to accept new product offerings. Some experiments were also performed in medical domain trying to find predictive rules linking patient's health condition information with the likelihood of the presence or absence of a disease [7].

The results of the analysis normally are presented in the text form, but they can be converted into visual display as well showing rules in the histogram form. In such a display, each rule corresponds to one bar of the histogram with the height of the bar being proportional to rule's predictive probability and width being proportional to rule's strength. The use of such a display helps in visual identification of strong and highly predictive rules.

The main advantage of KDD-R is its ability to extract strong rules from data, both numeric and categorical data. No formal comparison in that respect with other systems has been done, but author's experience with some other systems, in particular decision tree-based, indicates that the rules produced by KDD-R are on the average much stronger than "tree rules" corresponding to paths from the root to leaves of the tree. In other words, there is no "overfitting" problem with rules produced by KDD-R simply because weak rules are not extracted from the data, as opposed to other systems. The disadvantage of this approach is clearly the possible incomplete coverage of available data with rules, that is, some data records may not match any rules. This is the consequence of the underlying philosophy that it is better not to "mine" likely incorrect rules, focusing instead on identifying strong rules whose "credibility" is supported by a relatively large number of data points matching their preconditions.

Acknowledgments

The research reported in this paper was supported in part by a research grant from the Natural Sciences and Engineering Research Council of Canada.

References

1. Pawlak, Z.: Rough sets. International Journal of Information and Computer Sciences **11/5** (1982) 341–356
2. Pawlak, Z.: Rough classification. International Journal of Man-Machine Studies **20** (1984) 469–483
3. Pawlak, Z.: Rough sets - Theoretical aspects of reasoning about data. Kluwer Academic Publishers, Dordrecht (1991)
4. Ziarko, W.: Variable precision rough sets model. Journal of Computer and Systems Sciences **46/1** (1993) 39–59
5. Szladow, A.: Datalogic/R: Mining the knowledge in databases. PC AI **7/1** (1993) 40–41
6. Ziarko, W., Shan, N.: KDD-R: a comprehensive system for knowledge discovery using rough sets. In: T.Y. Lin (ed.), The Third International Workshop on Rough Sets and Soft Computing Proceedings (RSSC'94), San Jose State University, San Jose, California, USA November 10-12,(1994) 164–173
7. Tsumoto, S. Ziarko, W.: The application of rough sets-based data mining technique to differential diagnosis of meningoencephalitis. In: Z. W. Ras and M. Michalewicz (eds.), Ninth International Symposium on Methodologies for Intelligent Systems. Zakopane, Poland, June 9–13, Lecture Notes in Artificial Intelligence (ISMIS-96) **1079**, Springer-Verlag, Berlin (1996) 438–447

GPSR Compliance
The European Union's (EU) General Product Safety Regulation (GPSR) is a set of rules that requires consumer products to be safe and our obligations to ensure this.

If you have any concerns about our products, you can contact us on

ProductSafety@springernature.com

In case Publisher is established outside the EU, the EU authorized representative is:

Springer Nature Customer Service Center GmbH
Europaplatz 3
69115 Heidelberg, Germany

www.ingramcontent.com/pod-product-compliance
Ingram Content Group UK Ltd.
Pitfield, Milton Keynes, MK11 3LW, UK
UKHW021902190726
13853UKWH00003B/1382

* 9 7 8 3 6 6 2 1 2 9 3 6 4 *